BILATERAL AND REGIONAL TRADE AGREEMENTS

The stalling of the Doha Development Round trade negotiations has resulted in bilateral and regional free trade agreements (BRTAs) becoming an important alternative. These agreements have proliferated in recent years, and now all of the major trading countries are engaging in serious bilateral trade negotiations with multiple trading partners.

This second edition provides updated and comprehensive analysis of the contents and trends of recent BRTAs. It is unique in that it situates these agreements in their economic, international law and international relations contexts. It also comprehensively reviews the recent agreements in relation to each substantive topic covered (e.g. intellectual property, investment, services, social policy) so as to provide an overview of the law being created in these areas.

SIMON LESTER is President of WorldTradeLaw.net and a trade policy analyst with the Cato Institute's Herbert A. Stiefel Center for Trade Policy Studies.

BRYAN MERCURIO is Professor and Vice Chancellor's Outstanding Fellow of the Faculty of Law at the Chinese University of Hong Kong.

LORAND BARTELS is a University Senior Lecturer in Law and a Fellow of Trinity Hall at the University of Cambridge.

BILATERAL AND REGIONAL TRADE AGREEMENTS

COMMENTARY AND ANALYSIS

Edited by

SIMON LESTER

BRYAN MERCURIO

LORAND BARTELS

CAMBRIDGE
UNIVERSITY PRESS

University Printing House, Cambridge CB2 8BS, United Kingdom

Cambridge University Press is part of the University of Cambridge.

It furthers the University's mission by disseminating knowledge in the pursuit of
education, learning and research at the highest international levels of excellence.

www.cambridge.org
Information on this title: www.cambridge.org/9781107063907

First published 2015

Printed in the United Kingdom by TJ International Ltd. Padstow Cornwall

A catalogue record for this publication is available from the British Library

Library of Congress Cataloging in Publication data
Bilateral and regional trade agreements : commentary and analysis / edited by
Simon Lester, Bryan Mercurio, Lorand Bartels.
pages cm
Includes index.
ISBN 978-1-107-06390-7
1. Foreign trade regulation. 2. Commercial treaties. I. Lester, Simon Nicholas,
editor. II. Mercurio, Bryan, editor. III. Bartels, Lorand, editor.
K4600.B55 2015
382'.9–dc23
2015006480

ISBN 978-1-107-06390-7 Hardback

CONTENTS

CONTRIBUTORS

Lorand Bartels is a University Senior Lecturer in Law in the Faculty of Law and a Fellow of Trinity Hall at the University of Cambridge, where he teaches international law, WTO law and EU law. He holds degrees in English literature and law from the University of New South Wales and a PhD in law from the European University Institute. Dr Bartels is a member of the Executive Council of the Society of International Economic Law, which he helped to establish. He is a general editor of the Cambridge International Trade and Economic Law Series (CUP), an associate editor of the Journal of World Trade (Kluwer) and an editorial board member of several journals, including the Journal of International Economic Law (OUP), the Journal of International Dispute Settlement (OUP) and Legal Issues of Economic Integration (Kluwer). He has also acted as expert consultant to a number of countries and international organizations, including the Commonwealth Secretariat, ECOWAS, the EU and SADC.

Olivier Cattaneo is a Lecturer at the Jackson Institute, Yale University. As a lead expert on trade, he has previously worked at the World Bank, the OECD, and in a range of French ministries. He has taught WTO law and diplomacy at various institutions, including the Institut d'Etudes Politiques de Paris and the University of Paris I Panthéon Sorbonne. He was a World Fellow at Yale University and a Fellow with the Institute of International Economic Law at Georgetown University. A member of the New York Bar, he holds a PhD from the Graduate Institute of International Studies in Geneva, and is a graduate of the Georgetown University Law Center and Sciences-Po Paris.

Arwel Davies is an Associate Professor at the College of Law, Swansea University. His interests lie in the field of international economic law with particular emphasis on the intersection between the trade law and investment law regimes. He is also interested in international public procurement regulation. Dr Davies holds an LLB (Cardiff), LLM (Aberystwyth), and PhD (Nottingham).

Victoria Donaldson is Chief Legal Officer at the WTO Appellate Body Secretariat. Based in Geneva since 1999, she has worked with all of the current and former Appellate Body Members. From 1996 to 1999 she practised law with the Brussels office of Cleary, Gottlieb, Steen and Hamilton, and from 1995 to 1996 with

Russell & DuMoulin in Vancouver. Ms Donaldson obtained Bachelors' degrees in Law from the University of Oxford and the University of British Columbia, and a Master of Laws degree from Harvard Law School. She served as a law clerk to Mr Justice Peter de Carteret Cory at the Supreme Court of Canada in 1993–94. She has taught short courses on subsidies and WTO law for the masters' degree programs at the World Trade Institute and the University of Melbourne, respectively. Ms Donaldson has contributed to books on WTO dispute settlement, writing in particular on procedures for appellate review.

David Evans is Deputy Head of Mission at the New Zealand Embassy in Beijing. Previously, he served as a senior legal adviser to New Zealand's Ministry of Foreign Affairs and Trade, working on numerous WTO disputes and free trade agreement negotiations. From 2002 to 2005 he was legal adviser to the New Zealand Mission to the WTO in Geneva, including responsibility for DSU Review negotiations, Rules negotiations, the Committee on Regional Trade Agreements, and dispute settlement cases. During that time, Mr Evans chaired the WTO Committee on Anti-dumping Practices. He has served as a Panelist in two WTO disputes.

Michael Handler is an Associate Professor at the Faculty of Law, University of New South Wales. His research spans all areas of intellectual property law, with a particular focus on the legal regulation of geographical indications and on international and comparative trade mark and copyright law. He is the co-author, with Professor Robert Burrell, of *Australian Trade Mark Law* (Oxford University Press, 2010) and has published widely in journals and edited collections in the US, Europe and Australia. He teaches a range of undergraduate and postgraduate subjects in intellectual property law at UNSW, and is currently the Associate Dean (Education) in the Faculty.

Tim Josling was born in England and moved to California in 1978 to take a position as a professor in the Food Research Institute, Stanford University, Stanford, California. He previously taught at the London School of Economics and the University of Reading, England. His academic background includes a BSc in Agriculture from the University of London (Wye College), an MSc in Agricultural Economics from the University of Guelph, Canada, and a PhD in Agricultural Economics from Michigan State University. Dr Josling's research interests centre on industrial country agricultural policies, international trade in agricultural products, and the process of economic integration. He is currently involved in studies of the protection of intellectual property in the US and the EU; trade conflicts over food safety and animal health regulations; reform of the agricultural trading system in the WTO, including the progress in the current round of negotiations; the treatment of agriculture in free trade areas such as NAFTA and MERCOSUR; and the changes in the Common Agricultural Policy of the European Union (EU). Professor Josling is a member of the International Policy Council on Food and Agricultural Trade and former Chair of the Executive Committee of the International Agricultural Trade Research Consortium. He formerly held a Visiting Professorship at Imperial College at Wye (UK) and has held the post of President of the UK Agricultural Economics Association. He has also been a visiting scholar at the Institute for International Economics in Washington. In 2004, Professor Josling was made a Fellow of the American Agricultural Economics Association.

Pravin Krishna is Chung Ju Yung Distinguished Professor of International Economics and Business at Johns Hopkins University (School of Advanced International Studies and Department of Economics) and Research Associate at the National Bureau of Economic Research (NBER). Professor Krishna's fields of research interest are international economics, political economy and development. He has published articles in a number of scholarly journals including the *Journal of Political Economy*, the *Quarterly Journal of Economics*, the *Journal of International Economics* and the *Journal of Development Economics*. He is the author of *Trade Blocs: Economics and Politics* (Cambridge University Press, 2005). Professor Krishna holds a bachelors degree in engineering from the Indian Institute of Technology, Bombay and a PhD in economics from Columbia University. He has previously held appointments at Brown University, the University of Chicago, Princeton University and Stanford University and has served as a consultant to the World Bank and the International Monetary Fund.

Simon Lester is a trade policy analyst at the Cato Institute and the founder of WorldTradeLaw.net. Previously, he worked for the trade law practice of a Washington, D.C. law firm, and as a Legal Affairs Officer at the Appellate Body Secretariat of the World Trade Organization (WTO). He has written a number of law journal articles, which have appeared in such publications as the *Stanford Journal of International Law*, the *Journal of International Economic Law* and the *Journal of World Trade*. In addition, he has taught courses on international trade law at American University's Washington College of Law and the University of Michigan Law School.

Nicolas Lockhart is in private practice in the Geneva office of Sidley Austin LLP, focusing on WTO law and policy. Mr Lockhart has advised clients on a wide range of market access issues under WTO agreements on goods, services and intellectual property rights. He has counselled governments at all stages of WTO dispute settlement, from developing a case to securing effective implementation, and has made numerous appearances on behalf of complainants, respondents and third parties before WTO panels and the Appellate Body. Additionally, Mr Lockhart advises public and private sector clients on improvements to the WTO agreements in the context of the Doha Development Round of trade negotiations.

James Mathis is an Associate Professor in the Department of International Law and research fellow in the Amsterdam Center for International Law (ACIL), University of Amsterdam. His research interests include international trade law and the WTO, domestic regulation issues in regional trade agreements, transatlantic trade issues, and regional/international competition policies. James is the managing editor of *Legal Issues of Economic Integration* (Kluwer Law International), serves on the advisory board for the Trade Law Centre of Southern Africa (TRALAC), and is an occasional advisor on trade and competition issues for UNCTAD in Geneva.

Joshua Meltzer is a fellow in Global Economy and Development at the Brookings Institution and an adjunct professor at the Johns Hopkins School for Advanced International Studies. He works on international trade law and policy issues arising at the World Trade Organization and under free trade agreements such as the Trans-Pacific Partnership and the Transatlantic Trade and Investment Partnership negotiations. He focuses on international trade and climate change issues and on the significance of the Internet and cross-border data flows for international trade. Dr Meltzer has also been a consultant to the World Bank on trade and privacy issues. Prior to joining Brookings, Meltzer was a diplomat at the Australian Embassy in Washington D.C where he was responsible for trade, climate and energy issues and prior to that he was a trade negotiator in Australia's Department of Foreign Affairs and Trade. Meltzer holds an S.J.D. and LL.M. from the University of Michigan Law School and law and commerce degrees from Monash University.

Bryan Mercurio is a Professor and Vice Chancellor's Outstanding Fellow of the Faculty of Law at the Chinese University of Hong Kong. He also has been awarded a Hou-De Honorary Chair at the National Tsing Hua University (Taiwan), Research Center for Humanities and Social Services. Professor Mercurio has worked in both the public and private sector and is a frequent advisor and consultant to governments, aid agencies and non-governmental organizations on a variety of issues relating to international trade, investment and intellectual property rights. He is a member of the Asian WTO Research Network, a member of the Founding Committee and later the Executive Council of the Society of International Economic Law (SIEL), a founding member of the SIEL Intellectual Property Law Network and a founding member of the Asian International Economic Law Network.

Andrew Mitchell is a Professor at Melbourne Law School, Australian Research Council Future Fellow, Assistant Director Research at the Melbourne School of Government, Director of the Global Economic Law Network, a member of the Indicative List of Panelists to hear WTO disputes, and a member of the Energy Charter Roster of Panelists. He has previously practised law with Allens Arthur Robinson (now Allens Linklaters) and consults for States, international organisations and the private sector. Andrew has taught law in Australia, Canada and the

US and is the recipient of four major current grants from the Australian Research Council and the Australian National Preventive Health Agency. He has published over 100 academic books and journal articles and is a Series Editor of the Oxford University Press International Economic Law Series, an Editorial Board Member of the *Journal of International Economic Law* and a General Editor on the *Journal of International Dispute Settlement*. He has law degrees from Melbourne, Harvard and Cambridge.

Federico Ortino is Reader in International Economic Law at King's College London. He is a member of the ILA Committee on International Trade Law; founding Committee Member (and now co-Treasurer) of the Society of International Economic Law; consultative member of the Investment Treaty Forum; editorial board member of the Journal of International Economic Law; Yearbook on International Investment Law and Policy, Journal of International Dispute Settlement and Journal of World Investment and Trade. He is one of the editors of The Oxford Handbook of International Investment Law (Oxford, OUP, 2008) and the author of Basic Legal Instruments for the Liberalisation of Trade: a Comparative Analysis of EC and WTO Law (Oxford, Hart Publishing, 2004). Previously, he was Director, Investment Treaty Forum, British Institute of International and Comparative Law in London (2005-2007); Emile Noël Fellow and Fulbright Scholar at the NYU Jean Monnet Center in New York (2004); Legal Officer at the United Nations Conference on Trade and Development, Division on Investment and Enterprises (2003).

Krista Nadakavukaren Schefer is Professor of International Law at the University of Basel's Faculty of Law and is part of the World Trade Institute in Bern. Long interested in the intersection of international economic law and other areas of international law, her recent research has looked at poverty, corruption, human rights, and vulnerability. She is also actively pursuing research on the legal implications of obesity and the law of data protection. Professor Nadakavukaren is a native of the United States. She received her juris doctor from Georgetown University Law School, and her doctorate and 'habilitation' from the University of Bern.

Elizabeth Sheargold is a Ph.D. Candidate and Research Fellow at Melbourne Law School. She was previously an Associate Director at the Center for Climate Change Law at Columbia Law School, and practised law in the environment and litigation departments of Allens Arthur Robinson (now Allens Linklaters). She has taught in the Melbourne Law Masters program, and received her LLB (Hons.) from Melbourne Law School and her Master of Laws from Columbia Law School.

Tania Voon is Professor at Melbourne Law School and was Associate Dean (Research) until mid-2014. She is a former Legal Officer of the WTO Appellate Body Secretariat and has previously practised law with King & Wood, Mallesons and the Australian Government Solicitor and taught law at Georgetown University, the University of Western Ontario, and several Australian universities. Tania undertook her Master of Laws at Harvard Law School and her PhD at the University of Cambridge. She has published widely in the areas of public international law and international economic law and is Editor (International Economic Law) of *ASIL Insights* and Series Editor (with Professors John Jackson and Andrew Mitchell) of the *International Economic Law Series* of Oxford University Press. Tania is a member of the Roster of Panelists for the Energy Charter Treaty and of the Indicative List of Governmental and Non-Governmental Panelists for resolving WTO disputes. She has provided expert advice and training to entities such as the Australian Department of Foreign Affairs and Trade, the WTO, the World Health Organization, Telstra, and the McCabe Centre for Law and Cancer. In 2014 she was Senior Emile Noël Fellow at the Jean Monnet Center, New York University Law School.

FOREWORD

A sign of the times in trade is that the scholarship of some of the best thinkers on trade law is focused on new bilateral and regional trade agreements instead of on new multilateral trade agreements. This is not because they no longer care about multilateral agreements. It is because there are no new multilateral agreements. Since the conclusion of the Uruguay Round and the establishment of the World Trade Organization two decades ago, the Members of the WTO have, alas, failed repeatedly in their efforts to reach a consensus and conclude new global trade agreements.

Frustrated with years of endless impasse in the WTO Doha Development Round of multilateral trade negotiations, trading countries have turned increasingly to negotiating bilateral and regional deals, largely outside the legal framework of the WTO. During the past decade, these bilateral and regional deals have proliferated. Where once there were only a few, now there are a few hundred. Recently, these smaller bilateral and regional trade and investment deals have led to negotiations by major trading countries outside the WTO on so-called 'mega-deals' that, if concluded, would be beyond the shelter of the legal umbrella of the WTO.

These proposed mega-deals have drawn widespread support from those who see them as the only practical way forward from deadlocked multilateral WTO negotiations. The mega-deals could add much-needed new rules on many new issues in world trade. They could address a twenty-first century trade agenda ranging far beyond the traditional concerns of customs and tariffs. However, they could also exclude the vast majority of WTO Members, including most emerging and developing countries, from the benefits of these new arrangements. Stopping such discrimination in trade is much of what the WTO trading system is supposed to be about.

Simon Lester, Bryan Mercurio and Lorand Bartels are three of our leading thinkers on trade law. In editing this collection, they have come together to try to make some sense of the significance of this trend toward partial rather than global trade arrangements. The additional trade law thinkers they have chosen as their contributors help the editors succeed. They point to the positives and sound the right cautionary notes. They try to show how all that is happening can be stitched together legally if we should find the will to do so. Above all, they counsel us to study what is actually in these new agreements before rendering judgments.

Clearly, there are positives to partial deals. Historically, they have been shown to be excellent proving grounds for new approaches that have not yet attained a global

consensus. One example is the provision for investor-state dispute settlement pio-
neered in Chapter Eleven of the North American Free Trade Agreement and now
being considered for inclusion in some of the mega-deals. A more recent example is
the arrangement for dealing with the nexus between 'trade and environment' concerns in the free trade agreement between the United States and Peru. In these ways,
bilateral and regional deals can become models for moving forward. The experiments
conducted through them can be tried globally if they are tried bilaterally or regionally
and found to be true. The case studies found in the second volume of this collection
are all well worth pondering with this prospect in mind.

But how does all of this often worthy experimentation fit within the WTO? All of
the countries negotiating these partial deals are Members of the WTO. As such, they
each have an obligation to provide 'most-favoured-nation' treatment to all other
Members by not discriminating in their trade between and among the similar
products of other WTO Members. By definition, a decision to give a preference to
one country or to a handful of countries in a bilateral deal or a regional deal is a
decision to discriminate against other countries. How does this square with the basic
rule of non-discrimination that is at the very heart of the WTO treaty and trading
system?

Further, as a matter of equity and justice, how can such discrimination be justified
when the vast majority of those excluded from the mega-deals most prominent
among these proliferating initiatives are the poorer countries, who need better
connections to global value chains of the global economy? Representatives of some
of the smallest countries in the world have told how they have tried to gain entrée into
this new world of bilateral and regional negotiations but have found no takers. They
are too small economically to interest any of the larger countries in negotiating a deal
with them. How does this square with the professed desire of the leading trading
countries in their communiqués at G20 and other global summits to do much more
to include developing countries in the mainstream of the global economy?

Of course, as all good trade law thinkers know, these partial deals are legal for
WTO Members only if they meet the requirements of Article XXIV of the General
Agreement on Tariffs and Trade 1994, which is part of the WTO treaty and provides
an exception from the MFN obligation for 'customs unions and free-trade areas'. No
one claims that these bilateral, regional and mega-deals are 'customs unions'. More
ominously, no one knows what a 'free-trade area' is within the meaning of Article
XXIV.8(b) of the GATT – or really wants to know. The GATT/WTO trading system
has thrived for more than half a century without knowing the answer to this question.
As I have often said, and not entirely in jest, one of my greatest accomplishments as a
Member for eight years of the Appellate Body of the WTO was that I was able to get
out of Geneva alive without having to answer this question.

The current trend toward bilateral and regional deals makes it harder to avoid
answering this question. Eventually some Member of the WTO excluded from one of
these partial deals is going to think it 'fruitful' (as the WTO Dispute Settlement

Understanding puts it) to file a legal complaint alleging that the deal in question does not satisfy the requirements of Article XXIV. If the legal issue is then raised on appeal to the Appellate Body, then under the rules the Appellate Body 'shall address' that issue. And where will the trading system be then? With this legal eventuality in mind, I particularly commend to readers the thoughts essayed by Nic Lockhart and Andrew Mitchell on the legal requirements for FTAs under the WTO.

By far the better way to move forward partially is within the framework of the WTO through the negotiation of plurilateral agreements by 'coalitions of the willing' among the WTO membership as part of the WTO trading system. Such partial agreements within the framework of the WTO are inclusive, because they are open to the membership of all WTO Members willing to be bound by their terms. The Chapter by Krista Nadakavukaren Schefer and Arwel Davies on government procurement illustrates this option, which has also been pursued in information technology and, now, green goods, two of the most important 'new issues' in trade.

Some of the most significant trade issues can only be addressed multilaterally. Foremost among these is agriculture. Efforts to discipline agricultural support worldwide have been at the centre of GATT/WTO negotiations from the very beginning. Some aspects of agriculture can be dealt with bilaterally or regionally. But not the extent of overall domestic support that is the core of national agricultural regimes. A deal to discipline such support in any meaningful way can only be as part of a 'grand deal' done globally. Tim Josling explains and elaborates issues on the unfolding global trade agenda in his essay on the continuing centrality of agricultural trade.

Lastly, I would be remiss if I did not say a word on dispute settlement. One of the unanswered questions about all of these bilateral and regional deals is: how will their dispute settlement systems work? For the most part, they remain untried. Certainly they cannot compare to the 'security and predictability' offered for two decades now by the WTO dispute settlement system. It is worth examining these systems in their context. It is perhaps worth noting more that, in the context of negotiations on the proposed mega-deals especially, it has been suggested that dispute settlement might be entrusted to the WTO. That is an idea deserving of pursuit. But why not simply negotiate these mega-deals as plurilateral agreements within the WTO in the first place? Then they could fall by agreement under the jurisdiction of the WTO dispute settlement system. On this emerging issue, as a final observation, I commend to you the thoughts in these volumes of Simon Lester and Victoria Donaldson.

James Bacchus
Former Chair of the WTO Appellate Body

TABLE OF CASES

(1) *Index of WTO Dispute Settlement Panel and Appellate Body Reports*

Short title	Full title and citation
Argentina–Footwear Safeguards	Appellate Body Report, *Argentina–Safeguard Measures on Imports of Footwear*, WT/DS121/AB/R, adopted on 12 January 2000, DSR 2000: 1, 515
Argentina–Footwear Safeguards	Panel Report, *Argentina–Safeguard Measures on Imports of Footwear*, WT/DS121/R, adopted on 12 January 2000, as modified by the Appellate Body Report, WT/DS121/AB/R, DSR 2000: H, 575
Canada–Automotive Industry	Appellate Body Report, *Canada–Certain Measures Affecting the Automotive Industry*, WT/DS139/AB/R, WT/DS142/AB/R, adopted 19 June 2000, DSR 2000:VI, 2985
Canada–Automotive Industry	Panel Report, *Canada–Certain Measures Affecting the Automotive Industry*, WT/DS139/R, WT/DS142/R, adopted 19 June 2000, as modified by the Appellate Body Report, WT/DS139/AB/R, WT/DS142/AB/R, DSR 2000: VII, 3043
Canada – Continued Suspension (EC-Hormones)	Appellate Body Report, *Canada–Continued Suspension of Obligations in the EC – Hormones Dispute*, WT/DS321/AB/R, adopted 14 November 2008, DSR 2008:XIV, 5373
Canada – Continued Suspension (EC-Hormones)	Panel Report, *Canada–Continued Suspension of Obligations in the EC–Hormones Dispute*, WT/DS321/R and Add.1 to Add.7, adopted 14 November 2008, as modified by Appellate Body Report WT/DS321/AB/R, DSR 2008: XV, 5757

(1) (*cont.*)

Short title	Full title and citation
Canada–Periodicals	Appellate Body Report, *Canada–Certain Measures Concerning Periodicals*, WT/DS31/AB/R, adopted 30 July 1997, DSR 1997:1, 449
Chile–Alcoholic Beverages	Appellate Body Report, *Chile–Taxes on Alcoholic Beverages*, WT/DS87/AB/R, WT/DS110/AB/R, adopted 12 January 2000, DSR 2000:1, 281
China – Electronic Payment Services	Panel Report, *China – Certain Measures Affecting Electronic Payment Services*, WT/DS413/R and Add.1, adopted 31 August 2012, DSR 2012:X, p. 5305
EC – Approval and Marketing of Biotech Products	Panel Reports, *European Communities – Measures Affecting the Approval and Marketing of Biotech Products*, WT/DS291/R/WT/DS292/R/WT/DS293/R/Add.1 to Add.9 and Corr.1, adopted 21 November 2006, DSR 2006:III, 847
EC–Asbestos	Appellate Body Report, *European Communities–Measures Affecting Asbestos and Asbestos-Containing Products*, WT/DS135/AB/R, adopted 5 April 2001, DSR 2001: VH, 3243
EC–Bananas III	Appellate Body Report, *European Communities–Regime for the Importation, Sale and Distribution of Bananas*, WT/DS27/AB/R, adopted 25 September 1997, DSR 1997:11, 591
EC–Bananas III	Panel Report, *European Communities–Regime for the Importation, Sale and Distribution of Bananas*, WT/DS27/R/ECU, WT/DS27/R/GTM,HND, WT/DS27/R/MEX, WT/DS27/R/USA, adopted 25 September 1997, as modified by the Appellate Body Report, WT/DS27/AB/R, DSR 1997:111, 1085 (*Ecuador*); DSR 1997:11, 695 (*Guatemala and Honduras*); DSR 1997:11, 803 (*Mexico*); DSR 1997:11, 943 (*US*)
EC–Bananas III (Article 21.5–EC)	Panel Report, *European Communities–Regime for the Importation, Sale and Distribution of Bananas–Recourse to Article 21. 5 of the DSU by the European Communities*, WT/DS27/RW/EEC and Corr.1, 12 April 1999, unadopted, DSR 1999:11, 783

(1) *(cont.)*

(1) *(cont.)*

(1) *(cont.)*

Short title	Full title and citation
US–Continued Suspension (EC-Hormones)	Panel Report, *United States – Continued Suspension of Obligations in the EC–Hormones Dispute*, WT/DS320/R and Add.1 to Add.7, adopted 14 November 2008, as modified by Appellate Body Report WT/DS320/AB/R, DSR 2008:XI, p. 3891
US–Cotton Underwear	Appellate Body Report, *United States–Restrictions on Imports of Cotton and Man-made Fibre Underwear*, WT/DS24/AB/R, adopted 25 February 1997, DSR 1997:1, 11
US–Cotton Underwear	Panel Report, *United States–Restrictions on Imports of Cotton and Man-made Fibre Underwear*, WT/DS24/R, adopted 25 February 1997, as modified by the Appellate Body Report, WT/DS24/AB/R, DSR 1997:1, 31
US–Gambling Services	Appellate Body Report, *United States–Measures Affecting the Cross-Border Supply of Gambling and Betting Services*, WT/DS285/AB/R, adopted 20 April 2005, DSR 2005:XII, 5663
US–Gambling Services	Panel Report, *United States–Measures Affecting the Cross-Border Supply of Gambling and Betting Services*, WT/DS285/R, adopted 20 April 2005, as modified by the Appellate Body Report, WT/DS285/AB/R, DSR 2005:XII, 5797
US–Gasoline	Appellate Body Report, *United States–Standards for Reformulated and Conventional Gasoline*, WT/DS2/AB/R, adopted 20 May 1996, DSR 1996:1, 3
US–Lead and Bismuth II	Appellate Body Report, *United States–Imposition of Countervailing Duties on Certain Hot-Rolled Lead and Bismuth Carbon Steel Products Originating in the United Kingdom*, WT/DS138/AB/R, adopted 7 June 2000, DSR 2000:V, 2595
US–Line Pipe Safeguards	Appellate Body Report, *United States–Definitive Safeguard Measures on Imports of Circular Welded Carbon Quality Line Pipe from Korea*, WT/DS202/AB/R, adopted on 8 March 2002, DSR 2002:IV, 1403

(1) *(cont.)*

TABLE OF TREATIES AND INTERNATIONAL AGREEMENTS

(1) *International conventions and treaties*

Short title	Long title	Status
ACTA	Anti-Counterfeiting Trade Agreement	Signed in Tokyo on 1 October 2011 by United States, Australia, Canada, Korea, Japan, New Zealand, Morocco, and Singapore; not in force
Basel Convention	Basel Convention on the Control of Transboundary Movements of Hazardous Wastes and Their Disposal	Signed at Basel on 22 March 1989; in force 5 May 1992
Berne Convention	Berne Convention for the Protection of Literary and Artistic Works	Adopted in Berne on 9 September 1886; completed at Paris on 4 May 1896; revised 13 November 1908 (Berlin); completed 20 March 1914 (Berne); revised 2 June 1928 (Rome); revised 26 June 1948 (Brussels); revised 14 July 1967 (Stockholm); revised 24 July 1971 (Paris); amended 28 September 1979
Brussels Sugar Convention	Brussels Sugar Convention of 1902	Signed at Brussels on 5 March 1902; in force 1 September 1903
Cartagena Protocol	Cartagena Protocol on Biosafety to the Convention on Biological Diversity	Adopted in Montreal on 29 January 2000; in force 11 September 2003

(1) (*cont.*)

Short title	Long title	Status
CITES	Convention on International Trade in Endangered Species of Wild Fauna and Flora	Signed at Washington, DC, on 3 March 1973; in force 1 July 1975
CCAMLR	Convention for the Conservation of Antarctic Marine Living Resources	Signed at Canberra on 20 May 1980; in force 7 April 1982
	Convention for the Abolition of Import and Export Prohibitions and Restrictions	Signed 8 November 1927, never ratified
Cultural Expressions Convention	Convention on the Protection and Promotion of the Diversity of Cultural Expressions	Adopted in Paris by the United Nations Educational, Scientific and Cultural Organization (UNESCO) on 20 October 2005; in force 18 March 2007
Havana Charter	Havana Charter for an International Trade Organization	Signed at Havana on 24 March 1948; never ratified
IATTC	Convention for the Strengthening of the Inter-American Tropical Tuna Commission	Signed at Washington, DC on 31 May 1949; in force 3 March 1950; Protocol of Amendment adopted on 11 June 1999, not yet in force; Convention for the Strengthening of IATTC adopted on 23 July 2003, not yet in force
ICJ Statute	Statute of the International Court of Justice	Established by the UN Charter, signed 26 June 1945; in force 24 October 1945
ILO Constitution	Constitution of the International Labour Organisation	Part XIII of the Treaties of Versailles signed on 28 June 1919, in force 10 January 1920
ILO Declaration	International Labour Organization on Fundamental Principles and Rights at Work	Adopted in Geneva by the General Conference of the International Labour Organization (ILO) during its 86th Session on 18 June 1998

(1) *(cont.)*

Short title	Long title	Status
London Convention	Convention on the Prevention of Marine Pollution by Dumping of Wastes and Other Matter	Signed at London on 13 November 1972; in force 30 August 1975
Montreal Protocol	Montreal Protocol on Substances that Deplete the Ozone Layer	Signed at Montreal on 16 September 1987; in force 1 January 1989
Paris Convention	Paris Convention for the Protection of Industrial Property	Signed at Paris on 20 March 1883; revised at Brussels on 14 December 1900, at Washington on 2 June 1911, at The Hague on 6 November 1925, at London on 2 June 1934, at Lisbon on 31 October 1958, and at Stockholm on 14 July 1967 and as amended on 28 September 1979 Substantive provisions (Articles 1–12) in force generally on 26 April 1970 (for countries recognising the accession of the German Democratic Republic); 19 May 1970 (for countries not recognising the accession of the German Democratic Republic) Administrative provisions (Articles 13–30) in force generally on 26 April 1970
Ramsar Convention on Wetlands	Convention on Wetlands of International Importance, especially as Waterfowl Habitat	Signed at Ramsar on 2 February 1971; in force 21 December 1975
UN Charter	Charter of the United Nations	Signed at San Francisco on 26 June 1945; in force 24 October 1945
UNCLOS	United Nations Convention on the Law of the Sea	Signed at Montego Bay, Jamaica, on 10 December 1982; in force 16 November 1994

(1) (*cont.*)

Short title	Long title	Status
Vienna Convention	Vienna Convention on the Law of Treaties	Signed at Vienna on 23 May 1969; in force 27 January 1980
1986 Vienna Convention	Vienna Convention on the Law of Treaties Between States and International Organizations or Between International Organizations	Signed at Vienna on 21 March 1986; not yet in force
WCT	WIPO Copyright Treaty	Adopted in Geneva by the Diplomatic Conference on 20 December 1996; in force 6 March 2002
WPPT	WIPO Performances and Phonograms Treaty (1996)	Adopted in Geneva by the Diplomatic Conference on 20 December 1996; in force 20 May 2002
Whaling Convention	International Convention for the Regulation of Whaling	Signed at Washington, DC, on 2 December 1946; in force 10 November 1948; Protocol revising the Convention signed 19 November 1956

(2) *GATT/WTO Agreements*

Short title	Full title	Status/source
Agriculture Agreement	Agreement on Agriculture	Annex 1A of the WTO Agreement
Anti-dumping Agreement	Agreement on Implementation of Article VI of the General Agreement on Tariffs and Trade 1994	Annex 1A of the WTO Agreement
Customs Valuation Agreement	Agreement on Implementation of Article VII of the General Agreement on Tariffs and Trade 1994	Annex 1A of the WTO Agreement
DSU	Understanding on Rules and Procedures Governing the Settlement of Disputes	Annex 2 of the WTO Agreement

(2) (*cont.*)

Short title	Full title	Status/source
GATT 1947	General Agreement on Tariffs and Trade 1947	Signed 1 January 1948; provisionally applied
GATT 1994	General Agreement on Tariffs and Trade 1994	Annex 1A of the WTO Agreement
GATS	General Agreement on Trade in Services	Annex 1B of the WTO Agreement
GPA 1994	Agreement on Government Procurement 1994	Annex 4(b) of the WTO Agreement
Safeguards Agreement	Agreement on Safeguards	Annex 1A of the WTO Agreement
SCM Agreement	Agreement on Subsidies and Countervailing Measures	Annex 1A of the WTO Agreement
SPS Agreement	Agreement on the Application of Sanitary and Phytosanitary Measures	Annex 1A of the WTO Agreement
TBT Agreement	Agreement on Technical Barriers to Trade	Annex 1A of the WTO Agreement
TRIMs Agreement	Agreement on Trade-Related Investment Measures	Annex 1A of the WTO Agreement
TRIPS Agreement	Agreement on Trade-Related Aspects of Intellectual Property Rights	Annex 1C of the WTO Agreement
WTO Agreement	Marrakesh Agreement Establishing the World Trade Organization	Signed 15 April 1994; in force 1 January 1995

(3) *Preferential trade agreements*

Short title	Long title	Current parties (or membership immediately prior to extinction) (unless otherwise indicated)	Status
Agadir Agreement		Egypt, Jordan, Morocco and Tunisia	Signed in Rabat in February 2004; in force in March 2007
ALADI/LAIA	Latin American Integration Association (Asociación Latinoamericana de Integración)	Argentina, Bolivia, Brazil, Chile, Colombia, Cuba, Ecuador, Mexico, Paraguay, Peru, Uruguay, Venezuela	Signed 12 August 1980; in force 18 March 1981
Albania–Bosnia and Herzegovina FTA	Albania–Bosnia and Herzegovina Free Trade Agreement	Albania, Bosnia and Herzegovina	Signed 28 April 2003; in force 1 December 2004
AFTA	ASEAN Free Trade Area Agreement	Brunei, Cambodia, Indonesia, Laos, Malaysia, Myanmar, Philippines, Singapore, Thailand, Vietnam	Signed 28 January 1992; in force 28 January 1992
ANZCERTA (*also referred to as* CER)	Australia–New Zealand Closer Economic Relations Trade Agreement	Australia, New Zealand	Signed 28 March 1980; in force 1 January 1983
AP (*currently known as* CAN)	Andean Pact known since 1996 as the Andean Community of Nations (Comunidad Andina de Naciones)	Bolivia, Colombia, Ecuador, Peru, Venezuela	Signed 26 May 1969; in force 16 October 1969 Official codified text of the CAN signed 25 June 2003
Armenia–Kazakhstan FTA	Armenia–Kazakhstan Free Trade Agreement	Armenia, Kazakhstan	Signed 2 September 1999; in force 25 December 2001

Abbreviation	Full title	Parties	Status
ASEAN–China Framework Agreement	Framework Agreement on Comprehensive Economic Cooperation Between the Association of South East Asian Nations and the People's Republic of China	ASEAN states, China	Signed 4 November 2002; in force 1 July 2003 Agreement on Trade in Goods (ASEAN–China Goods Agreement) signed 29 November 2004; in force 1 January 2005 Agreement on Dispute Settlement Mechanism (ASEAN–China DSM) signed 29 November 2004; in force 1 January 2005
ASEAN–India Framework Agreement	Framework Agreement on Comprehensive Economic Cooperation Between the Republic of India and the Association of Southeast Asian Nations	ASEAN states, India	Signed 8 October 2003; in force 1 July 2004
ASEAN–Korea Framework Agreement	Framework Agreement on Comprehensive Economic Cooperation Among the Governments of the Member Countries of the Association of Southeast Asian Nations and the Republic of Korea	ASEAN states, South Korea	Signed 13 December 2005; in force 1 July 2006 Agreement on Dispute Mechanism (ASEAN–Korea DSM) signed 13 December 2005; in force 1 July 2006
AUSFTA	Australia–United States Free Trade Agreement	Australia, United States	Signed 18 May 2004; in force 1 January 2005
Australia–Chile FTA	Australia–Chile Free Trade Agreement	Australia, Chile	Signed 30 July 2008; in force 6 March 2009
Australia–Malaysia FTA	Australia–Malaysia Free Trade Agreement	Australia, Malaysia	Signed 22 May 2012; in force 1 January 2013

(3) (*cont.*)

Short title	Long title	Current parties (or membership immediately prior to extinction) (unless otherwise indicated)	Status
Benelux	Benelux Customs Union later known as the Benelux Economic Union	Belgium, Luxembourg, Netherlands	Signed 5 September 1944; in force 1 January 1948; Treaty of the Benelux Economic Union signed 3 February force 1958; in force 1 November 1960
BFTA	Baltic Free Trade Area	Estonia, Latvia, Lithuania	Signed 13 September 1993; in force 1 April 1994
BLEU	Belgium–Luxembourg Economic Union	Belgium, Luxembourg	Signed 25 July 1921; in force 22 December 1922
Bulgaria–Bosnia and Herzegovina FTA	Bulgaria–Bosnia and Herzegovina Free Trade Agreement	Bulgaria, Bosnia and Herzegovina	Signed 16 October 2003
CACM	Central American Common Market	Costa Rica, El Salvador, Guatemala, Honduras, Nicaragua	Signed 13 December 1960; in force 3 June 1961 (Guatemala, El Salvador, Nicaragua), 27 April 1962 (Honduras), 23 September 1963 (Costa Rica)
CAFTA–DR–US	Central America–Dominican Republic–United States Free Trade Agreement	Costa Rica, Dominican Republic, El Salvador, Guatemala, Honduras, Nicaragua, United States	Signed 5 August 2004; in force 1 March 2006 (El Salvador, United States), 1 April 2006 (Honduras, Nicaragua), 1 July 2006 (Guatemala), 1 March 2007 (Dominican Republic)
Canada–Chile FTA	Canada–Chile Free Trade Agreement	Canada, Chile	Signed 5 December 1996; in force 5 July 1997

Canada–Costa Rica FTA	Canada–Costa Rica Free Trade Agreement	Canada, Costa Rica	Signed 23 April 2001; in force 1 November 2002 Canada–Costa Rica Agreement on Environmental Cooperation (CCRAEC) signed 23 April 2001; in force 1 November 2002 Canada–Costa Rica Agreement on Labour Cooperation (CCRALC) signed 23 April 2001; in force 1 November 2002
Canada–Israel FTA	Canada–Israel Free Trade Agreement	Canada, Israel	Signed 31 July 1996; in force 1 January 1997
Canada–Panama FTA	Canada–Panama Free Trade Agreement	Canada, Panama	Signed 14 May 2010; in force 1 April 2013
Canada–Peru FTA	Canada–Peru Free Trade Agreement	Canada, Peru	Signed 29 May 2008; in force 1 August 2009
CARICOM (also known as Treaty of Chaguaramas)	Caribbean Community and Common Market	Antigua and Barbuda, the Bahamas, Barbados, Belize, Dominica, Grenada, Guyana, Haiti, Jamaica, Montserrat, St. Lucia, St. Kitts/Nevis/Anguilla, St. Vincent, Trinidad and Tobago	Signed 4 July 1973; in force 1 August 1973
CARICOM–Costa Rica FTA	CARICOM–Costa Rica Free Trade Agreement	CARICOM states, Costa Rica	Signed 9 March 2004; in force 15 November 2005 (Costa Rica, Trinidad and Tobago), 30 April 2006 (Costa Rica, Guyana), 1 August 2006 (Costa Rica, Barbados)

(3) (cont.)

Short title	Long title	Current parties (or membership immediately prior to extinction) (unless otherwise indicated)	Status
CARICOM–DR FTA	CARICOM–Dominican Republic Free Trade Agreement	CARICOM states, Dominican Republic	Signed 22 August 1998; in force 1 December 2001 (Trinidad and Tobago, Jamaica, Barbados), 5 February 2002 (Dominican Republic), 6 October 2004 (Guyana), August 2005 (Suriname)
CARIFTA	Caribbean Free Trade Area	Antigua, Barbados, Belize, Dominica, Grenada, Guyana, Jamaica, Montserrat, St. Kitts/Nevis/Anguilla, St. Vincent, Trinidad and Tobago	Signed 15 December 1965; in force 1 May 1968
CEAO/WAEC	West African Economic Community (Communauté Économique de l'Afrique de l'Ouest)	Benin (then Dahomey), Burkino Faso (then Upper Volta), Côte d'Ivoire, Mali, Mauritania, Niger, Senegal	Signed 3 June 1972; in force 1 January 1974
CEEAC/ECCAS	Economic Community of Central African States (Communauté Économiqué des États d'Afrique Centrale)	Angola, Burundi, Cameroon, Central African Republic, Chad, Democratic Republic of Congo, Republic of Congo, Equatorial Guinea, Gabon, Rwanda, São Tomé and Príncipe	Signed 18 October 1983; in force 18 December 1984

CEFTA	Central European Free Trade Agreement	*Parties to the original agreement:* Bulgaria, Croatia, Czech Republic, Hungary, Poland, Republic of Macedonia, Romania, Slovak Republic, Slovenia	Original agreement signed 21 December 1992; in force 1 March 1993
		Parties to the new enlarged agreement: Albania, Bosnia and Herzegovina, Croatia, Republic of Macedonia, Moldova, Montenegro, Serbia, UNMIK (on behalf of Kosovo)	New enlarged agreement signed 19 December 2006; in force 26 July 2007 (Albania, Kosovo, Macedonia, Moldova, Montenegro), 22 August 2007 (Croatia)
CEMAC	Central African Economic and Monetary Community/ Economic and Monetary Community of Central Africa (Communauté Économique et Monétaire de l'Afrique Centrale)	Cameroon, Central African Republic, Chad, Republic of Congo, Equatorial Guinea, Gabon	Signed 16 March 1994; in force June 1999
Central America–Chile FTA	Central America–Chile Free Trade Agreement	Chile, Costa Rica, El Salvador, Guatemala, Honduras, Nicaragua	Signed 18 November 1999 (Chile–Costa Rica; El Salvador–Chile), 20 November 2000 (Costa Rica–El Salvador); in force 14 November 2002 (Chile–Costa Rica), 3 June 2002 (El Salvador–Chile; Costa Rica–El Salvador)
Central America–Panama FTA	Central America–Panama Free Trade Agreement	Costa Rica, El Salvador, Guatemala, Honduras, Nicaragua, Panama	Signed 6 March 2002 (El Salvador and Panama), 15 June 2007 (Honduras and Panama); in force 11 April 2003 (El Salvador and Panama)

(3) (cont.)

Short title	Long title	Current parties (or membership immediately prior to extinction) (unless otherwise indicated)	Status
CEPGL	Economic Community of the Great Lakes Countries (Communauté Économique des Pays des Grands Lacs)	Burundi, Democratic Republic of the Congo, Rwanda	Established 20 September 1976
CETA	Comprehensive Economic and Trade Agreement	Canada, European Union	Signed 26 September 2014; not yet in force
Chile–China FTA	Chile–China Free Trade Agreement	Chile, China	Signed 18 November 2005; in force 1 October 2006
Chile–Colombia	Chile–Colombia Free Trade Agreement	Chile, Colombia	Signed 27 November 2006; in force 8 May 2009
Chile–Hong Kong FTA	Chile–Hong Kong Free Trade Agreement	Chile, Hong Kong SAR	Signed 7 September 2012; in force 9 October 2014
China–Hong Kong CEPA	China–Hong Kong Closer Economic Partnership Agreement	China, Hong Kong SAR	Signed 29 June 2003; in force 1 January 2004
China–Macao CEPA	China–Macao Closer Economic Partnership Agreement	China, Macao SAR	Signed 17 October 2003; in force 1 January 2004
China–New Zealand FTA	China–New Zealand Free Trade Agreement	China, New Zealand	Signed 7 April 2008; in force 1 October 2008
China–Pakistan FTA	China–Pakistan Free Trade Agreement	China, Pakistan	Signed 24 November 2006; in force 1 July 2007
China–Peru FTA	China–Peru Free Trade Agreement	Chile, Peru	Signed 28 April 28 2009; in force 1 March 2010
China–Singapore FTA (CSFTA)	China–Singapore Free Trade Agreement	China, Singapore	Signed 23 October 2008; in force 1 January 2009

Cobden–Chevalier Treaty	Cobden–Chevalier Treaty / France, United Kingdom	Signed 23 January 1860
COMESA	Common Market for Eastern and Southern Africa / Angola, Burundi, Comoros, Democratic Republic of Congo, Djibouti, Egypt, Eritrea, Ethiopia, Kenya, Libya, Madagascar, Malawi, Mauritius, Rwanda, Seychelles, Sudan, Swaziland, Uganda, Zambia, Zimbabwe	Signed 5 November 1993; in force 8 December 1994; free Trade Area established on 31 October 2000
Cotonou Agreement	ACP–EU Cotonou Partnership Agreement / ACP countries, European Union	Signed 23 June 2000; in force 1 April 2003; revised agreement signed 25 June 2005
Croatia–Albania FTA	Croatia–Albania Free Trade Agreement / Albania, Croatia	Signed 27 September 2002; in force 1 June 2003
CUSFTA	Canada–United States Free Trade Agreement / Canada, United States	Signed 2 January 1988; in force 1 January 1989
Deutscher Zollverein	Deutscher Zollverein (German Customs Union) / Majority of German Confederation states	Signed 22 March 1833; in force 1 January 1834
EAC	East African Community / Kenya, Tanzania, Uganda; *Parties to the re-established treaty*: Burundi, Kenya, Rwanda, Tanzania, Uganda	Originally established 6 June 1967; abolished 1 July 1977 Re-established 30 November 1999; in force 7 July 2000
EAC Customs Union	East African Community Customs Union / Burundi, Kenya, Rwanda, Tanzania, Uganda	Signed 2 March 2004; in force 1 January 2005
ECCM	East Caribbean Common Market / Antigua and Barbuda, Dominica, Grenada, Montserrat, St. Kitts and Nevis, St. Lucia, St. Vincent	Established 11 June 1968

(3) (*cont.*)

Short title	Long title	Current parties (or membership immediately prior to extinction) (unless otherwise indicated)	Status
ECOWAS	Economic Community of West African States	Benin, Burkina Faso, Cape Verde, Côte d'Ivoire, Gambia, Ghana, Guinea, Guinea-Bissau, Liberia, Mali, Niger, Nigeria, Senegal, Sierra Leone, Togolese	Signed 28 May 1975; in force 20 June 1975
EEA	European Economic Area	EFTA states (except Switzerland), European Union	Signed 2 May 1992; in force 1 January 1994
EFTA	European Free Trade Association	Iceland, Liechtenstein, Norway, Switzerland	Stockholm Convention: signed 4 January 1960, in force 3 May 1960; Vaduz Convention (amending the Stockholm Convention): signed 21 June 2001; in force 1 June 2002
EFTA–Canada FTA	EFTA–Canada Free Trade Agreement	Canada, EFTA states	Signed 26 January 2008, in force 2 July 2009
EFTA–Chile FTA	EFTA–Chile Free Trade Agreement	Chile, EFTA states	Signed 26 June 2003; in force 1 December 2004
EFTA–Croatia FTA	EFTA–Croatia Free Trade Agreement	Croatia, EFTA states	Signed 21 June 2001; in force 1 April 2002
EFTA–Egypt FTA	EFTA–Egypt Free Trade Agreement	EFTA states, Egypt	Signed 27 January 2007, in force 1 August 2007
EFTA–Hong Kong FTA	EFTA–Hong Kong Free Trade Agreement	EFTA states, Hong Kong	Signed 21 June 2011, in force 1 October 2012 with Iceland,

EFTA–Israel FTA	EFTA–Israel Free Trade Agreement	EFTA states, Israel	Signed 17 September 1992; in force 1 January 1993
EFTA–Jordan FTA	EFTA–Jordan Free Trade Agreement	EFTA states, Jordan	Signed 21 June 2001; in force 1 September 2002
EFTA–Korea FTA	EFTA–Korea Free Trade Agreement	EFTA states, Korea	Signed 15 December 2005; in force 1 September 2006
EFTA–Lebanon FTA	EFTA–Lebanon Free Trade Agreement	EFTA states, Lebanon	Signed 24 June 2004; in force 1 January 2007
EFTA–Macedonia FTA	EFTA–Macedonia Free Trade Agreement	EFTA states, Macedonia	Signed 19 June 2000; in force 1 May 2002
EFTA–Mexico FTA	EFTA–Mexico Free Trade Agreement	EFTA states, Mexico	Signed 27 November 2000; in force 1 July 2001
EFTA–Montenegro FTA	EFTA–Montenegro Free Trade Agreement	EFTA States, Montenegro	Signed 14 November 2011; in force 1 October 2012 with Iceland, Liechtenstein and Switzerland and 1 November 2012 with Norway
EFTA–Morocco FTA	EFTA–Morocco Free Trade Agreement	EFTA states, Morocco	Signed 19 June 1997; in force 1 December 1999
EFTA–Palestinian Authority FTA	EFTA–Palestinian Authority Free Trade Agreement	EFTA states, Palestinian Authority	Signed 30 November 1998; in force 1 July 1999
EFTA–SACU FTA	EFTA–SACU Free Trade Agreement	EFTA states, SACU states	Signed 26 June 2006; in force 1 May 2008
EFTA–Singapore FTA	EFTA–Singapore Free Trade Agreement	EFTA states, Singapore	Signed 26 June 2002; in force 1 January 2003

Liechtenstein and Switzerland and 1 November 2012 with Norway; Side Agreement on Labour between Hong Kong, China and the EFTA States

(3) (*cont.*)

Short title	Long title	Current parties (or membership immediately prior to extinction) (unless otherwise indicated)	Status
EFTA–Tunisia FTA	EFTA–Tunisia Free Trade Agreement	EFTA states, Tunisia	Signed 17 December 2004; in force 1 June 2005
EFTA–Turkey FTA	EFTA–Turkey Free Trade Agreement	EFTA states, Turkey	Signed 10 December 1991; in force 1 April 1992
EU/EC/EEC/European Treaties	Treaty of the European Union/ Treaty Establishing the European Communities	Austria, Belgium, Bulgaria, Cyprus, Czech Republic, Denmark, Estonia, Finland, France, Germany, Greece, Hungary, Ireland, Italy, Latvia, Lithuania, Luxembourg, Malta, Netherlands, Poland, Portugal Romania, Slovakia, Slovenia, Spain, Sweden, United Kingdom	EEC (Treaty of Rome): signed 25 March 1957; in force 25 March 1957 EU (Maastricht Treaty): signed 7 February 1992; in force 1 November 1993 EU Enlargement (25): accession 1 May 2004 EU Enlargement (27): accession 1 January 2007
EU–Algeria AA	European Union–Algeria Association Agreement	European Union, Algeria	Signed 22 April 2002; in force 1 September 2005
EU–CARIFORUM EPA	Economic Partnership Agreement between the CARIFORUM States and the European Community	European Union, Antigua and Barbuda, Bahamas, Barbados, Belize, Dominica, Dominican Republic, Grenada, Guyana, Haiti, Jamaica, St. Christopher and Nevis, St. Lucia, St. Vincent and the Grenadines, Suriname, Trinidad and Tobago	Signed 15 October 2008; in force 29 December 2008

EU–Central America AA	EU–Central America Association Agreement	European Union, Costa Rica, El Salvador, Guatemala, Honduras, Nicaragua, Panama	Signed 29 June 2012; provisionally applied since 1 August 2013 with Honduras, Nicaragua and Panama, since 1 October 2013 with Costa Rica and El Salvador, and since 1 December 2013 with Guatemala
EU–Chile AA	European Union–Chile Association Agreement	Chile, European Union	Signed 18 November 2002; in force 1 March 2005
EU–Colombia and Peru Trade Agreement	European Union–Colombia and Peru Trade Agreement	Colombia, Peru, European Union	Signed 26 June 2012; in force 1 August 2013
EU–Croatia SAA	European Union–Croatia Stabilisation and Association Agreement	European Union, Croatia	Signed 29 October 2001; in force 1 February 2005
EU–Egypt AA	European Union–Egypt Association Agreement	Egypt, European Union	Signed 25 June 2001; in force 1 June 2004
EU–FYROM SAA	European Union–Former Yugoslav Republic of Macedonia Stabilisation and Association Agreement	European Union, FYROM	Signed 9 April 2001; in force 1 April 2004
EU–Israel AA	European Union–Israel Association Agreement	European Union, Israel	Signed 20 November 1995; in force 1 June 2000
EU–Jordan AA	European Union–Jordan Association Agreement	European Union, Jordan	Signed 24 November 1997; in force 1 May 2002
EU–Korea	EU–Korea Free Trade Agreement	European Union, South Korea	Signed 15 October 2009; in force 1 July 2011
EU–Lebanon AA	European Union–Lebanon Association Agreement	European Union, Lebanon	Signed 17 June 2002; in force 1 April 2006

(3) (*cont.*)

Short title	Long title	Current parties (or membership immediately prior to extinction) (unless otherwise indicated)	Status
EU–MERCOSUR Framework Agreement	European Union–MERCOSUR Interregional Framework Cooperation Agreement	European Union, MERCOSUR countries	Signed 15 December 1995; in force 1 July 1999
EU–Mexico FTA	European Union–Mexico Economic Partnership, Political Co-ordination and Co-operation Agreement	European Union, Mexico	Signed 8 December 1997; in force 1 October 2000
EU–Morocco AA	European Union–Morocco Association Agreement	European Union, Morocco	Signed 26 February 1996; in force 1 March 2000
EU–Palestinian Authority Interim AA	European Union–Palestinian Authority Interim Association Agreement	European Union, Palestinian Authority	Signed 24 February 1997; in force 1 July 1997
EU–SA TDCA	European Union–South Africa Trade, Development and Co-operation Agreement	European Union, South Africa	Signed 11 October 1999; in force 1 May 2004
EU–Syria AA	EU–Syria Association Agreement	European Union, Syria	Initialled 19 October 2004; yet to be signed
EU–Tunisia AA	European Union–Tunisia Association Agreement	European Union, Tunisia	Signed 17 July 1995; in force 1 March 1998
Faroe Islands–Norway FTA	Faroe Islands–Norway Free Trade Agreement	Faroe Islands, Norway	Signed 28 August 1992; in force 1 July 1993
Hoyvik Agreement	Hoyvik Agreement	Faroe Island, Iceland	Signed 31 August 2005; ratified 2 May 2006 (Faroe Island) and 3 June 2006 (Iceland)

FTAA	Free Trade Area of the Americas	Antigua and Barbuda, Argentina, Bahamas, Barbados, Belize, Bolivia, Brazil, Canada, Chile, Colombia, Costa Rica, Dominica, Dominican Republic, Ecuador, El Salvador, Grenada, Guatemala, Guyana, Haiti, Honduras, Jamaica, Mexico, Nicaragua, Panama, Paraguay, Peru, St. Kitts and Nevis, St. Lucia, St. Vincent and the Grenadines, Suriname, Trinidad and Tobago, United States, Uruguay, Venezuela	Ministerial Declaration of Miami, 8th Ministerial Meeting, adopted 20 November 2003
G–3 FTA	Group of Three (G–3) Free Trade Agreement *now known as the Mexico–Colombia Free Trade Agreement after Venezuela's withdrawal 22 May 2006*	Colombia, Mexico, Venezuela	Signed 13 June 1994; in force 1 January 1995
GAFTA	Greater Arab Free Trade Area	Jordan, Bahrain, United Arab Emirates, Tunisia, Saudi Arabia, Syria, Iraq, Oman, Qatar, Kuwait, Lebanon, Libya, Egypt, Morocco, Sudan, Yemen, Palestinian Authority	Signed 19 February 1997; in force 1 January 1998
Georgia–Armenia FTA	Georgia–Armenia Free Trade Agreement	Armenia, Georgia	Signed 14 August 1995; in force 11 November 1998
India–Nepal FTA	India–Nepal Trade Treaty	India, Nepal	Signed 1951; last renewal 6 March 2002

(3) (*cont.*)

Short title	Long title	Current parties (or membership immediately prior to extinction) (unless otherwise indicated)	Status
India–Singapore CECA	India–Singapore Comprehensive Economic Co-operation Agreement	India, Singapore	Signed 29 June 2005; in force 1 August 2005
India–Sri Lanka FTA	India–Sri Lanka Free Trade Agreement	India, Sri Lanka	Signed 28 December 1998; in force 1 March 2000
Japan–Brunei EPA	Japan–Brunei Darussalam Economic Partnership Agreement	Japan, Brunei Darussalam	Signed in June 2007; in force 2008
Japan–Chile EPA	Japan–Chile Economic Partnership Agreement	Chile, Japan	Signed 27 March 2007; in force 3 September 2007
Japan–India CEPA	Japan–India Comprehensive Economic Partnership Agreement	India, Japan	Signed 16 February 2011; in force 1 August 2011
Japan–Malaysia EPA	Japan–Malaysia Economic Partnership Agreement	Japan, Malaysia	Signed 13 December 2005; in force 13 July 2006
Japan–Mexico EPA	Japan–Mexico Economic Partnership Agreement	Japan, Mexico	Signed 17 September 2004; in force 1 April 2005
Japan–Peru FTA	Japan–Peru Free Trade Agreement	Japan, Peru	Signed 31 May 2011; in force 1 March 2012
Japan–Philippines EPA	Japan–Philippines Economic Partnership Agreement	Japan, Philippines	Signed 8 September 2006; in force 11 December 2008
Japan–Singapore EPA	Japan–Singapore New-Age Economic Partnership Agreement	Japan, Singapore	Signed 13 January 2002; in force 30 November 2002
Japan–Thailand EPA	Japan–Thailand Economic Partnership Agreement	Japan, Thailand	Signed 3 April 2007; in force 1 November 2007

Abbreviation	Full name	Parties	Dates
JSFTEPA	Japan–Switzerland Free Trade and Economic Partnership Agreement	Japan, Switzerland	Signed 19 February 2009; in force 1 September 2009
KAFTA	Korea–Australia Free Trade Agreement	Australia, South Korea	Signed 8 April 2014, not yet in force
Korea–Chile FTA	Korea–Chile Free Trade Agreement	Chile, South Korea	Signed 15 February 2003; in force 1 April 2004
Korea–Singapore FTA	Korea–Singapore Free Trade Agreement	Singapore, South Korea	Signed 4 August 2005; in force 2 March 2006
KORUS FTA	Korea–United States Free Trade Agreement	South Korea, United States	Signed 30 June 2007; in force 15 March 2012
Kyrgyzstan–Moldova FTA	Kyrgyzstan–Moldova Free Trade Agreement	Kyrgyzstan, Moldova	Signed 26 May 1995; in force 21 November 1996
LAFTA	Latin American Free Trade Association	Argentina, Bolivia, Brazil, Chile, Colombia, Ecuador, Mexico, Paraguay, Peru, Uruguay, Venezuela	Signed 18 February 1960; in force 2 June 1961
Lomé Convention	Lomé Convention	ACP countries, European Union	First Lomé Convention: signed 28 February 1975; in force 1 April 1976

Second Lomé Convention: signed 31 October 1979; in force 1 January 1981

Third Lomé Convention: signed 8 December 1984; in force 1 May 1986

Fourth Lomé Convention: signed 15 December 1989; in force 1 March 1990 |

(3) (*cont.*)

Short title	Long title	Current parties (or membership immediately prior to extinction) (unless otherwise indicated)	Status
Macedonia–Romania FTA	Macedonia– Romania Free Trade Agreement	Macedonia, Romania	Signed 7 February 2003; in force 1 January 2004
MERCOSUR	Common Market of the Southern Cone (Mercado Común del Sur)	Argentina, Brazil, Paraguay, Uruguay	Signed 26 March 1991; in force 29 November 1991
Mexico–Bolivia FTA	Mexico–Bolivia Free Trade Agreement	Bolivia, Mexico	Signed 10 September 1994; in force 1 January 1995
Mexico–Central America FTA	Mexico–Central America Free Trade Agreement	Mexico, Costa Rica, El Salvador, Guatemala, Honduras and Nicaragua	Signed 22 November 2011, in force 1 January 2013 with Honduras, 1 July 2013 with Costa Rica, 1 September 2013 with Guatemala
Mexico–Chile FTA	Mexico–Chile Free Trade Agreement	Chile, Mexico	Signed 1 October 1998; in force 1 August 1999
Mexico–Costa Rica FTA	Mexico–Costa Rica Free Trade Agreement	Costa Rica, Mexico	Signed 5 April 1994; in force 1 January 1995
Mexico–Israel FTA	Mexico–Israel Free Trade Agreement	Mexico, Israel	Signed 10 April 2000; in force 10 July 2000
Mexico–Nicaragua FTA	Mexico–Nicaragua Free Trade Agreement	Mexico, Nicaragua	Signed 18 December 1997; in force 1 July 1998
Mexico–Northern Triangle FTA	Mexico–Northern Triangle (El Salvador–Guatemala–Honduras) Free Trade Agreement	El Salvador, Guatemala, Honduras, Mexico	Signed 29 June 2000; in force 14 March 2001 (Mexico), 15 March 2001 (El Salvador, Guatemala), 1 June 2001 (Honduras)

Abbreviation	Full name	Parties	Details
Mexico–Uruguay FTA	Mexico–Uruguay Free Trade Agreement	Mexico, Uruguay	Signed 15 November 2003; in force 15 July 2004
Mexico–Venezuela FTA	Mexico–Venezuela Free Trade Agreement	Mexico, Venezuela	Signed 22 May 2006; in force 19 November 2006
MRU	Mano River Union	Guinea, Liberia, Sierra Leone	Established 3 October 1973
NAFTA	North American Free Trade Agreement	Canada, Mexico, United States	Signed 17 December 1992; in force 1 January 1994 North American Agreement on Environmental Co-operation (NAAEC) signed 14 September 1993; in force 1 January 1994 North American Agreement on Labor Cooperation (NAALC) signed 14 September 1993; in force 1 January 1994
Nicaragua–Taiwan FTA	Nicaragua–Taiwan Free Trade Agreement	Nicaragua, Taiwan	Signed 16 June 2006; in force 11 July 2008
NZ–Australia FTA	New Zealand–Australia Free Trade Agreement	Australia, New Zealand	Signed 31 August 1965; in force 1 January 1966
NZ–China FTA	New Zealand–China Free Trade Agreement	China, New Zealand	Signed 7 April 2008, in force 1 October 2008
NZ–Malaysia	New Zealand–Malaysia Free Trade Agreement	Malaysia, New Zealand	Signed 26 October 2009; in force 1 August 2010: New Zealand–Malaysia Agreement on Labour Cooperation (side agreement) New Zealand–Malaysia Agreement on Labour Cooperation (side agreement)

(3) (*cont.*)

Short title	Long title	Current parties (or membership immediately prior to extinction) (unless otherwise indicated)	Status
NZ–Singapore CEPA	New Zealand–Singapore Closer Economic Partnership Agreement	New Zealand, Singapore	Signed 14 November 2000; in force 1 January 2001
NZ–Thailand CEPA	New Zealand–Thailand Closer Economic Partnership Agreement	New Zealand, Thailand	Signed 19 April 2005; in force 1 July 2005
Pakistan–Malaysia CEPA	Pakistan–Malaysia Closer Economic Partnership Agreement	Pakistan, Malaysia	Signed 8 November 2007; in force 1 January 2008
Panama–Taiwan FTA	Panama–Taiwan Free Trade Agreement	Panama, Taiwan	Signed 21 August 2003; in force 1 January 2004
PTA	Preferential Trade Area for Eastern and Southern African States	Angola, Burundi, Comoros, Djibouti, Eritrea, Ethiopia, Kenya, Lesotho, Madagascar, Malawi, Mauritius, Mozambique, Namibia, Rwanda, Seychelles, Somalia, Sudan, Swaziland, Tanzania, Uganda, Zambia, Zimbabwe	Signed 21 December 1981; in force 30 September 1982
Romania–Serbia–Montenegro FTA	Free Trade Agreement Between Romania and Serbia and Montenegro	Serbia and Montenegro, and Romania	Signed 4 September 1996; in force 16 October 1996
SACU	Southern African Customs Union	Botswana, Lesotho, Namibia, South Africa, Swaziland	Signed 11 December 1969; in force 1 March 1970

SADC	Southern African Development Community	Angola, Botswana, Democratic Republic of Congo, Lesotho, Madagascar, Malawi, Mauritius, Mozambique, Namibia, South Africa, Swaziland, Tanzania, Zambia, Zimbabwe	Signed 17 August 1992; in force 30 September 1993
SADCC	Southern African Development Co-ordination Conference	Angola, Botswana, Lesotho, Malawi, Mozambique, Swaziland, Tanzania, Zambia, Zimbabwe	Signed 1 April 1980; in force 20 July 1981
Singapore–Australia FTA	Singapore–Australia Free Trade Agreement	Australia, Singapore	Signed 17 February 2003; in force 28 July 2003
Singapore–Jordan FTA	Singapore–Jordan Free Trade Agreement	Jordan, Singapore	Signed 16 May 2004; in force 22 August 2005
Singapore–Panama FTA	Singapore Panama Free Agreement	Panama, Singapore	Signed 1 March 2006; in force 24 July 2006
Singapore–Taiwan FTA (also ASTEP)	Agreement between Singapore and the Separate Customs Territory of Taiwan, Penghu, Kinmen and Matsu on Economic Partnership	Singapore, Taiwan	Signed 7 November 2013; in force 19 April 2014
Thailand–Australia FTA	Thailand–Australia Free Trade Agreement	Australia, Thailand	Signed 5 July 2004; in force 1 January 2005
Trans-Pacific SEP (*also referred to as* P4 Agreement)	Trans-Pacific Strategic Economic Partnership	Brunei, Chile, New Zealand, Singapore	Signed 18 July 2005 (Chile, New Zealand, Singapore), 2 August 2005 (Brunei); in force 28 May 2006 (New Zealand, Singapore), 12 July 2006 (Brunei), 8 November 2006 (Chile)

(3) (*cont.*)

Short title	Long title	Current parties (or membership immediately prior to extinction) (unless otherwise indicated)	Status
Treaty of Balta Liman	Treaty of Balta Liman	Ottoman Empire, United Kingdom of Great Britain and Northern Ireland	Signed 16 August 1838
Treaty of Lisbon	Treaty of Lisbon	EU members	Signed 13 December 2007; in force 1 December 2009, modified the Treaty on the European Union(TEU) and renamed the Treaty establishing the European Community to Treaty on the Functioning of the European Union (TFEU)
T-TIP	Transatlantic Trade and Investment partnership	European Union, United States	Under negotiation
TTP	Trans-Pacific Partnership	United States, Australia, Brunei Darussalam, Canada, Chile, Japan, Malaysia, Mexico, New Zealand, Peru, Singapore, and Vietnam	Under negotiation
Turkey–Albania FTA	Turkey–Albania Free Trade Agreement	Albania, Turkey	Signed 22 December 2006; in force 1 May 2008
Turkey–Chile FTA	Turkey–Chile Free Trade Agreement	Chile, Turkey	Signed 14 July 2009; in force 1 March 2011
Turkey–Macedonia FTA	Turkey–Macedonia Free Trade Agreement	Macedonia, Turkey	Signed 7 September 1999; in force 1 September 2000
Turkey–Morocco FTA	Turkey–Morocco Free Trade Agreement	Morocco, Turkey	Signed 7 April 2004; in force 1 January 2006

Turkey–PLO FTA	Turkey–Palestine Liberation Organisation Free Trade Agreement	Palestinian Authority, Turkey	Signed 20 July 2004; in force on 1 June 2005
UDAO/WACU	West African Customs Union (Union Douanière des États de l'Afrique Occidentale)	Benin (*then* Dahomey), Burkina Faso (*then* Upper Volta), Côte d'Ivoire, Mali, Mauritania, Niger, Senegal	Established 9 June 1959
UDE/ECU	Equatorial Customs Union (Union Douanière Equatoriale)	Cameroon, Central African Republic, Chad, Republic of the Congo, Gabon	Established 23 June 1959
UDEAC/CACEU	Central African Customs and Economic Union/Customs and Economic Union of Central Africa (Union Douanière et Économique de l'Afrique Centrale)	Cameroon, Central African Republic, Chad, Republic of Congo, Equatorial Guinea, Gabon	Signed 8 December 1964; in force 1 January 1966
UDEAO/CUWAS	Customs Union of West African States/West African Customs and Economic Union (Union Douanière et Économique de l'Afrique de l'Ouest)	Benin (*then* Dahomey), Burkino Faso, Côte d'Ivoire, Mali, Mauritania, Niger, Senegal	Established 3 June 1966
UEMOA/WAEMU	West African Economic and Monetary Union/Economic and Monetary Union of West Africa (Union Économique et Monétaire Ouest-Africaine)	Benin, Burkina Faso, Côte d'Ivoire, Guinea-Bissau, Mali, Niger, Senegal, Togo	Established 10 January 1994
Ukraine–Montenegro FTA	Ukraine–Montenegro Free Trade Agreement	Ukraine, Montenegro	Signed 18 November 2011; in force 1 January 2013
US–Andean TPA	United States–Andean Countries Trade Promotion Agreement	Bolivia, Colombia, Ecuador, Peru, United States	Signed 12 April 2006 (Peru, United States), 22 November 2006 (Colombia, United States); in force 1 February 2009

(3) (*cont.*)

Short title	Long title	Current parties (or membership immediately prior to extinction) (unless otherwise indicated)	Status
US–Bahrain FTA	United States–Bahrain Free Trade Agreement	Bahrain, United States	Signed 14 September 2004; in force 1 January 2006
US–Chile FTA	United States–Chile Free Trade Agreement	Chile, United States	Signed 6 June 2003; in force 1 January 2004
US–Colombia TPA	United States–Colombia Trade Promotion Agreement	Colombia, United States	Signed 22 November 2006; in force 15 May 2012
US–Israel FTA	United States–Israel Free Trade Agreement	Israel, United States	Signed 22 April 1985; in force 1 September 1985
US–Jordan FTA	United States–Jordan Free Trade Agreement	Jordan, United States	Signed 24 October 2000; in force 17 December 2001
US–South Korea FTA (KORUS FTA)	United States–South Korea Free Trade Agreement	South Korea, United States	Signed 30 June 2007; in force 15 March 2012
US–Morocco FTA	United States–Morocco Free Trade Agreement	Morocco, United States	Signed 15 June 2004; in force 1 January 2006
US–Omar FTA	United States–Oman Free Trade Agreement	Oman, United States	Signed 19 January 2006; in force 1 January 2009
US–Panama TPA	United States–Panama Trade Promotion Agreement	Panama, United States	Signed 28 June 2007; in force 21 October 2011 United States Panama Agreement Regarding Certain Sanitary and Phytosanitary Measures and Technical Standards Affecting Trade in Agricultural Products (side agreement), in force 20 December 2006

US–Peru TPA	United States–Peru Trade Promotion Agreement	Peru, United States	Signed 4 December 2006; in force 1 February 2009
US–Singapore FTA	United States–Singapore Free Trade Agreement	Singapore, United States	Signed 6 May 2003; in force 1 January 2004
US–South Korea FTA	United States–South Korea Free Trade Agreement	South Korea, United States	Signed 30 June 2007; not in force

(4) *Bilateral investment treaties and international investment agreements*

Short title	Long title	Parties	Status
AIA Framework Agreement	Framework Agreement on the ASEAN Investment Area (AIA)	Brunei, Indonesia, Laos, Malaysia, Myanmar, Philippines, Singapore, Thailand, Vietnam	Signed 7 October 1998
CCIA Investment Framework Agreement	Investment Framework Agreement for the COMESA Common Investment Area	Angola, Burundi, Comoros, Democratic Republic of Congo, Djibouti, Egypt, Eritrea, Ethiopia, Kenya, Madagascar, Malawi, Mauritius, Rwanda, Seychelles, Sudan, Swaziland, Uganda, Zambia, Zimbabwe	Draft as of 2003
Germany–China BIT	Agreement between the People's Republic of China and the Federal Republic of Germany on the Encouragement and Reciprocal Protection of Investments	China, Germany	Signed 1 December 2003
Germany–Ethiopia BIT	Treaty between the Federal Republic of Germany and the Empire of Ethiopia	Ethiopia, Germany	Signed 21 April 1964
Italy–Jordan BIT	Agreement between the Government of the Hashemite Kingdom of Jordan and the Government of the Italian Republic on the Promotion and Protection of Investments	Italy, Jordan	Signed 21 July 1996

Spain–Argentina BIT	Agreement on the Reciprocal Promotion and Protection of Investments signed by the Kingdom of Spain and the Argentine Republic	Argentina, Spain	Signed 3 October 1991
Spain–Mexico BIT	Agreement on the Reciprocal Promotion and Protection of Investments signed by the Kingdom of Spain and the United Mexican States	Mexico, Spain	In force 18 December 1996
Sweden–Laos BIT	Agreement between the Government of the Kingdom of Sweden and the Government of the Lao People's Democratic Republic on the Promotion and Reciprocal Protection of Investments	Laos (Lao PDR), Sweden	Signed 29 August 1996
Sweden–Philippines BIT	Agreement between the Government of the Republic of the Philippines and the Government of the Kingdom of Sweden on the Promotion and Reciprocal Protection of Investments	Philippines, Sweden	Signed 18 August 1993
Switzerland–Iran BIT	Agreement between the Swiss Confederation and the Islamic Republic of Iran on the Promotion and Reciprocal Protection of Investments	Iran, Switzerland	Signed 8 March 1998

(4) (*cont.*)

Short title	Long title	Parties	Status
Switzerland–Jordan BIT	Agreement between the Hashemite Kingdom of Jordan and the Swiss Confederation on the Promotion and Reciprocal Protection of Investments	Jordan, Switzerland	Signed 11 November 1976
United States–Argentina BIT	Treaty between the United States of America and the Argentine Republic Concerning the Reciprocal Encouragement and Protection of Investments	Argentina, United States	Signed 14 November 1991; in force 20 October 1994

(5) *Wine and spirits agreements*

Short title	Full title	Parties	Status
EC–Australia Wine Agreement 1994	Agreement between Australia and the European Community on Trade in Wine	Australia, European Union	Signed 26 January 1994 (at Brussels) and 31 January 1994 (at Canberra); in force 1 March 1994, superseded by EC–Australia Wine Agreement 2008
EC–Australia Wine Agreement 2008	Agreement between the European Community and Australia on Trade in Wine	Australia, European Union	Signed 1 December 2008, in force 1 September 2010
EC–Canada Wine and Spirits Agreement	Agreement between the European Community and Canada on Trade in Wines and Spirit Drinks	Canada, European Union	Signed 16 September 2003; in force 1 June 2004
EC–Chile Spirits Agreement	Agreement establishing an association between the European Community and its Member States, of the one part, and the Republic of Chile, of the other part (Annex VI: Agreement on Trade in Spirit Drinks and Aromatised Drinks)	Chile, European Union	Signed 14 February 2006
EC–Chile Wine Agreement	Agreement establishing an association between the European Community and its Member States, of the one part, and the Republic of Chile, of the other part (Annex V: Agreement on Trade in Wines)	Chile, European Union	Signed 14 February 2006

(5) (cont.)

Short title	Full title	Parties	Status
EC–Mexico Spirits Agreement	Agreement between the European Community and the United Mexican States on the Mutual Recognition and Protection of Designations for Spirit Drinks	European Union, Mexico	Signed 27 May 1997
EC–South Africa Spirits Agreement	Agreement between the European Community and the Republic of South Africa on Trade in Spirits	European Union, South Africa	Signed 28 January 2002
EC–South Africa Wine Agreement	Agreement between the European Community and the Republic of South Africa on Trade in Wines	European Union, South Africa	Signed 28 January 2002
EC–Switzerland Spirits Agreement	Agreement between the European Community and the Swiss Confederation on Trade in Agricultural Products (Annex 8)	European Union, Switzerland	Signed 21 June 1999
EC–Switzerland Wine Agreement	Agreement between the European Community and the Swiss Confederation on Trade in Agricultural Products (Annex 7)	European Union, Switzerland	Signed 21 June 1999
EC–US Wine Agreement	Agreement between the European Community and the United States of America on Trade in Wine	European Union, United States	Signed 10 March 2006

ABBREVIATIONS

ACP	African–Caribbean–Pacific
ACTA	Anti-Counterfeiting Trade Agreement
AMS	Aggregate Measurement of Support
APEC	Asia–Pacific Economic Co-operation
ASEAN	Association of Southeast Asian Nations
BIT	Bilateral Investment Treaty
BTA	Bilateral Trade Agreement
CACM	Central American Common Market
CAFTA	Central America Free Trade Agreement
CAP	Common Agriculture Policy
CARICOM	Caribbean Common Market
CARIFORUM	Caribbean Forum
CCRAEC	Canada–Costa Rica Agreement on Environmental Co-operation
CCRALC	Canada–Costa Rica Agreement on Labour Co-operation
CEECs	Central and Eastern European Countries
CEFTA	Central European Free Trade Area
CEPT	Common Effective Preferential Tariff
CIS	Commonwealth of Independent States
CJEU	Court of Justice of the European Union
CMO	Common Market Organisation
CRTA	Committee on Regional Trade Agreements
CU	Customs Union
DCFA	Deep and Comprehensive Free Trade Agreement
DDA	Doha Development Agenda
DSB	Dispute Settlement Body
DSM	Dispute Settlement Mechanism
DSU	Understanding on Rules and Procedures Governing the Settlement of Disputes
EBA	Everything But Arms
EC	European Community
ECHR	European Court of Human Rights
ECJ	European Court of Justice

ECLA	Economic Commission for Latin America
ECOSOC	Economic and Social Council of the United Nations
EEC	European Economic Community
EFTA	European Free Trade Association
EIA	Economic Integration Agreement
EU	European Union
EU Treaty/EC Treaty	Treaty of the European Treaty/Union Establishing the European Communities
FNC	Friendship, Navigation and Commerce
FTA	Free Trade Agreement
GATS	General Agreement on Trade in Services
GATT	General Agreement on Tariffs and Trade
GCC	Gulf Cooperation Council
GDP	Gross Domestic Product
GI	Geographical Indications
GPA	Government Procurement Agreement
GSP	Generalised System of Preferences
Havana Charter	Havana Charter for an International Trade Organisation
ICJ	International Court of Justice
ICJ Statute	Statute of the International Court of Justice
ICSID	International Centre for Settlement of Investment Disputes
ICTSD	International Centre for Trade and Sustainable Development
ILC	International Law Commission
ILO	International Labour Organization
IMF	International Monetary Fund
IP	Intellectual Property
ISDS	Investor–State Dispute Settlement
ITO	International Trade Organization
MEA	Multilateral Environmental Agreement
MERCOSUR	Common Market of the Southern Cone
MFN	Most Favoured Nation
NAAEC	North American Agreement on Environmental Co-operation
NAALC	North American Agreement on Labor Co-operation
NAFTA	North American Free Trade Agreement
NGO	Non-Governmental Organisation
NT	National Treatment
OECD	Organisation of Economic Co-operation and Development
OECS	Organisation of East Caribbean States

OPEC	Organisation of Petroleum-Exporting Countries
ORC	Other Regulations of Commerce
ORRC	Other Restrictive Regulations of Commerce
PCIJ	Permanent Court of International Justice
PTA	Preferential Trade Agreement
RCEP	Regional Comprehensive Economic Partnership
RMP	Regional Margin of Preference
ROO	Rules of Origin
RTA	Regional Trade Agreement
RTAA	Reciprocal Trade Agreements Act
SACU	Southern African Customs Union
SCM	Subsidies and Countervailing Measures
SPS	Sanitary and Phytosanitary Agreement
TBT	Technical Barriers to Trade
TEU	Treaty on European Union
TFEU	Treaty on the Functioning of the European Union
TIFA	Trade and Investment Framework Agreement
TPA	Trade Promotion Agreement
TPP	Trans-Pacific Partnership Agreement
TRIMs	Agreement on Trade-Related Investment Measures
TRIPS	Agreement on Trade-Related Aspects of Intellectual Property Rights
TRQ	Tariff-Rate Quotas
TTIP	Transatlantic Trade and Investment Partnership
UK	United Kingdom
UN	United Nations
UN Charter	Charter of the United Nations
UNCITRAL	United Nations Commission on International Trade Law
UNCTAD	United Nations Conference on Trade and Development
UNESCO	United Nations Educational, Scientific and Cultural Organisation
US	United States of America
USSR	Union of Soviet Socialist Republics/Soviet Union
USTR	United States Trade Representative
Vienna Convention	Vienna Convention on the Law of Treaties, 1969
WIPO	World Intellectual Property Organisation
Working Procedures	Working Procedures for Appellate Review
World Bank	International Bank for Reconstruction and Development
WTO	World Trade Organization
WTO Agreement	Marrakesh Agreement Establishing the World Trade Organization

PART I

Introduction

1

Introduction

SIMON LESTER, BRYAN MERCURIO
AND LORAND BARTELS

The modern history of the world trading system, and in particular international trade agreements, is evidenced by shifts among bilateralism, regionalism and multilateralism. In the late nineteenth century and early twentieth century, bilateralism was clearly dominant. Trade agreements were negotiated on a bilateral basis between individual countries. In the 1860s and 1870s, England initiated much of this activity, pushing its trading partners to sign trade agreements that reciprocally lowered tariff rates. In the 1930s, it was the United States (US) that made a big push in this area through its Reciprocal Trade Agreements programme, although a number of other countries were also active in negotiating bilateral agreements to lower tariff rates.

However, immediately after World War II, multilateralism and regionalism replaced bilateralism as the dominant approach. From the late 1940s to the mid-1990s, multilateralism grew in strength as more and more nations joined the GATT or its successor, the WTO. The GATT, which began with 23 countries, unquestionably came to dominate the world trading scene. It did not, however, completely replace regional and bilateral trade agreements. Regionalism remained a competing model, as nations in Europe, North America, South America and elsewhere all formed trading blocs during this period. East Asia was the only region to eschew regionalism, while Western Europe was the clear leader in terms of both the timing and the scope of its economic integration, with other regions following behind. Bilateralism, on the other hand, diminished considerably during this period. Such agreements were extremely rare, and where they did exist could usually be explained mostly by political, rather than economic, factors.

More recently, though, bilateralism has returned with a vengeance. The initial return to bilateralism can be traced to the breakup of the Soviet Union and collapse of Communism in the early 1990s. The newly formed nations, along with several Eastern European economies in transition from a centrally planned to a market-based economy, led a mini-revival of bilateralism in the mid to late 1990s. Bilateralism, however, only significantly gained momentum following the failed WTO negotiations at the 1999 Seattle Ministerial Conference. Prior to 1999, it was rare for the major trading powers to negotiate and sign bilateral trade agreements. Following the failed Ministerial Conference, all major trading nations (including the East Asian nations) almost immediately launched multiple negotiations. A large number of such agreements have now been negotiated and signed, and many more are currently being negotiated. The rapid increase in the total number of agreements has created a competitive process among nations, with all of the major trading powers pushing hard to conclude these agreements so as not to lose particular markets to their competitors.

In addition to bilateral agreements, there are also a growing number of what could be termed 'loose' regional trade agreements (RTAs). These are concluded among several countries in the same 'region', with the term region more loosely defined than in previous eras. These agreements are, in essence, plurilateral agreements among countries which may or may not be in somewhat close proximity to each other, but do not necessarily include all countries from that area. For example, the North American Free Trade Agreement (NAFTA), a more traditional RTA, was signed in 1993 by Canada, the US and Mexico: three contiguous countries of North America. By contrast, in 2006 the Central America–Dominican Republic–United States Free Trade Agreement (CAFTA–DR–US) was signed by the US, a few Central American countries and the Dominican Republic. All are in the same general region, but there are many other countries within that region which were not included. On the other hand, the once-labelled Trans-Pacific Strategic Economic Partnership Agreement (P4) between Brunei, Chile, New Zealand and Singapore cannot be said to even remotely resemble nations in close proximity to one another (although admittedly all members are linked by the Pacific Ocean). Its successor, the Trans-Pacific Partnership Agreement (TPP), is currently being negotiated by countries as diverse as the US, Australia, Japan, Malaysia and Vietnam.

The TPP negotiations signal the latest trend in trade policy, that of the 'mega-regional' agreement between two or more large trading nations. Until recently, most trade agreements consisted of a larger partner and one or more smaller partner countries (the 'hub and spoke' model). The situation has now shifted, with economically powerful nations reaching agreements between and among themselves. Examples of current negotiations include the US–European Union (EU) and China–Japan–Korea. These follow completed 'blockbusters' such as US–Korea and EU–Korea, and the negotiated but not yet in force agreement between Canada and the EU.

The result of the proliferation of these agreements is that today's international trade rules now consist of a number of instruments. At the forefront, there is the multilateral WTO Agreement, which includes 161 countries or customs territories. In addition, there are the traditional regional trading blocs, each with their own agreements, some of which provide for deep integration or customs unions among the member countries. Then, there is the complex web of bilateral trade agreements between individual countries. Finally, there is a growing number of 'loose' regional agreements. All of these agreements – over 400 in total – exist together, creating a mish-mash of overlapping, supporting, and possibly conflicting, obligations.

Perhaps even more important than the sheer quantity of trade agreements are their scope and coverage. While the nineteenth- and early twentieth-century bilateral agreements were often narrowly focused on reducing tariffs, the more recent ones contain obligations that are wide-ranging and controversial, from investment provisions to intellectual property rights affecting access to medicines to protections for labour/human rights and the environment and against abuses from anti-competitive behaviour and state-owned enterprises. While the full impact that these agreements will have on domestic policy-making is uncertain, it is clear that a number of agreements are going beyond the coverage of the WTO as well as the regional and bilateral agreements negotiated prior to 1999, and reaching a new level of international policy-making.

Before turning to the structure of this volume, it is worth noting an important definitional point: What should this recent wave of agreements be called? Above, we have referred to 'bilateral trade agreements' and 'loose' 'regional trade agreements'. Most often, these agreements are referred to as 'free trade' agreements, and, in fact, many of the agreements have 'free trade' in the title (although others use more general terms such as 'economic partnership' agreements). Some commentators have also taken to referring to the collection of bilateral and regional trade agreements as 'preferential trade agreements'.

The term 'free trade agreements' (FTAs) has advantages in that it is the most commonly used term and is the term used in many agreements. On the negative side, it excludes customs unions, which these agreements sometimes are, and it perhaps puts the agreements in an overly positive, not to mention inaccurate, light. For instance, it could be argued that favouring certain countries in trade relations, as these agreements do, is not 'free trade' at all, but rather discriminatory trade. Moreover, the vast majority of these agreements do not actually create 'free' trade between partner countries. For these reasons, the term 'preferential trade agreements' (PTAs) was created. This term is not used as often, and is not used in any of the agreements themselves. On the other hand, it is a common term for these agreements, and it is arguably more accurate in describing what these agreements do (they establish preferences for some countries over others in trade relations). The term 'PTAs' also has the advantage in that it can include both free trade agreements and customs unions. In a sense, 'bilateral and regional trade agreements', as we have titled the book, is the most all-encompassing and accurate term. But it is wordy, and does not have an acronym that is commonly recognised (i.e., few people will be used to seeing the term BRTA). As a result, we preferred the use of the term PTA throughout this collection, but have given the authors the freedom to vary their terminology as they see fit. We do not intend there to be any negative connotations with the choice or use of any of the terms.

The structure of the book

As mentioned above, the expansion of PTAs as a key part of the world trading system is a fairly recent development. The nature of trade relations has evolved even since the first edition of this collection was published in 2007. As indicated in that edition, we always intended to continue expanding this study through future editions. For the chapters covering specific substantive areas, the contributors have provided updates to take into account new agreements and innovations in treaty drafting. We have also added seven additional case studies, which form the basis of the companion to this collection. In this way, we hope the books and their future editions will continue to serve as a comprehensive and essential resource for understanding the role of PTAs in the international trade regime.

The spread of PTAs raises a number of interesting questions in terms of politics, international relations, international law, economics and global governance:

- What are the reasons for the recent interest in and growth of these agreements?
- How do the benefits of bilateral trade liberalisation compare with those of multilateral trade liberalisation?
- How do these new agreements relate to existing multilateral and regional trade agreements, and to international law more generally?
- What is the substantive scope of these agreements? That is, what policies do they promote and what obligations do they contain?
- How are these agreements negotiated among the various governments, and what is the role of non-state actors who have an interest in the agreements?

The second edition of this book attempts to provide some updated, but still preliminary answers to these questions. We say 'preliminary' because the development of these agreements is still ongoing. The end does not appear to be in sight yet, especially as the Doha Round continues on (and on) with no set timetable for completion. Thus, the analysis offered here is necessarily limited to what has occurred so far.

The book is structured as follows. Parts II and III will put these issues in context by providing some general background on the economics, politics, international relations and international law aspects of PTAs. For instance, Part II contains a chapter by Pravin Krishna of Johns Hopkins University, School of Advanced International Studies, evaluating the economics of PTAs. More specifically, Professor Krishna expands upon existing literature to find that the welfare effects of PTAs are ambiguous at best. The chapter also provides, *inter alia*, an interesting analysis on the design of PTAs with welfare-improving effects. Part II also contains a chapter on the political and international relations considerations of PTAs. Written by Olivier Cattaneo of the Jackson Institute at Yale University, the chapter asks the question 'Why do countries conclude PTAs?' and provides a unique assessment of both the historical and present situation, ultimately concluding that the political economy of PTAs revolves more around politics than economics. The final chapter is a practical analysis of some of the differences between bilateral PTAs and multi-party ones. In the chapter, David Evans of the New Zealand Ministry of Foreign Affairs and Trade demonstrates how the 'new generation' of plurilateral PTAs are a break from traditional bilateral PTAs and offer some challenging procedural and substantive issues, such as how such agreements are to be negotiated and structured to meet the needs (and ambitions) of all parties.

Part III situates PTAs in the wider context in which they exist. There are two aspects to this: (1) How do PTAs fit with the WTO, which prohibits discrimination among WTO Members but has an exception for free trade agreements and customs unions? and (2) How do PTAs fit within international law more generally? Part III begins with a chapter by Andrew Mitchell of the University of Melbourne, Faculty of Law, and Nicolas Lockhart of the law firm of Sidley Austin, examining the nature of the exception for PTAs under WTO rules. It outlines, in substantial detail, the conditions of the exception and concludes with an assessment of the likelihood of legal challenge to a PTA if it did not meet all of the conditions of the exception. Chapter 6, by Andrew Mitchell, Tania Voon and Elizabeth Sheargold, all of the University of Melbourne, Faculty of Law, provides a comprehensive analysis of the under-explored and often murky relationship of PTAs to international law. More specifically, Mitchell, Voon and Sheargold provide examples of difficult and unsettled issues surrounding the overlap between PTAs and public international law, including the particularly thorny issues of conflicting norms between two treaties/agreements and multiple dispute settlement systems that are capable of hearing the same dispute. Chapter 7 is a new addition to this collection. Authored by James Mathis of the University of Amsterdam, the chapter argues that the newer 'regulatory' or behind-the-border type issues being negotiated into modern trade agreements are more complementary to the multilateral trade system than the old tariff barrier regionalism, before examining the economic and legal implications of this emerging trend.

Part IV provides a detailed look at specific subject areas that are part of PTAs. In essence, this part offers a comparison across the various agreements, examining the scope of the law that is being created in seven important policy areas. First, Timothy Josling of Stanford University, Food Research Institute, analyses the contentious area of agriculture with reference to historical data as well as differences between bilateral and regional PTAs. Next, Federico Ortino of King's College London provides a review of services in the multilateral forum before comprehensively detailing how certain PTAs are creating GATS-Plus obligations. Joshua Meltzer from the Brookings Institute then contributes a thorough and detailed chapter on investment, focusing on both the wide-ranging obligations undertaken in the area as well as those areas which have caused much disagreement and dispute. Krista Nadakavukaren Schefer of the University of Basel and Arwel Davies of Swansea University, Faculty of Law, next provide a chapter on government procurement which illustrates how many agreements are hesitant to move substantially beyond the WTO model. Michael Handler of the University of New South Wales, Faculty of Law and Bryan Mercurio of the Chinese University of Hong Kong, Faculty of Law, provide a chapter on intellectual property which looks at three TRIPS-Plus areas of intellectual property: copyright, geographical indications and patents. Lorand Bartels of Cambridge University then analyses the inclusion of social issues, such as labour, environment and human rights, into PTAs. Finally, Simon Lester of WorldTradeLaw.net and the Cato Institute and Victoria Donaldson of the WTO Secretariat conclude with a detailed review of various dispute settlement provisions in PTAs, finding a general, but not perfect, correlation to the WTO model set out in the Dispute Settlement Understanding.

The companion volume to this book will again be made up of seven case studies of various PTAs, and will serve to complement the seven previous case studies featured in the first volume. We have again attempted to select a group of PTAs that includes a good sampling in terms of countries and regions covered, and also a sampling of agreements that address key issues (such as intellectual property and agriculture). Authored by leading scholars, practitioners and governmental officials, each case study provides a comprehensive review of particular agreements. The first two case studies involve Korea, and can be read together to compare and contrast scope, ambition and content. The first case study, authored by Y. S. (Steve) Lee of the Law and Development Institute and Jeremy Record, analyses the Korea–US FTA (KORUS), while Colin Brown of the European Commission then reviews the EU–Korea FTA. The third case study, authored by William Watson of the Cato Institute, reviews the US–Colombia FTA. The next two case studies involve China, and again can be read together for comparison and context. Henry Gao of the Singapore Management University outlines the China–New Zealand FTA, and Pasha Hsieh, also of the Singapore Management University, reviews the China–Taiwan Economic Cooperation Framework Agreement. In the sixth case study, Henning Grosse Ruse-Khan of the University of Cambridge and Chantal Ononaiwu of CARICOM provide an overview of the EU–Cariforum EPA. In the final case study, Meredith Kolsky Lewis of the University of Buffalo and Victoria University of Wellington outlines the ASEAN–Australia–New Zealand FTA.

With each edition published, the case studies become a comprehensive resource which should be useful in a number of ways. For example, each study can serve as an in-depth study of a particular PTA. Moreover, the group of case studies can be used to compare and contrast the coverage of different PTAs, or to examine the PTAs signed by a particular country.

Together, the commentary, analysis and case studies found in the companion volumes are the most comprehensive resource available to assist those interested in understanding the role of PTAs in the international trade regime. As events continue to evolve, we will continue expanding and refining the collection through updates of the substantive chapters and additional case studies.

PART II

Economics and politics of PTAs

2

The economics of PTAs

PRAVIN KRISHNA*

I. Introduction

Strongly influenced by the perception that restricted commerce and preferences in trade relations had contributed to the economic depression of the 1930s and the subsequent outbreak of war, the discussions leading to the General Agreement on Tariffs and Trade (GATT) in 1947 were driven by the desire to create an international economic order based on a liberal and non-discriminatory multilateral trade system. Enshrined in Article I of the GATT, the principle of non-discrimination (commonly referred to as the most-favoured-nation or MFN clause) precludes member countries from discriminating against imports based upon the country of origin. However, in an important exception to this central prescript, the GATT, through its Article XXIV, permits its members to enter into preferential trade agreements (PTAs), provided these preferences are complete. In so doing, it sanctions the formation of Free Trade Areas (FTAs), whose members are obligated to eliminate internal import barriers, and Customs Unions (CUs), whose members additionally agree on a common external tariff against imports from non-members. Additional derogations to the principle of non-discrimination now include the enabling clause, which allows tariff preferences to be granted to developing countries (in accordance with the generalised system of preferences) and permits preferential trade among developing countries.

Such PTAs are now in vogue. Even as multilateral approaches to trade liberalisation – through negotiations organised by the GATT/WTO – have made substantial progress in reducing international barriers to trade, GATT/WTO-sanctioned PTAs have rapidly increased in number in recent years. Among the more prominent existing PTAs are the North American Free Trade Agreement (NAFTA), the European Economic Community (EEC), both formed under Article XXIV, and the MERCOSUR (the CU between the Argentine Republic, Brazil, Paraguay and Uruguay), formed under the Enabling Clause. All in all, hundreds of PTAs are currently in existence, with nearly every member country of the WTO belonging to at least one PTA.[1]

---

* This chapter draws substantially on my earlier research, particularly my works of 2004 and 2005 (cited below).

1 For a listing of all bilateral and regional trade agreements notified to the WTO, see www.worldtradelaw.net/databases/ftas.php.

That a country liberalising its trade preferentially against select partners is doing something distinct from multilateral liberalisation (where it eliminates tariffs against all imports regardless of country of origin) should be easy to see. What this implies for the liberalising country is a little more difficult to understand. Even a good half century after the economic implications of trade preferences were first articulated by Viner,[2] the differences between preferential and multilateral liberalisation (or free trade areas versus free trade) remain a nuance that most policy analysts (and occasionally even distinguished economists) appear to miss.

It is with a discussion of these issues concerning the distinction between preferential and non-discriminatory trade liberalisation that we begin the analytical section of this chapter, which is intended as a brief and accessible primer on the economics of PTAs. Specifically, Section II develops the classic analysis of Viner and demonstrates the generally ambiguous welfare effects of preferential trade liberalisation. Section III discusses the role geographic proximity ('regionalism') may play in this discussion. Section IV discusses the design of welfare-improving preferential trade agreements. Section V reviews GATT/WTO regulations concerning PTA formation and asks how the existing provisions compare with the welfare-improving designs for PTAs described in Section IV. Section VI concludes.

II. Welfare analysis

A. Trade creation and trade diversion

Does preferential trade liberalisation in favour of particular trading partners have the same welfare consequences as non-discriminatory trade liberalisation in favour of all imports? Does a simple proportion of the welfare benefits of non-discriminatory free trade accrue with preferential liberalisation?

A thorough answer to these questions would require the reader to take a deep plunge into the abstruse world of the second-best (whose existence and complexities were, indeed, first discovered and developed by analysts working on the economics of PTAs). But the idea may be introduced in a rudimentary fashion using the following 'textbook' representation of Viner's analysis: Consider the case of two countries, A and B, and the rest of the world W. A is our 'home' country. A produces a good and trades it for the exports of its trading partners B and W. Both B and W are assumed to export the same good and offer it to A at a fixed (but different) price. Initially, imports from B and W are subject to non-discriminatory trade restrictions: tariffs against B and W are equal. Imagine now that A eliminates its tariffs against B while maintaining its tariffs against W. This is preferential tariff reduction as opposed to free trade, since the latter would require that tariffs against W be removed as well. It is very tempting to think that this reduction of tariffs against B

---

2 Jacob Viner, *The Customs Unions Issue* (New York: Carnegie Endowment for International Peace, 1950).

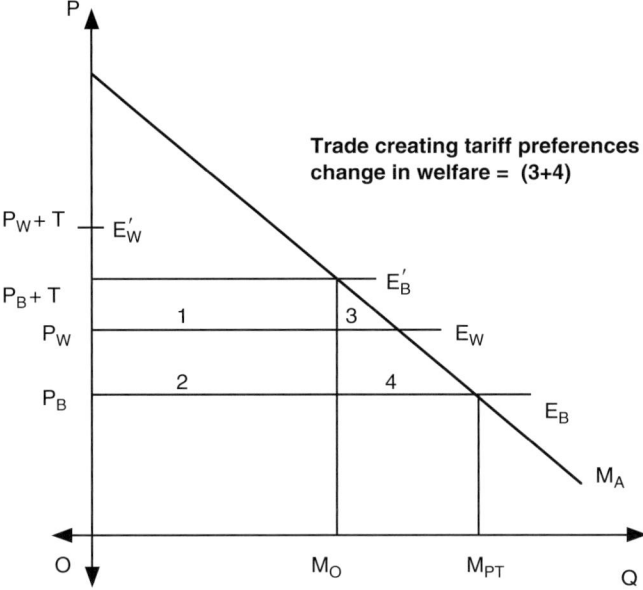

Figure 2.1

is a step in the direction of free trade and therefore that this ought to deliver to country A a proportionate fraction of the benefits of complete free trade. But Viner showed that this need not (and generally would not) be the case. Indeed, while a complete move towards free trade would be welfare-improving for country A, Viner demonstrated that the tariff preference granted to B through the FTA could in fact worsen A's welfare.

Figures 2.1 and 2.2 illustrate preferential tariff reform as respectively welfare-enhancing and welfare-worsening. The y-axes denote price and the x-axes denote quantities. M_A denotes the import demand curve of country A. E_B and E_W denote the price at which countries B and W are willing to supply A's demand; they represent the export supply curves of B and W respectively. In Figure 2.1, B is assumed to be a more efficient supplier of A's import than is W: E_B is drawn below E_W, and its export price P_B is less than W's export price P_W. Let 'T' denote the non-discriminatory per-unit tariff that is applied against B and W. This renders the tariff-inclusive price to importers in A as $P_B + T$ and $P_W + T$ respectively. With this non-discriminatory tariff in place, imports initially equal M_0 and the good is entirely imported from B. Tariff revenues in this initial situation equal the areas (1+2). When tariffs against B are eliminated preferentially, imports rise to M_{PT}. Imports continue to come entirely from B (since the import price from B now, P_B, is lower than the tariff-inclusive price of imports from W, $P_W + T$). The tariff preferences granted to B simply increase the

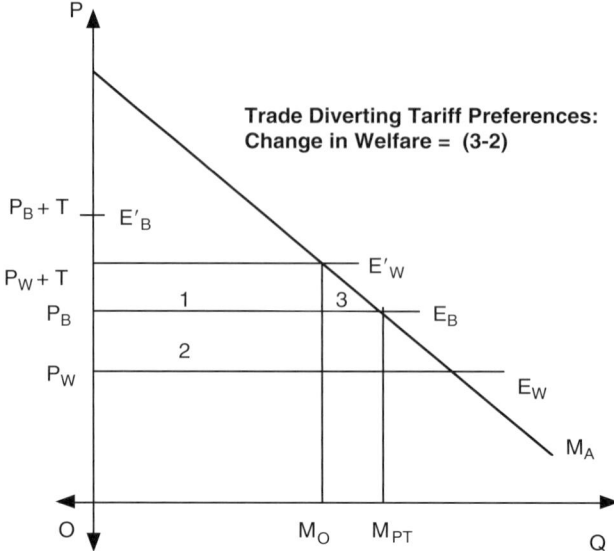

Figure 2.2

volume of imports. This increase in the volume of trade with the country whose exports were initially being purchased by A anyway (i.e., with the more efficient producer) when tariffs against it are preferentially reduced is referred to as 'trade creation'. Trade creation here can be shown to be welfare-improving. The increase in benefit to consumers (consumer surplus) in A following the reduction in consumption prices from $P_B + T$ to P_B equals the areas $(1 + 2 + 3 + 4)$. No tariff revenue is now earned and so the loss of tariff revenue equals areas $(1+2)$. The overall gain to A from this preferential tariff reduction equals areas $(1+2+3+4) - (1+2) =$ areas $(3+4)$, a positive number. The trade-creating tariff preference is thus welfare-improving.

In demonstrating that the tariff preference we have considered is welfare-improving for the home country, A, we have assumed that the partner which receives this tariff preference, B, is the more efficient supplier of the good. Figure 2.2 reverses this assumption, making W, the rest of the world, the more efficient supplier of the good. E_W is thus drawn below E_B. Initial imports are M_0. The tariff revenue collected is equal to the areas $(1+2)$. When tariffs are eliminated against B, the less efficient partner, the tariff-inclusive price of imports from W is higher than the tariff-exclusive price from B (this need not necessarily be the case; it is simply so as drawn). This implies that all trade is now 'diverted' away from W to B. What is the welfare consequence of this trade diversion? The increase in consumer surplus is equal to the areas $(1+3)$ since consumers now pay a price equal to P_B for this good. The loss in tariff revenue is (1+2). The overall gain to A equals the area (3−2), which may or may not be positive. Thus a trade-diverting tariff preference may lead to a welfare reduction.

The preceding examples illustrate a central issue emphasised in the academic literature on the welfare consequences of preferential trade. Preferential trade liberalisation towards the country from whom the good was imported in the initial non-discriminatory situation creates more trade and increases welfare; preferential liberalisation that diverts trade instead may reduce welfare. Subsequent analysis also developed examples of both welfare-improving trade-diversion and welfare-decreasing trade creation in general equilibrium contexts broader than those considered by Viner. However, the intuitive appeal of the concepts of trade creation and trade diversion has ensured their continued use in the economic analysis of preferential trade agreements, especially in policy analysis.[3]

Many recent empirical studies have quantified the adverse consequences of trade diversion and underscore the fact that trade diversion is not merely a theoretical concern. Yeats investigated the question of trade diversion within PTAs by performing an evaluation of trade patterns within MERCOSUR.[4] To describe the orientation of MERCOSUR trade, goods were characterised using two measures. The first measure is a 'regional orientation' index which is the ratio of the share of that good in exports to the region to its share in exports to third countries. The second measure is the 'revealed comparative advantage' measure which is the ratio of the share of a good in MERCOSUR's exports to third countries to its share in world exports (exclusive of intra-MERCOSUR trade). Yeats then compares the change in goods' regional orientation index between 1988 and 1994 (before and after MERCOSUR) with their revealed comparative advantage ranking. The results of his study are striking. As he notes, the goods with the largest increase in regional orientation are goods with very low revealed comparative advantage rankings. Specifically, for the 30 groups of goods with the largest increases in regional orientation, only two had revealed comparative advantage indices above unity. That is, the largest increases in intra-MERCOSUR trade have been in goods in which MERCOSUR countries lack comparative advantage, suggesting strong trade diversionary effects.

B. Internal terms of trade and revenue transfer effects

The Vinerian analysis illustrated in Figures 2.1 and 2.2 has assumed that the home country is small relative to both the partner country and the rest of the world, with the exportable goods from the partner and the rest of the world being perfect substitutes. Specifically, when consumption is switched from the rest of the world to the partner

---

3 For a comprehensive survey, see Arvind Panagariya, 'Preferential Trade Liberalization: The Traditional Theory and New Developments' (2000) 38(2) *Journal of Economic Literature* 287–331.
4 Alexander J. Yeats, 'Does MERCOSUR's Trade Performance Raise Concerns about the Effects of Regional Trade Arrangements?' (1998) 12(1) *The World Bank Economic Review* 1–28.

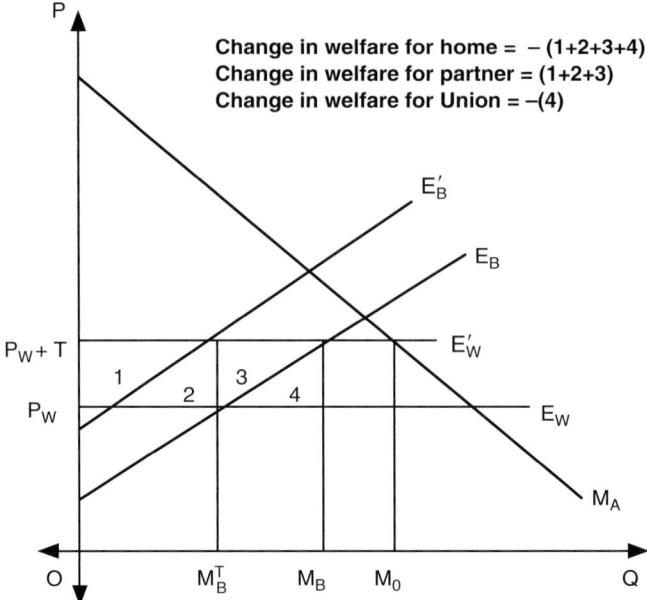

Change in welfare for home = − (1+2+3+4)
Change in welfare for partner = (1+2+3)
Change in welfare for Union = −(4)

Figure 2.3

country, the partner country is assumed to be able to satisfy all of the demand of the home country. What happens if B is so small that after receiving the tariff preference from A it is unable to satisfy all of A's demand for its imported goods? This implies that A continues to import some amount from the rest of the world W (which we assume for the moment is so large that it is able to handle all of the changes in A's demand without letting this affect its supply price) even after granting preferential access to B. Here, it can be shown that the home country loses unambiguously. The following example, provided by Panagariya,[5] illustrates this.

In Figure 2.3, the export supply curve of country B is shown to be rising. The tariff inclusive supply curve faced by the home country is E_B^T. Total consumption of the importable initially is M_0 and imports from B are M_B^T. A tariff preference in favour of B simply shifts the effective export supply curve to E_B and the imports from B to M_B. Total imports stay at M_0. The domestic price of the imported good in the home market in A is set by W (which continues to supply to A) and is the same as before (i.e., it stays at E_W^T). The outcomes in this case are quite stark. Since consumption of the imported good continues to be at M_0, there is no change in consumer surplus in the home country. There is, however, a direct tariff revenue loss since no tariff revenue is now earned on imports from the partner. The loss in tariff revenue

5 Panagariya, above n. 3.

(which is equal to the overall loss to A) equals the areas (1+2+3+4). In what can effectively be seen as a tariff revenue transfer to B, a gain of areas (1+2+3) accrues to B in the form of an increase in producer surplus. Thus, preferential tariff liberalisation leads to a loss in welfare for the liberalising country, a (smaller) gain in welfare for its partner and a net loss of area (4) to the union as a whole.

In general, in the context of an exchange in tariff preferences negotiated under a preferential trade agreement, we may expect that tariff revenue losses to the home country in some sectors are made up by gains in other sectors in which the home country gets preferential access to its partner's markets. Who gains more will depend upon the extent of tariff preferences exchanged and specific market circumstances (shapes of the supply and demand curves). The outcome is uncertain.

C. External terms of trade

Thus far, we have focused our discussion on the welfare consequences of preferential trade liberalisation on the countries undertaking the liberalisation. While we have not explicitly considered this so far, it should be easy to see that changes in demand by PTA members for the rest of the world's exports could lower the relative price of these exports (i.e., worsens the rest of the world's terms of trade). In general, the overall effect on the external terms of trade may be seen as a combination of income and substitution effects. The former represents the effect of real income changes due to the PTA on demand for imports from non-members and the latter reflects the substitution in trade towards partner countries (and away from non-members) due to the preferences in trade. In the case of a real-income reducing PTA, both effects would combine to lower demand from the rest of the world. This is also the case when substitution effects dominate the income effect.[6] The rest of the world experiences deterioration in its terms of trade and is therefore adversely impacted. Some indication of how the terms of trade may change for non-member countries in practice is provided by the empirical analysis of Chang and Winters who examine the impact of MERCOSUR (specifically, the exemption in tariffs that Brazil provided to its MERCOSUR partners) on the terms-of-trade (export prices) of countries excluded from the agreement.[7] Theory would suggest that trade diversion would worsen the terms of trade of excluded countries and this indeed is what they find. Specifically, their analysis reports a significant decline in the export prices of Brazil's major trading partners (the United States (US), Japan, Germany and Korea)

---

6 See Mundell for an analysis of how such extra-union terms of trade effects may complicate matters further for the tariff-reducing country, whose terms of trade with respect to the rest of the world may rise or fall following a preferential reduction in its tariffs against a particular partner: Robert A. Mundell, 'Tariff Preferences and the Terms of Trade' (1964) 32 *Manchester School of Economic and Social Studies* 1–13. On this point, see also the recent analysis by Panagariya: Arvind Panagariya, 'Preferential Trading and the Myth of Natural Trading Partners' (1997) 9(4) *Japan and the World Economy* 471–89.

7 Won Chang and L. Alan Winters, 'How Regional Trade Blocs Affect Excluded Countries: The Price Effects of MERCOSUR' (2002) 92(4) *American Economic Review* 889–904.

following MERCOSUR. These associated welfare losses sustained by the excluded countries are also significant – amounting to roughly 10 per cent of the value of their exports to Brazil.[8]

III. Geography and preferential trade agreements: Is regionalism 'natural'?

The previous section has discussed some of the reasons why economists have been divided on the wisdom of PTAs. Following Viner's demonstration that the net welfare effects of PTAs are unpredictable and possibly negative, many attempts were made to refine the theory and identify member country characteristics that would ensure welfare improvement and thus eliminate the welfare ambiguities associated with preferential trade. However, these efforts yielded results that did not have any greater direct operational significance than did Viner. This is to say that they did not yield any direct insights on what partner country characteristics would make trade creation rather than trade diversion a likely outcome.

More recently, however, increasing emphasis has been placed on geographic proximity as a criterion for membership in a PTA. Regionalism in preferential trade has been argued by some authors[9] as being key to generating better economic outcomes, with regional trading partners described as 'natural trading partners' in the context of preferential trade. The question of natural trading partners is immensely interesting for policy reasons. Many existing preferential trading arrangements are indeed regional. In addition, many extensions of existing arrangements along regional lines, such as the expansion of the NAFTA to include Chile, Argentina and other South American countries, or that of the European Union (EU) to include other regional countries are currently being debated and discussed in policy circles.

To evaluate the argument for geographic proximity as a membership criterion, we may start by noting that this argument itself rests on two economic hypotheses. First, that trade creation is greater and trade diversion lower when the initial volume of trade between the partners is higher (and trade with the rest of the world is lower) and second, that geographically proximate countries have larger volumes of trade with each other.

---

8 For instance, the United States is estimated to lose somewhere between $550 to $600 m on exports of about $5.5 bn with Germany losing between $170 and $236 m on exports of about $2 bn.

9 See, for instance, Paul Wonnacott and Mark Lutz, 'Is There A Case For Free Trade Areas?', in Jeffrey Schott (ed.), *Free Trade Areas and US Trade Policy* (Washington, DC: Institute for International Economics, 1989), pp. 59–84; Paul Krugman, 'The Move To Free Trade Zones', in Federal Reserve Bank of Kansas City, *Policy Implications of Trade and Currency Zones* (Kansas City: Federal Reserve Bank of Kansas City, 1991), pp. 7–41; and Lawrence H. Summers, 'Regionalism and the World Trading System', in Federal Reserve Bank of Kansas City, above, pp. 295–301.

As Bhagwati[10] and Bhagwati and Panagariya[11] have pointed out, however, these are not robust principles. For instance, the contention that geographically proximate countries trade more with each other is generally only valid as a conditional statement. That is to say, it is only after we 'control' for a variety of other variables (such as income levels of the partner country) that we are able to say that trade is higher between countries which are closer to each other. Importantly, however, the choice of partners in a PTA need not be conditioned on these same variables – diluting the relevance of proximity in discussions over trade preferences. An example may serve to clarify this point. In a hypothetical world, where the incomes of Japan and Mexico are equal (i.e., 'controlling' for income), US trade with Mexico may well be higher than trade with Japan. As it stands, however, Japan has a much higher income level than does Mexico. Its trade volume with the US is also much higher. Thus, even if initial trade volumes were to be used as a criterion by the US for choosing PTA members, the distant country (Japan) ought to be a preferred partner.

Furthermore it is incorrect to suggest that preferences towards the more significant partner are more likely to result in trade creation. Panagariya[12] offers a very clear argument on this point. Thus consider the economy discussed in section IIB and illustrated in Figure 2.3. Recall that when trade preferences towards country B result in a loss of welfare for the liberalising country A. Importantly, note that the losses (areas 1+2+3+4) are greater, the greater the initial volume of trade. Thus, with changing internal terms of trade, the argument that greater initial volumes of trade result in larger increases in welfare is directly contradicted.

Finally, it should be noted that the argument concerning trade creation and larger initial volumes of trade is not robust – even when internal terms of trade do not change. To see this, note that welfare gains with trade policy changes generally depend upon substitutions at the margin (changes in trade volumes – with partners and the rest of the world) as well as the initial levels of trade. This raises two issues. First, the relevant substitution elasticities do not generally depend on the initial volumes of trade. Differences in trade elasticities may therefore offset any differences in initial trade volumes. Second and more importantly, significant trading partners generally also compete to a greater extent with the rest of the world than do less significant trading partners. For example, Japan is a more significant trading partner of the US than is Ecuador, but it also competes in a wider range of markets and in larger volumes, say with EU suppliers, than Ecuador, which competes in a narrower and economically less significant set of markets. Importantly, while trade creation

10 Jagdish Bhagwati, 'Regionalism and Multilateralism: An Overview', in Jaime de Melo and Arvind Panagariya (eds.), *New Dimensions in Regional Integration* (Cambridge: Cambridge University Press, 1993), pp. 22–51.
11 Jagdish Bhagwati and Arvind Panagariya (eds.), *Free Trade Areas or Free Trade? The Economics of Preferential Trade Areas* (Washington, DC: AEI Press, 1996).
12 Arvind Panagariya, 'The Free Trade Area of the Americas: Good for Latin America?' (1996) 19(5) *World Economy* 485–515.

may be larger with significant partners, so may trade diversion. (In the preceding example, this implies that trade preferences granted by the US to Japan will divert larger volumes of trade – away from the EU – than trade preferences towards Ecuador). The empirical analysis of Krishna[13] finds evidence of just these effects in US data. In an econometric investigation of US trade, aimed at estimating trade creation and trade diversion effects under (hypothetical) trade preferences towards a variety of countries, trade creation and trade diversion are found to be correlated in their magnitudes. In his analysis, net welfare gains (i.e., gains from trade creation net of trade diversion losses) are found to be wholly uncorrelated with distance. All in all, arguments for regionalism in trade preferences do not appear to have a substantial basis in economic theory and are not supported by empirical analysis.

IV. Necessarily welfare-improving preferential trade areas

The generally ambiguous welfare results with trade preferences provoked an important question in the economic literature relating to the design of necessarily welfare-improving PTAs. A classic result due to Kemp and Wan[14] and Ohyama[15] provides a welfare-improving solution for the case of CUs. Starting from a situation with an arbitrary structure of trade barriers, if two or more countries freeze their net external trade vector with the rest of the world through a set of common external tariffs and eliminate the barriers to internal trade (implying the formation of a CU), the welfare of the union as a whole necessarily improves (weakly) and that of the rest of the world does not fall. The logic behind the Kemp-Wan theorem is as follows: By fixing the combined, net extra-union trade vector of member countries at its pre-union level, non-member countries are guaranteed their original level of welfare. Since there is no diversion of trade in this case, the welfare of the member countries is also not adversely affected. The PTA thus constructed has a common internal price vector, implying further a common external tariff for member countries. The Kemp-Wan-Ohyama design, by freezing the external trade vector and thus eliminating trade diversion, offers a way to sidestep the complexities and ambiguities inherent in the analysis of PTAs.

The Kemp-Wan-Ohyama analysis of welfare-improving CUs does not extend easily to FTAs since member-specific tariff vectors in the case of FTAs imply that domestic prices will differ across member countries. Panagariya and Krishna have, nevertheless, recently provided a corresponding construction of necessarily welfare-improving FTAs in complete analogy with the Kemp-Wan CU, with the essential difference that the trade vector of each member country with the rest of the world is

13 Pravin Krishna, 'Are Regional Trading Partners Natural?' (2003) 111(1) *Journal of Political Economy* 202–31.
14 Murray C. Kemp and Henry Wan Jr, 'An Elementary Proposition Concerning The Formation Of Customs Unions' (1976) 6(1) *Journal of International Economics* 95–7.
15 Michihiro Ohyama, 'Trade and Welfare in General Equilibrium' (1972) 9(1) *Keio Economic Studies* 37–73.

frozen at the pre-FTA level.[16] Since, in FTAs, different member countries impose different external tariffs, it is necessary to specify a set of rules of origin (ROO) to prevent a subversion of FTA tariffs by importing through the lower-tariff member country and directly trans-shipping goods to the higher-tariff country (which, if allowed, would bring the FTA arbitrarily close to a CU). The Panagariya-Krishna solution requires that all goods with any value added within the FTA are to be traded freely. Goods which enter the FTA as final goods are to be wholly prevented from trans-shipment by suitable ROO.

Theory thus suggests that ensuring welfare improvement requires that along with elimination of internal barriers, external tariff vectors should eliminate trade diversion – member countries should continue to import the same amounts from the rest of the world as they did initially. The next section examines how these theoretical prescriptions compare with WTO rules concerning the formation of PTAs.

V. PTA implementation and the WTO

The preceding discussion of necessarily welfare-improving CUs and FTAs provided a precise description of the tariff vectors that ought to be implemented in these agreements. Specifically, internal barriers are to be completely eliminated and the external tariff vector in both cases (i.e., the CU or the FTA) should eliminate trade diversion. Member countries should continue to import the same amounts from the rest of the world as they did initially. Can these be implemented in practice? And where do existing GATT/WTO provisions stand in relation to the theoretical specification?

Article XXIV of the GATT, which permits the formation of PTAs, also originally stipulated that internal preferences needed to be complete (i.e., that internal barriers between the members were to be completely eliminated) and that external trade barriers were not to be more restrictive than initially. As we will discuss below, a number of questions arose in connection with GATT regulations regarding both internal and external tariffs – some having to do with their economic merit, others to do with implementation and possible abuse given the ambiguous and imprecise wording adopted in the original text of the GATT. As we will discuss further, while the more recent 'Understanding on the Interpretation' of Article XXIV issued by the GATT in 1994 clarified some of these issues, other questions still remain.

A. Internal barriers to trade

On internal barriers to trade, two questions arise. The first relates to coverage – do GATT regulations require a removal of all internal barriers? The second relates to

---

16 Arvind Panagariya and Pravin Krishna, 'On the Existence of Necessarily Welfare Improving Free Trade Areas' (2002) 57(2) *Journal of International Economics* 353–67.

timing – how much time do countries have to comply with the rules? On the former issue, it should be stated that while the putative intent of the GATT was to require that internal barriers be eliminated completely, the actual text of the GATT only required that restrictions be eliminated on 'substantially all trade'. The ambiguous phrasing through the use of the qualifier 'substantially' opened up a number of possibilities for abuse. Whether 'substantially' should have been taken to imply a full 100 per cent or something smaller was not clear and has not yet been clarified. In this context, it is worth noting that for a given level of external tariffs, member country welfare is not necessarily maximised with zero internal barriers.[17] From a purely economic standpoint, given the level of external tariffs, welfare may well be maximised by maintaining some particular level of internal restrictions. It may therefore be argued that the ambiguous phrasing permitting non-elimination of internal barriers allowed member countries to aim at welfare-maximising outcomes. This, however, is quite unlikely. Any retention of internal barriers within PTAs is probably better explained by selective protectionist motivations on the part of country governments. Separately, it may be imagined that non-member countries would have an incentive to monitor and ensure the full dismantling of internal trade barriers within PTAs. However, it is also quite likely that the welfare of countries outside the union is higher when the discrimination against them is lower (i.e., when internal preferences are less than complete). *Ex post*, the external monitoring incentive is therefore minimal. On the question of the timing and the phasing out of internal barriers to trade, GATT rules, rather than requiring an immediate removal of internal barriers in a PTA, allowed for this to take place within a 'reasonable length of time', once again permitting substantial ambiguity in understanding and providing room for abuse.[18]

B. External barriers to trade

On external tariffs, the original GATT requirement was that external barriers not be more restrictive than initially. For FTAs, since countries retain individual tariff vectors, this could be taken to imply that no tariff was to rise. For CUs, since a common external tariff was to be chosen, and initial tariffs on the same good probably varied across countries, the tariff vector would necessarily change for each country. The expectation was then that the 'general incidence' of trade barriers would not be higher or more restrictive than before. Given the imprecise phrasing, there was once more substantial ambiguity as to what is implied – should the common external tariff

---

17 It is important to keep in mind here that the elimination of internal tariffs maximises the welfare of member countries for a given level of external trade (as in Kemp-Wan) and not for a given level of the external tariffs. With fixed tariffs, member country welfare may well be maximised with internal tariffs that are non-zero.

18 The more recent 'Understanding on the Interpretation' of Article XXIV issued in 1994 clarifies that the 'reasonable length of time' should exceed ten years in only 'exceptional cases'.

equal the unweighted mean of initial tariffs in the member countries? Should it be the trade-weighted mean? Or something else? As Dam,[19] Bhagwati[20] and several others have noted, it is clear that Article XXIV's ambiguity in this regard left plenty of room for opportunistic (i.e., protectionist) behaviour by member countries against non-members. The 1994 'Understanding on the Interpretation' of Article XXIV issued by the GATT provided substantial clarity on the issue of measurement and choice of the common external tariff – indicating that the GATT secretariat would compute weighted average tariff rates and duties collected in accordance with the methodology used in the assessment of tariff offers in the Uruguay round of trade negotiations and examine trade flow and other data to arrive at suitable measures of non-tariff barriers. While this relieves, at least partially, the issue of measurement of external barriers and the comparison with barriers in place initially, the economic concern regarding trade diversion is not addressed. Clearly, leaving external barriers at their initial level and removing internal barriers does not eliminate trade diversion (as theoretically required in the Kemp-Wan and Panagariya-Krishna constructions of welfare-improving PTAs). Indeed, with this configuration, trade diversion is practically guaranteed.

Having pointed to the deficiencies in existing GATT regulations in relation to the elimination of trade diversion, it may be noted that picking or designing tariff vectors *ex ante* that would ensure zero trade diversion, good by good, is a rather difficult task; the necessary measures of the exact sensitivity of external trade flows to external barriers of the CU or the FTA would be hard if not impossible to estimate accurately. So there is little prospect of identifying the exact trade-diversion-eliminating Kemp-Wan tariff vector and implementing it in practice.[21] Nevertheless, designing other disciplines to minimise diversion is less difficult; one can certainly say that lowering external barriers simultaneously with the formation of a CU or an FTA is likely to lower the degree of trade diversion (by minimising the substitution away from the goods supplied by the rest of the world to within-union goods). McMillan[22] has suggested as a test of admissibility of any PTA the measurement (estimation) of whether that PTA will result in less trade with the rest of the world.[23] In a similar

---

19 Kenneth W. Dam, *The GATT: Law and International Economic Organization* (Chicago: University of Chicago Press, 1970).

20 Bhagwati, above n. 10.

21 See, however, the paper by Srinivasan which attempts to identify and characterise the Kemp-Wan tariff vector in the context of a particular economic model: T. N. Srinivasan, 'Common External Tariffs of a Customs Union: The Case of Identical Cobb Douglas Tastes' (1997) 9 *Japan and the World Economy* 447–65.

22 John McMillan, 'Does Regional Integration Foster Open Trade? Economic Theory and GATT's Article XXIV', in Kym Anderson and Richard Blackhurst (eds.), *Regional Integration and the Global Trading System* (New York: St Martin's Press, 1993), pp. 292–310.

23 Of course, the Kemp-Wan and Panagariya-Krishna schemes both require that the PTA trade exactly the same amount as before. A PTA that trades no less, as in the McMillan test, is not necessarily welfare-improving, as Winters has argued: L. Alan Winters, 'Regionalism and the Rest of the World: The Irrelevance of the Kemp-Wan Theorem' (1997) 49 *Oxford Economic Papers* 228–34.

spirit, Bhagwati[24] has suggested that the requirement of a simultaneous pro rata reduction of external trade barriers with the progressive elimination of internal barriers could replace the current requirements.

C. Rules of origin

In free trade areas, importers have a potential incentive to import goods into the bloc through the member country imposing the lowest tariff on that good and then to tranship that good into higher tariff member countries by availing themselves of the duty free treatment within the bloc. To prevent this circumvention of the independent tariffs desired by member countries, however, FTAs need to be supported by ROO, which specify the circumstances under which a good may be given duty free treatment within the union.[25]

The discussion in the previous section has provided a welfare-theoretic basis for very simple rules of origin – goods which undergo any genuine value-added transformation within the union must be allowed to move duty free within the union. For any good entirely produced outside the union, trade deflection is to be prevented by imposing on direct imports and also any trans-shipped units the external tariff that is chosen by the member country where the good is eventually consumed. However, rules of origin are more complex in practice. They are differently concerned (depending on the good) with the fractional content of the good that is required to be produced within the union for the good to qualify for duty-free status.[26] More importantly, while the putative intention of rules of origin is simply to prevent deflection of trade, it has been argued that these rules have been used more flexibly as instruments of commercial policy.[27]

That the opportunity to set rules of origin would be abused to achieve other ends should come as no surprise to anyone even moderately familiar with the political economy of trade policy determination. While we may hope for FTA rules to be designed by welfare-maximising governments concerned with the enhancement of internal efficiency and equity towards non-members, in practice, the rules of origin are determined in intensely political contexts in which a variety of additional factors influence policy. Governments are under great pressure to deviate from the high path of choosing rules of origin to simply prevent trade deflection towards fixing rules that favour politically active and aggressive constituencies in the economy. Because in an FTA, there are no internal tariffs and because external tariffs themselves cannot be

---

24 See Bhagwati, above n. 10.
25 Since, in practice, at least some traded goods are not covered by the common external barriers of a CU, ROO are often used in CU as well.
26 For a detailed discussion of the different ways in which rules of origin are specified in practice, see Krishna, above n. 13.
27 See, for instance, Kala Krishna and Anne O. Krueger, 'Implementing Free Trade Agreements: Rules of Origin and Hidden Protection', in Alan V. Deardorff, James A. Levinsohn and Robert M. Stern (eds.), *New Directions in Trade Theory* (Ann Arbor: University of Michigan Press, 1995), pp. 149–87.

raised to further disadvantage non-member countries, it has been argued that, to please their constituencies and protect them from the economic changes that come about due to entry into the free trade area, governments manipulate rules of origin to protect both domestic suppliers of final and intermediate goods.[28] This may happen in the following ways:

(a) *Protection for final good suppliers*: Consider a final goods supplier in a member country facing greater competition from suppliers in other member countries due to the impending elimination of internal barriers of trade within the FTA. Consider further that this foreign competition uses in its production intermediates from outside of the FTA. Due to the political pressures brought to bear on the domestic government, whether it is from capitalists, affected voters or displaced workers, that government will have reason to negotiate intra-union content criteria severe enough to push those competing goods out of the duty-free category. In so doing they will insulate the home country supplier from that greater competition, but also undermine the intended competitive enhancement from joining an FTA.

(b) *Protection for intermediate goods suppliers*: Governments can negotiate for rules of origin that specify a high degree of domestic (i.e., within-bloc) content, significantly diverting demand from goods produced with foreign intermediates to goods produced using intermediates from within the FTA.

However, this use of rules of origin undermines the two key rules imposed by the WTO on its members for FTA formation. While complete internal liberalisation is sought by the WTO, this is negated by the selective use of rules of origin. Further, while the WTO requires that trade barriers against non-members cannot be raised by FTA members, the use of stringent rules of origin would divert imports of intermediates away from non-member exporters even if external tariffs are maintained at the same level as before.[29]

To what extent rules of origin are used to prevent trade deflection and to what extent they are politically motivated commercial policy instruments is ultimately an empirical question. While empirical research in this area is still in its infancy, Cadot, Estevadeordal and Suwa-Eisenmann[30] have recently provided some interesting results. They directly examined the possible use of rules of origin to achieve protection for final goods producers and the creation of a captive market for intra-union suppliers of intermediate goods. Specifically, they measured the effects of rules of

---

28 Of course, it may be just such protection that enables a government to generate enough political support for the FTA in the first place, as Duttagupta and Panagariya have argued: Rupa Duttagupta and Arvind Panagariya, 'Free Trade Areas and Rules of Origin: Economics and Politics', Mimeo, 2001.

29 Ironically, however, highly severe rules of origin may result in greater imports from the rest of the world than before, owing to the preference of importers to pay the external tariff rather than comply with demanding domestic-content standards.

30 Olivier Cadot, Antoni Estevadeordal and Akiko Suwa-Eisenman, 'Rules of Origin as Export Subsidies', Mimeo, 2003.

origin on Mexican imports to the US market and found that rules of origin were a large enough negative influence on intra-union trade flows so as to offset the tariff preferences granted by the trade agreement. Further, the creation of a protected market for intermediate goods producers also appears to be a key determinant of the rules of origin chosen.

D. Non-trade issues in preferential integration

Some proponents of preferential integration have argued[31] that PTAs achieve 'deep' integration. That is, rather than simply achieving trade liberalisation, as in multi-lateral liberalisation contexts, PTAs involve 'deep' integration through coordination, or harmonisation, of other non-trade policies such as competition policies, environmental policies, labour standards, product standards and investment codes. It is further argued that such harmonisation of policies will be efficiency enhancing and beneficial to member countries.

The proposition that harmonisation of policies is uniformly beneficial to all of the member countries in a PTA has been met with scepticism by others[32] who note that there are good reasons for diversity in domestic policies and standards and that harmonisation is not automatically a welfare-enhancing policy. For instance, the choice of optimal pollution levels and labour standards generally depends on income level. While every country may prefer lower pollution levels, countries may reasonably disagree on what the optimal pollution levels are, what costs they should bear to lower pollution and where these efforts are best directed (e.g., developing countries may prefer to lower water pollution, while air pollution may be a greater concern for richer countries). Similarly, countries may disagree on minimum wage levels, worker-safety issues and on the merits of permitting voluntary child labour. Thus, while harmonisation may indeed bring some forms of efficiency enhancement, it is far from clear that such harmonisation of policies will be beneficial overall or that any benefits will accrue uniformly to all the member countries. A practical concern is that under the guise of 'deep integration' the larger and more powerful countries in a PTA negotiation may be able to extract concessions not merely in trade but in other 'non-trade' matters as well.

VI. Conclusion

PTAs, while conceived originally as minor exceptions to the GATT's central principle of non-discrimination, and only to be permitted under strict conditions, now number in the hundreds. A half-century of research has advanced significantly our

31 See, for instance, Robert Z. Lawrence, *Regionalism, Multilateralism and Deeper Integration* (Washington, DC: The Brookings Institution, 1997).
32 See, for instance, Arvind Panagariya, 'The Regionalism Debate: An Overview' (1999) 22(4) *World Economy* 477–511.

understanding of the implications of trade discrimination even if the frequently equivocal theoretical and empirical results have established among economists and policy-makers an ambivalent attitude towards preferential trade agreements. However, concerns regarding the fragmentation of the world trade system have grown with the rapid proliferation of PTAs in recent years. Several hundred PTAs are currently in existence (with many countries belonging to multiple PTAs) and many more are in process. With this inexorable erosion of non-discriminatory disciplines within the trade system, research on preferential trade is certain to remain central to the field of international trade policy for many years to come.

3

The political economy of PTAs

OLIVIER CATTANEO

I. Introduction: Re-thinking the paradigm
of bilateral/regional trade agreements

Why do countries conclude bilateral/regional trade agreements? Numerous researchers have sought to answer this question, most often through creating a typology of the agreements. Such efforts, however, have been in vain. A bilateral/regional trade agreement is rarely, if ever, based on a single motive, and two or more parties to an agreement can often have different and sometimes even conflicting objectives (e.g., one seeking market access and the other political support). In fact, different actors within each country itself can also have different objectives (e.g., one sector seeking trade creation whilst another trade diversion). Thus, any typology is bound to create artificial categories, and would not necessarily give a proper or accurate answer to the original question.

Sometimes, countries fall into a similar trap by trying to explain the rationale behind their bilateral/regional trade policy. For example, in its 'Global Europe' Communication (2006), the European Commission acknowledged that it had been predominantly motivated by political considerations in concluding trade agreements with countries that were candidates for European Union (EU) membership (with the exception of Mexico, South Africa, and Chile). Although such a policy was in line with the EU's neighbourhood and development objectives, it did little to serve the EU's central trade interests.[1] The EU therefore designed a new strategy, where economics was restored as the chief criterion for future bilateral agreements. Future partners would be selected on the basis of:

- their market potential (economic size and growth),
- their level of protection against EU export interests (tariffs and non-tariff barriers), and
- the state of negotiations with EU competitors (to measure the likely impact of a bilateral agreement with a competitor on EU markets and economy, as well as the

---

1 European Commission, *Global Europe: Competing in the World. A Contribution to the EU's Growth and Jobs Strategy*, Communication to the Council, the European Parliament, the European Economic and Social Committee and the Committee of the Regions, COM/2006/0567 of 4 October 2006, Brussels, at p. 11.

risk of erosion of the preferential access to EU markets currently enjoyed by the EU's neighbouring and developing country partners).[2]

The Commission concluded that the Association of Southeast Asian Nations (ASEAN), Korea, and the Common Market of the Southern Cone (MERCOSUR) were 'priorities'; while India, Russia, and the Gulf Co-operation Council (GCC) were 'of direct interest'; and China, although meeting the criteria, 'required special attention' because of both the potential and risks it presented.[3] At the time, some commentators contested the objectivity of this selection: 'The fact that, on Commission's own numbers, its new targets for free trade agreements account for only a third of the potential markets in Asia, takes the shine off this argument.'[4] It was also perceived as an evolution of EU trade policy rather than an abrupt break with the past.[5] In practice, since 2006, the EU has continued to negotiate with neighbouring countries in Central and Eastern Europe and the Mediterranean, as well as with African, Caribbean and Pacific (ACP) Group of States in the context of the Economic Partnership Agreements (EPAs). New negotiations were launched also, among others, with the United States (US). The 2010 Free Trade Agreement with South Korea is the only agreement that was concluded in accordance with the 'economic' priorities set in 2006. Thus, apart from the re-packaging, the EU bilateral trade policy remains a combination of economic and other (political) factors.

The US offers a similar opinion. A 2004 report of the US General Accounting Office (GAO) lists six factors driving the selection of potential preferential trade agreement (PTA) partners:

- country readiness,
- economic/commercial benefit,
- benefits to the broader trade liberalisation strategy,
- compatibility with US interests,
- Congressional/private sector support, and
- US government resource constraints.[6]

These factors are vague enough to make the claim that decisions 'are not mechanical' and furthermore 'reflect US trade strategy, foreign policy, and foreign economic development goals'.[7] As a result, PTAs cannot be placed in clean-cut boxes, as it is widely recognised that they are not primarily driven by economics.

---

2 *Ibid.*   3 *Ibid.*
4 Simon J. Evenett, 'The New EU Trade Policy: Grand Strategy or Stop-Gap?', *WTO News from the Swiss Institute for International Economics and Applied Economic Research*, Issue No. 15, January 2007, at p. 1.
5 Simon J. Evenett, 'Global Europe: An Initial Assessment of the European Commission's New Trade Policy' (January 2007) 61(4) *Aussenwirtschaft* 377–402.
6 USGAO, *International Trade: Intensifying Free Trade Negotiating Agenda Calls for Better Allocation of Staff and Resources*, GAO-04-233 (January 2004), available at www.gao.gov/new.items/d04233.pdf.
7 *Ibid.*, at p. 2.

Questioning the objectives of US trade policy, the Ways and Means Committee of the House, at the end of January 2007, called for a hearing on trade and globalisation with a view to elicit responses from witnesses concerning: (1) the theory that more trade is always better, no matter its terms or contents; (2) recommendations on specific changes to US trade policy and international trading rules in order to maximise the benefits and minimise the costs of liberalisation; and (3) identifying some of the most important successes of US trade policy in the recent past.[8] In other words, the philosophy of trade agreements (bilateral, regional, and multilateral) is itself being brought into question. Far from being a 'mechanical decision' based on precise economic criteria, the negotiation of new trade agreements remains at the mercy of political and ideological arbitrages between advocates and opponents of free trade.

Based on these preliminary considerations, this chapter does not attempt to create yet another typology of trade agreements. Instead, it attempts to explain the key role of bilateral/regional trade agreements in international trade history (Part II); it argues for the revocation of the idea that trade agreements are strictly economically driven (Part III); and it stresses their political dimension (Part IV). It therefore challenges some basic assumptions on which the usual critics of bilateralism/regionalism are based. The first challenged assumption is that multilateralism is the rule and bilateralism/regionalism the exception; from a historical perspective, it is the opposite, and bilateral/regional agreements are the most common trade policy instruments. The second challenged assumption is that trade policy, and bilateral/regional agreements in particular, always have to make economic sense when in fact it is only a political arbitrage/compromise between free trade and protectionist views (two economic doctrines, but where economic rationale competes with ideology), driven by foreign or domestic policy considerations.

II. Multilateralism is the exception, not the rule

Bilateral/regional trade agreements are not new: they pre-date multilateral trade agreements by centuries. The proliferation of bilateral/regional trade agreements – the source of most comments and fears about PTAs today – is not a new phenomenon either. In the 1860s, following the conclusion of an FTA between France and Britain (the Cobden–Chevalier Treaty), trading nations rushed into a 'free trade epidemic'.[9] According to Accominotti and Flandreau, the 14 trading nations of the time

---

8 Hearing archives are available at http://waysandmeans.house.gov/calendar/eventsingle.aspx?EventID=246106 (Hearing on Trade and Globalization of 30 January 2007).
9 Olivier Accominotti and Marc Flandreau, 'Does Bilateralism Promote Trade? Nineteenth Century Liberalization Revisited', Center for Economic Policy Research Discussion Paper Series No. 5423 (December 2005), at p. 3.

concluded more than 50 bilateral treaties,[10] i.e., more than half of the technically possible combinations $(14 \times 13 \div 2 = 91)$.[11] By comparison, today, the 159 members of the WTO have notified roughly 430 physical trade agreements, i.e., 'only' 3 per cent of the technically possible combinations $(159 \times 158 \div 2 = 12{,}561)$.[12] Moreover, fewer than 250 of those notified agreements are currently in force.

Nor was the long history of bilateral/regional trade agreements meant to end with the emergence of multilateralism. Bilateralism/regionalism and multilateralism have long co-existed. Article I of the General Agreement on Tariffs and Trade (GATT 1947) excluded *existing* preferential schemes from the most-favoured-nation (MFN) treatment (grandfather rights). In addition, Article XXIV provided a legal framework for *future* bilateral/regional trade agreements, stressing their role in the trade-liberalisation process. Despite the emergence of a multilateral regulatory framework for trade, embodied in the World Trade Organisation (WTO) since 1995, countries have continued to use bilateral/regional agreements as a common tool of trade and foreign policy.

A. An historical perspective on the respective roles of bilateralism and multilateralism

History has consisted of successive waves of liberalism and protectionism, and bilateral/regional trade agreements have often served both purposes: some agreements securing trade monopolies, while some others liberalising trade, including on an MFN basis. These agreements have pre-dated modern states. In 1157, the Hanseatic League (an alliance of trading guilds representing German cities) negotiated a trade agreement with England, which included special trading privileges and market rights, exemptions from all London tolls, and the authorisation to trade at fairs throughout England.[13] While the globalisation of free trade was advocated early (e.g., Hugo Grotius published his *Mare Liberum* treatise in 1604, where he advocated open-use of the sea for the maritime trade of all nations), multilateral agreements appeared only at the end of the nineteenth century. At first they were confined to specific commodities (e.g., multilateral negotiations regarding international sugar trade started in the 1850s and led to the 1902 Brussels Sugar Convention)[14] or trade-related topics (e.g., the 1883 Paris Convention for the Protection of Industrial

---

10 United Kingdom, France, Zollverein, Austria–Hungary, Italy, Spain, Norway–Sweden, Belgium, Denmark, Russia, US, Portugal, Switzerland, and the Netherlands.

11 Accominotti and Flandreau, above n. 9, at p. 22.

12 Note that the 430 physical trade agreements notified to the WTO include regional (as opposed to bilateral) trade agreements, both increasing the number of technically possible combinations and the potential coverage of each of the agreements. The comparison therefore only gives a rough element of comparison.

13 Philippe Dollinger, 'The German Hansa', vol. 1 of *The Emergence of International Business, 1200–1800; with a new introduction by Mark Casson* (London: Routledge/Thoemmes Press, 1999).

14 Heitor Pinto de Moura Filho, 'Pioneering Multilateralism: The Sugar Agreements 1864–1914', Paper presented at the XIVth International Economic History Congress, Helsinki, 2006, Session 109.

Property or the 1886 Berne Convention for the Protection of Literary and Artistic Works). It was not until the next wave of trade liberalisation, in the aftermath of World War II, that a multilateral instrument (the GATT 1947) aimed to discipline all trade – with significant exceptions such as trade in agriculture or services (neither being properly addressed until 1995).

According to some authors, trade policy has long rested on bilateral negotiations, proving that they could be an effective instrument of liberalisation and trade promotion.[15] For others, however, trade liberalisation and growth have happened *in spite of* these bilateral agreements.[16] This controversy largely results from confusing the act of liberalising trade (signing an agreement and, for example, reducing tariffs) and the effects of such an action. It is therefore possible that during the period when free trade reached its peak in Europe in the 1860s (when dozens of PTAs were signed) there was a serious decline in trade (and economic) growth.[17] Some empirical studies on the 1860s suggest that bilateralism did not promote trade.[18] This is not a critique of bilateral trade agreements (BTAs) (as opposed to, for example, multilateral agreements) per se, it is merely a query of the impact of trade liberalisation on trade growth. Recent economic literature has similarly suggested that the WTO (and its predecessor GATT) do not actually promote trade.[19]

We do know that de facto FTAs corrupted the universal doctrine of free trade by introducing the concept of 'reciprocity'. These were in response to the findings of John Stuart Mill who suggested that more economic surplus from trade could accrue to a country following reciprocal, rather than completely free, trade policies. Compared to unilateral liberalisation, which had until then prevailed both in theory (models based on absolute or comparative advantages) and in practice (England, in the 1860s, bound some concessions in trade agreements it had unilaterally made since the 1840s), reciprocity was a backward step.[20] Some authors have even suggested that England at that time promoted FTAs with a view to preserving its technological advantage (acquired with the help of high tariff protection) – kicking away the ladder, so to speak, or confining its trade partners to the production of commodities and agricultural products (trade in which was promoted by the suppression of the Corn Laws) while flooding their markets with its manufactured goods.[21]

15 Douglas A. Irwin, 'Multilateral and Bilateral Trade Policies in the World Trading System: An Historical Perspective', in Jaime de Melo and Arvind Panagariya (eds.), *New Dimensions in Regional Integration* (Cambridge: Cambridge University Press, 1993), pp. 90–119.
16 See, e.g., Paul Bairoch, *Economics and World History, Myths and Paradoxes* (Chicago: University of Chicago Press, 1993), at pp. 44–5; and Accominotti and Flandreau above, n. 9.
17 See Bairoch above, n. 16, at pp. 46–7.   18 See Accominotti and Flandreau above, n. 9.
19 Andrew K. Rose, 'Do We Really Know that the WTO Increases Trade?' (2004) 94(1) *American Economic Review* 98–114.
20 Unless one country was forced into unilateral concession by another, e.g., in the so-called 'unequal treaties' presented in Part IV of this chapter, in which case reciprocity was a step forward.
21 Charles P. Kindleberger, *Economic Response: Comparative Studies in Trade, Finance, and Growth* (Cambridge MA and London: Harvard University Press, 1978).

Interestingly enough, the same critics are today opposed to the WTO and its most advanced members.

Nineteenth-century BTAs included an MFN clause: after two countries concluded a trade agreement, all additional concessions made by one of the countries to a third party in subsequent agreements would systematically be extended to its partner. In other words, the proliferation of agreements created a virtuous circle of tariff reductions, where new concessions would be automatically propagated through the entire web of PTAs.

This original version of the MFN clause has, however, been corrupted over time, once again by the concept of reciprocity. With the Great Depression of the last quarter of the nineteenth century, countries reverted to protectionism and high tariffs: in 1879, Bismarck abandoned the German free trade policy; in 1888, Benjamin Harrison won the US presidency on a protectionist ticket; and in 1892, France introduced the Méline Tariff. This 'tariff war' reached its peak in the aftermath of the 1929 crash, as famously illustrated by the adoption of the Smoot-Hawley Tariff Act that doubled US tariffs. In this difficult economic and political context, it became clear that countries would not give away concessions by making them available to all without some form of recompense. The concept of *conditional* MFN was thus introduced and followed for a time, for example by the US, where concessions would be generalised, but only at the price of *reciprocal* concessions.[22] This ideological transition was best illustrated by the adoption of the 1934 Reciprocal Trade Agreements Act (RTAA), which allowed for BTAs that did not include an MFN clause. However, this ideological shift created a greater complexity in negotiations, and discrimination became the rule. Aware of both these complications and the political vulnerabilities of offering unconditional MFN again, Cordell Hull and others found a motive for moving to a multilateral forum. In their minds, the conclusion of a multilateral deal could help to extract concessions from otherwise unreciprocating beneficiaries.[23] This strategic move is comparable to Arthur Dunkel's 1990 proposal to create a world trade organisation, in the hopes of unlocking the Uruguay Round negotiations (which started in 1986), forcing concessions from all in a package deal, and putting an end to the 'GATT-à-la-carte' discriminatory approach consecrated by the Tokyo Round (concluded in 1979).

In other words, the GATT 1947 was the only solution that could be found to restore unconditional MFN without having to give away concessions whilst receiving no benefit in return – and once again, the mandate of the US President was to negotiate *reciprocal* trade agreements. The GATT was therefore not fundamentally different in spirit from any of the bilateral PTAs concluded in the late nineteenth century. One could even say that the GATT was the largest PTA the US had ever

---

22 Kenneth W. Dam, 'Cordell Hull, The Reciprocal Trade Agreement Act, and the WTO', University of Chicago Law & Economics, Olin Working Paper No. 228 (October 2004), at p. 6.
23 *Ibid.*

concluded – history having changed the once pragmatic solution dictated by US domestic policy constraints into an icon of post-war solidarity spirit. For some commentators at the time, the motives of the US behind the conclusion of the GATT were quite similar to those of the United Kingdom (UK) in 1860 – to secure technological advances and market shares for a booming manufacturing sector:

> One should not forget that the US is in a peculiar position. After doubling its production capacities during the war, it will have, tomorrow, in order to avoid unemployment, to increase its exports in vast proportions. Some already quote numbers that are hard to believe. The US policy will therefore be a large scale expansionist trade policy, facilitated by the needs of countries hit by the war.[24]

It should also be remembered that only 23 countries participated in the first round of GATT negotiations (Geneva Round, 1947), and 13 in the second (Annecy Round, 1949) – fewer than the number of countries in the web of PTAs at the end of the nineteenth century. It is also worth noting that the 'regional' (and to some extent preferential) character of the GATT was reinforced by the non-participation of the Soviet countries; the GATT has historically been used as an instrument of reinforcement of economic (and political) solidarities within the Western bloc.

As mentioned earlier, the GATT 1947 did not ban bilateral/regional trade agreements, but instead granted grandfather rights to existing preferential schemes and secured the possibility of contracting parties concluding more such agreements in the future. The MFN clause became lost in the web of PTAs, however, with important consequences for the world trading system. While in the late nineteenth century the proliferation of PTAs resulted in a general lowering of tariffs, the current proliferation of PTAs simply creates more discrimination. Bilateralism/regionalism is not to blame: the GATT contracting parties have continuously tried to circumvent the MFN clause through the use of FTAs, among other avenues (e.g., the 1979 Enabling Clause authorised GATT contracting parties to maintain generalised systems of preferences in favour of developing countries). This has led some commentators to rename MFN treatment in the WTO 'least-favoured-nation' treatment.

In sum, the motivations behind PTAs and multilateral deals are not fundamentally different. In the past, different circumstances have led countries to opt for either one or the other instrument. When the free trade spirit blows over a country or a region, whatever instrument is most readily available will be instinctively used. In exceptional cases, multilateral deals – which are the most efficient method of trade acceleration – will be used but bilateral/regional trade agreements will remain the bread and butter of international trade policies.[25]

---

24 'Les Accords de Bretton-Woods', *Le Monde*, 26 July 1945, at p. 1 (author's translation).
25 An interesting topic for further research would be to investigate whether the GATT 1947 was closer in spirit to a PTA than it is to the WTO, justifying current disaffection for the latter and the proliferation of bilateral/regional trade agreements.

B. Multilateralism and bilateralism/regionalism:
supplements or substitutes?

The above conclusion is very pragmatic – when it comes to trade liberalisation, bilateral/regional and multilateral agreements have been interchangeably used (even if results differ). The partial shift from bilateralism to multilateralism in 1947 was primarily the result of a conjunction of exceptional political and historical circumstances. In practice, countries will use whichever instrument offers the best chance of success in the promotion of specific trade interests.

Naturally, countries first turn to the WTO, because of the potential higher return on negotiation time and costs. However, commitment to multilateralism ends there. This is perfectly illustrated by the EU trade strategy. The 'Global Europe' Communication of the Commission stresses that the EU remains committed to the WTO, but that the Doha Development Agenda (DDA) cannot be the only trade policy tool used to enhance the competitiveness of the EU economy.[26] According to the same document:

> FTAs, if approached with care, can build on WTO and other international rules by going further and faster in promoting openness and integration, by tackling issues which are not ready for multilateral discussion and by preparing the ground for the next level of multilateral liberalization.[27]

Issues of particular economic importance referred to by the EU (also qualified as 'new areas of growth') are, notably intellectual property, services, investment, public procurement, and competition.[28] The EU first turned to the WTO to address these issues, and became the main promoter of the so-called 'Singapore issues' (investment, competition, trade facilitation, and transparency in government procurement) in the DDA. However, absent any consensus on the modalities of negotiations, the ambition of the DDA on 'Singapore issues' was largely scaled down: the so-called 'July Package' (2004) removed three out of four issues from the Doha work programme.[29] Similarly, on the intellectual property front, the EU tried to promote the extension of rules on geographical indications at the WTO, but encountered serious opposition from other members (thereby vindicating the EU's assertion that the WTO could not be the only trade policy tool to promote its trade interests in certain new areas). Recently negotiated 'Deep and Comprehensive Free Trade Agreements' (DCFTAs) illustrate the role of regional trade integration in regulatory convergence, beyond WTO rules.

The EU is not the only actor to use 'new generation' bilateral/regional trade agreements that explore areas not covered, or insufficiently covered, by the WTO. The objective of these FTAs could be to break new ground and tackle new obstacles to trade (e.g., competition or investment rules), or to go further than the WTO on

---

26 European Commission, above n. 1, at p. 10.   27 *Ibid.*   28 *Ibid.*, at p. 7.
29 WTO, Decision Adopted by the General Council on 1 August 2004, WT/L/579, 2 August 2004.

certain topics (e.g., intellectual property, labour or environmental regulations). For example, most US trade agreements include provisions that go beyond WTO rules in patenting and other intellectual property rules (so-called 'TRIPS+' or 'WTO+' provisions) – e.g., the United States–Singapore Free Trade Agreement; the North American Free Trade Agreement (NAFTA), and the United States–Jordan Free Trade Agreement both contain labour standards and environmental regulations.[30] These 'WTO+' rules are important to the US and the EU for securing market access and fair competition of some specific products (e.g., European wines and US pharmaceutical products). The long-term objective is more subtle: some EU and US standards (e.g., genetically modified organisms) or rules (e.g., moral rights, geographical indications, and patenting of genes and certain organisms in intellectual property law, or competition law) are incompatible; thus, PTAs are designed by the US and the EU to lock as many countries as possible into a specific set of rules, and either prepare the ground for the next round of multilateral trade negotiations that would include these areas (i.e., build a coalition of like-minded countries), or secure the widest possible diffusion of these rules in the absence of multilateral disciplines (see Part IV below on the race for power between the major trading nations). The major challenge of the Transatlantic Trade and Investment Partnership (TTIP) will therefore be to reconcile those two sets of rules: whilst the gains to be expected from the TTIP are limited when it comes to the removal of barriers to trade at the border, they could be very significant in case of an ambitious regulatory convergence. However, such convergence will be hard to achieve, even at the bilateral level.

The flexibility of PTAs also allows trade to move faster in certain areas where a country has clear offensive interests (e.g., services), while slowing the pace of liberalisation in other areas where defensive interests prevail (e.g., agriculture). In the same vein, a PTA can be concluded with a country with a complementary production structure, with a view to avoiding conflicts of interest – although this significantly reduces the potential economic benefits of the agreement (from an economic perspective, the benefits of liberalisation and competition arise when the two countries trade similar products). Because of the MFN clause, this selectivity is not possible in a multilateral framework, and global deals necessarily imply more politically painful decisions. Examples of such selective agreements include the Japan–Singapore New-Age Economic Partnership Agreement (Japan–Singapore EPA), where the absence of a significant agricultural sector in Singapore facilitated the signing of an agreement; however, the Japan–Singapore EPA also excluded the very few agricultural products that Singapore does export, such as cut flowers and ornamental fish.[31] The downside, however, is that governments are more exposed to

---

30 See Chapters 11 and 12 of this volume.
31 Jayant Menon, 'Bilateral Trade Agreements and the World Trading System', Asian Development Bank Institute Discussion Paper No. 57 (28 November 2006), at p. 8.

lobby pressures, and might not be able to liberalise as much as they had initially intended, or as they could have in a multilateral forum (where they have the advantage of blaming international peer pressure). For this reason, some voices are being raised in the US Congress against FTAs, arguing that PTAs put US legislative and executive bodies under too much domestic pressure.

In sum, while history has shown that it could be argued that PTAs act as substitutes for multilateralism, the reverse is *not always* true. Countries may choose to supplement multilateral interaction with bilateral/regional agreements where (e.g., in new trade areas such as investment) and when a consensus cannot be reached at the multilateral level. Evidence suggests that there is no strong empirical link between multilateral and regional agendas, despite frequent allegations of the kind. For example, the US Trade Representative Robert Zoellick wrote a famous op-ed after the 2003 Cancun Ministerial, suggesting that 'America will not wait for the won't do countries' and will 'move towards free trade with can-do countries'.[32] The US had, however, already started most of its bilateral negotiations at the time, and these would probably have continued even if the Cancun Ministerial had been a success. Lack of progress in multilateral negotiations is more often a convenient *a posteriori* justification than a motive for moving trade policy in a bilateral direction.

III. Bilateral/regional agreements are the result of a political arbitrage between free trade and protectionist views, only partially driven by economic principles

The decision to negotiate a trade agreement of any kind is based on a political arbitrage between free trade and protectionist views. Here again, multilateral and bilateral/regional agreements are not fundamentally different. However, bilateral/regional agreements are more flexible than their multilateral counterparts. This makes the political cost of an arbitrage in favour of free trade lower in this context for two main reasons: (1) sensitive sectors can be carved out of the agreement (defensive interests); and (2) new disciplines can be promoted in some sectors of high interest where multilateral consensus is yet to emerge (offensive interests). In other terms, opposition to the conclusion of the agreement is likely to be lower while support is higher.

From an economic perspective, this level of political facility drives the agreement to far less than an optimal conclusion: interests of the most vocal lobbyists prevail over consumers' interest at large. This is already the case at the multilateral level, but even more so at the bilateral/regional level because of built-in flexibilities. Thus, while some political economy concepts (e.g., free trade), backed by economic theory (e.g., the theory of comparative advantages) are at the centre of the decision to

---

32 Robert B. Zoellick, 'America will not Wait for the Won't Do Countries', *The Financial Times*, 22 September 2003, p. 23.

negotiate trade agreements, in practice, political compromises can nullify or impair the positive economic impact of the agreements. This, in turn, supports the opponents of free trade in making their point that free trade can be harmful, creating a vicious circle: more concessions are likely to be made to groups representing defensive interests and, in the end, trade diversion overshadows trade creation.

A. A political decision with a varnish of economic rationale

The hypothesis that bilateral/regional trade agreements are driven by economics could be empirically tested. However, it is unclear what economic theory recommends as even PTAs have their fervent opponents and supporters among economists. A useful step was made in the 1950s, when Jacob Viner, followed by James Meade, articulated the concepts of trade creation and trade diversion.[33] Since then, theories of economic integration have flourished[34] and a certain number of conditions, which help trade creation effects outweigh trade diversion effects, have tentatively appeared. In the 1990s however, the belief remained that traditional trade theory did not adequately explain the attractiveness of bilateralism/regionalism (the theory was, incidentally, likewise unable to sufficiently explain the potential benefits of non-discriminatory trade liberalisation). As a result, a new trade theory began to explore the implications of imperfect competition in an increasingly integrated world economy.[35] Subsequently, a distinction was also made between deep and shallow integration.[36] Did, however, this vast economic literature and quest for the optimal FTA influence policy makers at any stage?

Jacob Viner intuitively provided an answer to this question when he concluded that:

> [Customs unions] are unlikely to yield more economic benefit than harm, unless they are between sizable countries which practice substantial protection of substantially similar industries. But customs unions of this character have always been extremely difficult to negotiate in a nationalistic and protectionist world.[37]

A few decades later, Viner's conclusion remains valid: without regard to economists' recommendations, countries have continued to negotiate PTAs with countries of different sizes and exclude sensitive sectors when doing so. Similarly, the model of

---

33 Jacob Viner, *The Customs Union Issue* (New York: The Carnegie Endowment for Development, 1950); and James E. Meade, *The Theory of Customs Unions* (Amsterdam: North Holland, 1955).
34 See, e.g., the literature review in Alfred Tovias, 'A Survey of the Theory of Economic Integration' (1991) 15(1) *Journal of European Integration* 5–23.
35 Dean A. DeRosa and John Gilbert, 'Technical Appendix. Quantitative Estimates of the Economic Impacts of US Bilateral Free-Trade Agreements', Background Paper Prepared For the Conference on Free-Trade Agreements and US Trade Policy, Washington, DC, Institute for International Economics, 7–8 May 2003, at p. 4.
36 *Ibid.*, at p. 5.   37 Viner, above n. 33, at p. 135.

deep integration is rarely adopted, despite the potentially higher welfare gains.[38] Put another way, most PTAs remain based on a model of 'shallow' integration. The best illustration of this disregard for economics (and any form of guideline for the conclusion of PTAs) is that of the WTO Committee on Regional Trade Agreements. While this committee was set up to review all agreements of which the WTO is notified, it has never properly functioned, and neither has it adequately ensured the adherence of PTAs to WTO rules.[39] These rules, as contained in Article XXIV of the GATT, were designed to ensure that bilateral/regional trade agreements facilitated trade between the contracting parties without raising barriers to trade with the rest of the world. Such rules transcribed an economic rationale that would be theorised just a few years later. But here again, members treated the implementation of these rules as a political issue (despite their logic and economic merits), and no agreement could ever be reached on their interpretation e.g., on the portion of trade that should be fully liberalised in PTAs.[40]

In sum, if bilateral/regional trade agreements were totally driven by economics, they would probably have a different shape or coverage and involve different groupings of countries. Members of the WTO would also be less fearful of the conclusions of the Committee on Regional Trade Agreements and decisions would remain mostly political. However, political and economical doctrines are intertwined. To quote John M. Keynes:

> [T]he ideas of economists and political philosophers, both when they are right and when they are wrong, are more powerful than is commonly understood. Indeed, the world is ruled by little else. Practical men, who believe themselves to be quite exempt from any intellectual influences, are usually the slave of some defunct economist.[41]

History is composed of a succession of phases of protectionism and trade openings with trade policies (including decisions to negotiate bilateral/regional agreements) varying according to the changes in political regimes and majorities of the day. For example, Louis Napoleon Bonaparte (Napoleon III) was exposed to the liberal model while in exile in England and, shortly after the restoration of the French Empire, he amended the Constitution so as to gain the power to conclude BTAs with legal effect.[42] This was the origin of the 1860 French trade agreement with England and

---

38 See, e.g., the recommendations made in David Evans *et al.*, *Assessing Regional Trade Agreements with Developing Countries: Shallow and Deep Integration, Trade, Productivity, and Economic Performance*, Report prepared for DFID by the University of Sussex (March 2006), DFID Project No. 045881.

39 See commentary by Simon Lester and Bryan Mercurio at www.worldtradelaw.net.

40 The WTO Members did agree, however, to clarify the rules on regional trade agreements as part of the DDA, and adopted a new transparency mechanism in 2006.

41 John M. Keynes, *The General Theory of Employment, Interest and Money* (New York: Harcourt, Brace and Company, 1936), at p. 383.

42 Article 6 of the 14 January 1852 Constitution and Article 3 of the 25 December 1852 Sénatus-consulte 'portant interprétation et modification de la Constitution du 14 janvier 1852' (texts available at www.conseil-constitutionnel.fr/textes/constitution/c1852.htm).

the 'free trade epidemic' that soon swept Europe. At the time, the opposition in France treated this move toward liberalism as a 'coup d'Etat douanier', revealing the strong ideological content of Napoleon III's decision.[43] A few years later, the next shift to protectionism in Europe also coincided with a change in political leadership (Bismarck in Germany). It was influenced less by liberal economic theories (Friedrich List, who suggested the use of tariff protection to allow Germany to catch up with England – free trade remained the objective, but protectionism was the way to reach it).[44] This fight between advocates and opponents of free trade goes on, and since then bilateral/regional trade agreements have been used, more or less successfully, by those in the free trade camp to anchor their reforms and bind future governments. For example, the NAFTA helped the Mexican government commit its country to liberalism.

As any change in either the terms or volume of trade has corresponding effects on every person's life in a country affected by the change, the liberalisation of trade (whether unilateral, bilateral/regional or multilateral) creates both winners and losers. The decision to liberalise trade and negotiate PTAs is thus necessarily a political one. In the US, this has in turn translated into the necessity for the President to obtain a delegation of power from Congress to negotiate trade agreements. Given the multiplicity of views on trade, the renouncement of Congress of its constitutional right to amend trade treaties was crucial to enable the President to make a political decision and conclude agreements. Recurrent debates concerning the renewal of the Trade Promotion Authority (previously known as 'fast-track') continue to reveal the lack of unanimity on the economics and politics of trade.

B. Trade diversion and the domino effect of bilateral/regional trade agreements

Because of the economic controversy over the desirability of trade liberalisation, bilateral/regional trade agreements have also been used to promote protectionism and segment markets. The most famous example is probably the 1834 *Deutscher Zollverein* (German customs union) where under the Prussian leadership, German states established a customs union with the aim of facilitating trade among themselves whilst simultaneously allowing the adoption of high common external tariffs to protect German infant industries from foreign competition, in particular that of England. Trade diversion was clearly the short-term objective, although in List's mind economic catch up would eventually facilitate free trade.[45] With this historical

---

43 Pierre Bezbakh, 'Napoleon III et le libre-échange', *Le Monde Economie*, 2 December 2003.
44 Friedrich List, *The National System of Political Economy* (London: Longmans, Green and Co, 1909) (translated 1885 from German, first published in 1841).
45 *Ibid.*, Book II, Chapter XXVI 'Customs Duties as a Chief Means of Establishing and Protecting the Internal Manufacturing Power'.

precedent in mind Article XXIV(4) of the GATT stipulates that 'the objective of a customs union or a free trade agreement should be to facilitate trade between the constituent territories and not to raise barriers to the trade of other contracting parties with such territories'. The absence of institutionalised reviews of modern FTAs contributed, however, to the survival of trade diversion effects.

These trade diversion effects, whether as the objective or just an undesired result of a bilateral/regional trade agreement, are the main factors for the proliferation of these agreements.[46] This is, in a way, an example of economics having the last laugh in that even where a bilateral/regional agreement is initially concluded for non-economic reasons, countries not originally party to the agreement will still have an incentive to join the agreement or conclude side agreements to restore market access (and remedy the effects of trade diversion). This is what some authors have called a 'domino effect'.[47] History abounds in examples of this effect of PTA proliferation. The above-mentioned *Zollverein* is a good illustration of the phenomenon, as initially only a few German states had formed the customs union but the threat of trade diversion to exporters within the *Zollverein* led to the eventual adhesion of all German states.[48] In the 1860s, the conclusion of a PTA between Europe's two major powers (France and England) led to a 'free trade epidemic'. In modern history, the progressive enlargement of the European Economic Community (EEC) and its subsequent transformation into the EU is yet another example, for although Britain initially stayed out of the EEC to maintain political independence, it eventually sought membership when its share of intra-European trade declined as a result of trade diversion. What began with only six original members now has twenty-seven.[49] The 2000 European Union–Mexico Free Trade Agreement had similar roots: as a result of the NAFTA, the share of the EU in Mexican trade dropped from 10.6% in 1991 to 6.5% in 1999, and the average Mexican tariffs on EU goods stood at 8.7%, compared to only 2% on US goods. The EU responded by concluding a PTA with Mexico, and less than a year after that agreement had entered into force, Mexican exports to the EU had grown by 40%, and EU exports to Mexico by 60%.[50] In other words, the trade-diverting effects of the NAFTA on the EU had been restricted through the latter's proactive response.

The proliferation of PTAs has, however, had very different effects at different times in history. In the nineteenth century, the proliferation of PTAs resulted in a general lowering of tariffs because of the MFN clause contained in the agreements. Modern PTAs do not include an MFN clause but are instead conceived as exceptions to the

---

46 David Lazer, 'The Free-Trade Epidemic of the 1860's and Other Outbreaks of Economic Discrimination' (1999) 51(4)*The Journal of World Politics* 447–83.
47 Richard E. Baldwin, 'Multilateralising Regionalism: Spaghetti Bowls as Building Blocks on the Path to Global Free-Trade' (2006) 29(11) *The World Economy* 1451–518.
48 Lazer, above n. 46, at 479.   49 *Ibid.*, at 480.
50 Pascal Lamy, 'La politique commerciale envers l'Amérique Latine: Priorité de l'Union européenne', Speech, Casa de America, Madrid, 26 July 2001.

MFN treatment granted by the WTO. Thus, the proliferation of PTAs does not necessarily offer a harmonising effect. On the contrary, the 'spaghetti bowl' effect prevails, and contributes to the increased differentiation of treatment among countries. This effect is further aggravated by the complexity of rules contained in modern PTAs, which no longer simply concern tariffs, but rather comprise a complex set of rules and disciplines on trade and trade-related issues. This proliferation of rules has itself come at the price of a reduction in the security of transactions and additional administrative burdens for exporters (e.g., to comply with different rules of origin). Eventually, it is likely that this will lead exporters operating in world markets to ask for a further harmonisation of rules – a 'multilateralisation of regionalism'.[51] While the WTO (multilateralism) will have an important role to play toward this end, bilateral/regional trade agreements will not disappear. The jury is still out on many issues where the US and EU positions remain irreconcilable. Since provisions contained in the agreements concluded by the US and the EU tend to be uniform, a likely intermediary step could therefore be the polarisation of the world through the use, by each trade superpower, of a web of bilateral/regional trade agreements. Enlargement of such spheres of influence will, however, take time, and the EU experience shows that the next stage of 'deepening' trade agreements will be a difficult one. Finally, the level of ambition and progress made on the negotiations of the TTIP will provide a good indication of the credibility of the 'multilateralisation' process.

In sum, bilateral/regional agreements are here to stay, and the proliferation of FTAs is likely to continue at a fast pace.

IV. Bilateral/regional agreements are primarily driven by political considerations and are an instrument of foreign policy

The 'domino effect' is the revenge of economics. It also reveals a fundamental inequality among countries vis-à-vis bilateral/regional trade agreements and explains why a typology of these agreements does not make sense: namely that the proliferation of bilateral/regional trade agreements is driven by the race for leadership for some, and the fear of exclusion for others. In other words, the motives behind PTAs are often quite different for two parties to the same agreement. This is only a partial revenge, however, as the domino effect does not explain why regional trading powers in the first place decide to negotiate trade agreements, nor, more importantly, how they choose their partners. It also does not explain the reason behind the use of bilateral/regional trade agreements between countries of the same economic size. Indeed, politics remains the main driver of FTAs both domestically and geopolitically.

51 See, e.g., Baldwin, above n. 47.

A. *The political objectives behind bilateral/regional trade agreements*

In the period of history that pre-dates the introduction of trade agreements, trade provisions were included in navigation acts – understandably since freedom to trade was predominantly concerned with the access of foreign merchants to ports and the open use of the sea. Trade policy was an appendage to geopolitics, and vice versa, and the control of main navigation roads was seen as a strategic objective from both a military/security and commercial perspective. For example, in 1580, Portugal's loss of independence to Spain created a monopoly on trade in spices from the Indies. Without competition, Spain could raise European prices and shut the free-trading Dutch out of the market. Similarly, Prussia's main objective for the German *Zollverein* was to create a unified Germany under its political influence whilst its deliberate decision to exclude Austria from the customs union was a purely geopolitical move. Since then, trade policy and geopolitics have remained intertwined, but the strategic focuses have changed.

The best illustration of the geopolitical dimension of trade, and the role of bilateral/regional agreements, is the race for power between the EU and the US. When the EU negotiates a trade agreement with Mexico, Chile, or MERCOSUR, it is partially to avoid trade diversion effects prompted by the similar negotiations of these states with the US (see above). Nonetheless, it is also a geopolitical decision:

> The success of MERCOSUR is in Europe's best interest. Let's remember the results of MERCOSUR: not so long ago, Brazil and Argentina were nuclear powers. With MERCOSUR, it is not the case anymore. Let's remember also the fundamental role played by MERCOSUR in the consolidation of democracy in the Southern Cone, for instance in Paraguay. The trade negotiations engaged by the EU with MERCOSUR fit into the frame: the objective is political ... During the last session of negotiations that took place in Montevideo at the beginning of July (2001), we presented concrete proposals to open our market to their industrial and agricultural goods and to their services. We could have waited because MERCOSUR was not ready. We choose to do it for political reasons. For posing a political act ... And this, a year before negotiations on the Free Trade of Americas Act (FTAA) is seriously discussed.[52]

Obviously, trade policy is no longer simply concerned with securing navigation routes, and neither is it only about reducing tariff protection. Instead, the trade policies of today appear to centre more on the race for leadership between the US and the EU to impose a set of rules (e.g., on competition, investment, and intellectual property) and standards (e.g., on agricultural products) on the rest of the world.[53] Bilateral/regional trade agreements have become the main vehicles of this

---

52 Lamy, above n. 50 (author's translation).
53 Olivier Cattaneo, *Quelles ambitions pour la politique commerciale de l'Union européenne?* (Paris: Institut Français des Relations Internationales, 2002), at pp. 22–3.

competition to extend normative and economic influence much in the same way the US and the Soviet Union (USSR) raced to conclude bilateral/regional 'pacts' in order to extend their respective spheres of influence during the Cold War. The current proliferation of FTAs could be referred to as a real 'pactomania'.[54] Referring again to the FTAA, then European Commissioner Pascal Lamy warned:

> With the Pan-American zone, the US has an opportunity to impose its regulatory system to the whole continent, which would cause a serious problem to the EU ... We are in competition with the US. On agriculture, services, investment regimes, intellectual property, and public procurement, offers will escalate. Ultimately, the countries of the Southern Cone will need to decide which type of 'geo-economic-political' equilibrium they desire between the US and the EU.[55]

For the two major trading powers, the political importance of bilateral/regional trade agreements goes beyond the competition for regulatory leadership. For the EU, it is obvious as the Union itself is based on a single market, that is a model of regional deep trade integration. The initial objective of the EEC was to create economic solidarities among European countries (starting with steel and coal production) that would make another war between France and Germany 'not only unimaginable, but also technically impossible'.[56] In the mind of its founding fathers, like Jean Monnet and Robert Schuman, building Europe was building peace. Trade integration (free movement of goods, services, capital, and people) was just a means whereas political stability was the end. This original concept largely shaped the bilateral trade policy of the EU, and in particular the so-called 'neighbourhood policy' where economic integration is seen as a preparatory step to political integration for some, or a gauge of prosperity, stability, and security for others.[57] Only recently, when the EU had integrated most of its like-minded neighbouring countries, could the Commission revert to an ostensibly more economically-driven bilateral/regional trade policy.

The organic peculiarity of the EU (not a sovereign state, but a union of countries, with common institutions and shared powers) makes its trade policy even more of a political tool. Indeed, the EU uses trade policy as a weapon to struggle for power abroad *and* domestically. Since 1970, trade policy has been the prerogative of the European Communities (EC); at the WTO or in bilateral trade negotiations, the EC represents its members and negotiates with a mandate. Qualified majority voting is used at the European Council upstream and downstream (i.e., one member alone

---

54 *Ibid.*
55 Pascal Lamy, 'Les règles de l'OMC doivent être revues', *La Tribune*, 14 May 2001 (author's translation).
56 See, e.g., the famous *Discours de l'horloge* given by Robert Schuman on 9 May 1950 at the Ministry of Foreign Affairs in Paris, France.
57 See, e.g., the Stability Pact concluded with the Balkan countries in 2001 (half of them have joined the EU already), or the European Neighbourhood Policy in place since 2004.

cannot block the decision to conclude an agreement). In other fields of foreign policy, members have not transferred their powers, and unanimity is required. While the EU is a main actor on the WTO/trade scene, it is absent at the United Nations (UN) or Bretton Woods institutions (International Monetary Fund, World Bank). The helplessness of the EU was illustrated during the war in former Yugoslavia and other major international political crises. As a result of these organic constraints, the European Commission has tended to use trade policy as a tool box for foreign policy: European FTAs and preferential schemes include provisions that far exceed the scope of (*stricto sensu*) trade policy.[58] For example, the Generalised System of Tariff Preferences (GSP) requires, for additional concessions (GSP+), the ratification and effective application of 27 key international conventions on sustainable development and good governance. As another example, the Cotonou Agreement promotes, among others, democracy, transparent and accountable governance, the fight against corruption and bribery, social dialogue and respect for basic rights including gender equity, environment protection, etc.[59] Thus, bilateral/regional trade agreements are a key foreign policy instrument for the EU, and at the same time an important instrument for domestic policy, extending the powers of the Commission *vis-à-vis* its members. For example, both the Amsterdam and Nice treaties extended the scope of trade policy to include intellectual property and services, and there was a similar attempt at the inclusion of investment in the prerogatives of the Commission under Article 133 of the EU Treaty.[60] In other words, motives behind the conclusion of trade agreements (including bilateral/regional) are only remotely trade related.

The US is in a different position. As a sovereign state, it has other instruments to promote foreign policy objectives. Bilateral/regional trade agreements can also be backed by other purely political treaties (e.g., on security). This did not, however, prevent the US from using PTAs as a foreign policy instrument. 'Compatibility with US interests' is one of the six factors that guide the discussion in selecting future PTA partners: 'A potential PTA partner is examined for its compatibility with broad US interests, including its support for US foreign policy positions.'[61] This compatibility criterion has proven prevalent in US trade relations and it is worth remembering that the first PTA concluded by the US since the creation of the GATT was with Israel in 1985 – an agreement that commentators observe has a special importance to US foreign policy that extends far beyond its trade coverage.[62] PTAs have been used, at the beginning of the twenty-first century, as an instrument of the 'war on terror' and a

---

58 Olivier Cattaneo, 'La politique commerciale, fer de lance de l'action extérieure de l'Europe' (May–June 2002) 99 *Défense* 53–4.

59 Olivier Cattaneo and Christian Pitschas, 'The Link Between the Trade and Development Policies of the European Union' (Autumn–Winter 2005) 3 *The European Enterprise Journal* 12–18.

60 Cattaneo, above n. 53, at p. 48.   61 USGAO, above n. 6, at p. 10.

62 Howard Rosen, 'Free-Trade Agreements as Foreign Policy Tools: The US–Israel and US–Jordan PTAs', in Jeffrey J. Schott (ed.), *Free-Trade Agreements: US Strategies and Priorities* (Washington: Institute for International Economics, 2004), pp. 51–77.

reward for countries supporting US efforts in Iraq (the 'coalition of the willing'); about half of the countries selected by the US for PTA negotiations supported the US policy in Iraq.[63] The US entered into an agreement with Australia (who is also part of the coalition) but not with its neighbour New Zealand (who is not part of the coalition and furthermore has an anti-nuclear position that caused friction with the US).[64] Summarising the motives behind the PTA with Morocco, the USGAO noted:

> Although a US–Morocco FTA would have a minimal trade benefit to the United States, one USTR official stated that this FTA would further the administration's goal of promoting openness, tolerance, and economic growth across the volatile Middle-East. Morocco, a moderate Muslim country, also signaled its readiness to enter into a comprehensive FTA by demonstrating its willingness to liberalize its economy and make domestic reforms.[65]

Similarly, for the United States–Bahrain Free Trade Agreement, the USGAO concluded: 'Although Bahrain represents a small share of US trade, an PTA with this US ally and moderate Muslim nation would support US security and political goals by fostering prosperity in the region.'[66] In 2009, the US concluded another PTA with Oman. Of course, motives behind PTAs are just as diverse as US foreign policy objectives; for example, the US could negotiate PTAs with members of the G20 with a view to weaken this coalition.[67]

Similar to Europe, these agreements can also serve *domestic* policy objectives. For example, the agreement with Mexico was partially aimed at containing migration pressures, and the insistence of the majority in Congress in 2007 to include more ambitious labour provisions in PTAs was meant to put pressure on domestic reforms. The vote on the Trade Promotion Authority is therefore only partially driven by trade considerations. But bilateral/regional trade agreements are just one of the available instruments that serve these domestic and foreign policy objectives. For example, unilateral trade preferences are also driven by political factors, as illustrated by the new denomination of the 2002 Andean Trade Promotion and Drug Eradication Act (previously known as the Andean Trade Preference Act first enacted in 1991 to combat drug production and trafficking in Bolivia, Colombia, Ecuador, and Peru). In 2009 and 2012, respectively, the US concluded PTAs with Peru and Colombia. Unilateral trade sanctions on Libya and Cuba have also long served strictly political objectives.

The use of bilateral/regional trade agreements as instruments of foreign policy is not, however, the privilege of the US and the EU. In recent years, the multiplication of PTAs in Asia has been one of the responses to the 'China challenge' with its economic (e.g., maintaining the capacity of neighbouring countries to attract foreign direct

63 Murray Gibbs and Swarnim Wagle, 'Fear of Exclusion: The Driving Force Behind North-South PTAs', UNDP Discussion Paper (2005), at pp. 6–7.
64 *Ibid.*   65 USGAO at p. 12.   66 *Ibid.*, at p. 11.   67 Gibbs and Wagle, above n. 63, at p. 7.

investment) and geopolitical dimensions (e.g., stability in the region).[68] Taiwan, thus far excluded from major regional agreements (such as ASEAN), is now urging the US to conclude a bilateral PTA:

> Taiwan's trading partners are looking for the leadership in the US before considering the negotiation of FTAs with Taiwan. As a consequence, Taiwan risks becoming isolated and weakened economically. Taiwan is an important force in maintaining peace and stability in the Asia Pacific. A marginalised and economically weakened Taiwan will not be in a position to contribute to the long-term stability of the region.[69]

Conversely, China has first become active in negotiating PTAs to isolate Taiwan. Other motives behind the Chinese PTAs include the decision by PTA partners not to apply provisions contained in its terms of accession to the WTO, which permit WTO members to impose restrictions against China that would otherwise be prohibited by WTO rules, including provisions specific to the 'non-market economy status' of China.[70] For instance, Singapore has used its PTAs as a 'door-opener' to gain access to 'other strategic, security-related agreements'.[71] Energy security is also a possible motive: for example, Japan is seeking security of supply commitments in its PTA negotiations with Indonesia, a member of the Organization of Petroleum-Exporting Countries (OPEC).[72] In India, foreign policy considerations prevail. Similarly, on the African continent, PTAs with little substance or economic sense proliferate, raising serious implementation issues.

The race for influence in Asia has crystallised in the negotiations of the Trans-Pacific Partnership Agreement (TPP) among APEC countries and the Regional Comprehensive Economic Partnership (RCEP) between China and the ten ASEAN countries together with India, South Korea, Japan, Australia, and New Zealand, but not the US. Seven countries currently participate in both sets of negotiations: Australia, Brunei, Japan, Malaysia, New Zealand, Singapore, and Vietnam. For the US, the TPP is clearly about reinforcing its political influence in Asia; for China, it is about ruling out some of the disciplines and standards promoted by the US and resisting the US encirclement strategy; for countries participating to both sets of negotiations, it is about protesting against the use of PTAs as foreign policy instruments and imperialistic rhetoric. In spite of these protests, given the incompatibility

---

68 Christopher Findlay, Mohd Hafleh Piei and Mari Pangestu, 'Trading with Favorites: Risks, Motives and Implications of PTAs in Asia Pacific', Background Paper to the Pacific Economic Co-operation Council (PECC) Trade Forum, 22–23 April 2003, Washington, DC, at p. 12.

69 Sheng-Cheng Hu (Minister of State and Chairman, Council for Economic Planning and Development, Executive Yuan), 'Taiwan's Economy and the Role of a US–Taiwan PTA', Speech to the Annual Board of Directors of the US–Taiwan Business Council (28 November 2006), p. 3.

70 Gibbs and Wagle, above n. 63, at p. 4.

71 Razeen Sally, 'FTAs and the Prospects for Regional Integration in Asia', European Centre for International Political Economy (ECIPE) Working Paper No. 1, Brussels (2006) at p. 5.

72 Gibbs and Wagle, above n. 63, at p. 6.

of the US and China's approach to PTAs, countries in the region will have to choose their geopolitical allegiance and economic paradigm.[73]

If PTAs were not primarily driven by politics, how could we explain the negotiation of an agreement between Singapore and Kuwait, Sri Lanka and Iran, Taiwan and Nicaragua, etc.? In the context of proliferation, both rational and irrational fear of exclusion and mimesis drive new negotiations. Sally summarises:

> [Most PTAs] tend to be driven by foreign policy aspirations, but with justifications that are all too often vague, muddled and trivial, having little relevance to commercial realities and the economic nuts and bolts of trade agreements. This can amount to little more than symbolic copycatting of other countries' FTA activity and otherwise empty gesture politics. In such cases economic strategy is conspicuous by its absence.[74]

B. The imbalance of powers resulting from the prevalence of political objectives

The fact that most PTAs are driven by politics has important consequences. First, it is difficult to assess the results – and even more so the success – of a PTA. Too often commentators judge PTAs in light of their economic effects, when the objective of the parties could have been purely political. How does one measure, for instance, the contribution of a trade agreement to the political stability of a region? On the other hand, the absence of economic evaluation helps to hide the imbalance of some agreements and the uneven sharing of their costs and benefits. Also worth noting is the fact that foreign policy ambitions and geopolitical power vary significantly from country to country – the effectiveness of PTAs as a means of achieving foreign policy objectives thus varies accordingly. While merely political gesticulations for some, PTAs can be an effective means of imposing extra-territorial reforms for others. This again can lead to significant imbalances.

Before reciprocity was introduced in bilateral/regional trade agreements, trade concessions were made unilaterally, either voluntarily or forced through so-called 'unequal treaties'. At the time, the link between geopolitics and trade was obvious: unequal treaties were signed with China as a result of the First Opium War (e.g., the Treaty of Nanking, 1842); similar treaties were concluded with Japan (between 1854 and 1858) and Korea (between 1876 and 1910). The objective was for the European powers to gain access to Asian ports and exhort lower tariffs for their exports. Similarly, Britain obtained important trade concessions from the Ottoman Empire in consideration for its military assistance, for example against Syria (Treaty of Balta Liman, 1838). Modern agreements cannot be compared to these instruments of

---

73 Jane Kelsey, *Hidden Agendas: What We Need to Know About the TPPA* (Wellington: Bridget Williams Books, 2013).
74 Sally, above n. 71, at p. 6.

imperialism – nonetheless, despite the introduction of the concept of reciprocity, some imbalances remain. While the regional or world trade superpowers can choose conditions attached to a PTA (rule-makers), smaller countries often have no choice but to accept these conditions (rule-takers) or run the risk of exclusion.

In their analysis of the process of accession to the WTO, Evenett and Braga concluded that, since 1995, 'the price of joining the WTO is steadily rising, [. . . and] now includes commitments that go beyond the GATT/WTO agreements'.[75] The question is whether the same logic applies to PTAs, in other words, whether the price to pay for PTAs (scope of commitments) increases with time, as the fear of exclusion and diversion effects reduce the bargaining power of a country. A positive answer would give a premium to the first mover(s), and explain the 'FTA epidemic'. In practice, however, there is no such evidence: for example, not all FTAs negotiated by the US included comparable (if at all) provisions on labour or environmental standards, and the content of the PTAs has fluctuated more with the majority in Congress at the time of negotiation than with time. On the other hand, it remains true that the US and the EU, as noted earlier, have 'pet' provisions that appear in all their PTAs (e.g., geographical indications for the EU, and TRIPS+ provisions on patents for the US). With time and the multiplication of non-tariff barriers to trade, PTAs have also become more sophisticated: for example, in its 'Global Europe' strategy, the EU called for a 'new generation' of EU competitiveness-driven PTAs that would include stronger rules in 'new trade areas' of importance to the EU, notably intellectual property, services, investment, public procurement, and competition.[76] In practice, it also appears that the EU expects from its future partners a level of concession at least equal to the one conceded to the US in earlier agreements: for example, the Central America–Dominican Republic–United States Free Trade Agreement (CAFTA–DR–US), which was the starting point of the European Economic Partnership Agreement (EPA) negotiations in the Caribbean region. Thus, the cost of PTAs is increasing with their proliferation, but does not discriminate between first movers and late comers.

Reciprocity in PTAs is largely illusory: concessions are reciprocal, but the 'anchor' country can choose the level and content of these concessions, and impose them on any country willing to join its PTA web. Often, in North–South agreements, the developing country also enters into the agreement with a view to ensuring the maintenance of tariff preferences that the anchor country had previously granted unilaterally. In other words, reciprocity consists in consolidating *old* concessions for the anchor and making *new* concessions for the developing country. The current negotiation of the EPAs is a good example: required by the WTO to reform its system of preferences in favour of the Africa Caribbean Pacific (ACP) countries, the

---

75 Simon J. Evenett and Carlos A. Primo Braga, 'WTO Accession: Lesson from Experience', World Bank Trade Note Series No. 22 (6 June 2005), at p. 2.
76 European Commission, above n. 1, at p. 7.

EU offered to negotiate a regional trade agreement (RTA) with each sub-section of the group.[77] While these agreements would restore reciprocity and compatibility with WTO law, many critics suggested that the ACP countries were the only ones paying the cost of these new regional agreements.[78] So far, the EU has only concluded one EPA with the CARIFORUM states, and interim EPAs with the Pacific, Eastern and Southern Africa, and some individual states of other groups. In August 2006, the US Administration also launched a review of its GSP programme, seeking comments on eligibility criteria and competitive need limitation (CNL) waivers.[79] The threat of possible removal of GSP eligibility might create an incentive for some countries to negotiate a PTA with the US with a view to preserving their access to the US market; these countries would, however, have to reciprocate the US concessions.

At different stages of development, countries seem to have different needs which are reflected in the sophistication of the bilateral/regional trade agreements they negotiate. The problem with the asymmetry of the bilateral/regional trade negotiations comes when agreements negotiated by the US or the EU might not best suit the needs of their partners. At an early stage of industrialisation and development in the nineteenth century, England negotiated PTAs that merely attempted to secure market access (see Part II above). With the 'new generation' of bilateral/regional trade agreements, market access is just one part of the deal and for most developing countries, participation in a 'new generation' agreement requires significant regulatory reforms, e.g., in the fields of competition, investment or intellectual property laws. Some of these reforms go further than what is required by the WTO and can be costly, e.g., the establishment of a sophisticated system of registry and monitoring of geographical indications. Here again, the cost of joining a 'reciprocal' agreement is uneven as the 'anchor' country does not need to reform in any way, given that its own regulatory framework serves as a model. PTAs of the kind negotiated by the European nations in the 1860s would therefore be better suited to the needs of developing countries, as current North–South FTAs are trapped in the paradox of being used by developed countries to go further than the WTO when developing countries already have problems implementing the reforms necessary for full compliance with their multilateral commitments.

South–South and North–North agreements should suffer less from this imbalance. Here again, however, the largely political dimension of bilateral/regional trade agreements alters this logic: a transatlantic PTA would make most sense from an economic perspective, but the political gaps between the US and the EU will not be easily bridged in the TPP negotiations. In the South, the number of bilateral/regional

---

77 See, e.g., www.ec.europa.eu/trade/issues/bilateral/regions/acp/index_en.htm, or www.acp-eu-trade.org for further details about the EPAs.
78 See, e.g., www.epawatch.eu, which contains documents prepared by state and non-state actors, and shows the diversity of views and concerns about the EPA negotiations.
79 Office of the USTR, 'Administration to Review Whether to Continue Trade Benefits under the GSP Program', *Press Release*, 7 August 2006.

trade agreements has flourished, but political will has often been lacking at the implementation stage. Most of these agreements have thus remained empty shells (e.g., the Greater Arab Free Trade Area (GAFTA), where the principle of free trade was adopted, but export licenses are hardly ever granted). In sum, given the political nature of PTAs, it is not surprising that the best results are obtained where *political integration* is as much an objective as *economic integration*. This helps to explain the success of European economic integration, both as an instrument of growth/development and political stability in the region.

V. Conclusion

There is no straight answer to the original question 'Why do countries conclude PTAs?', and the multiplicity of objectives assigned to PTAs makes a typology of the agreements largely impossible. It seems clear, however, that the political economy of bilateral/regional trade agreements revolves more around politics than economics. If this were not the case, the shape of the agreements and the participating countries themselves would be different – for example, the transatlantic partnership would be reinforced and most African RTAs would either disappear or be more thoroughly implemented. This does not exclude a role for economics in the decision-making process as the fear of exclusion and that of the negative trade diversion effects of PTAs largely explain the current proliferation of agreements. An agreement concluded on political grounds can give birth to a stream of agreements driven by economic considerations.

The fact that bilateral/regional trade agreements are primarily a political phenomenon explains the fact that they might be fashionable one day, and in disgrace the next. The free trade rush that Europe experienced in the 1860s was followed by a complete return to protectionism. In more recent US history, the arrival of the George W. Bush Administration coincided with an acceleration of the negotiation of FTAs in the name of the so-called 'competitive liberalisation'. Similarly, the content of FTAs can change with the majority in Congress – after the Democratic Party won the 2006 congressional elections, it asked for a re-negotiation of the FTAs with Peru and Colombia to include provisions on labour standards.

Despite all criticisms and fears, bilateral/regional agreements are here to stay. From an historical perspective, multilateralism is the exception rather than the rule. Taking a provocative stance, one could say that the GATT 1947 was only a hiccup of history, and probably the largest PTA the US has ever concluded. From the 23 original contracting parties of the GATT to the 159 members of the WTO, the practicality of multilateralism has diminished. The MFN clause that most commentators associate today with the multilateral trading system (and the WTO) was originally embodied in bilateral/regional trade agreements, but nowadays these agreements are perceived as exceptions to the MFN clause. This fundamental change has affected the desirability of PTAs: in the 1860s, their proliferation resulted in a virtuous circle of trade liberalisation, because they embodied an MFN clause. Today, however, the proliferation of bilateral/regional trade agreements creates a vicious circle, in which discrimination becomes the rule and the MFN treatment in the WTO a 'least-favoured treatment' of sorts. Accepting that the GATT was the largest PTA ever concluded and that every single agreement should include an MFN clause[80] would restore some equity and positive spin. That would require, however, a complete revolution of the system.

The continuous use of bilateral/regional trade agreements in history should not mask the fact that these agreements have dramatically changed over time. The suppression of the MFN clause is not their only mutation. Partially, the agreements changed with the needs of the trading nation: in the 1860s market access was the central goal (the opening of ports and the reduction of tariffs). Today non-tariff barriers play a more important role. It is common practice that modern PTAs tackle those barriers. Sometimes, however, countries use trade agreements to pursue objectives that are far removed from trade itself. As a result, these agreements can be poorly suited to the development needs of their poorest participants. The main problem here is that trade facilitation has the potential to equate to the adoption of more sophisticated rules and bodies to supervise the implementation of the rules: it is not only about removing barriers, but also adopting new laws or creating new administrative bodies. This requires significant technical assistance. If bilateral/regional agreements are to make sense and not be confined to political gesticulation, they should be accompanied by the transfer of technical and financial means that would help their implementation and enforcement. It should be remembered that the GATT, if treated as the largest PTA ever concluded by the US, was accompanied by the Marshall Plan and vast transfers of wealth to Europe. Similarly, the European integration was a success because of internal transfers in favour of lagging regions (European Regional Development Fund). The main challenge is therefore to develop a method of monitoring aid for trade in bilateral/regional agreements rather than exclusively focusing on multilateral issues, given that PTAs often demand much more extensive effort than do the WTO agreements from developing countries.

---

80 Often, the MFN clause is misinterpreted: it applies only to contracting parties to an agreement. For example, if the US concludes a PTA with Israel, and subsequently concludes a PTA with Canada, the application of the MFN clause would require that the US applies to both countries the most favourable conditions contained in either of the treaties. It does not mean that the US would have to extend any of these treatments to the rest of the world. Similarly, the MFN clause in the GATT applies only to WTO members, but the quasi-universal membership creates some confusion.

4

Bilateral and plurilateral PTAs

DAVID EVANS*

I. Introduction

The immense level of international effort being devoted to free trade agreements (FTA) negotiations shows no sign of abating. Negotiating preferential trade agreements (PTAs) has been elevated from a sideshow to the World Trade Organization (WTO) to centre stage in many countries' trade policies. The halting pace of the Doha Round has increased the pressure to find alternatives. Many of the obvious and easy deals and partnerships have been formed, but the search for new partners continues.

A significant portion of recent PTA activity is directed at negotiating plurilateral PTAs. This is nothing new. Many of the best-known and most successful PTAs are multipartite unions, such as the European Union (EU) and North American Free Trade Agreement (NAFTA). Likewise the phenomenon of the 'hub and spoke' pattern of agreements is also well recognised, whereby an established 'hub' such as the EU seeks out separate PTAs with a number of 'spoke' countries.

An examination of a number of recent plurilateral PTA negotiations, however, reveals that they do not fit so easily into this pattern. There seems to be a growing tendency to negotiate plurilateral PTAs amongst more tenuous groupings with looser underlying linkages. Some involve disparate countries that are unlikely ever to have the cohesion or concentration to operate as a hub. Others may bear a certain resemblance to the 'hub and spoke' pattern, but on closer examination show significant differences resulting from the fact that the 'hub' or the 'spoke' is comprised of a group of countries that is still in the process of pursuing internal economic integration at the same time as negotiating externally with third countries.

These 'new generation' plurilateral PTAs pose new complexities and challenges. Academic writing has tried to keep apace. A smorgasbord of food-related metaphors has emerged, and whether the preference is for Italian (spaghetti) or Asian (noodles), the general view is of a bowl beginning to overflow. Attempts are made to grapple with the important but complex question of whether this constitutes a building block or stumbling block to global economic well being. Analysis in that context, understandably, focuses on qualitative analysis of the nature and scope of PTA obligations.

---

* The views expressed in this chapter are those of the author alone and not of the New Zealand Ministry of Foreign Affairs and Trade.

However there are also more practical issues and complexities to address in the context of these 'new generation' plurilateral PTAs. How are such agreements to be negotiated? How are they to be structured so as to best reflect the negotiating objectives of the parties? How can differing levels of ambition and development be accommodated? How should existing and overlapping PTAs be handled? This chapter seeks to provide an initial examination of some of these issues, and starts to explore some options for addressing them.

II. The emergence of a 'new generation' of plurilateral PTAs

A. Traditional plurilateral PTAs

Plurilateral PTAs[1] constitute almost half of all PTAs notified to the WTO.[2] Indeed, some of the best-known PTAs, such as the NAFTA, the EU[3] and the European Free Trade Association (EFTA) are plurilateral. These long-established PTAs are characterised by close geographic proximity, and a reasonably high degree of economic (and in the case of the EU in particular, political) integration. Liberalisation under these traditional plurilateral PTAs tends to be broad in scope and run deep in terms of the level of commitments undertaken.

It is also clear from looking at a list of existing PTAs, that a substantial subset of plurilateral PTAs involve negotiations between a 'pre-existing bloc' of countries, such as the EU or EFTA, and a third country. These types of PTAs fall under the rubric of 'hub and spoke' agreements. The pre-existing bloc of (traditionally highly integrated) countries is the 'hub' that negotiates PTAs with other countries outside the sphere of the more integrated bloc, the 'spoke'.

The EU is the most prolific practitioner of this type of hub and spoke PTA. It has concluded over twenty PTAs with third countries ranging from Bulgaria and Norway to Egypt, South Africa and Chile.[4] Closely following (and in some respects shadowing) the EU is EFTA, which has concluded thirteen PTAs with third countries both inside and outside Europe.[5] Indeed, in combination, the hub and spoke PTAs of the

---

1 The term 'plurilateral PTA' is used in this chapter to mean a free trade agreement or customs union with more than two parties. The term is used in contrast to bilateral PTAs, which are PTAs with only two parties. The term 'plurilateral' is used rather than 'regional' as a number of the 'new generation' plurilateral PTAs discussed in this chapter reach beyond regional boundaries.

2 See 'Bilateral/Regional Trade Agreements Notified to the WTO', at www.worldtradelaw.net.

3 The EU is, of course, much more than simply a 'plurilateral PTA', but for the purposes of this chapter the term is used as useful shorthand. In the case of trade in goods, the EU comprises a customs union rather than a PTA. As we shall see, this affects the structure of PTAs concluded between the EU and third countries.

4 The EU has concluded similar agreements with: Algeria, Andorra, Bulgaria, Chile, Croatia, Egypt, Faroe Islands, Macedonia, Iceland, Israel, Jordan, Lebanon, Mexico, Morocco, Norway, OCTs, Palestinian Authority, Romania, South Africa, Switzerland, Liechtenstein, Syria, and Tunisia.

5 EFTA has concluded agreements with Bulgaria, Chile, Croatia, Macedonia, Israel, Jordan, Mexico, Morocco, Palestinian Authority, Romania, Singapore, Tunisia, and Turkey.

EU and EFTA account for just over one-fifth of all PTAs notified to the WTO and 40 per cent of all notified plurilateral PTAs.

A characteristic of these traditional plurilateral hub and spoke agreements is the degree of pre-existing integration of the 'hub'. As will be discussed in the next section, the intention of such 'hubs' is not to further liberalise amongst its own members. The intention, rather, is to offer certain trade preferences to a third country, in return for reciprocal trade preferences offered to the hub.

In many senses, then, this traditional type of hub and spoke agreement resembles a bilateral PTA, more than a truly plurilateral agreement. The negotiation takes place between two main 'actors' (the hub and the spoke), rather than an array of countries each negotiating solely on its own behalf,[6] and rights and obligations generally flow bilaterally, not multi-directionally between all parties to the PTA. The members of the pre-existing bloc (the hub) do not take on additional obligations *vis-à-vis* one another, only *vis-à-vis* the third country (the spoke).

B. Newer trends

It is widely recognised that the last decade has witnessed a surge in PTA negotiations, both bilateral and plurilateral.[7] Figures recently released by the Asian Development Bank (ADB) are particularly striking. In 1995 only three PTAs notified to the WTO involved developing member countries of the ADB. By 2005 there were twenty-seven such agreements, forty-two more were being negotiated, and another fifty-five potential agreements were the subject of feasibility studies.[8]

The reason for this increase in PTA activity is partially explained by the slow pace of multilateral trade reform at the WTO, punctuated by high-profile failures such as the 2003 collapse of talks in Cancún, and the break-down in mid-2006. And there is something of a 'domino effect' at play. As more countries engage in PTAs, the cost of staying on the sidelines increases.[9] Even countries that continue to advocate the benefits of multilateralism over bilateral or plurilateral alternatives have, out of necessity, focused increasingly on PTAs.[10]

---

6 Indeed, with respect to many areas of a negotiation, the 'hub' may have a single 'lead negotiator' that represents the interests of all members of the pre-existing bloc.

7 In fact, bilateral and plurilateral approaches to trade liberalisation have operated in tandem with multilateral approaches since the end of World War II. The dynamic between the two is complex. A recent article identifies a number of 'phases' over the last fifty years in which bilateral or plurilateral approaches to trade liberalisation have developed. See Richard E. Baldwin, 'Multilateralising Regionalism: Spaghetti Bowls as Building Blocks on the Path to Global Free Trade' (2006) 29(11) *The World Economy* 1451–518.

8 Asian Development Bank (ADB), *Asian Development Outlook 2006: Routes for Asia's Trade* (2006), at pp. 276–8, available at www.adb.org/publications/asian-development-outlook-2006-routes-asias-trades.

9 Baldwin also explains that as global tariffs are lowered, the small advantages created by relative tariff differentials matter more – another explanation for the recent surge in PTA activity. See Baldwin, above n. 7, at 1472.

10 For example, Japan, New Zealand, and Australia have traditionally been, and continue to be, staunch advocates of the multilateral process. At the time of writing all three countries are involved in multiple PTA negotiations.

As the ADB bank figures indicate, in the new millennium this trend has been nowhere more evident than in Asia.

While the current ebb in multilateral approaches to trade liberalisation continues, the pressure to find alternatives increases. One outcome of this is a push for new and more ambitious plurilateral PTAs. A recent high-profile example of this was the decision by Asia Pacific Economic Co-operation (APEC) leaders in late 2006 to undertake a study into the feasibility of a free trade agreement spanning the twenty-one economies making up APEC.

More generally, one can observe a proliferation of a 'new generation' of plurilateral free trade negotiations that differ in some important respects from their traditional counterparts. First, they are more likely to involve constellations of nations based less on immediate geography than on an assessment of economic and political mutual advantage. Second, plurilateral 'hub and spoke' agreements are being negotiated by groupings or blocs of countries that are less integrated than in the past.

An example of a PTA that differs in the first respect from traditional plurilateral PTAs is the Trans-Pacific Strategic Economic Partnership Agreement (Trans-Pacific SEP). The Trans-Pacific SEP was negotiated initially between three countries from three different regions – South America (Chile), Asia (Singapore), and Australasia (New Zealand). Brunei later joined the negotiations making it an example of a 'four-party' PTA (hence it is sometimes referred to as the P4). The ethos behind the Trans-Pacific SEP is that of open regionalism – it is open to accession by other countries, and this is actively encouraged.

Although currently stalled, another negotiation that falls into this category, but on a much grander scale, is the Free Trade Agreement of the Americas (FTAA). A full-blown FTAA would cover thirty-four countries and span the Western Hemisphere. The concept of an Asia–Pacific Free Trade Agreement also falls into this category of new generation plurilateral PTA. A twenty-one-member APEC Free Trade Area, stretching from the United States (US) and South America to Japan, China, and Australia, would represent roughly half of total world trade and 57% of global gross domestic product.

The Association of South East Asian Nations (ASEAN) provides an example of the second point of differentiation – a more recent group of countries first establishing itself as a regional bloc, and then going on to negotiate PTAs with third countries. ASEAN was first formed as a regional group in 1967. The ASEAN Free Trade Agreement (AFTA) came into force in 1992, and was originally negotiated between Brunei, Indonesia, Malaysia, Philippines, Singapore, and Thailand. AFTA has since expanded to accommodate the recently acceding ASEAN countries, Cambodia, Laos, Myanmar, and Vietnam. While ASEAN continues a programme of internal liberalisation amongst its own members, it also negotiates 'as a bloc' with third countries.[11]

---

11 In fact, for various reasons, very little intra-ASEAN trade occurs under AFTA's preferential arrangements. However, ASEAN has become sufficiently cohesive to hold itself out as a 'bloc' of countries ready to

ASEAN has already concluded a Framework Agreement,[12] a Goods Agreement,[13] and a Dispute Settlement Mechanism[14] with China, and is continuing to negotiate with China on services and investment. ASEAN is also currently negotiating PTAs with Australia and New Zealand (jointly), India, Japan, and Korea.

The European Commission has also recently sought a mandate to negotiate with ASEAN. This mandate is part of the Commission's strategy to negotiate a 'new generation' of PTAs, which includes a proposal to negotiate Association Agreements with the Central American and Andean countries. The EU is already negotiating with two regional groupings, the Common Market of the Southern Cone (MERCUSOR) and the Gulf Co-operation Council (the GCC). In the words of then Trade Commissioner Peter Mandelson, '[w]ith MERCOSUR and ASEAN, the Gulf Co-operation Council and the Central American and Andean countries, our goal is to reach agreement not with individual countries but with regional groupings who want, in their own ways, to draw the lessons of Europe's successful experience of economic integration'.[15]

The primary reason that groups of countries might want to negotiate as a 'bloc' is summarised in a recent publication by the EFTA Secretariat:

> The main reason why Iceland, Liechtenstein, Norway and Switzerland use EFTA as their common vehicle for free trade negotiations is that, as a trade grouping, the EFTA countries carry more weight as economic players and are thus more interesting for potential trade partners.[16]

As competition for PTAs intensifies, this logic suggests more countries may seek to group together to increase their attractiveness as negotiating partners, either as a 'hub', or as a 'plurilateral spoke'.[17] Examples of similar plurilateral PTAs might include the free trade agreement between Central American countries, the

---

negotiate PTAs with third countries. As noted, the first example of this was ASEAN's PTA negotiations with China.

12 Framework Agreement on Comprehensive Economic Cooperation Between the Association of South East Asian Nations and the People's Republic of China (ASEAN–China Framework Agreement).

13 Agreement on Trade in Goods of the Framework Agreement on Comprehensive Economic Co-operation between the Association of Southeast Asian Nations and the People's Republic of China (ASEAN–China Goods Agreement).

14 Agreement on Dispute Settlement Mechanism for the Framework Agreement on Comprehensive Economic Co-operation Between the Association of Southeast Asian Nations and the People's Republic of China (ASEAN–China DSM).

15 Speech by Peter Mandelson at the London School of Economics, London, 9 October 2006.

16 EFTA Secretariat, *This is EFTA* (2006), available at www.efta.int/publications/this-is-efta/this-is-efta-2006.

17 There is some academic debate about what characteristics define a 'hub'. Certainly market size is an important factor. Whether ASEAN would be considered a 'hub' or a 'spoke', for example, may depend on the negotiation. Negotiating with the EU it could perhaps be considered a 'plurilateral spoke'. Likewise when negotiating with China. Nevertheless, ASEAN certainly appears to be seeking to establish itself as an East Asian hub in its own right. For the purposes of this article, whether ASEAN, or other regional groupings such as the Central American countries, are characterised as 'hubs' or 'spokes' is less important than the fact that they are a grouping of partially integrated countries negotiating PTAs 'as a group' with one or more third countries.

Dominican Republic and the US (CAFTA–DR–US), the negotiations currently being conducted by the GCC and third countries, and negotiations by the South African Customs Union (SACU) and third countries.

These 'new generation' plurilateral PTAs present both new opportunities and new challenges. There is a large and growing literature analysing the merits of PTAs in terms of their contribution (or otherwise) to global welfare. This is often presented in terms of a building block/stumbling block dichotomy. The focus tends to be on the nature of obligations contained in any particular PTA. Some argue that the broader and deeper the commitments, and the more open and less 'reciprocal' or discriminatory such agreements are, the more likely they are to be building blocks to global economic welfare.[18]

The complexities that arise from different and overlapping rules of origin are central to this debate. One recent analysis suggests that the unbundling or fragmentation of manufacturing processes may create a political economy favourable to 'taming the tangle' of multiple rules of origin, and predicts the eventual harmonisation of such rules. The analysis is, therefore, cautiously optimistic regarding the spaghetti-bowl-as-building-block scenario.[19] Others are more sceptical.[20]

Whatever view one may take on these important matters, this 'new generation' of plurilateral PTAs unquestionably also presents new challenges at a more practical level. They raise a set of issues that are more complex than those raised by their traditional counterparts. For a start, the groupings of countries involved are often more diverse geographically and economically, encompassing countries at different levels of development, not to mention political and cultural differences. The groupings may already be partially integrated themselves, or still in the process of integration.

How are such agreements to be negotiated? How are they to be structured so as to best reflect the negotiating objectives of the parties? How can differing levels of ambition and development be accommodated? How should existing and overlapping PTAs be handled? These questions are addressed in the next section.

III. Issues, options and challenges in negotiating new generation plurilateral PTAs

This section will examine in more detail some of the particular negotiating issues that arise in the context of plurilateral PTAs, particularly where these differ from traditional types of plurilateral PTAs. It will look first at the negotiating process, and then consider some options for structuring plurilateral PTAs. Following that, the issue of how to deal with prior PTAs is considered, including in cases where agreements

---

18 See ADB, above note 8, at p. 290.   19 See Baldwin, above n. 7.
20 See, e.g., Razeen Sally, 'Free Trade Agreements and the Prospects for Regional Integration in East Asia', (2006) 1(2) *Asian Economic Policy Review* 306–21.

contain most favoured nation (MFN) provisions. Finally, some of the issues unique to plurilateral PTAs that arise in the context of dispute settlement provisions, institutional mechanisms, and final provisions will be examined.

A. The negotiating process

Whether bilateral or plurilateral, the broad process by which a PTA is negotiated is likely to be similar. A primary negotiating committee (often called the Trade Negotiating Committee or TNC) will usually be established that brings together the lead negotiators of each country. The detailed negotiating work will take place in smaller working groups or committees made up of representatives of the countries negotiating the PTA. The working groups are often divided according to subject area – so there will be a goods negotiating group which is responsible for drafting the goods chapter of the PTA, a services negotiating group which drafts the services chapter of the PTA, and so on. Typically, separate working groups are set up for each different topic or chapter in a PTA. In addition, a legal group made up of the international lawyers from each country will discuss the dispute settlement mechanism, the institutional framework for the agreement, the exceptions, and the final provisions.

Once these working groups have completed their work (say, in the form of a draft goods chapter), the TNC will be called upon to endorse the outcome. Issues that cannot be resolved in the detailed negotiating groups are also commonly referred to the TNC for resolution by lead negotiators of each country. If the TNC cannot resolve the issue, Ministerial involvement may be required to break the deadlock.

The process described above applies equally to the negotiation of bilateral and plurilateral PTAs – only that in the case of a plurilateral PTA there will be more countries around the table at each level of the negotiating process. This alone adds a layer of complexity to the negotiation. Generally speaking, the more countries involved, the more complex it will become.

Particular challenges are also faced where there are significant differences in the level of development amongst negotiating parties. This may affect not only levels of ambition, but also the ability of countries to fully participate in the negotiating process. PTA negotiations are extremely resource intensive and often involve highly technical and specialised discussions. For this reason, technical assistance and capacity building will need to become (and, in some cases, have become) important aspects of the actual negotiating process itself, as well as being reflected in substantive PTA commitments.

The situation is more complex still when it comes to negotiating specific market access commitments, which lie at the heart of PTA negotiations.[21] The practical focus

---

21 In order to be consistent with WTO rules, a PTA must meet certain thresholds regarding market access established in the GATT, GATS, and the Enabling Clause. For example, tariffs must be eliminated on substantially all the trade between the PTA parties (GATT Article XXIV(8)(b)).

of market access negotiations is the goods, services, and investment schedules of a PTA. These schedules contain the tariff reduction commitments, and services and investment market access and national treatment commitments.

In the context of a bilateral PTA, market access negotiations are, naturally, bilateral in nature. There is also an important bilateral component when negotiating plurilateral PTAs. Market access negotiations are typically driven by a bilateral 'request and offer' process. A country will make a specific bilateral request for market access to each negotiating partner. The content of each request is likely to differ for each negotiating partner, as it will reflect the particular trade profile between the two countries. The two countries then negotiate bilaterally, without the presence of the other countries, until agreement is reached between them. The various outcomes of these bilateral negotiations are usually 'plurilateralised' so that they apply to all countries in the negotiation. This is achieved by each country having a single identical tariff schedule, services schedule, and investment schedule that applies to every party to the PTA. In many ways, this reflects the way market access negotiations are conducted in the WTO.

Also mirroring WTO practice, 'negotiating modalities' can also be developed to assist market access negotiations. 'Negotiating modalities' generally refer to certain negotiated parameters or minimum requirements that guide or underpin the bilateral market access negotiations. The extent to which this occurs depends on the negotiation. The goods negotiation under the Trans-Pacific SEP, for example, relied primarily on bilateral request and offer negotiations rather than a pre-negotiated modality. The tariff schedules in the ASEAN–China Goods Agreement, by contrast, are based on a very complex and detailed modality, leaving more limited room for bilateral negotiations. Indeed, under that Agreement, it is primarily a *unilateral* decision for each party to determine exactly which tariff lines to place on the 'normal' track and which tariff lines to place on the 'sensitive' track (containing longer phase-out periods), provided such decisions conform with the parameters set out in the modalities. The modalities are themselves incorporated into the Agreement.[22]

How does the process described above relate to negotiations involving pre-existing blocs? As we have seen, when the EU reaches out to third countries to negotiate PTAs, it does so not so much as a group of individual countries, but as a pre-existing economic, political, and legal entity. If you ask a negotiator from Chile, for example, 'who were you negotiating with', they can answer with a single acronym (the EU), and not a list of the various Member States. As we shall see, this is particularly the case in the context of goods negotiations, where for reasons of competence, it is the European Commission that enters into bilateral goods agreements with third countries. The EFTA Secretariat is also heavily involved when EFTA negotiates with third countries, although unlike the European Commission it does not enter into agreements as a party in its own right.

22 Annexes 1 and 2 of the ASEAN–China Goods Agreement.

When it comes to plurilateral PTA negotiations involving less integrated or newer groupings of countries, the situation is likely to be more complicated. Of course, it is possible for such groups of countries to negotiate as a 'true' hub like the EU or EFTA, with a single voice reflecting a common position.[23] However, the less integrated the 'bloc' of countries is to begin with, the less likely that common positions on all issues will be possible. Common positions require pre-negotiation, and this can take considerable time and resources. The EU, for example, relies on a large and well-resourced institutional structure and the work of the Commission to arrive at common positions. Few other groupings have such resources at their disposal.

The result is likely to be a process that will take longer to complete, and require more flexible negotiating methods. Time may have to be allocated to allow for internal co-ordination, for example. It may be that on some issues a pre-existing bloc has a common position, while on others the individual members of the bloc will speak on their own behalf. There is also a close connection between the way the parties intend to structure the PTA, and the way the negotiating process will be conducted.

B. Structuring plurilateral PTAs

The exact scope of a PTA is often a matter for negotiation between the negotiating countries. Some PTAs contain little more than a broad commitment to co-operate and an undertaking to negotiate in the future. However, most PTAs will at least contain commitments relating to the liberalisation of trade in goods ('goods-only' agreements). And the trend is to go further. Many PTAs today also contain commitments on services, investment, non-tariff barriers (such as SPS and TBT), intellectual property, competition policy, government procurement, and co-operation. Some also deal with environment and labour issues.

Across these subject areas, a PTA will contain many different types of rights and obligations. These may range from very specific market access obligations (such as tariff reduction timetables or services market access commitments), to general requirements to conform with WTO commitments, to mechanisms designed to enhance and facilitate ongoing co-operation in certain fields. There may also be broader commitments to promote private sector co-operation in sectors of particular interest.

The question, in the context of negotiating a plurilateral PTA, is how to configure these rights and obligations and assign them amongst the parties – that is, how to structure the PTA. This question is inextricably linked to the objectives of the negotiating parties. It is also a question that can never be fully answered in the abstract. Each PTA negotiation has its own set of particular issues and sensitivities

---

23 As a matter of negotiating tactics, this is likely to be the preferred approach for such countries. A pre-negotiated common position is harder to negotiate against than a series of individual country positions.

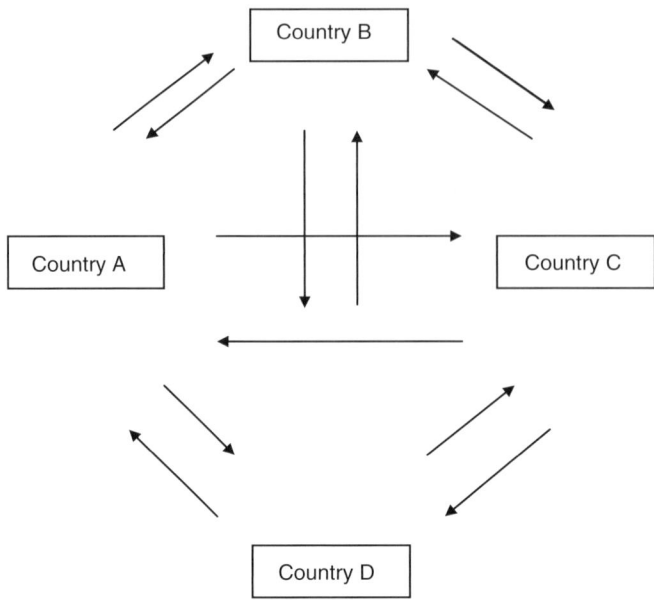

Figure 4.1   Model 1 Multiparty PTA

that will need to be addressed and accommodated. Nevertheless, it is possible to identify four general ways that rights and obligations could be assigned in a plurilateral PTA.

Under this model the rights and obligations flow between each and every party to the PTA. For example, under Model 1, Country A would have a goods schedule that applies to Countries B, C and D. Country B would have a goods schedule that applies to Countries A, C and D, and so forth. Such an approach could also be taken to services, investment, SPS, TBT – in fact any subject area covered by a PTA. This approach reflects an intention that each party should take on the same commitments and receive the same rights *vis-à-vis* each other party to the PTA.

The Trans-Pacific SEP is based upon this model. The obligations contained in the Trans-Pacific SEP are generally expressed as those of 'the Parties' and apply with respect to each other 'Party'. NAFTA is also based on this general model, although under NAFTA each country had two different goods schedules, one for each of its negotiating partners. This reflects the fact that NAFTA originated out of two bilateral processes – the Canada–United States Free Trade Agreement (CUSFTA) on the one hand, and negotiations toward establishing a Mexican–United States Free Trade Agreement on the other.

When it comes to negotiations with a pre-existing bloc, one of the key questions is whether the objective is to further liberalise amongst the members of the pre-existing bloc. If the answer is no, then Models 2 and 3 (below) provide possible approaches.

Model 2 can be appropriate where there is a high degree of integration already amongst the members of the pre-existing bloc. As can be seen, rights and obligations flow in just two directions. In this sense the situation is identical to a bilateral PTA.

The European Community's hub and spoke agreements provide a good example, most notably in the goods area. Because the European Community is a customs union with a common external tariff, in its hub and spoke PTAs it has a single 'Community tariff schedule' rather than separate tariff schedules for each of the EU member States. The objective is clearly to create commitments as between the EU and the third country, and not to create any obligations amongst the EU member States themselves. The pursuit of these types of PTAs is sometimes referred to as 'hub and spoke bilateralism'.[24]

In the services area things are a little more complex as there is no equivalent to a common external tariff, and there continue to be differences between the regulatory environments in the EU member States. Nevertheless, the EU does negotiate a common 'Community schedule' for services in its hub and spoke PTAs.[25] Many of the commitments in the Community schedule apply universally to all EU member States. However some country-specific limitations on commitments are also identified within the common schedule. As the Introductory notes to the Community's schedule in the EU–Chile Association Agreement (EU–Chile AA) makes clear:

> These commitments apply only to the relations between the Community and its Member States on the one hand, and non-Community countries on the other. They do not affect the rights and obligations of Member States arising from Community law.[26]

More generally, under the EU's hub and spoke agreements the extent to which the rights and obligations are assigned in accordance with Models 2 or 3 (below) depends on the subject area and issues of competence within the EU. A provision in the EU–Chile AA reflects the EU's approach:

> For the purposes of this Agreement, 'the parties' shall mean the Community or its Member States or the Community and its Member States, within their respective areas of competence as derived from the Treaty establishing the European Community, on the one hand, and the Republic of Chile, on the other.[27]

Rights and obligations under PTAs can only be assigned to 'parties' to the Agreement. This definition of 'parties' indicates that whether a particular obligation in a PTA involving the EU rests on the Community or on individual member States, or both, would require a situation-specific analysis.

---

24 See Baldwin, above n. 7, at 1483.   25 See, e.g., EU–Chile AA.
26 Paragraph 1 of the Introductory Notes to the EU's services schedule, EU–Chile AA.
27 Article 197 of the EU–Chile AA. See also Article 55 of the European Union–Mexico Economic Partnership, Political Coordination and Co-operation Agreement.

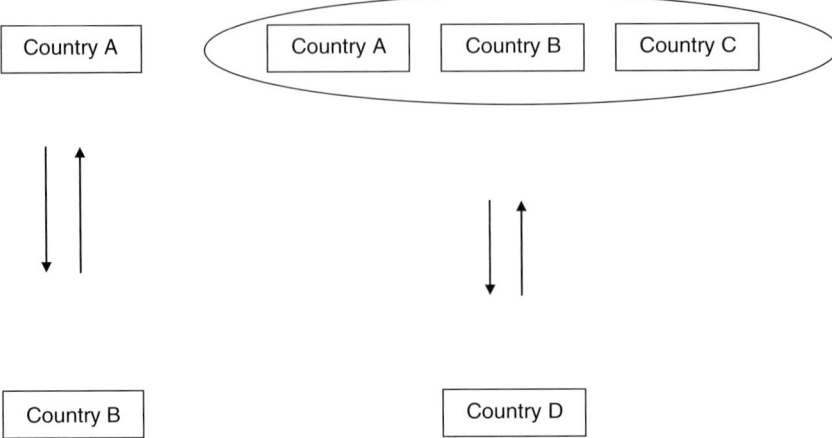

Figure 4.2   Model 2 Pre-existing bloc and a third country (option A)

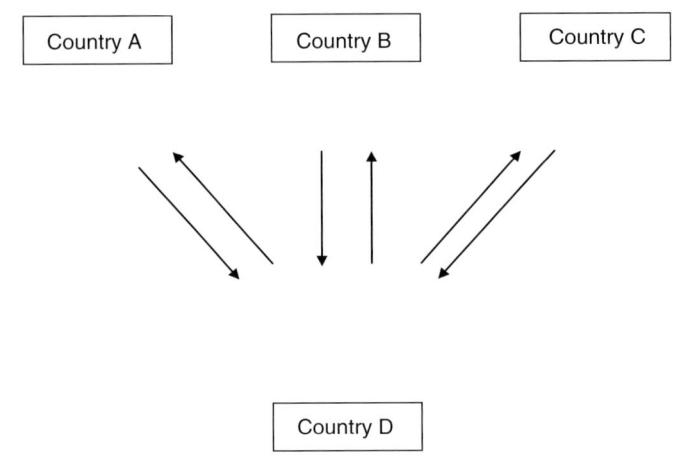

Figure 4.3   Model 3 Pre-existing bloc and third country (option B)

Absent the degree of integration in the EU, Model 2 is not likely to be appropriate. As has been seen above, even in the context of the EU there are areas where a universal Community-wide approach is not possible or appropriate. Model 3 provides an alternative approach. Again, the intention here is to not undertake further commitments *vis-à-vis* the members of the pre-existing bloc, only *vis-à-vis* a third country.

A key point from a legal (or drafting) perspective is that commitments in a PTA are generally expressed as those of 'the parties', and each state involved in the negotiation of a PTA will usually be a party in its own right.[28] As a result, if the objective is to limit the application of rights and obligations to certain parties and not others, this must be provided for expressly in the agreement.

The EFTA hub and spoke agreements provide an example. In the EFTA–Singapore Free Trade Agreement, Article 3 is headed 'Trade and Economic Relations Governed by this Agreement'. Article 3.1 provides that:

> The provisions of this Agreement apply to the trade and economic relations between, on the one side, the EFTA states and, on the other side, Singapore, but not to the trade relations between individual EFTA states, unless otherwise provided for in this Agreement.

This provision effectively reverses the default position mentioned above. Instead of having to expressly 'carve out' commitments where you do not want them to apply as between certain parties, as a result of this clause it would be necessary to expressly 'carve-in' provisions that do apply as between the EFTA states.[29] The general intention of the EFTA states is to create obligations only *vis-à-vis* each EFTA state and the third country, and not between EFTA states themselves.

Where one of the objectives of the members of a pre-existing bloc in negotiating with a third country is to further liberalise amongst its own members, then Model 4 provides an appropriate approach. Under Model 4, each party has rights and obligations *vis-à-vis* every other party. In fact, in this sense, this model is identical to Model 1. However under this model, there is a degree of pre-existing integration amongst some of the parties to the PTA negotiations. Such an approach might be called 'hub and spoke plurilateralism'.

CAFTA–DR–US provides an example.[30] In general, CAFTA–DR–US expresses obligations as applying between 'the Parties', and a party is defined as any State for which the Agreement is in force. So in the goods chapter, for example, the national treatment obligation is expressed in terms of 'each Party' providing national treatment to 'the goods of another Party'.[31] Likewise, 'no Party' may increase customs duties except as otherwise provided in the Agreement,[32] and 'each Party' shall progressively eliminate customs duties in accordance with Annex 3.3.[33] These provisions indicate a general intention to apply the primary goods commitments in CAFTA–DR–US not only *vis-à-vis* the US and the Central American states, but *vis-à-vis* the Central American states themselves.[34] Although the phrase 'except as

---

28 As we have seen above, the situation with respect to the EU is more complicated.
29 The ability to 'carve-in' areas where the PTA would apply to EFTA states arises from the phrase 'unless otherwise provided for in this Agreement'.
30 As noted above, the US is the 'hub' in this negotiation, and the Central American states are perhaps best thought of as a 'plurilateral spoke'.
31 CAFTA–DR–US, Article 3.2.1.   32 Ibid., Article 3.3.1   33 Ibid., Article 3.3.2.
34 Annex 3.3.6 appears to provide a special regime between the Dominican Republic and the Central American states that goes beyond the schedule commitments, and it has the options of claiming access under this Annex or the schedules.

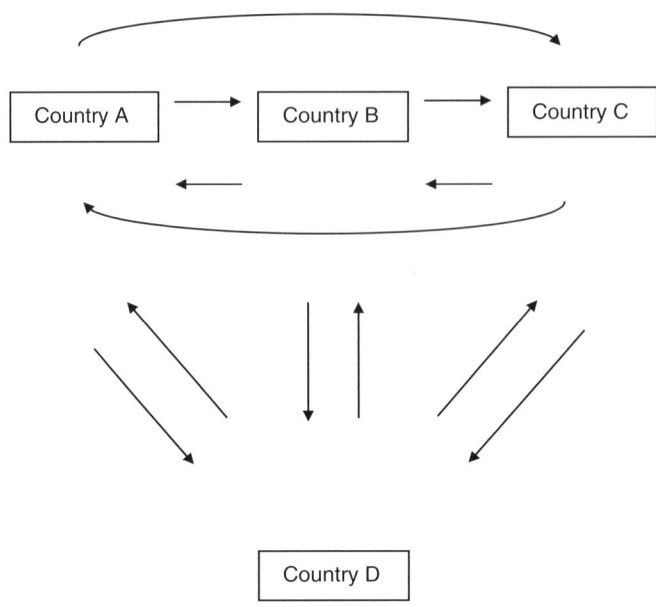

Figure 4.4   Model 4 Pre-existing bloc and third country (option C)

otherwise provided in this Agreement' preserves some flexibility to 'carve-out' the application of certain provisions in certain circumstances, the default position is universal application amongst all parties.

Likewise in the services[35] and investment chapters,[36] the key obligations are expressed in terms of 'each Party' owing obligations to 'any other Party'. While it would have been possible to exclude the application of these obligations for the Central American states *vis-à-vis* each other by taking out an appropriately worded reservation in the services and investment schedules, this does not appear to be have been done. The effect is that key commitments in the services and investment chapters undertaken by a Central American party apply not just *vis-à-vis* the US, but *vis-à-vis* every party to the PTA, including other Central American States.

1. Variations

Within each of the four general models discussed above there exists a number of possible permutations and variations. For example, as noted above, the approach taken to goods liberalisation in NAFTA contains an important variation. Rather than having an identical goods schedule applying to each other party, the countries have differentiated goods tariff phase-outs for each of the other two parties. Such an

35 CAFTA–DR–US, Chapter Eleven (Cross-Border Trade in Services).
36 CAFTA–DR–US, Chapter Ten (Investment).

approach is likely to become more unwieldy, however, the greater the number of parties that are negotiating the PTA.

The approach that ASEAN has taken to tariff reduction also warrants a brief mention in this context. In the context of AFTA a modality has been utilised based on a complicated notion of reciprocity. For example, as between two parties to the PTA, preferences are only granted on tariff lines that are not contained on either party's 'sensitive list' of products. The result is that 'market access is defined by the interaction of the two lists thus creating different market access for every one of 45 bilateral flows among the ten ASEANs'.[37] AFTA is therefore a rather complex variation to Model 1.

ASEAN's PTAs provide an example of another interesting variation to the models outlined above, in that they create legal distinctions between certain members of a pre-existing bloc. This creates flexibility to reflect different levels of economic development amongst members of ASEAN. For example, in the ASEAN–China Framework and Goods Agreements a distinction is made between the 'ASEAN 6' (which is defined as referring to Brunei Darussalam, Indonesia, Malaysia, the Philippines, Singapore, and Thailand), and the 'newer ASEAN Member States' (which is defined as referring to Cambodia, Lao PDR, Myanmar, and Vietnam). These two definitions then provide the tool by which newly acceded ASEAN nations are given greater flexibility in terms of, for example, timeframes to complete negotiations,[38] timeframes to phase out tariffs,[39] and the number of tariff lines that can be placed on the 'sensitive list'.[40] In the detailed Annexes containing the precise modalities for tariff reduction, a further distinction is made between Vietnam on the one hand, and Cambodia, Lao PDR, and Myanmar on the other.

Despite these distinctions *between* ASEAN countries, the actual obligations undertaken by each ASEAN country under the ASEAN–China Agreements appear to apply to all 'Parties' to the PTA.[41] That is, tariff reduction commitments undertaken by each ASEAN member State appear to apply not only *vis-à-vis* China, but also to each other ASEAN member State. If this interpretation is correct, it would be an example of a variation to Model 4.

Another variation that may become increasingly common is free trade negotiations between two pre-existing regional blocs. Depending on the degree of integration of each bloc, this could take the form of a variation of Model 2, Model 3, or Model 4. The failure to date of attempts to conclude a European Union–MERCOSUR Free Trade Agreement perhaps hints at some of the difficulties and complexities that arise in such a context.

---

37 See Baldwin, above n. 7, at note 32.   38 ASEAN–China Framework Agreement, Article 8.
39 ASEAN–China Goods Agreement, Annex 1.   40 Ibid., Annex 2.
41 ASEAN–China, Article 3.3, states that, 'Subject to Annex 1 and Annex 2 of this Agreement, all commitments undertaken by each Party under this Article shall be applied to all the other Parties'.

2. Mixing and matching models

Commonly, PTAs do not fall neatly within one model or another. While PTAs will often be *based* on one model, they may contain certain areas where rights and obligations are assigned in a different way. This reflects the fact that the parties' objectives may well be different regarding the application of different aspects of the PTA. Provided such differing intentions are clearly expressed in the Agreement, it is certainly possible to take a chapter-specific (or even obligation-specific) approach to assigning commitments in a PTA.

For example, the intention may be to apply some aspects of the PTA to members of a pre-existing bloc but not other aspects. Goods liberalisation is often the starting point for regional economic integration, and it may be that the pre-existing bloc already has a goods agreement in place amongst its members. If it did not want to use the opportunity of negotiations with a third country to further liberalise trade in goods amongst its own members, as noted above, it will need to insert a provision in the agreement that 'carves out' the goods chapter and related tariff schedules as between the members of the pre-existing bloc.

This could take the form of some alternative to the EFTA language discussed above, but limited in application to the goods chapter and schedule, rather than the entire agreement.[42] An alternative approach might be to limit the application of the tariff schedule only to certain parties – so for Model 3 above, the tariff schedules of Countries A, B, and C would apply only to Country D, whereas the tariff schedule of Country D would apply to Countries A, B, and C.

Similar approaches could be taken in services and investment. A general provision at the beginning of the relevant chapter could be used to ensure that the chapter only creates rights and obligations between the third country and each of the members of the pre-existing bloc, but does not create rights and obligations between the members of the bloc.

The alternative approach of limiting the application of the services/investment schedules to only certain parties (which could perhaps be specified in the headnote of the schedules) could also be used where commitments are scheduled on a positive list basis – that is, where the schedules set out the sectors where specific commitments are undertaken. This would operate in the same way as the exclusion of tariff schedules. Where a negative list approach is taken to scheduling however, it would be necessary to craft a reservation that expressly carves out the application of the market access and national treatment obligations *vis-à-vis* particular countries.[43]

---

42 If this approach is taken, and depending on the structure of the PTA, it may also be useful to clarify the extent to which other goods-related chapters would apply, for example the rules of origin and customs chapters.

43 A different approach is required because, unlike the positive list approach, under the negative list approach market access and national treatment obligations are not limited to 'scheduled sectors'. Rather, they apply to the extent that they are not 'carved out' through reservations contained in the services schedule. So the effect of not applying the schedules (i.e., the reservations) to a particular country would be to give unfettered market access and national treatment to that country – the very opposite of what is intended.

One further point to bear in mind in relation to excluding the application of schedules is that the obligations contained in the relevant chapter would still apply. While the specific tariff reduction or market access obligations are contained in *schedules* to the PTA, other obligations are contained in the relevant goods, services, or investment *chapters*. For example, in NAFTA, although different goods schedules apply to different parties, the same national treatment obligation, contained in the goods chapter, applies equally to all three parties.[44]

In contrast, there may be areas of the PTA where the members of the pre-existing bloc would like to *apply* the outcomes of the PTA with the third country, amongst its members. This may be so where, for example, the new PTA covers new ground not yet tackled by the pre-existing bloc, or goes significantly beyond the level of commitments amongst the members of the bloc.

For example, if the pre-existing bloc had only concluded a goods agreement amongst its members, it may wish to use the negotiations with a third country to establish services commitments amongst its members also. As mentioned, from a drafting perspective, this is easily achieved, as the default position is that such obligations would apply between all of 'the parties'.[45]

So far the focus has been on the goods, services, and investment chapters. As noted however, many PTAs today contain chapters covering areas such as non-tariff barriers to trade, intellectual property, competition policy, and transparency to name a few. Subject always to the intentions of the parties, it may be that some of these chapters lend themselves more easily to universal application between all the parties. For example, provisions on the prompt publication of laws, or providing for procedural fairness in administrative rulings.

In other areas, the creative use of institutional mechanisms could provide flexibility in terms of the application of certain chapters. For example a chapter on Technical Barriers to Trade may establish consultative frameworks designed to enhance future co-operation in areas including conformance requirements. As it may be difficult to say at the time that the PTA is negotiated whether any particular party will wish to make use of such provisions in the future, it probably will not make sense to exclude any parties from the chapter outright. An alternative might be to allow for voluntary participation in future initiatives by those countries that wish to do so. Provisions that allow parties to 'opt in' or 'opt out' of certain chapters, or parts of chapters, may also offer flexibility. Excluding a particular chapter from the dispute settlement

---

44 In addition to the national treatment obligation there will be other obligations in the goods chapter, such as those relating to administrative fees and formalities, export duties, and institutional arrangements, for example. In the services chapter there may well be obligations relating to transparency and monopolies. Under the 'exclusion of schedules' approach these would still apply between all parties for the simple reason that only the obligations in the schedules are excluded.

45 If an EFTA-style 'carve-in' provision is included in the agreement, however, then an express provision will be required applying the services commitments to the pre-existing bloc.

mechanism might be another response to concerns over the effect of applying the chapter to all parties.

In summary, there are a number of ways a plurilateral PTA can be structured, and a number of ways that rights and obligations can be assigned. Various legal mechanisms can be used to mix, match, and modify these general approaches so as to develop a structure for a PTA that best accords with the negotiating objectives of the parties.

C. Prior PTAs

One likely outcome of this proliferation of PTAs, some having a broad membership, is that new PTAs will often overlap with existing PTAs. Such an overlap can, of course, occur in the context of bilateral PTAs. However the issues are likely to be more complicated in the context of a plurilateral PTA.

In the absence of an express provision, the relationship between a pre-existing PTA and a subsequent PTA will be governed by customary international law, as codified in Articles 30 and 59 of the Vienna Convention on the Law of Treaties ('Vienna Convention'[46]).

In the context of a bilateral PTA being negotiated between two states that already have a pre-existing bilateral PTA in force between them, the situation is fairly straightforward. Either the earlier treaty will be terminated or suspended in accordance with Article 59 of the Vienna Convention,[47] or where this is not the case, 'the earlier treaty applies only to the extent that its provisions are compatible with those of the later treaty'.[48] In other words, the new PTA prevails over the pre-existing one to the extent of any conflict. In order to avoid any doubt however, express provisions are usually inserted into the new PTA to govern the relationship between it and a pre-existing PTA between the parties. Often, this is simply to terminate the pre-existing PTA.

In the plurilateral context, the situation can be more complicated in at least two ways. First, the pre-existing PTA may be in force between only some of the parties to the new plurilateral PTA. For example, in the context of the Trans-Pacific SEP, New Zealand had a pre-existing bilateral PTA with Singapore. In the absence of any contrary intention, under the Vienna Convention the situation would be as described above for bilateral PTAs – the new agreement would prevail to the extent of any conflict.

A second complication can arise where the pre-existing PTA includes states other than those that are parties to the new plurilateral PTA. The Trans-Pacific SEP again

---

46 Done at Vienna 23 May 1969, in force 27 January 1980, 1155 UNTS 331; (1969) 8 ILM 679, UKTS (1980) 58.
47 This will be the case where the treaty relates to the same subject-matter and it appears from the later treaty, or is otherwise established, that the parties intended that the matter should be governed by the later treaty, or the provisions of the later treaty are so far incompatible with those of the earlier one that the two treaties are not capable of being applied at the same time.
48 Article 30(3) of the Vienna Convention.

provides an example – Singapore and Brunei were already parties to AFTA, a wider plurilateral PTA with other ASEAN countries. In the absence of a contrary intention, under the Vienna Convention, rights and obligations *vis-à-vis* Singapore and Brunei would be governed by the same rules as those for bilateral PTAs (the agreement that is later in time, the Trans-Pacific SEP, would prevail in the event of conflict), rights and obligations *vis-à-vis* Singapore and Brunei on the one hand and Chile and New Zealand on the other would be governed by the Trans-Pacific SEP, and rights and obligations between Singapore and Brunei on the one hand and the other ASEAN member states on the other would be governed by AFTA.

Rather than relying on general international law, most countries prefer to insert an express provision in the new PTA that clarifies the relationship between it and pre-existing agreements. Where the intention is to apply both agreements simultaneously, it is best to state this expressly. The Trans-Pacific SEP, for example, specifies that nothing in that Agreement shall derogate from the existing rights and obligations under any other multilateral or bilateral agreement to which it is a party.

In addition, a separate bilateral exchange of letters between New Zealand and Singapore clarifies that:

> Where either the NZSCEP or the Trans-Pacific SEP provides different treatment for an exporter, service supplier or investor of New Zealand or Singapore, that exporter, service supplier or investor is entitled to claim the more favourable of the treatment accorded to that exporter, service supplier or investor under either Agreement.

Plurilateral negotiations involving a pre-existing bloc raise similar issues given that the members of the pre-existing bloc will almost certainly have some form of PTA already in force between them.[49] Deciding on the appropriate relationship between this pre-existing PTA and the new PTA will again turn on the objectives of the parties in undertaking negotiations with third countries. Is the objective to replace the pre-existing agreement in its entirety, or in part? Or is the objective to leave the pre-existing agreement in place and have the two live side-by-side (with the new agreement perhaps augmenting the old in some areas)?

CAFTA–DR–US provides an example of one possible answer to these questions. Article 1.3.2 provides:

> For greater certainty, nothing in this Agreement shall prevent the Central American parties from maintaining their existing legal instruments of Central American integration, adopting new legal instruments of integration, or adopting measures to strengthen and deepen these instruments, provided that such instruments and measures are not inconsistent with this Agreement.

---

49 The level of integration required before a group of countries would hold themselves out to negotiate as a bloc with third countries is almost certainly going to include economic integration in the form of preferential trade relations of some kind.

This provision clarifies that the existing legal instruments of Central American integration are not terminated by the CAFTA–DR–US, and nor will the CAFTA–DR–US prevent the adoption of instruments which bring about deeper integration for the Central American parties. At the same time, it makes clear that to the extent that any such existing or future instruments of integration conflict with the CAFTA–DR–US, the CAFTA–DR–US prevails.

1. Pre-existing PTAs and most-favoured-nation (MFN) treatment

The inclusion of MFN clauses in PTAs can have particular implications in the context of negotiations with a pre-existing bloc of countries.

MFN treatment is one of the fundamental building blocks of the international trading system, and is expressed in Article I of the General Agreement on Tariffs and Trade (GATT 1994) and Article II of the General Agreement on Trade in Services (GATS). PTAs that provide preferential treatment to the goods and services of particular states are recognised as exceptions to the fundamental requirement to treat all trading partners as equals, and are only consistent with the WTO if they meet certain stringent requirements regarding the scope and depth of commitments.

PTAs are, therefore, exceptions to a broad MFN obligation. However the use of MFN obligations *within* PTAs themselves is becoming more common, especially in services and investment, and has recently even appeared in goods.[50]

The basic concept of these PTA-specific MFN clauses is identical to their broader multilateral counterpart – if a party to the PTA extends more favourable treatment to any state it must extend that more favourable treatment to the other parties to the PTA. Whatever the merits of this type of clause in policy terms,[51] it does raise a potential issue with respect to pre-existing PTAs, and ongoing integration by a pre-existing bloc. In the absence of any other provision to the contrary, an MFN clause would mean that any integration amongst the members of the pre-existing bloc (whether extended before or after the conclusion of the new PTA), that goes beyond the benefits extended in the new PTA, has to be extended to the parties of the new PTA.

Again, whether this presents an issue or not depends upon the intentions of the parties. Such an outcome is consistent with an objective to pursue ongoing integration amongst the parties to the new PTA. Alternatively, a pre-existing bloc may prefer to preserve some flexibility to pursue deeper integration amongst its members only, without having to automatically extend the benefits of such integration to other PTA partners. If this is the intention, it will be necessary to provide for this expressly where a PTA contains an MFN clause.[52]

---

50 Agreements with MFN in goods include all EU EPAs as well as a soft-version in the PACER.

51 It could be argued that such clauses promote PTAs as building blocks because they operate to automatically extend benefits achieved in one limited context to a broader group of countries.

52 Because there is generally no MFN clause in goods chapters, it is not necessary to preserve this flexibility in that context. Interestingly, however, in the CAFTA–DR–US a provision has been inserted 'for greater

For example, in CAFTA–DR–US each Central American party took an Annex II reservation against the MFN commitment in the services and investment chapters. The reservation is in the following terms:

> [Name of Central American party] reserves, *vis-à-vis* the United States and the Dominican Republic, the right to adopt or maintain any measure that accords differential treatment to countries under any bilateral or multilateral international agreement in force or signed prior to the date of entry into force of this Agreement.

The effect of this clause is to allow Central American parties to continue to provide preferential treatment to each other (and indeed, to any other country) under any agreement in existence when CAFTA–DR–US enters into force. The US and the Dominican Republic took out similar reservations. Notably the provision is backwards-looking in that it does not cover measures taken under future instruments of integration. If the intention is to cover future integration as well, that would have to be made explicit in the reservation.

D. Dispute settlement provisions in plurilateral PTAs

A feature of modern PTAs is the inclusion of a binding dispute settlement mechanism for resolving disputes. This mirrors the development of a binding mechanism in the WTO, and dispute settlement chapters in PTAs are often modelled on the WTO's Dispute Settlement Understanding (DSU).

The core provisions relating to dispute settlement will be the same regardless of the number of parties to a PTA. However, there are some issues that arise only in the context of plurilateral PTAs, or that become more vexed in such a context.

One of these issues relates to the extent to which 'third parties' can participate in a dispute between other parties to the PTA. This question of 'third party rights' has received a lot of attention in the WTO negotiations aimed at reviewing the DSU. At present under the DSU third parties have limited rights to participate, whereby they only receive documents submitted prior to the first panel hearing, can provide only one written submission, and can attend only a special session scheduled during the first panel hearing.

A number of proposals to 'enhance' these existing rights have received good support from a broad cross-section of the WTO membership. However, disagreement remains over exactly how much third party rights should be enhanced. Most agree that some degree of third party participation is useful as it enables third parties to provide their views on the proper interpretation of the agreement. But this needs to

---

certainty'. Article 3.3.3 states: 'For greater certainty, paragraph 2 (progressive elimination of customs duties) shall not prevent a Central American party from providing identical or more favourable tariff treatment to a good as provided for under the legal instruments of Central American integration, provided that the good meets the rules of origin under those instruments.'

be balanced against the objective of providing an efficient mechanism for resolving a dispute between the primary disputing parties.

Plurilateral PTAs must address this issue. There are two stages of the disputes process where the rights of third parties need to be determined. The first is at the consultation phase, and the second is when the dispute has proceeded to arbitration by a panel. With regards the first, some of the options include: giving third parties an unfettered right to join consultations,[53] giving the complaining party the right to veto the participation of certain third parties (the situation currently in the DSU), giving the complaining party the right to veto the participation of third parties but only if it does so with respect to *all* potential third parties (i.e., not enabling it to pick and choose), and enabling third parties to join unless the complaining and responding party agree otherwise (i.e., where there is joint agreement that a third party should *not* join). The ASEAN–Korea DSM provides a further alternative in that it does not appear to contemplate third parties participating in the consultation phase at all.[54]

Once a dispute has proceeded beyond consultations to the arbitral phase, third parties are generally given an unfettered right to join the process.[55] The issues to consider here are the number of submissions a third party can make, the number of hearings it can attend, and which documents it should receive. For example, the Trans-Pacific SEP contemplates third parties making 'written submissions', attending 'hearings of the tribunal', and receiving all written submissions of the disputing parties. In CAFTA–DR–US third parties are 'entitled to attend all hearings, to make written and oral submissions to the panel, and to receive written submissions of the disputing parties'.[56] In the ASEAN–Korea DSM third parties only receive the submissions of the disputing parties at the first meeting of the arbitral panel.

A second issue that arises in the context of plurilateral PTAs is how to deal with multiple disputes on the same or similar issue. In the interests of efficiency and procedural fairness, the usual approach is to encourage multiple complainants to 'join' a dispute so that similar disputes are consolidated into a single disputes procedure. In the WTO this has become common and the process is facilitated by the WTO secretariat. In the context of plurilateral PTAs, where the same level of institutional support is not likely to exist, thought needs to be given to how these procedures will operate.

The possibility of more than one complainant raises other issues. For example, how will the process for choosing arbitrators be affected? Commonly, the complainant chooses one of the arbitrators. Where there is more than one complaining party, the complaining parties will presumably have to agree amongst themselves before

---

53 This is the position in CAFTA–DR–US, Article 20.4.3.
54 Agreement on Dispute Settlement Mechanism Under the Framework Agreement on Comprehensive Economic Co-operation Among the Member Countries of the Association of South East Asian Nations and the Republic of Korea (ASEAN–Korea DSM).
55 This is consistent with the position under the DSU.   56 CAFTA–DR–US, Article 20.11.

nominating an arbitrator. This may give rise to some difficulties given the fairly tight timeframes usually contemplated for the composition of arbitral tribunals.

Another issue that becomes more complicated where there are multiple complainants is that of 'choice of forum'. Choice of forum provisions operate where the same dispute could be taken either under the PTA or some other international agreement (most likely the WTO, although it could also be another overlapping PTA). The issues are difficult enough in the context of a bilateral PTA: should the complainant have to make an irreversible choice between alternate forums for pursuing a case, or should it have the freedom to pursue the case in both forums? The latter option gives the complaining party greater flexibility, but risks the development of inconsistent jurisprudence on the same issue, and allows a de facto appeal from one forum to another.

In the context of multiple complainants the issues become even more difficult. Should the decision of one complainant to use a particular forum restrict other potential complainants to using that same forum? If not, how should the risk of inconsistent jurisprudence be managed? From a respondent's perspective, how should the risk of multiple challenges in multiple forums on the same issue be managed? At present, while dispute chapters in PTAs are still relatively young and not widely used, these questions remain largely theoretical. However the image of the spaghetti bowl is never more appropriate than when contemplating the prospect of a tangled knot of inconsistent arbitral rulings on essentially the same issues.[57] It is difficult to see how such an outcome could contribute to the swift resolution of trade disputes – the very reason to have binding dispute settlement.

Finally, unlike a bilateral PTA where the obligations are purely reciprocal in nature, under a plurilateral PTA obligations may be considered either 'reciprocal' or obligations owed 'inter se' to all parties. Whether the nature of the different types of obligations should have an impact on the remedies available might also be considered. For example, in the context of the breach of a purely reciprocal obligation, the provision of bilateral compensation – even monetary compensation – may be considered more appropriate than where the breached obligation is owed equally to all parties.

E. Institutional provisions of plurilateral PTAs

The primary role of institutional mechanisms established under PTAs is to oversee the implementation of existing commitments, and facilitate ongoing co-operation, negotiation, and further integration by the parties. There is a fairly common approach across PTAs, whether bilateral or plurilateral. A primary Committee or

---

57 While the formal legal basis of the decisions would be different (as they would be based on provisions contained in different international agreements), the issues being ruled on would be substantially the same. This is particularly the case where PTA provisions simply mirror or cross-refer to language used in WTO provisions.

Commission is usually established, supported by a number of sub-committees that deal with particular areas (such as goods, services, TBT, and so on). The agreement will usually set out the functions and powers of the various committees and practical details such as how often they will meet and at what level.

Much like the negotiating process, the obvious difference in the plurilateral context is that there will be more countries represented in the various committees. At a very practical level, this represents a greater logistical challenge. Co-ordinating meetings between two countries is relatively straightforward; co-ordinating meetings between larger groups of countries tends to become exponentially more difficult. As a result, plurilateral PTAs are likely to require a greater level of institutional support.[58] Pre-existing blocs may already benefit from the support of a secretariat (e.g., the ASEAN secretariat and EFTA secretariat), and thought might be given to how these might best be used in the context of PTAs with third countries.

In plurilateral PTAs, an additional institutional layer is provided by the depositary. Unlike their bilateral counterparts, plurilateral PTAs often designate a depositary to carry out the functions specified in Article 77 of the Vienna Convention. In accordance with that Convention the depositary may be a state, a group of states or an international organisation.[59]

In terms of institutional processes, plurilateral PTAs also raise the question of how decisions by the committees should be made. Clearly the preference in international trade bodies will always be for consensus decision-making, and this is the standard approach taken in plurilateral PTAs. However, larger and more ambitious plurilateral PTAs may need to confront the questions faced in multilateral systems – what if consensus is not possible? Should provision be made for voting in the absence of consensus? If so, what kind of majority should be required? Should voting be limited to issues of a certain kind?

F. Final provisions in plurilateral PTAs

The final provisions of a PTA typically deal with signature and entry into force, amending the agreement, the relationship of the agreement to other agreements, accession, and withdrawal.

In a plurilateral PTA, special attention needs to be paid to the entry into force provisions. A bilateral PTA would usually enter into force when both parties have ratified it, or signalled that they have completed their internal procedures, often given

58 Although the focus here is on the institutions and institutional support following the entry into force of a PTA, the same basic point applies to the negotiating process itself. The practical and logistical challenges of negotiating a plurilateral PTA should not be underestimated.

59 For example, the Trans-Pacific SEP designates the Government of New Zealand as the depositary, the EFTA–Singapore PTA designates the Government of Norway as the depositary, CAFTA–DR–US designates the General Secretariat of the Organisation of American States as the depositary, and the EU–Chile AA designates the Secretary General of the Council of the European Union as Depositary.

effect through an exchange of notes between the two countries. In a plurilateral PTA not involving a pre-existing bloc of countries, the PTA would typically enter into force when at least two parties have deposited their instrument of ratification or acceptance, or otherwise notified the depositary that they have completed necessary internal procedures. The Trans-Pacific SEP provides an example of this type of entry into force provision.[60]

In a plurilateral PTA that does involve a pre-existing bloc, thought must be given to the conditions under which the agreement should enter into force. One option is to adopt the same approach as that described above, simply requiring two countries to have ratified it. It may, however, be preferable to require the third country and at least one member of the pre-existing bloc to have ratified it. Article 22.5 of the CAFTA–DR–US provides an example of this approach.

Another point to bear in mind is that a plurilateral PTA, in all likelihood, will enter into force on different dates for different countries. It may be desirable to set a limit on when a country can join the agreement beyond the date it first enters into force. In CAFTA–DR–US, for example, unless the parties otherwise agree, a signatory cannot take action to join the agreement later than two years after the date it enters into force.[61]

In addition, a provision may be required to clarify what happens if the agreement enters into force for a country after certain tariff reductions are already supposed to have taken place under that country's tariff schedule. Again, CAFTA–DR–US provides an example whereby the rates of duty are applied as if the agreement entered into force for that party on the date that it first entered into force.[62]

IV. Conclusion

Countries have turned to PTAs as a quicker and simpler alternative to the multilateral process. But while PTAs may be *relatively* quicker and simpler, this is not to say that they are (by any means) quick and simple. Negotiating bilateral free trade agreements is difficult enough. Plurilateral free trade agreements, especially 'new generation' plurilateral PTAs, offer additional complexities.

This chapter has explored some of the issues that arise in that context. It is worth noting that much of the discussion has been based on an idealised vision of how a PTA negotiation takes place. In reality, however, it is not always possible to follow a linear progression from the formulation of negotiation objectives to their perfect reflection in the architecture of the final agreement. In the pressure and 'fog' of a negotiating process things tend to occur somewhat more organically. Issues are grappled with as they arise, and in the particular circumstances of that negotiation.

---

60 Trans-Pacific SEP, Article 20.4.   61 CAFTA–DR–US, Article 22.5.2.
62 CAFTA–DR–US, Annex 3.3, Article 4.

All the more reason, however, to reflect further on these issues outside of that context. Exploring innovative and flexible approaches will be increasingly important as more ambitious PTAs are undertaken, and as countries or groups of countries pursue plurilateral PTAs with partners in different geographic regions and with differing levels of economic development.

PART III

Relationship with WTO and international law

5

Legal requirements for PTAs under the WTO

ANDREW D. MITCHELL AND NICOLAS J.S. LOCKHART*

I. Introduction

The global trading system is now comprised of an inter-locking, ever-growing, network of bilateral, plurilateral and multilateral trade agreements. It would be easy to assume that trade agreements, whether bilateral, plurilateral or regional, are necessarily beneficial for trade. After all, such agreements pursue the common goal of trade promotion through liberalisation. More trade agreements of whatever type might, therefore, translate into more trade liberalisation. The shortcoming of this assumption is, however, that bilateral, plurilateral and multilateral agreements pursue this goal in different and often conflicting ways. A core objective of the multilateral trading system is 'the elimination of discriminatory treatment in international trade relations'.[1] In pursuit of this objective, WTO Members must accord equal treatment to the goods and services of all other WTO Members (through 'most-favoured-nation' or 'MFN' treatment).[2] In contrast, bilateral and plurilateral trade agreements – preferential trade agreements (PTAs)[3] – pursue trade liberalisation through precisely this type of discrimination. The parties to a PTA liberalise trade solely among themselves, creating a network of special preferences within the PTA that are not available to other WTO Members. PTAs, therefore, entrench the very discrimination that WTO rules seek to eliminate. This key difference in approach makes the relationship between multilateralism and regionalism both complicated and controversial. In economic terms, it is still not clear whether maintaining an ever-growing network of PTAs alongside multilateral rules produces an overall increase or decrease in economic welfare. In legal terms, the coexistence of the WTO and PTAs

---

* This chapter expands on previous work by the authors in: 'Regional Trade Agreements Under GATT 1994: An Exception and its Limits', in Andrew D. Mitchell (ed.), *Challenges and Prospects for the WTO* (London: Cameron May, 2005), pp. 217–52; and 'The Relationship between the WTO and an Australia–China FTA', in Sisira K.W. Jayasuriya, Donald MacLaren and Gary B. Magee (eds.), *Negotiating a Preferential Trading Agreement: Lessons from Australia and China* (London: Edward Elgar, 2009), pp. 235–53. The authors would like to thank Professor Tania Voon (The University of Melbourne) and Dr Lorand Bartels (University of Cambridge) for their comments on an earlier version of this chapter.

1 WTO Agreement, Preamble. 2 GATT 1994, Article I; and GATS, Article II.
3 It is common in the WTO to refer to such agreements as regional trade agreements. However, many recent agreements lack any regional proximity, such as the United States–Jordan Free Trade Agreement.

among WTO Members creates a complex system of competing international rights and obligations.

As PTAs involve discrimination contrary to the general MFN obligation, they would normally give rise to inconsistencies with WTO rules. However, the WTO Agreements contain a series of exceptions for PTAs that allow limited derogation from WTO rules for PTAs meeting certain conditions. Only PTAs falling within one of these exceptions are valid under WTO law. In other words, a WTO Member must ensure that any PTA to which it is a party complies with the conditions of the relevant WTO exception. Otherwise, the Member risks acting inconsistently with its WTO obligations. The PTA exceptions are contained in: Article XXIV of GATT 1994; paragraph 2(c) of the Enabling Clause;[4] and Article V of GATS. The first two exceptions apply to Regional Trade Agreements (RTA) provisions relating to goods, while the third applies to RTA provisions relating to services. A PTA covering both goods and services would generally need to comply with the relevant exceptions for both goods and services.

Few provisions of the WTO Agreements have inspired as much controversy and disagreement as the PTA exceptions. The WTO Members themselves are divided on almost every issue of significance in these exceptions, with the result that the process for WTO review of PTAs has broken down. Although 241 PTAs have been notified to the WTO since it was established in 1995,[5] none has completed the GATT or GATS examination process to determine its WTO-consistency. Ironically, this systemic failure comes at a time when the WTO exceptions for PTAs should have taken on increasing importance because of the unprecedented proliferation of PTAs among WTO Members.[6] In addition, although the Appellate Body recently issued its first decision on the Enabling Clause,[7] it has provided very little substantive guidance on Article XXIV of GATT 1994 or Article V of GATS. Therefore, it is worth examining these exceptions to identify the main areas of controversy and uncertainty, particularly as they are subject to negotiation in the current Doha Round and may arise in future disputes.

This chapter addresses the substantive aspects of the exception for PTAs in relation to goods under Article XXIV, beginning with an explanation of its structure and scope. The chapter goes on to examine in detail the conditions with which PTAs must comply in order to fall within the exception – these conditions relate to the

---

4 Decision on Differential and More Favourable Treatment, Reciprocity, and Fuller Participation of Developing Countries, GATT Document L/4903, BISD 26S/203 (28 November 1979) (Enabling Clause). As a decision of the GATT Contracting Parties, the Enabling Clause forms part of GATT 1994: see para. 1(b)(iv) of the language incorporating GATT 1994 into the WTO Agreement.

5 See www.wto.org/english/tratop_e/region_e/summary_e.xls (calculated as the sum of notifications occurring after 1 January 1995 relating to the enabling clause, GATS Article V and GATT Article XXIV as at 7 June 2013).

6 In 1995 there were 62 operative PTAs, in 2000 that number had increased to 104 and by 7 June 2013 the number was 280: see www.wto.org/english/tratop_e/region_e/summary_e.xls.

7 See Appellate Body Report, *European Communities – Conditions for the Granting of Tariff Preferences to Developing Countries*, WT/DS246/AB/R, 7 April 2004 (*EC–Tariff Preferences*).

elimination of restrictions on trade between the parties to the PTA, and to the nature and level of restrictions that the parties to the PTA impose on trade with WTO Members that are not party to the PTA. The chapter then goes on to briefly consider the substantive aspects of the exception for PTAs in relation to services under Article V of the GATS. Finally, it discusses the activities of the Committee on Regional Trade Agreements as well as the lack of enforcement of the rules before WTO tribunals. This puts into context the likelihood of any legal challenge.

II. Scope of the GATT exception for RTAs: Article XXIV:5

A. Exception as defence

Article XXIV:5 of GATT 1994 provides an exception to certain WTO obligations for 'customs unions' and 'free-trade areas' (FTAs), which are the two possible types of PTAs for the purposes of this chapter. The opening paragraph, or chapeau, of Article XXIV:5 states:

> Accordingly, the provisions of this Agreement shall not prevent, as between the territories of Members, the formation of a customs union or of a free-trade area.

The Appellate Body has indicated that the words 'shall not prevent' in Article XXIV:5 mean that 'the provisions of the GATT 1994 *shall not make impossible* the formation of a customs union'[8] or, presumably, an FTA.[9] That is, Article XXIV:5 provides a justification for the adoption of certain PTAs and constitutes a 'defence' to a claim that such a PTA is inconsistent with any provision of GATT 1994.[10] According to the general jurisprudence of WTO panels and the Appellate Body regarding the burden of proof in WTO disputes, this means that it would be for the Member challenging a PTA to establish its inconsistency with a provision of GATT 1994, and for the responding Member to prove that the inconsistency is justified or removed[11] because the PTA falls within the exception in Article XXIV:5.[12]

B. Purpose of the exception

The WTO Agreements, including GATT 1994, are to be interpreted according to the words used in the treaty, read in their context, and in the light of the object and

---

8 Appellate Body Report, *Turkey – Restrictions on Imports of Textile and Clothing Products* (*Turkey–Textiles*), WT/DS34/AB/R, 22 October 1999, para. 45 (original emphasis).

9 In *Turkey–Textiles*, the Appellate Body was considering a customs union and not an FTA. However, the chapeau of Article XXIV:5 applies to both customs unions (under Article XXIV:5(a)) and FTAs (under Article XXIV:5(b)), so the same reading of the words 'shall not prevent' should also apply to FTAs.

10 Appellate Body Report, *Turkey–Textiles*, para. 45.

11 See Appellate Body Report, *EC–Tariff Preferences*, pp. 100–3.

12 See, e.g., Appellate Body Report, *United States – Measure Affecting Imports of Woven Wool Shirts and Blouses from India*, WT/DS33/R, 25 April 1997, p. 14; compare Appellate Body Report, *EC–Tariff Preferences*, paras. 87–8.

purpose of the treaty.[13] Article XXIV:4 sets out the purpose of the exception in Article XXIV:5 and therefore acts as a guide to understanding and applying that exception.[14] Article XXIV:4 states:

> The Members recognize the desirability of *increasing freedom of trade* by the development, through voluntary agreements, of closer integration between the economies of the countries parties to such agreements. They also recognize that the purpose of a customs union or of a free-trade area should be *to facilitate trade between the constituent territories* and *not to raise barriers to the trade of other Members* with such territories. (Emphasis added.)

This statement is complemented by the Understanding on the Interpretation of Article XXIV of the GATT 1994 (RTA Understanding), in which WTO Members expand further on the purpose of Article XXIV:5.[15] In the RTA Understanding, WTO Members:

- recognise 'the contribution to the expansion of world trade' that may be made through the establishment of customs unions and FTAs;
- recognise that the expansion of world trade 'is increased' if internal trade restrictions within an RTA are eliminated for 'all trade' and 'diminished if any major sector of trade is excluded'; and
- reiterate that the establishment of an RTA 'should to the greatest extent possible avoid creating adverse effects on the trade of other Members'.[16]

In *Turkey–Textiles*, the Appellate Body addressed Article XXIV for the first time. The Appellate Body noted that Article XXIV:4 'does not set forth a separate obligation itself but, rather, sets forth the overriding and pervasive purpose for Article XXIV'.[17] It added that the other provisions of Article XXIV 'must be

---

13 Article 3.2 of the DSU states that the WTO agreements are to be interpreted in accordance with the customary rules of interpretation of public international law. These rules were codified in Articles 31, 32 and 33 of the Vienna Convention on the Law of Treaties, done at Vienna 23 May 1969, in force 27 January 1980, 1155 UNTS 331. See Appellate Body Report, *United States–Standards for Reformulated and Conventional Gasoline*, WT/DS2/AB/R, 29 April 1996, p. 17.

14 One question that arises in relation to the object and purpose of the WTO Agreements is whether the object and purpose that is relevant is that of the WTO Agreements as a whole (given that they comprise one treaty) or of individual WTO Agreements. Article 31(1) may leave some scope for consideration of both kinds of object and purpose. The Appellate Body in *European Communities – Customs Classification of Frozen Boneless Chicken Cuts*, WT/DS269/AB/R, WT/DS286/AB/R, 12 September 2005, para. 238 concluded that the reference to 'its' object and purpose in Article 31(1) suggests that it is referring to the object and purpose of 'the treaty itself, in its entirety'. However, the Appellate Body also stated that Article 31(1) does not exclude consideration of the object and purpose of particular treaty terms, if doing so assists the interpreter in determining the treaty's object and purpose on the whole. See generally: Andrew D. Mitchell, *Legal Principles in WTO Disputes* (Cambridge: Cambridge University Press, 2008).

15 The RTA Understanding forms part of GATT 1994 pursuant to para. 1(c)(iv) of the language incorporating GATT 1994 into the WTO Agreement. The RTA Understanding was adopted at the conclusion of the Uruguay Round.

16 RTA Understanding, Preamble.   17 Appellate Body Report, *Turkey–Textiles*, para. 57.18.

interpreted in the light of the purpose' through a process of 'constant reference to this purpose'.[18]

How can we summarise the purpose of the PTA exception in GATT 1994? Perhaps unsurprisingly, the primary goal of the exception, as reflected in Article XXIV:4 and the RTA Understanding, is the promotion of trade. As noted earlier, the parties to a PTA grant each other special trade preferences that are not offered to other WTO Members. The establishment of a PTA, therefore, creates the potential for positive effects on *internal* trade between the parties (who benefit from the preferences) and negative effects on *external* trade with other Members (who are excluded from the preferences). To secure an overall expansion of world trade, the exception in Article XXIV:5 is designed to maximise the internal trade-liberalising effects of a PTA and to minimise its external trade-restricting effects.[19]

C. Exception for what?

1. PTAs covered

(a) Customs unions and free-trade areas The exception in Article XXIV:5 of GATT 1994 applies to customs unions and FTAs, as defined in Article XXIV:8(a) and (b) respectively. Broadly, a customs union means 'the substitution of a single customs territory for two or more customs territories',[20] so that almost all restrictions are eliminated with respect to substantially all trade between the parties (i.e., internal trade),[21] and the parties apply substantially the same restrictions to the trade of other countries (i.e., external trade).[22] Again, in broad terms, an FTA is 'a group of two or more customs territories' in which almost all restrictions are eliminated with respect to substantially all internal trade.

In essence, Article XXIV:8 establishes certain conditions with which an agreement must comply in order to fall within the definition of a customs union or an FTA. In addition, Article XXIV:5 describes certain conditions that a customs union or an FTA must meet in order to benefit from the exception.[23] The conditions imposed on customs unions and FTAs are similar in many respects, as discussed further below.

Many WTO agreements have special rules or flexibilities that apply less onerous disciplines to developing countries as compared to developed countries (an aspect of 'special and differential treatment'). In the context of PTAs, less onerous disciplines could have been applied to a customs union or an FTA between a developing country WTO Member and a developed country WTO Member.[24] For instance, in forming an FTA, a developing country could have been permitted to liberalise its own market

18 *Ibid.*   19 *Ibid.*   20 GATT 1994, Article XXIV:8(a).   21 GATT 1994, Article XXIV:8(a)(i).
22 GATT 1994, Article XXIV:8(a)(ii).
23 Certain special requirements regarding these conditions may apply under Article XXIV:9 in relation to preferences in respect of import duties or charges as described in Article I:2 of GATT 1994.
24 Certain RTAs concluded between developing countries are covered by the Enabling Clause.

to a lesser degree than a developed country partner (so-called 'asymmetrical' obliga-tions). However, the exception in Article XXIV:5 does not expressly include any such flexibilities.

(b) Interim agreements The formation of a PTA entails significant trade policy co-ordination among the parties, as well as extensive changes to domestic regula-tions affecting trade. Article XXIV recognises that WTO Members wishing to enter into a PTA may not be able to achieve the required level of economic integration immediately. Consequently, the exception for PTAs in Article XXIV:5 extends to 'interim agreements' necessary for the formation of customs unions or FTAs, subject to certain requirements. Under Article XXIV:5(c), an interim agreement must lead to the formation of a customs union or FTA 'within a reasonable length of time'. Paragraph 3 of the RTA Understanding specifies that this period 'should exceed 10 years only in exceptional cases'. Although such cases are not defined, where one of the PTA parties is a developing country, the level of development of that party might be an exceptional circumstance justifying an extended period of time for formation of a PTA.

There is some controversy as to when an interim agreement must meet the requirements of Article XXIV:5 and 8.[25] Some Members consider that these require-ments need to be fulfilled only at the end of the reasonable period for implementa-tion. Others argue that the requirements of Article XXIV:5 (not raising external barriers to trade) must be met at all stages of implementation.[26] This distinction seems to find support in a textual difference between the two paragraphs. Article XXIV:5 explicitly includes 'interim agreements' in the list of agreements that may not impose 'higher or more restrictive' external trade restrictions. In contrast, Article XXIV:8 does not state that 'interim agreements' are subject to the requirement to eliminate internal restrictions on substantially all trade. This suggests that interim agreements need not fulfil the requirements of paragraph 8 but must fulfil the requirements of paragraph 5. This reading of the text is consistent with the purpose of the PTA exception because it ensures that other WTO Members are not faced with increased barriers to trade at any stage of the implementation process but it allows Members time to eliminate internal trade restrictions.

2. Measures covered

(a) Measures adopted upon formation Article XXIV:5 states that GATT 1994 shall not prevent 'the formation of a customs union or of a free-trade area'. The Appellate Body has interpreted the word 'formation' to mean that measures imposed by WTO Members that would otherwise be inconsistent with GATT 1994 do not fall within the Article XXIV:5 exception unless they are 'introduced upon the formation of a

---

25 See e.g. Lorand Bartels, '"Interim agreements" under Article XXIV GATT' (2009) 8(2) *World Trade Review* 339–50.

26 WTO Committee on Regional Trade Agreements, *Synopsis of 'Systemic' Issues Related to Regional Trade Agreements: Note by the Secretariat*, WT/REG/W/37 (2 March 2000), para. 48(c).

customs union'[27] or, presumably, an FTA. Thus, WTO-inconsistent measures that are added to the terms of a PTA after the PTA has been formed would not fall within the exception.

In some situations, this limitation may create difficulties for PTA parties. One example arose in *US–Line Pipe Safeguards* in relation to safeguard measures, which are emergency actions taken to respond to particular market situations on a temporary basis.[28] The dispute in *US–Line Pipe Safeguards* concerned a specific safeguard measure on line pipe adopted by the United States (US). The US excluded imports from Canada and Mexico from the application of the safeguard measure because these three countries had agreed as a general matter, pursuant to the North American Free Trade Agreement (NAFTA), not to impose safeguard measures on each other.[29] Korea challenged the safeguard under several provisions of GATT 1994 and the Agreement on Safeguards.[30] The panel found that the line pipe measure fell within the exception of Article XXIV:5 of GATT 1994 because 'the mechanism providing for the exclusion of free-trade area partners from safeguard measures' was established upon the formation of NAFTA, even though the specific safeguard on line pipe was adopted after NAFTA's formation.[31] On appeal, the Appellate Body found it unnecessary to review these findings and declared them to be 'moot' and 'of no legal effect'.[32] Therefore, although the panel's reasoning is instructive, it has no formal legal value.

The panel's approach adds a dose of pragmatism to the understanding of the word 'formation' in Article XXIV:5. Often, the parties to a customs union or an FTA will be unable to provide specifically for every conceivable eventuality upon the formation of the agreement. Therefore, a distinction should be drawn between general framework provisions introduced upon formation and specific implementing measures adopted subsequently, pursuant to the framework provisions. The exception under Article XXIV:5 should extend to the framework provisions and the implementing measures. However, to improve transparency and to allow WTO Members to scrutinise a PTA at the time of its adoption, the framework provisions should make plain the nature of the WTO-inconsistent measures envisaged and the circumstances in which they are likely to be adopted.

(b) Measures necessary for formation In *Turkey–Textiles*, the Appellate Body specified that Article XXIV:5 can be used as a defence for inconsistent measures adopted in connection with a customs union 'only to the extent that the formation of the customs union would be prevented if the introduction of the measure[s] were not

---

27 Appellate Body Report, *Turkey–Textiles*, para. 46.

28 GATT 1994, Article XIX:1(a); and the Safeguards Agreement, Articles 6–7.

29 This situation also raised questions regarding the extension of the exception in Article XXIV:5 of GATT 1994 to the Safeguards Agreement, as discussed further in section II.D.2 below.

30 Panel Report, *United States – Definitive Safeguard Measures on Imports of Circular Welded Carbon Quality Line Pipe from Korea*, WT/DS202/R, 29 October 2001 (*US–Line Pipe Safeguards*), para. 3.1.

31 *Ibid.*, n. 128.

32 Appellate Body Report, *US–Line Pipe Safeguards*, WT/DS202/R, 15 February 2002, paras. 198–9.

allowed'.[33] Presumably this 'necessity test' would apply equally to FTAs. If applied broadly, this test would mean that a PTA can only depart from GATT 1994 rules if the departure is necessary to the formation of the PTA.

However, it is not clear whether the necessity test applies solely to inconsistencies arising from the imposition of *external* trade restrictions or also to inconsistencies arising from the elimination of *internal* trade restrictions. Although the Appellate Body drew no distinction between these types of restrictions in formulating the test, that dispute concerned an inconsistency resulting from the introduction of restrictions on the *external* trade of a customs union. In particular, Turkey introduced nineteen quantitative restrictions on imports from India on the formation of a customs union with the European Union (EU).

In *US–Line Pipe Safeguards*, the panel noted the specific facts addressed in *Turkey–Textiles* and suggested that the necessity test does not apply to inconsistencies arising from the elimination of *internal* trade restrictions. The panel stated:

> [T]he elimination of 'duties and other restrictive regulations of commerce' between parties to a free-trade area ... is the very raison d'être of any free-trade area. If the alleged violation of GATT 1994 forms part of the elimination of 'duties and other restrictive regulations of commerce', there can be no question of whether it is necessary for the elimination of 'duties and other restrictive regulations of commerce'.[34]

On appeal, the Appellate Body did not specifically address this finding, but it held that the panel's findings on Article XXIV were moot and of no legal effect.[35]

Nonetheless, there are good reasons for confining the Appellate Body's ruling in *Turkey–Textiles* to the facts before it and, therefore, applying a necessity test only to external trade restrictions. This approach is consistent with the purpose of the exception in Article XXIV:5. As discussed above, the exception in Article XXIV:5 aims to prevent increases in the level of external trade restrictions. Therefore it makes sense to impose an additional requirement of necessity on the introduction of any such restrictions. However, as reflected in the RTA Understanding, a key purpose of Article XXIV:5 is to promote the complete elimination of internal trade restrictions. The application of a necessity test to internal trade restrictions would undermine this purpose by requiring PTA parties to demonstrate that the elimination of each and every internal restriction is necessary to the formation of the PTA.

Moreover, as explained below, under Article XXIV:8, the parties to an FTA are required only to eliminate internal restrictions on 'substantially all' – but not all – trade. Therefore, under this provision, it is *never necessary* to eliminate *all* internal

---

33 Appellate Body Report, *Turkey–Textiles*, para. 46. That appeal concerned a customs union rather than an FTA. However, a similar necessity test presumably applies to FTAs as the chapeau of Article XXIV:5 applies to both types of RTA.
34 Panel Report, *US–Line Pipe Safeguards*, para. 7.148.
35 Appellate Body Report, *US–Line Pipe Safeguards*, paras. 198–9.

trade restrictions. The application of a necessity test, in this situation, could, there-fore, mean that parties would be required to maintain some internal restrictions. Yet, the stated purpose of Article XXIV, as set out in the RTA Understanding, seeks precisely to secure the elimination of *all* internal trade restrictions. The application of the necessity test would, therefore, prevent parties to a customs union or an FTA achieving the objectives of Article XXIV.

Moreover, it is difficult to see how WTO Members, panels or the Appellate Body could determine whether the elimination of a particular trade restriction among PTA parties was necessary for the formation of the PTA, or why they should have jurisdiction to review such questions. Article XXIV:8 of GATT 1994 simply requires a PTA to eliminate trade restrictions on 'substantially all' internal trade. It focuses on the *level* of internal trade restrictions rather than the *type* of trade affected. It does not prescribe which restrictions should be removed and which maintained; nor does it provide criteria in this regard. Thus, the PTA parties have discretion as to which internal trade restrictions to eliminate and in which circumstances,[36] provided that restrictions are eliminated on substantially all trade. It would go beyond the role of panels and the Appellate Body to second-guess such decisions.[37] In addition, the panel in *US–Line Pipe Safeguards* gave the following example of the practical difficulties of applying a necessity test to internal trade restrictions:

> [A]ssume that an FTA eliminates duties on peanuts, but not cars. In the context of a necessity test, third countries could claim that it was not necessary to eliminate duties on peanuts to meet the 'substantially all the trade' threshold of Article XXIV:8(b), as that threshold could have been met by eliminating duties on cars. In such cases, it is difficult to imagine how a necessity requirement could ever be fulfilled.[38]

D. Exception to what? Extending the exception beyond GATT 1994

1. Agreement on textiles and clothing

On its face, the exception in Article XXIV:5 of GATT 1994 applies solely to incon-sistencies with the provisions of 'this Agreement', that is GATT 1994 itself. The exception might not, therefore, justify PTA measures that are inconsistent with other WTO agreements. Remarking on this issue in a footnote in *Turkey–Textiles*, the Appellate Body observed that 'legal scholars' have taken the view that Article XXIV:5 provides an exception for inconsistencies with GATT provisions. It went on to note

---

36 For example, Article 802.1 of NAFTA limits the exclusion of Canada and Mexico from safeguard measures to situations where imports from these countries do not account for a 'substantial share of total imports' and do not 'contribute importantly' to serious injury. Article 5.3 of the United States–Israel Free Trade Agreement limits the exclusion of safeguard measures to situations where imports from Israel are not 'a substantial cause of the serious injury'.

37 See DSU, Articles 3.2 and 19.2.   38 Panel Report, *US–Line Pipe Safeguards*, n. 137.

that the chapeau 'refers only to the provisions of the GATT 1994'.[39] Nonetheless, the Appellate Body considered that Article XXIV:5 could provide an exception for an inconsistency with Article 2.4 of the Agreement on Textiles and Clothing (ATC) because Article 2.4 itself permits restrictions introduced under 'relevant GATT 1994 provisions'. The Appellate Body considered that this explicit reference to GATT 1994 in Article 2.4 means that the exception in Article XXIV is 'incorporated in the ATC'.[40]

So which WTO provisions, in which other WTO agreements, are covered by the exception in Article XXIV:5? The Appellate Body's reasoning in *Turkey–Textiles* suggests that the exception does not extend automatically to all WTO provisions. In *Turkey–Textiles*, the extension was based on an express reference, in another covered agreement, to GATT 1994. In all likelihood, other extensions will also depend on the wording and context of the relevant provisions. This approach is supported by the general interpretative note to the WTO goods agreements, found in Annex 1A of the WTO Agreement. The note states that 'in the event of a conflict' between provisions of GATT 1994 and provisions of one of the other goods agreements, the latter prevails. If the exception in Article XXIV:5 permits a PTA measure that is inconsistent with another goods agreement, a conflict exists between GATT 1994 and the other agreement. If a panel automatically applied the GATT 1994 exception to the other agreement, without examining the specific context, this would be contrary to Annex 1A of the WTO Agreement.

2. Agreement on safeguards

One fertile area of dispute over the scope of the PTA exception in Article XXIV:5 concerns the Agreement on Safeguards.[41] Safeguard measures are imposed by WTO Members pursuant to both Article XIX of GATT 1994 and the provisions of the Agreement on Safeguards.[42] Articles I, XIII and XIX of GATT 1994, as well as Article 2.2 of the Agreement on Safeguards, require that safeguard measures be applied on a non-discriminatory, MFN basis to imports of the relevant product from all sources. In some instances, a WTO Member has excluded PTA partner countries from the application of safeguard measures, claiming that such discriminatory application is permitted under Article XXIV. This situation may raise questions regarding the type of measures that benefit from the exception in Article XXIV:5, as discussed above,[43] and the requirement in Article XXIV:8 that PTAs eliminate internal trade restrictions on substantially all trade, as discussed below.[44]

---

39 Appellate Body Report, *Turkey–Textiles*, n. 13.   40 *Ibid.*
41 See, e.g., Joost Pauwelyn, 'The Puzzle of WTO Safeguards and Regional Trade Agreements' (2004) 7(1) *Journal of International Economic Law* 109–42; Dukgeun Ahn, 'Foe or Friend of GATT Article XXIV: Diversity in Trade Remedy Rules' (2008) 11(1) *Journal of International Economic Law* 107–33.
42 Appellate Body Report, *Korea – Definitive Safeguard Measure on Imports of Certain Dairy Products*, WT/DS98/AB/R, 14 December 1999 (*Korea–Dairy Safeguards*), para. 77.
43 See section II.C.2(a) and (b) above.   44 See section III.C and D below.

Another problematic aspect of this issue is whether the exception in Article XXIV:5 extends to the MFN obligation in Article 2.2 of the Agreement on Safeguards. So far, the Appellate Body has not answered this question. However, as foreshadowed above,[45] the panel in *US–Line Pipe Safeguards* ruled that Article XXIV:5 of GATT 1994 can provide a defence to Article 2.2 of the Agreement on Safeguards. The panel highlighted the 'close interrelation between Article XIX and the Safeguards Agreement', and the fact that 'safeguard measures subject to the provisions of the Safeguards Agreement are understood to be Article XIX measures'.[46] It noted that Article XXIV:5 provides a defence to the MFN obligations in Articles I, XIII, and XIX of GATT 1994[47] and that it would be 'incongruous' if it did not also provide a defence to the MFN obligation in Article 2.2 of the Agreement on Safeguards for the same measure.[48]

Although the Appellate Body declared the panel's findings on Article XXIV moot and of no legal effect,[49] the panel's reasoning on this issue is both compelling and faithful to the Appellate Body's rulings in *Turkey–Textiles* and in safeguard disputes. The panel extended the exception in Article XXIV:5 to a provision of another WTO agreement on the basis of specific language in the other agreement. Moreover, the Appellate Body has already recognised that the Agreement on Safeguards and Article XIX of GATT 1994 impose a single, cumulative set of obligations on the same measures – that is, safeguard measures.[50] The link is particularly strong in the case of the MFN obligation because this same obligation is imposed in both Article 2.2 of the Agreement on Safeguards and in Articles I, XIII and XIX of GATT 1994.

A further consideration in extending the exceptions in Article XXIV of GATT 1994 to the Agreement on Safeguards is the last sentence of footnote 1 to the latter agreement, which states:

> Nothing in [the Agreement on Safeguards] *prejudges* the interpretation of the relationship between Article XIX and paragraph 8 of Article XXIV of GATT 1994. (Emphasis added.)

The panel in *US–Line Pipe Safeguards* noted that this phrase deals with the relationship between *two provisions of GATT 1994* and *not* the relationship between the Agreement on Safeguards and Article XXIV. The panel, therefore, held that the footnote did not affect its conclusion that the application of Article XXIV to provisions of the Agreement on Safeguards should be determined by an examination of the Agreement on Safeguards itself, together with relevant provisions of GATT 1994.

3. Other WTO goods agreements

Similar questions could arise in relation to the effect of Article XXIV:5 of GATT 1994 on the provisions of other WTO agreements. For instance, a number of PTAs have

45 See section II.C.2(a) above.   46 Panel Report, *US–Line Pipe Safeguards*, para. 7.150.
47 *Ibid.*, para. 7.146.   48 *Ibid.*, para. 7.150.
49 Appellate Body Report, *US–Line Pipe Safeguards*, paras. 198–9.
50 Appellate Body Report, *Korea–Dairy Safeguards*, para. 77.

adopted harmonised rules that differ from the WTO disciplines in the SPS Agreement and the TBT Agreement. Based on the existing jurisprudence on Article XXIV:5, the extension of the exception to provisions of these or other WTO agreements will depend on whether there is a 'close interrelation' between the provisions and GATT 1994.

While the approaches of the panel and Appellate Body in *US–Line Pipe Safeguards* are firmly rooted in the language of Article XXIV:5, it may be questioned whether that provision, dating from GATT 1947, remains appropriate for a legal framework that now comprises twelve separate agreements dealing with goods, in addition to GATT 1994. Article XXIV expresses a policy decision by WTO Members to accept the inevitable positive discrimination that PTAs create in favour of the PTA parties. If Members accept this discrimination for all of the obligations in GATT 1994, as well as for certain obligations in other WTO goods agreements that have a 'close interrelation' with GATT 1994, what reason could there be not to extend the exceptions to all obligations in the WTO goods agreements?

The legal framework for goods may be contrasted with the framework for services where there is no doubt that the PTA exception applies to all services obligations.[51] Applying the PTA exception in Article XXIV:5 of GATT 1994 to only some goods-related obligations might imply the existence of a hierarchy of norms among the goods obligations, with some being subject to the exception but not others. However, it does not seem that the Members intended to establish such a hierarchy. Rather, the exception in Article XXIV:5 originally extended to all goods-related obligations – that is, to all obligations under GATT 1947. As negotiators gradually extended the number and scope of goods agreements, they did not expressly extend the exception in Article XXIV:5. In the absence of such express clarification, panels and the Appellate Body cannot apply the exception automatically to all goods-related obligations. Rather, they must strive to translate the ambiguous textual indications into a workable system of rights and obligations. The current climate of uncertainty, and possible dissatisfaction with the existing jurisprudence, may provide the necessary impetus for Members to reach a specific agreement on this question in the ongoing negotiations.

III. Eliminating restrictions on trade within the PTA: Article XXIV:8(a)(i) and (b)

A. Introduction

As already mentioned, Article XXIV:8 of GATT 1994 defines 'customs union' and 'free-trade area'. To benefit from the exception in Article XXIV:5, a PTA must meet one of these definitions. Both types of PTA are defined by the elimination of internal

---

51 GATS, Article V.

trade restrictions. For customs unions, this requirement is contained in Article XXIV:8(a)(i):

> duties and other restrictive regulations of commerce (except, where necessary, those permitted under Articles XI, XII, XIII, XIV, XV and XX) are eliminated with respect to substantially all the trade between the constituent territories of the union or at least with respect to substantially all the trade in products originating in such territories.

For FTAs, the corresponding requirement is contained in Article XXIV:8(b):

> duties and other restrictive regulations of commerce (except, where necessary, those permitted under Articles XI, XII, XIII, XIV, XV and XX) are eliminated on substantially all the trade between the constituent territories in products originating in such territories.

Thus, both customs unions and FTAs: (a) require the elimination of restrictions on 'substantially all the trade' between the PTA parties; (b) define the restrictions that must be eliminated as duties and 'other restrictive regulations of commerce' (ORRCs); and (c) expressly allow the maintenance of certain restrictions, 'where necessary', namely 'those permitted under Articles XI, XII, XIII, XIV, XV and XX' of GATT 1994.

Before turning to an examination of these three common elements, we point out a difference in these provisions regarding the origin of goods traded between PTA parties. In the case of customs unions, internal restrictions must be eliminated either on substantially all trade between the parties, or on substantially all trade in products originating in the parties. The first option is more trade-liberalising, because it entails the elimination of restrictions on trade in any goods, irrespective of where the goods originate. In contrast, the second option entails the elimination of trade restrictions only on goods originating within the customs union. In the case of FTAs, only the second of these options is available. That is, internal restrictions must be eliminated on substantially all trade 'in products originating' within the FTA.

B. Measuring 'substantially all the trade'

1. Members' views

The meaning of 'substantially all the trade' in Article XXIV:8 has given rise to much discussion over the years. To date, WTO Members have been unable to agree on the proportion of trade that amounts to 'substantially' all trade,[52] or how 'all the trade' within a PTA is to be measured.[53] However, two overlapping approaches have gained

---

52 New Zealand has even suggested, in view of the many difficulties surrounding the word 'substantially', that the word should be 'removed' from Article XXIV:8: WTO Committee on Regional Trade Agreements, *Note on the Meetings of 16–18 and 20 February 1998*, WT/REG/M/16 (18 March 1998), para. 115.
53 WTO Committee on Regional Trade Agreements, *Coverage, Liberalization Process and Transitional Provisions in Regional Trade Agreements: Background Survey by the Secretariat*, WT/REG/W/46 (5 April 2002).

currency. First, a *qualitative* approach, which would require the elimination of restrictions with respect to every major sector of the economies of the PTA parties. Second, a *quantitative* approach, which relies on a statistical threshold, for example requiring the elimination of restrictions with respect to a predefined percentage of trade.

The qualitative approach is designed to prevent PTA parties from maintaining restrictions to protect important sectors from competition within the PTA. The rationale would seem to be that an exception to WTO rules should only be granted when the parties to a regional agreement have shown commitment to closer economic integration. If the parties exclude major economic sectors from liberalisation, that commitment is deemed lacking. If this approach were adopted, it would be likely to operate in conjunction with a quantitative criterion, and rules would be required to determine what constitutes a major economic sector.

Under the quantitative approach, one suggestion is that internal restrictions should be eliminated on 95 per cent of all Harmonised Commodity Description and Coding System (HS) tariff lines at the six digit level. Tariff lines can be used as a criterion to ensure that liberalisation covers all possible or potential trade between the PTA parties, because all goods fall within a tariff line. However, using tariff lines may give a misleading impression of the extent to which trade has been liberalised, for instance where actual trade flows between the PTA parties are concentrated in a few tariff lines. If restrictions on these few tariff lines were maintained, a large share of current trade could escape liberalisation.[54] Conversely, a large number of tariff lines may be devoted to a small amount of actual trade. For example, around a quarter of all HS tariff lines deal with agricultural products, which may account for only a small portion of actual trade.[55]

Trade flows provide an alternative to tariff lines in establishing the threshold of trade for which restrictions must be eliminated. Thus, for example, the elimination of internal restrictions could be required with respect to 95 per cent of all trade flows between the PTA parties. However, using trade flows as a criterion is also problematic. First, actual trade flows are distorted by trade restrictions and do not necessarily reflect the likely trade volumes if restrictions were eliminated.[56] Second,

---

54 For instance, the European Union (formerly the European Communities) has pointed out that in agreements involving the Faroe Islands, 'well under 50 tariff lines accounted for about 80 per cent of the trade'. Norway, likewise, has observed that in a Faroe Islands–Norway Free Trade Agreement, all of the trade between the two parties was conducted under just ten tariff lines. WTO Committee on Regional Trade Agreements, *Note on the meetings of 16–18 and 20 February 1998*, WT/REG/M/16 (18 March 1998), paras. 118 and 125.

55 WTO Committee on Regional Trade Agreements, *Note on the Meetings of 23–24 September 1998*, WT/REG/M/19 (16 October 1998), para. 18.

56 See generally WTO Committee on Regional Trade Agreements, *Communication from Australia*, WT/REG/W/22 (30 January 1998) and Add.1 (24 April 1998). See also WTO Committee on Regional Trade Agreements, *Note on the meetings of 16–18 and 20 February 1998*, WT/REG/M/16 (18 March 1998), para. 112.

difficulties arise in applying this criterion. For example, a threshold of 95 per cent of all trade could be measured either as a proportion of aggregate trade flowing between the parties or as a proportion of each party's individual trade with the other. To take the simplest case, where there are only two PTA parties,[57] suppose that Country A exports to Country B are valued at US$95m, and Country B exports to Country A are valued at US$5m. Using an aggregate measure, the two countries would need to eliminate internal trade restrictions on 95 per cent of the total trade, valued at US$100m. The parties would have discretion as to which part of the total trade to liberalise,[58] and they could even agree simply that Country B would eliminate all restrictions on Country A imports. In contrast, using an individual measure, each country would have to eliminate trade restrictions on 95 per cent of the imports from the other country.

The question of how to calculate trade flows in applying a quantitative approach to 'substantially all the trade' could be of particular importance in the case of North–South agreements, where the parties may wish to liberalise trade unequally. Using an aggregate measure, developing countries might be able to benefit from the elimination of restrictions on a greater share of their exports to a developed country party. Alternatively, WTO Members might consider it preferable to prescribe individual measurement, in order to prevent one PTA party from forcing another, in a weaker bargaining position, to accept a lower degree of liberalisation.

In order to measure 'substantially all the trade' between FTA parties 'in products originating' in those parties under Article XXIV: 8(b), rules are required to determine whether goods 'originated' within the PTA. Such rules are also needed in connection with a customs union if the parties chose to eliminate restrictions not with respect to substantially all trade between them, but only with respect to substantially all trade in products originating in the parties' territories.

Rules of origin are used to decide in which country goods are produced and, therefore, in a PTA setting, whether they qualify for a tariff preference.[59] In FTAs, the parties often adopt special rules of origin to determine which goods qualify for preferential treatment in the PTA. The preferential rules may apply much stricter qualifying conditions than the rules of origin generally used in MFN trade.[60] Thus, goods that are deemed to originate in one PTA party under the general rules of origin may not be treated as originating in that party under preferential rules of origin. Such special rules of origin may, therefore, narrow the scope of trade that is liberalised within a PTA. This has led some Members to suggest that the

---

57 The situation becomes even more complicated for RTAs with three or more parties.
58 See WTO Committee on Regional Trade Agreements, *Communication from Australia – Addendum*, WT/REG/W/22/Add.1 (24 April 1998).
59 The WTO imposes limited disciplines on rules of origin under the Agreement on Rules of Origin.
60 Preferential rules of origin are not subject to the general obligations in the Agreement on Rules of Origin, although they are subject to certain transparency requirements in the Common Declaration with Regard to Preferential Rules of Origin in Annex II of that Agreement.

measurement of 'substantially all the trade' should take into account preferential rules of origin. For example, 'all the trade' within a PTA in products originating in the PTA parties could be measured using MFN rules of origin, while the proportion that is liberalised could be measured using the preferential rules of origin applying within that PTA.[61]

2. Interpretation in dispute settlement

Although the Members have yet to agree on a meaning for the term 'substantially all the trade', panels or the Appellate Body may be called upon to interpret the term in dispute settlement. So, far, neither the Appellate Body nor any panel has provided a detailed interpretation of this notion. In *Turkey–Textiles*, the Appellate Body noted that 'substantially all the trade' is not the same as all the trade, but that it 'is something considerably more than merely *some* of the trade'.[62] Therefore, the relevant amount of trade falls somewhere between some and all trade among the PTA parties. Beyond this, the disputes provide little guidance. In order to prove that NAFTA complied with Article XXIV:8(b) in *US–Line Pipe Safeguards*, the US submitted evidence that NAFTA eliminated 'duties on 97 per cent of the Parties' tariff lines, representing more than 99 per cent of the trade among them in terms of volume'.[63] After reviewing the evidence, and without offering any views on the meaning of 'substantially all the trade', the panel held that the US had established a *prima facie* case that NAFTA met the definition of an FTA under Article XXIV:8 (b).[64] The Appellate Body took the view that it need not address this finding and declared it to be of no legal effect.[65]

It is perhaps unrealistic and inappropriate to expect that panels or the Appellate Body will develop a refined formula for identifying 'substantially all the trade'. For instance, it would be difficult for a panel to find a textual basis for a finding that a precise threshold of 90 per cent is never 'substantial' but that a precise threshold of 95 per cent always is. If the clarification of this notion is left to panels and the Appellate Body, it is more likely that they will develop a flexible test premised on the word 'substantial', which indicates that the elimination of internal restrictions must cover a very considerable proportion of the trade between the parties. The words 'all trade' will also be important, as they identify the broad base against which internal liberalisation is to be measured. In each case, panels are likely to reach a conclusion based on the specific facts at issue, probably taking account of the qualitative and quantitative factors discussed by the Members.

---

61 See, e.g., WTO Committee on Regional Trade Agreements, *Note on the meetings of 6–7 and 10 July 1998*, WT/REG/M/18 (22 July 1998), para. 19.
62 Appellate Body Report, *Turkey–Textiles*, para. 48 (original emphasis).
63 Panel Report, *US–Line Pipe Safeguards*, para. 7.142.   64 *Ibid.*, para. 7.144.
65 Appellate Body Report, *US–Line Pipe Safeguards*, paras. 198–9.

C. Eliminating 'duties and other restrictive regulations of commerce'

A second question arising from the definitions of customs unions and FTAs is the question of which trade restrictions are to be eliminated. According to Article XXIV:8(a)(i) and (b), the parties to a customs union or an FTA must eliminate duties and ORRCs on substantially all the trade within the PTA. WTO Members have frequently discussed the words 'duties and other restrictive regulations of commerce', without reaching any agreement on their meaning. Similarly, no panel or Appellate Body reports to date have interpreted these words. While the words 'substantially all the trade' dictate how much trade must be liberalised within a PTA, the words 'duties and other restrictive regulations of commerce' describe the types of restriction to be eliminated. Evidently, elimination of a broader range of restrictive regulations will result in a higher level of liberalisation within the PTA, in accordance with the purpose of the exception in Article XXIV:5.

What seems important, in determining which regulations constitute ORRCs, is not the form of a regulation, but its effect on commerce. The requirement of elimination applies only to regulations that have a 'restrictive' effect on commerce, irrespective of whether the regulation imposes duties or takes some other form. Article XXIV:8 does not state expressly what kind of restrictive effect is intended. Virtually all regulations affecting goods have some kind of 'chilling' effect that restricts trade in those goods. This is equally true of border regulations, which chill imports, and marketplace regulations,[66] which chill trade in domestic and imported goods. It seems rather unlikely, though, that Article XXIV:8 was intended to encompass all regulations that have a restrictive effect on trade, however small. It is worth noting that the RTA Understanding refers to the 'elimination *between the constituent territories* of duties and other restrictive regulations of commerce' (emphasis added). This suggests that the regulations to be eliminated under Article XXIV:8 are those restricting the cross-border movement of goods between the PTA parties. The focus of internal liberalisation under Article XXIV:8 is, in other words, on restrictions that adversely affect imported or exported goods, with the goal being to create a market among the parties that is border-free rather than regulation-free.

So what types of restrictions are duties or ORRCs pursuant to Article XXIV:8? By definition, border restrictions apply solely to imports, imposing restrictions on the cross-border movement of goods, and they are certainly ORRCs. These include import bans, quantitative restrictions and the many administrative rules regulating importation. Sanitary and phytosanitary (SPS) measures prohibiting the importation of goods would also be ORRCs. ORRCs are also likely to include marketplace regulations that adversely affect imported goods, as compared with domestic goods, but such regulations would likely be already proscribed by the WTO national treatment obligation.[67]

---

66 Marketplace regulations regulate, for example, the distribution, transport, marketing or sale of goods.
67 GATT 1994, Article III.

Much discussion among academics and WTO negotiators has focused on whether trade remedy measures are ORRCs. Measures adopted under Article VI (anti-dumping and countervailing measures) or XIX (safeguard measures) of GATT 1994 are not expressly identified in the bracketed phrase in Article XXIV:8, ('except, where necessary, those permitted under Articles XI, XII, XIII, XIV, XV and XX'), which is discussed further below.[68] The exclusion of trade remedy measures from this phrase could mean that trade remedy measures are simply not ORRCs (in which case there was no need to include them in the brackets and they are not subject to the elimination requirement). However, it could also be that they are ORRCs and their exclusion from the brackets means there is no express right to maintain them (in which case they should be eliminated on substantially all the trade between the PTA parties).[69]

The text of Article XXIV:8 contains little support for excluding trade remedy measures from the measures that need to be eliminated, i.e., duties and ORRCs.[70] Anti-dumping and countervailing duties are described as 'duties' in Articles II and VI of GATT 1994, as well as in the Anti-Dumping Agreement and the SCM Agreement. These 'duties' are imposed, in addition to ordinary customs duties, on the importation of products. Moreover, the very purpose of these duties is to restrict imports of specific products. Under Article XIX of GATT 1994, safeguard measures involve the modification or withdrawal of a market access concession for imported goods. The purpose of safeguard measures is, therefore, also to restrict imports. The restriction on access takes the form of either a duty or a quantitative restriction. Again, there is little reason to suppose that safeguard measures are not ORRCs.[71]

D. Internal restrictions that may be maintained

1. Restrictions on an 'insubstantial' portion of trade

Under Article XXIV:8, the PTA parties need not eliminate all ORRCs; they must simply eliminate ORRCs on 'substantially all the trade' between the parties. On the remaining portion of trade, the parties are entitled to retain all ORRCs of any type

---

68 See section III.D.2 below.
69 WTO Negotiating Group on Rules, *Compendium of Issues Related to Regional Trade Agreements – Background Note by the Secretariat (Revision)*, TN/RL/W/8/Rev.1 (1 August 2002), para. 74.
70 Cf. Angela T. Gobbi Estrella and Gary N. Horlick, 'Mandatory Abolition of Anti-Dumping, Countervailing Duties and Safeguards in Customs Unions and Free-Trade Areas constituted between WTO Members: Revisiting a Long-Standing Discussion in Light of the Appellate Body's *Turkey–Textiles Ruling*' (2006) 40(5) *Journal of World Trade* 909–44.
71 The panel in *Argentina – Safeguard Measures on Imports of Footwear*, WT/DS121/R, 25 June 1999 (*Argentina–Footwear Safeguards*) assumed that safeguard measures are 'duties and other restrictive regulations of commerce' under Article XXIV:8: paras. 8.96–8.97. The Appellate Body reversed the panel's findings on Article XXIV: Appellate Body Report, *Argentina–Footwear Safeguards*, WT/DS121/AB/R, 14 December 1999, para. 110. However, this aspect of the panel's findings on Article XXIV was not examined by the Appellate Body nor specifically declared to be an erroneous interpretation of Article XXIV:8.

(provided that they are not otherwise inconsistent with WTO rules), including trade remedy measures and other measures not listed in the brackets. But difficult questions remain.

If the PTA parties decide to retain the possibility of imposing trade remedy measures on each other, the PTA is likely to include a general authority for each party to impose such measures in specific cases in the future. This general authority, of itself, might be regarded as an ORRC on all the products that are potentially subject to trade remedy measures at a later stage. In this case, restrictions would be deemed to remain on all the products potentially subject to trade remedy measures. To comply with the requirement to eliminate restrictions on substantially all the trade, PTA parties would have to confine the general authority to a defined group of products representing no more than an insubstantial portion of trade.

Alternatively, it could be argued that the general authority does not, in fact, restrict commerce; it merely enables a potential future restriction, which might never be realised. On that view, the general authority is not an ORRC and need not be limited to particular products representing an insubstantial portion of trade. Rather, specific measures imposed pursuant to the general authority are ORRCs and must be limited to such a portion.[72] This approach is also problematic. It would leave undefined and uncertain the number and type of ORRCs that could be imposed within the PTA and, hence, the proportion of trade subject to ORRCs. As a result, the consistency of the PTA with the conditions of the exception in Article XXIV:5 of GATT 1994 would vary, depending on the number and extent of trade remedy measures imposed at any given time. It would be impossible to state definitively, based merely on the PTA itself, whether it was justified under the exception.

2. Other restrictions expressly permitted

Although Articles XXIV:8(a)(i) and (b) state that, in a customs union or an FTA, restrictive regulations of commerce must be eliminated on substantially all internal trade, both paragraphs create an exception to this requirement, 'where necessary', for 'those' ORRCs 'permitted under Articles XI, XII, XIII, XIV, XV and XX'.

Some WTO Members have suggested that the bracketed list of measures is illustrative only. In other words, measures apart from those 'permitted under Articles XI, XII, XIII, XIV, XV and XX', such as trade remedy measures, may also be implicitly included in the list and maintained within a PTA.[73] This argument has not won the support of all Members. In any case, since the bracketed list provides an

---

72 This seems to be the approach suggested in Panel Report, *Argentina–Footwear Safeguards*, para. 8.97. See *ibid*.

73 WTO Negotiating Group on Rules, *Compendium of Issues Related to Regional Trade Agreements – Background Note by the Secretariat (Revision)*, TN/RL/W/8/Rev.1 (1 August 2002), para. 75. The WTO Secretariat has observed that '[t]he drafting history does not indicate why Articles XI–XV and XX were included in the list of exceptions while others, in particular Article XIX, were not included': WTO Committee on Regional Trade Agreements, *Systemic Issues Related to 'Other Regulations of Commerce': Background Note by the Secretariat (Revision)*, WT/REG/W/17/Rev.1 (5 February 1998), para. 6.

exception to the general rule of elimination of ORRCs, it would normally be interpreted in a manner precluding the addition of other measures. This approach is
consistent with the Appellate Body's statement in *Turkey–Textiles* that the bracketed
phrase allows parties to maintain measures 'otherwise permitted under Articles XI
through XV and under Article XX of the GATT 1994'.[74] While not a definitive ruling
on this issue, this statement suggests that the Appellate Body would read the
bracketed phrase as containing an exclusive list of the ORRCs that may be maintained
in a PTA.[75]

In *Turkey–Textiles*, the Appellate Body recognised that this exception to the
general requirement of elimination of ORRCs offers 'some flexibility' to the
parties to a customs union (and presumably also an FTA) to maintain certain
types of ORRCs.[76] However, the Appellate Body cautioned that this flexibility is
limited by the requirement that ORRCs be eliminated with respect to substantially all internal trade. In addition, the exception applies only 'where necessary',
although the text provides no guidance as to when it is necessary to maintain
restrictions. In *Turkey–Textiles*, the Appellate Body developed and applied a
necessity test to the exception for PTAs in Article XXIV:5 of GATT 1994.[77]
A similar test could also be applied to the bracketed phrase in Article XXIV:8. In
that context, to the extent that the formation of a PTA would be prevented if an
ORRC listed in that phrase were eliminated, it could be regarded as 'necessary' to
maintain the ORRC.

An interesting and, as yet, unresolved question is whether products subject to
ORRCs listed in the brackets are part of the 'substantial' or 'insubstantial' portion of
trade. The question can be illustrated by example. Suppose a WTO Member maintains quantitative restrictions, under Article XII, on imports of all steel products from
partner countries in a PTA. No duties or other restrictions are imposed on steel
imports. In measuring whether ORRCs have been eliminated on substantially all
the trade in the PTA, should steel products be counted as trade on which ORRCs
have been eliminated (the substantial portion of trade) or as trade on which ORRCs
have not been eliminated (the insubstantial portion of trade)?

The straightforward – and stricter – view is that trade in any product subject to an
ORRC has not been liberalised, and the product cannot form part of the substantial
portion of trade on which ORRCs have been eliminated. On this view, the substantial
portion of trade is confined to products that are subject to no ORRCs at all;

---

74 Appellate Body Report, *Turkey–Textiles*, para. 48.
75 It may be that certain measures permitted under Article XXI of GATT 1994 in connection with essential
    security interests are also permitted by Article XX, perhaps as necessary to protect human, animal or plant
    life or health, or even public morals.
76 Appellate Body Report, *Turkey–Textiles*, para. 48. The Appellate Body was examining a case involving a
    customs union and not an FTA. However, the text of Article XXIV:8 is the same in this regard for customs
    unions and FTAs.
77 See section II.C.2.(b) above.

conversely, a product that is subject to any ORRC, including an ORRC listed in the brackets, must form part of the insubstantial portion of trade.[78]

This reading is, however, problematic with respect to ORRCs that are justified under WTO law. For example, the list of ORRCs in brackets includes, among others, restrictions maintained pursuant to Article XX of GATT 1994. Article XX provides a general exception to all GATT 1994 obligations. In certain circumstances, Article XX allows Members to promote governance priorities – such as public health and environmental protection – that conflict with WTO rules. Other examples include WTO-consistent SPS measures (which are also covered by Article XX[79]) and WTO-consistent technical barriers to trade. There is broad recognition in the WTO agreements, and among WTO Members, that Members should have discretion to pursue these other priorities, subject to the conditions governing the exceptions to WTO rules. However, if a product subject to health restrictions permitted by Article XX necessarily formed part of the insubstantial portion of trade on which ORRCs had not been eliminated, this would constrain WTO Members' right to pursue health objectives. In a customs union or an FTA, a WTO Member would be able to promote health only through internal restrictions on the 'insubstantial' group of products. As well as being questionable in terms of state sovereignty, this reading of Article XXIV:8 would be at odds with the text of Article XX. Article XX(b) states that 'nothing in this Agreement shall be construed to prevent the adoption or enforcement by any Member of measures ... necessary to protect human, animal or plant life or health'. If Article XXIV:8 of GATT 1994 meant that Article XX health measures could only be maintained on the insubstantial portion of trade, that interpretation would 'prevent' the adoption or enforcement of health measures on 'substantially all the trade', contrary to Article XX.

An alternative reading follows from the structure of Articles XXIV:8(a)(i) and (b). These two sub-paragraphs require that a PTA eliminate all ORRCs – except those bracketed – on substantially all trade. The bracketed exception is located immediately after the phrase 'duties and other restrictive regulations of commerce' and, together with this phrase, defines the universe of restrictions that must be eliminated with respect to substantially all trade. Thus, for products comprising substantially all trade, all ORRCs must be eliminated except those listed in the brackets. This reading, therefore, creates, three categories of product under Article XXIV:8:

- First, products that are not subject to ORRCs at all. These products form part of the 'substantial' portion of trade with respect to which all ORRCs have been eliminated.

---

78 It is not clear whether the advocates of this approach take the view that the only restrictive regulations that may be applied to any product are those mentioned in the brackets. Contrary to this view, we have suggested that the parties are free to retain any restrictive regulations they wish on products representing an insubstantial portion of trade because Article XXIV:8 requires only the elimination of restrictions on the substantial portion of trade.

79 See SPS Agreement, Article 2.4.

- Second, products that are not subject to ORRCs, except for one or more of those listed in the brackets. These products also form part of the 'substantial' portion of trade with respect to which ORRCs, other than those listed in the brackets, have been eliminated.
- Third, products that are subject to ORRCs that are not listed in the brackets. These products must represent no more than an 'insubstantial' portion of trade, with respect to which ORRCs need not be eliminated. These products may also be subject to ORRCs listed in the brackets.

Under this reading, WTO Members would be entitled to maintain, 'where necessary', any of the ORRCs listed in the brackets with respect to any product. In addition, they would be entitled to maintain any ORRCs with respect to an insubstantial portion of trade. This reading of Article XXIV:8 would, therefore, avoid the problem of constraining Members from maintaining measures permitted under Article XX.

IV. Restrictions on the external trade of the PTA

A. Introduction

As we have seen in the previous section of this chapter, Article XXIV:8 of GATT 1994 imposes certain conditions on the restrictions imposed by PTA parties on trade within the PTA. In addition, as we shall see in the following sections, Article XXIV of GATT 1994 imposes two conditions on the restrictions applied by PTA parties in the external trade of the PTA.

First, under Article XXIV:8(a)(ii), the definition of a customs union requires each of the parties to the union to apply 'substantially the same duties and other regulations of commerce to the trade of territories not included in the union'.[80] This condition applies only to customs unions and not to FTAs.

Second, under Articles XXIV:5(a) and (b), a PTA will not qualify for the PTA exception under Article XXIV:5 if, broadly speaking, the 'duties and other regulations of commerce' imposed by the PTA parties on other WTO Members are higher or more restrictive than before the PTA was formed. The precise character of this condition differs for customs unions and FTAs. For customs unions, the condition is framed as follows under Article XXIV:5(a):

> [T]he duties and other regulations of commerce imposed at the institution of [a customs union] in respect of trade with [WTO Members] not parties to such union . . . shall not on the whole be higher or more restrictive than the general incidence of the duties and regulations of commerce applicable in the constituent territories prior to the formation of such union.

---

80 This requirement is expressly subject to Article XXIV:9, which relates to preferences in respect of import duties or charges as described in GATT 1994, Article I:2.

For FTAs, the condition is contained in Article XXIV:5(b):

> [T]he duties and other regulations of commerce maintained in each [of] the constituent territories and applicable at the formation of [an FTA] to the trade of [WTO Members] not included in such area . . . shall not be higher or more restrictive than the corresponding duties and other regulations of commerce existing in the same constituent territories prior to the formation of the free-trade area.

Sub-paragraphs 5(a), 5(b), and 8(a)(ii) of Articles XXIV all impose conditions on the 'duties and other regulations of commerce' imposed by PTA parties on external trade. We examine the meaning of these words before turning to the specific requirements of the different provisions.

B. The meaning of 'duties and other regulations of commerce'

1. Structure and context of the relevant provisions

In our view, it makes sense to interpret the words 'duties and other regulations of commerce' consistently in sub-paragraphs 5(a), 5(b), and 8(a)(ii) of Articles XXIV, mindful of the different context in which they appear.

The words 'duties and other regulations of commerce' in sub-paragraphs 5(a), 5(b), and 8(a)(ii) of Articles XXIV are reminiscent of the words 'duties and other restrictive regulations of commerce' in sub-paragraphs 8(a)(i) and 8(b) of Article XXIV, examined earlier in the context of the conditions imposed on internal trade restrictions. The key difference is that the word 'restrictive' is absent in the context of external trade. However, although this is not formally part of the definition of 'other regulations of commerce' (ORCs), sub-paragraphs 5(a) and 5(b) of Article XXIV are concerned with the 'restrictiveness' of ORCs.

Sub-paragraphs 5(a) and 8(a)(ii) form a coherent pair, both dealing with customs unions. Under sub-paragraph 8(a)(ii), the parties to a customs union must 'substantially' harmonise duties and ORCs applied to the trade of countries that are not party to the PTA (whether or not they are WTO Members); sub-paragraph 5(a) requires that the newly harmonised ORCs, plus any remaining un-harmonised ORCs, applied in respect of trade with WTO Members that are not party to the PTA, be no more restrictive than the ORCs previously applied in respect of such trade. Thus, the ORCs described in sub-paragraph 5(a) (i.e., ORCs applied to WTO Members) form a subset of the ORCs that must be harmonised under sub-paragraph 8(a)(ii) (i.e., all ORCs). Sub-paragraph 5(b) relates to FTAs and, like sub-paragraph 5(a), it addresses ORCs applied in respect of trade with WTO Members that are not party to the PTA. In the remainder of the discussion in this section of the meaning of 'duties and other regulations of commerce', we use the words 'external trade' or 'trade with third countries' as a convenient way of referring to the trade of countries that are not party to the PTA (in the context of Article XXIV:8(a)(ii)) and to trade with WTO Members that are not party to the PTA (in the context of Article XXIV:5(a) and (b)).

2. Examples of regulations of commerce

PTA parties could impose various measures that could potentially constitute ORCs, including:

- border measures regulating either the import of goods from third countries or the export of goods to third countries; and
- marketplace measures that may be applicable: solely to goods of third countries; to goods of both third countries and PTA parties; or solely to goods of PTA parties.

(a) Border measures It seems clear, and relatively uncontroversial, that the ORCs relevant to sub-paragraphs 5(a), 5(b), and 8(a)(ii) of Article XXIV include border measures applied to imports from third countries, as these measures are certainly imposed on, or applied to, external trade. These measures include customs duties and similar charges, import prohibitions, quantitative restrictions and administrative rules regulating importation. Administrative rules might include rules of origin used to distinguish between imports of goods originating in a PTA party and those originating in a third country, and prohibition of imports from third countries that do not comply with certain SPS or TBT standards. Moreover, these measures are ORCs whether they are applied individually by one PTA party or, in the case of a customs union, by all parties.

Border measures that restrict exports from PTA parties to third countries are more problematic. During the Uruguay Round, one proposal was that the words 'duties and other regulations of commerce' should be interpreted to cover 'all border measures taken in connection with importation or exportation which have a differential impact on imported products as compared to domestic products'.[81] This proposal was rejected due to, among other things, the inclusion of the word 'exportation'. This might suggest that the negotiators did not agree that ORCs included export measures.

A further difficulty with interpreting ORCs as including border measures on exports is that such measures are generally applied by PTA parties to their own goods when destined for third-country markets[82] and therefore cannot be described as being applicable or applied 'to the trade *of*' third countries within the meaning of Articles XXIV:5(b) and 8(a)(ii). However, in the context of customs unions, Article XXIV:5(a) refers to measures 'imposed . . . in respect of trade *with*' third countries. This language might be broad enough to encompass export measures. This could mean that, on the one hand, export measures are not relevant to the determination under Article XXIV:8(a)(ii) of whether the parties to a customs union apply

---

81 WTO Committee on Regional Trade Agreements, see above n. 61, para. 10.
82 Export measures may also restrict the re-exportation of (processed) goods imported from third countries.

substantially the same ORCs to other countries, nor to the determination under Article XXIV:5(b) of whether the parties to an FTA impose higher or more restrictive ORCs on other Members; but, on the other hand, export measures are relevant to the determination under Article XXIV:5(a) of whether the parties to a *customs union* impose higher or more restrictive ORCs on other Members. It is unclear whether the drafters intended this distinction.

(b) **Marketplace measures** During the Uruguay Round, a second proposal was for 'duties and other regulations of commerce' to be interpreted as covering 'all duties and charges and measures imposed on or in connection with importation or exportation'.[83] This proposal was also rejected, primarily because of differing opinions as to whether ORCs include internal measures such as sales taxes and price controls. In the end, no agreement was reached on an authoritative interpretation of 'duties and other regulations of commerce', and no explicit guidance was included as to whether these words cover internal or 'marketplace' measures.

The Appellate Body has read Article XXIV:8(a)(ii) as requiring the parties to a customs union to adopt 'a common external trade regime'.[84] In other words, it appears to be assumed that parties are not obliged by Article XXIV:8(a)(ii) to harmonise internal marketplace measures (in addition to eliminating internal restrictions on trade under Article XXIV:8(a)(i)). This approach is supported by the context and purpose of Article XXIV:8(a)(ii). Read together with the chapeau of Article XXIV:8, sub-paragraph 8(a)(ii) states that a 'customs union shall be understood to mean the substitution of a single customs territory for two or more customs territories, so that . . . substantially the same duties and other regulations of commerce are applied . . . to the trade of territories not included in the union'. The use of the word 'customs' in the chapeau indicates that the provision focuses on border measures. Moreover, it would be rather intrusive if WTO rules required parties to apply 'substantially the same' marketplace measures on goods, whether such a requirement was limited to goods from third countries or extended to goods from within the PTA. Such a rule would be particularly broad, given that Article XXIV:8(a)(ii) is not limited to 'restrictive' regulations of commerce, and it would also not necessarily further the purpose of maximising the liberalising effects of the PTA on trade between PTA parties and minimising the trade restrictive effects on other WTO Members.

The language of Articles XXIV:5(a) and (b) suggests that the ORCs that must not be 'higher or more restrictive' do not include marketplace measures. In relation to customs unions, as already noted, Article XXIV:5(a) refers to ORCs imposed 'in respect of trade with' other WTO Members. Thus, the focus is on trade between a PTA party and another Member, rather than on trade within the PTA party. In relation to FTAs, Article XXIV:5(b) refers to ORCs 'maintained in . . . and applicable . . . to the trade of' other WTO Members. This wording might more easily

---

83 WTO Committee on Regional Trade Agreements, see above n. 61.
84 Appellate Body Report, *Turkey–Textiles*, para. 49.

extend to marketplace measures. However, the use of the word 'trade' (as opposed to 'goods') may well signify that the focus is not on the treatment of goods of other Members within the PTA, but on the treatment of such goods at the border.

Some Members have argued that certain marketplace measures imposed by PTA parties solely on goods originating within the PTA might restrict external trade and therefore be relevant ORCs under these three sub-paragraphs.[85] Examples of such measures, drawn from existing PTAs, include the application of lower SPS or TBT standards[86] on internal PTA trade or the replacement of anti-dumping measures within the PTA with competition rules.[87] These harmonised rules apply solely to goods from PTA parties; the normal WTO rules apply to goods from third countries.[88]

It is difficult to know how to treat measures that apply solely to goods from PTA parties but may have a distortive effect on trade with third countries. ORCs are described as measures 'imposed ... in respect of' (Article XXIV:5(a)), 'applicable ... to' (Article XXIV:5(b)), or 'applied ... to' (Article XXIV:8(a)(ii)) the relevant trade. The verbs 'impose' and 'apply' suggest that relevant ORCs are measures that directly regulate trade with third countries and not measures that merely have an indirect effect on trade with third countries. This perhaps indicates that marketplace measures 'imposed' only on goods from PTA parties are not ORCs and, therefore, do not need to be harmonised in customs unions (under Article XXIV:8(ii)) or included in determining the level of restrictions on external trade in any PTA (under Articles XXIV:5(a) and (b)). Moreover, these harmonised rules arise from internal liberalisation within the PTA, which some have argued means that they should not be regarded as barriers to trade with third countries.[89] However, it is difficult to reconcile this with the twin purpose of the PTA exception in Article XXIV:5, given that these harmonised rules may well distort or restrict trade from third countries.

---

85 WTO Committee on Regional Trade Agreements, *Note on the Meetings of 6–7 and 10 July 1998*, WT/REG/M/18 (22 July 1998), paras. 40–6.
86 The application of two different SPS or TBT regimes – one for internal trade and another for external trade – may mean that the external regime is inconsistent with the SPS or TBT Agreement. For instance, if more stringent rules are applied externally than internally, that could well indicate that the external rules are more trade-restrictive than is necessary or that different restrictions are being applied in similar circumstances. See SPS Agreement, Articles 5.5, 5.6 and 6.1; and TBT Agreement, Article 2.2.
87 See WTO Committee on Regional Trade Agreements, *Inventory of Non-Tariff Provisions in Regional Trade Agreements: Background Note by the Secretariat*, WT/REG/W/26 (5 May 1998).
88 Canada has argued that preferential rules of origin cannot be ORCs because they are directed to the internal trade of the RTA and not the external trade (WTO Committee on Regional Trade Agreements, *Note on the Meetings of 6–7 and 10 July 1998*, WT/REG/M/18 (22 July 1998), para. 28). However, preferential rules of origin apply equally to all goods to determine their origin, even though the result will be preferential treatment for goods treated as originating in the RTA.
89 See WTO Committee on Regional Trade Agreements, *Note on the Meetings of 3–5 November 1997*, WT/REG/M/14 (24 November 1997), para. 8.

C. Substantially the same external restrictions in customs unions: GATT Article XXIV:8(a)(ii)

Article XXIV:8(a)(ii) requires the parties to a customs union to apply 'substantially the same duties and other regulations of commerce . . . to the trade of territories not included in the union'. This requirement has been described as creating 'a common external trade regime' or 'a common commercial policy'.[90] To achieve this, the parties must harmonise their respective external trade rules regulating trade with third countries; but to what extent must these restrictions be harmonised?

Discussions among Members have not focused on the meaning of 'substantially the same'. However, in the event of agreement on the meaning of 'substantially all the trade', the criteria adopted might also apply, *mutatis mutandis*, to the term 'substantially the same'. In dispute settlement, in *Turkey–Textiles*, the panel indicated that Article XXIV:8(a)(ii) describes 'a situation where constituent members have "comparable" trade regulations having similar effects with respect to trade with third countries'.[91] The Appellate Body rejected this interpretation,[92] suggesting that the word 'substantially' means 'something closely approximating "sameness"'.[93] Nevertheless, it stated that parties have 'a certain degree of flexibility' to retain individual restrictions on external trade.[94] They are not required to harmonise all external trade restrictions or to adopt an identical external trade regime.[95] Despite these statements by the Appellate Body, certain questions remain as to how to determine whether the parties to any particular customs union apply substantially the same duties and ORCs to other countries. Adopting a case-by-case approach, relevant factors could include: the number of ORCs that are fully or partially harmonised, as compared with the number of un-harmonised ORCs; the degree of partial harmonisation; and the products and value of trade affected by these different restrictions.

In order to harmonise external ORCs upon the formation of a customs union, a party to the union may need to increase a specific duty beyond the bound rate specified in its Schedule of Concessions under Article II of GATT 1994. In that event, Article XXIV:6 requires the party to enter into negotiations with affected Members following the procedure set forth in Article XXVIII of GATT 1994. Essentially, these negotiations are directed towards modification or withdrawal of concessions by affected Members[96] in order to 'maintain a general level of reciprocal and mutually advantageous concessions not less favourable to trade than that provided for in [GATT 1994] prior to such negotiations'.[97] Following the enlargement of the European Union (EU) from fifteen to twenty-five Member States on 1 May 2004, negotiations of this kind commenced. The EU recently extended the deadline for affected Members to withdraw concessions as a result of the

---

90 Appellate Body Report, *Turkey–Textiles*, paras. 49 and 50; Panel Report, *Turkey–Textiles*, para. 9.148.
91 Panel Report, *Turkey–Textiles*, para. 9.151.   92 Appellate Body Report, *Turkey–Textiles*, para. 50.
93 *Ibid.*   94 *Ibid.*   95 *Ibid.*, para. 49.   96 GATT 1994, Article XXVIII:1.   97 *Ibid.*, Article XXVIII:2.

withdrawal of concessions by certain new EC member States in connection with the enlargement.[98]

D. External restrictions not higher: Article XXIV:5

1. Customs unions: Article XXIV:5(a)

Article XXIV:5(a) of GATT 1994 states that the duties and other regulations of commerce imposed 'at the institution of' a customs union in respect of trade with other WTO Members 'shall not on the whole be higher or more restrictive than the general incidence of the duties and regulations of commerce applicable in the constituent territories prior to the formation of such union'. This provision therefore requires a comparison of the ORCs imposed before and after the institution of the customs union. Before forming the union, each party applies its own ORCs on trade with other Members. After forming the union, the parties largely replace these individual trade regimes with a common external trade regime. In keeping with the purpose of the PTA exception, the requisite comparison aims to ensure that the new external trade regime of the union does not raise barriers to trade with other Members.

First, the comparison requires an assessment of 'the general incidence of the duties and other regulations of commerce applicable in the constituent territories prior to the formation of' the customs union. The term 'general incidence' suggests a focus on the cumulative or combined effect of all ORCs imposed by the PTA parties rather than the specific effects of any individual ORC or the ORCs imposed by one PTA party. In any case, it would be difficult to compare specific ORCs before and after formation of the customs union because they are likely to be replaced by different ORCs under the new common external trade regime.

Second, the comparison requires an assessment of the 'duties and other regulations of commerce imposed at the institution of' the customs union. This includes all harmonised ORCs, as well as any un-harmonised ORCs that the parties to the union continue to apply on an individual basis. Such ORCs are not to be 'on the whole . . . higher or more restrictive' than before. The words 'on the whole', like the words 'general incidence', demonstrate that the comparison is based on the overall, cumulative impact of the ORCs, not on specific ORCs. As a result, certain specific ORCs imposed by one or more PTA parties may be more burdensome than before, while others may be less burdensome. However, if the ORCs 'as a whole' are more burdensome than before, the customs union cannot benefit from the PTA exception in Article XXIV:5.

The RTA Understanding provides a methodology for determining the cumulative impact of ORCs before and after the formation of the customs union, based on 'an

---

98 WTO Council for Trade in Goods, *Communication from the European Union: Article XXIV:6 Negotiations; Enlargement of the European Union*, G/L/695/Add.11 (10 May 2010).

overall assessment of weighted average tariff rates and of customs duties collected'. Paragraph 2 of the RTA Understanding states:

> This assessment shall be based on import statistics for a previous representative period to be supplied by the customs union, on a tariff-line basis and in values and quantities, broken down by WTO country of origin. The Secretariat shall compute the weighted average tariff rates and customs duties collected in accordance with the methodology used in the assessment of tariff offers in the Uruguay Round of Multilateral Trade Negotiations. For this purpose, the duties and charges to be taken into consideration shall be the applied rates of duty.

As regards ORCs other than duties and charges, the RTA Understanding is less explicit. Paragraph 2 recognises that for the 'overall assessment' of ORCs 'for which quantification and aggregation are difficult, the examination of individual measures, regulations, products covered and trade flows affected may be required'. This general guidance falls short of a methodology and leaves open precisely how to assess the impact of these ORCs. This process may be difficult because, unlike duties and charges, these restrictions do not take the form of a fixed amount or percentage that is applied to specific products.

2. Free-trade areas: Article XXIV:5(b)

Like Article XXIV:5(a), sub-paragraph 5(b) calls for a comparison between two sets of ORCs: those 'existing' prior to the formation of the FTA, and those 'applicable' at the formation of the FTA. For customs unions, we saw that the comparison under Article XXIV:5(a) is between the 'general incidence' of all ORCs applied before and after the formation of the union. For FTAs, Article XXIV:5(b) calls for a comparison between the ORCs applied after the formation of the FTA and the 'corresponding' ORCs applied before formation. The use of the word 'corresponding' suggests that specific ORCs should be compared as they applied before and after the formation of the FTA.

This view is consistent with the nature of economic integration in FTAs. As with parties to customs unions, FTA parties must eliminate most 'duties and other restrictive regulations of commerce' on substantially all internal trade. However, as stated above, FTA parties have no obligation to adopt common rules for external trade, and parties to an FTA typically continue to impose their own external trade regimes.[99] Therefore, Article XXIV:5(b) prevents an FTA party from using the formation of an FTA as an opportunity to increase the burden of any individual ORC it imposes on external trade. In Article XXIV, such an increase in burden is essentially deemed unnecessary to the formation of an FTA and is inconsistent

---

99 There may be situations where the formation of an FTA does result in modification to the external trade regimes of the parties. For instance, the parties to an FTA may harmonise certain internal restrictions, such as SPS measures, and in consequence modify the corresponding external restrictions.

with the purpose of Article XXIV of minimising the restrictive effects of PTAs on external trade.

Article XXIV:6 envisages increases in specific bound rates upon the formation of a customs union and provides a procedure for negotiating a 'compensatory adjustment' for the affected Member. In contrast, no provision in Article XXIV envisages any increase in specific duties upon the formation of an FTA. This supports the view that a WTO Member may not make any ORC more burdensome upon the formation of an FTA. Nevertheless, other provisions of GATT 1994 or other covered agreements could conceivably provide a justification for the introduction of new restrictions by FTA parties. For instance, if the parties to a PTA decide to harmonise the SPS/TBT framework within the PTA and, in the process, one or more of the parties introduces new SPS measures or technical regulations that are applied on an MFN basis, the parties could justify the new restrictions under the SPS Agreement or the TBT Agreement, even if these restrictions would normally be regarded as relevant ORCs under Article XXIV:5(b). The introduction on the formation of an FTA of a new ORC that is justified by other WTO provisions should not prevent the FTA concerned from benefiting from the PTA exception under Article XXIV:5 – WTO rules entitle the Member to adopt the ORC whether or not it joins the PTA.

V. The GATS exception for PTAs: Article V

Article V[100] of the GATS is the GATS equivalent of Article XXIV of the GATT. It does not make a distinction between FTAs and CUs, although the PTAs that it contemplates appear closest to GATT FTAs. Its provisions are similar to the GATT's[101] and it also has been the subject of only very limited consideration by WTO dispute settlement bodies.[102]

A. Eliminating restrictions on trade within the PTA

The first substantive requirement for a PTA in the GATS is substantial sectoral coverage and the elimination of substantially all discrimination. Article V:1 of the GATS states:

---

100 See generally, Christopher Findlay, Sherry Stephenson and Francisco J. Prieto, 'Services in Regional Trading Arrangements', in Patrick F.J. Macrory, Arthur E. Appleton and Michael G. Plummer (eds.), *The World Trade Organization: Legal, Economic and Political Analysis* (New York: Springer, 2005), Vol. 1, pp. 293–312.

101 Cf., e.g., GATS, Article V.5; and GATT, Article XXIV.6.

102 It has only been considered in Panel Report, *Canada–Automotive Industry*, paras. 10.265–10.272. In that case the Panel simply found that the measures at issue could not be considered part of NAFTA provisions on liberalisation of trade in services since they were only part of a 'specific exemption'. Further the measure's import duty exemption (i) was accorded to only a small number of US firms on a selective basis; and (ii) excluded other firms in another party to the economic integration agreement (Mexico). The Panel held that this was inconsistent with GATS Article V:1(b).

This Agreement shall not prevent any of its Members from being a party to or entering into an agreement liberalising trade in services between or among the parties to such an agreement, provided that such an agreement:

(a) has substantial sectoral coverage; and
(b) provides for the absence or elimination of substantially all discrimination, in the sense of Article XVII, between or among the parties, in the sectors covered under subparagraph (a), through:
   (i) elimination of existing discriminatory measures, and/or
   (ii) prohibition of new or more discriminatory measures, either at the entry into force of that agreement or on the basis of a reasonable timeframe, except for measures permitted under Articles XI, XII, XIV and XIV*bis*.

Footnote 1 to Article V:1 of the GATS states that the term substantial sector coverage is to be 'understood in terms of number of sectors, volume of trade affected and modes of supply. In order to meet this condition, agreements should not provide for the *a priori* exclusion of any mode of supply'. The 'substantial sectoral coverage' requirement is suggestive of the 'substantially all trade' requirement of Article XXIV of the GATT. Unfortunately, as we saw above, there is no agreement about the meaning of this requirement so we cannot use it to shed light on its context in the GATS.[103]

B. Restrictions on the external trade of the PTA

The second substantive requirement is a prohibition from erecting new trade barriers against those outside the PTA. Article V:4 of the GATS states:

Any agreement referred to in [Art V.1] shall be designed to facilitate trade between the parties to the agreement and shall not in respect of any Member outside the agreement raise the overall level of barriers to trade in services within the respective sectors or subsectors compared to the level applicable prior to such an agreement.

However, Article V:5 of the GATS makes it clear that compensation must be negotiated where commitments are to be modified:

If, in the conclusion, enlargement or any significant modification of any agreement under [Art V.1], a Member intends to withdraw or modify a specific commitment inconsistently with the terms and conditions set out in its Schedule, it shall provide at least 90 days advance notice of such modification or withdrawal and the procedure set forth in paragraphs 2, 3 and 4 of Article XXI shall apply.

---

103 See above section III.

VI. The likelihood of legal challenge

One might imagine that, given the uncertainties identified above and the enormous number of FTAs concluded or being negotiated, FTAs are at substantial risk of challenge. Certainly FTAs can be challenged, either through the Committee on Regional Trade Agreements (CRTA) or through the dispute settlement mechanism. However, neither mechanism looks likely to begin effectively enforcing the rules.

A. Committee on Regional Trade Agreements

WTO Members have a duty to notify the WTO of their decision to enter into FTAs.[104] These notifications are received by the Committee on Regional Trade Agreements (CRTA).[105] The CRTA is required to, among other things:

> (a) carry out the examination of agreements in accordance with the procedures and terms of reference adopted by ... and thereafter present its report to the relevant body for appropriate action.[106]

The CRTA has the power to determine that an FTA is inconsistent with the rules. It may:

> make such reports and recommendations to Members as they may deem appropriate.

However, the CRTA has never made a decision that an FTA was inconsistent with the rules. Indeed, the reports that the CRTA makes on the FTAs it reviews are adopted notwithstanding the often divergent views on their consistency with the rules.[107]

The only consensus that has been achieved on an FTA's consistency with the rules was the 1993 customs union between the Czech Republic and the Slovak Republic after the breakup of Czechoslovakia. Given that 241 notifications have been made, the sustained lack of serious enforcement suggests a systemic failure.

B. Dispute settlement

While WTO tribunals clearly have the competence to determine claims of the inconsistency of a PTA with the WTO Agreements,[108] a legal challenge is unlikely

---

104 GATT, Article XXIV:7(a). The language in this Article suggests that it is a prospective obligation, but for most of its history, notifications to the CRTA have been made after the establishment of the PTA.
105 The CRTA was established by a decision of the General Council on 7 February 1996: WTO Doc WT/L/127.
106 *Ibid.*
107 Mitsuo Matsushita, Thomas J. Schoenbaum and Petros C. Mavroidis, *The World Trade Organization: Law, Practice, and Policy*, 2nd edn (Oxford: Oxford University Press, 2006), p. 560.
108 PTA Understanding, Article 12: 'The provisions of Articles XXII and XXIIII of GATT 1994 as elaborated and applied by the Dispute Settlement Understanding may be invoked with respect to any matters arising from the application of those provisions of Article XXIV relating to customs unions, free-trade areas or

for a number of reasons. One is that Members may consider that WTO tribunals will avoid determining the ambiguities identified above and therefore not wish to engage in the costly process of bringing a dispute. Given:

> the uncertainty surrounding the precise legal frontiers between consistency and inconsistency with the multilateral rules, apart from exceptional cases, it is unlikely that a panel will find itself on firm legal ground to provide a definitive statement on the law itself. [For example, they might state] the burden of proof has not been met, or evidence provided has not been effectively refuted and request additional proof from the complainant.[109]

WTO tribunals are skilled at avoiding answering unnecessary questions and are likely to be able to avoid resolving some key questions where the WTO inconsistency of an FTA was at issue. A stronger reason is that, since all but one WTO Member is party to a FTA, and many FTAs could be WTO-inconsistent, a situation of 'co-operative equilibrium' has developed, where to avoid challenge, Members do not challenge other Members' FTAs.[110]

VII. Conclusion

In a global trading system, where PTAs have become a central tool of trade policy, and where they are growing rapidly in number and complexity, the exceptions in Article XXIV:5 of GATT 1994 and Article V of GATS play a crucial role in ensuring coherence between multilateral and regional trade policy. We have noted that these exceptions seek to ensure that PTAs work to the benefit of the global trading system by promoting a net increase in trade liberalisation. Yet questions remain on almost every issue of importance concerning this exception.[111] Without answers to these questions, the value of Article XXIV and Article V in shaping regional trade policy is diminished. Moreover, the risk that PTAs work to undermine trade liberalisation at the multilateral level increases. This chapter has explored some of the questions surrounding Article XXIV and Article V, evaluating possible options, always keeping in mind the underlying purpose of the PTA exception. We have examined the views expressed by Members, panels

---

interim agreements leading to the formation of a customs union or a free-trade area.' See also Lorand Bartels, 'WTO Dispute Settlement Practice on Article XXIV of the GATT', in Federico Ortino and Ernst-Ulrich Petersmann (eds.), *The WTO Dispute Settlement System 1995–2003* (The Hague: Kluwer Law International, 2004), pp. 263–73, at p. 268.

109 Matsushita *et al.*, above n. 107, at p. 585.   110 *Ibid.*, at p. 587.

111 For example, does the exception extend to GATT-inconsistencies arising from the elimination of internal trade restrictions only if these inconsistencies were necessary to the formation of the RTA? Does it justify a departure from the obligation under the Agreement on Safeguards to impose safeguards on all imports of the relevant product from all sources? How should 'substantially all the trade' between the RTA parties be measured in assessing whether internal trade restrictions have been sufficiently reduced? Do the parties to a customs union have to harmonise not only border measures but also marketplace measures applied to goods of other Members?

and the Appellate Body, as well as the text of WTO agreements. We have also drawn on the way PTAs work in practice. The conclusion must be that Article XXIV and Article V are mired in doubt. Until the WTO makes further progress in this area, the WTO-consistency of most PTAs will be uncertain and Members will have difficulty determining the best way of structuring PTAs in a WTO-consistent fashion.

6

PTAs and public international law

ANDREW D. MITCHELL, TANIA VOON
AND ELIZABETH SHEARGOLD*

I. Introduction

Since the first report of the Appellate Body of the World Trade Organization (WTO) in 1996,[1] commentators and practitioners alike have been grappling with the thorny relationship between the WTO and public international law.[2] More recently, problems in interpreting and applying WTO provisions in the light of customary international law and non-WTO treaties[3] have come to reflect a concern regarding 'fragmentation' of international law more generally.[4] One reason for this potential fragmentation lies in the disparate dispute settlement mechanisms under various

---

* This chapter was finalised from September to November 2013. For helpful comments on the original draft chapter for the first edition, we thank Joshua Meltzer, Bryan Mercurio, and David Morgan. For research and editorial assistance for the second edition, we thank Caroline Henckels. For helpful comments on the draft chapter for the second edition, we thank Lorand Bartels. We also acknowledge the generous funding provided by the Australian Research Council pursuant to the Discovery Project scheme (project number DP130100838). Any errors are ours.
1 Appellate Body Report, *US–Gasoline*, p. 17: 'the *General Agreement* is not to be read in clinical isolation from public international law.'
2 See Joost Pauwelyn, *Conflict of Norms in Public International Law: How WTO Law Relates to Other Rules of International Law* (Cambridge: Cambridge University Press, 2003). See also, e.g., Lorand Bartels, 'Applicable Law in WTO Dispute Settlement Proceedings' (2001) 35(3) *Journal of World Trade* 499–519; Michael Lennard, 'Navigating by the Stars: Interpreting the WTO Agreements' (2002) 5(1) *Journal of International Economic Law* 17–89; Gabrielle Marceau, 'WTO Dispute Settlement and Human Rights' (2002) 13(4) *European Journal of International Law* 753–814; Joel P. Trachtman, 'The Jurisdiction of the World Trade Organization' (2004) 98 *American Society of International Law Proceedings* 139–42; and Joel P. Trachtman, 'Jurisdiction in WTO Dispute Settlement', in Rufus Yerxa and Bruce Wilson (eds.), *Key Issues in WTO Dispute Settlement: The First Ten Years* (Cambridge: Cambridge University Press, 2005), pp. 132–43.
3 See, e.g., Appellate Body Report, *EC–Tariff Preferences*, para. 163; and Appellate Body Report, *EC–Sugar Subsidies*, paras. 310 and 312.
4 See, e.g., International Law Commission, *Fragmentation of International Law: Difficulties Arising from the Diversification and Expansion of International Law*, Report of the Study Group (finalised by Martti Koskenniemi), UN Doc. A/CN.4/L.682 (4 April 2006); and Campbell McLachlan, 'The Principle of Systemic Integration and Article 31(3)(c) of the Vienna Convention' (2005) 54 *International & Comparative Law Quarterly* 279–320.

international legal systems,[5] including preferential trade agreements (PTAs),[6] some of which also contain investment obligations and allow for investor–state dispute settlement.

As the future of the Doha Round remains uncertain,[7] PTAs have proliferated.[8] A large number of states are contemplating or commencing PTA negotiations, including the Trans-Pacific Partnership agreement (a trade and investment treaty involving 12 countries including Australia, the United States, Chile, and Singapore), the Regional Comprehensive Economic Partnership (a PTA developing from the Association of Southeast Asian Nations plus six other countries), and a Transatlantic Trade and Investment Partnership between the United States and the European Union. The burgeoning number of PTAs means that the relationship between them and other institutions and aspects of public international law becomes all the more crucial. States evaluating the benefits of PTAs must be fully aware of the broader international context into which they are born and the implications of international law as each PTA develops. Moreover, existing PTA members may seek additional certainty about their PTA rights and obligations and the likely outcome in the event of a dispute relating to other areas of international law. More broadly, an investigation into the relationship between public international law and PTAs provides an additional case study of the perceived problem of fragmentation of international law.

In this chapter, we focus on two primary sources of public international law, namely treaties and customary international law. We also take into account two other sources of public international law, namely general principles of law and judicial decisions and leading commentary. All four sources are included in Article 38(1) of the Statute of the International Court of Justice (ICJ Statute), which is often recognised as providing an informal list of the sources of international law.[9]

---

5 See, e.g., Joost Pauwelyn, 'Adding Sweeteners to Softwood Lumber: The WTO–NAFTA "Spaghetti Bowl" is Cooking' (2006) 9(1) *Journal of International Economic Law* 197–206; and Yuval Shany, *The Competing Jurisdictions of International Courts and Tribunals* (Oxford: Oxford University Press, 2003).

6 We use the term 'preferential trade agreements' to refer to bilateral and regional agreements between States or customs territories that focus at least in part on liberalising trade between the parties, as distinct from the multilateral system established under the WTO. 'PTAs' therefore include free-trade areas and customs unions within the meaning of Article XXIV of GATT 1994.

7 Pascal Lamy, 'Documents from the negotiating chairs: Cover note from TNC Chair', 21 April 2011, WT/TN/C/13; 'The Doha Round: Dead Man Talking', *The Economist*, 28 April 2011.

8 See, e.g., Report by the Consultative Board to the Director-General, 'The Future of the WTO: Addressing Institutional Challenges in the New Millennium', Geneva, 2004, para. 76; and World Bank, *Global Economic Prospects 2005: Trade, Regionalism, and Development* (Washington, DC: World Bank, 2005), at pp. 28–30. As of 10 January 2013, the WTO had received notifications of 546 PTAs (counting goods, services, and accessions separately), including 354 in force: see www.wto.org/english/tratop_e/region_e/region_e.htm.

9 See, e.g., Martti Koskenniemi, 'Introduction', in Martti Koskenniemi (ed.), *Sources of International Law* (Aldershot: Ashgate, 2000), p. xi; Gerald G. Fitzmaurice, 'Some Problems Regarding the Formal Sources of International Law' (1958) *Symbolae Verzijl* 153–76, at 173; and Robert Y. Jennings, 'What is International Law and How Do We Tell It When We See It?' (1981) 37 *Schweitzerisches Jahrbuch für Internationales Recht* 59–88, at 61.

Below, we examine three significant areas in which public international law interacts with PTAs: first, how various forms of public international law affect the interpretation of PTA provisions; second, the related issue of how PTAs contribute to customary international law and the extent to which customary international law applies to PTAs; and, finally, how to resolve conflicts between PTAs and other treaties. This final section examines both substantive conflicts and problems arising from overlapping jurisdictions of PTA tribunals and other international tribunals. This survey illustrates the complex web of links between PTAs and public international law and the readiness of PTA tribunals, particularly under Chapter 11 of the North American Free Trade Agreement[10] (NAFTA), to draw on other sources of international law in interpreting PTA provisions and otherwise determining PTA disputes. At the same time, no clear answers emerge about how best to deal with the likelihood of ever increasing conflicts between PTAs and other treaties.

II. Interpreting PTA provisions

In exploring how public international law influences the interpretation of PTA provisions, we first consider the role of the Vienna Convention on the Law of Treaties[11] (Vienna Convention), before moving on to the relevance of WTO law.

A. Impact of the Vienna Convention on the Law of Treaties

The Vienna Convention applies to 'treaties between States',[12] where a 'treaty' is defined as 'an international agreement concluded between States in written form and governed by international law, whether embodied in a single instrument or in two or more related instruments and whatever its particular designation'.[13] This would naturally include PTAs between any of the 114 parties of the Vienna Convention,[14] unless they were concluded before that convention's entry into force in 1980.[15]

At least some parts of the Vienna Convention are widely accepted as codifying customary international law or having attained the status of customary international law.[16] Articles 31 and 32 on the interpretation of treaties, in particular, are frequently

---

10 (1993) 32 ILM 289 and (1993) 32 ILM 605. Chapter 11 (Investment) regulates the conduct of states in terms of their treatment of investors from other states.

11 Done at Vienna 23 May 1969, in force 27 January 1980, 1155 UNTS 331; (1969) 8 ILM 679, UKTS (1980) 58.

12 Vienna Convention, Article 1. Accordingly, the Vienna Convention does not apply to treaties between States and international organisations or between international organisations: Ian Sinclair, *The Vienna Convention on the Law of Treaties*, 2nd edn (Manchester: Manchester University Press, 1984), at pp. 6–7. The Vienna Convention is adapted to international organisations by the Vienna Convention on the Law of Treaties Between States and International Organisations or Between International Organisations, opened for signature 21 March 1986, not yet in force, (1986) 25 ILM 543.

13 Vienna Convention, Article 2(1)(a).

14 UN, *Multilateral Treaties Deposited with the Secretary-General*, ST/LEG/SER/E/–, available at http://treaties.un.org.

15 Vienna Convention, Article 4.   16 We discuss customary international law further below in section III.

regarded as declaring or reflecting customary international law.[17] This means that the rules of interpretation in these provisions apply to all PTAs between States, whether or not those States are party to the Vienna Convention. This conclusion is fairly uncontroversial, just as few would argue that the WTO agreements should be interpreted other than by reference to Articles 31 and 32 of the Vienna Convention.[18]

In any case, although a PTA could conceivably dictate alternative rules for interpretation, the more common scenario would be that the PTA explicitly or implicitly confirms that the Vienna Convention rules apply. For example, Article 21.9(2) of the Australia–United States Free Trade Agreement (AUSFTA) provides:

> The panel shall consider this Agreement in accordance with applicable rules of interpretation under international law as reflected in Articles 31 and 32 of the *Vienna Convention on the Law of Treaties* (1969).[19]

Similarly, Article 102(2) of NAFTA provides that '[t]he Parties shall interpret and apply the provisions of this Agreement in the light of its objectives set out in paragraph 1 and in accordance with applicable rules of international law', which are read (by arbitral tribunals) to include Articles 31 and 32 of the Vienna Convention.[20]

Articles 31 and 32 of the Vienna Convention themselves provide an example of public international law (in this case, interpretative rules amounting to customary international law) influencing PTAs. Thus, the primary customary international law rule for interpreting treaties also applies to PTAs: 'A treaty shall be interpreted in good faith in accordance with the ordinary meaning to be given to the terms of the treaty in their context and in the light of its object and purpose'.[21]

In turn, various forms of public international law may affect the meaning of various terms in Articles 31 and 32 and how they should be applied. For example, Article 31(3) of the Vienna Convention states that, in interpreting a treaty:

> There shall be taken into account, together with the context:
>
> (a) any subsequent agreement between the parties regarding the interpretation of the treaty or the application of its provisions;
> (b) any subsequent practice in the application of the treaty which establishes the agreement of the parties regarding its interpretation;
> (c) any relevant rules of international law applicable in the relations between the parties.

---

17 See, e.g., *Case Concerning the Territorial Dispute (Libyan Arab Jamahiriya v. Chad) (Merits)* [1994] ICJ Rep. 6, pp. 21–2; Sinclair, above n. 12, at p. 19 (regarding Vienna Convention, Articles 30–3); Pauwelyn, above n. 2, at p. 245. See also *Gabcíkovo-Nagymaros Project (Hungary v. Slovakia) (Merits) (Gabcíkovo-Nagymaros Project)* [1997] ICJ Rep. 7 at p. 38 (regarding Vienna Convention, Articles 60–2).
18 See, e.g., Appellate Body Report, *US–Gasoline*, pp. 16–17; and DSU, Article 3.2.
19 See also NAFTA, Article 102(2).
20 See, e.g., NAFTA Ch 20 Panel Report, *Tariffs Applied by Canada to Certain U.S.-Origin Agricultural Products*, CDA-95-2008-01 (2 December 1996), paras. 118–19; and NAFTA Ch 11 Arbitral Tribunal, *SD Myers Inc v. Government of Canada ('Myers v. Canada')* (Partial Award of 13 November 2000), para. 200.
21 Vienna Convention, Article 31(1).

The words 'subsequent practice' have taken on a specific meaning in public international law,[22] and a correct interpretation in accordance with Article 31(3) should have regard to that meaning.

More importantly, Article 31(3)(c) of the Vienna Convention provides a concrete basis for examining non-interpretative rules of public international law in interpreting PTA provisions. In particular, other treaties to which the PTA members are party should be considered. For example, the NAFTA Chapter 11 Tribunal in *SD Myers* v. *Government of Canada* examined the Basel Convention on the Control of Transboundary Movements of Hazardous Wastes and their Disposal and the Canada–United States Transboundary Agreement on Hazardous Waste in interpreting NAFTA provisions in an arbitration between the Government of Canada and a United States (US) investor.[23] The WTO agreements (applicable to all WTO Members, numbering 159 at the time of writing) would also constitute rules of international law between the parties to a PTA created between WTO Members.

B. Relevance of WTO law

This leads to the question of the significance of WTO 'jurisprudence' in clarifying the WTO rules and, in turn, in interpreting PTA provisions. WTO case law itself, in the form of Panel or Appellate Body Reports adopted by the Dispute Settlement Body (DSB),[24] does not necessarily amount to or create rules of international law within the meaning of Article 31(3)(c) of the Vienna Convention, given that Panels, the Appellate Body and the DSB must not 'add to or diminish the rights and obligations provided in the covered agreements'.[25] It may nevertheless comprise 'judicial decisions' providing a 'subsidiary means for the determination of rules of law'.[26] Locknie Hsu even suggests that WTO provisions and cases may 'evolve into customary international law'[27] and on that basis be relevant sources of international law in

---

22 See, e.g., Arnold D. McNair, *The Law of Treaties* (Oxford: Clarendon Press, 1961), chapter XXIV; Sinclair, above n. 12, at pp. 135–8; Georg Nolte (ed.), *Treaties and Subsequent Practice* (Oxford: Oxford University Press, 2013); and Appellate Body Report, *Japan–Alcoholic Beverages*, paras. 12–13.

23 *Myers* v. *Canada*, paras. 205–8.

24 For general information about the WTO dispute settlement system, see WTO, *A Handbook on the WTO Dispute Settlement System* (Cambridge: Cambridge University Press, 2004); David Palmeter and Petros C. Mavroidis, *Dispute Settlement in the World Trade Organization: Practice and Procedure*, 2nd edn (The Hague: Kluwer Law International, 2004); Bryan Mercurio, Yang Guohua and Li Yongjie, *WTO Dispute Settlement Understanding: A Detailed Interpretation* (The Hague: Kluwer Law International, 2005); and Giorgio Sacerdoti, Alan Yanovich and Jan Bohanes (eds.), *The WTO at Ten: The Contribution of the Dispute Settlement System* (Cambridge: Cambridge University Press, 2006).

25 DSU, Articles 3.2 and 19.2.

26 ICJ Statute, Article 38(1)(d). As Brownlie notes, 'the practical significance of the label "subsidiary means" in Article 38(1)(d) is not to be exaggerated': Ian Brownlie, *Principles of Public International Law*, 6th edn (Oxford: Oxford University Press, 2003).

27 Locknie Hsu, 'Applicability of WTO Law in Regional Trade Agreements: Identifying the Links', in Lorand Bartels and Federico Ortino (eds.), *Regional Trade Agreements and the WTO Legal System* (Oxford: Oxford University Press, 2006), pp. 525–52, at p. 532.

interpreting PTAs.[28] At the least, even though the WTO's Ministerial Conference and General Council 'have the exclusive authority to adopt interpretations' of the WTO agreements,[29] the reasoning and conclusions in adopted Panel and Appellate Body Reports may shed light on the correct interpretation of particular WTO provisions, which may be relevant in interpreting related PTA provisions. The significance and precedential value of adopted Appellate Body Reports in particular has been emphasised in WTO case law in recent years.[30]

This conclusion is particularly apt where the PTA provision in question incorporates a WTO provision by reference or replicates the wording of the WTO provision, both of which are common techniques.[31] An example of a PTA incorporating a WTO provision by reference appears in Article 301(1) of NAFTA:

> Each Party shall accord national treatment to the goods of another Party in accordance with Article III of the *General Agreement on Tariffs and Trade* (GATT), including its interpretative notes, and to this end Article III of the GATT and its interpretative notes, or any equivalent provision of a successor agreement to which all Parties are party, are incorporated into and made part of this Agreement.

While this provision does not of itself incorporate subsequent WTO jurisprudence interpreting GATT Article III directly into the PTA, a tribunal applying the PTA would be likely to give some weight to interpretations of GATT Article III in adopted WTO Panel and Appellate Body Reports. An example of a PTA replicating the wording of a WTO provision[32] appears in Article 809 of the Thailand–Australia Free Trade Agreement, which is very similar to Article XVI of the WTO's General Agreement on Trade in Services (GATS).

The relevance of WTO law in interpreting these and other PTA provisions[33] is evidenced by a number of decisions by PTA tribunals. For instance, examining a NAFTA exception provision that 'closely track[ed] the GATT Article XX language', an Arbitral Panel established under NAFTA Chapter 20 found that 'the GATT/WTO jurisprudence proves helpful in determining what "necessary" means'.[34] The NAFTA *Myers* Arbitral Tribunal referred to WTO case law on 'like products' in interpreting

---

28 However, the so-called 'Baxter paradox' suggests that as the number of parties to a treaty increases, it becomes more difficult to establish that the same rule is also customary international law (as distinct from the treaty). See Richard R. Baxter, 'Treaties and Custom' (1970) 129 *Recueil des Cours* 27–105, at 64.

29 WTO Agreement, Article IX:2.

30 See, e.g., Appellate Body Report, *US–Stainless Steel (Mexico)*, paras. 160–2.

31 On the different ways in which PTA provisions may invoke WTO law, see Hsu, above n. 27, at p. 542.

32 See also AUSFTA, Article 17.9(3), duplicating TRIPS Agreement, Article 30.

33 Conversely, incorporation of WTO provisions in PTAs may have implications for the compulsory nature of the WTO dispute settlement system, given that the same issue may be litigated under a PTA instead of the WTO. This relates to the problem of overlapping WTO/PTA jurisdiction, as discussed further below, section IVB.

34 NAFTA Ch 20 Panel Report, *In the Matter of Cross-Border Trucking Services*, USA-MEX-98-2008-01 (6 February 2001), paras. 260 and 262.

the words 'like circumstances' in Article 1102 of NAFTA[35] (although a subsequent tribunal criticised this approach, given the different language used in the two treaties).[36]

Incidentally, citation by WTO Panels or the Appellate Body of PTA tribunal decisions as legal authority in interpreting WTO law is much rarer,[37] although Todd Weiler has argued that:

> should NAFTA tribunal jurisprudence in the fields of services and investment regulation continue to outstrip that of WTO panels, it would not seem too much to ask that NAFTA awards be considered by WTO panels in the adoption of an inductive approach to as-of-yet 'untested' GATS obligations.[38]

Weiler made this statement in 2003, before the release of several significant WTO cases on services (although these did not embrace PTA tribunal jurisprudence either).[39] A complication for WTO tribunals in referring to PTA provisions or jurisprudence arises from the uncertainty within the WTO context as to whether the reference to 'relevant rules of international law applicable in the relations between the parties' in Article 31(3)(c) of the Vienna Convention means rules applicable between all WTO Members or only between the parties to the relevant WTO dispute[40] (assuming that the rules in question are 'relevant' to the dispute at hand).

III. PTAs and customary international law

As already mentioned,[41] Articles 31 and 32 of the Vienna Convention reflect customary international law on treaty interpretation and therefore represent one way in which customary international law affects PTAs. Moreover, Article 31(3)(c) provides an avenue for various aspects of public international law (including customary

35 *Myers* v. *Canada*, paras. 243–6. See also NAFTA Ch 11 Arbitral Tribunal, *Pope & Talbot Inc* v. *Government of Canada* ('Pope & Talbot v. Canada') (Interim Award of 26 June 2000), paras. 45–7. For further discussion of the use of WTO law by NAFTA panels and tribunals, see Hsu, above n. 27, at pp. 543–9; Jürgen Kurtz, 'The Use and Abuse of WTO Law in Investor – State Arbitration: Competition and its Discontents' (2009) 20(3) *European Journal of International Law* 749–71.
36 NAFTA Ch 11 Arbitral Tribunal, *Methanex Corporation* v. *United States of America* (Award of 9 August 2005), Part IV, Chapter B, paras. 29–37. See also London Court of International Arbitration, *Occidental Exploration and Production Company* v. *Ecuador* (Award of 1 July 2004), paras. 174–6; *Continental Casualty Company* v. *Argentine Republic*, ICSID Case No. ARB/03/9 (Award of 5 September 2008), paras. 192–5 (both in the context of a bilateral investment treaty rather than a PTA).
37 Cf., e.g., Appellate Body Report, *EC–Chicken Classification*, paras. 310–45. See also Isabelle Van Damme, 'What Role is there for Regional International Law in the Interpretation of the WTO Agreements?', in Bartels and Ortino (eds.), above n. 27, pp. 553–75, at pp. 569–71, on the use by WTO Panels and the Appellate Body of PTAs (as opposed to PTA jurisprudence) in interpreting WTO law.
38 Todd Weiler, 'NAFTA Article 1105 and the Principles of International Economic Law' (2003) 42(1) *Columbia Journal of Transnational Law* 35–85, at 73.
39 See, in particular, Appellate Body Report, *US–Gambling*; and Panel Report, *Mexico–Telecoms*.
40 See Panel Report, *EC–Biotech*, para. 7.68; Appellate Body Report, *EC and certain member States–Large Civil Aircraft*, paras. 844, 846.
41 See above section IIA.

international law) to influence the interpretation of PTAs. In this section, we explore two additional issues regarding the relationship between PTAs and customary international law. To begin with, how might PTAs contribute to or influence customary international law? Conversely, how might customary international law affect the operation of PTAs other than in an interpretative sense? We address these intersecting questions in turn.

A. Contribution of PTAs to customary international law

Customary international law is an independent source of international law, as reflected in Article 38(1)(b) of the ICJ Statute, which refers to 'international custom, as evidence of a general practice accepted as law'.[42] In accordance with this description, customary international law is essentially created through the two elements of 'State practice' and 'opinio juris'[43] (i.e., belief among the relevant States that this practice accords with a binding norm). More particularly:

> Not only must the acts concerned amount to a settled practice, but they must also be such, or be carried out in such a way, as to be evidence of a belief that this practice is rendered obligatory by the existence of a rule of law requiring it . . . The States concerned must therefore feel that they are conforming to what amounts to a legal obligation.[44]

In 1990, before the creation of the WTO, Stephen Zamora canvassed the possibility of 'customary international economic law', suggesting that international economic law (including in the form of multilateral and bilateral treaties) could contribute to, or provide, evidence of both State practice and opinio juris.[45]

Let us consider an example of how this might occur. Under customary international law, a State is responsible for a 'denial of justice' where its courts or tribunals fail to accord a minimum standard of procedural or (more rarely) substantive fairness to aliens in the administration of justice.[46] Denial of justice is understood to form one of the elements of the international minimum standard of treatment of

---

42 For further discussion of customary international law, see Michael Byers, *Custom, Power and the Power of Rules* (Cambridge: Cambridge University Press, 1999); and Kristen Walker and Andrew D. Mitchell, 'A Stronger Role for Customary International Law in Domestic Law?', in Hilary Charlesworth, Madelaine Chiam, Devika Hovell and George Williams (eds.), *The Fluid State* (Sydney: Federation Press, 2005), pp. 110–35, at pp. 112–25.

43 See, e.g., *North Sea Continental Shelf (Federal Republic of Germany v. Denmark; Federal Republic of Germany v. Netherlands) (Merits)* ('*North Sea Continental Shelf* ') [1969] ICJ Rep. 3, at p. 41.

44 *North Sea Continental Shelf*, p. 44.

45 Stephen Zamora, 'Is There Customary International Economic Law?' (1990) 32 *German Yearbook of International Law* 9–42, at 18–23.

46 See, e.g., *Case Concerning Elettronica Sicula SpA (ELSI) (United States of America v. Italy) (Merits)* ('*Elettronica Sicula*') [1989] ICJ Rep. 15, pp. 66–7; Louis B. Sohn and Richard R. Baxter, 'Responsibility of States for Injuries to the Economic Interests of Aliens' (1961) 55 *American Journal of International Law* 545–84; Robert Y. Jennings and Arthur Watts (eds.), *Oppenheim's International Law*, 9th edn (London: Longman, 1992), Vol. I, at pp. 543–4; Jan Paulsson, *Denial of Justice in International Law* (Cambridge:

aliens.[47] Importantly, this 'minimum standard' may relate to the way the State treats its own nationals, but it operates independently of and supplements the 'national treatment' rule common in WTO agreements and PTAs.[48] This customary rule could be relevant in interpreting PTA provisions,[49] or it could apply independently to the conduct of PTA parties just as other customary rules may do, as discussed below. At the same time, the development of the rule in PTAs and PTA jurisprudence could affect the content or status of the customary rule. This is particularly likely given that PTAs including investment obligations frequently incorporate some form of the doctrine of denial of justice, and that disputes concerning the treatment of aliens, including in the courts, often arise in the context of PTAs.

For instance, Article 1105(1) of NAFTA provides:

> Each Party shall accord to investments of investors of another Party treatment in accordance with international law, including fair and equitable treatment and full protection and security.

The reference to international law in this provision highlights the dynamic relationship between NAFTA and other aspects of public international law. The mere inclusion of Article 1105(1) in NAFTA could provide some evidence of state practice and *opinio juris* in connection with the doctrine of denial of justice in customary international law. The NAFTA Free Trade Commission's interpretation of Article 1105(1) supports this suggestion, stating that '[t]he concepts of "fair and equitable treatment" and "full protection and security" do not require treatment in addition to or beyond that which is required by the customary international law minimum standard of treatment of aliens'.[50] Furthermore, NAFTA jurisprudence on Article 1105(1) could influence the meaning of denial of justice beyond the scope of NAFTA.

One of the most prominent cases interpreting Article 1105(1) of NAFTA is *Loewen Group Inc and Raymond L Loewen* v. *United States of America*, in which Canadian investors challenged, *inter alia*, a Mississippi State Court decision in a commercial dispute with a local business. The grounds for challenge included allegations of

---

Cambridge University Press, 2005); and Andrew D. Mitchell, 'Due Process in WTO Disputes', in Yerxa and Wilson (eds.), above n. 2, pp. 144–60, at pp. 148–9.

47 See Ronald Kläger, *Fair and Equitable Treatment in International Investment Law* (Cambridge: Cambridge University Press, 2011), pp. 51, 118.

48 Giorgio Sacerdoti, 'Bilateral Treaties and Multilateral Instruments on Investment Protection' (1997) 269 *Hague Academy, Recueil des Cours* 251–460, at 342.

49 In relation to the doctrine of denial of justice in interpreting investment treaty provisions, see Weiler, above n. 38, at 77 and 79–81; Rudolf Dolzer and Christoph Schreuer, *Principles of International Investment Law*, 2nd edn (Oxford: Oxford University Press, 2012), pp. 178–83.

50 NAFTA Free Trade Commission, *Note of Interpretation of Certain Chapter 11 Provisions* (2001). Article 133(2) NAFTA provides that notes of interpretation issued by the Commission shall be binding on arbitral tribunals. See *The Loewen Group, Inc. and Raymond L. Loewen* v. *United States of America* ('*Loewen* v. *US*'), ICSID Case No. ARB(AF)/98/3 (Award of 26 June 2003), paras. 125–6 and 128. The Commission's interpretation contrasts with the earlier decision in *Pope & Talbot* v. *Canada*, paras. 111–18, which held that the 'fair and equitable treatment' standard was separate from and supplementary to the customary international law standard.

procedural irregularities, and that the court 'permitted extensive nationality-based, racial and class-based testimony and counsel comments'.[51]

Discussing the concept of 'denial of justice', the Tribunal noted:

> [W]e take it to be the responsibility of the State under international law and, consequently, of the courts of a State, to provide a fair trial of a case to which a foreign investor is a party. It is the responsibility of the courts of a State to ensure that litigation is free from discrimination against a foreign litigant and that the foreign litigant should not become the victim of sectional or local prejudice[52] ...
>
> A decision which is in breach of municipal law and is discriminatory against the foreign litigant amounts to manifest injustice according to international law.[53]

The Arbitral Tribunal determined that the conduct of the trial amounted to a 'miscarriage of justice amounting to a manifest injustice as that expression is understood in international law'.[54] However, due to the failure to appeal the State Court decision and subsequent developments affecting its jurisdiction, the Arbitral Tribunal ultimately dismissed Loewen's claims,[55] a conclusion that has been criticised by many commentators.[56]

Another prominent dispute that raised allegations of a 'denial of justice' in the context of NAFTA Article 1105(1) was *Mondev International Ltd* v. *United States of America*.[57] Mondev, a Canadian company, had sought damages from a local authority in Massachusetts for tortious interference in contractual relations, although the State Supreme Court had denied the claim on the basis of a statutory immunity granted to the local authority. In these circumstances, the Arbitral Tribunal held that no denial of justice had occurred. In defining the standard required, the tribunal noted that the relevant question was whether, 'having regard to generally accepted standards of the administration of justice ... the impugned decision was clearly improper and discreditable, with the result that the investment has been subjected to unfair and inequitable treatment'.[58]

Despite the concerns regarding the outcome reached in *Loewen*, the broader discussions of the meaning of denial of justice in that decision and in *Mondev*

---

51 *Loewen* v. *US*, para. 39.   52 *Ibid.*, para. 123.   53 *Ibid.*, para. 135.   54 *Ibid.*, para. 54.
55 *Ibid.*, para. 240.
56 See, e.g., Campbell McLachlan, Laurence Shore and Matthew Weiniger, *International Investment Arbitration: Substantive Principles* (Oxford: Oxford University Press, 2007), at pp. 231–3; William S. Dodge, 'Loewen Group, Inc. v. United States, and Mondev International Ltd. v United States' (2004) 98(1) *American Journal of International Law* 155–63, at 161–3; Francesco Francioni, 'Access to Justice, Denial of Justice and International Investment Law' (2009) 20 *European Journal of International Law* 729–47, at 733–5; Jürgen Kurtz, 'Access to Justice, Denial and Justice and International Investment Law: A Reply to Francesco Francioni,' (2009) 20 *European Journal of International Law* 1077–85, at 1080.
57 *Mondev International Ltd* v. *United States of America* ('*Mondev International* v. *US*'), ICSID Case No. ARB(AF)/99/2 (Award of 11 October 2002).
58 *Ibid.*, para. 127.

could nevertheless clarify the scope of the doctrine under international law. Although the decisions do not provide binding directions, they could be seen to reflect the understanding of the NAFTA parties regarding the content of customary international law (potentially as evidence of *opinio juris*)[59] and perhaps as a guide to the development of that law.

Other international investment tribunals have indeed referred to NAFTA rules and jurisprudence in interpreting other international treaties and determining the content of international law rules such as the minimum standard of treatment of aliens. Many tribunals and commentators have equated this minimum standard with the concept of fair and equitable treatment, which appears in most international investment agreements, including PTAs with investment provisions.[60] For example, in *Tecnicas Medioambientales Tecmed SA* v. *United Mexican States*, an Arbitral Tribunal was established within the framework of the International Centre for Settlement of Investment Disputes (ICSID) to hear a dispute concerning a bilateral investment treaty between Spain and Mexico.[61] The tribunal cited as authority the NAFTA decisions in *Myers* and *Mondev International Ltd* v. *United States of America* in determining that the concept of fair and equitable treatment under the investment treaty was 'an expression and part of the *bona fide* principle recognized in international law, although bad faith from the State is not required for its violation'.[62] While not referring specifically to this passage of the decision, some commentators have criticised the findings of the tribunal in *Tecmed* as representing an overly broad interpretation of the concept of fair and equitable treatment.[63]

More recently, in *CMS Gas Transmission Company* v. *Argentine Republic*,[64] another ICSID Arbitral Tribunal considered a dispute arising under a bilateral

---

59 Here we emphasise that these decisions could provide *evidence* of States' beliefs and intentions to establish the existence or content of customary international law. We do not mean that the decisions would themselves constitute *opinio juris* or customary international law. As noted elsewhere in this chapter, judicial decisions may constitute a 'subsidiary means' for determining rules of international law.

60 Although this is the subject of debate and depends on the treaty provision at issue: see, e.g., the discussion in Kläger, above n. 47, at pp. 85–7; Martins Paparinskis, *The International Minimum Standard and Fair and Equitable Treatment* (Oxford: Oxford University Press, 2013), pp. 160–6.

61 See the Spain–Mexico BIT.

62 *Tecnicas Medioambientales Tecmed SA* v. *United Mexican States*, ICSID Case No. ARB(AF)/00/2 (Award of 29 May 2003), para. 153 (footnote omitted), citing *Myers* v. *Canada*, para. 134 and NAFTA Ch 11 Arbitral Tribunal, *Mondev International* v. *US*, para. 116. See also *Azurix Corporation* v. *The Argentine Republic*, ICSID Case No. ARB/01/12 (Award of 14 July 2006), para. 372.

63 See, e.g., Zachary Douglas, 'Nothing if Not Critical for Investment Treaty Arbitration: Occidental, Eureko and Methanex' (2006) 22 *Arbitration International* 27–51, at 28. In contrast to the *Tecmed* decision, other tribunals have held that bad faith is required to establish a breach of the minimum standard of treatment of aliens. For example, when interpreting NAFTA Article 1105, one tribunal held that the basic obligation imposed on states is 'to act in good faith and form, and not deliberately to set out to destroy or frustrate the investment by improper means': *Waste Management Inc* v. *United Mexican States*, ICSID Case No. ARB(AF)/00/3 (Award of 30 April 2004), para. 138.

64 *CMS Gas Transmission Company* v. *Argentine Republic* ('*CMS* v. *Argentina*'), ICSID Case No. ARB/01/8 (Award of 12 May 2005).

investment treaty between the US and Argentina.[65] Article II(2)(a) of the treaty provided that '[i]nvestment shall at all times be accorded fair and equitable treatment, shall enjoy full protection and security and shall in no case be accorded treatment less than that required by international law'.[66] Referring to the NAFTA Free Trade Commission's interpretation of Article 1105(1) of the NAFTA,[67] the Arbitral Tribunal in *CMS* concluded that the standard of fair and equitable treatment under the investment treaty was 'not different from the international law minimum standard and its evolution under customary law'.[68] However, the approach taken in *CMS* represents a minority view. Most arbitral panels that have considered the concept of fair and equitable treatment outside NAFTA have held that the treaty obligation is distinct from the standard under customary international law.[69]

The *CMS* case also demonstrates how PTA tribunal decisions may affect state practice. The Arbitral Tribunal noted that the NAFTA ruling in *Pope & Talbot Inc* v. *Government of Canada*[70] that 'the standard of fair and equitable treatment is separate and more expansive than that of customary international law'[71] prompted the Free Trade Commission's contrary interpretation[72] as well as clarifications in other treaties,[73] such as the United States–Chile Free Trade Agreement. Article 10.4.2 of that PTA provides additional guidelines regarding the obligations in Article 10.4.1, stating, '[f]or greater certainty', that '[t]he concepts of "fair and equitable treatment" and "full protection and security" do not require treatment in addition to or beyond that which is required by' the standard applicable under customary international law. A similar qualification appears in the AUSFTA, which requires treatment of covered investments 'in accordance with the customary international law minimum standard of treatment of aliens, including fair and equitable treatment and full protection and security'.[74]

The increasingly important role of NAFTA and other PTA tribunals in public international law may concern some commentators, who argue that they are not 'equipped to hear questions of international law that are normally submitted to the' International Court of Justice (ICJ).[75] On the other hand, the process of 'dialectic review' pursuant to NAFTA Chapter 11 may be especially valuable in the 'development of international norms of due process' and the 'refinement of existing norms'.[76] Interestingly, the Arbitral Tribunal in *Loewen* pointed out that Chapter 11 itself

65 See the United States–Argentina BIT.   66 As cited in *CMS Gas* v. *Argentina*, para. 266.
67 *CMS Gas* v. *Argentina*, para. 283. See above n. 50 and corresponding text.
68 *CMS Gas* v. *Argentina*, para. 284. See also *Alex Genin, Eastern Credit Limited, Inc and A.S. Baltoil* v. *Estonia*, ICISD Case No. ARB/99/2 (Award of 25 June 2001), para. 367.
69 Kläger, above n. 47, at 85.   70 See above n. 50 and corresponding text.
71 *CMS* v. *Argentina*, para. 282.   72 See above n. 50 and corresponding text.
73 *CMS* v. *Argentina*, para. 282.   74 AUSFTA, Article 11.5(1) (see also Article 11.5(2)).
75 Ari Afilalo, 'Towards a Common Law of International Investment: How NAFTA Chapter 11 Panels Should Solve Their Legitimacy Crisis' (2004) 17 *Georgetown International Environmental Law Review* 51–96, at 84.
76 Robert B. Ahdieh, 'Between Dialogue and Decree: International Review of National Courts' (2004) 79(6) *New York University Law Review* 2029–163, at 2124–5.

'represents a progressive development in international law whereby the individual investor may make a claim on its own behalf and submit the claim to international arbitration'.[77]

Each of the norms described above relates to the protection of foreign investors, an area in which customary rules of international law are well established. In contrast, customary international law relating to common trade norms is difficult to discern. For example, most-favoured-nation (MFN) treatment provisions are a ubiquitous feature of international trade agreements. In the 1960s and 1970s, the International Law Commission undertook a detailed study of MFN clauses, with its first Special Rapporteur for the subject concluding that '[a]lthough the grant of most-favoured-nation treatment is frequent in commercial treaties, evidence is lacking that this has developed into a rule of customary international law'.[78] The inability to establish that MFN treatment or other key trade obligations form part of customary international law may be an example of the so-called 'Baxter paradox', which suggests that more states being party to a treaty obligation makes it more difficult to establish that the obligation is also custom.[79] As a result of investment protections being recognised as customary norms more often than are trade obligations, the most prominent contributions of PTAs to the development of customary international law may be in the area of investment.

B. Non-interpretative impact of customary international law on PTAs

We turn now to the related question of how customary international law constrains or otherwise affects the operation of PTAs, in addition to its common influence in dictating rules of interpretation. Specifically, we consider the extent to which customary international law may impact on PTAs in the absence of a PTA provision that expressly incorporates or refers to a specific rule or principle of international law (such as the minimum standard of treatment of aliens).

Some PTA provisions may suggest that all aspects of customary international law (as well as other aspects of international law, such as treaties, as discussed further below) apply not merely in interpreting PTA provisions but more broadly in resolving PTA disputes. For instance, Article 1131 of NAFTA, the corollary of Article 102(2) mentioned above,[80] provides in relation to state-investor disputes under Chapter 11:

> Governing law
> 1. A Tribunal established under this Section shall decide the issues in dispute in accordance with this Agreement and applicable rules of international law.

---

77 *Loewen v. US*, para. 223.
78 Mr. Endre Ustor, Special Rapporteur, *Third report on the most-favoured-nation clause*, UN Doc A/CN.4/ 257 and Add.1 (31 March and 8 May 1972).
79 See above n. 28.   80 See above section IIA.

The reference to 'applicable rules of international law' encompasses all procedural or substantive rules of international law, as opposed to purely interpretative rules such as those found in Articles 31 and 32 of the Vienna Convention. Thus, Article 1131 may be viewed as widening the scope of the law applicable by the Tribunal to incorporate all of these procedural and substantive rules. Conversely, one might contend that Article 1131 has no impact on the Tribunal's applicable law, as it simply confirms or restates out of an abundance of caution what would be the case anyway. In other words, Article 1131 could arguably be seen as an acknowledgement that, pursuant to international law, certain rules not spelled out in NAFTA will apply to Chapter 11 disputes. Assuming that this latter interpretation is correct, or that we are discussing a PTA that contains no equivalent to Article 1131, we are faced with the question of whether or which customary international law rules would apply.

In the WTO context, few would dispute that Panels and the Appellate Body have jurisdiction to hear only claims under WTO law, as opposed to claims under any other body of domestic or international law.[81] Similarly, most PTAs that include dispute settlement provisions make clear the types of claims that the relevant tribunals may hear: typically those concerning the interpretation or application of the PTA in question.[82] A separate, more controversial question[83] in the context of both the WTO and PTAs is the extent to which a tribunal appointed to resolve a dispute has the power to apply customary international law.

On one view, put simply, each PTA is 'born into' public international law and therefore customary international law applies to it and the resolution of disputes under it to the extent that the PTA does not otherwise provide. This is the view espoused by Pauwelyn in relation to the WTO.[84] Joel Trachtman forcefully expresses the opposing position:

> It is important . . . to recognize the distinction between the law that applies to the conduct of states and the law that is applicable within WTO dispute settlement. [Pauwelyn] argues that because states are subject to the full range of their conventional and customary international legal obligations unless they contract out of them, WTO dispute settlement must apply all international legal obligations unless they are specifically precluded from application . . . This logic is fundamentally incorrect: it is a non sequitur. The opposite is true. International legal tribunals are authorized only to (1) hear cases and (2) apply law pursuant to their specific, positive mandates. They are not implicitly

---

81 See, e.g., Joost Pauwelyn, 'The Jurisdiction of the World Trade Organization' (2004) 98 *American Society of International Law Proceedings* 135–8, at 135; Trachtman, 'The Jurisdiction of the World Trade Organization', above n. 2, at 139; and Debra P. Steger, 'The Jurisdiction of the World Trade Organization' (2004) 98 *American Society of International Law Proceedings* 142–6, at 143.

82 See, e.g., Thailand–Australia FTA, Article 21.2. On 'non-violation' claims, as allowed under this provision and certain other PTAs as well as Article XXIII:1(b) of GATT 1994 and Article XXIII:3 of GATS, see Locknie Hsu, 'Non-violation Complaints – World Trade Organization Issues and Recent Free Trade Agreements' (2005) 39(2) *Journal of World Trade* 205–37.

83 International Law Commission, above n. 4, para. 45.   84 Pauwelyn, above n. 2, at pp. 460–1 and 466–7.

courts of general jurisdiction, either as to the cases they can hear *or* as to the law they can apply.[85]

Although this debate has so far taken place largely in the context of the WTO, the same issues arise in relation to PTAs and are equally difficult to resolve. Nevertheless, PTA provisions and case law provide some indication of how PTAs in practice deal with their relationship with other sources of international law, particularly custom and general principles.

At the outset, it is important to recognise that PTAs can neither 'contract out of' nor avoid by omission certain rules of international law, namely *jus cogens* norms. Article 53 of the Vienna Convention defines a *jus cogens* norm or 'a peremptory norm of general international law' as 'a norm accepted and recognized by the international community of States as a whole as a norm from which no derogation is permitted and which can be modified only by a subsequent norm of general international law having the same character'.[86] Under the same provision, '[a] treaty is void if, at the time of its conclusion, it conflicts with a peremptory norm of general international law'. Similarly, Article 64 of the Vienna Convention provides that '[i]f a new peremptory norm of general international law emerges, any existing treaty which is in conflict with that norm becomes void and terminates'.[87] These pronouncements as to *jus cogens* norms being above all others in the hierarchy of public international law apply not merely to States parties to the Vienna Convention, as '[t]he concept of *jus cogens* operates as a concept superior to both customary international law and treaty'.[88] Arguably, the implications for a treaty that conflicts with a *jus cogens* norm as set out in the Vienna Convention represent customary international law and are therefore also binding on all States.[89]

---

85 Joel Trachtman, 'Book Review. Conflict of Norms in Public International Law: How WTO Law Relates to Other Rules of International Law by Joost Pauwelyn' (2004) 98 *American Journal of International Law* 855–60, at 857–8 (emphasis in original).

86 See *Legality of the Threat or Use of Nuclear Weapons (Advisory Opinion)* [1996] ICJ Rep. 226, p. 258, referring to Vienna Convention, Article 53, as defining *jus cogens*.

87 Article X of the Treaty of Utrecht (1713) provides an interesting example revealing doubt as to the force of Article 64 of the Vienna Convention. Through Article X, Spain conceded sovereignty over Gibraltar, while Great Britain agreed, *inter alia*, that 'no leave shall be given, under any pretence whatsoever, either to Jews or Moors, to reside or have their dwellings, in the said town of Gibraltar.' Since this treaty was concluded, a prohibition on racial discrimination has come to be recognised as a peremptory norm of international law. In spite of this part of Article X not having been enforced for several years and being clearly inconsistent with the international law prohibition on racial discrimination, both Spain and Britain maintain that the grant of sovereignty over Gibraltar and related conditions established by Article X of the Treaty of Utrecht continue to be valid. See Vaughne Miller, *Gibraltar: Diplomatic and Constitutional Developments*, House of Commons Research Paper 06/84 (11 October 2006), which includes statements and correspondence between government officials of the United Kingdom, Spain and Gibraltar, containing their views on the continued validity of Article X of the Treaty of Utrecht.

88 *Application of the Convention on the Prevention and Punishment of the Crime of Genocide (Bosnia and Herzegovina v. Serbia and Montenegro) (Order on Provisional Measures)* [1993] ICJ Rep. 325, p. 440 (Separate Opinion of Judge Lauterpacht).

89 See Sinclair, above n. 12, pp. 17–18.

Norms generally recognised as having the character of *jus cogens* include, for instance, genocide,[90] crimes against humanity, war crimes,[91] and 'the prohibition of the use of force expressed in Article 2, paragraph 4, of the Charter of the United Nations'.[92] Therefore, peremptory norms may have minimal impact on PTAs in practice, given that few PTAs would ever be likely to conflict with these kinds of norms.

Aside from these non-derogable norms, several customary international law norms may apply to PTAs and PTA dispute settlement, either because the PTA designates them or customary international law more generally as part of the applicable law or because the PTA does not specify that they are inapplicable (taking the Pauwelyn approach). We now provide an example of international norms on state responsibility and consider how they might arise in a PTA dispute.

In the *Myers* case, the NAFTA Arbitral Tribunal held that a Canadian ban on certain exports to the US violated Canada's NAFTA obligations and that Canada therefore must pay compensation to the US investor Myers for the injury caused to its investment in Canada.[93] The Arbitral Tribunal therefore needed to consider the 'principles on which compensation should be awarded'.[94] Noting that it had to decide the matter, pursuant to Article 1131, in accordance with NAFTA 'and applicable international law', the Arbitral Tribunal first considered the NAFTA provisions on compensation but found no relevant guidelines. It therefore turned to international law for guidance.[95] Referring to[96] the *Factory at Chorzów* decision by the Permanent Court of International Justice[97] and to the (then draft) *Articles on Responsibility of States for internationally wrongful acts* of the International Law Commission (ILC Articles on State Responsibility),[98] it concluded that the approach to calculating compensation should 'reflect the general principle of international law that compensation should undo the material harm inflicted by a breach of an international obligation'.[99] Thus, the Arbitral Tribunal applied an aspect of the international law

---

90 *Reservations to the Convention on the Prevention and Punishment of Genocide (Advisory Opinion)* [1951] ICJ Rep. 15, p. 23.

91 *Application of the Convention on the Prevention and Punishment of the Crime of Genocide (Bosnia and Herzegovina v. Serbia and Montenegro)*, p. 440 (Separate Opinion of Judge Lauterpacht); M. Cherif Bassiouni, 'International Crimes: *Jus Cogens* and *Obligatio Erga Omnes*' (1996) 59(4) *Law and Contemporary Problems* 63–74, at 68; and *Restatement (3rd) of the Law: The Foreign Relations Law of the United States* (1987), vol. 2, § 702, pp. 161–2.

92 *Case Concerning Military and Paramilitary Activities in and against Nicaragua (Nicaragua v. United States of America) (Merits)* [1986] ICJ Rep. 14, pp. 100–1.

93 *Myers* v. *Canada*, para. 301.   94 *Ibid.*, chapter XI.   95 *Ibid.*, paras. 304–10.

96 *Ibid.*, paras. 311–12.

97 *Case Concerning the Factory at Chorzów (Claim For Indemnity) (Merits)* [1928] PCIJ (Ser. A) No. 17, pp. 4 and 47.

98 See UN General Assembly Resolution, *Responsibility of States for Internationally Wrongful Acts*, A/RES/56/ 83 (28 January 2002) Annex, Article 36; and James Crawford, *The International Law Commission's Articles on State Responsibility: Introduction, Text and Commentaries* (Cambridge: Cambridge University Press, 2002).

99 *Myers* v. *Canada*, para. 315.

rules on state responsibility either as a norm of customary law or as a general principle of law (as discussed further below). Application of the rules on state responsibility to determine compensation payable is relevant only to investor-state disputes under PTAs, and not to trade disputes between states, which typically do not provide for compensation as a potential remedy for breach.

Before turning to the issue of conflicts between PTAs and other treaties, we wish to make certain additional observations regarding the relationship between PTAs and 'general principles of law', which form a separate source of international law according to Article 38(1)(c) of the ICJ Statute. That provision directs the ICJ to apply 'the general principles of law recognized by civilized nations'. This is a complex area of international law that is explored elsewhere.[100] For the purpose of this chapter, it is worth noting that general principles of law may apply to PTAs and PTA disputes just as customary international law may do. To some extent these principles may overlap with customary international law, but as certain general principles may find no corollary in customary international law we should not forget this source of international law.

One important example of a general principle of law (as well as possibly a part of customary international law) that may be significant in a PTA dispute is the principle of good faith.[101] Indeed, Weiler describes good faith as a substantive principle of international economic law.[102] The scope and content of this principle is unclear, but some PTA provisions incorporate some form of it. For example, the AUSFTA requires parties, in the event of a dispute, to 'enter into consultations in good faith',[103] echoing the WTO's Understanding on Rules and Procedures Governing the Settlement of Disputes (DSU).[104] Depending on one's understanding of the applicable law in PTA disputes,[105] this and other aspects of the principle of good faith may operate independently of any PTA provision.

In the *Pope & Talbot* case, the NAFTA Arbitral Tribunal rejected Canada's claim that the US investor was estopped from bringing a challenge under NAFTA Chapter 11, because the elements of estoppel recognised under international law were not made out.[106] Although estoppel did not lie in this case, in ruling on Canada's claim with reference to international law, the Arbitral Tribunal applied one particularisation of the principle of good faith. The principle of good faith may also require parties to a PTA to perform the PTA in good faith (*pacta sunt servanda*, as reflected in

---

100 See generally Bin Cheng, *General Principles of Law as Applied by International Courts and Tribunals* (London: Stevens & Sons, 1953); and Andrew D. Mitchell, *Legal Principles in WTO Disputes* (Cambridge: Cambridge University Press, 2008).

101 *Certain Norwegian Loans (France* v. *Norway) (Jurisdiction)* [1957] ICJ Rep. 9, p. 53. See also Cheng, above n. 100, at pp. 105–60; John O'Connor, *Good Faith in International Law* (Aldershot: Ashgate, 1991); and Andrew D. Mitchell, 'Good Faith in WTO Dispute Settlement' (2006) 7 *Melbourne Journal of International Law* 339–71, at 341–51.

102 Weiler, above n. 38, at 77.   103 AUSFTA, Article 21.5(1).   104 DSU, Article 4.3.

105 See section IIIB.   106 *Pope & Talbot* v. *Canada*, paras. 111–12.

Article 26 of the Vienna Convention),[107] to exercise their rights under the PTA in good faith (in accordance with the doctrine of *abus de droit*),[108] and to fulfil any legitimate ('reasonable and justifiable') expectations created by their conduct.[109] While *Pope & Talbot* is an example of an investor-state dispute that considered good faith, the principle could also be applicable in relation to trade disputes under PTAs. The relevance of good faith in trade disputes between states can be seen from WTO cases where particularisations of the principle, such as estoppel, have been raised.[110]

From these examples concerning state responsibility and good faith, we can see that the practice of PTA tribunals (or at least those constituted under NAFTA Chapter 11) is to apply substantive and procedural aspects of customary international law and general principles of law in resolving disputes when relevant. Where the PTA expressly overrides such international law norms (other than *jus cogens* norms), the PTA will typically prevail. However, resolving conflicts between PTAs and other treaties is more complex.

IV. Resolving conflicts between PTAs and other treaties

We now explore the possibility of conflicts between PTAs and other treaties, recalling that Article 38(1)(a) of the ICJ Statute includes as a potential source of international law 'international conventions, whether general or particular, establishing rules expressly recognized by the contesting states'.

A. Substantive conflicts

Because of the expanding content of PTAs and their broadening geographical coverage, they are increasingly likely to include rights or obligations that conflict with those under other bilateral or multilateral treaties, including the WTO agreements, other PTAs, and conventions on issues from human rights and the environment to development and consular immunities. The possibility of these conflicts raises issues similar to those discussed above in relation to PTAs and customary international law.[111] In particular, for the purpose of resolving disputes within the framework of a PTA, if the applicable law includes public international law (either because the PTA does not specifically exclude public international law or because the PTA specifically incorporates it, depending on one's point of view), the PTA tribunal will need to

---

107 See also, e.g., *North Atlantic Coast Fisheries Arbitration (United States v. Great Britain)* (1910) 11 RIAA 167, p. 186; *Gabčíkovo-Nagymaros Project*, p. 79; and Arnold D. McNair, *The Law of Treaties* (Oxford: Clarendon Press, 1961), at p. 540.
108 See generally G. D. S. Taylor, 'The Content of the Rule against Abuse of Rights in International Law' (1972–3) 46 *British Yearbook of International Law* 323–52.
109 NAFTA Ch 11 Arbitral Tribunal, *International Thunderbird Gaming Corporation v. Mexico* (Award of 26 January 2006), para. 147.
110 See Mitchell, above n. 101, at 351–73.   111 See section IIIB.

decide whether the relevant PTA rule or the conflicting non-PTA rule should prevail. This will of course depend on the circumstances, but several common considerations and guidelines will apply to the decision, as we explain below. If the non-PTA rule is to prevail, this may mean it provides a defence to a PTA violation, independent of any PTA provision providing for this defence.

The rules on treaty interpretation as discussed above,[112] including Article 31(3) of the Vienna Convention, may assist in avoiding conflicts between PTAs and other treaties. If a conflict does arise and cannot be avoided through interpretation, we must look to the PTA or conflicting treaty to see if any specific provision indicates how to resolve it. Article 30(2) of the Vienna Convention provides: 'When a treaty specifies that it is subject to, or that it is not to be considered as incompatible with, an earlier or later treaty, the provisions of that other treaty prevail.' Accordingly, the impact of a conflict rule may depend on its content and the timing and nature of the conflicting treaty.

One example of a PTA conflict rule that is likely to fall within Article 30(2) of the Vienna Convention and therefore be effective in resolving conflicts with certain other treaties is Article 20.3(3) of the Korea–Chile Free Trade Agreement, which states:

> Nothing in this Agreement shall affect the rights and obligations of either Party under any tax convention. In the event of any inconsistency between this Agreement and any such convention, that convention shall prevail to the extent of the inconsistency.

In contrast, Article 103 of NAFTA sets out its 'relation to other agreements' as follows:

1. The Parties affirm their existing rights and obligations with respect to each other under the General Agreement on Tariffs and Trade and other agreements to which such Parties are party.
2. In the event of any inconsistency between this Agreement and such other agreements, this Agreement shall prevail to the extent of the inconsistency, except as otherwise provided in this Agreement.

This provision takes the opposite approach to that set out in Article 30(2) of the Vienna Convention, by stating that NAFTA prevails over other agreements to the extent of any inconsistency. However, it is consistent with the *lex posterior* rule reflected in Article 30(4)(a) of the Vienna Convention, as discussed further below, and it would be effective at public international law to ensure that NAFTA prevails over GATT and other previous agreements, at least as between the NAFTA parties.

In addition to the general conflict rule in Article 103, NAFTA contains some specific rules governing its relationship with other international agreements.

---

112 See section IIA.

Annex 702.1 of NAFTA incorporates, as between Canada and the United States, the rule contained in Article 710 of the earlier Canada–United States Free Trade Agreement:

> Unless otherwise specifically provided in this Chapter, the Parties retain their rights and obligations with respect to agricultural, food, beverage and certain related goods under the General Agreement on Tariffs and Trade (GATT) and agreements negotiated under the GATT, including their rights and obligations under GATT Article XI.

While not phrased as a conflict rule, Canada relied on this provision to justify increasing tariffs on various over-quota agricultural imports from the United States. The basis of the United States' claim was Article 302(1) of NAFTA, which prohibits any party from increasing customs duties or imposing new duties on imports from another party. Canada argued that the WTO Agreement on Agriculture required it to 'tariffy' certain quotas and other non-tariff barriers, and that the increased duties it had imposed formed part of this process.[113] Canada suggested that, by virtue of Annex 702.1 and Article 710 of the FTA incorporating 'agreements negotiated under the GATT', its rights under the WTO Agreement on Agriculture were also protected under NAFTA. In the alternative, Canada argued that if NAFTA conflicted with the WTO Agreement on Agriculture, the latter would prevail as it was later in time.[114] The Tribunal held that Annex 702.1 of NAFTA and Article 710 of the FTA effectively incorporated the relevant provisions of the WTO Agreement on Agriculture into NAFTA, replacing those rights and obligations under the PTA that had previously governed agricultural quotas.[115]

PTAs may also contain provisions that are not explicit conflict rules, but that provide exceptions for certain policy objectives or particular kinds of measures that may be promoted under other treaties (equivalent to, say, Article XX of GATT 1994 in the WTO context). The United States–Singapore Free Trade Agreement, for example, provides an exception for 'environmental measures necessary to protect human, animal, or plant life or health',[116] which could include measures undertaken pursuant to multilateral environmental agreements.

Article XXIV of GATT 1994 provides an example of a corresponding exception in another treaty that might conflict with a PTA (the WTO treaty). A PTA that meets the stringent requirements of this exception for 'customs unions and free-trade areas' would not conflict with WTO law, or at least not with GATT 1994. The same applies to the arguably less stringent requirements of Articles V and Vbis of GATS,[117] as regards a conflict with GATS. Unfortunately, the limited jurisprudence to

---

113 NAFTA Chapter 20 Panel Report, *Tariffs Applied by Canada to Certain U.S. Origin Agricultural Products*, CDA-95–2008-01 (2 December 1996), paras. 63–80.
114 *Ibid.*   115 *Ibid.*, paras. 199–201.   116 Article 13.4(1)(b) and (2).
117 Bernard Hoekman, 'Tentative First Steps: An Assessment of the Uruguay Round Agreement on Services', World Bank Policy Research Working Paper No. 1455 (May 1995), at p. 8.

date sheds little light on the meaning of these exceptions,[118] which are contested and by their terms ambiguous,[119] if not inherently flawed.[120] Although this uncertainty may create a practical disincentive for one WTO Member to challenge another's compliance with Article XXIV of GATT 1994 (particularly in view of the proliferation of PTAs across the WTO Membership), it means that Article XXIV does not provide a lasting, predictable solution to resolving conflicts between PTAs and WTO law.[121]

Lorand Bartels suggests that, while not conflict rules, Articles 3.2 and 19.2 of the DSU create a similar result through an indirect means, by delimiting the powers of WTO dispute settlement panels.[122] These two articles could potentially operate to resolve conflicts with PTAs, although they do not do so explicitly, and no consensus exists on any such rules. Language more clearly amounting to a conflict rule is found in non-trade treaties such as the Cartagena Protocol on Biosafety to the Convention on Biological Diversity,[123] the preamble of which states:

> *Recognizing* that trade and environment agreements should be mutually supportive with a view to achieving sustainable development,
> *Emphasizing* that this Protocol shall not be interpreted as implying a change in the rights and obligations of a Party under any existing international agreements,
> *Understanding* that the above recital is not intended to subordinate this Protocol to other international agreements.

These kinds of statements (which are followed in other treaties such as the draft Convention on the Protection and Promotion of the Diversity of Cultural Expressions adopted by the United Nations Educational, Scientific and Cultural Organization in 2005)[124] promote the positive notion of mutual

---

118 Sungjoon Cho, 'Breaking the Barrier between Regionalism and Multilateralism: A New Perspective on Trade Regionalism' (2001) 42(2) *Harvard International Law Journal* 419–66, at 421 and 437–50. See also Joel P. Trachtman, 'Toward Open Recognition? Standardization and Regional Integration under Article XXIV of GATT' (2003) 6(2) *Journal of International Economic Law* 459–92, at 473–7 and 481–9.

119 On the many difficult issues surrounding the exception in Article XXIV of GATT 1994, see generally Nicolas Lockhart and Andrew D. Mitchell, 'Regional Trade Agreements under GATT 1994: An Exception and its Limits', in Andrew D. Mitchell (ed.), *Challenges and Prospects for the WTO* (London: Cameron May, 2005), at p. 217. See also James H. Mathis, *Regional Trade Agreements in the GATT/WTO: Article XXIV and the Internal Trade Requirement* (The Hague: TMC Asser Press, 2002); and Joel P. Trachtman, 'International Trade: Regionalism', in Andrew T. Guzman and Alan O. Sykes (eds.), *Research Handbook in International Economic Law* (Cheltenham, UK: Edward Elgar, 2007), pp. 160–74.

120 Cho, above n. 118, at 450–2.

121 For an example of how Article XXIV of GATT 1994 might apply to a challenged measure in practice, see Lorand Bartels, 'The Legality of the EC Mutual Recognition Clause under WTO Law' (2005) 8(3) *Journal of International Economic Law* 691–720.

122 Bartels, above n. 2, at 507–8.

123 Adopted 29 January 2000, in force 11 September 2003, (2000) 39 ILM 1027.

124 Adopted 20 October 2005, in force 18 March 2007, CLT-2005/CONVENTION DIVERSITE-CULT REV (20 October 2005), Article 20.

supportiveness and allow some flexibility, while preventing the suggestion of any deliberate or blatant breach of WTO or PTA law. However, they may be ultimately too contradictory or unhelpful to resolve conflicts as they arise.

Especially where a PTA and another treaty 'relating to the same subject matter'[125] do not make clear how to resolve a substantive conflict between them (or where they conflict as to the proper way of doing so), the *lex posterior* rule as set out in Article 30 of the Vienna Convention comes into play:[126]

> 3. When all the parties to the earlier treaty are parties also to the later treaty but the earlier treaty is not terminated or suspended in operation under article 59, the earlier treaty applies only to the extent that its provisions are compatible with those of the later treaty.
> 4. When the parties to the later treaty do not include all the parties to the earlier one:
>   (a) as between States Parties to both treaties the same rule applies as in paragraph 3;
>   (b) as between a State party to both treaties and a State party to only one of the treaties, the treaty to which both States are parties governs their mutual rights and obligations.

In general, problematic PTA conflicts would involve Article 30(4), namely because the PTA conflicts with an earlier multilateral treaty that includes the PTA parties as well as non-PTA parties.[127] In a dispute between PTA parties (or one party and an investor of another) the PTA would generally prevail in accordance with Article 30(3) of the Vienna Convention. However, in a dispute between a PTA party and a non-PTA party (say, before the ICJ or a WTO Panel), Article 30(4) provides that the earlier multilateral treaty would prevail. Accordingly, as a matter of international law, the PTA party would be obliged to comply with all its obligations under that earlier treaty with respect to non-PTA parties.

What if none of these rules – in the PTA, the conflicting treaty, or the Vienna Convention – is able to resolve a particular conflict? Essentially, no hierarchy exists between treaties, unless a *jus cogens* norm[128] or Article 103 of the Charter of the

---

125 Vienna Convention, Article 30(1). See International Law Commission, above n. 4, paras. 253–6.
126 We leave to one side the possibility that the whole or part of a PTA might be 'illegal' by virtue of Articles 41 or 58 of the Vienna Convention, in which case a PTA conflict rule could not save it. See Pauwelyn, above n. 2, at pp. 302–15.
127 Of course, the dating of a multilateral treaty such as the WTO agreements may be difficult. Is the date of the WTO agreements 15 April 1994 (signing), 1 January 1995 (entry into force), 2 March 2013 (most recent accession), or some other date, given that negotiations on revising the agreements have occurred almost continuously since they entered into force? For further discussion, see Pauwelyn, above n. 2, at pp. 372–84.
128 See section IIIB.

United Nations[129] is involved.[130] The principle of *lex specialis derogat legi generali* may assist, although its precise meaning and status in international law remain uncertain.[131] Therefore, the results in any given instance are difficult to foresee.

B. Overlapping disputes

International tribunals may face difficulties in reconciling their role with the operation of domestic court systems or other international tribunals, particularly where a given dispute is litigated in different domestic and international fora, either simultaneously or in sequence. Some PTAs mitigate this problem by precluding resort to domestic dispute resolution in some circumstances. For example, Article 21.15 of the AUSFTA provides: 'Neither Party may provide for a right of action under its domestic law against the other Party on the ground that a measure of the other Party is inconsistent with this Agreement.'[132] Even in those agreements without a clause such as Article 21.15, the doctrine of state immunity would protect most non-commercial actions of a state from claims in the domestic courts of another country. However, a growing problem for PTAs and international tribunals more generally is the potential for conflict between dispute resolution fora at the international level, with given circumstances giving rise to potential claims under more than one treaty. This includes potential conflicts not only between rulings of the WTO's DSB and those of PTA tribunals, but also between rulings of one PTA tribunal and another, and between PTA tribunals and other specialised or general tribunals operating within public or private international law.

To combat this problem, many PTAs with dispute settlement mechanisms therefore include a 'choice of forum' clause. Article 21.4 of the AUSFTA thus states:

1. Where a dispute regarding any matter arises under this Agreement and under another trade agreement to which both Parties are party, including the WTO Agreement, the complaining Party may select the forum in which to settle the dispute.
2. Once the complaining Party has requested a panel under an agreement referred to in paragraph 1, the forum selected shall be used to the exclusion of the others.

A similar but more elaborate provision exists in NAFTA to prevent a complaining party from pursuing a remedy under both NAFTA Chapter 20 and the WTO dispute

---

129 Article 103 states: 'In the event of a conflict between the obligations of the Members of the United Nations under the present Charter and their obligations under any other international agreement, their obligations under the present Charter shall prevail.' Article 30(1) of the Vienna Convention provides that the usual rules in Article 30 regarding successive treaties are subject to Article 103 of the UN Charter.
130 Ignaz Seidl-Hohenveldern, 'Hierarchy of Treaties', in Jan Klabbers and René Lefeber (eds.), *Essays on the Law of Treaties: A Collection of Essays in Honour of Bert Vierdag* (The Hague: Martinus Nijhoff, 1998), pp. 7–18, at pp. 7–9; and International Law Commission, above n. 4, paras. 324–79.
131 See International Law Commission, above n. 4, paras. 56–122; and Pauwelyn, above n. 2, at pp. 385–409.
132 See also NAFTA, Articles 1121(1)(b) and (2)(b).

settlement system.[133] However, although these provisions may be effective within the PTA dispute settlement system, their impact outside that system may depend on the application of the VCLT rules as discussed above. In other words, a PTA party might bring a dispute first to a PTA tribunal and then to a different tribunal, despite the existence of a choice of forum clause preventing such action. Moreover, the complaining party might find the second tribunal amenable to hearing the dispute despite the existence of that clause.[134]

That conflicts between PTA tribunals and other international tribunals are more than mere possibilities is demonstrated by several WTO cases.[135] In particular, in *Mexico–Taxes on Soft Drinks*,[136] Mexico asked a WTO Panel to decline jurisdiction in order to enable the parties to resolve their dispute within NAFTA.[137] The Panel refused, and the Appellate Body upheld this decision.[138] However, the circumstances of the case were unusual, in that the dispute before the WTO was brought by the US against certain Mexican tax measures on soft drinks and other beverages, whereas the dispute that Mexico wanted heard before NAFTA would have been brought by Mexico against certain US measures limiting market access for Mexican cane sugar.[139] In addition, the US was stalling the NAFTA dispute by preventing panellist selection (indeed, this may have been part of Mexico's justification for imposing the measures that allegedly violated WTO law).[140] Hence, the NAFTA choice of forum clause did not apply to prevent the matter from proceeding before a WTO Panel.[141]

The result might have been different had Mexico or the US called on the WTO Panel to enforce or apply the NAFTA choice of forum clause by declining jurisdiction or accepting that it lacked jurisdiction. In other words, had Mexico requested a NAFTA panel to resolve the dispute under NAFTA and then

---

133 Article 2005 of NAFTA. Regarding factors for parties to consider in deciding whether to use NAFTA or WTO dispute settlement, see generally Rafael Leal-Arcas, 'Choice of Jurisdiction in International Trade Disputes: Going Regional or Global?' (2007) 16(1) *Minnesota Journal of International Law* 1–59.

134 Kwak and Marceau reach a similar conclusion: Kyung Kwak and Gabrielle Marceau, 'Overlaps and Conflicts of Jurisdiction between the World Trade Organization and Regional Trade Agreements' (2003) 41 *Canadian Yearbook of International Law* 83–152, at 106–7.

135 See, e.g., the cases discussed in Greg Anderson, 'Can Someone Please Settle This Dispute? Canadian Softwood Lumber and the Dispute Settlement Mechanisms of the NAFTA and the WTO' (2006) *World Economy* 585–610; Kwak and Marceau, above n. 134, at 91–5; and Gabrielle Marceau, 'NAFTA and WTO Dispute Settlement Rules: A Thematic Comparison' (1997) 31(2) *Journal of World Trade* 25–81, at 75–80.

136 Appellate Body Report, *Mexico–Taxes on Soft Drinks*; and Panel Report, *Mexico–Taxes on Soft Drinks*.

137 Panel Report, *Mexico–Taxes on Soft Drinks*, paras. 3.2, 7.11 and 7.12.

138 *Ibid.*, paras. 7.1, 7.18 and 9.1; and Appellate Body Report, *Mexico–Taxes on Soft Drinks*, paras. 57 and 85(a).

139 Panel Report, *Mexico–Taxes on Soft Drinks*, para. 7.14.

140 *Ibid.*, paras 8.170 and 8.200; Pauwelyn, above n. 5, at 198.

141 Several NAFTA Ch 11 disputes were brought by US investors in relation to the same subject matter: *GAMI Investments, Inc v. Mexico*, UNCITRAL (NAFTA) (Final Award of 15 November 2004); *Archer Daniels Midland Company and Tate & Lyle Ingredients Americas, Inc v. United Mexican States*, ICSID Case No. ARB (AF)/04/5 (Award of 21 November 2007); *Corn Products International, Inc v. United Mexican States*, ICSID Case No. ARB (AF)/04/1 (Decision on Responsibility of 15 January 2008).

subsequently requested the establishment of a WTO panel to resolve the same dispute under WTO law, the WTO panel might have concluded that the choice of forum clause in Article 2005 of the NAFTA prevented it from adjudicating the dispute. Perhaps this is what the Appellate Body had in mind when it stated: 'we express no view as to whether there may be other circumstances in which legal impediments could exist that would preclude a panel from ruling on the merits of the claims that are before it.'[142] An express choice of forum clause preventing resort to both the WTO and a PTA panel might be one such 'legal impediment'. According to Pauwelyn, a WTO Panel faced with such a clause would have to conclude that it lacked jurisdiction to hear a dispute brought in violation of it (i.e., in violation of the agreement already reached between the disputing parties about how to resolve their trade disputes).[143] On the other hand, Kyung Kwak and Gabrielle Marceau contend that '[i]t is doubtful whether this type of provision would suffice to allow a WTO panel to refuse to hear the matter in situations where the dispute settlement process of the free trade agreement has been triggered.'[144]

Other doctrines might also prevent a PTA tribunal or other international tribunal from hearing a dispute that overlapped with another tribunal, thereby avoiding contradictory rulings. This is a complex area that Yuval Shany has ably covered elsewhere.[145] Nevertheless, it is worth briefly examining some of the considerations to which PTA tribunals might have regard in the face of a potential conflict with another tribunal. First, in recognition of the principle of judicial comity (even though this may not have the force of international law),[146] a PTA tribunal might defer or decline to commence proceedings while another tribunal was hearing the same or a closely related dispute. On the same basis, a PTA tribunal might refuse to adjudicate a matter that another tribunal had already resolved. This kind of response would express respect for the other tribunal and discourage forum-shopping by disputing parties, while also potentially reducing the chances of substantive conflicts between treaties (e.g., due to interpretations without regard to other treaties).

More legally forceful principles could also govern a PTA tribunal's response in these circumstances. In particular, *res judicata*, recognised as part of customary international law or as a 'general principle of law' within the meaning of Article

---

142 Appellate Body Report, *Mexico–Taxes on Soft Drinks*, para. 54. See also Panel Report, *Mexico–Taxes on Soft Drinks*, para. 7.13.

143 Joost Pauwelyn, 'How to Win a World Trade Organization Dispute Based on Non-World Trade Organization Law: Questions of Jurisdiction and Merits' (2003) 37(6) *Journal of World Trade* 997–1030, at 1013.

144 Kwak and Marceau, above n. 134, at 90–1.

145 Shany, above n. 5. See also Vaughan Lowe, 'Overlapping Jurisdiction in International Tribunals' (1999) 20 *Australian Yearbook of International Law* 191–204.

146 Shany, above n. 5, at p. 262. See also Pauwelyn, above n. 5, at 202; Caroline Henckels, 'Overcoming Jurisdictional Isolationism at the WTO–FTA Nexus: A Potential Approach for the WTO' (2008) 19 *European Journal of International Law* 571–99, at 584–97; Andrew D. Mitchell and David Heaton, 'The Inherent Jurisdiction of WTO Tribunals: The Select Application of Public International Law Required by the Judicial Function' (2010) 31 *Michigan Journal of International Law* 559–619, at 596–602.

38(1)(c) of the ICJ Statute,[147] could prevent a PTA tribunal from hearing a dispute that had already been resolved by another tribunal. This could occur where the disputes before the two tribunals involved the same parties and issues.[148] Similarly, even in the absence of a choice of forum clause, a PTA tribunal might hold that a complainant was estopped from bringing before it a claim of a PTA violation having already brought essentially the same claim to another forum.[149] However, some have expressed doubts as to the suitability of the doctrine of *res judicata* on the basis that the cause of action before the two tribunals is not the same, such as where the two tribunals apply different law (for example, the law of the WTO agreements as opposed to the law of the relevant PTA).[150]

One difficulty that a PTA tribunal might perceive in determining whether it lacked jurisdiction due to a pre-existing proceeding would be that it might need to analyse non-PTA laws to answer that question. This difficulty is reflected in the WTO context in *Mexico–Taxes on Soft Drinks*, where the Appellate Body emphasised, '[w]e see no basis in the DSU for panels and the Appellate Body to adjudicate non-WTO disputes.'[151] However, a PTA tribunal would not need to decide anything as a matter of non-PTA law in order to determine whether the doctrines of *res judicata* or estoppel applied or to decide whether and how to give effect to a choice of forum clause. Although it might need to consider non-PTA law to assess the similarity between the issues and claims before the two tribunals, it would not thereby be resolving a non-PTA dispute. The meaning of the non-PTA law would be a question of fact, just as international tribunals frequently evaluate domestic laws as questions of fact.[152] In contrast to its comments in *Mexico–Taxes on Soft Drinks*, the WTO Appellate Body has previously been willing to engage in the interpretation of non-WTO international law (the Lomé Convention), when establishing the meaning of that agreement as a legal fact was necessary for the application of WTO law.[153] This demonstrates the important distinction between a tribunal making findings as to the meaning of

---

147 Cheng, above n. 100, at p. 336; and Shany, above n. 5, at pp. 245–6.
148 Shany, above n. 5, at pp. 24–5; and Pauwelyn, above n. 5, at 200.
149 Cf. NAFTA Ch 19 Panel Decision, *In the Matter of Certain Top-Mount Electric Refrigerators, Electric Household Dishwashers, and Gas or Electric Laundry Dryers*, CDA-USA-2000-1904-03 (15 April 2002), pp. 25–6. For further discussion of *res judicata*, issue estoppel, and collateral estoppel in the context of WTO versus PTA disputes, see Pauwelyn, above n. 143, at 1017–19; Joost Pauwelyn and Luiz Eduardo Salles, 'Forum Shopping Before International Tribunals: (Real) Concerns, (Im)possible Solutions' (2009) 42 *Cornell International Law Journal* 77–118, at 102–5.
150 Kwak and Marceau, above n. 134, at 103; Pauwelyn and Salles, above n.149, at 102–4.
151 Appellate Body Report, *Mexico–Taxes on Soft Drinks*, para. 56.
152 See Tania Voon and Alan Yanovich, 'The Facts Aside: The Limitation of WTO Appeals to Issues of Law' (2006) 40(2) *Journal of World Trade* 239–58, at 251–2.
153 The Appellate Body approved findings of the Panel concerning the interpretation of the Lomé Convention in the *EC–Bananas III* dispute. See Appellate Body Report, *EC – Bananas III*, para. 255(g)–(h); Lorand Bartels, 'Jurisdiction and Applicable Law Clauses: Where does a Tribunal Find the Principal Norms Applicable to the Case before it?', in Tomer Broude and Yuval Shany (eds.), *Multi-Sourced Equivalent Norms in International Law* (Oxford: Hart, 2011), at p. 140.

external law when necessary, and a tribunal inappropriately seeking to adjudicate a dispute that arises under another agreement.

V. Conclusion

Some aspects of the relationship between PTAs and public international law are much clearer than others. For example, few would question that the interpretative rules contained in the Vienna Convention guide the interpretation of PTA provisions unless the PTA provides otherwise. Through these interpretative rules, and specifically Article 31(3)(c) of the Vienna Convention, treaty law, customary international law and general principles of law may affect the meaning and development of PTAs. This includes, in particular, WTO rules and jurisprudence, which may shed light on PTA provisions, especially where the PTA provisions mirror those in the WTO agreements.

The relationship between PTAs and customary international law beyond the interpretative context is murkier, as is the existence and content of customary international law itself. Nevertheless, an examination of past PTA disputes, particularly under NAFTA Chapter 11, demonstrates that PTAs have the potential to contribute to customary international law. In addition, customary international law may apply to PTAs in a procedural and substantive rather than purely interpretative manner. Examples of this are found in the recognition of *jus cogens* norms and the international norms on state responsibility.

The trickiest issues surrounding the overlap between PTAs and public international law arise where a PTA conflicts with another treaty, either because of conflicting norms between the two treaties or because of dispute settlement systems that are capable of hearing the same dispute. The potential for conflicts is growing as the number and breadth of PTAs grow, and further complications can be expected as individual PTA dispute settlement systems become more active or developed. Public international law offers some methods for dealing with treaty conflicts and intersecting jurisdictions, while the judicial experience of decision makers on tribunals may also assist. As to the extent to which PTA tribunals will make use of principles such as judicial comity, *res judicata* and *lex specialis derogat legi generali* to avoid or resolve conflicts, we can only wait and see.

7

Regulatory regionalism in the WTO:
Are 'deep integration' processes compatible
with the multilateral trading system?

JAMES H. MATHIS

I. Introduction

This chapter assesses the proposition that regulatory provisions in preferential trade agreements (PTAs) are implemented on a most-favoured nation basis and therefore complementary to the multilateral trading system in the WTO. The subject is raised because of the documented prominence that regulatory cooperation has attained in later-generation trade agreements, together with an apparent relative decline of the importance of preferential tariff cuts as a primary motivating force for concluding trade agreements. This was documented by the WTO 2011 Annual Report on preferential trade agreements[1] in its survey of over 97 agreements concluded between 1958 and 2010, and reinforced (or perhaps foretold) by Richard Baldwin's analysis of tariffs and regulations in so-called 'deep integration' agreements.[2] As the reasoning goes, regulatory activities – whether they be WTO 'plus' or WTO 'extra'[3] – do not lend themselves to implementation approaches on a preferential basis. To give just one example, if a country establishes a new competition law, its enforcement will neither favour nor punish foreign firms on the basis of their country of origin. There is nothing inherently externally preferential in the design of a competition law, and it does not become preferential because its origins can be traced to a provision in a preferential trade agreement.[4]

---

1 WTO Secretariat, Economic Research and Statistics Division, 'The WTO and Preferential Trade Agreements: From Co-existence to Coherence' (2011) hereinafter, the '2011 WTO Report', available at, www.wto.org/english/res_e/reser_e/wtr_e.htm.
2 Richard Baldwin, '21st Century Regionalism: Filling the Gap between 21st Century Trade and 20th Century Trade Rules' (2011) WTO Staff Working Paper, ERSD-2011–08, available at www.wto.org/english/res_e/reser_e/wpaps_e.htm.
3 'WTO Plus' refers to treated policy areas that are already subject to some form of commitment in the WTO Agreements. 'WTO Extra' refers to policy areas that are outside the current mandate of the WTO. See, 2011 WTO Report, 128, and citing H. Horn, P. Mavroidis, A. Sapir, 'Beyond the WTO? An Anatomy of EU and US Preferential Trade Agreements' (2010) 33 The World Economy 1565–88. This chapter is limited to a discussion of WTO 'plus' regulatory policy subjects.
4 2011 WTO Report, 168–9.

This is the MFN thesis for regulatory regionalism. There is a variation on the theme for services market access commitments in the vein of GATS Article XVI. These restrictions are also notably eliminated by altering domestic regulatory policies. Here, the WTO Report finds that notified GATS V economic integration agreements contain significant levels of market access commitments in excess of those made by the same WTO Members in their GATS schedules.[5] This suggests a possible resulting preferential treatment on behalf of signatory service providers, similar to preferential tariff treatment for trade in goods. However, the WTO Report (and Baldwin) also make the point that it is difficult to establish the country of origin of a service in the first instance, and attempts to clarify or enforce origin, by reference to country of incorporation for example, tend to be sufficiently porous to allow foreign third-country affiliates and subsidiaries to derive the benefits from doing business in a trade agreement partner's territory.[6]

These examples make a good intuitive case for the proposition that the new regulatory regionalism is more complementary to the multilateral trade system than the old tariff barrier regionalism. If new policies introduced in any given PTA tend to benefit all, then everyone with a stake in the multilateral trading system should be satisfied.[7] While acknowledging this general proposition, this chapter examines the possibilities that might arise for preferential application of regional regulatory policies to determine if any of these activities might have a residual preferential character. If so, it will consider whether they would be subject to an applicable WTO MFN provision and then possibly qualify for an exception under either GATT Article XXIV or GATS Article V.[8]

Several factors motivate this inquiry. First, as the WTO Report notes, there is not much known about the de facto implementation of trade agreement regulatory policies, the manner by which country implementations actually occur. An example provided by the report is the granting of licenses. The process may be non-discriminatory on its face, but whether it is tilted in favour of certain applicants bidding for a limited number of licenses is not so discernible.[9] Unfortunately, any validation of a de facto pattern of discriminatory implementation is also not so discernible, buried as it would be within the practices of different agencies and not likely to be a matter of common documentation. Thus, the literature on country implementation of trade agreement regulatory policies is scarce and an inquiry along those lines, at this time, does not appear to be fruitful.[10]

---

5 *Ibid.*, 134.   6 *Ibid.*, 168, Baldwin, supra note 2, 27.

7 Except as Baldwin also notes, the WTO itself risks losing its pre-eminence as the 'rule maker' in the international trading system. Baldwin, supra note 2, 31.

8 This chapter does not consider preferential trade agreements notified under the 1979 Enabling Clause.

9 2011 WTO Report, 168. The Report notes that the opposite can also be the case, that a provision which is preferential on its face might not be preferential in implementation.

10 As has been noted for implementation of TBT provisions in bilateral free-trade agreements. C. Lesser, 'Do Bilateral and Regional Approaches for Reducing Technical Barriers to Trade Converge Towards the Multilateral Trading System?' (2007) OECD Trade Policy Working Paper No. 58, 26. For a case study

A second factor flows from the continuing drive by countries for more PTAs and raises the question: if it is a given that tariff preferences are no longer the motivation for forming them, and if we accept the thesis that the regulatory benefits from one trade agreement automatically accrue to all other WTO Members, then what is the continuing motivation for any country to seek a regulatory-enhanced PTA with any other country that is already in a pre-existing deep integration agreement? In other words, why would a country seek a new bargain to achieve what it already has received for free?

There may be good reasons for the continuing PTA drive that do not undermine the regulatory MFN proposition, including motivations that are more about politics than about trade,[11] or the fact that the policies from agreement to agreement are simply not the same. An example can be cited in the intellectual property (IP) WTO 'extra' area where the choice of subjects (and referenced international IP treaties) in a US trade agreement will vary from those covered in an EU trade agreement. Another example can be found in service-provider licensing provisions, in which different countries seek admission for different types of services that are also regulated by different agencies of a country government. This array of different policies across an array of trade agreements might raise its own headaches for the multilateral system, a sort of 'regulatory spaghetti bowl' if you like,[12] but again, it should not raise any MFN issue. A multiplicity of regulatory policies across a range of PTAs should, if the MFN thesis holds, be automatically transmitted to all other Members of the WTO. This would not necessarily occur by the operation of a governing WTO MFN provision, but by the non-discriminatory nature of the regulatory policy itself as implemented. The result should arguably be more a beneficial multilateral 'accumulation' of global regulatory enhancements than a system-damaging 'fragmentation'.

Thus, regulatory policy subject areas may not be the issue. A counter proposition posed here is that any discrimination determined is more the result of the *processes* that are taken up in current PTAs in their approaches to regulatory cooperation and mutual recognition, transparency and participation, and consultation and dispute settlement. Here, the discussion turns more to institutional questions than to the examination of substantive policies. What is suggested is that many of the regulatory processes – *inter alia*, the various committees and working groups, inclusion of economic operators, structured contact points and scheduled meetings – do not lend themselves very well to a multilateral application, nor are they designed for

---

dealing with transparency implementation in OECD countries, E. Moïsé, 'Transparency Mechanisms and Non-tariff Measures' (2011) OECD Trade Policy Papers No. 111, discussed in, L. Biuković, 'Transparency Norms, the World Trade System and Free Trade Agreements: The Case of CETA' (2011) 39 *Legal Issues of Economic Integration* 1, 93–107, 96, which also reviews EU and Canada transparency provisions in their respective regional trade agreements.

11 See for example, J. Ravenhill, 'The "New East Asian Regionalism": A Political Domino Effect' (2010) 17 *Review of International Political Economy* 2, 178–208.

12 Cf. J. Bhagwati. See also, WTO News, 'Lamy warns rise of regional trade agreements could lead to "policy fragmentation"' 20 September 2012, available at www.wto.org/english/news_e/sppl_e/sppl246_e.htm.

that. They are oriented instead to establishing closer bilateral relationships between the signatories in order to (hopefully) create effective processes that can reach existing and potential regulatory barriers. Whether any final results (the elimination of an internal barrier to trade) are also preferentially applied is a matter of case-to-case analysis and not examined here, but the processes by which regulatory cooperation is arranged are not necessarily 'open' for the participation of third countries, unless and until they negotiate their own separate regulatory-oriented trade agreement with those signatories. On that occasion, the pre-existing relationship is not necessarily enlarged to accommodate a new partner in a new plurilateral regulatory process, but is rather a new and additional bilateral relationship with all its processes commenced.

The chapter proceeds to distil these processes, from generally applied provisions for transparency, cooperation and dispute settlement, to selected subject areas, with an emphasis on WTO 'plus' subjects that have connections to underlying WTO agreements and their non-discrimination rules. These MFN provisions and possible regional exceptions will be considered as relevant. The trade agreement provisions examined are drawn from the four most recently ratified EU and US free-trade area agreements including their respective agreements with Korea,[13] the US agreement with Panama,[14] and the EU agreement with the CARIFORUM states.[15] The choice of EU and US agreements may be considered arbitrary, but it is based on the idea that they are both economically developed territories with advanced regulatory systems. Thus, their trade agreements could reasonably be expected to have an emphasis on regulatory issues, and they should offer some examples of advanced regulatory activities that appear in newer generation agreements.

II. General provisions affecting regulatory treatment

A. Transparency chapters and provisions

Both the US agreements and the EU–Korea agreement have separate chapters on transparency.[16] They cover the same subjects of publication, provision of

---

13 Respectively, Free Trade Agreement between the European Union and its Member States, of the one part, and the Republic of Korea, of the other part, (EU–Korea agreement) OJ L127/6, 14 May 2011; and, Free Trade Agreement Between The United States Of America And The Republic Of Korea (KORUS agreement), ratified in 2011. USTR available at www.ustr.gov/trade-agreements/free-trade-agreements/korus-fta/final-text.

14 United States–Panama Trade Promotion Agreement, (US–Panama agreement), ratified 2011. USTR available at www.ustr.gov/trade-agreements/free-trade-agreements/panama-tpa/final-text.

15 Economic Partnership Agreement between the CARIFORUM States, of the one part, and the European Community and its Member States, of the other part, (EU–CARIFORUM agreement), OJ L289/13, 30 October 2008.

16 KORUS agreement, Chapter Twenty One; US–Panama agreement, Chapter Eighteen; EU–Korea agreement, Chapter Twelve. This agreement defines 'interested persons' as natural or legal persons subject to rights and obligations under measures of general application, within the meaning of 'economic operators, especially small ones doing business in their territory'. EU–Korea agreement, Arts. 12.1, 12.2.

information, administrative proceedings, review and appeal. The US agreements
treat anti-corruption. With some minor differences, all three of them establish
regulatory transparency for the primary benefit of 'interested persons'.[17] They require
publication of existing laws of general application, and that the parties (to the extent
possible or by 'endeavouring') inform interested persons of proposals for such
general laws so that they may become acquainted with them and be given time
to provide the opportunity to comment.[18] The US agreements require parties to
provide information and to respond to questions by the requesting party, while the
EU agreement provides that opportunity to interested persons.[19] An emphasis on
persons is continued in similar fashion for the three agreements' articles on administrative and review proceedings. Wherever possible, persons directly affected by a
proceeding are to receive reasonable notice and have a reasonable opportunity to
present their arguments. The parties are obligated to insure proceedings for review
and the parties in these proceedings shall be given the opportunity to support or
defend their positions.[20]

The EU–Korea chapter concludes with a non-discrimination clause granting
national treatment, but also no less favourable treatment for transparency standards
accorded to interested persons of any third country or to a third country, 'whichever
are the best'.[21]

The EU–CARIFORUM agreement has a single Article 235 which obliges the
parties to ensure that laws of general application will be promptly published and
brought to the attention of the other party. There is no reference to persons. There are
no provisions governing administrative procedures, hearings and reviews, at the level
of general provisions.

The focus on interested persons in the agreements with transparency chapters
raises the question of whether treatment guaranteed for them need necessarily be
extended to the interested persons of third countries, those that have not bargained
for any reciprocal transparency treatment in their respective trade agreements.
Subjects such as publication and administrative proceedings would seem most easily
established and maintained on an MFN basis, since bifurcating these aspects among
the interested persons of different parties would seem difficult, if not impossible, to
organize and effectively operate. However, the focus on the treatment of interested

---

17 The US–Panama agreement has a provision for contact points and the KORUS agreement is shaded with
    additional detail for its treatment of central level regulations.
18 The KORUS agreement goes on to specify for central level regulations, required official journal publication
    with an explanation of their purpose and a 40-day period for comments. KORUS agreement, Art. 21.1.3.
    See also, transparency letters exchanged confirming Korea's commitment to a change of law to provide for
    the 40-day period.
19 The EU–Korea agreement does this by establishing 'appropriate mechanisms' for responding to enquiries
    from any interested person for laws proposed or in force. EU–Korea agreement, Art. 12.4.
20 KORUS agreement, Arts. 21.3, 21.4; US–Panama agreement, Arts. 18.4, 18.5; EU–Korea agreement, Arts.
    12.5, 12.6.
21 EU–Korea agreement, Art. 12.8.

persons in rights to comment and receive responses, or the availability of structured inquiry points for them, might generate a differentiation among interested persons on the basis of country origin.[22]

This differentiation may or may not in fact occur, but consider how a party with two agreements manages where the transparency provisions vary between them. The KORUS agreement has a provision of information requirements for the benefit of the other signatory party while the EU–Korea agreement extends this to interested persons, the economic operators doing business in 'their' territories. While it may seem more expedient to simply extend the additional treatment to all economic operators of any party doing business in the territory, the question still lingers: why extend that treatment to another party that has not bargained for it and is not required to grant it on a reciprocal basis? That the EU–Korea agreement also has an MFN provision for transparency treatment granted to interested persons of third parties does not close the point, but does suggest that preferential treatment in transparency procedures is possible.

GATT Article X provides the context for trade in goods. This requires transparency for prompt publication of trade regulations so that governments and traders can become acquainted with them. Review tribunals are also required for customs matters to be independent of agencies of enforcement. Reference is made to appeals lodged by importers, and private parties are therefore clearly contemplated. Each contracting party is to maintain its laws in a uniform, impartial and reasonable manner, inferring non-discriminatory treatment for trade transparency regulations. The GATT Article is narrower than the broader regulatory scope of the trade agreements discussed and it lacks material dealing with proposals for laws and for interested persons to engage that process. GATS Article III requires publication and notification to the Council for any measure of general application pertaining to or affecting the operation of the GATS agreement, and requires the establishment for inquiry points for Members (not interested persons) operated upon request. This broader transparency article still does not deal with proposals for laws and guarantees for private participation. General GATT and GATS Articles may however have some reach to equalize any differentiation generated by a trade agreement. Matters covered by GATT Article III.4 include any measure affecting the internal sale of an imported product and are subject to GATT Article I MFN. GATS Article II MFN refers to 'any measure covered by this Agreement', and as defined in GATS Article I, the agreement applies to measures 'affecting' trade in services. What one can conclude from this is that while there is a potential for preferential treatment in some transparency procedures, there is also possible scope for general GATT and GATS MFN Articles to reach that differential treatment. What remains unanswered is whether the

---

22 Moïsé states that for OECD countries, RTA provisions do not provide foreign stakeholders any additional opportunities of participation beyond what is already offered in those domestic frameworks. Supra notes 10, 11.

practical difficulties of implementing differential transparency treatment outweigh
the preferential opportunity to do so.

B. Dispute settlement chapters

While not entirely uniform, all four agreements conform to the well-known pattern
of state-to-state dispute resolution, from consultations to panel establishment, implementation of reports and compliance reviews. Without detailing dispute settlement
procedures, the scope of application of the chapters refers to matters covered by the
agreements as between the parties to the agreements. Dispute settlement provisions
in a regional trade agreement are an institutional remedy to which only the parties to
the agreement can avail themselves. This means that for whatever other MFN
characteristics that might attach to the regulatory policies engaged in the agreements
for the benefit of third states, de facto or de jure, they do not extend to creating any
rights of recourse for violations of those provisions in a state-to-state regional dispute
settlement forum. Thus, for example, while economic operators of a third state could
well be the beneficiaries of an enhanced administrative due process procedure as a
result of another territory's trade agreement, those economic operators cannot rely
on their home state to compel that treatment to be extended by the host state
according to the terms of any trade agreement. The power to engage consultation
and charge a violation before an arbitral panel – and to claim compliance review and
compensation – is wholly preferential to the parties of that trade agreement.[23] If there
is a parallel WTO obligation that may also be violated, then depending upon the
choice of forum clause used in the trade agreement, the WTO forum may be
exclusive[24] or be cumulative.[25] If cumulative, the trade agreement party has a choice
of forums that a non-signatory does not have. The cause of action may also be distinct
to the trade agreement. A WTO complaint may necessarily have to be formed on the
basis of discrimination. If the underlying trade agreement obligation does not have a
parallel WTO obligation, the non-party may have to form its WTO claim on the basis
of discriminatory effects of that policy measure. The trade agreement complainant
may, however, be able to fashion its claim on the basis of non-performance of the
trade agreement provision itself.

The EU–Korea agreement has an additional device besides the traditional con-
sultation/arbitration panel dispute settlement procedure. This is the 'Mediation
Mechanism for Non-Tariff Measures' that is to address measures believed to be

---

23 This is where the recourse allowed by the trade agreement is strictly state to state. It does not consider
    whether a party may grant direct effect to individuals of the agreement's provisions in the national courts,
    or any action brought in a national court under the domestic law.
24 I.e., that a party must choose one forum to the exclusion of the other or that the WTO forum is designated
    as the only available forum.
25 I.e., that a party may choose one of the forums without excluding the other for a later action, or employ
    both forums in parallel.

adversely affecting trade in goods other than customs duties.[26] This is a softer legal procedure than panel arbitration that allows for the appointment of an expert mediator to give an advisory opinion and proposed solution, and to facilitate a mutually agreed solution between the parties. The procedure itself is not compulsory, but the requested party shall 'favourably consider the request' to which a response is required.[27] The availability of this instrument is limited to the parties to the trade agreement and is wholly preferential.

III. Trade in goods, WTO 'plus' subjects

The most prevalent WTO 'plus' subjects are ranked by frequency in the 2011 WTO Report and include (in this order) industrial tariffs, agricultural tariffs, customs, anti-dumping, countervailing measures, export taxes, TBT, GATS, TRIPS, state aid, public procurement and SPS. Selecting for the more regulatory-oriented subjects, the list of customs, TBT, GATS, TRIPS, state aids, public procurement and SPS emerges. The order considered here will be customs, TBT and SPS, TRIPS, public procurement, state aids and then GATS. This bundles some related subject areas together for trade in goods and separates trade in services (GATS) for separate treatment.

A. Customs cooperation

The general approach to this subject is to emphasize transparency, efficiency and simplicity in the procedures, with attention to promoting electronic clearance technology. The EU agreements make repetitive reference to international protocols and accords as the context for bilateral cooperation between customs authorities.[28] While many of the expressions are set with some obligatory tone, their content can tend to be less so, as in, 'the parties shall cooperate'. Most activities are of a sort that one would assume would be implemented for all importers irrespective of origin; electronic clearance, for example. Each EU agreement establishes a bilateral committee charged with guiding the chapter's implementation and resolving differences and issues as they emerge. This is understood to be a more bilateral process as a part of facilitating the objectives of the free-trade agreements. Some other elements of enhanced cooperation might also be engaged on a bilateral basis, such as the exchange of customs officers, the harmonization of documents, and perhaps early notification of changes to rules, obligations for forming advanced rulings and the maintenance of contact points.

---

26 Mediation Mechanism for Non-Tariff Measures, EU–Korea agreement, Annex 14-A, L 127/1336–37.
27 *Ibid.*, Annex 14-A, Art. 3.2.
28 Generally, EU–Korea agreement, Chapter Six, Arts. 6.1–6.16; EU–CARIFORUM agreement, Chapter 4, Arts. 29–36.

The US agreements[29] provide for the same topics dealing with the release of goods, automation, advance rulings, etc., with the addition of provisions for information to assist investigations into possibly unlawful activities and provisions made for express shipments. The US agreements do not establish committees. Other than bilaterally agreed-upon definitions applied to facilitate the passage of information for unlawful activities, there otherwise appears to be little else projected in the manner of bilateral regulatory processes. This conclusion assumes that provisions to facilitate express shipments would also be generally applied and implemented for all foreign express shipment providers.

Summarizing, the customs cooperation subject area is quite benign in its preferential processes. Most of the processes that would be engaged in exclusively by the signatories are also softer law in content and therefore might have less legal traction in allowing for the effect of distinct preferential treatment. The subject area is also well captured by GATT Article I since the general MFN obligation extends to 'all rules and formalities in connection with importation and exportation'. This would include those matters treated in GATT Article X's provisions for *Publication and Administration of Trade Regulations* to the extent that they are able to be characterized as GATT Article I's 'rules and formalities'.

B. TBT and SPS measures

There is a pattern common to all the agreements surveyed in which the parties' rights and obligations under the WTO TBT and SPS Agreements are affirmed, and then supplemented with bilateral regulatory cooperation activities of varying levels of intensity.

1. TBT type provisions

The two US agreements are very similar. Both include a commitment to a process of joint cooperation, provisions for conformity assessment procedures and their potential recognition, transparency notifications, information exchanges, and the establishment of joint committees to facilitate the above.[30] The two US agreements have several points of administrative interaction where the process of cooperation is strengthened somewhat from what the WTO TBT Agreement contains. This includes a right to request and receive a response for an explanation when one party does not accept the results of a conformity assessment procedure in the other's territory,[31] and

---

29 Generally, KORUS agreement, Chapter Seven; US–Panama agreement, Chapter Five.
30 Generally, KORUS agreement, Chapter Nine, US–Panama agreement, Chapter Seven. The agreements are nearly identical and the example provisions in the text here are drawn from the KORUS Agreement. One difference noted is in the US–Panama agreement where there is an obligation to explain why one party has not accepted a technical regulation of the other as equivalent. US–Panama agreement, Art. 7.6. The sectoral provisions for automobiles in the EU–Korea and KORUS agreements are not covered here.
31 KORUS agreement, Art. 9.5.2. The US agreements do not contain provisions for mutual recognition of technical regulations.

a number of activities detailed for transparency including a right to allow persons of the other party to participate in the development of standards, technical regulations and conformity assessment procedures, coupled with a national treatment obligation for persons of the other party, and a separate bilateral notification to the other party when either notifies in accordance with WTO TBT Agreement notification requirements.[32] This separate notification is to provide an explanation of the objectives meant to be served by the proposal and a transmission of the proposal electronically to the established inquiry point of the other party.[33] The transparency provisions are concluded by a request and response paragraph whereby

> each Party shall provide the other Party with additional available information regarding the objective of, and rationale for, a standard, technical regulation, or conformity assessment procedure that the Party has adopted or is proposing to adopt. Such requests may include requests for information regarding the matter the technical regulation or conformity assessment procedure is designed to address, alternative approaches the Party considered, and the merits of the particular approach the Party chose.[34]

It may well be that these activities can be similarly accomplished in the WTO TBT Committee, but here the process of information and exchange is promoted on a bilateral basis with supervision by the regional agreement's designated committee. The emphasis in the notification process is upon early notice with an accorded right to participate to 'persons', and the right to receive the other party's statements on two elements critical to the application of the TBT Agreement provisions to a given technical regulation. The first is information regarding the objective sought to be accomplished, an element that is necessary to consider in applying both TBT Articles 2.1 and 2.2.[35] The second is an accounting of what alternatives were considered and the party's explanation of the merits of the approach adopted. This goes to the core of TBT Article 2.2 in determining whether lesser restrictive alternatives might have been considered, and if so, why they were not adopted.

After the usual affirmation of the WTO TBT Agreement, the two EU agreements go on to set forth some enhancements for regulatory cooperation, transparency and conformity assessment.[36] The agreements are, however, somewhat 'lighter' than the US examples discussed above, being less detailed and specific on cooperation and transparency activities, and notably less so in the EU–CARIFORUM agreement. Both establish 'coordinators' or 'contact points' rather than structured committees. Two points of clear detail are noted for the EU–Korea agreement. One is a stated timeline of 60 days for receiving the other party's comments for TBT Agreement notifications.[37]

---

32 *Ibid.*, Art. 9.6.   33 *Ibid.*, Arts. 9.6.3, 9.6.4.   34 *Ibid.*, Art. 9.7.
35 For national treatment and for prescribing that regulations shall not be unnecessary obstacles to trade, respectively.
36 EU–Korea agreement, Chapter Four; EU–CARIFORUM agreement, Chapter Six.
37 EU–Korea agreement, Art. 4.4.1(f).

The other is for information on technical regulations to be transmitted to the other party's 'economic operators' including 'written guidance on compliance with their technical regulations' upon request.[38] Neither of these activities is necessarily bilateral, although the second provision could be. As in the US agreements, there are no statements promoting or establishing processes for equivalency recognition of technical regulations and no on-going process is established for identifying possible priorities for equivalency.

2. SPS type provisions

The SPS chapters in the EU agreements are not similar to one another.[39] The EU–Korea agreement establishes an on-going committee and pays some detailed attention to determining pest- or disease-free areas by a two year 'confidence-building activity', to be eventually confirmed by the WTO SPS Committee.[40] In addition, the parties specify the possibility of consultations if a party rejects the determination of the other. Both agree to be open for inspection, testing and other procedures.[41] The EU–CARIFORUM agreement is more oriented to cooperation for technical assistance for SPS-type measures within the region and to promoting harmonization of standards with the possibility of bilateral equivalency agreements. No committee is created.

The SPS chapters of US agreements are fairly brief, primarily functioning to establish a bilateral committee for consultation and coordination for understanding one another's SPS measures and their implementation.[42] Both agreements exempt their SPS chapters from regional dispute settlement procedures, although the only actionable matters in the chapter relate to the responsibilities to establish the committee and hold its meetings. A single exception to the lightly cooperative approach of the US agreements is the side agreement between Panama and the US providing for Panama's recognition of US sanitary, phytosanitary and related regulatory systems as equivalent to Panama's for meat, poultry, dairy and processed products.[43]

3. SPS and TBT implications

The most detailed bilateral approach of the four agreements surveyed here is the KORUS TBT annex, with its bilateral notification requirements, the designated right for persons to participate in the rule-making process, and the right of request and response regarding objectives and alternatives considered. This is not to say that these aspects might not also be implemented on a multilateral basis in practice, but there is nothing inherently multilateral about them and they can be applied on a bilateral basis. Multilateral application or not, they do raise the application of the TBT

---

38 *Ibid.*, Art. 4.4.1(d).
39 EU–Korea agreement, Chapter Five; EU–CARIFORUM agreement, Chapter Seven.
40 EU–Korea agreement, Art. 5.8.3.   41 *Ibid.*, 5.8.4–5.
42 KORUS agreement, Chapter Eight, US–Panama agreement, Chapter Six.
43 Agreement Regarding Certain Sanitary and Phytosanitary Measures and Technical Standards Affecting Trade in Agriculture Products, dated 20 December, 2006, paras 2, 4.

Agreement's Article 2 provisions for the 'preparation, adoption and application of technical regulations'. It is not clear whether the broader scope of Article 2's title is captured in the actual scope of the MFN obligation of TBT Article 2.1, for which treatment no less favourable is required in respect of technical regulations for 'products imported from the territory of any Member'. Rather than referring to any measure 'affecting' the internal sale of a product, this TBT Article appears limited to existing and applied technical regulations rather than to their process of adoption. The subjects discussed above are more about the processes of considering and adopting technical regulations. GATT Article III.4 (as subject to GATT Article I MFN) arguably does have that broader scope of application for laws, regulations and requirements affecting internal sale, and if preferential notification provisions in a trade agreement were to be equated with 'regulations' or 'requirements' then perhaps a discriminatory measure could be identified, thus calling forth the possible defensive application of either GATT Article XX or GATT Article XXIV.

Both TBT and SPS regional measures present a somewhat protracted analysis for the application of most-favoured nation and subsequently the possible application of the Article XXIV regional exception. This has been visited periodically by a number of authors and is not going to be re-visited here, other than to note the trend in case law and opinion that GATT exceptions (Articles XX and XXIV) do not appear to be applicable to justify violations of obligations contained in other WTO Annex 1A agreements.[44] In addition, for a discriminatory technical regulation process violation of GATT Article I (as it applies to matters covered by GATT Article III.4) to be justified by invoking GATT Article XXIV would require that the measure was 'necessary' as an elimination of a restrictive regulation of commerce (ORRC) in the sense of Article XXIV paragraph 8. The opinion here is that it would be neither an ORRC nor necessary to eliminate in order to complete the regional formation.[45]

The agreements are otherwise about enhancing cooperation with the use of non-obligatory instruments. As such, while the cooperation is decidedly bilateral in nature (joint committees), there is a real question whether any of the provisions have a

---

44 Recent examples include J. Trachtman, 'The Limits of PTAs: WTO Legal Restrictions on the Use of WTO-Plus Standards Regulation in PTAs', in K. Bagwell and P. Mavroidis (eds.), *Preferential Trade Agreements: A Law and Economic Analysis*, (Cambridge: Columbia Studies in WTO Law and Policy, 2011), 115–49; J. Mathis, 'Multilateral Aspects of Advanced Regulatory Cooperation: Considerations for a Canada-EU Comprehensive Trade Agreement (CETA)' (2012) 39 *Legal Issues of Economic Integration* 1, 73–91; B. Rigod, 'TBT-Plus Rules in Preferential Trade Agreements' (2013) 40 *Legal Issues of Economic Integration* 3, 247–70, 269–70, noting also that Trachtman (*ibid.*) argues that Art. XXIV should apply to the TBT and SPS agreements by the principle of effective interpretation. Rigod, *ibid.*, at note 110. Trachtman however also concludes that TBT and SPS harmonization or recognition would not pass the GATT Art. XXIV necessity requirement. Trachtman, *ibid.*, 134.

45 On the necessity of TBT liberalizing measures (for EU mutual recognition), L. Bartels, 'The Legality of the EC Mutual Recognition Clause Under WTO Law' (2006) 8 *Journal of International Economic Law* 3, 691–720, 713; and generally, J. Mathis, 'Regional Trade Agreements and Domestic Regulation: What Reach for "Other Restrictive Regulations of Commerce"?', in L. Bartels and F. Ortino (eds.), *Regional Trade Agreements and the WTO Legal System* (Oxford: Oxford University Press, 2006) 79–108.

sufficient legal character in either obligatory requirements or specific content to summon any meaningful degree of preferential behaviour in the sense of the term 'discriminatory'. While the activities may be bilateral and therefore preferential, the legal obligatory quality of the cooperation would understandably be a consideration in determining whether the process is sufficiently discriminatory to constitute being a 'measure' in the sense of a WTO provision requiring non-discriminatory treatment. At the same time, this lighter preferential cooperative behaviour is intended to generate some ultimate effects on the trade relationship of the signatories to the agreements, in that the processes are set in place to facilitate the objectives of the agreement, and the primary objective is market access. In that sense, the activities, non-legal or 'softer law' as they may be, are potentially able to generate a market effect (better market access) and possibly a corresponding legal effect (discrimination). Aside from that possible and perhaps tenuous connector, it is otherwise difficult to assign a role for a WTO MFN provision in the absence of a measure upon which MFN would be able to attach. The establishment of a committee is not likely to be a measure (committees in trade agreements are ubiquitous) and it would seem that only the activities of the committee could be so designated to the extent they had legal effect. While the concept of a 'measure' is broad enough to include 'practices', it is questionable whether an 'obligation' to 'encourage understanding' of the parties' respective regulations, or to 'facilitate coordination' rises to that level.

C. Intellectual property (IP) rights

The discussion here is related to TRIPS 'plus' aspects, those IP subjects that are also treated in the WTO TRIPS agreement. This subject area demonstrates well the proposition that regulatory provisions tend to be applied on a multilateral basis. This is strongly characterized in IP laws where differential treatment of IP rights on the basis of origin is not practiced by national jurisdictions, as well as the TRIPS Agreement's MFN provision regarding the protection of intellectual property. Its scope is broad 'with regard to the protection of intellectual property', extending to all Members any advantage granted by a Member to the nationals of any other country.[46]

The trade agreements affirm existing TRIPS rights and obligations and go on to complement and specify the regimes, for definitional substance as well as enforcement procedures. There is little bilateral institutional structure for regulatory cooperation established in any of the agreements. The entire field of cooperation is wholly absent from the US agreements, while the EU agreements provide for exchange of information, experiences of enforcement and capacity building.[47] The

---

46 WTO TRIPS agreement, Art. 4, and subject to its listed exemptions. On TRIPS MFN application, see R. Valdés and R. Tavengwa, 'Intellectual Property Provisions in Regional Trade Agreements' (2012) WTO Staff Working Paper, ESRD-2012–21, 40, para 152.

47 EU–Korea agreement, Art. 10.69, for example. The agreement does establish a working group for geographical indications. *Ibid.*, Art. 10.25.

EU–CARIFORUM agreement places emphasis on regional capacity building and also has as an objective the harmonization of IP protection 'across their respective regions' which is taken to be a reference to the separate regions of each party.[48]

The EU–Korea agreement's section on geographical indications (GIs) should be noted as a possible deviation from the multilateral character of IP protection. This establishes a reciprocal recognition of the other party's GI list (as annexed) together with an undertaking to enforce the list.[49] This is based upon an acknowledgment that the elements of registration, verification, control and objection are met in the domestic system of each party.[50] While each of these territories employs a *sui generis* system for listing and protecting GIs that is open to non-territory applicants, the action here bypasses the process of individual producer applications by recognizing those already made and approved in the other territory.[51] A territory's GI enforcement policy is clearly subject to the TRIPS MFN obligation,[52] and the question arises whether MFN extends this recognition system either to third countries that request a reciprocal treatment on the same terms, or even to those that might request a unilateral recognition of their listed GIs. The recognition activity in this agreement can be compared to an equivalency recognition for technical regulations to the extent that the underlying quality of a national system is assessed and approved. This suggests a conditional form of MFN (as some argue the TBT Agreement might permit), but the TRIPS Agreement has no comparable article encouraging bilateral or preferential agreements for the extension of the substance or the enforcement of rights.[53] The Appellate Body ruled in *EC – Geographic Indications* that the conditioning of GI listing on reciprocal treatment was a violation of GATT Article III.4.[54] The issue there was one of national treatment because an EU member state did not have to meet the same conditions for protection under the EU Regulation. While the EU now registers individual non-EU products by application to the Commission without reciprocity, the issue presented here is whether a territory's listing of products would be recognized either reciprocally or unilaterally.

---

48 EU–CARIFORUM agreement, Art. 141.   49 EU–Korea agreement, Art. 10.18(1–5).
50 *Ibid.*, Art. 10.18(6)(a–f).
51 An individual producer application would need a local language translation and likely use of a local agent for facilitating the process. This is yet perceived as less burdensome than systems which rely on unfair competition or consumer protection laws. O'Connor and Company Report for the European Commission, 'Geographical Indications and TRIPs: 10 Years Later ... A roadmap for EU GI holders to get protection in other WTO Members' (2007) 13, available at, http://trade.ec.europa.eu/doclib/docs/2007/june/tra doc_135088.pdf.
52 The TRIPS MFN provision is not limited to IP protection as provided only in the TRIPS Agreement, nor is it even limited to the referenced subject areas covered by the TRIPS Agreement. See, footnote 3 to TRIPS Articles 3 and 4.
53 TRIPS Art. 4(d) MFN exempts only prior notified international agreements. TRIPS Art. 24 refers to negotiations to conclude bilateral or multilateral agreements, within the context of TRIPS Art. 23, for wines and spirits.
54 *EC–Protection of Trademarks and Geographical Indications for Agricultural Products and Foodstuffs*, WT/DS290/R, 15 March 2005, para 2.272.

In contrast, the KORUS agreement only provides that each party shall recognize that GIs are eligible as trademarks.[55] Further, if a party does have a system for recognition of GIs by trademark or otherwise (as Korea maintains), then as regards to the US, the KORUS agreement specifies an objection procedure and the grounds for refusing or cancelling registration if the GI is likely to cause confusion with a trademark that is in earlier pending application, or for a trademark that is 'well known' in the party's territory.[56] The EU agreement does not specify conditions for objection, but possibly renders the two separate regimes coherent where it provides that the GI protection accorded is without prejudice to the continued use of a trademark which has been applied for, registered or established, with certain conditions.[57]

This might be a benign example of multiple regulatory regimes being extended to all in the trading system by the operation of WTO MFN clauses or the inherent multilateral character of the regulatory activity. If so, it is not difficult to see the potential for conflict when one regime focuses on the protection of a subject area and the other focuses on the exceptions to that protection. If they do go into conflict, then the system of MFN extension would serve to spread that conflict rather than resolving it, since all Members would have access to both conflicting regimes. It is understood that one agreement cannot be a modification of the other in respect of a party who is not a signatory to the second agreement. Perhaps those facts are not present here, but a regulatory conflict could be conceptualized that could not be resolved other than by triggering a violation of the first agreement, and arguably the MFN rights to those regulatory provisions held by all other WTO Members by operation of the multilateral extension.

It becomes apparent from this example that the EU and Korea are not likely to envisage this GI regime as being applied in a multilateral manner. They appear to be of sufficiently like minds on the extension of the existing TRIPS provisions to provide for a more institutionalized bilateral system of GI protection and have made that exchange. The US is on record in the WTO negotiations as not supporting extension of the existing TRIPS GI protection for wines and spirits,[58] and perhaps carries the opinion that its trade agreement has either mollified (or modified) the characteristics of the Korea regime so that US trademarks and their (potential) registration remain safe. The US and Korea may view this as a multilateral provision where those exceptions as defined in the KORUS agreement would be applied by both to all WTO Members. On Korea's behalf, this assumedly is accomplished without raising any conflict in the agreed-upon GI regime with the EU.

A note on processes is raised also for GIs in the EU–Korea agreement's provisions for the establishment of a working group to 'intensify the cooperation' and manage

---

55 KORUS agreement, Art. 18.2.2.   56 *Ibid.*, Art. 18.2.15(a).   57 EU–Korea agreement, Art. 10.21.5.
58 See, WTO, Geographical Indications, 'Background of the current situation', updated November, 2008, available at, www.wto.org/english/tratop_e/trips_e/gi_background_e.htm#protection.

the regime by consensus decisions.[59] The group has the authority to add GIs to the regime and to remove those that are no longer recognized in the country of origin. This is another distinctly bilateral activity. Even if there was an extension of recognition of a GI regime to a non-signatory, this would not likely be accompanied with participation in this working group.

A final note is made about a regional exception that could rescue an MFN violation made within a trade agreement. The WTO TRIPS agreement does not have regional exception and the ability to link preferential IP protection to the terms of GATT Article XXIV would seem to require locating a separate violation of GATT Article I (as applying to matters within GATT Article III.4) or GATT Article III.4 by itself.[60] The regional exception of Article XXIV could be invoked by the respondent on the violation, but to be 'necessary' for the violation to fall within the Article XXIV exception, it would have to be demonstrated that the IP protection eliminated a 'restrictive regulation of commerce', a term that seems more fit for eliminating barriers to trade than for positive recognition and enforcement regimes.

D. Public procurement

Public procurement is a chapter subject in each of the four trade agreements. There is an initial distinction to be made in the preferential character of the agreements between those made by signatories to the WTO Agreement on Government Procurement ('a GPA party')[61] and those made with non-members to that WTO agreement.[62] The agreements with non-GPA parties install the same or similar commitments of the GPA agreement between them and thus establish a bilateral public procurement agreement.[63] All the processes that are referenced in the bilateral agreement remain wholly preferential on the side of the non-GPA party in favour of the other signatory to the extent that those activities fall under the GATT procurement exemption from the general GATT national treatment obligation[64] or the GATS Articles exempting procurement for trade in services.[65] Procurement undertakings incurred by the GPA member with a non-GPA member also remain preferential in respect to other WTO Members for the general GATT and GATS

59 EU–Korea agreement, Art. 10.25.
60 See discussion, supra note 44. Here the question is Art. XXIV's application *outside* of WTO Annex 1A. If GATT Art. XXIV applies to TRIPS violations, then arguably GATT Art. XX should also apply to excuse TRIPS violations. It seems increasingly clear that GATT exceptions do not apply to other Annex IA agreements unless referenced, and the argument to make the application outside of Annex IA would not seem to be an easier bridge to cross.
61 EU–Korea agreement, Chapter Nine; KORUS agreement, Chapter Seventeen.
62 EU–CARIFORUM agreement, Chapter Three; US–Panama agreement, Chapter Nine.
63 For an overview of procurement provisions in RTAs, J. Bourgeois, K. Dawar, S. Evenett, 'A Comparative Analysis of Selected Provisions in Free Trade Agreements' (2007) *DG Trade* 99–116, available at http://eulib.com/documents/tradoc_138103.pdf.
64 GATT Art. III.8(a).
65 GATS Art. XII, exempting government procurement from GATS Articles II, XVI and XVII.

Articles (as above) and also in respect of WTO GPA parties. This last point may seem incongruous, but the non-discrimination provision in the WTO procurement agreement only extends advantages to GPA parties that are accorded to other GPA parties.[66]

The WTO procurement agreement's non-discrimination obligations do reach to agreements made by WTO GPA members. However, there is also a limitation on the scope of the non-discrimination article, which refers to 'laws, regulations, procedures and practices regarding government procurement *covered by this Agreement*'.[67] Any additional procurement coverage in a bilateral trade agreement would therefore have to be assessed for whether or not it is 'covered' by the WTO procurement agreement.[68] Preferential results are therefore possible depending upon the determined scope of the WTO procurement agreement.

Institutionally, the agreements provide for working groups and/or contact points for the purpose of engaging in cooperation and information. These are relatively light provisions that do not set clear legal targets or provide for identifiable recourse.

E. State aids (and state owned enterprises/monopolies)

The US agreements do not treat state aids. There are references in the KORUS agreement to state monopolies and enterprises obliging the parties to render their conduct consistent with the obligations of the agreement and to act solely in accordance with commercial considerations.[69] These provisions should be seen as being applied in a non-preferential manner and they somewhat mimic the GATT agreement's commercial requirements for state-trading enterprises. The EU–CARIFORUM agreement also calls for the elimination of trade distortions by public and special or exclusive rights enterprises and for them to be subject to competition rules.[70] This would also seem to be a generally applicable provision that would not be preferentially implemented. An additional rule on state monopolies calls for them

---

66 WTO Agreement on Government Procurement, Art. III.1(b) refers to suppliers of any other 'Party'. The agreement's preamble refers to '*Parties to this Agreement (hereinafter referred to as "Parties")*'. Therefore an advantage given to another territory not a 'Party' to the procurement agreement need not be extended to other 'Parties' of the procurement agreement. This possibility of offering treatment 'better than' that accorded to WTO procurement parties may not be a likely occurrence in any trade agreement between a WTO procurement party and a non-party.

67 WTO procurement agreement, Art. III.1. Compare with the TRIPS agreement provisions which refer to treatment or advantages 'with regard to the protection of intellectual property'. TRIPS agreement, Arts. 3.1 and 4.

68 A possible example is drawn from the EU–Korea agreement for EU public works concessions and Korea 'build-operate transfer' (BOT) contracts. According to one source, this is an area 'not covered in the GPA'; European Commission, 'The EU–Korea Free Trade Agreement in Practice' (2011) 14 located at, http://trade.ec.europa.eu/doclib/docs/2011/october/tradoc_148303.pdf. See, EU–Korea agreement, Annex 9, L127/1317.

69 KORUS agreement, Arts. 16.2, 16.3.   70 EU–CARIFORUM agreement, Art. 129.2.

to operate in a commercial manner and without discrimination for the sale of goods and services as between the two territories.[71] As limited only to the trade of the parties, depending upon the nature of the discrimination eliminated, this requirement could conceivably be implemented in a preferential manner. Any recourse available to enforce a violation would be wholly preferential between the parties to the agreement.

State aids are only treated in the EU–Korea agreement and by primary reference to the WTO subsidies agreement. Supplementing that agreement is an elaboration of what is deemed to be specific and prohibited as according to Article 2 of the WTO agreement in regards to subsidies covering debts of certain enterprises and those for insolvent enterprises without credible restructuring plans.[72] Bilateral transparency reporting requirements are also applied for the specific subsidies affecting trade.[73] These requirements are not inherently multilateral. The definitions for specificity need not be applied to trade relations with third parties. While they are deemed to be specific for meeting the conditions of the WTO subsidies agreement, Article 11.11 states that they 'shall be prohibited for the purposes of this Agreement in so far as they adversely affect international trade of the Parties'. While the transparency requirements are very similar to the WTO subsidies agreement,[74] what is determined to be specific and therefore required to be notified to the WTO is subject to that agreement, not the EU–Korea agreement. The WTO subsidies agreement lacks a non-discrimination clause that would catch differential bilateral treatment.

F. Trade in goods conclusion

One can see the mixed bag that emerges on regulatory processes that splits between those that are clearly multilateral because of their character or applicable WTO rules, like customs cooperation, and those that target treatment on a bilateral basis and do not appear to be required to be extended by WTO rules, such as the state aid definitions for specificity or processes that apply only to the trade between the parties. The mixed bag has another splitting of elements between policies that are 'legal' enough to call forth obligations, such as some of the TBT provisions guaranteeing interested persons participation or requiring party responses to requests for information, and those that clearly remain softly cooperative and seem to be more about relationships than about law. The latter are being established on a bilateral basis but they do not appear preferential in the sense of triggering WTO rules. This is to say that a lighter form of cooperation may not qualify as a measure. If WTO rules cannot be invoked, then it is hard to conclude that any legal compatibility issues arise for the

---

71 *Ibid.*, Art. 129.3.   72 EU–Korea agreement, Art. 11.11(a) and (b).   73 *Ibid.*, Art. 11.12.
74 WTO Agreement on Subsidies and Countervailing Measures, Art. 25.

multilateral trading system. Between these two elements of preferentialism and legality, we can configure the possible combinations as follows:

– preferential and legal;
– preferential and non-legal;
– non-preferential and legal;
– non-preferential and non-legal.

If the WTO compatibility issue is only raised by the first category of preferential and legal measures, one can conclude that there are occasional points of process operating even within otherwise multilaterally applied regulatory policies that raise the possibility of preferential incompatibility with WTO rules and the multilateral trading system. Examples provided in the section above included preferential transparency notifications and dispute settlement provisions. An example that is preferential but perhaps straddles the line on legality is the non-tariff measure instrument found in the EU–Korea agreement. This is a softer law instrument (mediation) but with potential for having legal effects in the resolution of non-tariff barriers between Parties. Such a resolution may be multilaterally applied or may be specific to the product issue of the other party and preferential. This is not to suggest that the instrument is necessarily 'reachable' on an MFN claim in the WTO, but that its legal results may be.

It is also clear that the analysis repeatedly turns on the scope of the relevant WTO MFN provisions and the scope of GATT Article XXIV. For the latter, guidance is derived from WTO case law. Those arguing a broad scope for the Article XXIV exception must emphasize the liberalizing character of the trade agreement provisions in question, as in Article XXIV.4's statement that the purpose of a free-trade area or customs union is to liberalize trade between the constituent parties and not to raise barriers to the trade of non-members. Thus, anything in a trade agreement that assists liberalization while not harming non-members should fall within the exception granted by Article XXIV. A simple difficulty with this approach is that paragraph 4, 'contains purposive, and not operative, language'.[75] The legal requirements for an Article XXIV 'defence', which establish the scope of the Article XXIV exception, are actually located in paragraphs 5 and 8 of the Article.[76] This view of the regional exception may appear restrictive to some given the arguably liberalizing elements of new approaches possible for treating administrative participation, transparency, technical regulations and IP enforcement systems, and for the various arbitral possibilities to resolve non-tariff barriers. However, it also describes the WTO law

75 The Appellate Body, in reversing the panel's application of an 'effective interpretation' which gave a legal effect to paragraph 4. *Turkey – Restrictions on Imports of Textile and Clothing Products*, WT/DS34/AB/R, para 57.
76 *Turkey – Textiles, ibid.*, at para 58: 'that the measure at issue is introduced upon the formation of a customs union that fully meets the requirements of sub-paragraph 8(a) and 5(a) of Article XXIV'.

'as it is' and respects a principle that exceptions be narrowly rather than broadly construed.

One can finally identify an issue regarding the scope of Article XXIV as to institutional processes more generally. We tend to view the regional exception as dealing with substantive policies, first identifying a measure that is a GATT Article violation and then examining the possibility that the violating measure is eliminating either a tariff duty or an 'other restrictive regulation of commerce' (ORRC). We thus consider that what is 'necessary' for elimination between the regional parties is granted an exception by Article XXIV. What is suggested here is that if the policy is redeemed by the scope of elimination of duties or ORRC as applied, then the complementary processes to achieve that elimination would also fall within the exception. Thus, for example, a regional dispute settlement process to ensure the elimination of duty according to the agreement's schedule would understandably also fall within the Article XXIV exception. For an example contrary, if an enhanced regional participation policy for addressing non-tariff barrier product standards was found to violate GATT Article I (as applied to matters covered by Article III.4) and not validated as falling within the scope of ORRC, then it would seem to follow accordingly that the processes facilitating that enhanced participation would also not find validation under Article XXIV.

IV. Trade in services

All the agreements have fairly extensive chapters dealing with international trade services. In order to isolate the processes involved, they are treated here by considering, in turn, generally applicable provisions treating origin, transparency, regulatory cooperation, and then the distinctive processes relating to sectoral treatment. The point has been made by others that policies addressing liberalization in an economic integration agreement (EIA), centred as they are on domestic regulatory changes, tend to be less preferential in final effects than the comparable treatment of preferential border taxation which governs liberalization for trade in goods agreements.[77] Further, even if these domestic regulation regimes might provide for superior preferential treatment, the rules of origin provisions of GATS Article V.6 require services agreements (for a developed-country partner) to provide its benefits to juridical persons constituted under the laws of a regional party with 'substantial business operations' within the territory. This is understood to limit the preferential effect that could otherwise be generated by imposing national control and ownership rules as a condition of origin.[78]

---

[77] P. Sauvé and A. Shingle, 'Reflections on the Preferential Liberalization of Services Trade' (2011) 45 *Journal of World Trade* 5, 953–63, 958–9. Although, agreements on trade in goods also treat regulatory issues.

[78] Sauvé and Shingle, *ibid.*, 959–60. The lack of restrictive origin rules may offset the preferential nature of a first mover advantage for network and infrastructure service sectors. See also, P. Latrille and J. Lee, 'Services Rules in Regional Trade Agreements – How Diverse and How Creative as Compared to the GATS Multilateral Rules' (2012) WTO Staff Working Paper, ERSD-2012–19, 15–17.

This suggests that while there is much attention in economic integration agreements to domestic regulations and their processes, the ability to render them preferential is arguably more limited and a more multilateral liberalization occurs as a matter of course. Thus, the approach here is to survey the selected agreements for their origin rules and their accompanying 'denial of benefits' provisions to confirm that compliance with GATT Article V.6 is or is not the on-going practice. Two caveats are noted. First, an open origin rule for enterprises does not pre-judge whatever preferential possibilities of regulatory benefits might occur when accorded to 'parties' to the agreements rather than to their operators. In those cases, how a party chooses to extend those benefits or represent enterprises of its choice would be more a matter of domestic law and practice than a matter governed by the origin definitions of the trade agreement.[79] Second, an open origin rule does not say anything about whether there may be territorial characteristics that would limit the ability for non-party enterprises to establish substantial business operations in a party territory. If a party maintains restrictions on foreign ownership of domestic enterprise sectors, foreign operators are not going to be established as substantial business operations in the territory no matter what the origin rule says in the trade agreement.

A. Service provider origin

The US agreements follow the GATS V.6 origin rule with some variations, allowing denial of benefits for service supplies of the other party, whether controlled or owned by a non-party, when the denying party does not maintain diplomatic relations with the non-party[80] or 'normal economic relations' with the non-party,[81] or the denying party maintains a prohibition on transactions that would be circumvented by granting the benefits of the services chapter. These conditions have more the sense of security or economic sanction exceptions. The rest of the denial of benefits provisions are made subject to the substantial business operations rule and are not more restrictive than GATS V.6.[82] The EU agreements also have a general definition for 'juridical person' that denies that status for a registered company not engaging in substantial business operations in the territory.[83] Except as perhaps otherwise modified in more specialized sections of the agreements, the preferential character of the

---

79 This also depends on whether the agreement is given direct effect in domestic law.
80 US–Panama agreement, Art. 11.11.   81 KORUS agreement, Art. 12.11.
82 The KORUS agreement has some difficult phrasing on this requirement where the placement of the word 'or' could also suggest that non-ownership or control is alone sufficient to deny the benefit. 'A Party may deny the benefits of this Chapter to a service supplier of the other Party if the service supplier is an enterprise owned or controlled by persons of a non-Party *or* of the denying Party that has no substantial business activities in the territory of the other Party.' Latrille and Lee do not however note this agreement as one deviating from the GATS V.6 rule. Supra note 78, 16–17.
83 EU–CARIFORUM agreement, Art. 61(e); EU–Korea agreement, Art. 7.2(f)(i), with a notation permitting an 'effective and continuous link' as equivalent to substantial business operations.

provisions in the services chapters have an inherently 'porous' character, allowing benefits to be extended to non-party operators with substantial business operations in one of the parties.

B. Transparency and regulatory cooperation for services

The EU agreements follow the form of providing a 'regulatory framework' section (or chapter),[84] containing 'provisions of general application', which include mutual recognition and transparency, with the EU–CARIFORUM agreement containing an article for procedures, and in the EU–Korea agreement, articles for domestic regulation and governance. Regulatory aspects are then put in detail for particular service sectors.[85] The US agreements place these regulatory topics in their respective chapters for cross-border services and both of them include transparency, domestic regulation and mutual recognition. Separate annexes then treat the sectors.[86]

1. Transparency

EU agreements provide for response to requests by parties, but the EU–Korea agreement goes on to refer to the rights of applicants to be informed of the status of an application and the reasons for denial. A time provision is also inserted requiring an authority to rule on a pending application within 120 days or provide notification to the applicant.[87] US agreements establish mechanisms for responding to inquiries from interested persons. The agreements then vary; the KORUS agreement requires a party to address in writing the reasons for not allowing advance notice and opportunity for comments on proposed regulations, while the Panama agreement indicates that at the time of final adoption, a party shall (to the extent possible) also address in writing the substantive comments received from interested persons. The variations in these provisions, as subtle as they may be, raise again the question of whether this kind of treatment can be bifurcated in respect of the different parties' rights with a common signatory, and if not, then how is the baseline (assumedly the more liberal) treatment to be accorded to all?

2. Domestic regulation

The subject of domestic regulation is covered in three of the agreements. The US agreements are nearly identical; both compel applications to be decided within a reasonable time, and recite a portion of GATS Article VI.4, ensuring that

---

84 EU–Korea agreement, Section E, Arts. 7.21–7.24; EU–CARIFORUM agreement, Chapter 5, Arts. 85–7.
85 These include for both of the EU agreements, computer, postal and courier, telecommunications, financial, maritime transport and E-commerce. The EU–CARIFORUM agreement has an additional section for tourism services, not covered here.
86 US–Panama agreement, Chapter Seven, Arts. 11.7–11.9; KORUS agreement, Chapter Twelve, Arts. 12.7–12.9. The US agreements' annexes treat financial services, telecommunications and electronic commerce.
87 EU–Korea agreement, Art. 7.22 (4–6).

qualification requirements, *et. al.*, shall not constitute unnecessary barriers to trade. Any results from WTO negotiations related to Article VI of the GATS shall be incorporated into the trade agreement.[88] The EU–Korea agreement tracks these provisions nearly verbatim, with some additional recitation from GATS Article VI.[89] Because these agreements add nothing to the material that is already provided in GATS Article VI, they have no preferential character, other than that they adopt the proposed disciplines of Article VI.4(a–c) as operative between the parties.[90]

3. Recognition

The two EU agreements and the KORUS agreement follow a very similar approach to recognition of certificates and qualifications for professional services. They encourage the professional associations to develop recommendations on mutual recognition, and for the trade committee of the agreement to review and approve those recommendations if consistent with the agreement. The parties (or the appropriate bodies) then go on to negotiate a mutual recognition agreement.[91] The EU agreements both indicate that any recognition negotiated will be in conformity with GATS Article VII, which requires notification and the possibility for other WTO Members to join the negotiation and potentially join the agreement.

One can imagine that this area could be quite fruitful for preferential treatment if an institutional process was set in motion with the authority to obtain results. However, the processes involved here are highly voluntary, and while perhaps results will be derived over time from these encouraged relationships, they certainly have little if any preferential traction based on the provisions alone. If agreements are realized and not relegated to the GATS Article VII process (the EU agreements appear to pledge notification according to GATS Article VII), then there would be a different preferential discussion to be had over whether GATS Article V can accommodate recognition within its requirements and thereby excuse the regional parties from violating the GATS Article VII participation rights of other WTO

---

88 US–Panama agreement, Chapter Seven, Art. 11.8; KORUS agreement, Chapter Twelve, Art. 12.7.
89 EU–Korea agreement, Section E, Art. 7.23.
90 Whereas GATS Art. VI refers to future disciplines with those elements. It has been noted that the US agreements extend the disciplines to services other than those subject to commitments. Latrille and Lee, supra note 78, 27–8. The absence of ambitious domestic regulatory treatment in the US and EU agreements with Korea has been discussed elsewhere. E. Laurenzo and J. Mathis, 'Regulatory Cooperation for Trade in Services in the EU and US Trade Agreements with the Republic of Korea: How Deep and How Compatible?' (2013) 14 *Melbourne Journal of International Law* 1, 171–204.
91 The US–Panama agreement does not have professional service recognition provisions. Slight differences among the EU agreements include the identification of priority sectors in the EU–CARIFORUM agreement (architecture, engineering and tourism), and establishment of a working group for recognition in the EU–Korea agreement. Generally, EU–CARIFORUM agreement Art. 87; EU–Korea agreement, Art. 7.21. The KORUS agreement provisions for professional service recognition are found in ANNEX 12 – A to the cross-border services chapter.

Members. At least for these agreements and the results obtained thus far, that discussion is premature and may remain so for quite some time.[92]

C. Sector treatment

The regulatory material in the sectoral annexes or sections is too plentiful to detail for the purposes of this chapter. What can be expediently done is to apply the rule of origin analysis discussed above to determine whether the scope of origin and the denial of benefits provisions apply generally through the sectoral agreements.[93] To the extent that they remain 'open' in the sense that the GATS Article V.6 definition is respected, then we can say that for the benefits extended on behalf of economic operators, the sectoral agreements continue the MFN liberalizing demeanour. The same caveats made above for benefits extended to parties rather than operators and for any domestic limitations on the establishment of foreign providers apply here as well.

1. Financial services

Both US financial services annexes expressly incorporate definitions (or other provisions) from the cross-border services chapters. Both incorporate the denial of benefit definitions and therefore apply the substantial business operations test without a nationality or control requirement. The EU agreements refer to financial service suppliers and define that term as any natural or juridical person of a party seeking to provide services.[94] A juridical person is defined by the general services chapter definitions and, as noted above, the agreements incorporate the substantial operations test as per GATS Article V.6.

2. Telecommunications

The US annexes do not have an express incorporation provision and cross-border chapter definitions would therefore apply unless otherwise modified, including the denial of benefits provision, which is not modified by the telecommunications annex. Benefits of the annex are extended to 'service suppliers of the other party' which in the KORUS agreement is defined as a party that is either a covered investment in the territory of the party or a person of the other party that seeks to supply or supplies services in or into the territory.[95] This definition appears consistent with the general definition applied in the cross-border services

---

92 This is not to say that the subject of qualifying MRAs under GATS Art. V has not otherwise been raised. See for example, C.M. Cantore, 'How Does It Feel to Be on Your Own? – Mutual Recognition Agreements and Non-discrimination in the GATS: A Third Party's Perspective' (2010) 11 *German Law Journal* 11, 706. For a discussion of whether GATS Article XVIII might serve to qualify MRAs under GATS V, see Mathis, supra note 44, 84.

93 Also for expediency, and unless stated otherwise, only the US and EU agreements with Korea are used for this sectoral section.

94 EU–Korea agreement, Art. 7.37.   95 KORUS agreement, Art. 14.24.

chapter.[96] The EU sections for telecommunications also do not modify the general definition of suppliers.

3. Electronic commerce

The annexes or sections of both US and EU agreements refer to the WTO Agreement on electronic commerce and prohibit the charging of customs duties on deliveries by electronic means. Neither agreement provides definitions of origin for digital products, although the KORUS agreement annex incorporates any relevant provision of the cross-border services chapter.[97] However, if that electronic commerce is about products rather than service providers, the origin concepts from the general services chapters would not apply. Rather, the origin rules from the chapters on goods would apply. Thus, to the extent that regulatory provisions in the electronic commerce sections here could be preferential in character, discrimination may not be diffused by the porous nature of services origin rules. The EU electronic commerce section sets out a dialogue for regulatory cooperation and closes the section with a listing of general exceptions as also found in GATS Article XIV and GATT Article XX. There is no highly beneficial preferential treatment being accorded here by either party.

4. Additional sectors, EU–Korea agreement

The other sectoral sections are not covered in US annexes so only the EU sections are reviewed.[98] These sections include computer services, in which a set of agreed-upon definitions, but not referring to the origin of the services or their providers, is established; and postal and courier services, in which a three-year period to set out a regulatory framework for competition in those markets is established. Maritime services are accorded non-discrimination (national treatment) status on behalf of ships flying the flag of the other party or operated by service suppliers of the other party. Even if a party is accorded its flags on the basis of nationality, the general service supplier definitions would apply to allow operators with substantial business operations in the territory to have access to the provisions in this section.

D. Trade in services conclusion

This is an admittedly brief pass over a very extensive subject area that contains a large number of different party processes. As limited to a survey of the applicable origin rules, the results here for general subjects and sectoral treatment support the MFN thesis, that the regulatory subjects and the processes open to operators are not being established on the basis of restrictive origin rules. Since this section has not treated party benefits explicitly, no conclusion is rendered on any aspects that only benefit the parties rather than the service providers. For example, the section has not detailed

---

96 *Ibid.*, Art. 12.13.   97 *Ibid.*, Art. 15.2.
98 EU–Korea agreement, computer services from Art. 7.25 and maritime services from Art. 7.47.

any dispute settlement provisions in favour of parties. On mutual recognition, we see the commencement of a process rather than a mutual recognition agreement. If and when such agreements flow from the processes established, they will either be notified under GATS Article VII or they will not be. To the extent they are not, then the opinion here is that a GATS violation can be framed that is not salvageable by a reference to the exceptional requirements of GATS Article V.[99]

V. Conclusion

While this inquiry has located some points of likely or possible preferential regulatory treatment, the results are necessarily ambivalent both for those identified as preferential and for those found not to be so preferential in character. This is for two reasons. First, as noted in the introduction, there is not sufficient secondary source material describing the way domestic agencies actually implement regulatory provisions. Thus, while one can identify the possibility of preferential transparency provisions in favour of interested persons of another party, this still does not say anything about what actually happens in the application of those rules and whether domestic treatment is ever bifurcated or not.

Second is the somewhat opaque nature of deep integration provisions themselves. It is evident that the purpose of the regulatory agreements in many instances is to frame expectations for the future rather than to prescribe applicable legal regimes. The term 'soft law' comes to mind when a provision is located that is firm in obligation but soft in content (or the other way around). But sometimes even soft law is absent, suggesting that the regulatory relationships may not be about law at all, but rather about creating (again) 'frameworks of expectations'. Sometimes one discerns that the nature of the expectation framed may ultimately result in a legal act, an analysable measure if you will. At other times it seems that no legal result of any kind is intended and that the expectation to be realized is to 'discuss' and 'cooperate'.

This puts the question of compatibility with the multilateral trading system in a slightly different light, suggesting that the exercise of assessing compatibility could be somewhat premature. That a later assessment might bear more legal fruit would be based on an optimistic view that the regulatory processes in these agreements might result in identifiable legal acts or regimes. If one takes the more pessimistic view that the agreements have only a low potential to realize legal results, then another conclusion comes forward. This would hold that the question of compatibility with the multilateral trading rules is irrelevant because the agreements are too weak to cross the initial threshold of providing anything for those multilateral rules to examine.

---

99 One argument to consider for the GATS Art. V scope to include MRA's within its exception is by reference to GATS Art. XVIII for 'Additional Commitments', which is also located in Part III of the GATS for 'Specific Commitments'. See for discussion, Mathis, supra note 44, 85–6.

The view here is that the regulatory agreements are generating both low and high sets of expectations and that more could be coming in the way of legal outcomes from these processes. It is also likely that what we perceive now as the 'state of the art' moves along over time. One can imagine stronger mediation instruments to address non-tariff barriers, additional participation rights for private actors and stronger mutual recognition processes. These types of process enhancements would present more interesting compatibility issues for the multilateral trading system.

For now, what can be said of the regional regulatory processes and the multilateral trading system is that while some of them might translate well to a larger group exercise in the WTO, they instead remain exclusive to the bilateral relationships established by the trade agreement parties. If non-party WTO Members might wish, for whatever reasons, to be a part of those processes, the mechanisms for opening or duplicating them for the larger group will have to be commenced by WTO Members themselves. To the extent they choose not to engage with more advanced regulatory processes in the larger club, this omission will also contribute to widening a gap of compatibility as regulatory regionalism continues to develop.

PART IV

Legal aspects of PTAs: A comparative analysis

8

Agriculture

TIMOTHY E. JOSLING

I. Introduction

Agricultural trade is regarded as a sub-category of trade in goods for the purposes of bilateral, regional and multilateral trade agreements. But in virtually all such agreements, it is subject to special treatment. This treatment in bilateral and regional trade agreements can range from exclusion from the schedule of tariff reductions to import restrictions by quota over a transition period, and often includes specific safeguards and new institutions such as committees to which problems can be referred. In multilateral agreements specific treatment for agricultural products has also been the rule: exceptions for primary products were included in the General Agreements on Tariffs and Trade (GATT 1947) and an Agreement on Agriculture was negotiated in the Uruguay Round that perpetuates the special treatment of the sector.

The reason for such exceptional treatment lies in the sensitive nature of agricultural imports. Most governments share a concern for the security of their country's food supply and the level and stability of the income of their rural sector. This concern has translated itself in importing countries into caution about relying on imports for basic foodstuffs and a conviction that protection from overseas competition is necessary for the health of the rural economy. Those countries with export potential in the agriculture sector have long decried such sentiments, arguing that they can provide a regular supply of foodstuffs at lower prices and that supporting inefficient domestic production is not a sound basis for development. But, as one might expect in a sector where governments still have considerable control over markets, negotiations to open up trade in farm products have tended to proceed at the pace of the most reluctant importers.

Within the past two decades, this cautious attitude towards trade in farm goods has begun to give way to a more confident approach that sees imports as complementary to domestic production and exports as a natural extension of domestic markets. Consumers are becoming used to the greater choice of foodstuffs that comes with trade, and producers are setting their sights increasingly on foreign markets for new sources of revenue. Developed countries still have 'sensitive' sectors that, for political reasons, need to be sheltered, from both local and global competition. Developing countries, too, are concerned about opening up markets and putting their own producers' livelihoods at risk. But even in these cases regional and bilateral trade agreements are slowly constraining the ability of governments to maintain a high level of protection for agricultural producers.

For the purposes of this chapter, a distinction will be made between Regional Trade Agreements (RTAs) and Bilateral Trade Agreements (BTAs).[1] Regional Trade Agreements involve more than two countries and are generally concluded among countries in the same geographical region. Such RTAs share a number of characteristics that make them of interest in the area of agriculture. They are reciprocal, involving trade liberalisation by all parties, though some have different treatment for low-income partner countries. This reciprocal nature implies that agricultural sectors are inevitably brought into the complex trade-offs that are needed in a regional negotiation. Indeed, RTAs often have an underlying rationale of increasing regional cohesion and political integration, making the treatment of the agricultural sector of interest beyond the commercial advantage. Food security can be enhanced and economic stability improved by co-ordination of food policies and marketing infrastructure. Export patterns are often similar, limiting the immediate impact of regional liberalisation on agricultural trade flows, but trade possibilities are enhanced by proximity to markets. Of the two types of RTAs, those that involve a common external tariff (Customs Unions) and those where the members retain their existing external tariffs (Free Trade Agreements (FTAs)), agricultural problems tend to be easier to solve in the latter. External protection can remain the province of domestic authorities. But in FTAs, rules of origin are necessary to prevent excessive trade deflection. As agricultural products are often undifferentiated, making such rules of origin enforceable or effective is not always easy.

Bilateral Trade Agreements include those between two countries that may or may not be in the same region. These BTAs also usually include reciprocal obligations, though often phased to avoid problems in one or other party. Such bilaterals are commonly aimed directly at expanding trade between the countries concerned, though sometimes have a political rationale in addition. Agriculture poses both problems and opportunities in BTAs. Relations between the bilateral partners are often asymmetric, with smaller countries seeking assured access into larger markets, while the larger country is likely to be able to shelter sensitive import-competing sectors and to impose an agreement that favours its export interests. Thus BTAs

---

1 Also of relevance to agricultural trade are Preferential Trade Agreements (PTAs) that involve asymmetric obligations. These usually grant non-reciprocal market access into the preference-giving country. Commonly such preferences are granted by developed countries seeking to assist certain developing countries to expand or maintain their exports. However, such access is often constrained when sensitive domestic industries (such as agriculture) are involved. Generalised preference schemes offered by industrial countries to most developing countries (GSPs) and the asymmetric treatment of Least Developed Countries within the WTO and by some developed countries are also forms of PTA. Agricultural trade is often constrained under these schemes. However, this chapter only discusses reciprocal free-trade agreements (RTAs and BTAs).

involving a country that is a significant agricultural exporter will inevitably have provisions for improved market access for those goods.[2]

An examination of the treatment of agriculture in regional and bilateral trade agreements (RTAs and BTAs) suggests certain patterns. It is likely to be easier for agriculture to be fully included in an RTA if the parties to the agreement have similar production costs (whether high or low). Regional trade partners are more likely to have similar climatic and soil constraints and thus have similar production patterns, though disparate policies and production structures can lead to different cost structures among neighbours.[3] This gives the incentive for some degree of co-ordination within the region to take advantage of specialisation and scale opportunities and to avoid conflicts. For those regional groups with sufficient political cohesion, there is a tendency to develop common polices for agriculture (including a common level of tariff protection), but many such common policies lack operational significance. Bilateral trade pacts, by contrast, do not appear to venture down the path of common policies for agriculture. Production patterns are likely to be different, leading to greater possible gains from trade (trade creation) and less possibility of sheltering high cost production within the bilateral agreement (trade diversion).

One of the issues in evaluating trade agreements for their consistency with WTO rules (specifically with Article XXIV of GATT 1994) is their product coverage. Article XXIV requires 'substantially all trade' to be covered, and the level of preference to be 100 per cent. Though there has as yet been no firm agreement on the interpretation of 'substantially all trade', agriculture is the sector most often excluded or treated differently. A simple measure of the difference between the inclusion of agriculture and manufacturing tariff lines in discriminatory trade agreements is given by the relative margin of preference (RMP) ratio. The striking difference in the sectoral coverage as given by this measure is shown in Figure 8.1, drawn from a WTO Secretariat presentation on RTAs.[4] Manufactures are far more likely to benefit from tariff reductions in RTAs than are agricultural goods. On the other hand, the prospect of competing exporters challenging the exclusion of agriculture in an RTA is remote: they benefit from the exclusion. And exporters within the RTA have implicitly agreed to the exclusion, and would be reluctant to make a challenge against a partner in respect of mutually agreed decisions.

How have sensitive sectors of agriculture been protected from competition from regional and bilateral partners? A review of the various ways that agriculture has been treated shows that this is most often done by quantitative restrictions on imports. On some occasions the sensitive sector is excluded altogether. More

---

2 BTAs are usually in the form of free-trade agreements rather than customs unions. One party (or both parties) to a BTA can itself (themselves) be an RTA.
3 The original six countries of the EEC differed in their costs, but were able to offset this by adopting a high level of protection that was geared to the least efficient.
4 Roberto V. Fiorentino, 'Regional Trade Agreements and the WTO: Theory and Practice of WTO Provisions on RTAs', Presentation given to Workshop, Rome, 10–14 October 2005.

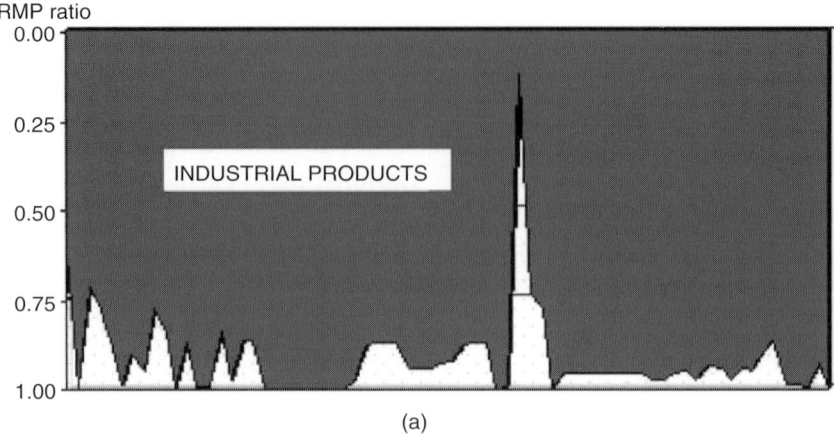

(a)

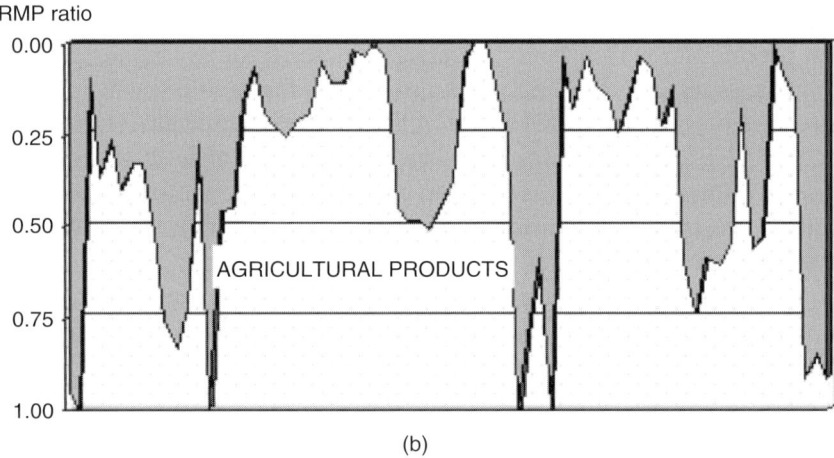

(b)

Figure 8.1   Comparison of the depth of liberalisation of industrial versus agricultural products

frequently, the tariff on imports from partners is reduced more slowly than that for other goods.[5] This chapter explores how the issue of agricultural trade is addressed in regional and bilateral trade agreements. The first section looks at regional trade agreements, grouping them by continent. The second section discusses bilaterals, particularly those being negotiated by the European Union (EU) and the United States (US). A third section looks at the prospects for future regional trade agreements and networks among such agreements in regard to the inclusion of agricultural trade.

5 Typically, the tariff schedule of each partner is divided into categories (A, B, C, etc.) corresponding to different reduction paths.

II. Agriculture as an issue in regional trade agreements

This brief survey focuses on the emergence of RTAs since the 1950s in the major trading regions of the world, Western Europe, the Americas, Africa and Asia, and their treatment of agricultural trade. It does not try to be comprehensive: instead it illustrates the range of ways that agricultural trade has been incorporated into these regional trade agreements.[6]

A. Agriculture in the RTAs of Western Europe

One of the first regional trade agreements of the modern era was the economic union between Belgium and Luxembourg (BLEU) that came into effect in 1922.[7] This pact integrated the smaller Luxembourg economy into the larger Belgian market and included bilateral free trade, the adoption of the Belgian external tariff, the use of the Belgian franc in Luxembourg and the development of common institutions. Agriculture was a problem area for the formation of the Union, as Luxembourg feared direct competition from Belgian farmers.[8] Special payments were made to Luxembourg farmers to compensate for the reduction of prices and later that country was allowed to re-impose quantitative limits on farm imports from Belgium.

The agricultural problems of the BLEU were exacerbated when the Netherlands entered the Union in 1948. The Benelux Union faced the problem that Dutch agriculture was more efficient than that of its partners. As a result, import restrictions were allowed within the Benelux market as an exception to free internal trade and the three countries essentially ran their own agricultural policies. The Netherlands continued to argue for the full inclusion of agriculture into the free trade zone, and it was eventually agreed that by 1962 the three countries should have a common policy and agricultural goods would circulate freely between Belgium and Holland, though the Luxembourg market was still protected. A fund was set up for adaptation of agriculture in the region, in essence to help Belgian and Luxembourg agriculture

---

6 One region not discussed below is the Middle East. This does not imply that there has been no activity in this region. For example, in February 1997, the Arab League launched a free-trade programme, known as the Greater Arab Free-Trade Area (GAFTA), in which member states were asked to come up with specific commitments regarding elimination of tariffs, non-tariff measures and rules of origin. GAFTA currently has seventeen member states. In the area of agriculture, the programme offered members the opportunity to suspend tariff reductions on some produce during the peak harvest seasons. Each GAFTA country was allowed to submit ten produce items for tariff suspension. So far, ten GAFTA countries have submitted a list of thirty fruits and vegetables. The exclusion of certain agricultural products during the crop/harvest seasons for the full transitory period of ten years will however substantially limit the trade creation effect. Within GAFTA, a sub-group of countries with strong trade ties to the EU (Jordan, Egypt, Tunisia and Morocco) negotiated the Agadir Agreement in 2004 that does include considerable liberalisation of agricultural trade.

7 The nineteenth century was a period of extensive regional trade agreements, in the absence of any multi-lateral framework for trade rules. Most of these agreements were shattered by the events leading up to World War I.

8 Michael Tracy, *Government and Agriculture in Western Europe*, 3rd edn (Hemel Hempstead: Harvester Wheatsheaf, 1989), at p. 243.

compete with the Dutch producers.[9] But events overtook this experiment in economic integration, as the three Benelux countries joined the European Economic Community (EEC) in 1957, and their agricultural policies were subsumed in the Common Agricultural Policy (CAP) of the EEC.

1. The EEC/EC/EU

The countries of continental Western Europe experimented in the 1950s with deep political and economic integration. In the context of rapid reconstruction of the war-torn economies, this regional integration played a strong role in the recovery of the European economies, and led directly to the formation of the EEC. Decisions made at that time with respect to the treatment of agriculture have had a lasting effect on Western Europe and on the world trading system.

The lessons of the Benelux Union were fresh in the minds of the architects of the EEC. The Spaak Report of 1956, which formed the basis for the Treaty of Rome that set up the EEC in the following year, emphasised the necessity to include agriculture in the common market. This was intended both to gain the advantage from the rationalisation of Western European farming and to make the EEC acceptable to the agricultural exporting countries (France, the Netherlands and Italy) in exchange for allowing German industrial products access into their markets. The Treaty established the principle of free movement for farm goods within the internal market but mandated 'market organisations' at the EEC level, at the insistence of the French, to manage the competition. The price for free internal trade was adequate external protection against third country imports (known as 'Community Preference').

The formation of the EEC in 1957 set the scene for the integration of Western European agricultural markets. A common market organisation (CMO) was developed for each of the main commodities. Administered prices were related to a 'target' price level for each commodity. Imports were only allowed in at 'threshold' price, calculated on the basis of the target price and transport costs, and excess production would be taken off the market at 'intervention' prices again fixed relative to the target price.[10] Prices were to be set each year by the Council of Ministers on the proposal from the European Commission.

The CAP was a major part of the EEC, and in fact was one of the few active 'common' policies (as opposed to the more passive removal of internal barriers to trade). The CAP dominated the work of the Commission, the spending of the common budget and the foreign trade policy of the emerging EU for its first three decades. Later, the CAP became a 'safe haven' against the instability of world market prices, but by the 1990s it proved increasingly difficult to sustain this isolation.

---

9 *Ibid.*, at p. 245.
10 This terminology was used for the cereal market regime: some differences in instruments and nomenclature were introduced in the other commodity marketing organisations.

European integration has developed by 'widening' the EU to encompass new members as well as 'deepening' to embrace new functions. In the act of widening, the full incorporation of agriculture was maintained though progress was vastly complicated by the existence of the CAP. The countries of Central and Eastern Europe included agriculture fully in the Baltic Free Trade Area (BFTA) and in a more limited way in the Central European Free Trade Area (CEFTA), both intended as precursors to EU membership by the countries concerned. The Europe Agreements that aimed for free trade between the Central and Eastern European countries and the EU also included agriculture, initially with quantitative limits on products that threatened the operation of the CAP. Even these restrictions were relaxed as the process of integration developed. These countries became members of the EU, in May 2004, and they fell within the orbit of the CAP and thus their agricultural sectors have been essentially absorbed into that of the EU.

2. EFTA

The role that agricultural trade played in the architecture of post-war European integration is shown by the contrast between the EEC and the European Free Trade Association (EFTA), concluded in 1960 by seven of the countries that had opted out of the EEC. The position of the UK as a large importer of agricultural products from the British Commonwealth conflicted with the desire of the Six to expand internal trade behind tariff walls. Other countries (Sweden, Finland, Austria and Switzerland) had high-cost farming sectors as a result of climate or topography and did not wish to compete directly with Dutch or French producers. So the EFTA countries chose to exclude agriculture (and fisheries) from the free-trade provisions. Each country was able to maintain its own agricultural policy, through its tariff provisions and domestic support.[11]

The decision to leave agriculture (and fisheries) out of the EFTA agreement led to the exclusion of the sector from the terms of the European Economic Area (EEA), the set of bilaterals that the EU negotiated with the EFTA members as a way of keeping them compatible, in terms of economic regulation and price levels, with the EU. The EEA allowed free trade in manufactured goods and co-operation in regulatory issues: in effect it extended the previous bilaterals to include several aspects of trade that had been incorporated in the 1992 Single Market. Though some quotas on agricultural goods were expanded, there was no progress toward the incorporation of the rural sector in economic integration such as would have been stimulated by enlargement. The EFTA countries still did not have a say in EU decisions, and thus were unable to influence regulations that would apply to them. The political stance of neutrality that had prevented several EFTA countries from having too close a tie with the EU countries became of less importance with the end of the Cold War. So, before the

---

11 A side agreement guaranteed access for Denmark to the British market for pigmeat products and limited quantities of dairy goods.

ink was dry on the EEA, Sweden made the decision to apply for full membership, and three other EFTA countries followed suit. Thus, with the entry of Austria, Sweden and Finland into the EU in 2004. EFTA currently comprises Norway, Iceland, Switzerland and Liechtenstein, and the exclusion of agricultural products in the market access provisions has been maintained.

B. Agriculture in the RTAs of the Americas

1. LAFTA

Agriculture played a lesser role in the development of regional trade agreements in Latin America. The sector was largely excluded from the Latin American Free Trade Area (LAFTA) that was formed in 1960 and covered most of the subcontinent.[12] LAFTA, though in some respects following the European model, chose a quite different integration strategy. Rather than agreeing that all tariffs and trade barriers on internal LAFTA trade would be abolished, subject to a negotiated 'negative list', the decision was taken to offer a 'positive list' of sectors that would benefit from free trade. Not surprisingly, agricultural products were virtually absent from the list of sectors to be liberalised. Countries with export interests in farm products were not able to persuade their trade partners to open up their markets. Manufactured trade expanded in the region for the first few years, before also succumbing to the reluctance of countries to open their borders.

The nature of economic development in South America has tended to emphasise trade across the water rather than by land. Old colonial trade patterns linked port cities with European destinations. Development of internal transportation emphasised the movement of goods to the ports. The stimulus for the LAFTA came from the prevailing economic view of the early 1960s, as articulated by the Economic Commission for Latin America (ECLA) under the intellectual guidance of Raul Prebisch. This view held that trade with the industrial countries of Europe and North America was on increasingly disadvantageous terms, as prices for agricultural exports fell relative to the manufactured imports. It followed that industrialisation through import substitution was the key to economic development. Regional trade agreements fit into this pattern of development by promising the realisation of some economies of scale in the development of protected industries, through their location in one or more trade partners.

The timetable for liberalisation of trade in LAFTA slipped, and countries withheld offers to liberalise the sectors which were most sensitive. Agriculture was singled out as a sector which was not appropriate for liberalisation. The attitude towards agriculture reflected the generally prevailing development paradigm for the region. Import substitution in areas of manufacture was seen as the main thrust of trade

---

12 The seven original signatories were: Argentina, Brazil, Chile, Mexico, Paraguay, Peru and Uruguay. Colombia and Ecuador joined in 1961, followed by Bolivia and Venezuela.

policy, along with attempts to raise and stabilise the prices of raw materials on world markets. Regional import substitution was thus the aim of free-trade areas. Agriculture remained an exportable good, usually controlled by para-statal institutions and often taxed for revenue purposes. Intra-regional agricultural trade did not fit easily into this paradigm. Perhaps as a result of a misreading of the experience of the European Communities (EC), the inspiration for much of the economic integration in the 1960s, agriculture was not considered an essential part of a free-trade area.[13]

Andean Pact The Andean Pact (AP) arose from dissatisfaction with the workings of the LAFTA. There was a general feeling that the largest part of the benefit of the LAFTA had fallen to the largest countries, namely Argentina, Brazil and Mexico. The smaller economies were not receiving the benefits of industrial development, as both political weight and economic market size tended to pull these new industries to the big three countries. In addition, the poorer countries felt that making offers of tariff reductions in favour of the larger and richer nations would be exposing their own nascent industries to dangerous competition. As a result, Chile, Colombia, Bolivia, Ecuador, and Peru set up another trade group in 1969, known as the Andean Pact, which they felt was more suited to their own economic conditions. Attempts were made to avoid incompatibilities between the Andean Pact and LAFTA, but the effect was a mortal blow to the place of LAFTA in regional economic policy.

The Cartagena Agreement (1969), which established the Andean Pact, stated that the objectives of the AP should extend 'beyond' trade liberalisation to promote capital-intensive projects and to facilitate regional economic planning. Trade among the countries of the Andean Pact was to be free of all customs duties. The process of liberalisation was to be 'automatic and irrevocable' and include all products. Total liberalisation was initially set for the end of 1980 'at the latest', though this was extended for three years by the Lima Protocol of 1976.[14] A Common External Tariff was also to be agreed. Venezuela joined the AP in 1973, and Chile left in 1976.

Free trade among the AP countries was supposed to include agricultural products. However, in practice, the governments of the region chose not to allow agricultural goods to be traded freely. One of the first acts of the Andean Pact Commission was to enter a list of exceptions to free trade, including meat, dairy products, fruit, vegetables, cereals, rice, seeds, tobacco, hides and skins, timber, wool and cotton. Most countries in the region had centralised purchasing and marketing structures for the basic agricultural products. Rigid price controls had been the norm, and countries were reluctant to allow regional trade to undermine the control of the domestic market. Agriculture in most of the AP countries was adversely influenced by

---

13 It was sometimes stated in discussions of Latin American integration that the EC had excluded agriculture from free internal trade (see, for instance, Sidney Dell, *A Latin America Common Market?* (New York: Oxford University Press, 1966)); in fact, there was no exemption from the free movement of goods internally in the case of agriculture, as mentioned above.

14 Beverly M. Carl, *Economic Integration Among Developing Countries: Law and Policy* (New York: Praeger, 1986), at p. 227.

restrictive government polices, including export taxes and the effect of overvalued exchange rates. Investment was therefore discouraged in the domestic sector, whether for export or local consumption. Foreign foodstuffs, particularly from the US, were often underpriced as a result of macroeconomic policies. Some agro-industrial activities were sponsored under the Andean Multinational Enterprise scheme.

The Andean Pact recovered some of its momentum in the 1980s and developed, among other activities, a Common Agricultural Policy. The Presidents of the AP countries, meeting in La Paz, Bolivia in November 1990, indicated that the Andean Common Agricultural Policy would include the following elements: the equalising of conditions for competition in sub-regional markets; a stronger boost for joint development programmes; the adoption of sole stands in international forums; a common system for the treatment of food donations; the harmonisation of export incentives and policies and of mechanisms for stabilising the cost of imports from third countries; the progressive elimination of elements leading to price distortions; the consolidation of the free trade zone; and the strengthening of health activities. Such plans were by no means without substance. An Andean Pact price band to stabilise domestic prices was introduced, though not all countries adopted it. In effect, the AP (now the Andean Community) became primarily a vehicle for trade policy between Colombia and Ecuador and Venezuela: Bolivia and Peru were increasingly impacted by the economies of the Mercado Commun del Sur (MERCOSUR). Venezuela became a member of MERCOSUR in 2005 and chose to leave the AC in 2006 (in part as a reaction to the closer trade ties between the AC members and the US).[15] The current membership of the AC includes Colombia, Ecuador, Bolivia and Peru.

2. MERCOSUR

The most significant step in recent years towards trade integration in the region has been the creation of MERCOSUR (the Common Market of the Southern Cone), in 1991. MERCOSUR negotiations were initiated in the mid-1980s by Argentina and Brazil, building upon an earlier agreement between those two countries. The four original members were Argentina, Brazil, Paraguay and Uruguay. This pact is one of the new 1980s variety of trade agreements that emphasised free internal trade over the *dirigiste* planning of the internal market, and emphasises the need for a low common external level of protection to prevent the cosseting of uncompetitive domestic industries.

The objectives of MERCOSUR are the acceleration of economic growth in the region by establishing free trade within its borders, and by co-ordinating economic policies for further integration. The Treaty of Asuncion aimed for the elimination of both tariff and non-tariff internal trade barriers by 1994, and the adoption of a Common External Tariff. The free internal market was delayed, but now covers 90

---

15 Venezuela's full membership of MERCOSUR was completed in 2012.

per cent of intra-bloc trade: the common tariff was agreed in 1994 and came into operation in 1995. The common tariff was set between zero and 20 per cent for most goods. A list of exceptions to the free internal trade has been drawn up, and some of these have yet to be removed. Macroeconomic instability and political tensions have also hindered the integration of the MERCOSUR economies. Some harmonisation of standards has already taken place, and discussions have taken place on such trade issues as investment protection, antidumping and intellectual property rights. Though eventually envisioned, the free movement of labour and capital has not yet been achieved.

Among the countries of the MERCOSUR, agricultural trade is nominally free. MERCOSUR has relatively few provisions that apply specifically to agriculture. Two reasons are likely to account for this relatively liberal treatment of agriculture. First, MERCOSUR includes major exporters of temperate agricultural products, each of whom would like to strengthen their agricultural industry and promote regional exports. Second, as a result of sweeping structural reforms, the countries concerned have eliminated many of the state marketing monopolies that previously controlled trade.[16] This, together with the reduction of subsidies and support prices, has allowed a fuller incorporation of agriculture within MERCOSUR than in many other RTAs.

In the case of MERCOSUR there was no real alternative to including agriculture in the provisions of the free trade treaty. Brazilian farmers were initially anxious about competing with the Argentinean producers, who had higher yields and lower costs, but this concern proved groundless. Argentina had removed many agricultural programmes that would have interfered with free trade, including the National Grain Board, the National Meat Board and the sugar and tobacco boards. Brazil also removed the government monopoly on wheat marketing and trading, and cut producer subsidies in 1991, though Brazil retained many programmes for price regulation, and government storage. Uruguay still controls the import and export of wheat, but in general participates in regional agricultural trade. Paraguay, somewhat more remote from the coastal ports and transportation hubs, sells less of its products overseas, and is largely dependent on internal trade with MERCOSUR and Andean Pact countries. Agricultural trade issues have arisen largely over the widespread use of export taxes in Argentina and some recent protectionist measures in Brazil.

Agriculture is thus a significant feature in intra-bloc agricultural trade in MERCOSUR, as contrasted with the situation in the Andean Pact. This gives it much more potential importance in trade policy developments in the region. But in addition, the fact that member countries are significant exporters to the rest of the

---

16 Argentina removed export taxes on agricultural goods, long a source of government revenue, in 1991. A small tax on oilseed exports remained, together with a fee to pay for research. Argentina has essentially liberalised imports of agricultural goods, though some export taxes have reappeared in recent years.

world complicates relationships with other trade blocs, such as the North American Free Trade Agreement (NAFTA) and the EU.

3. CUSFTA/NAFTA

As a first step in the direction of greater market integration in North America, Canada and the US signed an FTA in 1987 that took effect in January 1989. This agreement, the Canada–United States Free Trade Agreement (CUSFTA), liberalised trade between two countries of similar income levels who were already each the largest trading partner of each other. It was relatively easy to agree on a set of mutually agreeable steps to remove trade barriers.

Agriculture was included to the extent that it created no political problems. This meant essentially that Canada was able to exclude its supply-managed sectors, primarily dairy and poultry, which were managed largely by provincial marketing boards. Neither the US nor Canada wished to face the task of harmonising marketing systems for these products, and it was felt that the operation of the boards required control of all imports, including those from the US. As a result, the integration of these sectors was delayed. However, cereal trade did benefit from an agreement in the CUSFTA to allow imports from the other partner if the level of protection on the domestic market was not higher than that in the partner country. As a result of fluctuations in support levels over the first two years, trade barriers were essentially removed on grains moving across the border.

The request by Mexico to have a trade agreement with the US posed more significant problems for agriculture. In June 1990, Mexico initiated negotiations with the US, and in February 1991 these negotiations were expanded to include Canada. By August 1992, negotiations for a free trade area between the three countries were announced as completed. The agreement was subsequently ratified by the legislature in all three countries and went into operation on 1 January 1994.

Agricultural trade was evident in the motives for NAFTA negotiations. The US looked to gain market access in Mexico for grains and livestock products: Mexico wanted to be able to increase sales of fruits and vegetables in the US and reduce the chance that US trade barriers and health and safety standards would not be used to restrict such trade. On the other hand, Mexican growers of corn, in particular those in the low-productivity *ejido* sector, feared that US grain would sweep them out of business, and fruit and vegetable growers in Florida (and to a lesser extent, California) were concerned that their own sales into the US market would be undercut.

NAFTA set in progress the removal of all trade barriers to goods moving between countries in North America, and freed up trade in services except where sensitive regulatory issues precluded agreement. The time period for most sectors to achieve market integration was ten years, though the markets for some sensitive agricultural products were given fifteen years to adjust. NAFTA also set up some common institutions for settling disputes, and includes protocols on labour conditions and environmental legislation. A fund was established to help Mexico improve environmental conditions, in particular in border regions.

Agriculture figured prominently in both the NAFTA negotiations and the debate over the ratification of the final agreement. As in the CUSFTA, it is one of a small number of sectors that is given the attention of a separate Chapter (Chapter Seven). The Chapter was structured to include a trilateral component, of relevance to all three countries and all agricultural commodities, and two separate bilateral trade agreements covering US–Mexico and Canada–Mexico agricultural trade. The general free-trade provisions of NAFTA (Market Access) apply to all trade, including agricultural trade, and the schedule of tariff reductions, along with the conversion of non-tariff barriers to tariffs, is contained in an Annex to that Chapter.[17] With few exceptions, all agricultural tariffs are subject to elimination on the schedules agreed in the NAFTA accord. The schedule of tariff reductions identifies categories of products subject to different rates of reduction.

As from the date of entry into force of the Treaty, no agricultural non-tariff barrier can remain unless specifically allowed by the GATT (under Article XI) or specifically included in the NAFTA text. Existing non-tariff barriers were converted into tariffs, as specified in the new tariff schedules, with tariff-rate quotas as agreed in the negotiations. Each country declared and was granted a set of exceptions to the provisions of the NAFTA.

The trilateral component of the agricultural agreement was relatively modest. It anticipated the existence of a GATT agreement in the Uruguay Round that was to cover the same areas of trade policy. It contains a statement on market access, that 'Parties shall work together to improve access to their respective markets through the reduction or elimination of import barriers to trade between them in agricultural goods', leaving the main action in this area to the bilaterals. Under Article 703.3, countries can invoke 'special' safeguards for selected (national) lists of commodities, representing the items judged to be most import-sensitive.

On domestic support, the NAFTA also contains the injunction to 'endeavor to work towards domestic support measures' that have minimal trade distorting effects, or that would be exempt under a future GATT agreement (the so-called 'Green Box' policy instruments). However, it recognises the right of Parties to change domestic support measures subject to GATT obligations. This light treatment of a contentious area enabled negotiators to say that they were not altering domestic policy.

On export subsidies, the text states that Parties 'share the objective of the multilateral elimination of export subsidies for agricultural goods' and promises cooperation in the GATT to this end. However, the zeal for multilateral elimination of such policies does not extend to their internal use. Article 705.2 of the NAFTA

---

17 The Agriculture Chapter, however, has priority over the Agreement's 'general' chapters where they affect the agricultural sector. If there is an inconsistency in tariff provisions between Chapter Three (Market Access) and Chapter Seven (Agriculture), the latter chapter prevails.

merely holds it 'inappropriate' for a Party to grant export subsidies on sales to another Party unless the importing country is benefiting from export subsidies paid by other countries.[18] In other words, matching EU export subsidies in Mexico is allowable by the US and Canada, until such practices are stopped multilaterally. Indeed, if the exporting and importing parties agree to an export subsidy on intra NAFTA trade, such a subsidy is allowed. This no doubt was included to take account of the considerable importance to the US of retaining the means to stay competitive with EC export subsidies in the Mexico market.

The trilateral agricultural agreement also set up some institutional mechanisms for administering the arrangements (a Committee on Agricultural Trade) and a new committee for dealing with private disputes (an Advisory Committee on Private Commercial Disputes regarding Agricultural Goods). The FTA Panel Review process is extended to include Mexico, adding procedures to be followed to address non-compliance or negation of a NAFTA Panel Ruling.

The trade aspects of NAFTA were included in three bilateral pacts and one trilateral agreement. The US–Canada bilateral pacts essentially continued the modest market opening in agricultural products that had been in the CUSFTA of 1986. An opening of the cereal trade across the Canadian border was ingeniously tied to the level of relative protection: neither side could maintain quantitative import restrictions if its own support level was higher than that of its neighbour.[19] Fluctuations in the level of support did in fact open up the grain trade, as both partners lost the right to protect their market in the first few years of the agreement. Attempts to integrate the US–Canada meat market proved less successful, and both pork and beef have been the subject of numerous bilateral disputes over the years. The sensitive sectors of dairy and poultry ('milk and feathers') were deliberately left off the table in the US–Canada talks, and so trade between the US and Canada in these products remained restricted in the NAFTA.[20]

In sharp contrast to the cautious approach taken in the US–Canada bilateral, the US and Mexico decided on a bold initiative to move to a tariff- and quota-free market for all agricultural goods. Instead of permanent exceptions for sensitive products, long transition periods were agreed to put off for up to fifteen years the full impact of free access. For Mexico, the longest transition period was reserved for corn and beans, and for the US the sensitive products included citrus and tomatoes.

For sugar, the US and Mexico negotiated a complicated path toward free access into the US market by the end of fifteen years. Mexico retained its quota of 7,258 tons of raw sugar. If Mexico produced a surplus (at that time imports exceeded exports) a

---

18 This is much softer language and treatment of export subsidies than was found in the CUSFTA where the use of export subsidies between the two countries was banned.

19 For this comparison the Producer Subsidy Equivalent (PSE) was used, though as it included direct payments, it was not the ideal measure of trade advantage.

20 Canada's bilateral agreement with Mexico mirrored that with the US: imports of dairy and poultry products were not included in the liberalisation schedules, but Canada gained access to the Mexican market at a rate similar to the US.

fixed amount of sugar, set at 25,000 tons, could enter the US duty free for each of the first six years. Thereafter, the quantity increased annually, jumping to 150,000 tons in the seventh year and rising by 10 per cent thereafter. If, however, Mexico should become a consistent net exporter of sugar, as actually happened, then the quantitative restrictions would eventually be removed altogether. The prospect of a single sugar market between the US and Mexico in 2008 was of concern to cane sugar producers in the US South and to other sugar producers throughout the States. Just as the Everything But Arms (EBA) agreement in the EU put pressure on the internal sugar regime (and the traditional preferred suppliers overseas) so the free importation of Mexican sugar could eventually erode the effectiveness of the high-price regime for sugar in the US.

Central America Five Central American countries agreed to form a free-trade area in June 1958, the Central American Free Trade Area. Two years later this was strengthened to become the Central American Common Market, under the General Treaty of Central American Economic Integration. The founding members were Costa Rica, El Salvador, Guatemala, Honduras and Nicaragua.[21] Panama was admitted first as an observer and then attained the status of a full member in July 1991. The CACM flourished in the 1960s, floundered in the 1970s and practically disappeared in the 1980s. By 1970, the members had liberalised 94 per cent of intra-regional trade, and 80 per cent of external trade was subject to a common external tariff. After 1970, political problems among the members, as well as domestic strife within many of them, caused intra-bloc trade to decline.

The push toward regionalism has revived in Central America in recent years, as in other parts of Latin America. In 1990 the treaty was resuscitated and the decision was made to move to a common market by the end of 1992. The tariff rates on internal trade were to follow. A schedule was established of 5, 10, 15 and 20 per cent tariffs on different categories of inter-bloc imports. Most agricultural products traded within the CACM were to be free of duties by the end of 1991, with the rest being removed by June 1992.[22] Thus intra-bloc free-trade was finally to be extended to include agriculture.

As with the countries of the Andean Pact and MERCOSUR, the region of the CACM is on balance an exporter of agricultural products. Such exports declined slowly in the last decade although periodic booms in coffee prices interrupted this trend in 1994. Along with the reduction in exports of agricultural produce there has been a rise in imports of agricultural products, associated with the modest growth in the region. Fruit and vegetables constitute the major export items, along with sugar. Cereals and live animals are imported into the region.

There are however some significant differences between the situation in Central and South America. Central America is tied by trade links more closely to the US than

---

21 Honduras left in 1967 and rejoined in 1991.
22 Augusto De la Torre and Margaret R. Kelly, *Regional Trade Agreements*, IMF Occasional Paper No. 93 (Washington, DC: IMF, 1992), at p. 7.

are the countries to the south. The economies, being small, are relatively open: with trade amounting to 80 per cent of GDP in Costa Rica, 50 per cent in Honduras, El Salvador and Nicaragua, and 40 per cent in Guatemala. Well over 40 per cent of all trade is with the US. Twenty per cent of regional exports go to the EU, mainly coffee and bananas, and 11 per cent of imports come from Europe. Thus the security of trade pacts with the US and the EU has been a major aim of the region. The successful completion of BTAs with the US (see below) has provided a stronger basis for developing export sectors and diversifying the product composition.

4. CARICOM

The Caribbean Common Market (CARICOM) was established by the Treaty of Chaguarmas in 1973, to replace the Caribbean Free Trade Area (CARIFTA) of 1968. The original membership of CARICOM included Barbados, Belize, Dominica, Grenada, Guyana, Jamaica, Montserrat, St Kitts and Nevis, St Lucia, St Vincent and the Grenadines, and Trinidad and Tobago. Antigua and Barbuda, and the Bahamas joined in 1983, and the British Virgin Isles and the Turks and Caicos Islands became associated with CARICOM in 1990. Belize and Suriname also have become members. Within the CARICOM there exists another free-trade grouping, the Organization of East Caribbean States (OECS), which includes seven of the smaller island members of CARICOM; Antigua, Dominica, Grenada, Montserrat, St Kitts, St Lucia and St Vincent. These countries established the East Caribbean Common Market in 1968, a prelude to the OECS Treaty of 1981. Recent developments in CARICOM have included the plans for a single internal market and a judicial body. Uneven country size and income levels have hampered the region in its quest for true integration but efforts continue in this direction.

The countries of the Caribbean region are among the most open of economies, and among the smallest in the hemisphere. Prior to gaining political independence and statehood these countries exported a limited range of traditional crops and imported not only manufactured products but significant proportions of their domestic food supply. The colonial legacy is still evident in the trade statistics today. Trade is heavily oriented towards the European market, in particular the UK. Trade with the US is large, but the volume of agricultural exports to that country is overshadowed by the imports of US temperate zone farm products. The US and the EC are the source of more than 55 per cent of CARICOM's imports and receive more than 60 per cent of its exports. There is a small but growing trade with Latin America, particularly as a destination for CARICOM's exports.

Agricultural commodity trade has traditionally been the lifeblood of the Caribbean economies. With few exceptions, agricultural trade has been critical to the overall development of the economy. Agricultural exports provide more than 75 per cent of the foreign earnings for four of the Caribbean states and greater than 40 per cent for all but three of the states. The direction of agricultural export trade is strongly linked to the preferential trade agreements enjoyed by the region. In the case of the US these agreements come under the US Sugar Act and the Caribbean Basin Initiative (CBI). The former sets quotas on the amount of sugar that can be exported into the US market, while the latter eliminates import duties on a broad cross-section of imports from CBI countries. In the case of the EU the preferences were enshrined in successive Lomé Conventions, and subsequently in the Cotonou Agreement under which the Caribbean exported sugar and bananas at preferential rates. The Cotonou Agreement led to the negotiation of an Economic Partnership Agreement that subsumes the existing market access for these countries in the EU but adds reciprocal preferences for EU goods in the Caribbean countries.

These preferential arrangements have been economically advantageous to the Caribbean. According to a World Bank study, 'in the period 1980–1986, preferential arrangements relating to sugar were worth an average of US$90m per year to Caribbean countries, and those relating to bananas an average of US$28 million per year.'[23] For bananas this benefit accrues mainly to the Commonwealth Caribbean. However, for sugar the benefits extend to the Dominican Republic, which in terms of both volume and value accounts for approximately 54 per cent of the region's sugar exports to the US.

The Caribbean Basin Economic Recovery Act, which gave substance to the CBI, was passed in the Congress of the United States in July 1983. The CBI is an integrated programme incorporating aid, trade and investment provisions promoting greater economic co-operation between the US and the Caribbean Basin countries (twenty-one islands in the Caribbean and seven Central American countries). Trade expansion is considered a centrepiece of this agreement and is promoted through the elimination of US import duties on all but selected categories of imports from CBI countries. In August 1990, the CBI legislation was extended indefinitely.

C. Agriculture in Sub-Sahara African RTAs

Africa has a long history of RTAs, dating back to the desire to preserve some of the trade patterns among countries that had developed before independence. The goal of an African Economic Union has been espoused over the years. The reality, at least for agriculture, is that trade has not expanded along with the growth of RTAs. Trade patterns are still dominated by exports to the EU and by imports from European and American sources. Internal African food trade has been hampered by all manner of problems from political conflicts to inadequate roads. However, several trade agreements have emerged, not least as a result of the need to negotiate more effectively with outside institutions. Some of these are mentioned below.

---

23 World Bank, *Caribbean Region: Current Economic Situation, Regional Issues and Capital Flows*, 1992 (Washington, DC: World Bank, 1993).

1. ECOWAS

West Africa has had extensive experience in negotiating and operating free trade areas and customs unions among countries in the region. The first of these regional trade groupings stemmed from the early days of independence and followed the structures set up by the colonial authorities. Several francophone countries joined together to form in 1959 the West African Customs Union (UDAO/WACU) to preserve the customs union that had existed from before independence. Members of this group were Benin, Burkina Faso, Côte d'Ivoire, Mali, Mauritania, Niger and Senegal. They not only inherited a free-trade area but also benefited from a single currency tied to the French franc. The UDAO treaty called for common institutions and harmonisation of tax legislation, but proved to be too ambitious. The UDAO evolved in 1966 into the less demanding Customs Union of West African States (UDEAO/CUWAS). Trade at first rose rapidly within the UDEAO, but then fell back somewhat. Non-tariff barriers began to re-emerge, prompted by problems over the distribution of benefits within the region.[24] The UDEAO had virtually collapsed by 1972, when it was reorganised into the West African Economic Community (CEAO/ WAEC). The CEAO enjoyed some success, but intra-bloc trade fell from 11.6 to 6.5 per cent of total (recorded) trade between 1983 and 1986. Non-tariff barriers re-emerged and the external tariff was never harmonised.

In 1975, the members of the CEAO joined with Nigeria and other English-speaking countries in the region to form ECOWAS. These included the three countries that had formed the Mano River Union (MRU) in 1973, Guinea, Liberia and Sierra Leone, as well as Gabon, the Gambia, Ghana, Guinea-Bissau and Togo. This grouping of almost 200 million people aimed initially at liberalising the trade in agricultural and handicraft trade, to be followed later by manufactured trade liberalisation, the removal of non-tariff barriers and the establishment of a common tariff. The Economic Community of West African States (ECOWAS) also sought to promote 'harmonisation' of agricultural policies, including export price structures, and to curb (unofficial) trade in these commodities among member countries.

Agricultural trade is of paramount importance to the ECOWAS countries, but most of that trade is in tropical products for the European market. Intra-bloc trade in agricultural products is spasmodic, seasonal and often moves against the wishes of the authorities. Much of this illicit trade is an attempt to circumvent the normal marketing channels, usually run by parastatal marketing agencies. Some is 'normal' patterns of trade superimposed on 'artificial' national boundaries. Estimates of the extent of unrecorded trade reach as high as 30 per cent of recorded (total) trade, and would thus bring the level of intra-bloc trade up to that achieved for some other trade areas. Much of this unrecorded trade is in agricultural goods, responding to seasonal

---

24 For a discussion of the problems of these agreements, see Ulrich Hiemenz and Rolf J. Langhammer, *Regional Integration Among Developing Countries: Opportunities, Obstacles, and Options* (Teubingen, Germany: Westview Press, 1990).

production fluctuations, climatic advantage and arbitrage possibilities. Until this trade can be transformed into legal, sanctioned economic transactions, the ambivalence of authorities toward such activities will always impede liberalisation.

The ECOWAS treaty places particular emphasis on the need for policy co-operation in agriculture. Unlike many regional RTAs, the Lagos Treaty calls explicitly for a Common Agricultural Policy (Article 35). This policy is to co-ordinate the exploitation of natural resources in the area, as well as share research findings and harmonise internal and external agricultural policies. The ECOWAS Commission has produced a number of proposals and reports on the implementation of this policy, but as yet, little action has been taken.

2. CEEAC

In Central Africa, the Equatorial Customs Union (UDE/ECU) started in 1959, was replaced in 1966 by the Central African Customs and Economic Union (UDEAC/CACEU). The six members, the Republic of Cameroon, Central African Republic, the Republic of the Congo, Chad, Equatorial Guinea and Gabon, were francophone countries with relatively strong economies and the advantage of a history of monetary co-operation. The UDEAC aimed to set up a full customs union and set a timetable for the reduction of duties on regional trade. However, member states were allowed to introduce other barriers to intra-bloc trade. Intra-bloc trade stagnated, a victim of general slowdown in trade and reduction in income levels. More recently, an attempt has been made to expand and strengthen the agreement and encourage intra-bloc trade. This entailed the adoption of the Treaty establishing the Economic Community of Central African States, (CEEAC/ECCAS) in 1983. Besides the UDEAC countries, signatories included the members of the Economic Community of the Great Lakes Countries (CEPGL), the three former Belgian colonies of Burundi, Rwanda and Zaire, whose own free-trade area had been unsuccessful at generating internal trade flows, and the former Portuguese colony of São Tomé e Principe. CEEAC aimed for a free-trade area over a period of twelve years, with the final stage being the establishment of a customs union. As with other similar groupings, the timetable proved optimistic, and trade barriers still remain among the countries.

The CEEAC countries have experienced declining sales of agricultural produce over the years, while total merchandise exports have risen steadily. The countries concerned have somewhat similar agricultural conditions and production patterns. Expanded trade in the region is unlikely without a renewed effort to reduce the administrative and political impediments to market integration.

3. EAC, PTA and SADC

Trade agreements are somewhat less numerous in Eastern and Southern Africa. In East Africa, the East African Community (EAC) was established in 1967 to take over from the colonial common market that had existed before independence. The EAC, with members Kenya, Tanzania and Uganda, also comprised a monetary union and had a common tariff against third countries. The EAC finally broke up in 1977, unable to reconcile political differences between the members. More recently, two overlapping but rather different economic groupings have developed in southern and eastern Africa. In 1980, a number of states formed the Southern African Development Co-ordination Conference (SADCC), aimed at co-ordinating development in the region. Membership was primarily the States bordering South Africa, and had as an aim the reduction in dependence on transport facilities in that country. SADCC co-ordination extends to infrastructure, including transportation systems, and to agricultural research. It has proved attractive to donor organisations as a way of avoiding competing development strategies in the various member countries. The members created a new body, the Southern African Development Community (SADC), to extend operations more into trade matters.

More orthodox as a trade grouping, the Preferential Trade Area for Eastern and Southern African States (PTA) was set up in 1982 to promote liberalised trade, albeit with rules of origin which favour local manufacture. Members of the PTA include Burundi, Comoros, Djibouti, Ethiopia, Kenya, Lesotho, Malawi, Mauritius, Rwanda, Somalia, Swaziland, Tanzania, Uganda, Zambia and Zimbabwe. The original plan called for a common market by 1992, but few parts of the liberalisation schedule have been adopted. A wide dispersal of incomes makes market opening difficult. The decision by the SADCC countries to extend their co-operation in the trade area put the two blocs in potential conflict. The PTA, after a slow start, has expanded in membership and scope. Renamed COMESA in 1994, it now includes among its members Libya and Egypt, as well as nineteen other countries in the region.[25] However, the free-trade area only involves eleven of these countries, and ten of the COMESA members are also part of SADC.

Agricultural exports have been slipping in recent years, along with a general weakening of total merchandise exports. A sharp rise in agricultural imports over the past decade has eliminated the net exports from the region. Though one would not expect a high degree of intra-bloc agricultural trade in such a widely scattered region, opportunities undoubtedly exist for expanded commerce.

4. SACU

The South Africa Customs Union (SACU) has functioned for over ninety years among South Africa and the states in the immediate area. These presently include Botswana, Swaziland, Lesotho and Namibia. South Africa is the dominant economy, and the smaller states rely on that country for most of their trade. SACU is active in negotiating bilateral agreements, and this may have a positive impact on the development of the region as a whole. Agricultural trade is well integrated in the region, though each country still has autonomy in agricultural policy.

---

25 Two countries (Namibia and Swaziland) are members of the South African Customs Union (SACU). Tanzania has closer ties with the SADC countries, as well as a trade agreement with SACU.

D. Agriculture in the RTAs in Asia and the Pacific

1. ANZCERTA

The Closer Economic Relations Trade Agreement between Australia and New Zealand (ANZCERTA) came into effect in January 1983. It replaced an earlier agreement, the New Zealand–Australia Free Trade Agreement that had been introduced in 1966.[26] The first agreement had been somewhat limited in scope, covering a narrow range of manufactured products and trade in forest products.[27] The objectives of the ANZCERTA, besides broad co-operation in economic matters, included the removal of trade barriers between the two countries on an agreed timetable. Agriculture was to be included in the process of trade liberalisation, though some of the more difficult issues of parastatal marketing bodies were to be postponed.

A review of the working of the ANZCERTA in 1988 led to an acceleration of the process of liberalisation, and set the date of July 1990 for the removal of remaining tariff and non-tariff barriers. In addition, export subsidies on intra-bloc trade were to be removed, and many service sectors were included in the free-trade area. A further review was held in 1992, which added several new elements to the increasingly liberal economic relations between the two countries. The ANZCERTA takes the two countries further towards effective market integration than the NAFTA agreement in North America, though by no means as far as the EU.

One aspect of the ANZCERTA that is notable is the extent to which agricultural trade is now fully incorporated. The countries are major agricultural exporters. The product mix of exports is somewhat similar, reducing the scope for trans-Tasman trade, but there are natural trade flows based on climatic differences, such as sales of Australian wheat to New Zealand and exports of New Zealand dairy goods to Australia. These flows were hampered by tight restrictions on trade as a part of domestic marketing legislation. It took a bold political decision, coupled with a significant reduction in the power of the marketing agencies, to allow trade in agricultural products to flow freely.

2. ASEAN

The formation of ASEAN in 1967 was a manifestation of the desire to improve co-operation in a volatile region of the world. Such co-operation was more successful in the security than in the economic area. Though Singapore, in particular, had pushed for a free trade area, Indonesia was unwilling to travel as far in the direction of regional integration. At the Bali summit meeting in 1976 the leaders of the ASEAN

---

26 There had been earlier, unsuccessful attempts to establish a free-trade area between Australia and New Zealand in the 1870s. New Zealand even considered joining the new Australian federation when it was formed in 1901. In the 1920s, the two countries granted each other mutual preferences as members of the British Empire: see Peter J. Lloyd, *The Future of CER: A Single Market for Australia and New Zealand*, Monograph No. 96 (Committee for Economic Development of Australia, Melbourne, and Institute for Policy Studies, Wellington, 1991), at p. 18.

27 *Ibid.*, at p. 12.

nations expanded the scope of their co-operation to include regional tariff preferences (Preferential Tariff Arrangements), allowing intra-bloc imports to enter at a
lower tariff rate, as well as promoting industrial development through ASEAN
Industrial Projects and private firm co-operation on complementary ventures. The
five founder members of ASEAN (Indonesia, Malaysia, the Philippines, Singapore
and Thailand) were joined by Brunei in 1984 and more recently by Myanmar,
Cambodia, Laos and Vietnam.

The lack of a commitment to free internal trade left ASEAN without a strong
economic objective. The list of goods falling under the PTA expanded, but still
covered only a small share of the members' total trade. Increases in intra-bloc trade
have been small, due in part to the heavy reliance by countries on administered
protection, and the continued opposition of local interests threatened with increased
competition.[28]

With the renewed interest in regional trade liberalisation in recent years, an
attempt has been made to turn ASEAN into a free-trade area along the lines of
those in other regions. A plan for an ASEAN Free Trade Area (AFTA) was
agreed by the six governments in 1992, with the objective of eventual free
internal trade. Countries agreed to reduce tariffs on industrial goods and processed agricultural products on intra-ASEAN trade to a level of 0–5 per cent by
2008. The reductions are to be operationalised by establishing a Common
Effective Preferential Tariff (CEPT) for each country that will be reduced on
the basis of an agreed schedule. These tariffs are to be reduced to 20 per cent in
the first eight years, with the remaining reductions coming in the final seven
years of the transition. The reduction of non-tariff barriers to trade in manufactures is also mandated. However, expansion to include the four less developed
economies has delayed realisation of the AFTA. Currently the target date for the
completion of the free trade area was 2010 for the six more advanced members
and 2015 for the remaining four. Though there has been an expansion in
agricultural trade, many agricultural goods, foodstuffs and other primary products are still excluded from full liberalisation within ASEAN.[29]

Agricultural trade is important to the countries of ASEAN. The countries of the
region account for 85 per cent of the world's rubber exports and 80 per cent of
the palm oil trade, as well as significant quantities of copra and other raw materials.
Agricultural trade within the region is less significant, though Singapore relies heavily
on neighbouring countries for food supplies. Vulnerability to shortages of agricultural products on world markets has always been a concern of ASEAN countries. This
aspect of agricultural trade was tackled in 1979, with the establishment of an
emergency food stockpile, to which all would in principle contribute and from

---

28 Dean A. DeRosa, *Regional Trade Arrangements among Developing Countries: The ASEAN Example*,
   Research Report 103 (Washington, DC: International Food Policy Research Institute, 1995), at p. 3.
29 *Ibid.*, at p.4.

which each could withdraw in times of need. The initial stockpile consisted of 50,000 tons of rice, a small but useful reserve in times of shortage.[30]

The ASEAN region is a net exporter of agricultural products, with rising agricultural exports keeping ahead of rising imports. ASEAN countries have been active members of the Cairns Group (advocates of more open agricultural markets), the Group of 20 (agricultural exporters) and the Group of 33 (primarily agricultural importers). They can be expected to continue to push for further trade liberalisation at an international level, with an emphasis on maintaining policy flexibility at home. There is no doubt that increased trade among these countries would also be possible if agricultural liberalisation were to be fully included in the AFTA.

III. Agriculture as an issue in bilateral trade agreements

In contrast to the treatment of agriculture in RTAs, the way in which agriculture is treated in BTAs is a little more straightforward. RTAs grapple with the problem of the regional development of agriculture, balancing the benefits of rationalisation and efficiency against the interests of producers likely to be under pressure. Most BTAs have little interest in the development of regional agricultural competitiveness, but involve more the direct commercial exchange of goods, including agricultural products. The extent to which these BTAs include agriculture, then, is predominantly a matter of whether one or the other partner has specific commercial interests in such trade.

The nature of the agricultural component of BTAs can broadly be gauged by the policy of the largest of the trade partners: size of market allows considerable scope for setting parameters at an early stage in the talks. Thus there is a difference between BTAs negotiated with the EU and those with the US, and these are in turn different from those that involve China or Japan. The US has been persistent in arguing for the inclusion of agriculture in the BTAs that it has negotiated, and most of its negotiating partners have concurred, subject to safeguards and transition periods. However, the US has also been concerned to shelter some of its own sensitive sectors, such as sugar, from open competition in BTAs. It has negotiated bilaterals with Chile, Central America, Colombia, Peru, Panama, Dominican Republic and Australia that give those countries preferred, though not free, access to US agricultural markets (see below). Negotiations with countries that are not major suppliers of agricultural goods, such as Morocco, Jordan, Korea, Singapore and Kuwait, have generally been easier to conclude and have only marginally impacted agricultural trade.

The EU has been more defensive in its approach, and is often under pressure by the negotiating partner to include agricultural products more fully in the BTA. The EU gives limited access to sensitive agricultural products to the many countries that have signed such agreements, including the Mediterranean countries, the ACP, South

---

30 However useful this reserve is, it has rarely been used.

Africa and Mexico, as described below. Negotiations with MERCOSUR, that have been put on hold for the duration of the WTO Doha Round, were also approaching an agreement involving specific access to EU markets for grains, oilseeds and live-stock products from South America.[31]

Japanese BTAs are even more cautious than those involving the EU with respect to entry of farm products. Negotiations on the bilateral with Mexico stalled for many months on the issue of imports of pig meat and oranges from Mexico. Eventually, the Japanese market was opened by a series of tariff rate quotas for beef, chicken and oranges and a reduction of tariffs for pig meat and orange juice. Japan has also negotiated a bilateral with Thailand (2007), an efficient regional producer of rice and some other agricultural goods. Several farm exports to Japan are covered by the agreement, albeit with transition periods: free trade in rice, dairy products and wheat is not included. Japan has also agreed to lower trade barriers to many agricultural exports from the Philippines, under a BTA which came into effect in 2007, but the sensitive sectors of rice and sugar are not included in this agreement. An agreement between Japan and Chile will eventually allow imports of most of Chile's agricultural products, but these are generally not in competition with domestic production. The Japanese BTA with Singapore was not hampered by issues of agricultural trade. In addition to bilaterals with other regional countries, Japan has trade agreements with India, Switzerland and Peru: in none of these cases was free access given to sensitive domestic farm products. Current negotiations with countries such as the US, Canada, New Zealand and Australia (see below) are likely to challenge this protection. On the other hand, the launch of talks with the EU in March 2013 poses somewhat less of a challenge to Japanese farmers.

Korea has also negotiated a number of BTAs, often with the same countries as has Japan. Agriculture is even more of a sensitive issue in these agreements. Korean farmers have successfully argued that they cannot compete with imports. Thus, when Korea and ASEAN agreed an FTA in 2006, Thailand declined to sign the agreement, and has continued to argue for a significant tariff-rate quota (TRQ) for its rice exports to Korea. The bilateral with Chile has an emergency clause for agricultural products. Korea signed a bilateral with EFTA that went into effect in 2006 which excluded agricultural products. The bilateral with Singapore was similarly painless for agri-cultural interests. Discussions have been underway with Canada for several years, and are still stalled on issues related to access to the Korean market for livestock products and to the Canadian market for cars. Meanwhile, an FTA with the EU came into effect in 2011 that opened up trade in many agricultural products, though not for rice. Negotiations with the US were concluded in April 2007, but had to wait until 2011 for

---

31 This is made easier by the negotiation of tariff-rate quotas (TRQs) in the Uruguay Round that assured continued access for those countries with negotiated quotas. Allocation of TRQs allowed in WTO schedules to preferred partners is a main link between the multilateral and discriminatory trade regimes. These allocations appear contrary to the spirit of Article XIII of the GATT, which indicated that the distribution of quotas should be non-discriminatory and reflect market conditions.

Congressional ratification. This includes some limits on market access for sensitive products and minimal liberalisation in the case of rice.

China has also been active in negotiating bilateral trade pacts with countries in the region and beyond. Unlike Japan, China has considerable export potential in agricultural products. Tariffs on farm imports into China are in general lower than in many other countries in the region. So, one condition of a trade agreement with China appears to be that agricultural trade is included. The negotiation of an FTA between China and ASEAN, that came into effect in 2010, included improved market access for many agricultural goods. Indeed, agricultural trade was designated as one of the 'Priority' areas for trade expansion. This followed an earlier partial BTA with Thailand, signed in 2004, that also emphasised agricultural trade. Indeed, Thailand experienced a surge in agricultural imports from China, leading to concerns about the impact of exchange rates and of the possibility of subsidies to Chinese export sectors. Agriculture was included with few exceptions in the China BTAs with Chile (2006), Pakistan (2007), New Zealand (2008) and Peru (2010), though none of these countries represented a major threat to Chinese agricultural plans. Negotiations with India, currently under consideration, may be particularly difficult with respect to agriculture. Concerns with a rapid expansion of Chinese exports are already being expressed by Indian farm interests.

India itself has become a desirable partner for a trade agreement. Besides the talks with China, India has concluded a BTA with ASEAN (as well as with several ASEAN countries individually). Agricultural sensitivities have proved a problem, with both sides introducing 'negative lists' of goods to be excluded from liberalisation. Tropical products, particularly palm oil, rubber, coconuts, tea and pepper will feature prominently in remaining trade restrictions among these countries (as indeed they are within ASEAN). India has also negotiated a BTA with Japan (with fewer problems over agricultural market access) and is in discussions with Canada and EFTA. Ongoing negotiations with the EU have proved difficult to conclude, though agriculture is not the main stumbling block in this case.

The agricultural exporters that are the most active in seeking BTAs are Chile, Australia and New Zealand, with Canada and South Africa also showing an interest. However, the importer's sensitivities generally provide the parameters for the treatment of agriculture. Chile signed a BTA with EFTA in 2003 that omitted agricultural goods (Chapters HS1–24 of the tariff code), though it negotiated a 'complementary agreement on trade in agricultural goods' with each of the four current EFTA members that improved access marginally for Chile without any threat to domestic production for the importer. Australia has a bilateral agreement with the US (but had to agree to the exclusion of sugar and long transition periods for beef and dairy products) and is actively pursuing a BTA with Japan (where it is meeting similar resistance). New Zealand has not negotiated an agreement with the US but does have a BTA with several of the countries in the Asia-Pacific region. New Zealand has been the first developed country to complete a BTA with China, and though it has agreed to accept China's agricultural sensitivities it clearly relishes extensive access to China's growing market for agricultural goods.

South Africa has made an effort to keep up with other exporters of temperate zone products in exploring BTAs that include agricultural goods. Once again, the results have differed depending on the sensitivities of the import markets. A BTA with the EU (mentioned below) was completed in 1999 and negotiations continue toward a deeper 'Economic Partnership Agreement'. A BTA with EFTA came into effect in 2006, and a trade agreement with MERCOSUR was signed in 2005. Negotiations continue for an agreement with India. Agriculture may not be the driving force behind such cross-regional agreements, but domestic support for such policies will require some inclusion of agricultural market access.[32]

Even where limits are put on the extent of the liberalisation of agricultural trade in these bilaterals, over time substantial amounts of agricultural trade face barriers that are less restrictive than MFN tariffs. Some of this trade is undoubtedly diverted from lower-cost suppliers, but trade creation is also likely to occur. Detailed empirical analyses of each agreement would be necessary to judge whether the BTAs as a whole are consistent with more liberal trade or mere trading of access into protected markets with little impact on resource allocation and expansion of consumer choice.

One result of the growth in BTAs is however clear: the agricultural marketplace is becoming a web of different rules governing access and safeguards. Multipart tariff schedules are becoming the norm, and rules of origin are themselves taking on increased significance. Although a detailed look at these issues in each of the bilaterals is clearly beyond the scope of this chapter, some further discussion of a selection of such agreements gives a view of the complexities that are emerging. The focus will be on the EU and the US bilaterals as being not only the most numerous, but also the most significant, for other countries.

A. Treatment of agriculture in EU bilateral agreements

In the network of agreements involving the EU and non-members, agriculture is still treated as being largely outside the realm of unrestricted free trade. The Euro-Mediterranean agreements between the EU and the countries of North Africa have avoided including unrestricted access for sensitive agricultural products, as did the customs union that was negotiated with Turkey. The negotiation of an FTA between the EU and South Africa was held up by the reluctance of the EU to grant improved

---

32 Bilaterals are not confined to Asia, Europe and the Americas. Israel has complemented its BTAs with the US and the EU (see below) with pacts with Canada, EFTA, Romania, Bulgaria, Egypt, Jordan, Turkey, Mexico and MERCOSUR. The members of the Gulf Co-operation Council (GCC), separately or individually, have negotiated BTAs with Australia, China, MERCOSUR, Japan, Jordan, Turkey, New Zealand, India and the EU. Agriculture was not a major item on the agenda in these talks.

Table 1 *Bilateral trade agreements involving the EU*

Country/Agreement	Date/Status	Country/Agreement	Date/Status
EEA with EFTA countries (except Switzerland)	1992	Central America	2010
Cotonou Agreement with 78 African, Pacific and Caribbean countries (ACP)	2000	Andean Community	2010
Euro-Med	Agreements with most countries signed (except Syria and Libya)	India	Under negotiation
South Africa	1999 (broadened in 2004)	Gulf Co-operation Council	Under negotiation
Western Balkans	Unilateral trade agreements with Albania, Serbia-Montenegro; FTAs with Croatia (now an EU member), Macedonia	EPA Pacific	2011 Interim EPA
Mexico	2005	EPA Caribbean	2009
Chile	2006	EPA West Africa	Under negotiation
MERCOSUR	Negotiations underway	EPA Central Africa	Under negotiation
Korea	2011	EPA Southern Africa	Under negotiation
ASEAN	Negotiations with ASEAN stalled: agreements signed with Singapore and Malaysia	EPA Eastern and Southern Africa	Under negotiation
Canada	2014	EPA East African Community	Under negotiation

Source: EU Commission, DG External Trade

access to goods that would have directly competed with those covered by the CAP. The agreement between the EU and Mexico was also difficult to negotiate, until Mexico abandoned its attempt to get easy access for a full range of agricultural products into the EU market.

Similarly, talks between MERCOSUR and the EU are finding it difficult to over-come the problems that improved access to the EU market would seem to pose for European agriculture. These talks were discontinued for a time but could move forward in the absence of progress in the Doha Round. The Cotonou Agreement between the EU and the African, Caribbean and Pacific countries (ACP), that mandated the negotiation of a change in the existing non-reciprocal agreements into full free-trade areas after eight years, has attempted to address agricultural trade issues, but these negotiations pose little threat to EU agricultural producers. The trade agreement between the EU and the Least Developed Countries (called the Everything But Arms agreement) broke significant new ground in this respect, by providing duty- and quota-free access for agricultural goods, with only temporary derogations for the most sensitive commodities – rice, sugar and bananas.

1. Euro-Mediterranean partnership agreements

Traditionally, the EU has used the policy of trade preferences as a strategy of co-operation for development. Trade concessions have been granted by the EU on a unilateral basis to other countries. Now, Europe–Mediterranean agreements take further steps for trade liberalisation on a bilateral and reciprocal basis. Since the first Euro-Mediterranean Conference in November 1995, the EU and twelve Mediterranean countries have been engaged in negotiating Association Agreements (the Barcelona Process). The overall objective was to form, by 2010, one Euro-Mediterranean free-trade area from the separate agreements in place. The collapse of communism in Central and Eastern European countries (CEECs) and the conclu-sion of FTAs between these countries and the EU raised concerns that the Mediterranean Arab countries might be 'marginalised' in EU markets, as the compe-titive advantage that they used to enjoy in those markets would be eroded. To date, bilateral Association Agreements have been concluded with eight trade partners: Tunisia (1995), Israel (1995), Morocco (1996), Jordan (1997), the Palestinian Authority (1997), Algeria (2002), Egypt (2002) and Lebanon (2002).

Agriculture is a key sector in the debate between these trade partners as it is seen as necessary to establish a balance of commercial opportunities through the increase in both industrial and agricultural export from the region. However, trade in agri-culture is subjected to weak liberalisation, within the present framework of the Association Agreements. No specific liberalisation roadmap has been defined for the agricultural sector as a whole. Only for certain products have specific concessions for liberalisation been determined.

The deferment of substantive negotiations of liberalisation of trade in agricultural products has been a constant feature of the Euro-Mediterranean partnership. This is largely explained by the political difficulties of reforming the EU's CAP and by the resistance on the part of European farmers who compete with non-EU member Mediterranean countries. The southern enlargement of the EC in the 1980s redefined its relation with the Mediterranean partners. Spain, Greece and Portugal compete directly in agricultural products with the countries of North Africa, and these countries' political influence largely explains the limits to trade concessions through tariff quota and reference quantities.[33]

The other problem that needs to been considered by Mediterranean countries is a lack of diversification and competitiveness of their production structure. Several Mediterranean countries show a very similar product composition of exports. This is the case with Cyprus, Algeria, Spain, Israel and Morocco, all of them with an agriculture sector orientated to 'speciality products', mainly fresh fruit and nuts, olive oil and wine. The similarity of agricultural products makes supplies from non-member Mediterranean countries easily replaced by EU member countries, especially in the context of the enlargement of the EU to include Greece, Spain and Portugal as well as Malta and Cyprus.

2. EPAs

The current negotiations between the EU and the countries of the ACP (the signatories to the Lomé and Cotonou Agreements) are proceeding in separate regional talks. The EU negotiated with the ACP countries in the Caribbean region through CARICOM and their Regional Negotiating Mechanism. The Pacific ACP countries have also reached an agreement with the EU on an EPA. In the case of the African countries, negotiations are being channelled through the main regional agreements. ECOWAS, in collaboration with the West African Economic and Monetary Union (UEMOA/WAEMU), is the negotiating partner for sixteen West African states. Eight Central African states are negotiating through the Economic and Monetary Community of Central Africa (CEMAC) in conjunction with CEEAC with which it has merged. The countries of the East African Community are negotiating as a group. Several Southern African states are negotiating with the EU through SADC (though some of those states are not SADC members) and another fifteen are represented by COMESA, even though some of these countries do not participate in other COMESA activities. Though some interim agreements have been reached, the negotiations are still ongoing with the African country groups.

B. Treatment of agriculture in US bilateral agreements

US policy towards regional and bilateral trade agreements changed dramatically in the mid-1980s. Long a champion of the multilateral system, and of non-discrimination, the US has now become an active supporter of bilateral trade agreements as a complement to its commitment to the WTO and its membership of NAFTA. The US has completed, or is currently in the midst of, trade negotiations

33 Jose-Maria Garcia-Alvarez-Coque, 'Agricultural Trade and the Barcelona Process: Is Full Liberalization Possible?' (2002) 29(3) *European Review of Agricultural Economics* 399–422.

with thirty-one other countries aimed at creating about twenty-two separate
FTAs.[34] The US strategy is to expand its commercial ties with countries for both
economic and geopolitical reasons: the attraction to other countries is to secure
preferred access to the large US market.[35]

The first of these recent FTAs was signed with Israel in 1985, as an expression of
political and economic support for that country. The FTA with Canada followed in
1986, largely at the request of Canada, and was designed to consolidate existing sector
agreements, encourage US investment north of the border and give Canadian firms
some protection from aggressive use of trade remedy (anti-dumping and countervailing duty) provisions. But in 1990, Mexico requested similar conditions, to assure
overseas investors of their access to the large US market. Canada opted to join the US
and Mexico in the trilateral NAFTA which incorporated the earlier bilateral with
Canada. An FTA with Jordan was agreed in 2001, again as a show of political support
and economic assistance.

The US began to negotiate more bilaterals in 2002, as an expression of a policy of
'competitive liberalization' as articulated by the United States Trade Representative
(USTR). This policy consisted of offering swift negotiations to any country that was
willing to conform to the terms consistent with the mandate of the US
Administration as specified in the Trade Promotion Authority. The list of willing
trade partners included Singapore, Morocco and Bahrain. Among the other bilateral agreements with a more significant agricultural component were those with
Chile and Australia. Bilaterals were agreed with Peru and Oman in 2009 and with
Panama, Colombia and Korea in 2011. Talks with Malaysia, Thailand, Ecuador,
Bolivia, the South African Customs Union (SACU) and the United Arab Emirates
(UAE) are in various stages of suspension.[36] The list in Table 2 shows the BTAs that
are either in operation or have been under active discussion. Recent agreements
have often been designed as 'templates' for future BTAs within a region. Thus the
BTAs with Bahrain and Oman are seen as building blocks toward a Middle-East
Free Trade Area, and the negotiations with Malaysia and Thailand (along with that
already in place with Singapore) could pave the way for other bilaterals with
ASEAN countries. The BTAs themselves usually follow from Trade and
Investment Framework Agreements (TIFAs) and Bilateral Investment Treaties
(BITs). The US has a considerable number of TIFAs and BITS in place that would
form the basis for bilateral FTAs.

What agricultural provisions do these BTAs contain? All of the BTAs have provisions for tariff reductions that affect many food and agricultural goods. However,

---

34 It is worth recalling that the US trade policy in the late 1930s took a similar direction. The Reciprocal Trade
   Agreements (RTA) Act was an open-ended mandate to sign bilateral trade agreements with other
   countries. Some thirty such agreements were signed.

35 In many cases the access is already covered by existing agreements, but the negotiation of a formal FTA
   reduces the uncertainty concerning the continuation of these references.

36 SACU includes the Republic of South Africa as well as Botswana, Namibia, Lesotho and Swaziland.

Table 2 *Current bilateral trade agreements involving the US*

Country/Agreement	Date/Status
Israel	1985 (Agricultural Agreement 1996)
Canada (CUSFTA)	1986 (Grandfathered into NAFTA)
NAFTA (Mexico and Canada)	1994
Jordan	2001
Singapore	2004
Chile	2004
Australia (AUSFTA)	2005
CAFTA (Costa Rica, Honduras, Nicaragua, El Salvador, Guatemala)	2006
Dominican Republic (added to CAFTA)	2006
Morocco	2006
Bahrain	2006
Oman	2006
Colombia (TPA)	2011
Peru (TPA)	2011
Panama (bilateral)	2011
Korea	2011
South Africa (SACU)	Negotiations on hold
Thailand	Negotiations on hold
Malaysia	Negotiations on hold
Ecuador	Negotiations on hold
Bolivia	Negotiations on hold
UAE	Negotiations on hold

Source: Author's compilation based on USTR website

with few exceptions, the agreements control trade in a range of products considered politically sensitive in one or both partners. For the US these sensitivities include sugar, citrus fruits, peanuts and dairy products, and for the partners the list includes corn and beans along with rice.

Three current agreements have the most actual or potential impact on US agricultural markets and hence on the environment in which policy is formed: the recent BTAs with Chile and Australia, along with the CAFTA–DR–US agreement. Table 3 gives a summary of the main characteristics of each agreement.

1. CAFTA–DR–US

The US and five Central American countries – Costa Rica, El Salvador, Guatemala, Honduras and Nicaragua – began negotiations for a Central American Free Trade Agreement (CAFTA) in 2003. President Bush notified the US Congress of his

Table 3 *Summary of United States–Chile Free Trade Agreement (US–Chile FTA), Australia–United States Free Trade Agreement (AUSFTA) and CAFTA–DR–US arrangements for agriculture, and comparison with NAFTA*

	NAFTA	US–Chile FTA	AUSFTA	CAFTA–DR–US
Tariff cuts	Some tariffs eliminated: Others staged over 5, 10 and 15 years	Some tariffs eliminated: others staged over 4, 8, 10 and 12 years. Some cuts delayed for 2 and 4 years	Most tariffs eliminated: others staged over 4, 10 and 18 years	Some tariffs eliminated: others staged over 5, 10 and 15 years. Other cuts delayed for 6 or 10 years: duty free after 15 or 20 years
TRQs	Introduced during transition period for sensitive products (Annex 703.3)	No use of TRQs introduced	TRQs for avocados, cotton, peanuts, tobacco, beef and dairy products into the US expanded. Above-quota duties for beef phased out over 18-year period. Current Sugar TRQs not increased: no cuts in above-quota tariff	TRQs for sensitive products in Annex 3.3. Rules on administration of TRQs (in addition to GATT Article XIII)
Agricultural safeguards	TRQs allowed as special safeguard for horticultural crops (Annex 703.3)	Additional duties linked to price trigger (Article 3.18) for goods listed in Annex 3.18 Total duties not to exceed MFN rate. Safeguard not operative after 12 years, or when zero-duty stage reached	Additional customs duties linked to price trigger for horticultural products (Annex 3-A Section A) and to quantity triggers for beef (Annex 3-A Section B): price triggers used for beef in 19th year	Additional duties linked to trigger quantities (Article 3.14) for products listed in Annex 3.14. Total duties not to exceed MFN rate. Safeguard not operative when zero-duty stage reached

Other safe-guards	Safeguards (Chapter 8A): snapback to previous year's tariff on bilateral trade or MFN tariff	Trade remedies (Chapter 8) GATT 1994 Article XIX Safeguards	of agreement (Annex 3-A section C). Safeguard not operative when zero-duty stage reached Safeguards (Chapter 9) GATT 1994 Article XIX Safeguards	Trade Remedies (Chapter 8) GATT 1994 Article XIX Safeguards
Export subsidies	Agreement to avoid use of export subsidies on bilateral trade unless third countries subsidised exports to NAFTA markets. Agreement to work together for elimination in the GATT	Agreement to avoid use of export subsidies on bilateral trade unless third countries subsidised exports to Chile or the US. Agreement to work together for elimination in the WTO	Agreement to avoid use of export subsidies on bilateral trade unless third countries subsidised exports to Australia. Agreement to work together for elimination in the WTO	Agreement to avoid use of export subsidies on bilateral trade unless third countries subsidised exports to CAFTA–DR–US markets. Agreement to work together for elimination in the WTO
Domestic support	Agreement to work together in GATT for the reduction of domestic support levels and shift to less trade-distorting instruments	Agreement to work together in WTO for the reduction of domestic support levels and shift to less trade-distorting instruments	Agreement to work together in WTO for the reduction of domestic support levels and shift to less trade-distorting instruments	Agreement to work together in WTO for the reduction of domestic support levels and shift to less trade-distorting instruments
SPS measures	Precursor of WTO SPS Agreement (Chapter 7B)	Affirm commitment to SPS Agreement	Work to resolve trade conflicts over SPS barriers	Affirm commitment to SPS Agreement

Table 3 (*cont.*)

	NAFTA	US–Chile FTA	AUSFTA	CAFTA–DR–US
Dispute settlement	Dispute settlement mechanism for matters arising from Agreement (Chapter 20). Separate procedures for review of anti-dumping and countervail actions (Chapter 19)	Dispute settlement mechanism for matters arising from Agreement (Chapter 22)	Dispute settlement mechanism for matters arising from Agreement (Chapter 21). Provision for monetary penalties	Dispute settlement mechanism for matters arising from Agreement (Chapter 20)
Institutions	Committee on Agricultural Trade; Working Group on Agricultural Subsidies; Advisory Committee on Private Commerce; Disputes regarding Agricultural Goods	Working Group on Agricultural Trade; Committee on Sanitary and Phytosanitary Matters	Committee on Agriculture; Standing Technical Working Group on Animal and Plant Health Measures	Committee on Agricultural Trade; Agricultural Review Commission; Committee on Sanitary and Phytosanitary Matters

Source: Author's compilation from FTA texts

intention to enter into the CAFTA on 13 February 2004, and it was approved by Congress, under the Trade Promotion Authority granted to the President in 2002. CAFTA–US took effect in 2006. Negotiations with the Dominican Republic were concluded on 15 March 2004 that would fully integrate that country into the CAFTA. In addition, bilateral negotiations are underway with Panama, which if completed will conclude the establishment of FTAs between the US and almost all of the countries in Central America.[37]

The CAFTA–DR–US is intended to help foster economic growth and improved living standards in the Central American region by reducing and eliminating barriers to trade and investment. It essentially converts the non-reciprocal and discretionary benefits that these countries get from the CBI into permanent and reciprocal access to the US market. Though covering all trade, the agricultural component is one of the most important aspects of the FTA. The main agricultural provisions of CAFTA–DR–US are summarised in Table 3. The key to the agricultural agreement is market access, with relatively few provisions in the areas of export subsidies and sanitary and phytosanitary regulations. Domestic subsidies are not covered by the agreement.

The CAFTA–DR–US has improved market opportunities for US agricultural products and related goods and services. Agricultural trade barriers in the Central American countries are higher than those for manufactured goods. CAFTA–DR–US locks in the applied duty rates for many products and ensures that permanent US access to the market is preserved. However the short-term impact on US exports of the CAFTA–DR–US may be modest as the terms of the agreement delay the full benefits of increased access to the countries of the region for US agricultural products of interest. The lengthy phase-in period for increased market access and back-loading of commitment levels suggest the benefits of the agreement may only be realised many years from now.

Increased market access for Central American goods to the US will also be a consequence of CAFTA–DR–US. However, the impact here is likely to be even more limited, as most CAFTA–DR countries have had permanent duty-free access to the US market since the late 1960s under the Generalised System of Preferences (GSP), and, since 1990, under provisions of the CBI and the CBERA that implements the CBI. The CBI was enhanced in 2000 under the terms of the Caribbean Basin Trade Partnership Act (CBTPA) to give access more equivalent to that enjoyed by Mexico under the NAFTA. In fact, approximately 99 per cent of CAFTA–DR–US exports already enter the US market duty free. Duties are paid only on over-quota imports as part of the US tariff-rate quota regimes for sugar, dairy, cotton, meats and peanuts.[38]

---

37 Mechel S. Paggi, Fumiko Yamazaki and Timothy E. Josling, 'The Central American Free Trade Agreement: What's at Stake for Californian Agriculture?' (2005) Center for Agricultural Business, California State University, Fresno.

38 For more details on CAFTA and its potential impact on US agriculture, see *ibid*.

Chile The bilateral FTA with Chile was easier to negotiate than either NAFTA or CAFTA–DR–US. Chile is an important exporter of agricultural products, particularly fruits and vegetables and wine, but the different seasonality makes the produce complementary to rather than competitive with US production. So the beneficiaries were the supermarkets that could ensure year-round supplies. Moreover, Chile is one of the more liberal of the Latin American countries, even on agricultural products, implying that opening up to the US exporters was not such a big move for the Chilean farmer. Besides some controversy over wine labels, the talks went smoothly. It may have helped that Chile is not a significant sugar exporter.

Australia The Australian agreement also involved a country from the Southern Hemisphere, and thus offered some advantages of complementary production. But Australia is a major exporter of meats, dairy products, cereals and sugar, so tight rules had to be built in to the FTA to protect US farmers from competition from Australia. Reluctantly, Australia accepted a long transition period for dairy production and beef, as well as an exclusion altogether of any relaxation of protection for the US sugar sector. This decision may have an impact on the politics of future bilaterals.

2. KORUS FTA

The most ambitious bilateral to have been negotiated since NAFTA is that with Korea. The agreement was confirmed by Congress in 2011. The Korea–United States Free Trade Agreement (KORUS FTA) would establish a free trade area between the US and a major economy in East Asia. There was no doubt from the beginning of the talks that agriculture would be a stumbling block, with the Korean government in particular not wishing to open up the highly-protected rice market to US exports. However, the US position had been to include rice, even if access for US rice is introduced slowly over a transition period. In the end, the rice sector was excluded from the agreement. This establishes a precedent if the KORUS FTA were to act as a template for an agreement with Japan.

IV. RTAs, BTAs and the WTO: Key issues for agriculture

Regional and bilateral trade agreements coexist, if somewhat uneasily, with multilateral trade rules as enshrined in the WTO. One of the most significant issues facing negotiators of regional and bilateral pacts is their relationship with the WTO. In the case of agricultural trade, this interaction is more than usually pertinent. This section discusses the interaction between the treatment of agriculture in RTAs and BTAs and the rules of and negotiations under the WTO. This relationship is often one of symbiosis rather than antagonism. Many of the problems that make the incorporation of agriculture in a regime of free regional or bilateral trade exist to complicate moves towards multilateral trade liberal-isation. So the solution of these problems at one level can assist with their solution at another.

As prelude to this discussion, it is useful to recall the tangled history of the incorporation of agricultural trade into the multilateral trade system. The GATT, as it emerged in 1947, applied to agricultural trade but also included two articles that specifically modified the impact of the general provisions relating to trade in goods. Article XI, which established the principle that non-tariff trade barriers could only be used under specific circumstances, made way for some types of agricultural programmes. The article recognised the case where an agricultural product is subject to quantitative restrictions on domestic production (Article XI:2 (c)): under such circumstances quantitative import restrictions were allowed.[39] Many countries relied on this clause to restrict imports by quantitative trade barriers when domestic markets were being managed. The other agricultural 'exception' was to specify different rules for export subsidies of manufactures and primary pro-ducts. Though the original GATT subjected both primary and manufactured product export subsidies to the same notification and consultation procedures, in 1955 it was agreed to add an explicit prohibition on export subsidies on manufac-tured goods (Article XVI). Agricultural export subsidies were constrained only by the obligation not to use such subsidies to capture 'more than an equitable share' of world markets. Successive GATT panels failed to come up with a satisfactory definition of this concept, and agricultural export subsidies in effect escaped any disciplines.[40]

The Uruguay Round attempted to address these issues directly. Non-tariff trade barriers were to be converted to tariffs and bound in the WTO schedules. A schedule of tariff reductions for agricultural goods was agreed.[41] TRQs were introduced in cases of tariffication to ensure current market access and open up

---

39 Timothy E. Josling, Stefan Tangermann and Thorald K. Warley, *Agriculture in the GATT: Past, Present and Future* (Basingstoke: Macmillan Press, 1996).

40 Timothy E. Josling and Stefan Tangermann, 'Production and Export Subsidies in Agriculture: Lessons from GATT and WTO Disputes Involving the US and the EC', in Ernst-Ulrich Petersmann and Mark Pollack (eds.), *Transatlantic Economic Disputes: The US, the EU and the WTO* (New York: Oxford University Press, 2003). Even these two exceptions did not constrain farm policy in developed countries. A prominent example of this was the imposition of quotas by the US under s 22 of the Agricultural Adjustment Act (as amended) that mandated quantitative restrictions on imports of a number of goods whenever domestic programs were 'materially interfered with' by imports. This required a waiver of the US obligations under Article XI, a waiver that was renewed annually until made irrelevant by the Uruguay Round outcome. The EU also avoided restraints on its Common Agricultural Policy (CAP), which used 'variable levies' to stabilise the duty-paid price of imports. Such an instrument was not easily classified as either a customs duty or a quantitative restriction. The Uruguay Round Agreement on Agriculture specifically bans such variable levies.

41 Developing countries were allowed to use 'ceiling bindings' often at arbitrarily high levels and across many commodities. Actual tariffs applied have generally been well below these ceilings, giving countries ample scope for granting preferential access and for modifying tariff levels with world price changes.

additional markets. These TRQs were increased from 3 to 5 per cent of consumption over the implementation period. Export subsidies were not totally
eliminated, but new ones were banned, and existing subsidies declared and
entered into country schedules. In addition, domestic subsidies paid to farmers
were classified, depending on their notional level of trade distortion, into three
categories, which have become known as the Amber Box, the Blue Box, and the
Green Box.

Amber Box measures were those tied to output or input prices or to current output
levels: their magnitude was calculated as an 'Aggregate Measurement of Support'
(AMS). Total AMS has to be reduced by 20 per cent over the implementation period.
The Blue Box contained subsidies that were tied to supply control programmes: such
subsidies were regarded as less obviously output-increasing. No reduction was
required for Blue Box policies, though there were constraints on their increase.
Green Box subsidies were defined as those unrelated to price and output
('decoupled') and included research and extension, payments designed to compensate farmers for the cost of compliance with environmental regulations, and domestic
food assistance programmes. 'Green Box' policies were unconstrained, as having
minimal trade distorting effects.

The main contribution of the Uruguay Round Agreement on Agriculture
(URAA) was to bring disciplines to bear on agricultural trade and domestic
agricultural policies. In addition, future negotiations would be made easier as a
result of the simplification of market access restrictions and the categorising of
domestic support. A side effect of that contribution was to make regional and
bilateral trade agreement easier to negotiate. Conflicts over the opening up of
markets to imports were not themselves resolved, but the fact that tariffs had
replaced non-tariff trade barriers made the negotiation of a schedule of preferential reductions more straightforward. Even the TRQs became useful, as they
provided a way of granting preferences to partner exporters without necessarily
increasing the level of imports. Thus the potential rents accruing to suppliers of
goods within the TRQ could be used as an inducement to joining an RTA or
negotiating a BTA.

Two issues persist in the discussions about the relationship between the
treatment of agriculture in regional and bilateral trade agreements and that in
WTO. One is the extent to which adherence to Article XXIV of the GATT
obliges countries to include agricultural trade in the free-trade provisions. If
countries contemplating a regional or bilateral agreement can reasonably argue
that agricultural trade is an insignificant part of their trade relations then there
would be no compelling motive for including such products in the free-trade
arrangements. So far, there has been no definitive ruling from a panel on the
question of defining 'substantially all trade'. Clearly, if agricultural trade between
two (or more) countries is small because of high trade barriers, the use of

current trade flows is circular: agriculture could be left out of the agreement because it is highly protected. So RTAs and BTAs would be denied some benefits from opening up trade flows in farm products. The use of tariff lines, or other such measures, would be much more likely to oblige countries to include agriculture among the sectors for tariff-free trade.

The second issue is the extent to which one can include disciplines on domestic farm subsidies in regional and bilateral agreements. It is often assumed that the conduct of domestic policy is outside the realm of the FTAs, but this is not always the case. The movement towards 'decoupled' policies, encouraged by the URAA, has the advantage of making it easier to have free trade in a commodity and still maintain domestic support policies. Nevertheless, the existence of an active domestic support policy, involving subsidies and market management, complicates the negotiation of free trade in those products.

The issues are clearly connected. If one can omit agricultural trade from the FTA provisions then the question of domestic support does not arise. Conversely, if one cannot exclude agriculture without violating WTO provisions, then the potentially problematic issue of domestic support is unavoidable.

Allied to the issue of the application through RTAs and BTAs of disciplines on domestic support is that of the treatment of export subsidies. Various trade agreements have tried to include provisions that countries may not use export subsidies in mutual trade. This sounds like a logical provision. However, in practice it is not easy to ban subsidies paid on internal trade without creating an incentive to import from outside and a disincentive to export within the free-trade area. So in effect export subsidies have also to be controlled at the WTO level.

The current Doha Round of WTO talks would, if successfully completed, make a significant difference to the ease at which agricultural trade could be opened up within RTAs and BTAs. Tariff levels would come down by at least 50 per cent and TRQs for sensitive commodities would be expanded. This reduces the degree of preference for partner suppliers (and hence the risk of trade diversion) but it also reduces the shock of adjustment for import-competing sectors. With an agreed schedule of WTO tariff reductions, the marginal impact of faster reductions for regional or bilateral partners may be more tolerable. Additionally, export subsidies would finally be eliminated, a step that RTAs and BTAs have found difficult to accomplish. But the main contribution that the WTO negotiations on agriculture can make to the process of regional and bilateral trade liberalisation could be to further push countries to abandon price supports in domestic markets and embrace direct payments for public goods or for income relief. Such policies will be more compatible with preferential trade agreements as well as good for multilateral trade arrangements.

With WTO talks on agriculture grinding slowly, regional negotiations may, however, take the brunt of attempts to further liberalise agricultural trade and to gain access to new markets for agricultural exports. Thus in agriculture there is a strong degree of complementarity in trade negotiations. Plurilateral talks can erode market access barriers but set up trade flows encouraged by discrimination among suppliers. Multilateral talks can reduce the scope for such trade diversion. The multilateral process can handle subsidy reduction, which in turn makes it easier for countries to agree to opening up regional or bilateral trade. This complementarity, however, depends on progress at the multilateral level. Currently that is the stumbling block.

V. Prospects for the future

A new type of regionalism emerged in the mid-1990s as attempts were made to transform existing free-trade networks into actual or potential supra-regional trade agreements that span the continents. This new breed of supra-regional network agreements included both the Asia-Pacific Economic Cooperation forum (APEC) and the Free Trade Area of the Americas (FTAA). These two agreements were different from traditional regional trade blocs, as well as from each other. APEC and the FTAA have overlapping membership (several countries participate in both) and hence tend to join rather than isolate continents. The fact that a country can be a member of more than one such agreement is the key in this regard. This property makes these regional pacts more like networks than closed blocs. In this way they can build on current agreements (FTAA, which builds upon NAFTA and the ALADI agreements) or be neutral toward them (APEC, which includes members of ASEAN, the ANZCERTA, MERCOSUR and NAFTA, as well as countries that belong to no bloc, such as Japan). Even though they differ in certain crucial ways, in particular in their treatment of trade with third countries, both these supra-regional networks represent essentially new ways of negotiating reductions in trade barriers. They would certainly have to include provisions for freer trade in agricultural products.

Not long after the agreement on NAFTA, discussions began on a broader initiative to expand US economic relations with other Latin-American countries. This led ultimately to the declaration at Miami in 1994 of the intention to work toward an FTAA by 2005. There have been sporadic negotiations on the establishment of an FTAA covering thirty-four countries in the hemisphere since 1996. The development of the FTAA slowed at the end of the last decade as Brazil chose to strengthen its economic ties with South American countries before negotiating with the NAFTA countries. At the Miami summit of 2003 the scope for the FTAA was significantly revised. Sensitive issues such as domestic farm support and anti-dumping actions were by agreement left to the WTO. As a consequence, the US became less interested in the FTAA and negotiations have lapsed.

The attraction of the APEC talks to the US has been based on the broad range of issues that were addressed, but the prospect of APEC becoming a free trade area seems to have receded into the distance. In its place has emerged a new model of trade agreement that includes countries that already have BTAs with each other or would welcome a framework that encompasses more countries. The agreement that is in the final stage of negotiation is the Trans-Pacific Partnership (TPP), involving twelve countries around the Pacific Rim (Australia, Brunei, Chile, Malaysia, New Zealand, Peru, Singapore, Vietnam, Canada, Japan, Mexico and the US). Should this negotiation succeed, a significant proportion of world trade would fall under regulations additional to that in the WTO. Agriculture would certainly be included, though certain sensitive commodities would no doubt be shielded for some years.

The TPP would not in itself encompass all the countries in the region. China has also been considering the benefits of bilateral agreements and has actively supported a plan for a Regional Cooperative Economic Partnership (RCEP) including the ten ASEAN countries and six countries that already have BTAs with ASEAN (Australia, New Zealand, China, India, Japan and Korea). Negotiations are at an early stage, but the inclusion of China and India in an ambitious free trade area would signal a major shift in trade relations and pose issues for the US, the EU and Latin America. Though one might expect agricultural trade issues to be muted to avoid serious political tensions, inevitably there would be a major impact on trade flows of such a pact.

The other locus for significant trade agreements is in the Atlantic. The EU has negotiated a BTA with Canada that is almost complete, and the EU MERCOSUR talks could restart at any time (once the parties are convinced that no progress will be made in the WTO Doha negotiations). But the major activity in the coming months will be the negotiation of a Transatlantic Trade and Investment Partnership (TTIP) between the EU and the US. This negotiation will focus on reducing trade barriers and setting trade rules for almost one-third of world trade. The initial position of the two sides has been to avoid 'exceptions' to market access opening, though some transition periods are likely for sensitive products. In terms of agricultural trade the implications are significant. Though domestic support measures are unlikely to be part of the talks, removal of tariffs for those products that are currently protected by high tariffs could substantially increase trade. More importantly, if the EU and the US can agree on a number of regulatory issues to do with health and safety, biotech products and geographical labelling, it is likely that these agreements would form a template for other countries.

The future of the trade system, both multilateral and regional/bilateral, will be stamped by the outcome of the TPP, RCEP and TTIP negotiations. Not least will be the effect on agricultural trade. Many of the major exporters and importers of agricultural products will be included, putting pressure on excluded countries and regions (such as Latin America and Africa) to join. The days when agricultural products could be ignored in negotiating trade agreements are undoubtedly in the past. The actors in the global food and commodity markets are demanding open trade whether the locus of discussions be multilateral, bilateral or plurilateral. Exceptional treatment for agriculture appears to be on the way out.

9

Regional trade agreements and trade in services

FEDERICO ORTINO

I. Introduction

The services sector accounts today for two-thirds of global output (63% of GDP in 2012; 45% of GDP in 1960) and represents the fastest growing sector of the global economy. In a world where competitiveness is key to economic development, services play a vital role in ensuring a competitive economy. Service industries provide the infrastructure allowing modern economies to function by linking geographically dispersed economic activities or supplying crucial inputs into products competing in the domestic and global markets.

However, the share of services in global trade has been relatively low as certain characteristics of services, such as intangibility and nonstorability, affect their tradability.[1] Recent advances in information technology have nonetheless made trade in certain services now feasible or have greatly reduced its costs. Between 2000 and 2008, trade in commercial services (including in particular transport, travel, communications, financial, professional services) rose by 12% on average per year,[2] with the share of global export from a few developing countries steadily increasing (China, India, Hong Kong and Singapore are among the top fifteen exporters of services). Following the financial crisis, the growth of global trade in commercial services has decreased (in 2013 it reached 6%). In 2013 (as in the past few years), commercial services have accounted for 19–20% of total world trade and global trade in commercial services has averaged 10–11% of GDP.[3]

The growing internationalization of services also presents, in particular for developing countries, certain challenges. For example, these include the need to undertake necessary investments in modern IT networks, adapt educational systems to the information age, and design appropriate domestic and regional regulatory structures for service sectors.[4]

---

1 B. Hoekman and A. Mattoo, 'International trade: trade in services' in A. Guzman and A. Sykes (eds.) *Research Handbook in International Economic Law* (Edward Elgar, 2007) at 115.

2 WTO Secretariat, 'A Review of Statistics on Trade Flows in Services: Overview of Trade Flows in Commercial Services 2000–2010', S/C/W/329/Add.1 (7 January 2011).

3 WTO, *International Trade Statistics 2013* (Geneva, WTO, 2013) and WTO, 'Modest trade growth anticipated for 2014 and 2015 following two year slump', Press/721 (14 April 2014).

4 See Dominique Njinkeu and Bruno Powo Fosso, 'Intra-African Trade and Regional Integration' 11 November 2006 (copy with author); UNCTAD, 'Trade in services and development implications', TD/B/COM.1/85 (21 December 2006).

In recent years the number of international agreements purporting to liberalize and promote trade in services has increased dramatically. While the General Agreement on Trade in Services (GATS), negotiated as part of the Uruguay Round in the late 1980s/early '90s, has represented the pioneer – and often the model – in the field,[5] much of the recent and current international treaty-making addressing trade in services (as well as trade in goods and foreign investment) has occurred at the regional and bilateral levels.[6] The outlook stemming out of this almost frenetic treaty-making activity is a complex and multilayered network of international rules regulating the transnational movement of services and service providers in essential sectors such as the financial, telecommunication, business and professional sectors.

It should be emphasized at this stage that international trade rule-making does not always go hand in hand with actual, immediate liberalization of trade. As it has been in the case for trade in goods, trade rules function as the underlying framework against which effective liberalization can gradually occur. This is very much true also for trade in services. However, as it will be discussed in the following sections, a slightly different approach has been adopted in the area of trade in services given the different types of trade barriers restricting the flow of services compared with those restricting trade in goods.

This chapter is divided into two main parts. Section II describes the basic features of the GATS focusing in particular on the following issues: (a) scope of application, (b) general obligations and disciplines, (c) specific commitments and (d) sectoral disciplines. Focusing broadly on these same issues, section III will analyze the services chapters of the Regional Trade Agreements (RTAs) that have been notified to the WTO Council for Trade in Services on the basis of Article V GATS.[7] This chapter does not address the issue of the level of liberalization that these RTAs have actually accomplished[8] or the issue of the compatibility of these agreements with GATS.[9]

---

5 Earlier attempts to provide rules for trade in services are the Codes and Declaration concluded within the Organization for Economic Cooperation and Development (OECD) in the 1970s and '80s. Cf P. Raworth, *Trade in Services – Global Regulation and the Impact on Key Service Sectors* (New York, Oceana Publications, 2006) Chapter III.

6 For an account of this development see J. Crawford and R. Fiorentino, 'The Changing Landscape of Regional Trade Agreements', WTO Discussion Paper No. 8 (2005).

7 There are a total of 121 notifications from 1 January 1995 until 1 July 2014 on the basis of Article V GATS (including 117 new RTAs and four accessions). See WTO Document at http://rtais.wto.org/ui/publicsum marytable.aspx. Section III will principally focus on free trade agreements and economic cooperation agreements leaving aside a detailed analysis of custom unions (such as the European Treaty).

8 For a recent analysis of the liberalization impact of RTAs beyond the GATS see Martin Roy, Juan Marchetti and Hoe Lim, 'Services Liberalization in the New Generation of Preferential Trade Agreements (PTAs): How Much Further than the GATS?', Staff Working Paper ERSD-2006–07 (September 2006).

9 For an analysis of the compatibility of RTAs (and bilateral investment treaties) with GATS see F. Ortino and A. Sheppard, 'International Agreements Covering Foreign Investment in Services: Patterns and Linkages' in L. Bartels and F. Ortino, *Regional Trade Agreements and the WTO Legal System* (Oxford, OUP, 2006) at 201 et seq.

II. Trade in services and the GATS

The GATS represents one of the innovative features of the WTO 'single undertaking' stemming out of the Uruguay Round as it provides for the first multilateral, legally enforceable disciplines covering international trade (and investment) in services. The GATS architecture is composed of a three-layered structure: (1) a framework Agreement; (2) eight Annexes addressing sector-specific issues; and (3) individual Members' Schedules of Specific Commitments.

As the GATS is usually employed as a possible model or starting point for regional agreement regulating trade in services, it is worthwhile to set out a few basic features.

A. Scope of application

GATS rules apply to 'measures by Members affecting trade in services' (Article I:1). A 'measure' is defined very broadly in the GATS to embrace any action by a Member in any form such as a law, regulation, rule, procedure, decision, administrative action (Article XXVIII(a)). In theory, 'measures by Members' means measures taken by central, regional or local governments and authorities as well as non-governmental bodies in the exercise of powers delegated by central, regional or local governments or authorities.[10] However, GATS only requires Members to take such reasonable measures as may be available to them to secure compliance with GATS rules by sub-central and non-governmental bodies (Article I.3(a)).[11]

'Measures by Members affecting trade in services' include measures in respect of (i) the purchase, payment or use of a service; (ii) the access to and use of, in connection with the supply of a service, services which are required by those Members to be offered to the public generally; (iii) the presence, including commercial presence, of persons of a Member for the supply of a service in the territory of another Member (Article XXVIII(c)). This list being indicative, the inquiry centers around the term 'affecting'. WTO jurisprudence has interpreted broadly the term 'affecting'. A measure affects trade in service when the measure 'modifies the conditions of

---

10 On the related issue of attribution for non-mandatory governmental measures as well as for government-endorsed or authorized private measures, see Sharif Bhuiyan, 'Mandatory and Discretionary Legislation: The Continued Relevance of the Distinction under the WTO', (2002) 5(3) *Journal of International Economic Law* 571–604.

11 If this limitation is read in conjunction with Article 22.9 of the DSU, it may be argued that while the implementation obligations of the responsible Member are limited to such reasonable measures as may be available to it to ensure observance of WTO law, the dispute settlement provisions relating to compensation and the suspension of obligations do apply where the Member concerned has not been able to secure the observance of the WTO Agreement in its territory. In any event, the limitation found in Article I.3(a) GATS is a specific and limited exception to the principle that subjects of international law are responsible for the activities of all branches of power within their system of governance, including all regional levels or other subdivisions of government and thus should not be generalized and extrapolated to other authorities of a Member enjoying a degree of independence.

competition in supply of a service'.[12] In other words, GATS disciplines apply, in principle, to any measure of a Member to the extent it affects the supply of a service, regardless of whether such measure directly governs the supply of a service, or whether it regulates other matters but nevertheless affects indirectly trade in services.[13] Furthermore, in line with GATT/WTO jurisprudence, in order to determine whether a measure 'affects' trade in services, there is no need to determine actual effects, rather it is enough to demonstrate a potential effect on trade.[14] Accordingly, in determining the coverage of the GATS, it is sufficient to show that a governmental measure has the potential to affect (i.e., to have an effect on) trade in service.[15]

'Trade in services' is defined as the supply of a service (a) from the territory of one Member into the territory of any other Member (cross-border supply); (b) in the territory of one Member to the service consumer of any other Member (consumption abroad); (c) by a service supplier of one Member, through commercial presence in the territory of any other Member (commercial presence); and (d) by a service supplier of one Member, through presence of natural persons of a Member in the territory of any other Members (temporary presence of natural persons) (Article I.2).

'Natural persons of another Member' (whether for purpose of modes 2 or 4) means a natural person who resides in the territory of that other Member or any other Member and who under the law of that other Member is a national of that other Member or has the right of permanent residence in that other Member (if the Member in which he/she resides accords substantially the same treatment to permanent residents as it does to its own citizens) (Article XXVIII(k)). 'Juridical person of another Member' (whether for purpose of modes 2 or 3) means a juridical person which is either (i) constituted under the law of that other Member and is engaged in substantial business operations in the territory of that Member or any other Member or (ii) in the case of the supply of a service through commercial presence, owned or controlled by natural persons of that Member or juridical persons of that other Member identified under subparagraph (i) (where 'ownership' is defined as a holding

---

12 See Panel Report, *EC – Bananas III*, para. 7.281; Appellate Body Report, *EC – Bananas III*, para. 220. Also GATT Panel Report, *Italian Discrimination Against Imported Agricultural Machinery*, adopted 23 October 1958, BISD 7S/60.

13 Werner Zdouc, 'WTO Dispute Settlement Practice Relating to the General Agreement on Trade in Services' in Federico Ortino and Ernst-Ulrich Petersmann (eds.), *WTO Dispute Settlement System: 1995–2003* (London, Kluwer Law International, 2004), chapter 21. Cf Aaditya Mattoo, 'MFN and the GATS' in Thomas Cottier, Petros Mavroidis and Patrick Blatter (eds.) *Regulatory Barriers and the Principle of Non-Discrimination in World Trade Law* (Ann Arbor, University of Michigan Press, 2000) at 53.

14 Panel Report on *Canada – Autos*, paras. 10.80 and 10.84. See GATT Panel Report, *Italian Discrimination Against Imported Agricultural Machinery*, adopted 23 October 1958, BISD 7S/60, para. 12: 'The selection of the words "affecting" would imply, in the opinion of the Panel, that the drafters of the Article intended to cover . . . any laws or regulations which *might* adversely *modify the conditions of competition* between [like products]' (emphasis added).

15 In *US – Gambling*, however, the Panel and Appellate Body clarified that invoking a total prohibition is not enough for a complaining Member to prevail unless that Member does not also identify the specific measure(s) that is the source of the alleged prohibition. See Appellate Body Report, *US – Gambling*, paras. 120–6.

of more than 50% of the person's equity interest and 'control' is defined as the power to name a majority of the person's directors or otherwise to legally direct its actions) (Article XXVIII(m) and (n)).

'Commercial presence' is broadly defined as any type of business or professional establishment, including through (i) the constitution, acquisition or maintenance of a juridical person, or (ii) the creation or maintenance of a branch or a representative office within the territory of a Member for the purpose of supplying s service (Article XXVIII(d)).

As specified in the 'Annex on Movement of Natural Persons Supplying Services under the Agreement', the Agreement shall not apply to measures affecting natural persons seeking access to the employment market of a Member, nor shall it apply to measures regarding citizenship, residence or employment on a permanent basis (paragraph 2).

The GATS covers all services except those supplied in the exercise of governmental authority, that is any service which is provided on a non-commercial (non-profit) and non-competitive basis (Article I.3(b) and (c)). In order for a service to be excluded from the scope of application of the GATS both conditions must be met. Although there exists some uncertainty with regard to the cumulative requirements of non-profitability and non-competitiveness, it appears that the nature of the service itself or the characteristics of the service supplier are irrelevant for purposes of deciding the scope of the 'services supplied in the exercise of governmental authority' exception. Accordingly, one can conclude that apart from a limited set of governmental services (such as the police and military), the notion of 'services' in the GATS applies to all services.[16]

B. General obligations and disciplines

Part II of the GATS provides for certain general obligations, in particular the 'most-favoured-nation (MFN) treatment' (Article II), 'transparency' (Article III), 'domestic regulation' (Article VI), and 'recognition' (VII) as well as exceptions such as 'economic integration' (Article V), 'restrictions to safeguard the balance of payments' (Article XII), general exceptions' (Article XIV), and 'security exceptions' (Article XIV *bis*).

The scope of application of these *general* provisions may however be limited in two alternative ways.[17] First, each provision may apply only to *specific service sectors or*

---

16 Markus Krajewski, *National Regulation and Trade Liberalization in Services: The Legal Impact of the General Agreement on Trade in Services (GATS) on National Regulatory Autonomy* (The Hague/London/New York, Kluwer Law International, 2003) at 73. Cf E. Leroux, 'What is a "Service Supplied in the Exercise of Governmental Authority" Under Article I:3(b) and (c) of the General Agreement on Trade in Services?', (2006) 40 *JWT* 3, at 348.

17 Those provisions that employ both limitations concurrently are referred to as 'specific commitments' and are analyzed in the following section.

sub-sectors (usually listed in a Member's schedule of specific commitments).[18] These provisions may be referred to as 'sector-specific conditional obligations'.[19] On the other hand, if these provisions apply regardless of the existence of specific commitments, they are referred to as 'sector-specific unconditional obligations'.[20] In several cases, the same GATS article contains both sector-specific unconditional and conditional obligations.

Alternatively, the scope of application of these provisions may be limited by allowing each Member to exclude *specific measures* from the reach of the provision (usually by listing the non-conforming measures in an annex to the Agreement).[21] These provisions may be referred to as 'measure-specific conditional obligations'. The MFN provision is the only general obligation of this kind in the GATS as it permits WTO Members to maintain measures inconsistent with the MFN principle provided that such measures are listed in the Annex on Article II Exemptions.[22]

Part II of the GATS also includes four provisions mandating further negotiations relating to aspects on which the negotiators of the Uruguay Round could not reach consensus: further disciplines on domestic regulation (Article VI:4); emergency safeguard measures (Article X:1); government procurement (Article XIII:2); and subsidies (Article XV:1). With one small exception,[23] these negotiations have not produced any substantive outcome.

1. Most-favoured-nation treatment

The principal purpose of the MFN provision in GATS is to ensure equality of opportunity for services and service suppliers from all WTO Members.[24] The MFN provision sets out a three-part test of consistency: (a) whether the measure at issue is a 'measure covered' by the GATS;[25] (b) whether the services or service suppliers concerned are 'like' services or service suppliers;[26] and (c) whether the Member

---

18 As described in the following section, this follows a 'positive-list' approach, as only sectors that parties have expressly identified are subject to these provisions.

19 See, for example, the 'administrative due process requirements' in Article VI:1 GATS.

20 See, for example, the MFN obligation in Article II:1 GATS and the Transparency obligation in Article III:1 GATS.

21 This follows a 'negative-list' approach, as only the measures listed in the annex are exempted from the scope of application of the relevant provision.

22 No new exemptions can be added unless recourse has been made to the waiver provisions of the WTO Agreement. Moreover, the MFN exemptions are in principle valid for a period of 10 years from the entry into force of GATS. See M. Matsushita *et al.*, *The World Trade Organization – Law, Practice and Policy* (Oxford, Oxford University Press, 2006).

23 See the Accountancy Disciplines developed within the Article VI:4 mandate on domestic regulation.

24 Peter Van den Bossche and Werner Zdouc, *The Law and Policy of the World Trade Organization – Text, Cases and Materials* (Cambridge, Cambridge University Press, 2013).

25 See the discussion above regarding the scope of application of the GATS.

26 The GATS does not contain a definition of the term 'like' service providers. The issue of likeness under Article II GATS has only been addressed twice in GATS/WTO jurisprudence, albeit very briefly. In *EC – Bananas III* and *Canada – Autos*, the relevant statement by both Panels was that 'to the extent that entities provide like services, they are like service suppliers'. See Panel Report, *EC – Bananas III*, para. 7.322 and

accords 'less favourable treatment' to the services or service suppliers of another Member (the MFN obligation in GATS thus extends also to the treatment afforded to services and service providers of non-WTO Members).[27]

2. Transparency

Article III GATS provides for certain transparency requirements with regard to 'all relevant measures of general application, which pertain to or affect the operation of this Agreement'. First, Members shall publish promptly and at the latest by the time of their entry into force all relevant measures. However, this publication requirement does not arise when publication is 'not practicable' (although even in this case, the information shall nevertheless be made 'publicly available'). Despite the vagueness implicit in the criterion of 'practicability', this provision arguably allows WTO Members lacking the financial resources to publish all measures of relevant application the flexibility to avoid having to incur the full costs of publication (including the wide dissemination of certain material). With regard to the meaning of 'measures of general application', the Panel and Appellate Body in *US – Underwear* have noted (within the context of a similar provision in GATT Article X) that they are meant to encompass those measures that affect 'an unidentified number of economic operators'.[28]

Second, Members shall inform (at least annually) the Council for Trade in Services of the introduction of new, or any changes to existing laws, regulations or adminis-trative guidelines which significantly affect trade in services covered by specific commitments (Article III:3). Moreover, Article III:4 requires Members to establish enquiry points to facilitate transparency, with each enquiry point providing informa-tion to other Members in response to requests for specific information or in connec-tion with information that is to be provided pursuant to the notification provisions.

Certain notification requirements are imposed on Members for the benefit of private parties. Article VI:3 of the GATS provides that 'where authorization is

---

Panel Report, *Canada – Autos*, para. 10.248. Looking at the extensive jurisprudence on the issue of the likeness of products under GATT (Appellate Body Report, *EC – Asbestos*, para. 101), it may be said that the likeness test in the GATS should be based *inter alia* on the following factors: (a) service's end-uses in a given market; (b) consumer habits and preferences regarding the service or the service supplier; (c) characteristics of the service or the service supplier; and (d) classification and description of the service in the UN CPC system. Cf A. Mattoo, 'National Treatment in the GATS – Corner Stone or Pandora's Box', (1997) 31 *JWT* 107–36, at 128; Van den Bossche and Zdouc, *The Law and Policy of the World Trade Organization – Text, Cases and Materials* (Cambridge, Cambridge University Press, 2013).

27 In *EC – Bananas III*, the Appellate Body took the view that 'treatment no less favourable' in Article II:1 of the GATS should be taken to include both de jure and de facto discrimination (see Appellate Body Report in *EC – Bananas*, paras. 231–4). Furthermore, from the early GATT practice, the phrase 'no less favourable' has been described as an expression of the underlying principle of *effective* equality of treatment between different foreign products. Accordingly, a measure affords less favourable treatment if it adversely modifies the conditions of competition between imports from two different countries. See GATT Panel Report on *Italian Agricultural Machinery*, above, paras. 11–12 and GATT Panel Report in *United States – Section 337*, L/6439, adopted on 7 November 1989 BISD 36S/345, para. 5.10.

28 See Panel Report, *US – Underwear*, para. 7.65 and Appellate Body Report, *US – Underwear*, at 21.

required for the supply of a service ... the competent authorities of a Member shall ... inform the applicant of the decision concerning the application'.

Transparency requirements are not applicable to confidential information, the disclosure of which 'would impede law enforcement, or otherwise be contrary to the public interest, or which would prejudice legitimate commercial interests of particular enterprises, public or private' (Article III *bis*). The component of this exception allowing confidentiality on grounds of public interest raises issues of definition; for it is possible to argue that, without qualification, an exception to transparency on the basis of public interest could give a WTO Member a wide margin of discretion, and reduce considerably the scope of the transparency provisions.

3. Domestic regulation and recognition

Article VI GATS sets out certain good governance (or administrative due process) standards, in particular a duty to 'ensure that all measures of general application affecting trade in services are administered in a reasonable, objective and impartial manner' (Article VI:1) and a duty to 'maintain or institute as soon as practicable judicial, arbitral or administrative tribunals, or procedures which provide, at the request of an affected service supplier, for the prompt review of, and where justified, appropriate remedies for, administrative decisions affecting trade in services' (Article VI:2).[29]

The GATS provides for a normative mandate to the Council for Trade in Services to develop, through subsidiary bodies, any disciplines on domestic regulation in order to ensure 'that measures relating to qualification requirements and procedures, technical standards and licensing requirements do not constitute unnecessary barriers to trade in services'. Furthermore, these disciplines shall aim to ensure that such regulations are, *inter alia*, '(a) based on objective and transparent criteria, such as competence and the ability to supply the service; (b) not more burdensome than necessary to ensure the quality of the service; (c) in the case of licensing procedures, not in themselves a restriction on the supply of the service' (Article VI:4). Although this provision has so far only been applied once with regard to the accountancy sector,[30] it evidences that liberalization of trade in services, even more than in the case of goods, requires the adoption of *ad hoc* approaches with regard to a specific service sector, in particular when one moves from more shallow to deeper forms of economic integration.[31]

---

29 For an attempt to distinguish between 'substance' and 'administration' of a given measure (within the context of Article X GATT) see Appellate Body Reports, *EC – Selected Customs Matters*. More generally, see Panagiotis Delimatsis, *International Trade in Services and Domesic Regulations* (Oxford, Oxford University Press, 2007).

30 *Disciplines on Domestic Regulation in the Accountancy Sector*, S/L/64, adopted by the Council for Trade in Services on 14 December 1998.

31 Cf the work carried out within the WTO first by the Working Party on Professional Services (S/WPPS) and currently by the Working Party on Domestic Regulation (S/WPDR). See the latest Annual report of the WPDR (2013), S/WPDR/W/52 (15 October 2013) highlighting recent discussions on a list of potential technical issues covering in part 'verification and assessment of qualifications; identification of deficiencies

The GATS also envisages the possibility for a Member to recognize the education or experience obtained, requirement met, or licenses or certification granted in a particular country for purposes of the fulfilment of its standards or criteria for the authorization, licensing or certification of services suppliers. Such recognition may be based upon an agreement or arrangement with the country concerned or may be accorded autonomously (Article VII:1). Such recognition shall not constitute a means of discrimination between countries or a disguised restriction on trade in services (Article VII:3). Wherever appropriate, recognition should be based on multilaterally agreed criteria and Members shall work in cooperation with relevant intergovernmental and non-governmental organizations towards the establishment and adoption of common international standards and criteria for recognition and common international standards for the practice of relevant services trades and professions (Article VII:5).

From the above, three issues appear to be prominent in the discussion of future disciplines on domestic regulation affecting trade in services: necessity test, international standards and recognition of equivalence.[32]

4. Exceptions

There are several provisions in the GATS setting out exceptions to GATS obligations including an Economic Integration exception (Article V), a Balance of Payments exception (Article XII), a General Exception (Article XIV), and a Security Exception (Article XIV *bis*).

C. *Specific commitments*

Contrary to the general obligations analyzed in the previous section, part III of the GATS provides for a further set of obligations, which are however dependent on the level of commitments undertaken by each Member. These obligations are in particular the market access (Article XVI) and national treatment (Article XVII) obligations. Accordingly, the market access and national treatment obligations do not apply generally to all measures affecting trade in services, but only come into play if Members choose to commit service sectors or sub-sectors in their Schedules of Specific Commitments. In other words, with regard to market access and national treatment, GATS follows the so-called 'positive list' approach, whereby market access and national treatment obligations extend only to those *service sectors* that Members have actually (i.e., positively) inscribed in their individual schedules of commitments (service-specific limitation). However, even in those sectors or sub-sectors that Members have inscribed in their schedules, Members are allowed to reserve the

---

of qualifications; examinations; technical standards; general provisions and development-related aspects of the disciplines'.

32 See Markus Krajewski, 'Services Liberalization in Regional Trade Agreements' in L. Bartels and F. Ortino (eds.) *Regional Trade Agreements and the WTO Legal System* (Oxford, Oxford University Press, 2006) at 180.

right to maintain or adopt *measures* inconsistent with the market access and national treatment obligations (measure-specific limitation). This is done by specifying in their schedules any conditions on their market access and national treatment commitments.[33] Accordingly, it is more correct to describe the GATS approach as a 'positive/negative list' or hybrid approach.[34]

As mentioned above, the difference between the general provisions in part II and the specific commitments in part III is apparently in their scope of application: while general provisions may be limited by *either* sector-specific limitations *or* service-specific limitations, the latter provisions may be limited by *both* limitations.

1. Market access

With regard to the market access provision, Article XVI:2(a)–(f) identifies, in an apparently exhaustive manner, a number of measures (mostly of a quantitative nature), which Members should not maintain or adopt in the sectors where specific commitments have been undertaken, unless otherwise specified.[35]

In *US – Gambling*, the Panel and Appellate Body have given a seemingly broad reading to the market access limitations listed in Article XVI, which would include any measure having an *effect similar* to that of any market access limitations listed in Article XVI:2, regardless of form.[36]

2. National treatment

Article XVII requires each Member to 'accord to services and service suppliers of any other Member, in respect of all measures affecting the supply of services, treatment no less favourable than that it accords to its own like services and service suppliers' (Article XVII:1). Subject to each Member's specific commitments, Article XVII GATS sets out a three-tier test of consistency, which requires the examination of

---

33 A WTO Member may choose to describe either how trade in services is restricted ('No limitation, except') or what types of services transactions are allowed in a listed sector ('Unbound, except').

34 Some commentators have referred to this as the 'hybrid' approach because the fixing of the level of openness involves elements of both negative and positive listings. See Carsten Fink and Martin Molinuevo, 'East Asian Free Trade Agreements in Services: Roaring Tigers or Timid Pandas?' World Bank (June 2007).

35 Article XVI:2 GATS reads in part as follows: 'In sectors where market-access commitments are undertaken, the measures which a Member shall not maintain or adopt either on the basis of a regional subdivision or on the basis of its entire territory, unless otherwise specified in its Schedule, are defined as: (a) limitations on the number of service suppliers whether in the form of numerical quotas, monopolies, exclusive service suppliers or the requirements of an economic needs test.'

36 The Panel found, and the Appellate Body upheld, that the US ban is (1) a limitation on the number of service suppliers in the form of numerical quotas within the meaning of Article XVI:2(a) 'because it *totally prevents* the use by service suppliers of one, several or all means of delivery that are included in mode 1' and (2) a limitation on the total number of service operations or on the total quantity of service output in the form of quotas within the meaning of Article XVI:2(c) 'because it ... *results* in a "zero quota" on one or more or all means of delivery include[d] in mode 1'. Panel Report, *US – Gambling*, paras. 6.338 and 6.355; Appellate Body Report, *US – Gambling*, paras. 239 and 252. For a critique of this decision see Federico Ortino, 'Treaty Interpretation and the WTO Appellate Body Report in *US – Gambling*: A Critique', (2006) 9 *JIEL* 1, 117–48.

whether (1) the measure at issue affects trade in services, (2) the foreign and domestic services and service suppliers are 'like' services or service suppliers,[37] and (3) the foreign services or service suppliers are granted treatment no less favourable.[38]

Article XVII specifies further the content of the national treatment clause: 'A Member may meet the requirement of paragraph 1 by according to services and service suppliers of any other Member, either formally identical treatment or for-mally different treatment to that it accords to its own like services and service suppliers' (Article XVII:2). 'Formally identical or formally different treatment shall be considered to be less favourable if it modifies the conditions of competition in favour of services or service suppliers of the Member compared to like services or service suppliers of any other Member' (Article XVII:3).[39]

3. Additional commitments: Reference paper on basic telecommunications

Members may negotiate commitments with respect to measures affecting trade in services not subject to scheduling under Articles XVI or XVII, including those regarding qualifications, standards or licensing matters (Article XVIII). The Reference Paper on regulatory principles in basic telecommunications, the result of

---

37 With regard to the concept of 'like services', the Panel in *China – Electronic Payment Services* noted that 'a likeness determination should be based on arguments and evidence that pertain to the competitive relationship of the services being compared' (Panel Report, para. 7.702). With regard to the concept of 'like service suppliers', the Panel noted that 'the fact that service suppliers provide like services may in some cases raise a presumption that they are "like" service suppliers. However, we consider that, in the specific circumstances of other cases, a separate inquiry into the "likeness" of the suppliers may be called for. For this reason, we consider that "like service suppliers" determinations should be made on a case-by-case basis' (Panel Report, para. 7.705). See, more generally, Nicolas Diebold, *Non-Discrimination in International Trade in Services: Likeness in WTO/GATS* (Cambridge, Cambridge University Press, 2010).
38 Cf Van den Bossche and Zdouc, *The Law and Policy of the World Trade Organization* (Cambridge, Cambridge University Press, 2013).
39 The wordings of these two paragraphs draw heavily on the reasoning of two well-known GATT panel reports: *US – Section 337* and *Italian Agricultural Machinery*, respectively. Both panels addressed claims under Article III:4 GATT, which include a prohibition against discriminatory non-fiscal regulation very similar to Article XVII:1 GATS. In line with the GATT/WTO jurisprudence on Article III GATT, the *EC – Bananas* Panel Report application of the 'less favourable treatment' test in Article XVII GATS rested on the determination of *adverse effects* of the national measure under review *predominantly* on foreign service suppliers. Focusing on the combined effect of the structural features of the regulation under review (differentiating distributors according to their past marketing records) and the actual market shares of service suppliers of EC and non-EC origin (most of the suppliers of Complainants' origin were classified in Category A, while most of the suppliers of EC origin were classified in Category B), the Panel found that the EC regulation operated in such a way as to modify the conditions of competition to the detriment of foreign (non-EC) service suppliers (Panel Report, *EC – Bananas III*, para. 7.335). See also Appellate Body Report, *EC – Bananas III*, paras. 239–40. More recently, the Panel in *China – Publications and Audiovisual Products* confirmed that 'a measure that prohibits foreign service suppliers from supplying a range of services that may, subject to satisfying certain conditions, be supplied by the like domestic supplier cannot constitute treatment "no less favourable", since it deprives the foreign service supplier of any opportunity to compete with like domestic suppliers' (Panel Report, WT/DS363/R, 12 August 2009, paras. 7.978–7.979). Along the same lines, Panel Report, *China – Electronic Payment Services*, para. 7.687.

post-Uruguay Round negotiations on telecommunications, is an example of an 'additional commitment'. Building on Articles VIII and IX GATS, the Reference Paper is aimed to strengthen competition disciplines in the area, in particular to ensure that the market power of a former public monopoly service provider is not used to the detriment of new market entrants.

D. Sectoral disciplines

As mentioned above, next to the framework agreement (with its general and specific provisions), the GATS system provides also for several annexes addressing sector-specific issues[40] as well as an Understanding on Commitments in Financial Services. These additional sectoral agreements have different functions: to limit the scope of the GATS (e.g., to exclude air transport services), to set out rules and timetable for further negotiations in certain sectors (e.g., maritime transport services and basic telecommunications), or to provide for additional rules and disciplines for certain sectors (e.g., telecommunications, financial services).

While it is not possible here to examine in details these sectoral agreements, it should be emphasized at least that with regard to the latter function (to provide for additional disciplines) a few of these agreements do go well beyond the provisions set out in the framework agreement. Particularly, those instruments dealing with telecommunication and financial services provide for a set of rules and disciplines that go well beyond those provided in the framework agreement. These additional disciplines may either go beyond the framework agreement in terms of further trade liberalization or in terms of granting Members more leeway to restrict trade. For example, the 'Understanding on Commitments in Financial Services' and the 'Annex on Financial Services' provide for additional rules dealing with monopoly rights, government procurement, commercial presence and non-discriminatory measures that may be categorized as pro-liberalization measures as well as additional rules dealing with domestic regulation granting Members the prerogative to take measures for prudential reasons (the so-called 'prudential carve-out' in the Annex on Financial Services).

III. Services in Regional Trade Agreements

Up to end of 2013, 116 regional trade agreements have been notified to the Council of Trade in Services pursuant to Article V GATS.[41] This section, which is the core of the chapter, addresses certain key issues in the services chapters of RTAs.

---

40 See, for example, Annex on Movement of Natural Persons Supplying Services under the Agreement, Annex on Air Transport Services, two Annexes on Financial Services, Annex on Negotiations on Maritime Transport Services, Annex on Telecommunications, Annex on Negotiations on Basic Telecommunications.

41 Thirty services RTAs were notified up to 1994 and 87 between 1995 and 2013. Among the parties with the highest share of these services RTAs are Chile (18), Singapore (including those signed by ASEAN) (16), the EU (including the 1957 EC Treaty) (13), the United States (12), Japan (12), China (including those signed

A. Scope of application

The first issue to be considered is that of the scope of application of the services chapter in RTAs. This section will be broken down according to the following sub-issues: 'mode of supply', 'bodies', 'beneficiaries', 'excluded categories of services' and 'excluded government activities'.

1. Mode of supply

Regional trade agreements principally take two approaches with regard to the scope of application of the services chapter based on the mode of supply.[42] One approach follows the *GATS 'trade in services' model* and extends the coverage of the services chapter to the four modes of supply defined in Article I GATS (cross-border trade; consumer abroad; commercial presence; movement of natural persons). For example, Article 3.1 of the 2006 EFTA–Korea FTA (on the scope and coverage of the chapter on trade in services) states that the chapter 'applies to measures affecting trade in services' and Article 3.3 (on definitions) incorporates into the FTA the definition of 'trade in services' provided for in Article I GATS.[43]

A second approach follows the *NAFTA 'cross-border trade in services' model* and extends the coverage of the services chapter to 'measures affecting cross-border trade in services', which includes modes 1, 2 and 4. The service chapter in these RTAs does not cover the provision of a service through FDI, which is usually instead covered by a specific chapter on investment. Article 1201 NAFTA provides that Chapter 12 on 'Cross-Border Trade in Services' applies to measures relating to cross-border trade in services where 'cross-border trade in services' is defined as the

> provision of a service (a) from the territory of a Party into the territory of another Party, (b) in the territory of a Party by a person of that Party to a person of another Party, or (c) by a national of a Party in the territory of another Party, but does not include the provision of a service in the territory of a Party by an investment, as defined in Article 1139 (Investment – Definitions), in that territory.[44]

by Hong Kong) (11), Mexico (9), New Zealand (9), Korea (8), Malaysia (including those signed by ASEAN) (8), Australia (7), EFTA (7), Colombia (7), Canada (5).

42 For a review of the regulation of 'investment' in RTAs see the relative chapter in this volume.
43 See, for example, EFTA–Korea FTA ('Measures affecting trade in services' and GATS definition of 'trade in services'); Mexico–Nicaragua FTA (GATS four modes of supply); EC–Chile FTA (GATS four modes of supply); Thailand–Australia FTA (GATS four modes of supply); EFTA–Chile FTA (GATS four modes of supply); Singapore–Australia FTA (Articles 7.1 and 7.2); EFTA–Singapore FTA (Article 22); Jordan–Singapore FTA (Article 4.1); Japan–Singapore FTA (Articles 57–8); US–Jordan FTA (no chapter on investment); New Zealand–Singapore FTA (Articles 16–17); EFTA–Mexico FTA (no real obligations for investment); Mercosur; Caricom (chapter on establishment and services overlapping).
44 Article 1213, paragraph 2, NAFTA. See also 2013 Canada–Panama FTA (Articles 10.01–02); 2006 US–Bahrain FTA ('Measures adopted or maintained by a Party affecting cross-border trade in services (modes 1, 2, 4, but not 3) by service suppliers of the other Party'); CAFTA+DR (Article 11.1); US–Morocco FTA (Article 11.1); Korea–Singapore FTA (Article 9.2); Japan–Mexico FTA (Articles 97.1 and 106); US–Australia FTA (Articles 10.1 and 10.14, but see exception in Article 10.3); Korea–Chile FTA (Articles 11.1 and 11.2); US–Singapore FTA (Articles 8.1 and 8.2); US–Chile FTA; EC–Mexico FTA (chapter 10);

The GATS 'trade in services' model may have two variants (in respect to the coverage of investment in services): one where the service chapter covers investment in services on an exclusive basis (whether or not the RTA includes a chapter on investment)[45] and one where both the service and investment chapters apply simultaneously to investment in services.[46]

2. Bodies

As in the GATS, a 'measure by a Party' is usually defined very broadly in RTAs to include measures taken by central, regional or (even local)[47] governments and authorities as well as non-governmental bodies in the exercise of powers delegated by central, regional or local governments or authorities.[48] However, contrary to the GATS, several RTAs do not contain the provision found in Article I.3(a) GATS that Members need only take such reasonable measures as may be available to them to secure compliance with GATS rules by sub-central and non-governmental bodies.[49] On the contrary, a few RTAs expressly provide for a stricter obligation to ensure the observance of all obligations and commitments by regional and local governments and authorities.[50]

Canada–Chile FTA. However, in most of these FTAs, certain provisions in the service chapter do apply to measures affecting investment in services (usually the obligations on Market Access; Domestic Regulation and/or Transparency) as in the US–Singapore FTA (Article 8.2.2) or Canada–Panama FTA (Article 9.03.4).

45 2012 EFTA–Ukraine (Article 4.1.1); 2006 EFTA–Korea (Article 2.2: this Chapter 'shall not apply provided that the sector concerned is covered by chapters on trade in services or financial services'); 2004 EFTA–Chile FTA (Article 32); 2005 EC–Chile FTA; 2004 Thailand–Australia FTA (Article 903: 'This Article applies to measures adopted or maintained by a Party relating to: direct investments of investors of the other Party; and investors of the other Party, unless the measure is a measure by that Party affecting trade in services').

46 See, for example, 2008 Brunei Darussalam–Japan EPA (although Article 55.3 provides that in the event of any inconsistency, the chapter on services will prevail with respect to national treatment, MFN treatment and performance requirements, while the chapter on investment will prevail on any other matter); 2005 Mexico–Nicaragua FTA (although in case of inconsistency, the chapter on services will apply to the extent of the inconsistency); 2003 Singapore–Australia FTA; 2001 New Zealand–Singapore FTA (although certain provisions in the chapter on investment do not apply to measures 'adopted pursuant to' the chapter on trade in services; see Article 26).

47 Most RTAs include measures by 'local' government, such as the US–Bahrain FTA (Article10.1.2), EFTA–Korea FTA (Article 3.1.1), CAFTA+DR (Article 11.1.2), US–Morocco FTA (Article 11.1.2), Thailand–Australia FTA (Article 802). The Japan–Mexico FTA includes measures taken by 'federal or central government, state, or prefecture or any other local authority' (Article 106(b)). On the other hand, some RTAs exclude measures taken by local government from the scope of the service chapter. For example, Article 1213 NAFTA provides that, for purposes of the service chapter, 'a reference to a federal, state or provincial government includes any non-governmental body in the exercise of any regulatory, administrative or other governmental authority delegated to it by that government'. See also Chile–Mexico FTA (Article 10.02); Chile–Canada FTA (Article H-12).

48 For example, US–Singapore FTA (Article 8.2.1(c)); EFTA–Korea FTA (Article 3.1.1).

49 For example, ibid.

50 See EFTA–Korea FTA (Article 1.6): 'Each Party shall ensure within its territory the observance of all obligations and commitments under this Agreement by its respective regional and local governments and authorities, and by non-governmental bodies in the exercise of governmental powers delegated to them by central, regional and local governments or authorities.'

3. Beneficiaries

As RTAs extend trade benefits to signatory parties only, they provide rules determining which 'service providers of the other party' are covered by the agreement.[51] This is usually done by defining the 'natural person' and 'juridical person' of a party supplying the service (which are the relevant criteria for modes 2, 3 and 4).[52]

A natural person of a party is usually defined on the basis of both residence and nationality requirements. For example, Article 802 of the Thailand–Australia FTA defines natural persons (for purposes of the coverage of the services chapter) to include natural persons who reside in the territory of that party and who, under the law of that party, are nationals of that party. At times, this definition (coverage) is expanded to include either nationals or permanent residents.[53] Other times, the relevant definition of natural person only requires nationality without residency.[54]

A juridical (or legal) person of a party is at a minimum defined as a juridical person, which is constituted or organized under the law of that party.[55] Often, and in order to exclude from the beneficiaries of a RTA so-called mailbox companies, the relevant definition also includes the requirement that the juridical person be 'engaged in substantive business operation in the territory' of any party[56] or that its operations 'possess a real and continuous link with the economy' of any party.[57] Those services chapters that extend their coverage to mode 3 (i.e., commercial presence) provide for a specific definition of a juridical person of a party for purposes of this particular mode of supply. For example, the EFTA–Singapore FTA states that a juridical person of another party means 'a juridical person which is . . . (ii) in the case of the supply of a service through commercial presence, owned or controlled by: 1. natural persons of that other Party; or 2. juridical persons [constituted or organized under the law of that

---

51 A similar point can be made for 'services' of the other party. Services chapters in RTAs in fact apply to services that are supplied 'from the territory of the other party', as this is implicit in the definition of mode 1, which is found in both 'trade in services' and 'cross-border trade in services' model RTAs.

52 Using the parallel in trade in goods, some commentators refer to these rules as the 'rules of origin' for trade in services. Cf Fink and Molinuevo, above n. 34.

53 For example, Singapore–Australia FTA (Article 1(k)) states as follows: '"natural person of a Party" means a natural person who resides in the territory of the Party or elsewhere and who under the law of that Party: (i) is a national of that Party; or (ii) has the right of permanent residence in that Party.' Similarly, EFTA–Singapore FTA (Article 22(j)).

54 See EFTA–Korea FTA (Article 3.3.3), which, however, extends the coverage not only to nationals but also to 'permanent residents' of a party if that party accords substantially the same treatment to its permanent residents as to its nationals in respect of measures affecting trade in services. Also, EFTA–Mexico FTA (Article 20).

55 Singapore–Australia FTA (Article 1(f)); NAFTA (Articles 201 and 1213), which expands the coverage of the services chapter not just to 'an enterprise constituted or organized under the law of a Party' but also to 'a branch located in the territory of a Party and carrying out business activities there'.

56 2009 Japan–Switzerland EPA (Article 44(g)); EFTA–Singapore FTA (Article 22(l)). As noted above, this requirement is also found in Article XXVIII(m) GATS.

57 EFTA–Mexico FTA (Article 20).

other party and engaged in substantive business operations in the territory of any Party].'[58]

On the other hand, certain RTAs do not provide for exhaustive definitions of these terms and instead rely on 'denial of benefits' provisions to limit the scope of the beneficiaries of the trade preferences granted in these agreements. According to these provisions a party *may* deny the benefits of the services chapter to a service supplier of the other party (or parties) if the judicial person is owned or controlled by nationals of a non-Party with which the denying party does not maintain diplomatic relations[59] or if the service is being supplied by an enterprise that has no substantial business activities in the territory of the other party and it is owned or controlled by persons of a non-party or the denying party.[60] Some of these agreements condition the applicability of the denial of benefits option to certain prior notification and consultation requirements.[61]

4. (Excluded) categories of services

While in principle all types of services are included in the service chapter of RTAs, it is very often the case that services chapters exclude certain categories of services from their coverage on a vertical (sector-specific) and/or horizontal (across all sectors) basis.

There are a few service sectors that are often excluded from the coverage of the service chapter. This is either because the agreement contains a specific chapter addressing that particular service sector or because the agreement as a whole does not cover it. For example, service chapters (as well as investment ones) in several RTAs do not cover trade in financial services as this is usually the subject matter of a specific chapter.[62] Another service sector that is usually excluded from the services

---

58　See also Singapore–Australia FTA (Article 1(f)(ii)); EFTA–Korea FTA (Article 3.3.4(b)); Thailand–Australia FTA (Article 802); EFTA–Singapore FTA (Article 22(l)).

59　For example, Article 1211(a) allows a NAFTA party to deny the benefits of the services chapter to a service provider of another NAFTA party where the party establishes that: 'the service is being provided by an enterprise owned or controlled by nationals of a non-Party, and (i) the denying Party does not maintain diplomatic relations with the non-Party, or (ii) the denying Party adopts or maintains measures with respect to the non-Party that prohibit transactions with the enterprise or that would be violated or circumvented if the benefits of this Chapter were accorded to the enterprise.'

60　See US–Singapore FTA (Article 8.11) and similarly Canada–Chile FTA (Article H-11). Some agreements include both specific definitions of the meaning of a 'juridical person of a party' and a denial of benefits provision, such as the 2007 United States–Korea FTA including a definition of 'enterprise of a Party' (Article 12.13) and a denial of benefits clause (Article 12.11).

61　See for example, Canada–Chile FTA (Article H-11.2 stating as follows: 'Subject to prior notification and consultation in accordance with Articles L-03 (Notification and Provision of Information) and N-06 (Consultations), a Party may deny the benefits of this Chapter to a service provider of the other Party where the Party establishes that the service is being provided by an enterprise that is owned or controlled by persons of a non-Party and that has no substantial business activities in the territory of the other Party.')

62　See, for example, US–Bahrain FTA; CAFTA+DR FTA; US Morocco FTA; Korea–Singapore FTA; US–Singapore FTA; US–Chile FTA. The service chapter in the Korea–Chile FTA expressly excludes application to financial services despite there being no chapter on financial services in the agreement (Article 11.2.3). Similarly, the Chile–El Salvador FTA and Chile–Costa Rica FTA exclude financial services from the coverage of the agreement.

chapter (as well as from the entire agreement) is 'air services', including domestic and international air transportation services, whether scheduled or non-scheduled, and related services in support of air services, other than aircraft repair and maintenance services and speciality air services (that is non-transportation air services such as aerial firefighting, sightseeing, mapping, glider towing, etc).[63]

Services chapters often exclude from their coverage on a horizontal manner 'services supplied in the exercise of governmental authority', which are usually defined as 'any service which is supplied neither on a commercial basis nor in competition with one or more service suppliers'.[64] This is the same approach followed by the GATS. On the other hand, NAFTA takes a different approach as it lists the categories of services that the services chapter in NAFTA does not prevent a NAFTA party from providing, albeit in a manner not inconsistent with the chapter itself.[65]

5. (Excluded) government activities

Most RTAs exclude certain types of governmental activities from the coverage of the chapter on services either because these activities are covered in other chapters or because they are excluded from the agreement as a whole. The most recurrent ones are 'government procurement' and 'subsidies and grants provided by a party'.[66]

---

63 See for example, 2011 Ukraine–Montenegro FTA (Article 25.2), 2008 China–Singapore FTA (Article 60.4–5), 2007 Pakistan–Malaysia EPA (Article 68.2(d)), US–Bahrain FTA (Article 10.1.4(b)), CAFTA+DR FTA (Article 11.1.4(b)), US–Morocco FTA (Article 11.1.4(b)), Japan–Mexico FTA (Article 97.2(c)), US–Australia FTA (Article 10.1.4(c)), EFTA–Chile FTA (Article 22.2 extending the limited coverage of the services chapter also to the 'selling and marketing of air transport services and computer reservation system services'), Korea–Chile FTA (Article 11.2.3(b)), US–Singapore FTA (Article 8.2.3(c)), US–Chile FTA (Article 11.1.4(b)), Singapore–Australia FTA (Article 22.2–3), EFTA–Singapore FTA (Article 21.2), Canada–Chile FTA (Article H-01.2(b)), NAFTA (Article 1201.2(b)).
64 See for example, 2008 China–Singapore FTA (Article 60.2(a)), 2008 China–New Zealand FTA (Article 105.2(b)), US–Bahrain (Article 10.1.6), Japan–Mexico FTA (Article 97.2(g)), US–Morocco (Article 11.1.6), Thailand–Australia FTA (Article 803). At times this is done through incorporation of the relevant provision in the GATS: see, for example, Article 4.4 of the Jordan–Singapore FTA. On the other hand, certain agreements do not provide for such an exclusion: see, for example, 2010 Canada–Panama FTA and 2005 EFTA–Korea FTA.
65 Article 1201.3 provides as follows: 'Nothing in this Chapter shall be construed to: ... (b) prevent a Party from providing a service or performing a function such as law enforcement, correctional services, income security or insurance, social security or insurance, social welfare, public education, public training, health, and child care, in a manner that is not inconsistent with this Chapter.'
66 See for example, 2010 Canada–Panama FTA (Article 10.05.2), US–Bahrain FTA (Article 10.1.4(c) and (d)), CAFTA+DR FTA (Article 11.1.4(c) and (d)), Korea–Singapore FTA (Article 9.2.3(b) and (c)), US–Morocco FTA (Article 11.1.4(c) and (d)), Thailand–Australia FTA (Article 803), US–Australia FTA (Article 10.1.4(b) and (d)), Korea–Chile FTA (Article 11.2.3(c) and (d)), US–Singapore FTA (Article 8.2.3(b) and (d)), US–Chile (Article 11.1.4(c) and (d)), Canada–Chile FTA (Article H-01.2(c) and (d)), EFTA–Mexico (Article 19.4 and 5), EC–Chile FTA (Article 95.3 and 4). Only procurement: EFTA–Singapore (Article 21.4). Only subsidies or grants: 2005 India–Singapore EPA (Article 7.2.2) and 2003 Singapore–Australia FTA (Article 2.2(a) of Chapter 7). Contrary to subsidies and grants, exclusion of procurement from the coverage of the services chapter is usually accompanied by the chapter dealing with procurement in services.

Another area which is excluded in basically all RTAs relates to the movement of natural persons, and in particular to 'measures pursuant to immigration laws and regulations',[67] affecting 'natural persons seeking access to the employment market or employed on a permanent basis in the territory of a party',[68] or 'regarding citizenship, residence or employment on a permanent basis'.[69] The 2003 Singapore–Australia FTA strengthens this exclusion by expressly providing that:

> Nothing in this Chapter shall prevent a Party from applying measures to regulate the entry of natural persons of the other Party into, or their temporary stay in, its territory, including those measures necessary to protect the integrity of, and to ensure the orderly movement of natural persons across its borders, provided that such measures are not applied in such a manner as to nullify or impair the benefits accruing to the other Party under the terms of this Chapter.[70]

B. Main obligations and disciplines

This section addresses four main obligations and disciplines: 'national treatment', 'market access', 'transparency' and 'domestic regulation'. Given the different approaches followed by RTAs compared with the GATS approach, there is no justification in this section to distinguish between 'general' and 'specific' obligations.

1. National Treatment

The National Treatment obligation is certainly a central obligation regulating trade in services. It is no surprise that it is found in almost all services chapters of RTAs. National treatment obligations, however, differ depending on their 'formulation' and/or their 'scope of application'.

With regard to their **formulation**, two models may be identified (once again stemming from the national treatment obligations in the NAFTA services chapter and in the GATS). Article 1202.1 NAFTA provides that:

> Each Party shall accord to service providers of another Party treatment no less favorable than that it accords, in like circumstances, to its own service providers.[71]

On the other hand, as examined above, Article XVII:1 GATS provides that:

> each Member shall accord to services and service suppliers of any other Member, in respect of all measures affecting the supply of services, treatment no less favourable than that it accords to its own like services and service suppliers.[72]

---

67 2004 Japan–Mexico FTA (Article 97.2(f)).   68 2003 US–Singapore FTA (Article 8.2.4).
69 2003 Singapore–Australia FTA (Article 2.3 Chapter 7).
70 2003 Singapore–Australia FTA (Article 2.4 Chapter 7).
71 2003 Singapore–US FTA (Article 8.3), 1996 Canada–Chile FTA (Article H-02).
72 See, for example, 2009 Japan–Switzerland EPA (Article 47). Some RTAs also follow a hybrid approach, which refers the comparator 'in like circumstances' to both 'services and service providers'. See, for example, the 2011 Mexico–Central America FTA (Article 12-04: '1. Cada Parte otorgará a los servicios y

The two key differences relate to (a) the *beneficiaries* of the provision ('service providers' vs 'services and service suppliers') and (b) the *comparator* ('in like circumstances' vs 'like'). These textual differences may have relevant implications in the protection afforded by the national treatment provision. The interpretations rendered by NAFTA and WTO dispute settlement panels/tribunals with regard to the national treatment obligation in the context of trade in services (as well as in other contexts such as trade in goods and investment) shows the relevance of these textual differences. For example, the phrase 'in like circumstances' has been employed by NAFTA tribunals not just to determine the competitive relationship between foreign and domestic enterprises (as the phrase 'like' has been interpreted by WTO panels) but also as a *de facto* public policy justification mechanism.[73]

With regard to the **scope of application**, the national treatment obligation is almost never applicable on a general and unconditional basis; rather its application depends on the extent of the parties' specific commitments or reservations, which are usually attached to and incorporated into the agreement itself. Once again, the two models adopted by RTAs follow the different approaches of the NAFTA services chapter and the GATS.[74] While the national treatment obligation in Chapter 12 NAFTA applies to any measure of a party with respect to any service sectors or sub-sectors *unless* they are expressly listed in that party's schedule ('negative list' approach),[75] the national treatment obligation in the GATS *only* applies in sectors inscribed in Members' schedules and subject to any conditions and qualifications set out therein ('positive/negative list' approach).[76]

Those RTAs that follow the NAFTA model usually allow a party to exclude both certain measures and certain sectors/sub-sectors/activities. For example, Article 8.7 of the 2003 US–Singapore FTA provides that the national treatment obligation does not apply to (1) 'any existing non-conforming measure that is maintained by a Party at the central level of government [and] at a regional level of government as set out by that Party in its Schedule to Annex 8A' and (2) 'any measure that a Party adopts or

prestadores de servicios de la otra Parte, un trato no menos favorable que el que otorgue, en circunstancias similares, a sus propios servicios y prestadores de servicios'). See also 2008 Australia–Chile FTA; 2005 Korea–Singapore FTA, 2004 Japan–Mexico EPA, 2003 Chile–Korea FTA.

73 See *In the matter of Cross-border Trucking Services*, No. USA-MEX-98–2008-01, Final Report, 6 February 2001, at para. 258. Cf Federico Ortino, 'From "Non-discrimination" to "Reasonableness": A Paradigm Shift in International Economic Law?', (2005) *Jean Monnet Working Paper Series* 1, at 17–32.

74 For a somewhat different approach see Article 37 on the 'Removal of Restrictions on Provision of Services' of the Revised CARICOM Treaty ('1. Subject to the provisions of this Treaty, Member States shall abolish discriminatory restrictions on the provision of services within the Community in respect of Community nationals. 2. Subject to the approval of the Conference, COTED, in consultation with other competent Organs, shall, within one year from the entry into force of this Treaty, establish a programme for the removal of restrictions on the provision of such services in the Community by Community nationals.').

75 This is the 'negative list' approach as the relevant obligation will apply unless the party does not list any relevant *non-conforming measures* and/or any relevant *uncommitted services sectors or sub-sectors*.

76 We refer to the GATS approach as a 'positive/negative list' approach because the relevant obligation applies only to those sectors that are listed or committed in the Member's schedule (positive listing) and subject to any conditions and qualifications set out therein (negative listing).

maintains with respect to sectors, sub-sectors or activities as set out in its Schedule to Annex 8B'.[77] The difference between the two set of reservations is that, at least in principle, the exclusion of 'non-conforming measure' can apply only to *existing* measures:[78] provisions such as Article 8.7 of the US–Singapore FTA seems to imply that once the non-conforming measure is eliminated, the party's policy will automatically be bound at the more liberal level. On the other hand, the exclusion of certain sectors/sub-sectors/activities applies to both existing and future measures.[79] Moreover, it is common that in the NAFTA model 'negative list' agreements, the national treatment provision does not apply to any existing non-conforming measure maintained by a *local government* of the party independently of their express inclusion in the party's schedule.

On the other hand, those RTAs that follow the GATS model condition the applicability of the national treatment obligation to the specific commitments of the party both in terms of sectors (positive element) and conditions (negative element). For example, Article 4.3.1 of the 2003 Jordan–Singapore FTA takes the GATS model 'positive/negative list' approach as it provides that

> In the sectors inscribed in its Schedule of specific commitments, and subject to any conditions and qualifications set out therein, each Party shall accord to services and service suppliers of the other Party, in respect of all measures affecting the supply of services, treatment no less favourable than that it accords to its own like services and service suppliers.[80]

For all these agreements, in order to determine the level of actual liberalization, it is necessary to examine each party's schedule of commitments as well as its laws and regulations.[81]

2. Market access

A market access provision is also very common in services chapters of RTAs, albeit it may take different forms. Usually, these provisions are aimed at prohibiting a set of governmental measures restricting the provision of services apparently whether or not they are discriminatory in nature. The approach to market access in services

---

77 See also Japan–Mexico EPA (Article 101), Korea–Chile FTA (Article 11.5).
78 This exclusion usually extends to the 'continuation or prompt renewal' of any non-conforming measure as well as 'an amendment to' any non-conforming measure (to the extent that the amendment does not decrease the conformity of the measure).
79 For an approach that provides reservations for 'existing measures' and future measures without focusing on any specific sector or subsectors, see 2009 Japan–Switzerland EPA (Articles 47 and 57).
80 See also Thailand–Australia FTA (Article 810), EFTA–Chile FTA (Article 26), US–Jordan (Article 3.2(b)).
81 For an in-depth study assessing the level of actual liberalization with regards to trade in services in RTAs, see Martin Roy, Juan Marchetti and Aik Hoe Lim, 'The Race towards Preferential Trade Agreements in Services: How Much Market Access Is Really Achieved?', in M. Panizzon et al. (eds.) *GATS and the Regulation of International Trade in Services* (Cambridge, Cambridge University Press, 2008) and several contributions in Juan Marchetti and Martin Roy (eds.) *Opening Markets for Trade in Services Countries and Sectors in Bilateral and WTO Negotiations* (Cambridge, Cambridge University Press, 2008).

chapter of RTAs differ depending on (1) the list of measures in principle covered by the prohibition, (2) the normative content of the provision (i.e., what the provision would require), and (3) the actual scope of application (i.e., whether and the extent to which the market access provision is subject to specific commitments, conditions and/or reservations).

With regard to the **measures in principle covered** by the market access prohibition, they may include (a) restrictions of a quantitative nature, (b) restrictions on the type of legal entity required in order to provide a service, and (c) restrictions on foreign equity participation. These correspond to the measures listed in Article XVI:2 (a)–(f) GATS. Several RTAs follow exactly this approach by either reproducing Article XVI GATS verbatim[82] or by incorporating it into the agreement.[83] Other RTAs, including most of the recent United States RTAs, follow a very similar list but omit reference to restrictions on foreign equity participation.[84] As rightly noted by Fink and Molinuevo, this omission does not, however, appear to modify the liberalization nature of the agreement as foreign equity restrictions would, at least in principle, be caught by the national treatment provision.[85]

Other older RTAs, such as NAFTA, on the other hand, do not have a specific provision on 'market access' but include a similar provision addressing 'quantitative restrictions', which are defined as

> non-discriminatory measures that impose limitations on: (a) the number of service providers, whether in the form of a quota, a monopoly or an economic

82 See, for example, Thailand–Australia FTA (Article 809), EFTA–Chile FTA (Article 25), EFTA–Singapore FTA (Article 24).
83 See, for example, 2011 Ukraine–Montenegro FTA (Article 29), 2005 EFTA–Korea FTA (Article 3.5), Jordan–Singapore FTA (Article 4.2), US–Jordan FTA (Article 3.2(a)).
84 See, for example, Article 10.4 of the 2005 US–Bahrain FTA which states as follows:

'1. Neither Party may adopt or maintain, either on the basis of a regional subdivision or on the basis of its entire territory, measures that:
   (a) impose limitations on:
       (i) the number of service suppliers whether in the form of numerical quotas, monopolies, exclusive service suppliers, or the requirement of an economic needs test;
       (ii) the total value of service transactions or assets in the form of numerical quotas or the requirement of an economic needs test;
      (iii) the total number of service operations or on the total quantity of services output expressed in terms of designated numerical units in the form of quotas or the requirement of an economic needs test; or
       (iv) the total number of natural persons that may be employed in a particular service sector or that a service supplier may employ and who are necessary for, and directly related to, the supply of a specific service in the form of numerical quotas or the requirement of an economic needs test; or
   (b) restrict or require specific types of legal entity or joint venture through which a service supplier may supply a service.'

See also 2007 US–Korea FTA (Article 12.4), 2004 CAFTA+DR (Article 11.4), 2004 US–Morocco FTA (Article 11.4), 2004 US–Australia FTA (Article 10.4).
85 Fink and Molinuevo, above n. 34.

needs test, or by any other quantitative means; or (b) the operations of any service provider, whether in the form of a quota or an economic needs test, or by any other quantitative means.[86]

Depending on the interpretation of the term 'limitations on the operations of any service supplier', this apparently more limited list of restrictions may have a similar or broader coverage compared to the GATS-based list of market access restrictions. Only very few RTAs do not have any type of market access provision.[87]

With regard to the **normative content** of the market access provisions in services chapters, this is usually fairly unproblematic as a market access provision at least in principle (i.e., subject to its actual scope of application) prohibits parties from adopting or maintaining the measures listed in the market access provision itself. For example, Article 8.5 of the 2003 US–Singapore FTA provides that 'A Party *shall not adopt or maintain* ... measures that (a) limit (i) the number of service suppliers ... and (b) restrict or require specific types of legal entity'.[88]

However, in some of the older RTAs, such as NAFTA, the only express rule provided for with regard to the 'quantitative restrictions' covered by the services chapter is a mere listing and notification requirements as well as a non-binding obligation to negotiate the liberalization and removal of those restrictions. Article 1207 NAFTA on 'Quantititative Restrictions' provides as follows:

1. Each Party shall set out in its Schedule to Annex V any quantitative restriction that it maintains at the federal level.
2. Within one year of the date of entry into force of this Agreement, each Party shall set out in its Schedule to Annex V any quantitative restriction maintained by a state or province, not including a local government.
3. Each Party shall notify the other Parties of any quantitative restriction that it adopts, other than at the local government level, after the date of entry into force of this Agreement and shall set out the restriction in its Schedule to Annex V.
4. The Parties shall periodically, but in any event at least every two years, endeavor to negotiate the liberalization or removal of the quantitative restrictions set out in Annex V pursuant to paragraphs 1 through 3.[89]

Nevertheless, even these types of agreements included the possibility for parties to commit to the liberalization (i.e., the elimination) of non-discriminatory quantitative restriction. For example, Article 1208 NAFTA on 'Liberalisation of Non-Discriminatory Measures' provided that 'Each Party shall set out in its Schedule to Annex VI its commitments to liberalize quantitative restrictions, licensing requirements, performance requirements or other non-discriminatory measures.'[90]

86 Article 1213 NAFTA. See also Canada–Chile FTA (Article H-12).
87 See, for example, 2004 Japan–Mexico EPA.   88 Emphasis added.
89 See also the 2007 Panama–Costa Rica FTA (Article 11.09.1–2), the 2003 Chile–Korea FTA (Article 11.6), the 1996 Canada–Chile FTA (Article H-07).
90 See also the 2007 Panama–Costa Rica FTA (Article 11.09.3), the 2003 Chile–Korea FTA (Article 11.8), the 1996 Canada–Chile FTA (Article H-08).

Finally, significant differences also exist with regard to the actual **scope of application** of the market access provision. Like for the national treatment obligation, the market access provisions in services chapters is never applicable on a general and unconditional basis; rather its application depends on the extent of the parties' specific commitments or reservations, which are usually attached to and incorporated into the agreement itself. As noted with regard to national treatment, a market access provision may either take a NAFTA-based 'negative list' approach[91] or a GATS-based 'positive/negative list' approach.[92]

3. Transparency

Transparency requirements are generally very common in RTAs whether they are provided for in a separate chapter applying across the agreement (such as in NAFTA and the recent FTAs concluded by the United States and Canada)[93] or as specific provisions found in individual chapters (such as the services chapter). Also with regard to transparency requirements, these agreements follow in general either a GATS-based approach[94] or a NAFTA-based approach, albeit the difference is simply that the latter agreements provide for a marginally broader set of transparency obligations compared to the former.

Transparency requirements differ depending principally on two key features: (1) the mechanisms employed to implement transparency and (2) the items of information subject to the transparency requirements.

The principal **mechanisms employed to implement transparency** applicable *inter alia* to trade in services include (a) publication requirements, (b) provision of information requirements, (c) notification requirements and (d) transparency requirements in administrative proceedings.

Most agreements setting out transparency obligations applying to trade in services include at least a so-called 'publication' requirement, whereby, similarly to Article III:1 GATS, each party is required to promptly publish or otherwise make available certain measures respecting trade in services.[95] A few agreements simply incorporate the relevant provisions of the GATS.[96] Several publication requirements, however, differ from the publication obligation in the GATS as they specifically require parties to make their measures available in such a manner as to enable the other Party and

---

91 See, for example, 2010 Canada–Panama FTA (Article 10.07), 2005 US–Bahrain FTA (Article 10.4), CAFTA+DR (Article 11.4), US–Morocco FTA (Article 11.4), US–Australia FTA (Article 10.4), Singapore–Australia FTA (Article 3, Chapter 7).
92 See, for example, 2008 New Zealand–China FTA (Article 109), 2004 Thailand–Australia FTA (Article 809), 2003 EFTA–Chile FTA (Article 25), 2002 EFTA–Singapore FTA (Article 24).
93 See, for example, the 2010 Canada–Panama FTA (Chapter 20 on Transparency).
94 See, for example, Singapore–Australia FTA (Article 9).
95 See 2009 Japan–Switzerland FTA (Article 59); 2007 Pakistan–Malaysia EPA (Article 78), 2005 EFTA–Korea FTA (Article 3.18), 2004 Japan–Mexico FTA (Article 160), 2003 EFTA–Chile FTA (Article 82.1), 2003 Korea–Chile FTA (Article 17.3.1), 2003 Singapore–Australia FTA (Article 9.1).
96 See 2010 EFTA–Ukraine FTA (Article 3.11).

interested persons to become acquainted with them. For example, Article 14.1.1 of the 2005 Thailand–New Zealand FTA provides that:

> Each Party shall ensure that its laws, regulations, administrative rulings, procedures and policies and any amendment thereto of general application pertaining to trade in goods, services and investment are promptly published or otherwise made available in such a manner as to enable interested persons from the other Party to become acquainted with them.[97]

Reference to 'interested persons' other than the contracting parties may arguably have an influence on the publication mechanisms that need to be chosen in order to comply with the publication requirements of the treaty.[98]

Differently from the publication requirements under the GATS, some agreements also include the obligation to publish *in advance* any proposed measure and to provide interested persons with a reasonable *opportunity to comment* on such proposed measures.[99] Some of those agreements based on the NAFTA-model also include a provision in the services chapter requiring a party, which does not provide advance notice and opportunity to comment pursuant to the disciplines in the chapter on transparency, to address in writing the reasons therefore.[100]

Like Article III:4 GATS, most RTAs include provisions requiring parties to provide information and respond to questions from the other party ('provision of information' requirements). Some RTAs also include 'proposed measures' under the scope of these requirements. For example, Article 18.3.2 of the 2004 Dominican Republic–Central America–US FTA (CAFTA+DR) provides that 'On request of another Party, a Party shall promptly provide information and respond to questions pertaining to any actual or proposed measure.' In addition to these general obligations to provide

---

97 See also Article 18.03 of the Panama–El Salvador FTA stating: 'Cada Parte se asegurará que sus leyes, reglamentos, procedimientos y resoluciones administrativas de aplicación general que se refieran a cualquier asunto comprendido en este Tratado, se publiquen a la brevedad o se pongan a disposición para conocimiento de las Partes y de cualquier interesado.' Cf 2010 Canada–Panama FTA (Article 20.02), 2008 New Zealand–China FTA (Article 168), 2004 Thailand–Australia FTA (Article 1402.1), 2004 US–Australia FTA (Article 20.2.1), Chile–El Salvador FTA (Article 17.03.1), US–Singapore FTA (Article 19.3.1), US–Chile FTA (Article 20.2.1), US–Bahrain FTA (Article 17.1.1).

98 Interestingly, Article 1402.3 of the 2004 Thailand–Australia FTA specifies that a party may comply with the publication requirements of the agreement 'by publication on the internet'.

99 See, for example, Article 14.1.3 of the 2005 Thailand–New Zealand FTA which states: 'When possible, a Party shall publish in advance any measure referred to in Paragraph 1 that it proposes to adopt and shall provide, where applicable, interested persons with a reasonable opportunity to comment on such proposed measures.' Cf 2003 EFTA–Chile FTA (Article 83.2).

100 See, for example, 2008 New Zealand–China FTA (Article 168.2, limiting such requirements 'to the extent possible') and 2004 US–Australia FTA (Article 10.8.2). Interestingly, Article 10.8.3 of the US–Australia FTA also requires parties at the time of adoption of final regulations relating to trade in services, to the extent possible, to address in writing substantive comments received from interested persons with respect to the proposed regulations. See also Article 11.08 of the 2008 Nicaragua–Chinese Taipei FTA providing that 'at the time it adopts final regulations relating to the subject matter of this Chapter [cross-border trade in services], each Party shall, to the extent possible, including on request, address in writing substantive comments received from interested persons with respect to the proposed regulations'.

information, several agreements provide for the establishment of permanent enquiry or contact points in order to facilitate communications between the parties and to provide information on relevant matters.[101]

Equally common are 'notification' requirements (in particular in agreements following the NAFTA-based approach to transparency), whereby parties are required to notify the other party of certain proposed or actual measures. Article 18.3.1 of the 2004 CAFTA+DR provides that 'To the maximum extent possible, each Party shall notify any other Party with an interest in the matter of any proposed or actual measure that the Party considers might materially affect the operation of this Agreement or otherwise substantially affect that other Party's interests under this Agreement.'[102]

A further form of transparency provisions, which may be found in a few RTAs (but excluded from the transparency requirements in GATS), requires parties to follow certain transparency/due process requirements in administrative proceedings. For example, Article 18.4 of the CAFTA+DR provides that:

> each Party shall ensure that in its administrative proceedings ... (a) wherever possible, persons of another Party that are directly affected by a proceeding are provided reasonable notice, in accordance with domestic procedures, when a proceeding is initiated, including a description of the nature of the proceeding, a statement of the legal authority under which the proceeding is initiated, and a general description of any issues in controversy; (b) such persons are afforded a reasonable opportunity to present facts and arguments in support of their positions prior to any final administrative action, when time, the nature of the proceedings, and the public interest permit.[103]

It should be noted that, although they generally adopt mandatory language, all these transparency requirements may at times be limited by wording such as 'wherever possible',[104] 'to the extent possible',[105] 'to the maximum extent possible',[106] 'when possible'.[107] Undoubtedly, these limitations leave some discretion to parties in implementing transparency requirements.

The **items of information** that are subject to transparency requirements may differ depending on the specific transparency mechanism.

With regard to 'publication' requirements, reference is usually made to 'measures of general application' either with respect to any matter covered by the agreement (for those agreements with a separate chapter on transparency) or affecting the operation

---

101 See, for example, 2008 Nicaragua–Chinese Taipei (Article 11.08(a)); 2004 CAFTA+DR (Article 18.1).
102 See also 2008 New Zealand–China FTA (Article 172). On the other hand, no notification requirements may be found in the agreements following a GATS-based approach to transparency such as EFTA–Chile FTA, Singapore–Australia FTA, Japan–Mexico FTA, Jordan–Singapore FTA, EFTA–Korea FTA.
103 See also 2008 New Zealand–China FTA (Article 169).
104 See, for example, US–Australia FTA (Article 20.4).
105 See, for example, Panama–El Salvador FTA (Article 18.4).
106 See, for example, Korea–Chile FTA (Article 17.4.1).
107 See, for example, Thailand–Australia FTA (Article 1401.4).

of the services chapter. In particular, those agreements that follow the broad NAFTA-based approach to transparency requirements make express reference to 'laws, regulations, procedures, and administrative rulings of general application' with regard to publication requirements. Most of these agreements also provide for a definition of 'administrative rulings of general application'. For example, Article 18.6 of 2004 CAFTA+DR provides that:

> For purposes of this Section: 'administrative ruling of general application' means an administrative ruling or interpretation that applies to all persons and fact situations that fall generally within its ambit and that establishes a norm of conduct but does not include: (a) a determination or ruling made in an administrative or quasi-judicial proceeding that applies to a particular person, good, or service of another Party in a specific case; or (b) a ruling that adjudicates with respect to a particular act or practice.[108]

Even some of the agreements following the narrower GATS-based approach to transparency specify the items of information that are subject to publication requirement. For example, Article 160 of the 2004 Japan–Mexico FTA refers to 'laws, regulations, administrative procedures and administrative rulings and judicial decisions of general application as well as international agreements to which the Party is a party'.

On the contrary, notification and provision of information requirements in the NAFTA-based agreements seem to refer generally to 'measures' that the party considers might materially affect the operation of the agreement or otherwise substantially affect the other party's interests under the agreement.[109] Interestingly, these agreements tend to limit the scope of the notification/provision of information requirements by qualifying the otherwise broad term 'affect' with terms such as 'materially' and ' substantially'.[110]

4. Domestic regulation

Rules on domestic regulation may be found in several RTAs covering services trade.[111] These rules may require parties to (a) administer domestic laws in a

108 Similarly, Article 14.1.2 of the 2005 Thailand–New Zealand FTA provides that 'For the purposes of this Chapter, "administrative ruling of general application" means an administrative ruling or interpretation that applies to all persons and fact situations and that is relevant to the implementation of this Agreement.'

109 Article 18.3.1 of 2004 CAFTA+DR. Following the approach in Article III:4 GATS, other agreements refer to 'measures of general application' in their provision of information requirements. See, for example, 2012 EU–Central America Association Agreement (Article 178.1), 2005 EFTA–Korea FTA (Article 3.18), 2004 Jordan–Singapore FTA (Article 4.14.3), 2003 Singapore–Australia FTA (Article 9.3).

110 See, for example, Article 20.03.1 of the 2010 Canada–Panama FTA which provides as follows: 'To the maximum extent possible, a Party shall notify the other Party of an existing or proposed measure that the Party considers might materially affect the operation of this Agreement or substantially affect the other Party's interests under this Agreement.' Cf UNCTAD, *Transparency: UNCTAD Series on Issues in International Investment Agreements* (Geneva, United Nations, 2004).

111 Several RTAs also include provisions on mutual recognition, which for the most part replicate Article VII GATS. A few of these RTAs include at times more detailed provisions on the recognition of professional qualifications and registration procedures (see, for example, Article 4.8 of the 2004 Jordan–Singapore

reasonable, objective and impartial manner, (b) establish review and appeal mechanisms for administrative decisions, (c) ensure that measures relating to qualification requirements and procedures, technical standards, and licensing requirements do not constitute unnecessary barriers to trade in services (so-called 'necessity requirement'), and (d) use relevant international standards.[112] While Article VI GATS include all four rules (albeit subject to certain limitations), RTAs vary in their approach to domestic regulation, most of them not going beyond what is provided by GATS.[113]

With regard to the obligation to **administer domestic laws in a reasonable, objective and impartial manner**, several services chapters in RTAs follow the GATS approach either by reproducing Article VI:1 language[114] or by making express reference to the relevant GATS provisions.[115] In the case of the 2001 EFTA–Mexico FTA, such an obligation is found in Article 25 on the 'Right to Regulate'.[116] A few other agreements, following the NAFTA, do not provide for such a general obligation.[117]

FTA, Article 806 of the 2004 Thailand–Australia FTA, and Article 23 of the 2003 Singapore–Australia FTA), and higher education qualification (Annex 11.13 of the 2002 Panama–El Salvador FTA). At times mutual recognition provisions are included in annexes dealing specifically with professional services. See infra next section.

112 Occasionally, RTAs simply provide for non-discrimination obligation with regard to similar domestic laws. For example, Article 9.1 of the 1988 Australia–New Zealand Closer Economic Relations Trade Agreement requires, on a hortatory basis, that 'licensing and certification measures shall not have the purpose or effect of impairing or restraining, in a discriminatory manner, access of persons of the other Member State to such licensing or certification'.

113 For those RTAs that do not contain rules on domestic regulation applicable generally to trade in services, see, for example, the 1997 EU–Mexico FTA.

114 See, for example, 2011 Ukraine–Montenegro FTA (Article 32), 2003 Singapore–Australia FTA (Article 11), Protocol of Montevideo for the Trade in Services of Mercosur (Article 10.1).

115 See, for example, 2006 EFTA–Korea FTA (Article 3.8), 2005 Jordan–Singapore FTA (Article 4.9), 2001 US–Jordan FTA (Article 3.2(c)(ii)).

116 '1. Each Party may regulate, and introduce new regulations, on the supply of services within its territory in order to meet national policy objectives, in so far as regulations do not impair on any rights and obligations arising under this Agreement. 2. Each Party shall ensure that all measures of general application affecting trade in services are administered in a reasonable, objective and impartial manner.' Article 25.1–2, 2001 EFTA–Mexico FTA.

117 As mentioned above in the section on transparency, NAFTA does however include a more limited obligation addressing the administration of domestic laws, often contained in a stand-alone chapter on Transparency. Article 1804 provides: 'With a view to administering in a consistent, impartial and reasonable manner all measures of general application affecting matters covered by this Agreement, each Party shall ensure that in its administrative proceedings applying measures referred to in Article 1802 to particular persons, goods or services of another Party in specific cases that: (a) wherever possible, persons of another Party that are directly affected by a proceeding are provided reasonable notice, in accordance with domestic procedures, when a proceeding is initiated, including a description of the nature of the proceeding, a statement of the legal authority under which the proceeding is initiated and a general description of any issues in controversy; (b) such persons are afforded a reasonable opportunity to present facts and arguments in support of their positions prior to any final administrative action, when time, the nature of the proceeding and the public interest permit; and (c) its procedures are in accordance with domestic law.' See also 2007 US–Korea FTA (Article 21.3), 2004 Japan–Mexico FTA (Article 162),

With regard to the scope of application, this obligation may apply either only in the service sectors and sub-sectors where commitments have been undertaken (similarly to Article VI:1 GATS) or in principle to all service sectors and sub-sectors except as provided in the relevant annex on reservations or non-conforming measures (i.e., negative-list approach). For example, of the nine RTAs concluded by Singapore which include such a provision,[118] six follow the GATS positive/negative-list approach,[119] while three follow a negative-list approach.[120] Only in very few instances does the obligation to administer domestic laws in a reasonable, objective and impartial manner apply generally and unconditionally.[121]

Most RTAs include provisions requiring parties to **establish and maintain review and appeal mechanisms for administrative decisions** either as part of the services chapter or as part of the chapter on transparency.[122] For example, Article 163.1 of the 2004 Japan–Mexico FTA on 'Review and Appeal' (following a very similar provision in NAFTA) provides that:

> Each Party shall maintain judicial or administrative tribunals or procedures for the purpose of prompt review and, where warranted, correction of administrative actions regarding matters covered by this Agreement. Such tribunals or procedures shall be impartial and independent of the authorities entrusted with the administrative enforcement.[123]

Similarly, most RTAs include a **necessity requirement** with regard to certain measures affecting trade in services. Following the Article VI:5 GATS model, certain RTAs require parties to ensure that 'licensing and qualification requirements and technical standards' are based on objective and transparent criteria and not more burdensome than necessary to ensure the quality of a service. However, as mentioned above when analyzing GATS rules on domestic regulation, necessity requirements following the GATS model are subject to two important limitations: they can be

2003 Chile–Korea FTA (Article 17.6), 2003 US–Singapore FTA (Article 19.5), 2002 Panama–El Salvador FTA (Article 18.06).

118 As noted above, like NAFTA, some RTAs do not contain the obligation to administer domestic laws in a reasonable, objective and impartial manner but with regard to RTAs concluded by Singapore, see 2010 Costa Rica–Singapore FTA (Article 15.5), 2008 Peru–Singapore FTA (Article 15.5), 2003 Singapore–US FTA.

119 2008 China–Singapore FTA (Article 65.1), 2005 India–Singapore FTA (Article 7.10), 2004 Singapore–Jordan FTA (Article 4.9.1), 2002 Singapore–Japan FTA (Article 64.1), 2002 Singapore–EFTA FTA (Article 28.1), 2000 Singapore–New Zealand FTA (Article 21.1).

120 See, for example, 2006 Panama–Singapore FTA (Articles 10.9.1 and 10.7.3), 2005 Singapore–Korea FTA (Articles 9.11.1 and 9.6.3), 2003 Singapore–Australia FTA (Articles 11.1 and 5.3).

121 See, for example, the Protocol of Montevideo for the Trade in Services of Mercosur (Article 10.1).

122 Again here, Article VI:2 GATS, on the one hand, and Article 1805 NAFTA, on the other, provide the two models that are followed by subsequent RTAs.

123 See also 2003 Panama–El Salvador FTA (Article 18.07.1). Those agreements that follow the NAFTA provision also include a due process-type of procedural right by requiring that parties to such administrative proceedings be provided with 'the right to (a) a reasonable opportunity to support or defend their respective positions; and (b) a decision based on the evidence and submissions of record or, where required by domestic law, the record compiled by the administrative authority'. Cf Article 1805.2 NAFTA.

invoked only if the relevant regulatory measures nullify or impair specific commitments *and* could not reasonably have been expected when specific commitments were made.[124]

Those agreements that follow the NAFTA model with regard to the rules on domestic regulation usually differ from GATS necessity requirements in two respects. First, the necessity requirements found in the services chapter apply only on a best endeavour basis.[125] Second, they usually cover only 'requirements and procedures to the licensing or certification' of service providers of the other party (leaving out 'technical standards').[126] However, a few of these agreements (like NAFTA) contain a chapter on 'technical barriers to trade', which extends its coverage to 'standards-related measures' that affect both trade in goods and services[127] and provide *inter alia* for mandatory (WTO TBT Agreement-like) necessity requirements.[128]

Finally, requirements to **use relevant international standards** may take two forms depending on whether they are found in the provision on domestic regulation in the services chapter or in the chapter on standards-related measures. First, relevant international standards are taken into account to determine whether domestic measures (such as licensing and qualification requirements) comply with the necessity requirements in the RTA. This is the Article VI:5 GATS model.[129] A variance to this approach is taken by those RTAs expressly providing that 'domestic regulation prepared, adopted and applied in accordance with international standards shall be

---

124 One notable exception is the necessity requirement found in Article 10.4 of the Protocol of Montevideo for the Trade in Services of Mercosur, which does not include either of the two limitations.

125 For example, Article 1210.1 NAFTA provides: 'With a view to ensuring that any measure adopted or maintained by a Party relating to the licensing or certification of nationals of another Party does not constitute an unnecessary barrier to trade, each Party shall endeavor to ensure that any such measure: (a) is based on objective and transparent criteria, such as competence and the ability to provide a service; (b) is not more burdensome than necessary to ensure the quality of a service; and (c) does not constitute a disguised restriction on the cross-border provision of a service.' See also 2008 Canada–Peru FTA (Article 909.2), 2004 Japan–Mexico FTA (Article 104.1), 2003 Chile–Korea FTA (Article 11.10), 2003 US–Singapore FTA (Article 8.8.1).

126 See NAFTA (Article 1210.1), Chile–Korea FTA (Article 11.10), Japan–Mexico FTA (Article 104.1), Central America–Panama FTA (Article 11.07), Chile–EC FTA (Article 102.1). However, the US–Singapore FTA and the 2008 Canada–Peru FTA extend their non-mandatory necessity requirements to 'technical regulations' as well (Articles 8.8.1 and 909.2, respectively).

127 NAFTA (Article 901), Central America–Panama FTA (Article 9.03), Chile–Mexico FTA (Article 8–03.1; it should be noted, however, that Annex 8–01 limits the applicability of the chapter on standards-related measures de facto to computer and related services, only). On the other hand, a few agreements that exclude 'technical regulations' from the scope of the necessity requirements do not extend the chapter on technical barriers to trade to measures affecting trade in services. See for example, Chile–Korea FTA (Article 9.3).

128 For example, Article 9.04.2 of the Central America–Panama FTA provides: 'No Party may prepare, adopt, maintain or apply any standards-related measures, approval procedures and metrology-related measures with the purpose or effect of creating an unnecessary obstacle to trade with the other Party.'

129 See for example, 2009 Japan–Switzerland EPA (Article 48.4(b)), 2003 Singapore–Australia FTA (Chapter 7, Article 11.7), 2002 Japan–Singapore FTA (Article 64.6).

rebuttably presumed to comply with the [rules on domestic regulation]'.[130] This is also similar to the approach employed in Article 3.2 of the WTO SPS Agreement.

Secondly, other RTAs require parties to use international standards as a basis for preparing or applying their standards-related measures.[131] This approach is very similar to that characterizing Article 2.4 of the WTO TBT Agreement.

C. Sectoral disciplines

Several RTAs set out additional disciplines for specific service sectors in separate chapters (or annexes).[132] Financial services and telecommunications are the two areas for which these agreements include most often additional disciplines. Individual chapters (or annexes or sections) on 'transport', 'professional services' or 'temporary entry of business persons' may also be found in RTAs. Unsurprisingly, all these areas are subject to specific disciplines also within the GATS, mostly in annexes, understandings and reference papers.

The extent and content of the additional disciplines within RTAs may vary from a few provisions replicating the rules generally applicable to trade in services to a set of comprehensive and/or additional disciplines distributed among several articles (the latter most often in the case of financial services and telecommunications). For example, the chapter on **financial services** in the EC–Mexico FTA (which is more detailed than the chapter setting out the general provisions on trade in services) includes provisions very similar to the GATS 'Understanding on commitments in financial services' and 'Annex on financial services', such as provisions on establishment of financial service suppliers, cross-border provision of financial services, national treatment, most-favoured-nation treatment, regulatory and prudential carve outs, data processing, consultations and dispute settlement.

For example, the chapter on **telecommunications** in the Chile–Korea FTA includes many of the rules provided by the 'WTO Reference paper on basic tele-communications' such as 'access to and use of public telecommunications transport networks and services', 'conditions for the provision of enhanced or value-added services', 'standards-related measures', 'monopolies', and 'transparency'.

With regard to **professional services**, some RTAs provide specific annexes aimed at facilitating the provision of services by foreign professionals in particular through development of mutually acceptable standards and criteria for licensing and

---

130 Article 21.4 of the 2000 New Zealand–Singapore EPA. See also, 2003 EFTA–Chile FTA (Article 28.6), 2002 EFTA–Singapore FTA (Article 28.6), 1998 Chile–Mexico FTA (Article 8–04.4(b)).
131 See, for example, Central America–Panama FTA (Article 9.02.4), Central America–Chile FTA (Article 9.04.4).
132 Other agreements may instead provide for specific provision(s) dealing with certain services sectors. See, for example, Articles 4.16–4.18 of the Singapore–Jordan FTA dealing with Telecommunications, Financial Services Cooperation and Transport Cooperation, respectively.

certification of professional service providers. Additionally, certain RTAs set out specific sections for 'foreign legal consultants' and the 'temporary licensing of engineers' requiring parties, for example, to consult with their relevant professional bodies in order to develop common standards and criteria for the authorization of foreign legal consultants and the temporary licensing of foreign engineers.[133]

IV. Brief conclusions

From the perspective of the different approaches that RTAs have adopted in regulating trade in services, the present chapter shows that, despite the fact that all these agreements adopt more or less different rules ('there isn't one agreement like another'), most of them follow in principle the NAFTA and GATS models.[134] And these two models do not take two diametrically opposite approaches to the liberalization of trade in services. However, the differences are there, as the chapter has emphasized, for example, with regard to the 'scope of application' of the services chapters, the 'formulation' of the national treatment standard, the transparency requirements and the disciplines on domestic regulation. These differences have not really come to the surface as there has not been much adjudication with regard to all these provisions.[135] And a similar faith has been reserved to the GATS.

The question that thus arises is whether these RTAs are functioning only as pro-liberalization instruments, that is to get countries to increase the level of market access in the service sector. This is certainly part of the rationale of the services chapters in RTAs (as well as beyond services). However, one cannot deny other structural benefits of such agreements. For example, any discipline dealing with services regulation that is provided for in an RTA (such as transparency requirements, disciplines on domestic regulation, competition-oriented disciplines in the telecommunications sector) will bring certain benefits not just to the service providers of the other party to the RTA but in principle to all service suppliers. Many barriers to trade in services are in fact embedded in regulatory regimes and governments will often not put in place different regulatory regimes for different supplier countries.[136]

Looking ahead, one strategy to increase the (currently very slow) pace of the liberalization of trade in services (both at the regional and multilateral levels) may be to strengthen the 'regulatory' agenda of these agreements. In other words, it may be useful to make sure that the liberalization of trade and investment in services

---

133 See, for example, Annex 11.9 on Professional Services in the US–Chile FTA.

134 The third model is that provided by the EC Treaty, which this chapter has not addressed. Similarly, P. Latrille and J. Lee, 'Services Rules in Regional Trade Agreements: How Diverse and How Creative as Compared to the GATS Multilateral Rules?' *WTO Working Paper*, ERSD-2012–19 (October 2012) at 32.

135 The only exceptions are certainly the EC Treaty and to a much limited extent Mercosur and NAFTA.

136 See Martin Roy, Juan Marchetti and Hoe Lim, 'Services Liberalization in the New Generation of Preferential Trade Agreements (PTAs): How Much Further than the GATS?', Staff Working Paper ERSD-2006–07 (September 2006) at 55.

(including several very crucial and sensitive service sectors) are accompanied by a (stronger) international programme of regulatory reforms (involving both regulators and industries) to be implemented at the domestic level. Particularly with regard to services, sustainable liberalization cannot go ahead in any meaningful way without proper regulation.

10

Investment

JOSHUA P. MELTZER[*]

I. Introduction

This chapter provides an analysis of the investment commitments in Bilateral and Regional Free Trade Agreement (FTA) investment chapters.[1]

Part II commences with an examination of the history of treaty-based legal protections for foreign investment. This Part traces the evolution of investment provisions, from Treaties of Friendship, Navigation and Commerce (FNC), through to Bilateral Investment Treaties (BITs), and their most recent incorporation into investment chapters in Free Trade Agreements (FTAs).

Part III discusses the scope of investment provisions and analyses how the different definition of phrases such as 'investor' and 'investment' determines the scope of FTA Investment Chapters. This Part therefore inquires into whom the investment chapter applies to, and what will constitute an investment for the purpose of the chapter.

Part IV continues the analysis of States' commitments in the FTA Investment Chapter, but with a focus on their substantive commitments.

Part V focuses on investor-state dispute settlement (ISDS) provisions in FTA Investment Chapters and outlines the main elements and differences between the ISDS provisions in different FTA Investment Chapters. It also explains how these ISDS provisions use, and rely on, the United Nations Commission on International Trade Law (UNCITRAL) Arbitration Rules and the International Centre for Settlement of Investment Disputes (ICSID) Convention, Regulations and Rules ('ICSID Convention').

Part VI outlines the market access provisions in various FTA Investment Chapters, with a focus on whether States schedule their market access commitments in the form of either a positive or negative list. This Part looks at the differences between positive and negative lists, and considers the argument for and against each approach.

---

[*] The author would like to thank Jurgen Kurtz, Tania Voon, Andrew Mitchell, Federico Ortino and William Dodge for their useful feedback on a first edition of this chapter.

1 For the purposes of this chapter, a reference to an FTA Investment Chapter will, unless otherwise stated, include investment chapters in bilateral or regional FTAs.

Finally, Part VII discusses the main issues likely to arise under FTA Investment Chapters and considers the implications of the proliferation of FTAs with investment chapters for progress on investment at the WTO.

II. International investment law – from FCNs to FTAs

Investment provisions in international agreements have a long history. During the seventeenth and eighteenth centuries, a combination of capital and expertise led to significant foreign investment from United States (US) and European investors in large infrastructure projects such as railroads and telegraph systems in areas such as Latin America. However, the perceived national interest character of these investments also caused host States, from time to time, to expropriate these investments, thereby highlighting to investors the need for mechanisms to protect their overseas investments.[2]

As a result, in the eighteenth century the US began entering into what have been described as treaties of 'Friendship, Commerce and Navigation' (FCN). As their name suggests, investment was only one component of FCN treaties, which also included commitments on trade, navigation and friendship. The earlier FCN treaties also limited their investment protections to 'special protection' or 'full protection and security'. By the late nineteenth century, however, these treaties included provisions protecting against expropriation, and Most-Favoured-Nation (MFN) and National Treatment (NT) commitments. Some of the FCN treaties negotiated in the early part of the twentieth century also included currency protection provisions. In this way, the FCN treaty project presaged the modern BIT.[3]

Despite the proliferation of FCN treaties, their often broad principles and lack of enforcement mechanisms underscored the disagreement between capital-exporting and capital-importing States over what obligations were owed to foreign investors. The view of capital-importing States was expressed in the so-called 'Calvo doctrine' – developed by Carlos Calvo, an Argentinian lawyer – and which held that foreign investors were only entitled to the level of protection afforded to nationals.[4] And in the event of a dispute over whether appropriate protection had been afforded to the foreign investment, the matter was to be determined by domestic courts.

The capital-exporting view was expressed in the Hull Rule – named after Cordell Hull, former US Secretary of State.[5] According to the Hull Rule the protection host

2 Raymond D. Bishop, James Crawford and Michael W. Reisman (eds.), *Foreign Investment Disputes: Cases, Materials, Commentary* (The Hague: Kluwer Law International, 2005), at p. 3.
3 Kenneth J. Vandevelde, 'The Bilateral Investment Treaty Program of the United States' (1988) 21 *Cornell International Law Journal* 201 76, at 208.
4 See Donald R. Shea, *The Calvo Clause. A Problem of Inter-American and International Law and Diplomacy* (Minneapolis: Minnesota University Press, 1955), at p. 17.
5 Henry J. Steiner, Detlev F. Vagts and Harold H. Koh, *Transnational Legal Problems: Materials and Text*, 4th edn (Westbury, New York: Foundation Press, 1994), at pp. 456–7.

States owed foreign investors and their investments was defined by international law. As a result, it operated independently of the host State's treatment of its own citizens.

The end of World War II led to the recognition of 'the need for international economic institutions to prevent the type of "beggar-thy-neighbour" policies that had been so disastrous to world trade and economics during the interwar period and which, in the minds of many leaders, were responsible to a great degree for World War II itself'.[6] This led to the establishment of the World Bank and the IMF, and a proposal to establish an International Trade Organisation (ITO). The ITO was to include provisions on investment, but an inability to get US Congressional support led to its abandonment in 1950, leaving the GATT as the surviving multilateral agreement governing trade.[7]

While the establishment of the GATT meant that trade relations were conducted on a multilateral basis, investment remained to be pursued bilaterally. Therefore, after World War II, the US continued to pursue FCNs with stronger investment protection provisions, and these treaties also often included agreement by the parties to resolve disputes before the International Court of Justice (ICJ).

During the 1960s the rise of the Soviet Union and socialism in developing countries, combined with intense nationalism within recently de-colonised States, led to opposition to foreign investment as either an extension of an ideological battle against capitalism, or by viewing foreign investment as a form of neo-colonialism.[8] This ideological opposition was reinforced by development economics theory which encouraged import substitution and the building of an industrial base behind high tariff walls as the policy prescription that would allow least developed economies to industrialise.[9]

This opposition to foreign investment led to a number of significant expropriations. For example, in the 1970s Libya nationalised its petroleum industry and Chile nationalised its copper mining industry. The 1979 Iranian Revolution led to the expulsion of US companies and the nationalisation of their assets, and in early 1980 Kuwait nationalised its petroleum industry.

At the same time, the developing world, as capital-importing States, sought to have its views of the obligation of host States reflected internationally. The main success here was two UN General Assembly Resolutions, the 1974 Declaration of the New

---

6 John H. Jackson, *World Trade and the Law of the GATT* (Indianapolis: Bobbs-Merrill Company, 1969), at p. 37. See, however, Robert E. Hudec, *Essays on the Nature of International Trade Law* (London: Cameron May, 1999), at p. 315 (arguing that the experience of the post-World War II era is that 'without the underlying political animosities, discrimination itself seems to have no necessary effect on the peace of the world').

7 Jackson, above n. 6, at p. 50.

8 Kenneth J. Vandevelde, 'A Brief History of International Investment Agreements' (2005) 12(1) *University of California Davis Journal of International Law & Policy* 157–94, at 166.

9 Robert Gilpin, *Global Political Economy: Understanding the International Economic Order* (Princeton: Princeton University Press, 2001), at p. 308.

International Economic Order which recognised State sovereignty over natural resources, including a right to transfer ownership of these resources to their nationals.[10] The second Resolution was the 1974 Charter of Economic Rights and Duties of States, which affirmed a State's right to expropriate and have compensation assessed according to the expropriating State's national laws.[11] The capital-exporting States did not support these Resolutions.

During these decades of the twentieth century, foreign investment increased and capital-exporting States focused on negotiating bilateral agreements on investment protection. West Germany became the first country to commence negotiating BITs in 1959, followed closely by other major capital-exporting States such as the UK, France, Italy, Switzerland, The Netherlands and Belgium. By 1980, Europe had negotiated approximately 150 BITs with developing States. The US commenced its own BIT programme in 1981, but by 1990 only eight BITs had been signed and ratified by the US Senate.[12]

The US's BITs differed from the FCN treaties in that they focused solely on investment, they were largely with developing States, and their provisions also reflected the objective that 'investment matters should be regulated by the market rather than political forces'.[13] The same could be said for those BITs entered into by European States. In this way the BITs negotiated by Europe and the US sought to depoliticise investment matters by including absolute obligations regarding expropriation, a requirement to provide fair and equitable treatment, and a commitment to allow currency transfers. The attempt to separate foreign investment from foreign policy was assisted by the establishment of the World Bank International Centre for the Settlement of Investment Disputes in 1966, which allowed BITs to also include the right for investors to have their investment disputes settled by international tribunals, thereby avoiding the reliance of foreign investors on their government to assert their claim.[14]

The OECD supported the push by capital-exporting States to affirm these international investment obligations by adopting the Code of Liberalisation of Capital Movements and the Code of Liberalisation of Current Invisible Operations in 1961. Under these Codes, each OECD country committed itself to liberalise on a non-discriminatory basis, measures that restricted the movement of capital, including, as a

10 Declaration of the Establishment of a New Economic Order, General Assembly Resolution 3201 (S-VI), UN GAOR, 6th Special Session, 2229th Plenary Meeting, UN Doc. A/RES/3201 (S-VI), 1 May 1974.
11 Charter of Economic Rights and Duties of States, General Assembly Resolution 3281 (XXIX), UN GAOR, 29th Session, 2315th Plenary Meeting, UN Doc. /RES/3281(XXIX), 12 December 1974.
12 Jeswald W. Salacuse, 'BIT by BIT: The Growth of Bilateral Investment Treaties and Their Impact on Foreign Investment in Developing Countries' (1990) 24 International Law 655–75, at 657.
13 Kenneth J. Vandevelde, 'Of Politics and Markets: The Shifting Ideology of the BITS' (1993) 11 International Tax & Business Law 159–86, at 182.
14 Christoph H. Schreuer, The ICSID Convention: A Commentary (Cambridge: Cambridge University Press, 2001), at pp. 391 and 398.

result of subsequent amendments to these Codes, measures restricting foreign direct investment.

The international debt crisis in the 1980s revealed the structural challenges developing countries faced when seeking to repay their foreign debt. The perceived need for developing economies to undertake structural reform was mandated by the use of conditional loans from the IMF.[15] These conditions, referred to as the 'Washington Consensus', which included trade liberalisation and opening their economies to competition from the outside world, had an important impact on the receptiveness of developing countries to foreign investment.

The fall of the Berlin Wall in 1989 and the subsequent collapse of the Soviet Union also led to the unravelling of the ideological opposition to capitalism and foreign investment. States that had previously opposed foreign investment or international investment commitments became party to BITs. As a result, while 400 BITs were concluded between 1959 and 1989, by 2013 there were 2,370 BITs and FTAs with investment chapters.[16]

Furthermore, economic development in the developing world, particularly in Asia, resulted in countries that were traditionally importers of capital becoming exporters as well. Therefore, BITs became viewed offensively by a larger number of countries.[17]

Another consequence of the end of the Cold War for foreign investment was that it became possible again to seek to deal with investment multilaterally. While the establishment of the WTO in 1995 did not include comprehensive investment provisions, some investment disciplines were included. For instance, commercial presence for the delivery of services is regulated as a mode 3 discipline under the GATS, and the TRIPS Agreement also includes protections for intellectual property rights, also considered an investment under BITs. The WTO also contains the TRIMS Agreement, which prohibits Members from conditioning foreign investment on compliance with certain export or import conditions.

While the WTO witnessed the re-emergence of some multilateral rules on investment, failure to adopt a comprehensive approach led to the attempt to negotiate a Multilateral Agreement on Investment (MAI). The OECD was chosen as the forum, with the premise being that the negotiation of such an agreement would be easier amongst developed like-minded countries. It was anticipated that the treaty would be open for accession by developing countries.[18] However, negotiations were discontinued in the late 1990s. While disagreement amongst the OECD countries over issues such as culture and labour was already slowing the negotiating process, a

15 Gilpin, above n. 9, at pp. 314–5.   16 http://investmentpolicyhub.unctad.org/IIA.
17 UNCTAD 2006 World Investment Report, *FDI From Developing and Transition Economies: Implications for Development* (New York and Geneva: UN, 2006), at p. 228.
18 Jürgen Kurtz, 'A General Investment Agreement in the WTO? Lessons from Chapter 11 of NAFTA and the OECD Multilateral Agreement on Investment' (2002) 23(4) *University of Pennsylvania Journal of International Economic Law* 713–89.

confidential draft, released to NGOs in 1997, led to an effective grass-roots campaign against the MAI and killed the initiative.[19]

The failure to negotiate an MAI within the OECD led to further attempts to include investment in the WTO. However, even though the Singapore Declaration (1996) established a Working Group on the Relationship between Trade and Investment to consider the scope for multilateral rules on investment,[20] a lack of support amongst WTO members, including from the US, led to its abandonment in the Doha Round.[21]

As is demonstrated throughout this book, slowness in concluding the Doha Round has led to a number of countries pursuing their trade interests through FTAs. The rationale is, in part, that FTAs could be concluded faster than WTO trade negotiations and provide opportunities for countries to make commitments in areas currently not on the WTO agenda, such as investment.

This has led to a rapid growth in the number of FTAs containing investment provisions. In fact, by 2015, 282 FTAs included investment provisions, with approximately 90 per cent of these agreements having been concluded since the 1990s.[22]

III. Scope of the investment chapter

This Part considers the scope of FTA Investment Chapters by inquiring to whom and to what they apply, and focuses on how important terms in an investment chapter are defined. For example, an FTA's definition of an 'investor' determines to whom the investment chapter applies. Additionally, there are other provisions in an FTA Investment Chapter that affect its scope and which this Part considers. For example, a denial of benefits provision allows a Party to the FTA to avoid having to apply FTA Investment Chapter commitments to particular investors, thereby also affecting the scope of the chapter.

A. Definition of an investment

1. The 'asset-based' or 'enterprise-based' definition

The definition of an 'investment' is an important determinant of the scope of an FTA Investment Chapter. Most FTA Investment Chapters use an asset-based

---

19 See Michael J. Trebilcock and Robert Howse, *The Regulation of International Trade*, 3rd edn (London: Routledge, 2005), at pp. 457–60 for an overview of the MAI negotiations; see also Kurtz, above n. 18, at 756–61.
20 WTO, 1996 Singapore Ministerial Declaration, WT/MIN(96)/DEC, 13 December 1996, para. 20.
21 WTO General Council Decision of 31 July 2004, WT/GC/W/535, p. 3.
22 UNCTAD, *International Investment Arrangements: Trends and Emerging Issues* (New York and Geneva: UN, 2006), at p. 8; see also UNCTAD, above n. 16, at p. 8: http://investmentpolicyhub.unctad.org/IIA/ (visited 10 March 2015).

definition by defining an investment as 'every kind of asset'.[23] However, the definition of an investment as 'every kind of asset' begs the question of what constitutes an 'asset'. Most FTA Investment Chapters assist with this inquiry by providing an open-ended list of the types of assets that are investments.[24]

An alternative approach to the open-ended definition of an investment is to use a comprehensive but finite definition of what constitutes an investment. This is the approach taken in the Draft COMESA Common Investment Area (CCIA) Investment Framework Agreement where, in Article 1.7 paragraphs (a)–(e), there is a specific and finite list of what constitutes an investment.

Still yet, other FTA Investment Chapters, such as the North American Free Trade Agreement (NAFTA) and the Canada–Chile Free Trade Agreement, define an investment using an asset-based and enterprise-based definition. For example, the Canada–Chile FTA defines an investment as including an enterprise, an equity security of an enterprise, or a debt security of an enterprise.

An important underlying policy challenge is how to limit the benefits of the investment chapters to investors of the other party, and prevent investors from non-parties to the FTA from establishing shell companies in an FTA party to gain access to the FTA's investments protections and improved market access in the other country to the FTA. Some FTA Investment Chapters have addressed this issue by requiring that assets have the characteristics of an investment, including such characteristics as the commitment of capital or other resources, the expectation of gain or profit, or the assumption of risk.[25]

2. Foreign direct investment and portfolio investment

Another key issue regarding the scope of an investment chapter is whether it covers only foreign direct investment (FDI) or also extends to include portfolio investment such as shares and other securities. Shares which can be liquidated quickly may not need investment protection in FTAs. Additionally, countries have become cautious about according treaty level investment protections to short-term capital inflows, which the 1997 East Asia financial crisis demonstrated can quickly turn to capital outflows with potentially significant negative economic impacts. In this event, governments are concerned that responses to such capital outflows could rise to a breach of an investment commitment. On the other hand, even if there are good reasons not

---

23 See, e.g. United States–Chile Free Trade Agreement, Article 10.27; Singapore–Australia Free Trade Agreement, Chapter 8, Article 1.1(c); and India–Singapore Comprehensive Economic Cooperation Agreement (India–Singapore CECA), Article 6.1.1.

24 See, e.g., US–Chile FTA, Article 10.27; and Singapore–Australia FTA, Chapter 8, Article 1.

25 US–Chile FTA, Article 10.27; Korea–Chile FTA, Article 10.1; and CAFTA–DR–US, Article 10.28. See also *Salini Costruttori S.p.A. and Italstrade S.p.A.* v. *Kingdom of Morocco*, ICSID Case No. ARB/00/4, Decision on Jurisdiction (23 July 2001), where the tribunal, interpreting the reference to an 'investment' in ICSID Article 25(1) stated that an investment implies the presence of (a) a contribution of money or other assets of economic value; (b) a certain duration; (c) an element of risk; and (d) a contribution to the host State's development.

to accord investment protection to all forms of capital inflow, distinguishing between the types of capital that should be protected is difficult.

For now, most FTA Investment Chapters cover both FDI and portfolio investment.[26] This coverage is achieved by using an asset-based definition of an investment that lists as an asset, 'shares, stock and other forms of equity participation in an enterprise'.[27] In those FTAs that use an enterprise-based definition of an investment, direct and portfolio investment is covered by defining an investment as including equity in an enterprise.[28]

The European Union–Chile Association Agreement (EU–Chile AA) also includes, in Title III, Chapter III, limited commitments with regards to 'establishment' in the non-services sectors.[29] The definition in this Agreement of 'establishment' would also extend the scope of these commitments to FDI and portfolio investment.

Not all FTAs cover portfolio investment. For instance, the Framework Agreement on the ASEAN Investment Area (AIA) states in the 'scope' part of the AIA that the Agreement does not cover portfolio investment,[30] while the Thailand–Australia Free Trade Agreement also limits its pre-establishment investment commitments to FDI only.[31]

3. 'Direct' and 'indirect' investment

What constitutes an 'investment' in FTA Investment Chapters is often defined as including assets that are owned or controlled 'directly or indirectly' by the foreign investor.[32] What constitutes direct ownership or control of an investment is an absence of an intermediary between the investment and the investor. Therefore, indirect ownership or control refers to the existence of one or more intermediaries (regardless of nationality) between the investors and the investment.[33] An investment in the territory of an FTA Party can be owned or controlled by investors of the other FTA Party through investments established in third countries that are not party to the FTA.

Finally, the ability for an investment to be owned or controlled, directly or indirectly, also allows for the existence of more than one owner or controller of an investment.[34] For example, an investment could be directly owned or controlled by Company A as well as Company B through Company A.

---

26 See the Canada–Chile FTA, Article G-40; Japan–Singapore New-Age Economic Partnership Agreement (Japan–Singapore EPA), Article 72; India–Singapore CECA, Article 6.1.1; Korea–Singapore FTA, Article 10.1; and US–Chile FTA, Article 10.27.
27 US–Singapore FTA, Article 15.1.13(a).   28 See, e.g., Canada–Chile FTA, Article G-40.
29 The EU–Chile AA also includes commitments on mode 3 services in the services chapter.
30 AIA Framework Agreement, Article 2.   31 Thailand–Australia FTA, Article 903.
32 See, e.g., Japan–Singapore EPA, Article 72; and US–Chile FTA, Article 10.27.
33 *Aguas del Tunari S.A.* v. *Republic of Bolivia*, ICSID Case No. ARB/02/3, Decision on Respondent's Objections to Jurisdiction, para. 236.
34 *Ibid.*, para. 237.

4. Ownership and control

In most FTAs, ownership or control is left undefined.[35] This largely reflects the difficulty of providing a definition of ownership and control that does not lead to an over- or under-inclusion of investments within its scope.[36] Some FTAs provide guidance to treaty interpreters on how to define ownership or control. For example, the Japan–Singapore New-Age Economic Partnership Agreement (Japan– Singapore EPA) and Thailand–Australia FTA define ownership as 50 per cent of the equity interest of an enterprise, and control as 'the power to name a majority of [the enterprise's] directors or otherwise to legally direct its actions'.[37]

The issue of whether an investment is owned or controlled normally arises when the investment is an enterprise rather than, for example, the equity in that investment. This is because ownership of equity is easily established. However, whether the possession of, say, 25 per cent equity in an enterprise constitutes control of that enterprise is less clear. Therefore, even where FTAs do define control, definitions are broad and serve more as directions than bright lines. This approach has also been followed by arbitral tribunals, who have defined control broadly by finding that whether a minority shareholder controls an enterprise requires an inquiry into 'legal rights conveyed in instruments or agreements such as the articles of incorporation or shareholders' agreement or a combination of these'.[38]

B. Definition of an investor

The definition of what constitutes an investor also determines the scope of an FTA Investment Chapter. This is because this definition determines not only who falls within the scope of the investment chapter commitments. How an investor is defined also determines whether the substantive investment chapter commitments apply to the pre- and post-establishment phase of an investment, or to the post-establishment phase only.

1. An investor as a 'natural person'

Most FTA Investment Chapters define an investor as both a natural person and an enterprise or juridical person.[39] These FTAs define a natural person as a citizen or

---

35 See, e.g., US–Chile FTA and the Korea–Singapore FTA.
36 *Aguas del Tunari S.A.* v. *Republic of Bolivia*, para. 246.
37 Japan–Singapore EPA, Article 72; and Thailand–Australia FTA, Article 103(o).
38 *Aguas del Tunari S.A.* v. *Republic of Bolivia*, para. 264.
39 See AUSFTA, Article 11.17; US–Chile FTA, Article 10.27; Canada–Chile FTA, Article G-40; and Japan–Singapore EPA, Article 72.

national of a Party, and the laws of that Party regarding citizenship and nationality define whether a person is in fact a citizen or national. For example, according to Annex 2.1 of the US–Chile FTA, whether a person is a Chilean is determined according to Article 10 of the Constitucion Politica de la Republica, and a US citizen is defined according to the existing provisions of the US Immigration and Nationality Act.

Most FTAs broaden the scope of a 'natural person' to include permanent residents.[40] For instance, in the Japan–Singapore EPA, Singapore extends the definition of an investor to include a permanent resident, while Japan limits the definition to its citizens.[41]

Another issue is how to deal with dual citizens. Some FTAs define citizenship broadly, thereby including those persons with dual citizenship.[42] Other FTAs limit the scope of the FTA by requiring dual citizens to establish residency,[43] or limit citizenship to their dominant and effective nationality.[44]

2. An investor as an 'enterprise'

Most FTA Investment Chapters also define an investor as an enterprise and use the 'place of incorporation' to establish whether the enterprise is an investor of an FTA Party.[45] For example, the US–Chile FTA defines an enterprise, *inter alia*, as 'any entity constituted or organized under applicable law ... including a branch of an enterprise'.[46]

Many FTA Investment Chapters also include a branch of an enterprise within the definition of an enterprise. For example, the US–Chile FTA, Australia–United States Free Trade Agreement (AUSFTA) and Canada–Chile FTA include within the investment chapter a definition of an enterprise that draws on the definition of an enterprise in the 'general definition' part of the FTA, and extends the definition, for the purposes of the investment chapter, to include 'a branch of an enterprise'.

However, in these FTAs, the investment chapter also qualifies the extent that a branch of an enterprise will be an enterprise for the purposes of the FTA. This is done by defining 'an enterprise of a Party' as only applying to 'a branch located in the territory of a Party and carrying out business activities there'.[47] In the

---

40 See, e.g., Australia–United States Free Trade Agreement AUSFTA, Article 1.1 and Annex 1-A; CAFTA–DR–US, Article 2.1 and Annex 2.1; Canada–Chile FTA, Article B-01; Korea–Singapore FTA, Chapter 2; and Korea–Chile FTA, Article 2.1.
41 Japan–Singapore EPA, Article 72(f).
42 See, e.g., Korea–Singapore FTA, Chapter 2; India–Singapore CECA, Article 6.1, para. 5; and Canada–Chile FTA, Article B-01.
43 Japan–Singapore EPA, Article 72(f).   44 US–Chile FTA, Article, 10.27; and AUSFTA, Article 11.17.6.
45 See, e.g., Canada–Chile FTA, Article B-01; and Korea–Singapore FTA, Chapter 2.
46 US–Chile FTA, Articles 2.1 and 10.27.
47 US–Chile FTA, Article 10.27; AUSFTA, Article 11.17.2; and Canada–Chile FTA, Article G-40.

India–Singapore Comprehensive Economic Co-operation Agreement (India–Singapore CECA), an enterprise does not include 'any legal entity, which is established and located in the territory of a Party with negligible or nil business operations or with no real and continuous business activities carried out in the territory of that Party'.[48]

C. Pre- and/or post-establishment investment

Another important issue affecting the scope of an FTA Investment Chapter is whether its commitments cover measures that apply to the post-establishment stage of an investment only or extends to measures that affect the pre-establishment investment stage.

All FTA Investment Chapters apply to measures that affect the post-establishment phase of an investment. However, not all FTA Investment Chapters apply to measures that affect the pre-establishment investment stage.[49]

A measure that applies to the pre-establishment stage of an investment extends the investment chapter's substantive commitments to laws that affect the ability of an investor from the other FTA Party to make an investment in its territory. For example, a measure that only made it more difficult for foreign investors to invest in a particular company or sector could breach the investment chapter's national treatment commitment.

A measure that applies to the post-establishment stage affects an FTA Party's investor or its investment once established in the territory of the other FTA Party. For example, a measure that requires an investment of an FTA Party to employ local staff would constitute a measure affecting the post-establishment stage of an investment.

An FTA Investment Chapter applies to pre-establishment measures where the definition of an 'investor of a Party' extends coverage to an investment that an investor by the phrase 'that attempts to make',[50] or 'seeks to make'.[51] In the case of the Korea–Chile FTA, it is determined by the phrase 'that makes a juridical act in the territory of the other Party towards materializing an investment within it'.[52]

Even where Parties extend the scope of the FTA Investment Chapter to measures that affect pre-establishment investments, they can limit this to only some of the investment commitments most commonly being national treatment, MFN and

---

48 India–Singapore CECA, Article 6.1.6.
49 See, e.g., Singapore–Australia FTA, Chapter 8, Article 1; AUSFTA, Article 11.17.5; and Japan–Singapore EPA, Article 72(c).
50 See, e.g., Canada–Chile FTA, Article G-40; and US–Chile FTA, Article 10.27.
51 See, e.g., Korea–Singapore FTA, Article 10.1; and Thailand–Australia FTA, Article 1(m).
52 Korea–Chile FTA, Article 10.1.

performance requirements. For example, where the NT commitment applies to the 'establishment, acquisition, expansion' of an investment, this includes pre- and post-establishment.[53] In contrast, Thailand–Australia FTA is limited to post-establishment investments by applying the NT commitment to the 'management, conduct, operation and sale or other disposition of investments', limits it to post-establishment matters.[54]

Further, some FTAs include pre-establishment commitments for limited sectors, while maintaining a broader post-establishment commitment for a broader range of sectors. For example, the India–Singapore CECA investment chapter divides the NT commitment into two separate paragraphs, one dealing with the 'establishment, acquisition or expansion' of investments, namely, a pre-establishment commitment, and the other with the management, conduct, operation, liquidation, sale and transfer, namely, a post-establishment commitment.[55]

D. Denial of benefits

A denial of benefits provision gives a Party a right to deny the benefits of the investment chapter to an investor of the other Party. For example, a number of FTAs Investment Chapters exclude from the scope of the Investment Chapter investors of the other Party that are enterprises owned or controlled by investors from non-Parties and are established for the sole purpose of being used as a vehicle for getting the benefits of the FTA Investment Chapter.[56]

Arbitral decisions have also found that it is an abuse of international investment protections to restructure an investment only to gain the protection of an investment treaty. Factors the tribunal will look at to determine whether that has occurred are: (i) whether the dispute existed at the time of the corporate restructuring; and (ii) whether the dispute was reasonably foreseeable at the time of the restructuring.[57]

Various FTA Investment Chapter require such enterprises to have 'substantial' or 'substantive' business activities in the territory of an FTA Party.[58]

---

53 See, e.g., NAFTA, Article 1102.1; US–Chile FTA, Article 10.2; Canada–Chile FTA, Article G-02.1; and Singapore–Australia FTA, Chapter 8, Article 3.
54 Thailand–Australia FTA, Article 906(b).   55 India–Singapore CECA, Article 6.3.
56 See, e.g., US–Chile FTA, Article 10.11; Canada–Chile FTA, Article G-13.2; Singapore–Australia Free Trade Agreement, Chapter 8, Article 18; and AUSFTA, Article 11.12. See also Japan–Singapore EPA, Article 72 (a)(h), which excludes from the definition of an enterprise of a Party, 'an enterprise owned or controlled by persons of non-Parties and not engaging in substantive business operations in the territory of the other party'.
57 Tidewater Inc., et al v. The Bolivarian Republic of Venezuela (ICSID Case o ARB/10/5), Decision on Jurisdiction, 8 February 2013, para 146.
58 Singapore–Australia FTA, Chapter 8, Article 18, refers to 'substantive business operations', whereas the phrase 'substantial business activities' is used in US–Chile FTA, Article 10.11; AUSFTA, Article 11.12; and Canada–Chile FTA, Article G-13.

However, arbitral tribunals have found that a host State cannot deny the benefits of an investment chapter to an investor retrospectively, namely after the commencement of arbitration proceedings.[59]

IV. The substantive commitments in an FTA Investment Chapter

Part IV analyses the main substantive commitments found in an FTA Investment Chapter and considers how arbitral tribunals have interpreted these commitments in BITs and under NAFTA.

A. National treatment

The non-discrimination norm that underpins the multilateral trading system is also an important pillar of FTA Investment Chapters. In the WTO context, the non-discrimination norm is reflected in numerous provisions, most famously in the Article I MFN provision and Article III NT provisions of the GATT.

Whether a measure is inconsistent with a State's FTA Investment Chapter NT commitment usually requires establishing of three main issues. First, the foreign and domestic investors and/or their investments must be in 'like circumstances'? Second, the foreign investor/investment has to have received less favourable treatment than the like domestic investor/investment, like. And third, the less favourable treatment cannot be justified by the need to achieve a legitimate government policy?[60]

1. Is the domestic and foreign investor/investment in 'like circumstances'?

Similar to the WTO context, the NT obligation in an FTA Investment Chapter requires that the domestic and foreign investor/investment be in 'like circumstances' before differences in treatment can be deemed discriminatory.[61] Other FTA Investment Chapters use the phrase 'like economic activity',[62] while some do not use any comparator at all.[63]

---

59 *Anatolie Stati et al.* v. *Kazakhstan (SCC)*, Award, 19 December 2013, para 745.
60 NAFTA Ch 11 Arbitral Tribunal, SD Myers Inc. v. *Government of Canada* (*'Myers* v. *Canada'*) (Award of 10 April 2001), para. 250; and NAFTA Ch 11 Arbitral Tribunal, *Pope & Talbot Inc* v. *Government of Canada* (*'Pope & Talbot'*) (Award on the Merits of Phase 2, 10 April 2001), para. 78.
61 See AUSFTA, Article 11.3; CAFTA–DR–US, Article 10.3; Canada–Chile FTA, Article G-02.1; Korea–Chile FTA, Article 10.3; Japan–Singapore EPA, Article 73; and India–Singapore CECA, Article 6.3.
62 EU–Chile AA, Title III, Chapter III, Article 132.
63 Draft CCIA Investment Framework Agreement, Article 8.

When a foreign and domestic investor/investment are in 'like circumstances', any less favourable treatment accorded to the foreign investor constitutes discrimination.[64]

Whether foreign and domestic investments are in like circumstances requires comparing investors in the same economic sector. For instance, in *S.D. Myers* v. *Canada* and *Pope & Talbot Inc.* v. *Government of Canada*, the tribunal found that foreign and domestic investors/investments are in 'like circumstances' when they are in the same 'sector' as the national investor, where 'sector' includes the concepts of 'economic sector' and 'business sector'.[65] In *United Parcel Service of America* v. *Government of Canada*, the tribunal inquired into whether UPS was 'competing in the same market for the same market share' as Canada Post.[66] However, the tribunal in *Methanex* stated that 'it would be perverse to ignore identical comparators if they were available and to use comparators that were less "like"', thereby narrowing the 'like circumstances' inquiry.[67]

2. Is there less favourable treatment?

Tribunals have established that the requirement of no less favourable treatment in Article 1102 of the NAFTA means treatment that is 'equivalent to, not better or worse than, the best treatment accorded to the comparator'.[68] FTAs such as the US–Chile, US–Singapore, CAFTA–DR–US and the India–Singapore CECA use the legally equivalent phrase 'treatment no less favourable'.[69]

In the investment context, investors and their investments are to be accorded the best treatment provided to the class of investments in like circumstances with the foreign investment. For instance, the tribunal in *Pope & Talbot* found that any differences in treatment would violate NAFTA's national treatment commitment.[70] In *Methanex*, the tribunal also found that a foreign investment is entitled to the best treatment 'accorded to some members of the domestic class'.[71]

It is also the case that any difference in treatment is enough to find a breach of the requirement to provide no less favourable treatment.[72]

---

64 See Robert E. Hudec, 'GATT/WTO Constraints on National Regulation: Requiem for an "Aim and Effects" Test' (1998) 32 *The International Lawyer* 619–49, at 623, where Hudec observes that, '[f]or a regulatory measure to produce any difference in treatment at all, the regulation must divide products subject to the regulation into two or more categories. The finding of discrimination ultimately rests on a finding that the product distinction is illegitimate.'

65 *Myers* v. *Canada*, para. 250; and *Pope & Talbot*, para. 78.

66 NAFTA Ch 11 Arbitral Award, *United Parcel Service of America* v. *Government of Canada*, ('UPS') Award on the Merits of the Arbitral Tribunal, 24 May 2007, para. 83.

67 *Methanex*, Part IV, Chapter B, p. 8; see also *Feldman*, Final Award 16 December 2002, para. 171.

68 *Myers* v. *Canada*, para. 42; *Pope & Talbot*, paras. 41 2; and *Methanex,* Part IV, Chapter B, para. 21.

69 US–Chile FTA, Article 10.2; US–Singapore FTA, Article 15.4; CAFTA–DR–US, Article 10.3; and India–Singapore CECA, Article 6.3.

70 *Pope & Talbot*, para. 78.   71 *Methanex* Jurisdiction & Merits, Part IV, Chapter. B. para. 21.

72 *Pope & Talbot*, para. 79.

3. The search for a legitimate government policy

Some FTA Investment Chapters include an exceptions provision modelled on either Article XX of the GATT or Article XIV of the GATS.[73] In order to satisfy such an exceptions provision, the defending government would need to show that the offending measure was necessary to achieve one of the enumerated policy exceptions and that the measure satisfies the chapeau.

Other FTAs do not allow exceptions to the FTA Investment Chapter commitments.[74] Tribunals have responded to the absence of an exceptions provision by finding that where the less favourable treatment accorded to foreign investors/investments can be justified by the pursuit of legitimate policy goals, the domestic and foreign investors/investments are not in 'like circumstances' and therefore there is no national treatment violation. For example, in Marvin Roy Feldman Karpa (CEMSA) v. United Mexican States, the tribunal explained that where there is less favourable treatment,[75] the onus is then on the defendant to show that there is a 'rational justification' for the less favourable treatment.[76]

In *Myers* v. *Canada*, the tribunal quotas with approval the OECD Declaration on International and Multinational Enterprises 1976 and the review by the OECD in 1993, to conclude that:

> the assessment of 'like circumstances' in Article 1102 must take into account the general principles that emerge from the legal context of the NAFTA, including both its concern with the environment and the need to avoid trade distortions that are not justified by environmental concerns. The assessment of 'like circumstances' must also take into account circumstances that would justify governmental regulations that treat them differently in order to protect the public interest.[77]

Here the inquiry was into what is in the public interest, and whether distinguishing between domestic and foreign investors in leading to the less favourable treatment of the domestic investor is necessary to achieve that public interest goal.

In terms of what is in the public interest, the tribunal in *Myers* found that this includes legitimate policy goals such as protecting the environment. And the *Pope & Talbot* tribunal inquired into whether the measure relates to any 'rational government policy'.[78]

Regarding the relationship of the measure to the policy goal, the tribunal in *Pope & Talbot* stated that it will require a 'reasonable nexus' between the structure and design of the measure and the goal of the measure.[79] In the later case of *Marvin Roy Feldman Karpa (CEMSA)* v. *United Mexican States*, the tribunal explained that where there is

---

73 See, e.g., India–Singapore CECA, Article 6.11; Singapore–Australia FTA, Chapter 8, Article 19; Korea–Singapore FTA, Article 21.2; and Japan–Singapore EPA, Article 83.
74 See, e.g., CAFTA–DR–US, Article 21.1; Korea–Chile FTA, Article 20.1; Canada–Chile FTA, Article O-01; and AUSFTA, Article 22.1.
75 *Feldman*, Final Award 16 December 2002, para. 181.
76 *Pope & Talbot* Phase 2, (NAFTA Ch. 11 Arb. Trib. Apr. 10, 2001, para. 18-29.
77 *Myers* v. *Canada*, para. 250.   78 *Pope & Talbot*, para. 98.   79 *Ibid.*, para. 98.

less favourable treatment, the onus is then on the defendant to show that there is a 'rational justification' for the less favourable treatment.

Finally, while NAFTA tribunals have sought to address the absence of a list of exceptions to the investment chapter, there remains the issue of the operation of a GATT Article XX- or GATS Article XIV- type chapeau. Both contain the discipline that measures not 'be applied in a manner which would constitute a means of arbitrary or unjustifiable discrimination between countries where like conditions prevail, or a disguised restriction on international trade'.[80] The WTO Appellate Body has interpreted the chapeau as embodying:

> the recognition on the part of WTO Members of the need to maintain a balance
> of rights and obligations between the right of a Member to invoke one or other
> of the exceptions of Article XX specified in paragraphs (a) to (j), on the one
> hand, and the substantive rights of the other members under the GATT 1994,
> on the other hand.[81]

Therefore, in those FTAs that are without an exceptions provision, the absence of a chapeau to discipline discrimination in the application, rather than the design of a measure, means that a measure deemed consistent with some FTA Investment Chapters' NT commitments could be found to be inconsistent with the same NT provision in FTAs where the measure is also assessed through the disciplines of an exceptions provision's chapeau.[82]

B. Most-favoured-nation treatment

An MFN clause requires the host government to accord to investors if an FTA party no less favourable treatment accorded, in like circumstances, to investments by investors of any non-Party.[83] An MFN clause in an FTA Investment Chapter avoids the privileges accorded under the FTA being eroded when one of the FTA parties offers better concessions in future FTAs. An MFN clause thereby seeks to ensure equality of competitive opportunities between foreign investors and their investments.

However, an MFN clause can create an incentive for a State to make only minimal investment protections and liberalisation commitments in order to free-ride off any

---

80 GATS Article XIV refers to 'services' instead of 'international trade'.
81 Appellate Body Report, *US–Shrimp*, para. 156; see also Robert Howse, 'The Appellate Body Ruling in the Shrimp/Turtle Case: A New Legal Baseline for the Trade and Environment Debate' (2002) 27(2) *Columbia Journal of Environmental Law* 491–521, at 503.
82 Note that in those FTA Investment Chapters that do not include an exceptions provision, the commitment of performance requirements includes an in-built list of exceptions, including a GATT Article XX-style chapeau.
83 Hudec, above n. 6, at pp. 284–8. However, see Jürgen Kurtz, 'The MFN Standard and Foreign Investment – An Uneasy Fit?' (2005) 5(6) *Journal of World Investment and Trade* 861–86, at 867, who argues that in contrast to the GATT MFN clause an MFN provision in an FTA Investment Chapter will also apply to behind-the-border measures. Therefore, the argument that MFN provisions in FTA Investment Chapters are necessarily welfare-enhancing is harder to establish than in the trade context.

more favourable commitments the other FTA Party may offer in future FTAs.[84] Therefore, the decision of whether to include an MFN clause can reflect one FTA Party's satisfaction with the level of commitments undertaken by the other FTA Party and the likelihood of making more favourable commitments under a future FTA.[85]

A number of FTA Investment Chapters, such as the Korea–Singapore Free Trade Agreement, India–Singapore CECA and the Japan–Singapore EPA, include NT provisions but do not include MFN provisions. In contrast, NAFTA, AUSFTA, US–Chile FTA, US–Singapore FTA, Korea–Chile FTA, Canada–Chile FTA and CAFTA–DR–US include NT and MFN clauses.

Similar to the national treatment commitment in FTA Investment Chapters, the MFN commitment requires a party to establish that it is in 'like circumstances', but this time the comparison is with another foreign investor. The investors then also needs to show that the FTA Party accorded it less favourable treatment compared with the other similarly situated foreign investor. In addition, tribunals will look at whether there is a legitimate policy justification for the less favourable treatment.[86]

1. *Ejusdem generis* – the scope of an MFN clause

The principle of *ejusdem generis* refers to the rule that the scope of the MFN clause is to be determined by the subject matter to which it refers. This principle is reflected in Article 9 of the International Law Commission (ILC) Draft Article on Most-Favoured-Nation Clauses 1978, which states that '[u]nder a most-favoured-nation clause the beneficiary State acquires, for itself or for the benefit of persons or things in a determined relationship with it, only those rights which fall within the limits of the subject matter of the clause'.[87] The ILC commentaries to this Article, referring to the *Anglo-Iranian Oil Company Case*, describe the rationale for this principle as resting on the common intention of the parties – 'that the clause can only operate in regard to the subject matter which the two States had in mind when they inserted the clause in their treaty'.[88] This means that an MFN clause in an FTA can only be used to incorporate more favourable

84 Warren F. Schwartz and Alan O. Sykes, 'The Economics of the Most-Favoured-Nation Clause', in Jagdeep S. Bhandari and Alan O. Sykes (eds.), *Economic Dimension in International Law: Comparative and Empirical Perspectives* (Cambridge: Cambridge University Press, 1997), at p. 59.

85 See Hudec, above n. 6, at p. 307, where he observes that under the treaty system governing trade in the period 1860–1914, that 'almost every tariff agreement was exposed to the risk of having its value undercut by significant discriminatory concessions made to other parties in subsequent negotiations.'

86 *Parkerings-Compagniet AS v. Republic of Lithuania*, ICSID Case No. ARB/05/8, Award, 11 September 2007, para. 369.

87 *Yearbook of the International Law Commission*, 1978, vol. II, Pt Two, p. 27.

88 *Anglo-Iranian Oil Company Case (Jurisdiction)*, The Judgment of the International Court of Justice in the case of *The United Kingdom v. Iran*, rendered on 22 July 1952, ICJ Reports 1952, p. 110.

treatment accorded another foreign investor under an agreement also dealing with investment protection and promotion issues.

An unresolved issue is whether a Party to an FTA can rely on an MFN provision in the investment chapter to incorporate more favourable dispute settlement provisions that the other Party to the FTA accords to another country. One line of cases, comprising *Emilio Agustin Maffezini v. The Kingdom of Spain*,[89] *Siemens A.G. v. The Argentine Republic*,[90] *and Suez, Sociedad General de Aguas de Barcelona S.A. and InterAguas Servicios Integrales del Aguas S.A. v. The Argentine Republic*,[91] has understood the scope of an MFN clause as not being limited to the 'substantive' protections provided to investment, and therefore being capable of referring to dispute settlement provisions as well. The other line of cases, comprising *Salini Contruttori S.p.A and Italstrade S.p.A. v. The Hashemite Kingdom of Jordan*,[92] *Plama Consortium Limited v. Republic of Bulgaria*,[93] and *Telenor Mobile Communications v. The Republic of Hungary*,[94] has interpreted largely identical MFN clauses as not extending to more favourable dispute settlement provisions in other investment agreements, unless it is expressly made clear that this is the intended scope of the MFN clause.

Starting with the text, in *Maffezini*, the MFN clause referred to 'all matters' while in *Siemens* and *Aguas* the MFN clause referred to 'treatment'. Despite the textual differences, they were both considered wide enough to include dispute settlement provisions.[95]

In contrast, all the MFN clauses in *Salini* (*Jordan*), *Plama* and *Telenor* referred to 'treatment'; however, in these cases the tribunals reached the opposite conclusion, that according to the ordinary meaning of the terms of the MFN clause 'there is no warrant for construing the above phrase (the MFN clause) as importing procedural rights'.[96]

In FTAs such as US–Chile, Canada–Chile and US–Singapore, the type of 'treatment' covered by the MFN clause is limited to the 'establishment, acquisition, expansion, management, conduct, operation and sale or other disposition' of the investment. Therefore, the 'treatment' in these FTA MFN clauses is not as

89 *Emilio Agustin Maffezini v. The Kingdom of Spain* (*Maffezini*), Decision of the Tribunal on Objections to Jurisdiction, ICSID Case No. ARB/97/7 (25 January 2000).

90 *Siemens A.G. v. The Argentine Republic* (*Siemens*), Decision on Jurisdiction, ICSID Case No. ARB/02/8 (3 August 2004).

91 *Suez, Sociedad General de Aguas de Barcelona S.A. and InterAguas Servicios Integrales del Aguas S.A. v. The Argentine Republic* (*Aguas*), Decision on Jurisdiction, ICSID Case No. ARB/03/17 (16 May 2006).

92 *Salini Contruttori S.p.A and Italstrade S.p.A. v. The Hashemite Kingdom of Jordan* (*Salini* (*Jordan*)), Decision on Jurisdiction, ICSID Case No. ARB/02/13 (12 November 2004).

93 *Plama Consortium Limited v. Republic of Bulgaria* (*Plama*), Decision on Jurisdiction, ICSID Case No. ARB/03/24 (8 February 2005).

94 *Telenor Mobile Communications v. The Republic of Hungary* (*Telenor*), ICSID Case No. ARB/04/15 (Award of 13 September 2006).

95 *Maffezini*, para. 56; *Siemens*, para. 103; and *Aguas*, para. 55.

96 *Telenor*, para. 92. See also *Plama*, para. 204; and *Salini* (*Jordan*), para. 119.

open-ended as in the MFN clauses in the BITs, and the failure to refer to dispute settlement in the FTAs arguably reveals an intention to exclude dispute settlement from the scope of the MFN clause.

What constitutes 'treatment' also needs to be assessed in light of whether it is in fact more favourable treatment. As the tribunal noted in *Plama*: 'what if one BIT provides for UNCITRAL arbitration and another provides for ICSID? Which is more favourable?'[97] The tribunal in *Plama* for instance, suggested that a choice is better than no choice.[98]

The inconclusiveness of the text of the MFN clause led these tribunals to use other justifications for their decisions. One justification was that access by investors to dispute settlement provisions is essential for protecting investors' rights accorded under investment agreements.[99] Another was that the purpose of the BITs revealed in their preambles and titles an intention of States to protect and promote investments.[100]

The tribunals in *Telenor* and *Plama*[101] argued that the preamble and title are 'legally insufficient' to show that the MFN clause extends to dispute settlement provisions in other treaties.[102] Modern FTAs include comprehensive commitments on a range of areas in addition to investment, such as on goods, services, intellectual property and telecoms. As a result, establishing the scope of an MFN clause by reference to a single goal of an FTA Investment Chapter would ignore the fact that FTAs embrace a multitude of goals and purposes that represent an 'overall balance of rights and obligations'.[103]

The *Maffezini* tribunal sought to limit the effect of its broad application of the MFN clause by introducing policy exceptions, and these were endorsed by the tribunals in *Siemens* and *Aguas*.[104] These policy exceptions would not allow the dispute settlement provisions in the original treaty to be upset when shown that they were 'envisaged as fundamental conditions for the acceptance of the agreement in question'.[105]

Other tribunals have refused to follow this approach in *Maffezini* and instead have emphasised interpreting BITs using 'the ordinary cannons of interpretation, not to displace, by reference to general policy consideration concerning investor protection, the dispute resolution mechanisms specifically negotiated by the Parties'.[106] In *Wintershall* v. *Argentina*, the tribunal refused to allow the claimant to rely on the MFN clause in the Germany–Argentina BIT to avoid having to pursue litigation in

97 *Ibid.*, para. 208.   98 *Ibid.*, para. 208.   99 *Maffezini*, paras. 54–5; and *Aguas*, para. 60.
100 *Siemens*, para. 43; and *Aguas*, para. 57.   101 *Telenor*, para. 95; and *Plama*, para. 192.
102 *Plama*, para. 192.   103 US–Singapore FTA, Preamble.
104 *Maffezini*, para. 62; and *Siemens*, para. 109.
105 *Maffezini*, para. 62: This was outlined in *Maffezini* as including instances where consent to arbitration was conditioned on exhaustion of local remedies, a fork-in-the-road provision, where the agreement provided for a particular arbitration forum such as ICSID, and highly institutionalised dispute settlement provisions such as in NAFTA.
106 *Telenor*, para. 95.

the Argentine courts for eighteen months before proceeding to international arbitration. The tribunal reasoned that the eighteen-month rule was part of Argentina's consent to international arbitration. The tribunal was unwilling to overturn State consent unless the MFN clause clearly and unambiguously indicated that it should be extended in such a way.[107]

More recent cases have also shown divergent approaches to this issue. For instance, the arbitral tribunals in *Garanti Koza, Hochtief* and *Impregilo* allowed the claimant to rely on the MFN clause to avoid the eighteen-month rule, though in each of these cases there were dissenting opinions.[108] In contrast, in *Kilic* and *ICS Inspection*, the arbitral tribunals refused to allow the MFN clause to be extended to access dispute settlement provisions in other investment agreements.[109]

One way of understanding the different approaches of the tribunal to the scope of the MFN clause is to focus on the different facts of each case.

In *Maffezini, Siemens* and *Aguas*, the tribunals addressed the same provision in the Spain–Argentina BIT, namely, the requirement that local courts be given eighteen months to resolve a dispute before it could be referred to international arbitration. In all these cases the investors were seeking to avoid this requirement by relying on the MFN clause in the Spain–Argentina BIT to access the referring dispute settlement provisions in other BITs that allowed for a period of only six months of negotiation before the dispute could be referred to international arbitration.

In contrast, the investors in *Salini (Jordan)*, *Plama* and *Telenor* were asking the tribunals to interpret the MFN clause in a manner that would have extended the jurisdiction of the tribunal. For example, in *Salini (Jordan)* the investor sought to use the MFN clause to extend the scope of the jurisdiction of the tribunal under the Italy–Jordan BIT to include contractual disputes, pointing to other BITS to which Jordan was a Party and which allowed for the arbitration of contractual disputes before international tribunals. In *Plama* and *Telenor*, the BIT dispute settlement provisions were limited to claims of expropriation. In these cases the investors sought to extend the jurisdiction of the tribunal by reference to the dispute settlement provisions in other BITs to which these States were a party that did not limit the jurisdiction of tribunals in this manner.

2. Temporal scope of the MFN clause

The extent that an MFN clause requires a State to extend the benefits in an FTA chapter to other States also depends on the temporal application of the MFN clause.

---

107 *Wintershall Aktiengesellschaft* v. *Argentina Republic*, ICSID Case No. ARB/04/14, Award, 8 December 2008, para. 167.
108 *Garanti Koza LLP* v. *Turkmenistan* (ICSID Case No. ARB/11/20), Decision on the Objection to Jurisdiction for Lack of Consent, 3 July 2013, para. 41; *Hochtief* v. *Argentina*, Decision on Jurisdiction, 24 October 2011, para. 72; *Impregilo S.p.A.* v. *Argentina*, Award, 21 Jun 2011, paras. 103 and 108.
109 *Kilic* v. *Turkmenistan* (ICSID Case No ARB/10/1), Award, 2 July 2013, para. 7.9.1; *ICS Inspection and Control Services Limited (United Kingdom)* v. *The Republic of Argentina* (UNCITRAL, PCA Case No. 2010-9), Award on Jurisdiction, 10 February 2012, para. 280.

In this regard, most FTAs exclude from the scope of the MFN clause international agreements in force or signed prior to that FTA. In the case of the US–Chile FTA, Canada–US Free Trade Agreement (CUSFTA) and NAFTA, this limitation is captured in Annex II, which is where each Party lists those sectors where it wishes to maintain the flexibility to introduce measures that either liberalise or restrict its commitments under the FTA.

C. Fair and equitable treatment and full protection and security

The obligation to provide fair and equitable treatment and full protection and security is an absolute standard because, in contrast to NT and MFN treatment obligations, it is not defined by how the host State treats its nationals. This obligation thereby provides a floor for the treatment of foreign investors below which host States agree not to go. The development of this standard can be understood as a response to the claims of the Calvo doctrine which made the standard of investor protection relational – depending on the treatment accorded to investors within each State.

Three approaches can be identified in FTA Investment Chapters to the commitment to provide fair and equitable treatment and full protection and security. One approach, taken in FTAs such as US–Singapore, CAFTA–DR–US, US–Chile, AUSFTA and Korea–Singapore, describes the obligation to provide fair and equitable treatment and full protection and security as part of the minimum standard of treatment under customary international law.[110] For example, the US–Singapore FTA makes it clear that 'the concepts of "fair and equivalent treatment" and "full protection and security" do not require treatment in addition to or beyond that which is required by that standard, and do not create additional substantive rights'.[111] These FTAs also include provisions that prohibit a claimant from relying upon a breach of another provision of the FTA to establish a breach of the obligation to provide fair and equitable treatment.[112]

A second approach requires States to accord fair and equitable treatment in accordance with international law. This approach is followed in NAFTA and Canada–Chile.[113] A third approach is simply to refer to a commitment to provide 'fair and equitable treatment' without limiting it to the minimum standard of treatment or to international law. This approach is taken in the Thailand–Australia FTA.[114]

---

110 US–Singapore FTA, Article 15.5; CAFTA–DR–US, Article 10.5; US–Chile FTA, Article 10.4; AUSFTA, Article 11.5; and Korea–Singapore FTA, Article 10.4.
111 US–Singapore FTA, Article 15.2.
112 *Ibid.*, Article 15.5; CAFTA–DR–US, Article 10.5; US–Chile FTA, Article 10.4; AUSFTA, Article 11.5; and Korea–Singapore FTA, Article 10.4.
113 NAFTA, Article 1105; and Canada–Chile FTA, Article G-05.
114 Thailand–Australia FTA, Article 909.2.

Finally, some FTAs, such as the India–Singapore CECA and the Singapore–Australia Free Trade Agreement, do not include a commitment to provide fair and equitable treatment or full protection and security.

The following section looks at how tribunals have interpreted these three formulations of the commitment to provide fair and equitable treatment. It is worth noting that there is overlap in the scope of each of these fair and equitable treatment commitments. For instance, some international tribunals have interpreted a stand-alone commitment to provide fair and equitable treatment as being substantially the same as the customary international law minimum standard of treatment,[115] while others have interpreted the obligation to provide fair and equitable treatment at international law as being equivalent to fair and equitable treatment as a stand-alone commitment.[116]

1. The customary international law minimum standard of treatment

First articulated in the 1926 *United States* v. *Mexico General Claims Commission* (*'Neer Claim'*), the international minimum standard was understood as follows:

> [T]he propriety of governmental acts should be put to the test of international standards ... the treatment of an alien, in order to constitute an international delinquency should amount to an outrage, to bad faith, to wilful neglect of duty or to an insufficiency of governmental action so far short of international standards that every reasonable and impartial man would readily recognize its insufficiency. Whether the insufficiency proceeds from the deficient execution of a reasonable law or from the fact that the laws of the country do not empower the authorities to measure up to international standards is immaterial.[117]

The customary international law minimum standard of treatment has, however, evolved since its formulation in the Neer Claim, and the scope of the obligation remains contested.[118]

Some FTAs provide non-exhaustive definitions of the customary international law standard. For example, the US–Chile FTA states that "'fair and equitable treatment" includes the obligation not to deny justice in criminal, civil or

---

115 Judge Asante in his dissenting opinion in *Asian Agricultural Products Ltd. (AAPL)* v. *Republic of SriLanka*, ICSID Case No. ARB/87/3 (Award of 27 June 1990), equated the 'fair and equitable treatment' standard with the international minimum standard of treatment; *American Manufacturing & Trading (AMT) (US), Inc.* v. *Republic of Zaire*, ICSID Case No. ARB/93/1 (Award of 21 February, 1997), p. 29; *Alex Genin, Eastern Credit Limited, Inc. and A.S. Baltoil (US)* v. *Republic of Estonia*, ICSID Case No. ARB/99/2 (Award of 25 June 2001); and *Azurix Corp.* v. *Argentina*, ICSID Case No. ARB/01/12 (Award of 26 July 2006), para. 364.
116 *Tecnicas Medioambientales Tecmed, S.A.* v. *United Mexican States* (*'Tecmed'*), ICSID Case No. ARB(AF)/00/2 (Award of 29 May 2003), para. 155.
117 *United States* v. *Mexico General Claims Commission* (*'Neer Claim'*) (1926) 4 RIAA 60.
118 *ADF Group Inc.* v. *United States of America*, ICSID Case No. ARB(AF)/00/1 (Award of 9 January 2003), para. 179; and *Mondev International Ltd* v. *United States of America* (*'Mondev'*), ICSID Case No. ARB (AF)/99/2 (Award of 11 October 2002), para. 125.

administrative adjudicatory proceedings in accordance with the principle of due process embodied in the principle legal systems of the world'.[119] Other FTAs, such as the Korea–Singapore, also adopt this elaboration of the meaning of 'fair and equitable treatment', but without reference to 'the principle legal systems of the world'.[120]

In NAFTA, the commitment to provide fair and equitable treatment is tied to international law. However, in 2001 the NAFTA Free Trade Commission, comprising all NAFTA member States, issued the following Note of Interpretation:

1. Article 1105(1) prescribes the customary international law minimum standard of treatment of aliens as the minimum standard of treatment to be afforded to investments of investors of another Party.
2. The concepts of 'fair and equitable treatment' and 'full protection and security' do not require treatment in addition to or beyond that which is required by the customary international law minimum standard of treatment of aliens.
3. A determination that there has been a breach of another provision of the NAFTA, or of a separate international agreement, does not establish that there has been a breach of Article 1105(1).

This interpretative Note has formed the basis for the 'fair and equitable treatment' commitment in those FTAs that tie this commitment to the minimum standard of treatment. As a result, decisions of NAFTA tribunals that post-date this Note also shed important light on the content of this standard.

In *Thunderbird* v. *Mexico* the tribunal found that a breach of the minimum standard of treatment is a high threshold and would require 'gross denial of justice or manifest arbitrariness'.[121] In *Glamis Gold* v. *Mexico*, the tribunal found that to fall below the *Neer* standard would require 'an act sufficiently egregious and shocking – a gross denial of justice, manifest arbitrariness, blatant unfairness, a complete lack of due process, evident discrimination, or a manifest lack of reasons'.[122]

More recently, in an investment dispute under the Central American Free Trade Agreement – *Teco* v. *Guatemala* – the arbitral tribunal, following *Thunderbird* and *Glamis*, found that the minimum standard of treatment prohibits State conduct that is 'manifestly arbitrary, idiosyncratic, or that show a complete lack of candor in the conduct of the regulatory process'.[123]

The NAFTA minimum standard of treatment has also been found to include protection of investor's legitimate expectations. According to the tribunal in *Mobil & Murphy*, to establish a breach of this standards requires '(i) clear and explicit

119 US–Chile FTA, Article 10.4.2(a).   120 Korea–Singapore FTA, Article 10.5.2.
121 *International Thunderbird Gaming Corporation* v. *Mexico*, UNCITRAL (NAFTA), Award, 26 January 2006, para. 194.
122 *Glamis Gold, Ltd.* v. *United States*, UNCITRAL (NAFTA), Award, 8 June 2009, para. 616.
123 *TECO Guatemala Holdings, LLC* v. *Republic of Guatemala* (ICSID Case No, ARB/10/23), Award 19 December 2013, para. 492.

representations made by or attributable to the NAFTA host State in order to induce investment, and (ii) were, by reference to an objective standard, reasonably relied open by the investor, and (iii) were subsequently repudiated by the NAFTA host State'.[124]

2. Fair and equitable treatment as defined by international law

Article 1105 of the NAFTA describes the standard as 'fair and equitable treatment in accordance with international law', and therefore the approach of several NAFTA tribunals prior to the FTC Interpretative Note sheds light on the content of this obligation. Article G-05 of the Canada–Chile FTA also describes the standard as 'fair and equitable treatment in accordance with international law'.[125]

The significance of defining fair and equitable treatment according to international law is that tribunals have been prepared to interpret this commitment by reference to all sources of international law, including treaties such as BITs, customary international law and other general principles of international law.[126]

As a result, tribunals have treated this as a broader commitment than when it is framed as part of the minimum standard of treatment at customary international law. For instance, the tribunal in *Metalclad* included an obligation of transparency as part of the fair and equitable treatment commitment.[127] And the tribunal in *Myers v. Canada* found that a breach of the NAFTA NT provision could constitute a violation of the obligation to provide fair and equitable treatment.[128] The tribunal in *Pope & Talbot* appeared to uncouple the standard from international law entirely, by stating that 'investors are entitled to the international law minimum, plus the fairness elements'.[129]

For example, the tribunal in *Waste Management, Inc. v. United Mexican States*, reviewing decisions of former NAFTA tribunals on the 'fair and equitable treatment' standard, stated that conduct infringes the standard when it is:

> arbitrary, grossly unfair, unjust or idiosyncratic, is discriminatory and exposes the claimant to sectional or racial prejudice, or involves a lack of due process leading to an outcome which offends judicial propriety – as might be the case with a manifest failure of natural justice in judicial proceedings or a complete lack of transparency and candor in an administrative process. In applying the

124 *Mobil Investments Canada Inc. and Murphy Oil Corporation* v. *Canada* (ICSID Case No. ARB(AF)/07/4), Decision on Liability and Principles of Quantum, 22 May 2012, para. 152.
125 Note that the heading of Article G-05 is 'Minimum Standard of Treatment', which suggest that Canada does not consider there to be a distinction between fair and equitable treatment at international law and when defined as part of the customary international law minimum standard of treatment.
126 OECD, 'Fair and Equitable Treatment Standard in International Investment Law', OECD Working Papers on International Investment No. 2004/3 (September 2004), at p. 20.
127 *Metalclad Corporation* v. *United Mexican States* ('*Metalclad*'), ICSID Case No. ARB(AG)/97/1 (Award of 30 August 2000), para. 99.
128 See *Myers* v. *Canada*, para. 266.   129 See *Pope & Talbot*, para. 110.

standards it is relevant that the treatment is in breach of representations made by the host Sate which were reasonably relied on by the claimant.[130]

The tribunal in *Mondev* also made it clear that 'a State may treat foreign investment unfairly and inequitably without necessarily acting in bad faith'.[131] The tribunal in *Tecmed* further elaborated on the content of the standard by referring to the good faith principle.[132] Here, the tribunal stated that this requires the host State to 'act in a consistent manner, free from ambiguity and totally transparently in its relations with the foreign investor'.[133]

This trend towards a broad formulation of the standards in international law was also evident in *Tecmed*. In that case, the tribunal referred to the 'basic expectations' of the investor when it stated that the fair and equitable treatment standard requires the host State 'to act consistently, i.e. without arbitrarily revoking any pre-existing decisions or permits issued by the State that were relied upon by the investor to assume its commitments as well as to plan and launch its commercial and business activities'.[134] This approach has been criticised as raising an investor's 'basic expectation' into a treaty commitment.[135]

3. Fair and equitable treatment as a stand-alone commitment

The obligation to provide fair and equitable treatment, stated as a stand-alone commitment, is not legally equivalent to the obligation to provide fair and equitable treatment when stated as part of the minimum standard of treatment at customary international law.[136] This is because such a commitment should be understood as self-contained and interpreted in light of whether 'a particular treatment meted out to that investor is both "fair" and "equitable"'.[137]

Other tribunals have interpreted the obligation to provide fair and equitable treatment as entitling investors 'to the international law minimum plus the fairness elements'.[138] One commentator has gone so far as to observe that an obligation to provide fair and equitable treatment 'is likely to be sufficient to cover all conceivable cases, and it may well be that other provisions of the Agreements affording substantive protection are no more than examples or specific instances of this overriding duty'.[139]

---

130 *Waste Management, Inc. v. United Mexican States* ('*Waste Management*'), ICSID Case No. ARB(AF)/98/2 (Award of 2 June 2000), 43 ILM 967, paras. 98–9.
131 See *Mondev*, para. 161.   132 See *Tecmed*, para. 154.   133 *Ibid.*   134 See *Tecmed*, para. 154.
135 *MTD Equity Sdn Bhd & MTD Chile S.A. v. Chile*, ICSID Case No. ARB/01/7 (21 March 2007), para. 67.
136 UNCTAD, *Investment Provisions in Economic Integration Agreements* (New York and Geneva: UNCTAD, 2006), at p. 105; however, see *Tecmed*, para. 155; *Inmaris Perestroika Sailing Maritime Services GmbH and Others v. Ukraine* (ICSID Case No. ARB/08/8), Award, 1 March 2012, para. 264.
137 *Saluka Investments BV (The Netherlands) v. The Czech Republic* ('*Saluka v. Czech Republic*'), UNCITRAL Arbitral Tribunal (Partial Award of 17 March 2006), para. 282; and UNCTAD, *Fair and Equitable Treatment*, UNCTAD Series on Issue in International Investment, vol. 3 (New York and Geneva: UNCTAD, 1999).
138 *Pope & Talbot* (Award on The Merits of 10 April 2001), para. 110.
139 F.A. Mann, 'British Treaties for the Promotion and Protection of Investments' (1981) 52 *British Yearbook of International Law* 241–54.

The requirement to provide fair and equitable treatment was initially defined in Article II.2 of the 1948 Havana Charter for an International Trade Organisation[140] as a requirement to afford international investments 'just and equitable treatment'. The US's FNC treaties, as precursors to BITs, also included an obligation to provide 'fair and equitable' treatment.

The Thailand–Australia FTA refers to a requirement to accord fair and equitable treatment[141] while the Japan–Singapore EPA states that '[e]ach Party shall accord to investments in its territory of investors of the other Party fair and equitable treatment and full protection and security'.[142] These formulations of the 'fair and equitable treatment' standard are also reflected in numerous BITs, such as those used by Switzerland, Germany and Sweden.[143]

When the fair and equitable treatment standard is phrased as a stand-alone commitment, one approach to interpreting this standard has been to regard it as an autonomous standard not linked to international law and to be interpreted according to its plain meaning,[144] taking into account the treaties' object and purpose and circumstance of its conclusion.[145]

Relying on the terms of the treaty to give the fair and equitable treatment standard its content without reference to other sources of international law and other arbitral decisions provides significant scope for it to become a subjective standard reflecting a particular tribunal's sense of what is fair and equitable on that day. Conflicting interpretations of this standard are therefore inevitable,[146] which will undermine one of the goals of FTA Investment Chapters, namely, increased certainty and predictability in the investment conditions of the Parties to the treaty.[147] As a result of these problems, even where the standard is framed without reference to international law, tribunals often seek to interpret the commitment applying the applicable law, as defined in either the Agreement under which the

---

140 Done at Havana on 24 March 1948, never ratified.   141 Thailand–Australia FTA, Article 909.

142 Japan–Singapore EPA, Article 77.1.

143 See, e.g., Switzerland–Iran BIT, Article 4; Switzerland–Jordan BIT, Article 2; Germany–China BIT, Article 4; Germany–Ethiopia BIT, Article 1; Sweden–Laos BIT, Article 3; and Sweden–Philippines BIT, Article 3.

144 See Mann, above n. 139.

145 *Saluka* v. *Czech Republic*, para. 294; and *Ronald S. Lauder* v. *The Czech Republic* ('*Lauder* v. *Czech Republic*'), UNCITRAL Arbitral Tribunal Final Award of 3 September 2001.

146 See *Lauder* v. *Czech Republic*; and *CME Czech Republic B.V.* v. *The Czech Republic*, UNCITRAL Arbitral Tribunal Partial Award (Merits) of 13 September 2001, where these two tribunals applied the same stand-alone clause to the same facts and reached conflicting outcomes. However, the tribunal in *Saluka* v. *Czech Republic*, at paras. 284–5, argued that a stand-alone fair and equitable treatment standard does not 'invite the tribunal to decide the dispute in a way that resembles a decision *ex aequo et bono* . . . it does not set out totally subjective standards which would allow the Tribunal to substitute, with regard to the Czech Republic's conduct to be assessed in the present case, its judgement on the choice of solutions for the Czech Republic's [sic]'.

147 *Occidental Exploration and Production Company* v. *Republic of Ecuador*, LCIA Case No. UN3467, Final Award of 1 July 2004, para. 183, where the tribunal notes, referring to the BIT preamble, that 'the stability of the legal and business framework is thus an essential element of fair and equitable treatment'.

dispute arises or in ICSID or UNCITRAL.[148] The following outlines how tribunals have interpreted the obligation.

First, commentators and tribunals have recognised that it includes an obligation of due process and not to deny justice. A denial of justice in international law has been described as 'a denial, unwarranted delay or obstruction of access to courts, gross deficiency in the administration of judicial or remedial process, failure to provide those guarantees which are generally considered indispensable to the proper administration of justice or a manifestly unjust judgement'.[149] This conception of denial of justice has been found by arbitral tribunals to be an element of the obligation to accord investors fair and equitable treatment.[150]

Arbitrariness, understood as a 'willful disregard of due process of law, an act which shocks, or at least surprises, a sense of judicial propriety',[151] has been seen by tribunals as inconsistent with the obligation of due process and therefore an element of the fair and equitable treatment standard.[152]

Tribunals have also found the 'fair and equitable treatment' standard as requiring transparency. For instance, in *Tecmed* the tribunal described the standard as requiring the State 'to act in a consistent manner, free from ambiguity and totally transparently in its relations with the foreign investor'.[153] This obligation of transparency was also emphasised by the tribunals in *Metalclad* and *Waste Management*.[154]

Regarding the protection of legitimate investor expectations, some tribunals have understood this broadly. For instance, the tribunal in *Electrabel* v. *Hugary* found that the protections investor's reasonable and legitimate expectation is the most important function of the fair and equitable standard.[155] In that case the tribunal did not require specific assurances by the State to establish a reasonable expectation that any changes to the State's legal framework would be done 'fairly, consistently and predictably'.[156] In contrast, the tribunal in *Ulysseas* v. *Ecuador*

---

148 Where the Parties to the FTA fail to specify the applicable law, ICSID Article 42.1 directs the tribunal to apply 'the law of the Contracting States party to the dispute (including its rules on conflict of laws) and such rules of international law as may be applicable'. UNCITRAL Arbitration Rules, Article 33.2, does not refer to international law but does not allow a decision ex aequo et bono unless expressly authorised by the Parties; see also *MTD Equity Sdn. Bhd. & MTD Chile S.A.* v. *Chile*, ICSID Case No. ARB/01/7 (21 March 2007), para. 44.

149 Draft Convention Prepared By the Research in International Law of the Harvard Law School, Supplement to (1935) 29 *American Journal of International Law*.

150 *Mondev International Ltd* v. *United States*, ICSID Case No. ARB(AF)/99/2 (Award of 11 October 2002); and *Robert Azinian and others* v. *The United Mexican States*, ICSID Case No ARB(AF)/97/2 (Arbitral Award 1 November 1999), paras. 102–3.

151 *Ibid.*, p. 76.

152 *Electronic Sicula S.p.A. (ELSI) (United States of America* v. *Italy) ('Electronic Sicula')* [1989] ICJ Reports 15 (20 July 1989), p. 30.

153 *Tecmed*, para. 154; see also *Saluka* v. *Czech Republic*, para. 307.   154 *Waste Management*, paras. 98–9.

155 *Electrabel S.A.* v. *Republic of Hungary* (ICSID Case No. ARB/07/19), Decision on Jurisdiction, Applicable Law and Liability, 30 November 2012, para. 7.75.

156 *Ibid.*, para. 7.77.

followed the approach of the tribunal in *Mobil & Murphy* and found that specific promises by the State are necessary before an investor can have a legitimate expectation that there will be no change in the State's legal framework.[157]

D. Full protection and security

FCN treaties first articulated an obligation to provide full protection and security. Today, most FTAs include a commitment to provide fair and equitable treatment and also full protection and security.

The scope of the obligation to provide full protection and security depends on whether it is defined as limited to the customary international minimum standard of treatment or phrased as being a separate stand-alone commitment.[158] The obligation to provide full protection and security is commonly understood as an 'obligation for the host State to adopt all reasonable measures to physically protect assets and property from threats or attacks which may target particularly foreigners or certain groups of foreigners'.[159]

Tribunals have made it clear that the obligation to provide full protection and security is not an obligation of strict liability.[160] Instead, they have defined this obligation as one of 'due diligence', described as 'the reasonable measures of prevention which a well-administered government should be expected to exercise under similar circumstances'.[161] For example, the tribunal in *American Manufacturing & Trading, Inc* v. *Zaire* found a breach of Zaire's obligation to provide full protection and security due to its failure to stop the looting of AMT by Zairian armed forces. In this case, the tribunal refused to define this either as an obligation of conduct or result and instead relied on the additional obligation in the BIT on the Parties to provide compensation in cases of strife as confirming the responsibility of Zaire for losses and damages by AMT.[162]

In recent cases, tribunals have conflated the obligation to provide full protection and security with the fair and equitable treatment standard, stating that 'treatment that is not fair and equitable automatically entails an absence of full protection and security'.[163] In defining this obligation as part of the fair and equitable treatment standard, these tribunals have also extended this obligation beyond providing

157 *Ulysseas, Inc.* v. *The Republic of Ecuador* (UNCITRAL), Final Award, 12 June 2012, para. 248.
158 *Asian Agricultural Products Ltd* v. *Republic of Sri Lanka*, ICSID Case No. ARB/87/3 (Final Award of 27 June 1990), para. 50.
159 Georgio Sacerdoti, 'Bilateral Treaties and Multilateral Instruments on Investment Protection' (1997) 269 *Recueil des Cours* 251–460, at 347.
160 *Asian Agricultural Products Ltd* v. *Republic of Sri Lanka*, para. 50; *Ronald S. Lauder* v. *The Czech Republic*, para. 308; and *Saluka* v. *The Czech Republic*, para. 484.
161 *Asian Agricultural Products Ltd* v. *Republic of Sri Lanka*, paras. 76–7.
162 *American Manufacturing & Trading, Inc.* v. *Zaire* ('*AMT* v. *Zaire*'), ICSID Case No. ARB/93/1 (Award of 21 February 1997), paras. 6.08–6.14.
163 *Occidental Exploration and Production Company* v. *Republic of Ecuador*, para. 187.

physical protection.[164] It is, however, unlikely that tribunals will conflate the commitment to provide fair and equitable treatment with the commitment to provide full protection and security in FTAs such as US–Singapore where the full protection and security standard is limited to 'police protection required under customary international law'.[165]

E. Expropriation

The expropriation obligation is one of the most important and arguably most controversial of the protections afforded in FTA Investment Chapters. Traditionally, the expropriation debate focused on how a State could lawfully expropriate an investment and how the level of compensation was to be valued.[166] On the one hand, the Hull Rule required 'prompt, adequate and effective' compensation while on the other hand, the Calvo doctrine argued that it was only necessary to provide 'appropriate compensation, in accordance with the rules in force in the State taking such measures in the exercise of its sovereignty'.[167]

As discussed above, growing appreciation of the important development benefits of investment has led countries to accept that instances of expropriation should be subject to an international law standard regarding the payment of compensation. Therefore, the main debate today regarding the expropriation obligation is over the scope of what constitutes indirect expropriation (discussed below).[168]

1. Lawful expropriation

Under customary international law, an expropriation is prohibited unless it fulfils four conditions: (1) the measure is for a public purpose; (2) it is non-discriminatory; (3) it is in accordance with due process; and (4) compensation is paid.[169]

---

164 *Azurix* v. *Argentine Republic*, ICSID Case No. ARB/01/12 (Award of 14 July 2006), para. 408; however, see *PSEG Global Inc., The North America Coal Corporation and Konya Ilgin Elektrik Üretim ve Ticaret Limited Sirketi* v. *Republic of Turkey*, ICSID Case No. ARB/02/05 (Award 19 January 2007), para. 258, where the tribunal sought to limit those cases when a breach of the 'fair and equitable treatment' commitment would also constitute a breach of the 'full protection and security' commitment, to an 'exceptional situation'.

165 US–Singapore FTA, Article 15.52(b).

166 Rudolf Dolzer, 'Indirect Expropriations: New Developments?' (2002) 11 *New York University Environmental Law Journal* 64–93, at 64.

167 Steiner, Vagts and Koh, above n. 5, at p. 418. See Green H. Hackworth, *Digest of International Law* (Washington, DC: Government Printing Office, 1940–44), vol. 3, Sec. 228, at pp. 655–65, for the notes exchanged during the dispute in 1938 between the US and Mexico concerning expropriation by Mexico of US-owned properties.

168 See Dolzer, above n. 166, at 64.

169 See *Restatement of the Law Third, Foreign Relations Law of the United States* (1987), Section 712; and *Antoine Goetz and others* v. *Republic of Burundi*, ICSID Case No. ARB/95/3 (Award of 10 February 1999).

Most FTA Investment Chapters reflect these conditions for a lawful expropria-tion.[170] When referring to expropriation being in accordance with 'due process of law', many also require that an expropriation be carried out consistently with the minimum standard of treatment as defined in the investment chapter. This approach is followed in US–Singapore, US–Chile, Korea–Chile, Canada–Chile and Korea–Singapore.[171]

Other FTAs adopt slightly different formulations regarding how a State can lawfully expropriate. For instance, the India–Singapore CECA refers to 'a purpose authorized by law' rather than a 'public purpose', and makes it clear that any expropriation of land shall always be deemed 'a purpose authorized by law'.[172] However, given that the latitude tribunals normally extend to a State's assessment of what constitutes a 'public purpose', this provision was likely included to provide certainty for the Parties and does not alter the scope of their expropriation obligation.[173]

All of these disciplines on expropriation reflect customary international law, and in some FTA Investment Chapters this is made explicit. For example, Annex 11-B of the AUSFTA, the exchange of letters under the India–Singapore CECA, Annex 10-C of the CAFTA–DR–US, the side letter to the US–Singapore FTA and Annex 10-D to the US–Chile FTA state that the expropriation provisions are intended to reflect cus-tomary international law.

Public purpose The requirement that an expropriation be for a public purpose is based on the proposition that:

> if international law recognizes the undoubtedly very wide power of the State to appropriate the property of aliens on the ground that, as under municipal law, the interests of the individual must yield to the general interest and public welfare, the least that can be required of the State is that it should exercise power only when the measure is clearly justified by the public interest.[174]

While the requirement that expropriation be in accordance with a 'public purpose' seeks to prohibit the 'abusive exercise of power to expropriate and to give legal sanction to manifestly arbitrary acts of expropriation',[175] international law also

---

170 See, e.g., US–Singapore FTA, Article 15.6; AUSFTA, Article 11.7; Canada–Chile FTA, Article G-10; Japan–Singapore EPA, Article 77; CAFTA–DR–US, Article 10.7; Korea–Chile FTA, Article 10.13; and the Draft CCIA Investment Framework Agreement, Article 16.
171 US–Singapore FTA, Article 15.6; US–Chile FTA, Article 10.9; Korea–Chile FTA, Article 10.13; Canada–Chile FTA, Article G-10; and the Korea–Singapore FTA, Article 10.13.
172 India–Singapore CECA, Article 6.5.
173 See, e.g., *Tippets, Abbett, McCarthy, Stratton* v. *TAMS-AFFA Consulting Engineers of Iran* ('*Tippets v. TAMSAFFA*'), Iran–US Claims Tribunal (Award No. 141–7–2 of 22 June 1984), 6 Iran-US CRT 219, pp. 225–6.
174 Fourth Report on States Responsibility by F.V. Garcia-Amador, Special Rapporteur, 'State Responsibility', in *Yearbook of the International Law Commission 1959* (New York: UN, 1960) vol. II, UN Doc. A/CN.4/ 119, para. 59.
175 *Ibid.*

recognises that what constitutes a 'public interest' is to be assessed according to the domestic law of the expropriating State and at the time of the expropriation.[176] Therefore, in practice, the discipline that an expropriation be for a public purpose still provides States with a wide degree of latitude to expropriate.

What constitutes a public purpose is not defined in these FTAs. A plain text reading of the texts, however, suggests that expropriations for a private benefit will not constitute a public purpose.[177]

Non-discriminatory All FTA Investment Chapters require expropriation to be non-discriminatory. In the expropriation context, one commentator has described discrimination as entailing two concepts:

> [F]irst, the measures directed at a particular party must be for reasons unrelated to the substance of the matters, for example, the company's nationality. Second, discrimination entails like persons being treated in an inequivalent manner.[178]

This standard was followed in *Amoco International Finance Corp.* v. *Islamic Republic of Iran*, where the claimant argued that the expropriation was discriminatory because the Japanese share of the investment was not expropriated. In this case, the defendant argued that the expropriation of the American share in the investment was not based on nationality, but instead on other legitimate factors, such as the Japanese share not being an operational concern at the time of the expropriation.[179] The tribunal accepted these as justifiable grounds for drawing a distinction between the American and Japanese investment, and as a result, the tribunal found that the expropriation was not discriminatory.[180] Similarly, in *GAMI Investments* the tribunal found that the expropriation was connected to a legitimate government policy and for reasons other than the investor's nationality.[181]

Due process of law The Japan–Singapore EPA, NAFTA, US–Chile FTA, Canada–Chile FTA and AUSFTA all require that an expropriation be conducted in accordance with due process of law.[182] This requirement disciplines the manner in which the expropriation is conducted.

What constitutes 'due process' is not defined in these FTAs, though it would appear to include the requirement that the process of expropriation be fair,

---

176 *Siag and Vecchi* v. *Egypt*, Award, 1 June 2009, para. 432.
177 As outlined above, Article 6.5.3 of the India Singapore CECA clarifies that an expropriation of land shall be deemed as being for a public purpose.
178 Abul F.M. Maniruzzaman, 'Expropriation of Alien Property and the Principle of Non-Discrimination in International Law of Foreign Investment: An Overview' (1998) 8(1) *Journal of Transnational Law & Policy* 57–78, at 69.
179 *Amoco International Finance Corp.* v. *Islamic Republic of Iran*, Iran–US Claims Tribunal (Award 310–56–3 of 14 July 1987) (Chamber 3), 15 Iran–US CTR 189, paras. 140–2.
180 *Ibid.*   181 *GAMI Investments* v. *Mexico*, Award, 15 November 2004, para. 114.
182 Japan–Singapore EPA, Article 77; NAFTA, Article 1110; US–Chile FTA, Article 10.9; Canada–Chile FTA, Article G-10; and AUSFTA, Article 11.7.

transparent, subject to judicial review and participation by the affected investor.[183]

International law has allowed States significant discretion to determine what constitutes due process, only intervening when the process falls below the minimum standard of treatment.[184] In fact, a failure to accord 'due process' when expropriating may only arise when there is discrimination.[185] In the absence of discrimination, State actions that are consistent with their domestic law do not breach international law. Others have argued, however, that arbitrariness will constitute a breach of the due process requirement.[186]

Finally, it is worth recalling that a number of FTAs require expropriation to be in accordance with the minimum standard of treatment and that this standard also incorporates due process required.[187] Thus, a breach of the minimum standard of treatment commitment could not lead to an expropriation consistent with the FTA.

Compensation Once a Party to an FTA establishes that the expropriation was (1) for a public purpose; (2) non-discriminatory; and (3) done in accordance with due process of law, an obligation of compensation arises.

Public knowledge of an intended expropriation Most FTAs require that compensation be 'paid without delay at the date of expropriation', and that compensation be paid at the 'fair market value'.[188] However, because an expropriation can arise as a result of a series of acts over time, this raises the possibility of an intended expropriation becoming public knowledge, thereby reducing the value of the investment prior to the date of expropriation. The Canada–Chile FTA addresses this situation by stating the compensation paid 'shall not reflect any change in value occurring because the intended expropriation had become known earlier'.[189]

Assessing the value of the expropriated investment Most FTAs require compensation to be equivalent to the fair market value of the investment.[190] Some FTAs also outline how a Party to the FTA is to assess the fair market value of the expropriated asset. For example, the Canada–Chile FTA states that 'valuation criteria shall include going concern value, asset value including declared tax value of tangible property, and other criteria, as appropriate, to determine fair market value'.[191]

---

183 *Waste Management*, paras. 98–9.   184 See Garcia–Amador, above n. 174, para. 61.
185 *Sedco, Inc.* v. *National Iranian Oil Company*, Iran–US Claims Tribunal (Award ITL 59–129–3 of 27 March 1986), 10 Iran–US CTR 189.
186 See Garcia–Amador, above n. 174, para. 62.   187 See *Waste Management*, paras. 98–9.
188 See, e.g., Japan–Singapore EPA, Article 77.4; and Canada–Chile FTA, Article G-10.3.
189 See also, Korea–Singapore FTA, Article 10.13; Japan– Singapore EPA, Article 77; and AUSFTA, Article 11.17.2.
190 US–Singapore FTA, Article 15.6; AUSFTA, Article 11.7; Canada–Chile FTA, Article G-10; Japan–Singapore EPA, Article 77; CAFTA–DR–US, Article 10.7; Korea–Chile FTA, Article 10.13; Draft CCIA Investment Framework Agreement, Article 16; US–Chile FTA, Article 10.9; and Korea–Singapore FTA, Article 10.13.
191 Canada–Chile FTA, Article G.10.2.

In other FTAs, such as the Japan–Singapore EPA and the US–Chile FTA, the expropriation provision does not address how fair market value is to be assessed, leaving it to the Government (or an arbitral tribunal) to make this calculation.[192]

Currency of payment FTA Investment Chapters also address the currency in which compensation is to be paid and the related issues of which exchange rate is to be used. For example, the US–Chile FTA requires compensation to be in 'a freely usable currency.[193] The Canada–Chile FTA requires payment to be made in a G7 currency.[194] In the case of the AUSFTA, compensation can be designated in a freely useable currency or the Australian dollar.[195]

Those FTA Investment Chapters that allow the fair market value of the investment to be designated in a currency that may not be freely transferable also address the situation when that currency is not transferable. For example, under the AUSFTA, if the Australian dollar is not transferable on the date of payment then the compensation paid cannot be less than the fair market value of the investment converted into a freely useable currency.

Other FTAs, such as the Japan–Singapore EPA, do not address the issue of changes in exchange rates when compensation is denominated in a currency other than a freely useable currency, effectively shifting the risk of currency fluctuations onto the investor.

Interest In FTA Investment Chapters, interest is usually to be paid from the date of expropriation to the date when compensation is paid. The US–Chile FTA defines this interest rate as a 'commercially reasonable rate' and links the interest rate to the currency of compensation by requiring the interest rate to also be a 'commercially reasonable rate for that currency'.[196] A similar approach is also taken in the Canada–Chile FTA.[197] In contrast, the Japan–Singapore EPA requires only an 'appropriate interest'.[198]

2. Direct and indirect expropriation

All FTA Investment Chapters include disciplines on direct and indirect expropriation. However, different FTAs use different formulations to express this commitment. For example, the Japan–Singapore FTA Investment Chapter refers to 'measures equivalent to expropriation or nationalization'.[199] In contrast, the Korea–Singapore FTA Investment Chapter states that 'neither Party may, directly or indirectly, nationalize or expropriate an investment of an investor of the other

---

192 See Japan–Singapore EPA, Article 77; and US–Chile FTA, Article 10.9.
193 US–Chile FTA, Article 10.27.   194 Canada–Chile FTA, Article G-10.4.   195 AUSFTA, Article 11.7.
196 US–Chile FTA, Article 10.10.3.   197 Canada–Chile FTA, Article G-10.4.
198 Japan–Singapore EPA, Article 77.4.   199 *Ibid.*, Article 77.2.

Party'.[200] The Canada–Chile FTA Investment Chapter takes a similar approach to the Korea–Singapore FTA,[201] but includes the phrase, 'or take(s) a measure tantamount to nationalization or expropriation of such an investment'.[202] The only major departure from these formulations is in the Draft CCIA Investment Framework Agreement, which largely follows the 1967 OECD Draft Convention on the Protection of Foreign Property, and defines expropriation as including 'any measures attributable to the government of a member State which have the effect of depriving an investor of the ownership or control of, or a substantial benefit from, the investment and shall be interpreted to include all forms of expropriation such as nationalization and attachment as well as creeping expropriation'.[203]

Another group of FTA Investment Chapters include text that elaborates on the commitment not to directly or indirectly expropriate. These include CAFTA–DR– US, US–Singapore, US–Chile, India–Singapore and the AUSFTA.[204] All of these elaborations on the meaning of direct and indirect expropriation are substantially similar, and therefore the following analysis regarding this test is applicable to all these FTAs.

There has yet to be tribunal interpretation of the FTA Investment Chapter provisions that include text which elaborate on what constitutes direct or indirect expropriation. All of these FTA Investment Chapters state that these provisions 'reflect customary international law concerning the obligation of States with respect to expropriation'.

3. Direct expropriation

Annex 10-D to the US–Chile FTA is a representative example of those FTAs that address how to assess when direct or indirect expropriation arises. Firstly, paragraph 2 clarifies what will need to be established to show an expropriation, namely interference with a tangible or intangible property right or property interest in an investment.

Paragraph 3 then addresses what constitutes a direct expropriation, namely a nationalisation or formal transfer of title or outright seisure. Nationalisation may be understood as referring to changes or measures that affect an entire sector or country, whereas the term expropriation is applied to more discrete acts.

The description of direct expropriation in Annex 10-D largely reflects the position at customary international law.[205] For instance, the reference to property as

---

200 Korea–Singapore FTA, Article 10.13.   201 Canada–Chile FTA, Article G-10.
202 For a discussion, see *Myers* v. *Canada*, paras. 285–6; see also *Tecmed*, para. 114, which clarified that measures 'tantamount to nationalization or expropriation' do not address a type of expropriation in addition to direct and indirect expropriation.
203 Draft CCIA Investment Framework Agreement, Article 1.5.
204 AUSFTA, Annex 11-B; US–Chile FTA, Annex 10-D; India–Singapore CECA, Annex 3; CAFTA–DR–US, Annex 10-C; and US–Singapore FTA, Side-Letter on Expropriation.
205 OECD, '"Indirect Expropriation" and the "Right to Regulate" in International Investment Law', OECD Working Papers on International Investment No. 2004/4 (September 2004), at p. 3.

constituting a tangible or intangible property right is consistent with the approach in NAFTA, as well as many other BITs.[206]

The reference to expropriation of a 'property interest in an investment' in paragraph 2 of Annex 10-D indicates that a business may comprise numerous property rights, each of which may be subject to an expropriation. This is consistent with the approach of NAFTA tribunals in *Pope & Talbot* and *Myers* v. *Canada*, which both considered that a right to sell into a market can be a property interest separate from the investment.[207] However, in determining whether there is an expropriation, property rights in things like goodwill have been valued as part of the overall investment rather than as individual investments that can be subject to an expropriation.[208]

Therefore, there is likely to be no difference in the scope of the obligation not to directly expropriate between those FTAs that include text equivalent to Annex 10-D of US–Chile, and those that do not include such a provision.

4. Indirect expropriation

Regarding the definition of indirect expropriation, Annex 10-D of the US–Chile FTA, defines it as arising when 'an action or series of actions by a Party has an effect equivalent to direct expropriation without formal transfer of title or outright seizure'.

Paragraph 4 of Annex 10-D then establishes the following guidelines for determining when there is an indirect expropriation:

(a) The determination of whether an action or series of actions by a Party, in a specific fact situation, constitutes an indirect expropriation, requires a case-by-case, fact-based inquiry that considers, among other factors:
  (i) the economic impact of the government action, although the fact that an action or series of actions by a Party has an adverse effect on the economic value of an investment, standing alone, does not establish that an indirect expropriation has occurred;
  (ii) the extent to which the government action interferes with distinct, reasonable investment-backed expectations; and
  (iii) the character of the government action.
(b) Except in rare circumstances, non-discriminatory regulatory actions by a Party that are designed and applied to protect legitimate public welfare objectives, such as public health, safety, and the environment, do not constitute indirect expropriations.

What constitutes an indirect expropriation requiring compensation, as distinct from a regulatory non-compensable measure, is ultimately a question about the scope of the expropriation obligation. This is because most regulations or series of

206 See UNCTAD, above n. 180.
207 See *Pope & Talbot* (Interim Award of 26 June 2000), para. 96; and *Myers* v. *Canada*, paras. 292–6.
208 *Methanex*, para. 17; *Chemtura* v. *Canada*, Award, 2 August 2010, para. 258.

regulations can have an impact on the economic value of an investment. For example, an environmental regulation can impose significant costs on business, and in some cases render that business unviable. Alternatively, changes in a State's taxation regime can also impose large costs on business. The point at which the impact of a measure becomes severe enough to amount to an indirect expropriation has important implications on a Government's scope to regulate. This has led commentators to argue that too broad an expropriation obligation could lead to regulatory chill.[209]

As a result, international tribunals have long recognised that an assessment of whether a measure is an indirect expropriation or merely regulation that does not require compensation is largely determined by the particular facts of each case, thereby defying clear rules on how to draw this distinction.[210] The statement in Annex 10-D paragraph 4(a) that an assessment of what constitutes indirect expropriation requires 'a case-by-case, fact-based inquiry' is consistent with this.[211]

Where to draw the line between indirect expropriation and non-compensable regulation reflects debate over the rationale for prohibiting expropriation. One approach is that the distinction between indirect compensation and noncompensable regulation is a question of when the cost of regulation should be borne by the individual instead of the State,[212] or that the expropriation obligation is justified by the principle of unjust enrichment.[213] Others have argued that the expropriation obligation is justified by a need to ameliorate a foreign investor's lack of 'voice' in the host States' political process, and the difficulty of exit due to the nature of direct investment, which makes foreign investors particularly susceptible to incurring the costs of State laws.[214] Another more general rationale is that the expropriation obligation, like all other investor protection provisions in an FTA Investment Chapter, allow developing countries to commit to a level of protection in order to attract foreign investment.[215]

---

209 Vicki L. Been and Joel C. Beauvais, 'The Global Fifth Amendment? NAFTA's Investment Protections and the Misguided Quest for an International "Regulatory Takings" Doctrine' (2003) 78 *New York University Law Review* 30–143, at 132.

210 See *Saluka* v. *Czech Republic*, para. 265.

211 George C. Christie, 'What Constitutes a Taking of Property Under International Law?' (1962) 38 *British Yearbook of International Law* 307–38, at 338.

212 Rosalyn Higgins, 'The Taking of Property by the State: Recent Developments in International Law' (1982–III) 176 *Recueil des Cours* 259–392, at 276.

213 Andrew Newcombe, 'The Boundaries of Regulatory Expropriation in International Law' (2005) 20(1) ICSID *Review–Foreign Investment Law Journal* 1, at 34.

214 *Ibid*. See also Been and Beauvais, above n. 209, at 100–8, where they argue against this 'political process failure theory' as providing adequate justification for the expropriation obligation in NAFTA.

215 Rudolf Dolzer, 'The Impact of International Investment Treaties on Domestic Administrative Law' (2004–2005) 37(4) *New York University Journal of International Law & Politics* 953–72, at 954.

5. The economic impact of the government action

Under FTA Investment Chapters, the economic impact of the government action on the investment is one of the main determining factors of when an indirect expropriation has occurred.[216] The extent of the economic impact is also to be assessed in light of both its effect on legal title as well as the ability of the owner to use and enjoy their property.[217]

This was recognised in *Starrett Housing*, where the tribunal, assessing whether the appointment of Iranian managers to an American housing project constituted expropriation, stated that, 'it is recognized by international law that measures taken by a State can interfere with property rights to such an extent that these rights are rendered so useless that they must be deemed to have been expropriated, even though the State does not purport to have expropriated them and the legal title to the property formally remains with the original owner'.[218] The duration of the regulation is also relevant.[219] More recently, arbitral tribunals have focused on the extent of economic loss of the investment.[220]

In addition, a mere temporary takings will, under customary international law, not constitute expropriation.

Debate remains, however, over whether economic impact is the sole criteria for assessing whether a measure constitutes indirect expropriation, or whether other factors, such as the intent of the government, can be taken into account. These two approaches are referred to here as the 'sole effect doctrine' and the 'government purpose doctrine'.

According to the 'sole effect doctrine', the effect of the measure on the investment is the dominant criteria.[221] Under the 'government purpose doctrine', a tribunal is able to take into account the purpose and context of the measure as well as its economic impact, allowing a tribunal to balance the goal of the measure with the harm to the property interest.[222] Rudolf Dolzer frames the issue as follows:

> [I]s there any specific point within the spectrum of diverse effects of governmental measures on property at which and beyond which compensation is required regardless of the objective and the nature of the governmental measure, or does the taking doctrine require a balance of interests which weighs the effect of the property on the one hand and the objective of the governmental measure on the other?[223]

---

216 See OECD, above n. 205, at p. 10.   217 See Dolzer, above n. 215, at 79.
218 *Starrett Housing Corp. v. Islamic Republic of Iran* ('*Starrett Housing v. Iran*'), Iran–US Claims Tribunal (Award No. ITL 32–24–1 of 19 December 1983), 4 Iran-US CRT 122, p. 154.
219 See *Tecmed*, para. 116; and *Myers* v. *Canada* (Partial Award of 13 November 2000), para. 284.
220 *Burlington Resources Inc.* v. *Republic of Ecuador* (ICSID Case NO. ARB/08/05), Decision on Liability, 14 December 2012, para. 396; *Vivendi* v. *Argentina II*, Award, 20 August 2007, para. 7.5.11.
221 See Dolzer, above n. 215, at 79.
222 OECD, 'Indirect Expropriation and Governmental Measures Affecting Property of Nationals Not Requiring Compensation: Criteria to Articulate the Difference', DAFFE/IME/WD/(2004)2 (26 March 2004), para. 28.
223 See Dolzer, above n. 215, at 80.

The balancing approach has been used by the European Court of Human Rights (ECHR) when applying Article 1 of Protocol 1 of the European Convention of Human Rights. For example, the ECHR has required that the measure be proportionate to its goals and balances between the interests of the community in the measure and the private interests of the person who is bearing the cost of the measure.[224]

Customary international law does not prescribe one particular approach. A range of cases support either the sole doctrine approach or alternatively, have taken into account the purpose and object of the impugned measure. Cases that have taken the sole doctrine approach include the Permanent Court of International Justice in the *Factory at Chorzow* case[225] and tribunals in *Tippets v. TAMS-AFFA, Metalclad,* and *Antoine Biloune and Marine Drive Complex Ltd* v. *Ghana Investments Centre and The Government of Ghana.*[226] In contrast, the tribunals' decisions in *Myers v. Canada, Seal-Land Services, Inc.* v. *The Government of the Islamic Republic of Iran, Ports and Shipping Organization,*[227] *CME Czech Republic B.V.* (*The Netherlands*) v. *The Czech Republic,*[228] and *Revere Copper & Brass, Inc.* v. *Overseas Private Investment Corp*[229] have approached the expropriation analysis in a manner that took into account the intent of the government in enacting the measure.

As a result of the divergence of case law on this matter, one commentator has argued that 'it is so far impossible to characterize either alternative approach as dominant or as representing the mainstream of international thinking'.[230]

In light of this uncertainty at customary international law, the US–Chile FTA Annex 10-D and all other equivalent provisions in the other FTA Investment Chapters have effectively taken a position on the appropriate weight to be given by a tribunal to economic impact. In this regard, Annex 10-D paragraph 4(a)(i) directs a tribunal that when considering the economic impact of government action:

---

224 Helen Mountfield, 'Regulatory Expropriations in Europe: The Approach of the European Court of Human Rights' (2002) 11(1) *New York University Environmental Law Journal* 136–47, at 141; see also *Tecmed,* para. 122.

225 *Factory at Chorzow* (*Germany v. Poland*), 1928 PCIJ (Series A) No. 17 (Judgment of 13 September 1928).

226 *Antoine Biloune* (*Syria*) *and Marine Drive Complex Ltd* (*Ghana*) v. *Ghana Investments Centre and The Government of Ghana,* UNCITRAL Arbitral Tribunal (Award on Jurisdiction and Liability of 27 October 1989), 95 ILR 183.

227 *Sea-Land Services, Inc.* v. *The Government of the Islamic Republic of Iran, Ports and Shipping Organization,* Iran–US Claims Tribunal (Award No, 135–33–1 of 22 June 1984), 6 Iran-US CTR 149.

228 *CME Czech Republic B.V.* (*The Netherlands*) v. *The Czech Republic* (The Netherlands/Czech Republic BIT) (UNCITRAL Partial Award of 13 September 2001).

229 *Revere Copper & Brass, Inc.* v. *Overseas Private Investment Corp.*('*Revere Copper* v. *OPIC*') (Award of 24 August 1978), 17 ILM 132 1 (1978).

230 See Dolzer, above n. 215, at 90.

> [A]lthough the fact that an action or series of actions by a Party has an adverse effect on the economic value of an investment, standing alone, does not establish that an indirect expropriation has occurred.

As a result, these FTA Investment Chapters make it clear that the sole effect doctrine is not to be used when establishing whether indirect expropriation has occurred, and instead, other factors, also elaborated on in the FTA Investment Chapter Annex, are to be taken into account. For those FTAs that do not include such provisions, the uncertain state of customary international law in this area means that tribunals have greater discretion to decide whether to focus on the economic impact as the sole criteria for assessing whether an indirect expropriation has occurred, or to weigh the economic impact with the intent of the measure.

6. Reasonable investment-backed expectations

The requirement in FTA Investment Chapters that a tribunal assess the 'extent to which the government action interferes with distinct, reasonable investment-backed expectations' is also a reflection of customary international law. The possibility that an investor's reasonable investment-backed expectations could effectively create an obligation on a State not to act in a particular manner has been analogised to the domestic law of estoppel, which similarly imports an inquiry into good faith.[231] While international tribunals have yet to explicitly equate an inquiry into reasonable expectation with an estoppel-like analysis, it has been recognised that 'the principle of good faith is the corollary in public international law of the principle of protection of legitimate expectations'.[232]

Other international tribunals have described this as an inquiry into whether 'undertakings or assurances [were] given in good faith to such aliens as an inducement to their making the investment affected by the action',[233] or whether 'the treatment is in breach of representations made by the host State which were reasonably relied upon by the claimant'.[234]

In *Methanex*, the tribunal relied in part on an equity-based argument – that of clean-hands – to find that because Methanex understood and used lobbying, it was prevented from claiming that it did not understand the role of lobbying in forming regulation in the US.[235]

International tribunals have also made it clear that the principle of reasonable expectations does not insulate an investor from risk associated with an investment in a foreign country. Therefore, changes of regulation in response to changing economic, social or political circumstances that impact on an investment will not necessarily be considered expropriations.[236]

---

231 See Been and Beauvais, above n. 209, at 72.
232 *Opel Austria GmbH* v. *Council of the European Union*, Case T-115/94, Court of Justice of the European Communities – Fourth Chamber, 22 January 1997, para. 93.
233 See *Revere Copper* v. *OPIC*, p. 1331.   234 See *Waste Management*, para. 98.
235 See *Methanex*, Part IV Chapter D, para. 9.   236 See *Starrett Housing* v. *Iran; and Feldman*.

7. Character of the government action and the police powers exception

The character of the government action refers to the right of a government to promote recognised social purposes and general welfare such as public health and safety. The extent to which a tribunal focuses on such purposes, will, at least to some extent, be a product of whether they consider economic impact the sole determinative criteria or whether they are prepared to balance economic impact with other legitimate government purposes.

When a State can show that the measure falls within its police powers, then no obligation to provide compensation will be deemed to have arisen.[237] The scope of the police powers exception remains open to debate.[238] A common starting point is the American Law Institute's Restatement (Third) of Foreign Relations Law of the United States, which includes within the scope of the police powers exception general taxation, regulation, forfeiture for crime, or other action of the kind that is commonly accepted as within the police power of the States.

There are two distinct conceptions of the role of the police powers exception. One conception is to understand the police powers exception as a controlling element that once established, provides a complete defence to any claims for compensation. An alternative approach is to include the police powers as a factor that is considered in the weighing and balancing of the measure. Allen Weiner notes that a tribunal needs to examine 'whether a regulation is an exercise of the police power or is directed at a public welfare purpose, as opposed to a protectionist one'.[239] Under this approach, the distinction between a measure taken pursuant to the police powers and measures to pursue legitimate social purposes or welfare objectives blurs, and instead, a tribunal will need to examine the economic impact, and whether the measure is an exercise of its police powers or is directed at a public welfare objective.[240]

Those FTA Investment Chapters that include provisions equivalent to Annex 10-D of the US–Chile FTA have adopted this later approach. This is because not only do these provisions state that economic impact cannot on its own establish expropriation, but also paragraph 4(b) states that 'non-discriminatory regulatory actions by a Party that are designed and applied to protect legitimate public welfare objectives, such as public health, safety, and the environment, do not constitute indirect expropriations'. Read together, these provisions make it clear that when interpreting Annex 10-D, a tribunal is required to assess not only the economic impact and the legitimate investment-backed expectation of the investor, and will need to take into account the purpose of the measure, including what goals it seeks

---

237 See *Tecmed*, para. 19.   238 See *Saluka* v. *Czech Republic*, para. 263.
239 Allen S. Weiner, 'Indirect Expropriation: The Need for a Taxonomy of "Legitimate" Regulatory Purposes' (2003) 5(3) *International Law Forum (Du Droit International)* 166–75, at 175.
240 *Saluka* v. *Czech Republic*, para. 263, observed that 'international law has yet to identify in a comprehensive and definitive fashion precisely what regulations are considered "permissible" and "commonly accepted" as falling with the police or regulatory power of States and, thus, noncompensable.'

to achieve. Certainly, where a measure is about health, safety and the environment, it is likely that a tribunal will find that there is no indirect expropriation, even where there has been a complete taking of the investor's property.

However, Annex 10-D paragraph 4(b) of the US–Chile FTA is qualified by the phrase 'in rare circumstances'. This phrase operates is such that once it is established that the measure falls within paragraph 4(b), the burden of proof shifts to the investor to establish that this was nevertheless as 'rare circumstance', where the measure is still an indirect expropriation that requires compensation. No guidance is given in the FTA Investment Chapter provisions regarding what could constitute a rare circumstance. Drawing on the approach of the ECHR and *Tecmed*, a lack of proportionality between the means employed to achieve the government's aim could constitute a rare circumstance.[241]

In those FTA Investment Chapters that do not contain these indirect expropriation provisions, then customary international law will apply. Even though Annex 10-D states that it is intended to reflect customary international law, uncertainty regarding the role of the police powers exception and whether it is a controlling factor or merely one that is part of the overall assessment of whether the government action constitutes expropriation, makes it 'plausible that a balancing concept may ... yield results different from those reached under an analysis focused only on the effect of the measure'.[242] For example, in the *Metalclad* case, the tribunal refused to consider the purpose for which the Mexican Government enacted the Ecological Decree.[243] Instead, the tribunal found that the Decree's effect of barring work at the landfill site constituted an expropriation.[244] Under the approach required by Annex 10-D, a different outcome might have been reached.

F. Performance requirements

An agreement to prohibit performance requirements is a common feature of FTA Investment Chapters.[245] Provisions on performance requirements in FTA Investment Chapters are derived from the WTO TRIMS agreement. Under these provisions, the Parties agree not to condition the ability of investors from the other FTA from making an investment in their territory on that investor undertaking various acts, such as exporting a given amount of goods or services or using a certain amount of domestic goods or services in their investment.

---

241 See *Tecmed*, para. 122; and Mountfield, above n. 224, at 141; see also *Azurix* v. *Argentina*, Decision on Liability, 14 July 2006, para. 312.
242 See Dolzer, above n. 215, at 80.   243 See *Metalclad*, para. 111.   244 *Ibid.*, para. 109.
245 US–Chile FTA, Article 10.5; AUSFTA, Article 11.9; Korea–Chile FTA, Article 10.7; CAFTA–DR–US, Article 10.9; Japan–Singapore EPA, Article 75; Korea–Singapore FTA, Article 10.7 and India–Singapore CECA, Article 6.23.

A number of FTA Investment Chapters such as the US–Chile, AUSFTA, CAFTA–DR–US, Korea–Chile and Japan–Singapore[246] include prohibitions on performance requirements that extend to services, and include commitments not to require an investment to transfer 'technology, a production process or other proprietary knowledge to a person in its territory'.[247]

Certain FTAs, such as Canada–Chile and Korea–Chile, performance requirements extend these towards all investments in its territory.[248] The Korea–Singapore FTA (Footnote 10-3) requires an investor from the FTA party to show that they have suffered 'loss through the imposition of performance requirements to an investment or investor [sic] of a non-party', before the obligation not to impose performance requirements on investments from non-Parties arises. Therefore, while the legal commitment is bilateral only, failure to apply the performance requirements commitments to investments of non-parties would breach the FTA.

The rationale for including 'multilateral' performance requirement commitments within an FTA is to avoid the otherwise adverse incentive that would arise. Should an FTA Party remain free to impose performance requirements on all investments other than those from the other Party to the FTA, an incentive to prefer investments from non-Parties would be created as these investments could be required to comply with performance requirements.

Many of these TRIMS-Plus performance requirements are nevertheless subject to a range of exceptions. For example, under the Canada–Chile FTA, either Party can condition receipt of an advantage in connection with an investment in its territory on compliance with a requirement to do the following in its territory: (i) locate production; (ii) provide a service; (iii) train or employ workers; (iv) construct or expand particular facilities; (v) carry out research and development.[249]

The India–Singapore CECA is an example of an FTA that includes commitments on performance requirements that do not go beyond their TRIMS commitments. However, because the TRIMS Agreement only includes an indicative list of what constitutes a TRIMS, there is nothing in the text of the TRIMS Agreement that prohibits a WTO Member arguing for the TRIMS disciplines to be applied to requirements not in the indicative list; an outcome apparently confirmed by the Panel in *Canada–Automotive Industry*.[250]

This lack of certainty regarding the scope of the TRIMS Agreement is why many FTA Investment Chapters that are TRIMS-Plus also include a provision clarifying

---

246 US–Chile FTA, Article 10.5; AUSFTA, Article 11.9; CAFTA–DR–US, Article 10.9; Korea–Chile FTA, Article 10.7 and Japan–Singapore CECA, Article 75.
247 Canada–Chile FTA, Article G-06.
248 *Ibid.*, Article G-01.1(c); and Korea–Chile FTA, Article 10.2.1(c).
249 Canada–Chile FTA, Article 6–06.4.   250 Panel Report, *Canada–Automotive Industry*, para. 10.89.

that the performance requirements listed therein 'do not apply to any other requirement other than the requirements set out in those paragraphs'.[251]

V. Investor-State dispute settlement (ISDS) provisions in FTA Investment Chapters

This Part looks at the different types of ISDS provisions in FTA Investment Chapters.
ISDS provisions are a common feature of BITs and have been incorporated into most
FTA Investment Chapters. However, the scope and substance of ISDS provisions in
FTAs differ widely. As a general matter, the different approaches can be classified
broadly into those that adopt the NAFTA approach to ISDS and those that continue
to follow the BIT approach to ISDS. There are also a few FTA Investment Chapters,
such as the AUSFTA, that do not include ISDS provisions.[252]

Under the BIT approach, ISDS provisions are generally limited to confirming
that the Parties consent to international arbitration and to providing investors
with a right to commence arbitration under either the ICSID Convention or the ad
hoc UNCITRAL Arbitration Rules.[253] This approach has been continued in FTA
Investment Chapters such as the Korea–Singapore FTA.

The NAFTA-style approach goes beyond the BIT approach to ISDS by specifying
in detail the arbitration procedures to be followed by a tribunal, including a number
of provisions not found in ICSID or UNCITRAL. For example, provisions for
consolidation of claims, procedural mechanisms avoiding frivolous claims, commitments regarding transparency, appointment of experts and the right for the tribunal
to accept amicus briefs are additional ISDS provisions which are absent from the
ICSID and UNCITRAL arbitration rules.[254]

Some FTA Investment Chapters, such as the Japan–Singapore EPA, have adopted a
middle-of-the-road approach or NAFTA-lite, whereby they have incorporated only

---

251 US–Chile FTA, Article 10.5.4.
252 Note that AUSFTA Article 11.16 does include a commitment to enter into consultations with a view
    towards allowing an ISDS claim and establishing ISDS procedures upon request from a Party based on a
    change of circumstances affecting the settlement of disputes within the scope of the FTA Investment
    Chapter; see also William S. Dodge, 'Investor-State Dispute Settlement Between Developed Countries:
    Reflections on the Australia–United States Free Trade Agreement' (2006) 39(1) *Vanderbilt Journal of
    Transnational Law* 1–38, at 22, who argues that an optimal approach in AUSFTA would require the
    investor to exhaust local remedies after which it could resort to international arbitration; see also
    Ann Capling and Kim R. Nossal, 'Blowback: Investor-State Dispute Mechanisms in International
    Trade Agreements' (2006) 19(2) *Governance: An International Journal of Policy, Administration, and
    Institutions* 151–72, who present reasons why Australia and the US agreed not to include an investor-State
    dispute mechanism in AUSFTA and its implications for future FTA Investment Chapters.
253 See, e.g., Korea–Singapore FTA, Article 10.19.
254 Followed by the US–Chile FTA, Articles 10.14–10.26; CAFTA–DR–US, Articles 10.15–10.27; and Korea–
    Chile FTA, Article 10.19–10.42. See also UNCTAD, *Dispute Settlement: State–State*, UNCTAD Series on
    Issues in International Investment Agreements (New York and Geneva: UN, 2003).

some of these more detailed ISDS procedural provisions. The following is an analysis of the more significant FTA/ISDS provisions.

A. Scope of the ISDS provisions

In most cases, those persons that can claim under an FTA ISDS provision will be the investor of the other FTA Party. For example, the US–Chile FTA allows a claim to be made by an investor of the other Party on its own behalf or on behalf of its investment in the territory of the other Party.[255]

FTA ISDS provisions in Canada–Chile and Korea–Chile further limit the scope of their ISDS provisions by not allowing an investment (i.e., the domestic legal entity created by the investor) to make a claim under the ISDS provisions.[256] These provisions ensure that it is the investor of the other Party that is the party to the ISDS action. A similar outcome is achieved in the India–Singapore CECA where 'an enterprise duly organized under the law of a Party shall not be treated as an investor of the other Party, but any investments in that enterprise by investors of that other Party shall be covered under this Chapter'.[257] Prohibiting the investor from bringing a claim avoids a host Government being engaged in international arbitration against a company that is its own national.[258]

1. Frivolous claims

Several FTA Investment Chapter ISDS provisions seek to reduce the possibility that investors may raise frivolous claims. For example, the US–Singapore FTA and US– Chile FTAs state that 'a tribunal shall address and decide as a preliminary question any objection by the respondent that, as a matter of law, a claim submitted is not a claim for which an award in favour of the claimant may be made.'[259] These ISDS provisions also allow a tribunal in these instances to award costs and attorney fees against the losing party.[260]

B. Appointment of arbitrators under ICSID and UNCITRAL

The ISDS provisions in FTA Investment Chapters allow an investor of either Party to submit a claim to arbitration under either the ICSID or UNCITRAL rules.[261]

---

255 US–Chile FTA, Article 10.15.
256 Canada–Chile FTA, Article G–18.4; and Korea–Chile FTA, Article 10.21.
257 Singapore–India CECA, Article 6.2.2.
258 UNCTAD, *Investment Provisions in Economic Integration Agreements* (New York and Geneva: UN, 2006), at p. 119.
259 US–Singapore FTA, Article 15.19.4; and US–Chile FTA, Article 10.19.4.
260 US–Singapore FTA, Article 15.19.6; and US–Chile FTA, Article 10.19.6.
261 See, e.g., US–Singapore FTA, Article 15.15.5; Canada–Chile FTA, Article G–21; and India–Singapore CECA, Article 6.21.3.

ICSID and UNCITRAL both contain detailed provisions on the appointment of arbitrators.[262] Under those FTAs that adopt the BIT-style approach, such as the India–Singapore CECA and Korea–Singapore FTA, the process for appointing arbitrators is determined solely by whether the investor chooses to submit a claim under the ICSID or UNCITRAL arbitration rules.[263]

In contrast, those FTAs that use the NAFTA-style ISDS provisions, such as Korea–Chile, US–Chile, Canada–Chile and the Japan–Singapore EPA, include detailed provisions regarding the appointment of arbitrators that operate in conjunction with the ICSID or UNCITRAL processes.[264]

2. Number of arbitrators

Where an investor submits a dispute for settlement under the UNCITRAL Arbitration Rules, Article 5 provides that should the parties to the dispute fail to agree on one arbitrator, then the tribunal is to comprise three arbitrators. Arbitration under ICSID is not limited to either one or three arbitrators as under Article 37.1 a tribunal can comprise one or any uneven number of arbitrators. However, Article 37.2(b) requires a tribunal to consist of three arbitrators when the parties fail to agree on the number of arbitrators.

The ISDS provisions in both the Korea–Singapore FTA and the India–Singapore CECA do not specify whether a tribunal is to comprise either one or three arbitrators. Therefore, it is possible that arbitration under these FTAs that use the ICSID Convention could be before a Panel comprising more than three arbitrators.

Those FTA Investment Chapters that provide greater direction on the appointment of arbitrators all require a tribunal to comprise three arbitrators unless the disputing parties otherwise agree.[265] This forecloses the option in ICSID of a tribunal comprising more than three arbitrators.

3. Appointment of arbitrators

UNCITRAL and ICSID also provide different processes for the appointment of arbitrators. Under Article 7.1 of the UNCITRAL Arbitration Rules, each Party is required to appoint an arbitrator and for these two arbitrators to agree on the third arbitrator. In contrast, Article 37.1(2) of the ICSID Convention requires each disputing party to appoint an arbitrator and for the disputing parties to agree on the appointment of the third and presiding arbitrator.

262 See ICSID Convention, Articles 27–40; and UNCITRAL Arbitration Rules, Articles 5–8.
263 India–Singapore CECA, Article 6.21; and Korea–Singapore FTA, Article 10.19.
264 Korea–Chile FTA, Chapter 10, Section C; US–Chile FTA, Chapter 10, Section B; Canada–Chile FTA, Chapter G, Section II; and Japan–Singapore EPA, Article 82.
265 See, e.g., Canada–Chile FTA, Article G–24; Korea–Chile FTA, Article 10.27; and US–Chile FTA, Article 10.18.

Under ICSID, if either Party to the dispute fails to appoint an arbitrator, the ICSID Chairman, defined as the President of the World Bank, appoints those arbitrators not yet appointed from the Panel of Arbitrators.[266]

In contrast, UNCITRAL adopts different approaches for appointing an arbitrator that a Party to the arbitration failed to appoint, and for appointing the third arbitrators that the other two arbitrators failed to appoint. In the first case, the appointing authority, to be agreed upon by the parties, is to appoint the arbitrator/s not appointed by the Parties to the arbitration. In the event the Parties fail to agree on an appointing authority, Article 7.2(b) requires the Secretary-General of the Permanent Court of Arbitration at The Hague to designate an appointing authority. This appointing authority can then be requested by a party to appoint the second arbitrator. The use of the word 'request' indicates that there is no legal relation or obligation created by the UNCTIRAL Arbitration Rules between the party to the dispute and the appointing authority, and therefore no guarantee that the person so designated will agree to act.

In the second case, Article 6 of the UNCITRAL Arbitration Rules requires the appointing authority to use a 'list-procedure' unless that person decides that this process is not appropriate. Should this be the case, however, no guidance or provision is made for how the third arbitrator is to be appointed. The 'list-procedure' requires the appointing authority to provide each Party a list of three identical names. Each Party 'may' return the list with names they object to being removed from the list and those names not objected to being listed in order of preference. The appointing authority is then to select the arbitrator from the names 'approved on the lists returned to it and in accordance with the order of preference indicated by the parties'. Should all names on the list be rejected or the list not be returned to the appointing authority, then that person is given the discretion to appoint the third arbitrator, but again, this is not an obligation, leaving it open to the appointing authority to refuse to exercise that discretion.

In those FTA Investment Chapters that adopt the NAFTA-style approach to ISDS, each Party commits to appointing an arbitrator, and the third arbitrator is to be appointed by agreement between the disputing parties.[267] The ICSID Secretary-General is also designated as the appointing authority under all these FTAs and has also agreed to act as appointing authority for disputes under ICSID or UNCITRAL arbitration rules. Therefore, where either of the disputing parties fail to appoint their own arbitrator, the ICSID Secretary-General is required to appoint these arbitrators using his or her discretion, but subject to the requirements of nationality, as outlined above, in UNCITRAL or ICSID.

---

266 ICSID Convention, Article 38.
267 See, e.g., the Canada–Chile FTA, Article G–24; Korea–Chile FTA, Article 10.27; and US–Chile FTA, Article 10.18.

This approach in FTA Investment Chapter ISDS provisions removes the potentially lengthy process under UNCITRAL for finding the appointing authority and uncertainty over whether that appointing authority will act to appoint arbitrators. It is also a departure from ICSID which designates the President of the World Bank as the appointing authority.[268]

One of the potential consequences of this departure from the ICSID approach is that whereas the President of the World Bank, pursuant to Article 40(1) of the ICSID Convention, is required to appoint arbitrators from the Panel of Arbitrators, the ICSID Secretary-General would appear free to appoint an arbitrator from outside the Panel.

As a result of this greater freedom granted to the ICSID Secretary-General to appoint arbitrators, some FTA Investment Chapter ISDS provisions also direct how the ICSID Secretary-General is to exercise discretion to appoint the presiding arbitrator.[269] In these FTAs, the ICSID Secretary-General is to appoint the presiding arbitrator from a roster of thirty arbitrators, appointed by agreement between the FTA Parties. Should no arbitrator on this roster be available to serve, the ICSID Secretary-General has the authority to appoint arbitrators from the ICSID Panel of Arbitrators.

In contrast, other FTAs do not establish a roster of panellists and indeed do not provide any direction on how the ICSID Secretary-General is to exercise their power to appoint an arbitrator. Therefore, by default, the applicable arbitration rules under either ICSID or UNCITRAL will apply.[270]

Interestingly, the Japan–Singapore EPA, while content to largely rely on the provisions in the applicable arbitration rules for the appointment of arbitrators, contains limitations on how the Chairman under ICSID can exercise its authority to appoint arbitrators. This is achieved in Article 82.4(b) by conditioning each Party's consent to arbitration under ICSID on the Chairman allowing the disputing parties to indicate three nationalities whose appointment to a tribunal would be unacceptable to it, and by not appointing persons of these nationalities to a tribunal.

In the event that the Chairman acts inconsistently with this direction, then the Parties' consent to arbitration under ICSID only is vitiated; however, arbitration under the other arbitration rules listed in that FTA, namely UNCITRAL, is able to proceed. This approach therefore seeks to incorporate the UNCITRAL 'list-procedure' for selecting arbitrators under ICSID.

C. Consolidation

Some FTAs now provide for the consolidation of different investment disputes under the same agreement regarding the same measure.[271] There is no provision for the

---

268 ICSID Convention, Article 37(2)(b).
269 See, e.g., Canada–Chile FTA, Article G–25; and Korea–Chile FTA, Article 10.28.
270 See, e.g., US–Chile FTA, Article 10.18.
271 *Ibid.*, Article 10.24; CAFTA–DR–US, Article 10.25; and US–Singapore FTA, Article 15.24.

consolidation of investment disputes under either ICSID or UNCITRAL, and therefore it is only possible where provided for by the ISDS provisions in the FTA.

The NAFTA-style ISDS provisions usually include consolidation provisions. For
example the US–Chile FTA allows for consolidation '[w]here two or more claims
have been submitted separately to arbitration under Article 10.15(1) and the claims
have a question of law or fact in common and arise out of the same events or
circumstances'.[272]

These consolidation provisions usually require a party to request a consolidation of
claims, after which a third tribunal is established to consider the request and to either
assume jurisdiction and to hear and determine together all the claims in the request,
to determine part of a claim that will assist in the resolution of the other claims, or to
instruct one of the original tribunals to assume jurisdiction and hear and determine
all of the claims.

D. Transparency of arbitral proceedings

There are a number of different approaches to the transparency and openness of
tribunals under the ISDS provisions in FTA Investment Chapters. Whether an ISDS
process is open and transparent is a function of the extent to which tribunal hearings
are open to the public, and there is access of the public to documents in a dispute,
including the tribunal's award.

One approach is not to address these issues of transparency and openness in the
ISDS provisions, and instead to rely on the procedures, where they exist, in the
applicable arbitration rules. This is the approach taken in numerous FTAs, such as
Korea–Singapore, India–Singapore CECA, Japan–Singapore EPA and the Thailand–
Australia FTA.[273] Some FTAs allow either Party to the dispute to publish the
award.[274]

With respect to the publication of tribunal awards, both UNCITRAL and ICSID
require the consent of the Parties. However, under ICSID Rule 48(4), the centre will
publish 'exerpts of the legal reasoning of the tribunal'. Some FTAs allow either Party
to the dispute to publish the award. Further, neither ICSID nor UNCITRAL allow for
non-parties to the dispute to attend hearings.

An alternative approach being taken in FTA Investment Chapter ISDS provisions,
such as the US–Chile FTA, CAFTA–DR–US and NAFTA, is to include detailed
obligations regarding the transparency and openness of tribunals that are significant
departures from the limited transparency and openness that currently exists under
ICSID or UNCITRAL.

---

272 US–Chile FTA, Article 10.24.
273 Korea–Singapore FTA, Article 10, Section C; India–Singapore CECA, Article 6.21; Japan–Singapore EPA,
      Article 82; and Thailand–Australia FTA, Article 917.
274 See Korea–Chile FTA, Article 10.41.4 and Annex 10.41.4.

These FTAs require the parties to the dispute to make all documents in an ISDS dispute to be made available to the public, subject to a right to remove confidential information. All hearings of the tribunal are to be open to the public, with provision for closing these hearings for presentation of confidential information.

E. Amicus briefs

Those FTAs' Investment Chapters ISDS provisions that emphasise the transparency and openness of the ISDS process also tend to expressly include a right for a tribunal to accept amicus briefs. This approach is also consistent with how tribunals have understood the scope of their power under both the UNCITRAL arbitration rules and ICSID arbitration rules. For instance, the tribunals in *Methanex* and *UPS*, constituted under the UNCITRAL Arbitration Rules, interpreted Article 15.1 as providing them with the procedural power to accept amicus briefs.[275] However, they also made it clear that receipt of amicus does not confer rights, procedural or substantive, on the persons submitting the amicus briefs. The tribunals also noted that in deciding whether to accept or reject amicus briefs, they would consider whether the substantive matters in the dispute had a public interest dimension.

Similarly, the tribunal in *Vivendi Universal, S.A.* v. *The Argentine Republic*, constituted under the ICSID Convention, found that it has the power to receive amicus briefs pursuant to ICSID Convention Article 44.[276] The tribunal also noted that in determining whether to accept amicus, the tribunal shall consider the appropriateness of the subject matter as a basis for amicus submissions, whether the case involves matters of significant public interest, and that the tribunal will only accept amicus from persons who establish that they have the expertise, experience and independence to be of assistance. Similar to the *Methanex* tribunal, the tribunal in *Vivendi* noted that it would not accept amicus on jurisdictional issues.

VI. The architecture of FTA Investment Chapters

This Part outlines the different ways that States can make market access commitments to their FTA Investment Chapter commitments, and considers the arguments for and against each approach.

---

275 See *Methanex*, para. 47; and *UPS* v. *Canada*, Decision of the Tribunal on Petitions for Intervention and Participation as Amicus Curiae (17 October 2001), para. 67.

276 *Aguas Argentinas, S.A., Suez, Sociedad General de Aguas de Barcelona, S.A. and Vivendi Universal, S.A.* v. *The Argentine Republic* ('*Vivendi*'), ICSID Case No. ARB/03/19, Order in Response to a Petition for Transparency and Participation as Amicus Curiae (12 February 2007), para. 14.

A. Investment liberalisation

1. A negative or positive list

All FTA Investment Chapters include schedules wherein parties make their market access commitments to which the substantive commitments in the investment chapter apply. There are two main approaches for listing market access commitments in an FTA, namely through use of a positive or a negative list of commitments.

The positive list is a GATS-style approach, whereby member States list those sectors which they are prepared to subject to the FTA Investment Chapter commitments.[277] There are a number of FTAs that have adopted a positive list approach to scheduling commitments on investment, such as the Thailand–Australia FTA and the Japan–Singapore EPA.[278]

In contrast, under the negative list approach to scheduling FTA Investment Chapter commitments, all measures affecting investment in all sectors of the economy are required to be in conformity with the FTA Investment Chapter unless otherwise specified in a list of reservations to the FTA. Numerous FTA Investment Chapters have adopted the negative list approach to scheduling commitments, including AUSFTA, Canada–Chile, Korea–Singapore and CAFTA–DR–US.[279]

The negative list approach also normally includes two lists or annexes. Under Annex I, States list those non-conforming measures that they agree not to make any more non-conforming or restrictive. This is often referred to as a standstill commitment. Some FTA Investment Chapters, such as Korea–Singapore, Canada–Chile, and the Japan–Singapore EPA, also subject measures listed in Annex I to a 'ratchet mechanism', whereby any future amendment to a measure in that Annex that brings it into greater conformity with the FTA automatically becomes an international commitment or binding; the effect being that the measure cannot then be returned to its original non-conforming state without being in breach of the FTA.

In Annex II, States list those sectors with non-conforming measures they may wish to maintain or make more restrictive in the future. Annex II can also be used by a State to list those sectors in which it desires the flexibility to introduce new measures which may not conform to its FTA commitments.

---

277 Note that the GATS is a positive list for the national treatment and market access commitments, but that it adopts a negative list approach for the MFN commitment.

278 India–Singapore CECA, Article 6.16, Annexes 6A and 6B; and Japan–Singapore EPA, Article 76, Annexes VA and VB. The Thailand–Australia FTA uses a hybrid approach, whereby a positive list is used to make market access commitments to the pre-establishment NT commitment (see Article 904), and a negative list is used to make market access commitments to the post-establishment NT commitment (see Article 907).

279 AUSFTA, Article 11.13, Annexes I and II; Canada–Chile FTA, Article G–08, Annexes I and II; Korea–Singapore FTA, Article 10.9, Annexes I and II; and CAFTA–DR–US, Article 10.13, Annexes I and II.

2. Assessing investment liberalisation under positive and negative lists

In theory, the same level of liberalisation is achievable under either a positive or negative list approach to the scheduling of commitments. Under a positive list approach, the schedule reflects those sectors in which commitments (with their limitations) are taken, and by extension it can be assumed that those sectors without commitments contain a State's non-conforming measures. Under a negative list approach, those non-conforming measures are listed in either Annex I or Annex II, and there is a legal obligation that all other measures not listed are consistent with the FTA Investment Chapter commitments.

However, empirical evidence suggests that States that use a negative list approach are more likely to make more extensive commitments with less carve-outs than under a GATS style positive list approach.[280] In addition, under a negative list approach, unless provision is made in Annex II to the FTA Investment Chapter, new investment regulation is automatically bound by the FTA Investment Chapter commitments.

Significant from the perspective of increasing investor confidence and certainty, a negative list also provides greater transparency because all relevant investment restrictions are contained in the reservations. This is in contrast to the positive list approach, which only shows investors those sectors where commitments are taken, but does not reveal the range of non-conforming measures that remain. Further, where a State, in order to retain policy flexibility, chooses not to make a treaty level commitment by binding a measure, there may be measures that are consistent with its FTA Investment Chapter commitments that are not included in a positive list.

States, however, may prefer a positive list approach due to the administrative costs associated with preparing a negative list. Because under a negative list all measures are bound unless listed, States need to do a stock-take of all measures and assess those measures' conformity with the investment (and services) chapter. Where the measures are not in conformity a further decision needs to be taken whether to list that measure as a standstill commitment in Annex I, or when flexibility to increase the non-conformity of the measure is required, in Annex II.

In contrast, a positive list approach only requires States to consult with affected stakeholders. In most cases, many of these consultations may have taken place in the GATS context, and therefore States only have to consult with those stakeholders where GATS (mode 3)-plus and investment commitments in the non-services sectors are being made.

---

280 WTO Economic Research and Statistics Division, 'Services Liberalization in the New Generation of Preferential Trade Agreements (PTAs): How Much Further than the GATS?', Staff Working Paper ERSD-2006–07 (September 2006), at p. 55.

B. Investment in services – the investment or services chapter?

In a number of FTAs, the services chapter also contains important rules on investment. This will depend on whether the provision of a service through a commercial
presence, or mode 3 in WTO speak, is included within the FTA's services or investment chapter.

FTAs such as Japan–Singapore, Thailand–Australia, EU–Chile and India–
Singapore all include mode 3 provision of service in their services chapters.[281] In
contrast, FTAs such as AUSFTA, CAFTA–DR–US, Korea–Chile, US–Singapore and
Korea–Singapore do not include mode 3 in the Services Chapter, with the result that
these types of investments are captured by the broad definition of an 'investment' in
the investment chapter.[282]

VII. Prospects for FTA Investment Chapters

Looking forward, the trend towards comprehensive investment provisions as part of
bilateral and regional FTAs will continue. This reflects an appreciation of the
synergies gained from a comprehensive regulatory approach to trade and investment
and is consistent with the economic literature that shows trade and investment not
necessarily as substitutes, but also as complements.[283]

The use of increasingly complex and comprehensive investment provisions
in FTAs is nevertheless going to raise a number of challenges for States. In
particular, a number of specific investment provisions are, and will remain,
controversial.

A key issue for countries looking to negotiate FTAs – particularly with the
US – is whether to include ISDS provisions in these agreements. In the two
large FTA negotiations involving the US – the Trans-Pacific Partnership (TPP)
negotiations and the Transatlantic Trade and Investment Partnership (TTIP)
negotiations – including ISDS provisions is controversial. For instance, in the
TPP a range of developed and developing countries such as Australia and Malaysia
have concerns about ISDS. In the TTIP negotiations, Germany is opposed to
including ISDS provisions. The reason for this opposition to ISDS varies but the

---

281 Japan–Singapore EPA, Article 58; Thailand–Australia FTA, Article 802; EU–Chile AA, Article 96; and
India–Singapore CECA, Article 7.1.
282 AUSFTA, Article 10.14; CAFTA–DR–US, Article 11.14; Korea–Chile FTA, Article 11.1; US–Singapore
FTA, Article 8.1; and Korea–Singapore FTA, Article 9.1.
283 See OECD, 'Linkages Between Foreign Direct Investment, Trade and Trade Policy: An Economic
Analysis with Application to the Food Service in OECD Countries and Case Studies in Ghana,
Mozambique, Tunisia and Uganda', OECD Trade Policy Working Paper No. 50 (2 March 2007), at
p. 19; and UNCTAD, *Trade and Development Report 2006* (New York and Geneva: UN, 2006), at pp. 157–8;
see generally UNCTAD, *World Investment Report 1996: Investment, Trade and International Policy
Arrangements* (New York and Geneva: UN, 1996).

main issues are worries about investors using ISDS provisions to challenge legitimate government health and environmental regulation. As a result, governments in these FTAs negotiations are considering ways to limit the scope of ISDS provisions, for instance by including stricter rules to limit frivolous claims and clearer rules carving out legitimate government regulation from the scope of international arbitration.

There are also a range of issues concerning the substantive protections that FTA Investment Chapters offer that will continue to be a focus for stakeholders going forward. One of these is the commitment on expropriation and specifically the meaning of indirect expropriation. As traditionally capital-exporting States increasingly become defendants, either in State-to-State, though more often in investor-State arbitrations, the need to balance investment protection with ensuring adequate policy space for governments to regulate will become increasingly important.

As discussed above, a number of FTAs, such as AUSFTA, US–Chile FTA and the India–Singapore CECA, include detailed provisions on what constitutes indirect expropriation.[284] These expropriation provisions were initiated by the US in the FTAs it entered into after NAFTA and can therefore be understood as a response to concerns that legitimate government regulation was being challenged as inconsistent with the NAFTA expropriation commitment. In this regard, it is interesting to note that expropriation claims under NAFTA against the US involved claims of indirect expropriation. These concerns over the proper scope of expropriation provisions are not necessarily only a developed country issue. Therefore, to the extent that these provisions on indirect expropriation strike the appropriate balance between the right of Governments to regulate and the obligation to compensate investors for an expropriation, it is likely that such provisions will become increasingly prevalent in future FTAs.

The scope of the fair and equitable treatment standard is another ongoing area of concern due to its uncertain scope. The NAFTA Interpretative Note regarding the fair and equitable treatment standard reflects the NAFTA Parties' experience being the defendant in investor-State dispute settlement action. The controversy over this provision is similar to that raised with regard to the expropriation commitment, in that they are fundamentally about the appropriate balance between investment protection on the one hand and the ability of governments to regulate, on the other.

Another issue is the increasing potential for conflicting decisions amongst international tribunals. As discussed above, such cases already exist in areas such as

---

284 AUSFTA, Annex 11–B; US–Chile FTA, Annex 10-D; and India–Singapore CECA, Annex 3.

application of the MFN clause to more favourable dispute settlement provisions. Such decisions undermine, rather than enhance, the certainty and predictability that these provisions seek to create.[285] Consistency of arbitral decisions on investment could be addressed by establishing an appellate mechanism, something the Parties to CAFTA–DR–US have already agreed to do.[286]

285 International Law Commission, *Fragmentation of International Law: Difficulties Arising from the Diversification and Expansion of International Law*, Report of the Study Group (finalised by Martti Koskenniemi), UN Doc. A/CN.4/L.682 (4 April 2006), para. 419.
286 CAFTA–DR–US, Annex 10–F; the Parties to the US–Singapore FTA Article 15.26 and the Exchange of Letters on an Appellate Mechanism have agreed to consider within three years of entry into force of the FTA whether to establish an appellate mechanism to review ISDS rewards; see generally Susan D. Franck, 'The Nature and Enforcement of Investor Rights under Investment Treaties: Do Investment Treaties have a Bright Future?' (2005) 12(1) *University of California Davis Journal Of International Law & Policy* 47–100, at 62–6, for an outline of the implications of inconsistent decisions for investment treaty arbitration.

11

Government procurement

ARWEL DAVIES
AND KRISTA NADAKAVUKAREN SCHEFER

I. Introduction

When governments purchase goods or services from private parties for governmental use, it is referred to as "government procurement" or "public procurement". Examples of government procurement include the awarding of contracts to build roads and buildings, the installation of communications systems and the maintenance of information technology networks. Because governments around the world spend a significant percentage of their budgets on such purchases, government procurement markets are valuable. At the same time, because government officials may use their purchasing behaviour to achieve goals beyond the mere functioning of government, procurement markets can be discriminatory, inefficient, and lack transparency.

As trade in goods and services have become subject to rules on market access and non-discrimination, public procurement practices have likewise come under liberalization pressures. Today, an overwhelming majority of bilateral and regional preferential trade agreements (PTAs) seek to regulate these activities, or at least set out a commitment to do so. While several references to procurement only set forth a goal of procurement market liberalization, many refer to the fuller obligations of the multilateral rules of the WTO's Agreement on Government Procurement (GPA). A small number of other PTAs set out an autonomous regulatory system for procurement trade that includes market access obligations and detailed rules on how governments should seek offers for contracts and the processes by which the offers should be assessed and awarded. These latter agreements even contain rules providing for challenge procedures that can be invoked by disappointed applicants.

Part II sets out in more detail why procurement is subject to international regulation. At a certain level, the rationale for international regulation can be easily explained and understood. Discrimination against foreign suppliers in procurement markets can amount to a significant barrier to trade. International regulation therefore seeks to address distortions in the conditions of competition between domestic and foreign suppliers which can be caused by "buy national" tendencies and measures. Beyond this explanation however, understanding the rationale for international regulation and its relationship with national regulation throws up some challenging conceptual issues. The principles of non-discrimination contained in PTA procurement provisions serve the same purpose as they do in any other trade context: helping all market participants face the same conditions of competition in order to provide consumers with the broadest choice of goods and services at the lowest prices. However, there is room to question whether, in the procurement context, the identity of the purchaser as a public body not directly subject to market forces means that international rules need to be concerned with value for money – something which is generally regarded as an objective of only national procurement regulation – as well.

Part III turns to the content of international procurement rules. There are wide variations on the extent of liberalization among the government procurement provisions of PTAs, but most provisions can be grouped in one of three categories – objectives only, reliance on the GPA and autonomous regimes. Within those categories, the content is substantially the same. The common elements will therefore be examined.

Part IV turns to the GPA's influence on the development of procurement disciplines in PTAs, and concludes the chapter by questioning whether international procurement regulation through trade provisions is better served by detailed rules or general principles.

II. Why is public procurement subject to international regulation?

A. The market

The range of goods and services purchased by governments to carry out their functions is of course vast. Governments spend on the same goods and services that private firms and consumers purchase (such as computers, construction of buildings or landscaping) as well as making purchases of goods and services that only government needs (such as defense systems or national transportation infrastructure).

Global estimates of procurement spending are difficult to make with any accuracy, and governments can have significant differences in levels of public spending going to such purchases. One estimate indicates that industrialized countries spend 15–20% of their national budgets on government procurements while developing country governments spend even larger percentages – in the area of 20–30% of their total spending.[1] In terms of absolute spending, an estimate of $7 trillion per year is likely perhaps even, on the conservative side.[2]

For most government purchases, the nationality of the supplier is unrelated to the functionality of the product or quality of the service. Yet, domestic political pressures often result in competitive disadvantages for foreigners. In some jurisdictions, government procurement is wholly removed from the ordinary rules of trade, permitting facial discrimination against foreign suppliers. In others, the discrimination is

---

1 WTO, Government Procurement (Update November 2012).
2 Colin Cram, '$3.5tn global spend on local procurement "woefully" mismanaged', *The Guardian* 22 October 2012 (available at www.guardian.co.uk/local-government-network/2012/oct/22/colin-cram-local-government-global-procurement).

disguised. Whether it is in "buy national" legislation, contract specifications that work to the benefit of local producers or confidential selection procedures that ensure that particular local firms will be granted the contract, discrimination in government procurement processes can be a significant barrier to trade.

As a result, trade agreements that aim to ensure open markets and equal conditions of competition have begun comprehensively covering government procurement. While recognizing that governments may have certain legitimate preferences for selecting the suppliers of particular goods and services, government procurement negotiators strive to level the playing field as much as possible for global competitors. The resulting trade agreements have opened markets and reduced de facto discrimination.

B. Governance

A more recent concern involving government procurement is the governance of procurement activities. Because states' purchasing activities require officials to make decisions relating to the outlay of public funds, poor procurement decision-making has wide-ranging negative impacts on societies. Higher costs and poor quality goods and services are the most tangible of these negative impacts, but a dampening of innovation may also be an effect.

Developments in political thought and international law have led to increased pressure on governments to demonstrate that they are responsive to their citizens' needs, responsible in their use of financial resources, and willing to enforce these good governance principles throughout the government. To ensure that government officials are accountable, official decision-making must be open to review by national and international stakeholders. Citizens, but also potential foreign suppliers, have an interest in knowing on what basis government purchases were made from particular sources. Did the purchasing decision rest on economic efficiency considerations or other grounds? If other grounds, were they legitimate public interests or were they the results of personal favouritism or even corruption?

The fact that trade liberalization can be used to foster good governance has led to efforts to make this a secondary goal of trade agreements. As trade agreements have begun to incorporate an implicit goal of good governance, the rules on government procurement have begun to further emphasize the transparency of purchasing processes. Where it exists, the explicit incorporation of transparency principles underlines PTA parties' commitments to ensuring that liberalized trade is pursued for a higher aim.

III. Content of procurement regulations in the different types of PTA provisions

As mentioned above, a large majority of PTAs contain some form of reference to trade in government procurement. That being the case, the provisions differ according to the level of commitment to procurement liberalization, so each must be evaluated in context. Nevertheless, for purposes of understanding procurement regulation, one can categorize the provisions' content into three main groupings: a statement of an objective; deference to multilateral rules on procurement trade; and autonomous regulation of procurement activities. The following will briefly explain the general content of each approach.

A. Statement of objectives

Some PTAs contain a provision on government procurement which merely expresses the Parties' recognition of procurement liberalization as one goal of their relationship. These provisions can be a single paragraph, but often include several paragraphs within a single article to set forth the objective. Often using hortatory language, such provisions do not set forth any binding obligations for the Parties, and therefore cannot be subject to formal dispute settlement procedures. They may, however, be considered a basis for further negotiations and indicate an openness toward further economic integration. A basic version of the objective type government procurement provision is that found in the PTA between the EFTA countries and Egypt. The sole paragraph states:

> The Parties agree on the objective of a progressive liberalisation of public procurement. The Joint Committee will hold consultations on the implementation of this objective.[3]

The clear goal of liberalization is underscored by a commitment to further cooperate on the issue, but holds no indication of the direction of such efforts. A similar model is one, such as in the Turkey–PLO FTA, in which the statement of the objective is followed by a commitment to offer the partner's suppliers most-favorable treatment if advantages are offered to third party suppliers.[4]

A more elaborate objectives-type clause is that contained in Article 24 of the PTA between Romania and Macedonia:

> 1. The Parties consider the liberalization of their respective public procurement markets as an objective of this Agreement.
> 2. The Parties shall progressively adjust their respective rules, conditions and practices in the field of public procurement with a view to grant suppliers of the other Party upon request access to contract award procedures on their respective public procurement markets.

---

3 EFTA–Egypt FTA, Art. 33.
4 See Turkey–PLO FTA, Art. 27:
  1. The Parties consider the opening up of the award of public contracts on the basis of non-discrimination and reciprocity, to be a desirable objective.
  2. As of the entry into force of this Agreement, both Parties shall grant each other's companies' access to contract award procedures a treatment no less favourable than that accorded to companies of any other country.

3. The Joint Committee shall examine developments related to the achievements of the objectives of this Article and may recommend practical modalities of implementing the provisions of the Paragraph 2 so as to ensure free access, transparency, full balance of rights and obligations and mutual opening of their respective public procurement markets.[5]

In this example, the Parties clearly indicate a desire to avoid binding obligations, but do use mandatory language in the second and third paragraphs. This shows a commitment to future obligations of market access, with transparency following later.

B. Deference to multilateral rules

A number of PTA texts go beyond the mere objective approach, but do not set out their own rules on procurement or individual obligations for the Parties. Instead, this second category of PTAs defers to the WTO's rules regulating public purchasing. These provisions, like objectives-only provisions, are often found in a single article. Such articles often contain several paragraphs, including one that sets out liberalization of procurement markets as an objective, but then a following paragraph which may either refer to the application of GPA rules as a goal of the Parties or one that explicitly obliges the Parties to apply the rules of the GPA, and/or one that emphasizes that the Parties' obligations under the GPA are to be adhered to as a part of the PTA.

The first type (GPA adherence as a goal) is a variation of the objectives-only provision, but one which indicates a stronger commitment to liberalization of procurement. An example is that found in the agreement between Turkey and Albania:

Article 27 Public Procurement

1. The Parties consider the liberalization of their respective public procurement markets as an objective of this Agreement. The Parties aim at opening up of the award of public contracts on the basis of non-discrimination and reciprocity.
2. The Parties will progressively develop their respective rules, conditions and practices on public procurement with a view to granting suppliers of the other Party access to contract award procedures on their respective public procurement markets not less favorable than that accorded to companies of any country or territory.
3. The Joint Committee shall examine developments related to the achievement of the objectives of this Article and may recommend practical modalities of implementing the provisions of paragraph 2 so as to ensure free access, transparency and mutual opening of their respective public procurement markets.
4. During the examination referred to in this paragraph 3, the Joint Committee may consider, especially in the light of international developments and regulations in this area, the possibility of extending the coverage and/or the degree of the market opening provided for in paragraph 1.

---

5 Romania–Macedonia FTA, Art. 24. See also Romania– Serbia and Montenegro FTA, Art. 23; EFTA–Tunisia FTA, Art. 30.

> 5. The Parties shall endeavor to accede to the relevant Agreements negotiated under the auspices of the GATT 1994 and the Marrakesh Agreement, establishing the WTO.[6]

Here, the first paragraph puts forth the objective of liberalization, while the following ones underline the steps they will take to realize their objectives. The incorporation of references to the international legal developments, and in particular to the GPA, allows the Parties the flexibility to increase their liberalization obligations without having to set out firm details too soon.

Other PTAs use references to the GPA more strongly, bringing the obligations of that agreement into the framework of the PTA as binding on the Parties. Canada and Israel used such an approach, with Chapter 6 on Government Procurement stating simply:

> Article 6.1: Government Procurement
>
> The rights and obligations of the Parties relating to government procurement shall be governed by the *Agreement on Government Procurement*, Annex 4 of the *WTO Agreement*, as of the date of its entry into force for the Parties.
>
> Article 6.2: Further Liberalization
>
> The Parties will endeavour to negotiate further liberalization of access by suppliers of the other Party to their government procurement.[7]

Such an incorporation of the GPA provisions is an efficient method for PTA Parties to ensure a minimum of market access and non-discrimination of their producers and suppliers in their partners' procurement markets while avoiding the need to conduct separate negotiations on the subject.

Incorporation of another treaty's provisions does, however, bring up a question of general treaty law: do the obligations of the PTA change with changes in the GPA rules? This can be debated, as typically the PTA provisions do not explicitly set forth the Parties' intention on this issue. The general rule of treaty interpretation found in Article 31 of the Vienna Convention on the Law of Treaties, taking an objective approach to interpretation, may indicate that the current version of the GPA would apply to any PTA referring merely to the "Agreement on Government Procurement" without a particular date or further reference to modifications of the text. Yet, the concept of finding the Parties' intent could be used to support a position freezing the content of the incorporated GPA at the time of the PTA's conclusion. Where the objective approach might be more reasonable for the specific rules of the GPA, the subjective expectations of the Parties might well be the more appropriate approach for application of PTA provisions that were concluded prior to significant additions to GPA basic principles. This could be the case for provisions that came into effect prior to the establishment of the GPA as a separate agreement in the WTO system. Consider the following provision from the FTA between Iceland and the Faroe Islands:

---

6 See Republic of Turkey–Republic of Albania FTA, Art. 27; see also EFTA–Macedonia FTA, Art. 15.
7 Canada–Israel FTA, Chapter 6.

Article 18: Public Procurement

1. The Contracting Parties consider the effective liberalization of their respective public procurement markets as a desirable and important objective of this Agreement.

2. As of the entry into force of this Agreement, the Contracting Parties shall grant each others' companies access to contract award procedures on their respective public procurement markets according to the Agreement on Government Procurement of 12 April 1979, as amended by a Protocol of Amendments of 2 February 1987, negotiated under the auspices of the General Agreement on Tariffs and Trade.[8]

While the liberalization of procurement markets is set out as an "objective", the Parties clearly commit themselves to offering market access and non-discrimination to the extent reflected in the then-GATT related agreement on Government Procurement. Not saying anything about how the FTA provisions would relate to changes to the GATT for any amendments post-1987, it is unclear whether the further multilateral developments would add to the commitments taken bilaterally.

Given the changes to the multilateral rules on procurement since 1987, the Parties' intent to adhere to the current GPA provisions may be questioned. The consideration of what the PTA Parties could have legitimately expected is particularly important when examining their agreements in light of the enhanced transparency obligations and anti-corruption duties of the latest GPA revision. These changes, which will be further discussed below, add a significant new principle to the GPA which may or may not be agreed to by PTA Parties.

C. Autonomous regulation

A number of PTAs incorporate fully fledged chapters on government procurement that may or may not be patterned on the GPA.[9] These multi-article sections typically regulate the specifics of how procurement procedures are to take place, as well as how disappointed foreign producers and suppliers can respond to negative decisions by Party officials. The following briefly describes the main elements of autonomous government procurement chapters as found in PTAs.[10]

---

8 Agreement Between the Government of Denmark and the Home Government of the Faroe Islands, of the One Part, and the Government of Iceland, of the Other Part, on Free Trade Between the Faroe Islands and Iceland, Art. 18.

9 The New Zealand–Singapore FTA and the New Zealand–Thailand FTA, for example, both emphasize their adherence to the principles of the APEC Non-Binding Principles on Government Procurement (NBPs) rather than to the GPA approach. The NBPs approach stresses transparency instead of market access in a search for "value for money", accountability, non-discrimination and competition. See generally Review of the APEC Non-Binding Principles (NBPs) on Government Procurement, 2006/SOM3/GPEG/005 (8–9 September 2006).

10 The European Union's system of procurement regulation, aiming to create a "public market" for procurements, has been the subject of detailed analysis, the depth of which is beyond this chapter. For more, see Christopher H. Bovis, *EU Public Procurement Law* (Cheltenham: Edward Elgar Publishing, 2012).

D. Scope: Limits on procurement liberalization

Parties to a PTA with provisions on government procurement liberalization aim to ensure that government contracts are granted to the most efficient producer or supplier, independent of nationality. The objective is usually one of deepening the commitments undertaken in other areas of the agreement – with a higher goal of assuring the consumer (in this case the government) that the widest choice of goods and services at the lowest price, producers and service suppliers from other Parties have equal opportunities to compete for government contracts. For various reasons, however, international rules on government procurement do not apply to all government purchases.

First, government procurement regulation in PTAs is generally limited to the granting of government contracts in a normal course of business. Non-contractual agreements, including grants and loans or other fiscal incentives, or contracts made under advantageous short-term conditions as well as employment contracts are usually exempted from the scope of such provisions.[11]

Even for contracted purchases, liberalization applies only partially. The limited scope of government procurement obligations is generally reflected in the structure of the procurement chapters into obligations and annexes setting forth which procurements are covered. The limits are generally of two main types – limitations as to which governmental entities' purchases are covered; and limitations as to which purchases are covered.

The first type of limitation is to include only the purchases made by certain governmental entities within the coverage of the PTA government procurement regime. While international law generally presumes that any part of the government is to be bound by the state's international obligations,[12] government procurement provisions may be conceived so as to bind the parties only to the extent they set forth explicitly. Where there is a "schedule" of commitments, there is space for the parties to identify those offices whose purchases will be subject to the procurement provisions.

It is also usual for international rules on government procurement to specify financial thresholds. This second type of limitation means that only contracts which have a value of at least those thresholds will fall within the rules on purchasing.[13] While this limits the openness of a procurement system, it protects governments against the possibility of having to expend disproportionate amounts of administrative resources on evaluating bids from multiple would-be contractors on small projects.

---

11 See, e.g., Singapore–Panama FTA, Art. 8.2(5).
12 See ILC, 'Responsibility of States for Internationally Wrongful Acts' (2001), Art. 4 (text found in the Annex to General Assembly resolution 56/83 of 12 December 2001, as corrected by document A/56/49(Vol. I)/Corr.4.
13 The GPA financial thresholds are indicated in the Appendix I of each Party. For central government entities, the thresholds for supplies and services are generally set at SDR 130,000 (approximately USD $196,000) and at SDR 5m for construction services. Thresholds vary considerably at the sub-central level particularly for construction services. The US threshold at sub-central level for construction services is SDR 5m, but it is 15m for Korea. In the AUSFTA, the threshold for central government goods and services contracts is AUD$81,800. The same threshold at the regional level is AUD$666,000.

Given thresholds, full PTA chapters on government procurement also have a provision on valuation of contracts. Generally, such clauses attempt to ensure that Party entities do not write out their contract offers in a way so as to illegitimately avoid the thresholds for applying the PTA rules. Thus, all costs relating to a procurement are to be combined in the valuation, offered projects should not be broken into several contracts, and any optional purchases that might be included in a procurement are to be calculated with the base price to determine whether the offer is over the threshold.[14] These are important to ensure that the Parties are applying the same standards to procurement tenders.

The Chile–Japan Free Trade Agreement Chapter on Government Procurement offers a typical example of a structurally limited-scope agreement. It begins with a statement limiting the scope of the parties' obligations:

> Article 136: Government Procurement
>
> Scope
>
> 1. This Chapter shall apply to any measures adopted or maintained by a Party relating to government procurement, by any contractual means, including through such methods as purchase or as lease, rental or hire purchase, with or without an option to buy:
>   (a) by entities specified in Part 1 of Annex 14;
>   (b) of goods specified in Part 2 of Annex 14, services specified in Part 3 of Annex 14, or construction services specified in Part 4 of Annex 14; and
>   (c) where the value of the contracts to be awarded is estimated to be not less than the thresholds specified in Part 5 of Annex 14 at the time of publication of a notice of procurement.[15]

Thus, in order to assess whether the Parties have adhered to their obligations, a preliminary evaluation of the annex provisions is required to find out the extent to which they have promised liberalizations. Only then are the substantive treatment requirements relevant.

The PTA may also have exceptions from the scope for certain types of procurements or other spending projects. Non-contractual agreements, for instance, are often excluded, as are foreign assistance, hiring of employees and governmental financial services.

1. Note on market access

A significant trade law element of public procurement liberalizations is market access. As with other sectors of trade, government procurement trade liberalization is ultimately only as strong as the principle of market access the particular agreement incorporates. For without permitting the goods and services of foreign producers and

---

14 See, e.g., NAFTA Art. 1002.
15 Agreement between Japan and the Republic of Chile for a Strategic Economic Partnership, Chapter 12.

suppliers to reach the governmental purchasers, there can be no trade in government procurement to which to apply any further rules. Interestingly, however, market access is rarely explicitly set forth in PTA provisions. Instead, market access is subsumed in the scope provision and any reciprocity requirements that might exist.

E. Non-discrimination

Found throughout trade law, the non-discrimination principle in procurement law aims not only at protecting suppliers from discrimination, but also at protecting consumers by helping market forces function unimpeded toward the goal of ensuring that the most efficient suppliers will be selected as the government's contract partner (the "value for money" concept).[16] Of course, where social goals other than market efficiency are taken into account, these two approaches to non-discrimination may collide. Such is the case in domestic procurement regulations that work to counter the discrimination faced by disadvantaged groups of suppliers as a social equality measure.[17]

Non-discrimination in international procurement law has a different function. In PTAs, the trade goals of non-discrimination are dominant. Thus, while policy space for social regulation can be carved out in general exceptions provisions, non-discrimination obligations are the primary tool for ensuring that government procurement markets are accessible by foreign producers and suppliers on equal competitive terms. A typical and central part of procurement trade regimes, non-discrimination can come in two forms for government procurement (as it does in the general trade in goods and trade in services provisions): national treatment and most-favored nation treatment.

F. National treatment

National treatment provisions in PTAs are often worded similarly, including the language providing for "treatment no less favorable" than that of domestic goods and services to foreign goods and services. The obligation extends to the procedures as well as procurement laws and practices, although tariffs and other charges on the goods to be supplied are generally not going to be abolished by virtue of the non-discrimination provision. The Japan–Mexico Agreement is typical:

> National Treatment
>
> 1. With respect to any measures regarding government procurement covered by this Chapter, each Party shall provide immediately and unconditionally to the goods, services and suppliers of the other Party offering goods or services of the

---

16 For a further explanation of the relationship between value for money and non-discrimination, see *I*, p. 311–312.
17 See Christopher McCrudden, *Buying Social Justice: Equality, Government Procurement, & Legal Change* (New York: Oxford University Press, 2007), 512–515.

other Party, treatment no less favorable than that accorded to domestic goods, services and suppliers.

2. With respect to any measures regarding government procurement covered by this Chapter, each Party shall ensure:

   (a) that its entities shall not treat a locally-established supplier less favorably than another locally-established supplier on the basis of the degree of affiliation to, or ownership by, a person of the other Party; and

   (b) that its entities shall not discriminate against locally-established suppliers on the basis of the country of production of the goods or service being supplied, provided that the country of production is the other Party in accordance with the provisions of Article 121.

3. The provisions of paragraphs 1 and 2 above shall not apply to customs duties and charges of any kind imposed on or in connection with importation, the method of levying such duties and charges, other import regulations and formalities, and measures affecting trade in services other than measures regarding government procurement covered by this Chapter.

G. MFN

Most-favored nation treatment is less widely found in PTA government procurement chapters than are national treatment obligations. While some provisions exist in multi-party PTAs (such as those found in NAFTA Article 1003), MFN obligations extending beyond the PTA Parties themselves are rare where the national treatment obligation exists.[18] The Japan–Mexico FTA Chapter contains an interesting provision in this respect. Although there is a firm national treatment obligation, the Chapter's "Miscellaneous Provisions" also grants conditional MFN in the case of any procurement preferences being offered by one of the Parties to GPA partners' producers or suppliers.[19]

---

18 Where bilateral PTAs have only government procurement objectives, as opposed to any obligations, however, MFN obligations sometimes to exist. For example, Article 23(1) of the Albania–Bosnia and Herzegovina Free Trade Agreement provides for MFN in Article 23(2), despite having no binding national treatment obligation:

> The Contracting Parties will progressively develop their respective rules, conditions and practices on government procurement and shall grant suppliers of the other contracting party access to contract award procedures on their respective public procurement markets not less favourable than that accorded to companies of any third country.

The probable motivation for this approach is that MFN treatment alone amounts to a dormant commitment, which is only activated in the event of favourable treatment being granted to a third country.

19 Japan–Mexico FTA, Art. 130. See also EC–Mexico FTA, Art. 37: "In the case that the Community or Mexico offer a GPA or NAFTA Party, respectively, additional advantages with regard to the access to their respective procurement markets beyond what has been agreed under this Title, they shall agree to enter into negotiations with the other Party with a view to extending these advantages to the other Party on a reciprocal basis."

H. Further aspects of non-discrimination

Along with the national treatment (and possible MFN) provisions, PTAs often have accompanying obligations to reduce the possibilities of discrimination.

1. Rules of origin

One is a prohibition on applying different rules of origin on procured goods and services than would apply in a non-procurement context. This ensures that tenders by Party suppliers are not artificially less competitive. Such provisions may include or be accompanied by a denial of benefits provision that ensures that the benefits of the liberalization remain within the PTA Parties.[20]

2. Offsets

An "offset" is something a supplier can offer the community in which it is hoping to gain a contract in exchange for getting the contract. Like a "local content" in investment law, offsets typically include contributions to the economic development of a target community through the use of local products or services or through the hiring of local individuals in the performance of the contract. The term can also cover the use of sub-contracts or efforts to bring in foreign investment.

While offsets may be beneficial for the community, if a procuring entity requires that such offsets be given in order to consider a tender, it reduces the potential pool of tenderers and possibly gives a competitive advantage to local suppliers. Thus, the prohibition of offsets is another common provision of PTA chapters on procurement.

Supporting the national treatment provision in particular, such provisions restrict Parties' ability to force suppliers to promise benefits to the local economy in order to qualify or win a contract. An offset provision may resemble that of the EC–Mexico FTA's agreement by prohibiting the use of offsets and defining "offset":

> Each Party shall ensure that its entities do not, in the qualification and selection of suppliers, goods or services, in the evaluation of bids or the award of contracts, consider, seek or impose offsets. For purposes of this Article, offsets means conditions imposed or considered by an entity prior to, or in the course of, its procurement process that encourage local development or improve its Party's balance-of-payments accounts, by means of requirements of local content, licensing of technology, investment, counter-trade or similar requirements.[21]

While the prohibition of offsets is common to PTAs with full procurement regimes, the frequent use of offsets for defense procurements remains problematic.

20 The NAFTA has a rules of origin provision (Art. 1004) and a separate denial of benefits provision (Art. 1005), while the EC–Mexico FTA has a paragraph on each combined in its Art. 27.
21 EC–Mexico FTA, Art. 28.

The general exception from the procurement liberalization rules enjoyed by defense purchasing works to keep offsets in use in the military sector.[22]

I. Open question: How do value for money and non-discrimination relate to each other?

Good governance, it was mentioned above, is now widely regarded as a goal of regulating government procurement in trade agreements. Governance concerns are also goals of national procurement laws. A main aspect of good governance is the government's receiving "value for money" when it expends public funds.

This "value for money" term is imprecise, but can be taken to refer to the avoidance of unnecessary expenditure. Thus, it would be natural that procurement regulations (whether international or national rules) would aim to ensure that the procurement process leads to the most suitable goods and services being acquired at the lowest price.

Yet, although national and international rules strongly resemble each other in demanding competitive tendering procedures, some commentators assert that the value for money criteria is absent from international rules whereas it is frequently the overwhelming concern of national ones.[23] Instead, international rules are claimed to be interested in affording foreign producers and service suppliers non-discriminatory access to markets.[24]

One of the authors of this chapter insists that this is a false distinction, one based on a view of non-discrimination as an end in itself rather than an instrument of trade liberalization. Recognizing that non-discrimination aims to create conditions in the marketplace that will lead to the benefits of competition – including that of value for money – this latter view sees non-discrimination and value for money as following from each other: a rational economic actor, when making a purchasing decision, will favor the lowest price goods and services which can fulfil its requirements regardless

---

22 See Directorate General Internal Markets and Services, 'Directive 2009/81/EC on the award of contracts in the fields of defence and security Guidance Note: Offsets' (available at http://ec.europa.eu/internal_market/publicprocurement/docs/defence/guide-offsets_en.pdf); see also European Defence Agency, 'A Code of Conduct on Offsets' (version approved on 3 May 2011) (on file with author).

23 Sue Arrowsmith, *Government Procurement in the WTO* (The Hague: Kluwer Law International, 2003), 172–174. Arrowsmith, Linarelli and Wallace point out that national rules tend to require that the financial and technical capacity of suppliers *actually be ascertained*, while international rules only require the absence of discrimination in any verification process which *actually occurs*. Sue Arrowsmith, John Linarelli and Don Wallace Jr, *Regulating Public Procurement, National and International Perspectives* (The Hague: Kluwer Law International, 2000), 234.

24 Peter-Armin Trepte, *Regulating Procurement: Understanding the Ends and Means of Public Procurement Regulation* (Oxford: Oxford University Press, 2004), 284 ("the focus of the international system is limited primarily to securing non-discriminatory and reciprocal access to the procurement markets of their members. To the extent that the procedures adopted reflect those which already existed in the national systems of their membership, those systems will 'fortuitously' promote economic efficiency or, at least, not impede it").

of the origin and nationality of these goods and services. Of course, the principle–agent problem (that the governmental agent has "no direct interest in the outcome of the procurement in terms of 'profitability'") cautions against merely assuming that this necessarily holds true for public as well as private purchasers, but there is evidence to suggest that it in fact does.[25]

But should value for money become a value pursued by international regulation of procurement? Purchasing policies that involve preferences for local suppliers, for instance, entails both discrimination and the possibility of unnecessary expenditure and so might violate either principle. Other preferred procurement procedures might not involve discrimination, but might nonetheless be less likely than other available procedures to result in the best value for money.[26] A rule limiting discretion of procurement officials in order to reduce the opportunities for corruption, for instance, might secure the absence of discrimination but not foster value for money decision-making. Should international review bodies be able to question such policies? Or what if a state grants very broad discretion to procuring entities in order to enhance value for money, but by doing so risks violating non-discrimination rules? These are all questions that need to be taken up more fully in future work.

J. Methods of procurement

One aspect of government procurement that is of critical importance to determining the competitive opportunities of foreign producers and suppliers is the method by which the government calls for offers on contracts, or "tenders". PTAs with government procurement regulations often set out rules permitting Parties to use any of three different tender offer methods: open, selected and limited.

1. Open tender

Under the open procedure, any interested supplier can submit a tender, as governmental entities are not permitted to impose any conditions for participation or operate any kind of qualification system before tenders are submitted. Thus, this procedure is the one that promises the widest field from which to choose, and is therefore optimal from the perspective of liberalization and is often set out as the preferred method in FTAs.

---

25 Trepte, *ibid.*, 119 (Trepte points out that there is little empirical evidence which demonstrates that public procurement is conducted on a less efficient basis than private firms operating in a competitive market); John Linarelli, 'The WTO Agreement on Government Procurement and the UNCITRAL Model Procurement Law: A View From Outside the Region' (2006) 1 *Asian Journal of WTO and Health Law and Policy* 61–84, at 69 (noting officials' "reputational, career and programmatic incentives to be efficient").

26 This point is exemplified by the *Sintesi* case discussed below. Case C-247/02, *Sintesi SpA v. Autorità per law Viglinaza sui Lavori Pubblici* [2004] ECR I-09214.

2. Selected tender

Under the selected procedure, the procuring government invites suppliers to submit a tender. By allowing the government to choose the number and identity of potential contractors, selected tendering eliminates the administrative burden of putting out an invitation to tender and reviewing all the submissions. It also, of course, reduces the competition among tenderers. In order to balance the competing interests in competition and administration, selective tendering is sometimes subject to conditions relating to, for instance, an emergency situation requiring urgent supplies, a failure of open procedures to result in satisfactory bids, a limited number of potential suppliers with the requisite technology or intellectual property rights, or for contracts to replace parts or offer services on existing contracts.[27] In some PTAs, Parties would have to report on their choice of selected procedures, explaining why it was necessary to use them. Under the US–Bahrain FTA, the provision reads as follows:

> For each contract awarded under paragraph 2, a procuring entity shall prepare a written report that includes the name of the procuring entity, the value and kind of goods or services procured, and a statement indicating the circumstances and conditions described in paragraph 2 that justify the use of a limited tendering procedure.

The NAFTA Chapter on Government Procurement extends the regulation of selected tendering to include a right of Party suppliers to request to submit a tender despite not having been invited to do so.[28] Unless the Party can "promptly provide pertinent information concerning its reasons not to do so",[29] the tender is to be considered on a non-discriminatory basis.

3. Limited tender

A third method that may be included in a PTA is limited tendering. This is a non-competitive process under which the entity contacts suppliers individually. Essentially an extreme form of selected tendering, it is only to be used under limited circumstances as set forth in the agreement. The EFTA–Chile FTA demonstrates the narrow possibilities of using limited tendering, including the following words before listing the conditions under which it can be used:

> Provided that the tendering procedure is not used to avoid maximum possible competition or to protect domestic suppliers, entities shall be allowed to award contracts by means other than an open or selective tendering procedure in the following circumstances and subject to the following conditions, where applicable:[30]

27 E.g., Republic of Korea–Chile FTA, Art. 15.6(2).   28 NAFTA Art. 1011(3).   29 NAFTA Art. 1011(4).
30 EFTA–Chile FTA, Art. 56(1).

Reporting requirements, often the same as for selected tendering procedures, are also commonly included. Under US–Bahrain FTA, the relevant provision reads as follows:

> For each contract awarded under paragraph 2, a procuring entity shall prepare a written report that includes the name of the procuring entity, the value and kind of goods or services procured, and a statement indicating the circumstances and conditions described in paragraph 2 that justify the use of a limited tendering procedure.[31]

K. Tender proceedings

In order to ensure that the openness of the tender process actually fosters increased access to procurement markets, government procurement provisions will generally set out a framework for the government's conveyance of information regarding the tender. This generally covers the publication of the notice, the tender documents and the award.

The publication of either an invitation to submit tenders or a notice of a tender offer is typically required by PTAs. Such invitation or notice is to be made well in advance of the time limit for the tender to permit suppliers to prepare their bids sufficiently. In the interest of ensuring access to this information, the invitation or notice is to be placed in a publication that is specified by the Party in advance or on a platform that is available to interested suppliers without unreasonable efforts. Increasingly, invitations to tender are issued electronically. As such, suppliers have equal access to the notice for tender.

The invitation or notice itself is to provide all relevant information about the tender offer. This includes not only the substance of the call – a description of the items to be procured, the price, the award criteria, the relevant deadlines, and any specific technologies to be used – but also procedural information about the tender process such as the submission address of the selecting entity, the language of eligible submissions, whether the call is an open or select tender, and the final date for submission. Seemingly obvious, the offering of such information is not always practiced,[32] but is necessary to ensure that all suppliers have equal opportunities to compete.

Finally, PTA procurement frameworks generally contain rules calling for contracts to be awarded on the basis of the best offer and that the results be notified to all participants.

Some of the more complete frameworks for government procurement, such as the NAFTA's Chapter 10, also contain more specific requirements regarding the form of tender submissions, minimum time limits for tender preparation and explicit rules as

---

31 US–Bahrain FTA, Art. 9.8(3).

32 See generally OECD, *Integrity in Public Procurement: Good Practice from A to Z* (Paris: OECD, 2007) (containing several boxes and tables pointing to failures of OECD Member States to apply non-discriminatory and transparency-enhancing procurement procedures).

to what Parties may take into account when assessing bids. There is, additionally, language as to the circumstances under which a Party may negotiate with bidders and when they may refuse to disclose certain information. Such detail, however, is exceptional for PTAs, many of which remain focused on setting out only the general framework within which Parties are to regulate.

L. Challenge procedures

While the regulation of participants and tender proceedings, with the broadening of the pool of potential applicants and the making available of information, goes quite far in assisting foreign suppliers attain access to procurement markets, a key feature of government procurement frameworks in trade agreements is their inclusion of challenge procedures for unhappy bidders. Giving suppliers the opportunity to directly challenge Party entity procurement choices, challenge procedures encompass both deterrent and remedial functions.[33] For bidders, PTAs that contain challenge procedures move away from the traditional state-to-state dispute resolution that characterizes the other areas of trade law and toward the more rapid and direct complaint mechanism that national legal systems provide. For Parties, the challenge procedures work as a deterrent, as any violation of the procurement rules can subject them to court-like proceedings and a duty to remedy the violation.

Where challenge procedures exist, there is a variation among PTAs in terms of the level of detail with which they are regulated. At a minimum, challenge procedures are to provide the complaining bidder with the opportunity to make a formal complaint against a procuring entity,[34] receive a considered review of the matter by an impartial authority, and have the opportunity for such authority's decision to be subjected to judicial review. Some PTAs, such as the EU regulations, also require that the review authority have the competence to order remedies if it determines that the agreement was violated.[35] Others, like the NAFTA,[36] only give the review committee a power to recommend remedies. The review, it must be emphasized, need not be limited to PTA-regulated procurements. Rather, the process may be (and indeed generally is)

---

33 Erik A. Troff, 'The United States Agency-Level Bid Protest Mechanism: A Model for Bid Challenge Procedures in Developing Nations' (2005) 57 *A.F. L. Rev.* 113, 119.

34 See e.g., *Commission v. Austria*, C-212/02 (finding that Austria had violated its obligations under European Council Directive 89/665/EEC of 21 December 1989 and Council Directive 92/13/EEC of 25 February 1992 because not all of the subnational-level procurement regulations required tenderers to be given the opportunity to bring a challenge to a review committee).

35 Council Directive of 21 December 1989 on the coordination of the laws, regulations and administrative provisions relating to the application of review procedures to the award of public supply and public works contracts, 89/665/EEC, Art. 2.1; Council Directive of 25 February 1992 coordinating the laws, regulations and administrative provisions relating to the application of Community rules on the procurement procedures of entities operating in the water, energy, transport and telecommunications sectors, 92/13/EEC, Art. 2.1. See also Bovis, at 194–199.

36 NAFTA Art. 1017(1)(m). See also Troff, *supra* n. 33 at 136.

established at the national level for the benefit of all procurement participants of whatever nationality.[37]

In setting up a challenge procedure, each Party may limit the opportunity given the bidder to bring a complaint. Often this will be a temporal limitation in order to ensure that the procurement process as a whole is not unreasonably delayed. The United States, for example, gives tenderers a maximum of ten days after the basis for the complaint could have been known (for most types of challenges).[38]

The remedies are, of course, a very interesting aspect of the challenge. This is particularly so given that the remedy goes from the government Party to the bidder as a private person rather than to the bidder's own government. The forms of remedy for breaches of PTA governmental procurement provisions generally include "correction" or compensation. Whereas the latter term is familiar in international law, referring to loss or damages suffered, the former is not. Examining the provisions of a number of PTAs that provide for correction, it appears that it is intended to permit reviewing authorities to require that procuring entities suspend their processes and reconsider the violated bid. If the results of such action would cause disproportionately adverse consequences, correction might be disregarded in favor of offering compensation. Compensation, it is frequently noted, may be limited to the costs incurred in preparing the tender and in challenging the award.[39]

A fundamentally different means of resolving disputes is set out in Article 54 of the NZ–Singapore CEPA, in that suppliers have considerably less direct control over the process. Supplier complaints are first heard by way of consultations between the aggrieved supplier and the procuring government body. If the complaint is not resolved at this level, it then takes on an intergovernmental character since the next stage is for the supplier to seek the assistance of its national "designated body".[40] The complaint may be "processed informally" if this is deemed appropriate by the complainant and its national body.[41] No guidance is given on how the complaint might be informally processed although it is reasonable to suppose that the supplier's national body will enter into consultations with the complained-of procuring entity. If the complaint is not resolved via informal means, the supplier's national body then notifies the complaint to its counterpart in the other Party "for investigation of any alleged breach ... and for a report by it

---

37 For an overview of the national review bodies of the EU Member States see OECD, *Public Procurement Review and Remedies Systems in the European Union, Sigma Papers, No. 41* (OECD Publishing: Paris, 2007), 15–21.

38 *Ibid.* at 145–146 (explaining Federal Acquisition Regulation 33.103).

39 E.g., Japan–Mexico FTA, Art. 125.8(c); Korea–Chile FTA, Art. 15.13(4). But see Mexico–Israel FTA, Art. 6.17.7(c) (providing that compensation "shall [rather than may] be limited to costs for tender preparation or protest").

40 These bodies are the Ministry for Economic Development in New Zealand and the Ministry of Finance for Singapore.

41 Art. 54:2.

in writing".[42] The intergovernmental character of the complaint is reinforced by Article 54:4 which effectively provides for the complaint to lapse if the response to the written report is satisfactory to the complaining supplier's national body. If the complaint does not lapse, the complaining supplier's national body may refer the matter to the Minister responsible for procurement in the other Party "for further investigation and decision".[43] Article 30:6 envisages a thirty-day period for resolving the dispute which runs from the date the supplier notifies the complaint to its national body. This period is sufficiently short for interim measures to operate in order to preserve opportunities, although these are not expressly required. Finally, if the dispute is not resolved within thirty days, it can be subject to strictly intergovernmental proceedings under Part 10 of the Agreement.

M. Exceptions

The final characteristic of government procurement chapters in PTAs is the frequent (though not ubiquitous) appearance of a general exceptions clause. Such clauses tend to be shorter than their parallels in general trade in goods or services chapters, often listing only five grounds upon which a Party can justify its violation of a provision. The most frequently cited substantive grounds of exception to procurement rules are national security or defense concerns. The exclusion of defense contracts from the scope of non-discrimination rules is a typical feature of trade agreements, but leaves a large gap in ensuring that governments look primarily to economic value in their procurement practices.[44]

The public order or public morals exception is also common, and would permit governments to ignore the rules to ensure social goals of safety and the protection of reigning values. This could involve the exclusion of a supplier on grounds of it being a member of a suspected criminal organization or on account of an involvement in morally offensive activities.

A further exception may be granted to measures necessary to protect life and health. This will extend to the well-being of animals and plants as well as humans, and may also encompass general environmental concerns. Invoking this exception would permit procuring officials the policy space to, for example, incorporate

---

42 Art. 54:3. It is unclear from the wording which designated body must draft the written report. However, when para. 3 is read with para. 4, the impression created is that the report is drafted by the complaining supplier's national body. This is also the better interpretation as the supplier's national body can be expected to be more independent and impartial than its counterpart; a point which takes on extra significance where the counterpart happens to be the procuring entity complained of.

43 Art. 54:5.

44 The extent of irregularities in defense procurements cannot be known with any precision, but voices from inside the military have spoken out on the topic, which supports a conclusion that distortions are widespread. See, e.g., Marlin D. Paschal, 'Getting Beyond "Good Enough" in Contingency Contracting by Using Public Procurement Law as a Force to Fight Corruption' (2012) 213 *Mil. L. Rev.* 65.

environmental offsets into a procurement procedure or specify technical requirements to secure low emissions.

Some PTAs will include the protection of intellectual property rights as a ground to
avoid the Parties' commitments. This could be used to limit the information issued
following an award as well as to permit limited tendering where a particular technology is desired.

Finally, there are a number of PTAs that allow measures "relating to goods and
services of handicapped persons, of philanthropic institutions or of prison labor" to
override the general obligations of the government procurement provisions. Besides
finding the same words in the WTO's Revised GPA,[45] there are likely to be historical
grounds for permitting such "social justice" exceptions,[46] and their existence can be
seen as recognition of the legitimacy of governments wanting to pursue broader
social goals even at the cost of economic efficiency.

Like the exceptions for general trade, the PTA procurement exceptions provisions
have a three-part structure, with the substantive element, the relational limitation
(requiring, for instance, that the violative measures be "necessary" to achieving the
public aim), and an introductory paragraph circumscribing the invocation of such
measures to applications that are not disguised restrictions on trade nor arbitrary and
unjustifiable discriminations. Given the similarity of language between such provisions and the wording of the GATT Article XX, one can expect that these will be
similarly interpreted.

Note, however, that even where an exception may be considered suitable for avoiding
some provisions of a procurement provision, it may not be considered an exemption
from all of the relevant rules. Even where, for instance, a government's use of environmental (in addition to economic) considerations in assessing which tender offer will
receive the contract is permissible, the exception for human life and health would not
relieve the Party's obligation to publish the invitation to tender. Similarly, even where a
public safety exception could justify the use of a selected tender, it would not relieve the
contracting entity of making a non-discriminatory choice for the award.

IV. PTA rules on government procurement and the GPA

A. The influence of the GPA on PTA procurement rules

The WTO's GPA has clearly had a significant impact on how PTAs regulate government procurement, whether or not the Parties are also Parties to the GPA. As was
mentioned above, a large number of FTAs either incorporate some or all of the GPA
obligations or express accession to the GPA as an objective of the Parties. Even where

---

45 Revised GPA, Art. III.2(d).
46 For a historical background to the exception for persons with disabilities in national procurement
    legislation, see McCrudden, *supra* n. 17, 56–62.

the Parties establish autonomous procurement trade regimes, the content of their PTAs and the GPA is generally similar.[47]

Because the GPA aims at liberalizing procurement markets in order to foster non-discriminatory trade, the overlap of the main features of PTA rules and GPA rules should not be surprising. From the use of entity and threshold schedules to limit the scope to the qualification of calls for tender into open, select and limited (and the preference for open calls) to the rules about notifications, procedures, award-making and challenges, the GPA rules and PTA rules are different mainly in the details. These details, of course, can make a difference in practice, but familiarity with the principles of one permits working with the other without much difficulty. A noticeable difference is that most PTA procurement regimes are significantly less detailed than the GPA.[48] There are exceptions to this, such as the NAFTA's Chapter 10 and the European Union's public procurement regime. Even there, however, there are very few examples of general rules contained in PTAs which do not feature in the GPA.

Until recently, the one main difference between regional and multilateral rules lay in the extent to which procurement rules were suited to addressing concerns about the integrity of the public purchasing process. International legal attention to corruption has grown over the past fifteen years, and the extent of economic damage stemming from officials' misappropriation of funds in public purchasing has been revealed. The numbers are striking: even conservative estimates of corruption put the price societies are paying for government goods and services that are overpriced, of substandard quality or that are simply never delivered at hundreds of *billions* of dollars per year.[49] The structure of procurement processes – with large outlays of money and significant discretion of the procuring official – offers a lucrative and low-risk setting for corruption. Procurement liberalization, focusing on increasing foreign access to processes, if coupled with enhanced transparency, could raise the likelihood of corruption detection and presumably reduce it. Nationally, the United States led the anti-corruption in procurement campaign with the passage of the Procurement Integrity Act. This 1988 law prohibits corruption in all government purchasing activities and provides

---

47 Robert D. Anderson, Anna Caroline Müller, Kodjo Osei-Lah, Josefita Pardo de León, and Philippe Pelletier, 'Government Procurement Provisions in Regional Trade Agreements: A Stepping Stone to GPA Accession?' in Sue Arrowsmith and Robert D. Anderson (eds.), *The WTO Regime on Government Procurement: Challenge and Reform* (Cambridge: Cambridge University Press, 2011), 561–656, 618.

48 There are numerous descriptions of the elaborate set of rules contained in the GPA. For a recent analysis of the Agreement in its multiple aspects, see Arrowsmith and Anderson, *ibid.*

49 Transparency International, *Corruption and Public Procurement* 2 (TI Working Paper #05/2010) (estimating the percentage of procurement fund losses due to corruption at 10–25% of the total annual expenditure).

for severe punishment in cases of violation.[50] The OECD strongly encouraged its Members to implement anti-corruption measures in public procurements as well,[51] and certain steps were taken by governments to move in the direction of making corruption by procurement officials illegal.

On the multilateral level, however, governments did not seem ready to take up the anti-corruption cause. Negotiations for a Transparency Agreement to accompany the GPA were put on indefinite hold in 2004 when the WTO Members declared that these talks would not be made a part of the Doha Round agenda,[52] and on their own, the GPA rules' lack of an explicit reference to corruption of procurement officials was a problem.[53] This left governments without a clear mandate to address the governance issues of procurement through the international trade system.

It was here that a few PTAs went further. One restriction on corruption is found in provisions that permit governments not to consider bids by suppliers who have been convicted of corruption or participation in criminal activities.[54] A second possibility is a general call to make bribery in procurement illegal. This is the approach taken by the US and Australia, with Article 15:10 containing the following provision:

> Ensuring integrity in procurement practices
>
> 1. Each Party shall ensure that criminal or administrative penalties exist to sanction:
>   (a) a procurement official of that Party who solicits or accepts, directly or indirectly, any article of monetary value or other benefit, for that procurement official or for another person, in exchange for any act or omission in the performance of that procurement official's procurement functions;
>   (b) any person who offers or grants, directly or indirectly, to a procurement official of that Party, any article of monetary value or other benefit, for that procurement official or for another person, in exchange for any act or omission in the performance of his or her procurement functions; and
>   (c) any person intentionally offering, promising or giving any undue pecuniary or other advantage, whether directly or through intermediaries, to a foreign procurement official, for that foreign procurement official or a third party, in order that the foreign procurement official act or refrain from acting in relation to the performance of procurement duties, in order to obtain or retain business or other improper advantage.

---

50 For more on the law, see Timothy M. Cox, 'Should the United States Incorporate the Procurement Integrity Act into its Free Trade Agreements? A Look at the Australian–United States Free Trade Agreement' (2011) 17 *Sw. J. Int'l L.* 111, 118–121.

51 See, e.g., OECD, *Integrity in Public Procurement, supra* n. 32.

52 WTO, Decision Adopted by the General Council, WT/L/579, para. 1(g) (2 August 2004).

53 See generally, Krista Nadakavukaren Schefer, 'Corruption and the WTO Legal System' (2009) 43:4 *J. World Trade* 737, 742–746.

54 E.g., EC Public Service Directive 2004/18, Art. 45(1).

Given the United States' lead in pushing for anti-corruption initiatives worldwide, it is unsurprising that it was willing to place a clear, head-on tackling of corruption in a trade agreement with a like-minded partner. Together with the Australian government, the negotiators for the US were able to place the sensitive issue of corruption into an international trade treaty.

Recent developments at the WTO have brought the GPA closer to the level of the AUSFTA in the matter of procurement integrity. The Revised Text of the GPA, agreed to in December 2012, contains new language calling for Parties to fight corruption. Found not only in the Preamble but also in a substantive provision, the explicit reference to "corrupt practices" is a first for the WTO system. Article IV GPA (Revised) states that a "procuring entity shall conduct covered procurement in a transparent and impartial manner that (c) prevents corruption".[55] While there is some question as to whether this provision places a duty on Parties to actually take steps to detect corruption, the recognition of the problem is itself an element that could shift the focus of the Agreement toward ensuring good governance as well as non-discrimination and market access.[56]

How will this affect PTA Parties that have incorporated GPA references into their procurement provisions? The general international law rules on treaty interpretation leave substantial room for determining whether references to the GPA should bind Parties to any subsequent changes to the GPA. If Party intent is taken to be determinative, then at least for PTA Parties that are not GPA signatories the answer might be "no". From an objective viewpoint, the answer would be different. The GPA evolves, as to all treaties, and the PTA Parties could be expected to have limited their obligations to the GPA as it existed had they not wanted the evolutionary changes to affect them.

B. Which model for PTA government procurement regulation?

It can be questioned whether the influence of developments at the WTO level on the procurement content of PTAs is to be welcomed. Overall, it is submitted that the answer is yes, albeit some concerns can be identified.

At an early stage in the development of international procurement regulation it was realized that general obligations of non-discrimination would need to be supplemented with minimum procedural obligations to tackle the widespread use of discriminatory practices as opposed to readily identifiable laws and

---

55 Revised GPA, Article IV:4(c). See Adoption of the Results of the Negotiations under Article XXIV:7 of the Agreement on Government Procurement, Following their Verification and Review, as Required by the Ministerial Decision of 15 December 2011 (GPA/112), Paragraph 5: Action Taken by the Parties to the WTO Agreement on Government Procurement at a Formal Meeting of the Committee, at the Level of Geneva Heads of Delegations, on 30 March 2012, GPA/113 (2 April 2012).

56 See generally, Krista Nadakavukaren Schefer with Mintewab Gebre Woldesenbet, 'The Revised Agreement on Government Procurement and Corruption' (2013) 47 *Journal of World Trade* 1129.

measures.[57] There is now a view that the pendulum has swung too far in the direction of regulation by detailed rules. In particular, Arrowsmith's work calls for serious consideration to be given to a swing of the pendulum somewhat back towards regulation by general principles alone. Accepting this view would have clear implications for the future development of procurement disciplines in PTAs. It would follow that PTAs which presently do not set out detailed procedural rules should not be seen as inferior instruments, and ought not necessarily to pursue the objective of alignment with the GPA. This would apply particularly to the minority of PTAs which do not envisage this objective.[58] A number of reasons for regulation by general principles have been reflected in this chapter.

A second possible reason for regulation by general principles alone is that detailed rules have to respond continuously to changes in procurement methods at the national level; for example, to make use of electronic purchasing methods. There is a danger of the rules becoming ever more technical and difficult to apply, particularly as drafting errors inevitably creep in. It is possible that these problems are not sufficiently offset by any increased transparency achieved by detailed rules as opposed to general principles.

These are clearly not insurmountable problems, and the human urge to supplement general principles with specific rules is not something which can be easily suppressed. However, there is a third and more fundamental reason for a move away from the detailed regulation of award procedures. There are examples of developed country governments beginning to focus more on the outcome of the procurement process rather than the process itself. Such initiatives involve the exercise of broad discretion by entities as to how the procurement is conducted, coupled with audit mechanisms to assess the extent to which value for money has been achieved.[59] The exercise of this discretion for a covered contract would

---

57 Blank and Marceau report that a consensus emerged on this point during an information-gathering exercise on discriminatory measures and practices undertaken by the Trade Committee of the OECD in the early 1960s: Annet Blank and Gabrielle Marceau, 'The History of the Government Procurement Negotiations since 1945' (1996) 5 *Public Procurement L. Rev.* 77, 159.

58 Chapter 16 of the Chile–Costa Rica FTA exemplifies the approach of regulation through general principles which are not supplemented by detailed award procedure rules. There also does not appear to be any link with WTO developments.

59 One of the leading examples of this approach is the UK's "Best Value" regime which applies to local authorities and which was introduced by the Labour government partly in order to replace Compulsory Competitive Tendering. On the "Best Value" regime, see Stephen Cirell and John Bennett, *Best Value Law and Practice* (London: Sweet & Maxwell, 1999). Best Value is itself presently the subject of legislative reform. It is interesting to note an observation recently made by Cirell and Bennett: "Best Value did not succeed in delivering the outcomes planned by the Government. The reason for this may well be the way Best Value was introduced, meaning that a procedural 'machinery' of Best Value grew up which distracted from the main aim." This perhaps indicates that it is difficult to pinpoint when and how general principles should be supplemented with detailed guidance. See Stephen Cirell and John Bennett, 'Best Value, The White Paper and the New Local Government Bill' (15 February 2007), available at www.info.gov.za/greenpapers/1997/publicproc.htm (visited 27 February 2007).

breach some procurement provisions unless the preferred procedures happened to correspond with those of the text. Arrowsmith therefore suggests the possibility of Parties or entities having the "choice between the traditional rule-based approach . . . or an approach based on principles backed up by additional enforcement measures".[60]

60 Arrowsmith, *supra* n. 23, 437.

12

Intellectual property

MICHAEL HANDLER AND BRYAN MERCURIO

I. Introduction

The Agreement on Trade-Related Aspects of Intellectual Property Rights (TRIPS Agreement) forever changed the relationship between intellectual property (IP) and international trade. While there had always been a link between IP and international trade, the TRIPS Agreement formally integrated the two areas at the multilateral level for the first time. The TRIPS Agreement is comprehensive in its coverage of IP: it deals with copyright and related rights, trademarks, geographical indications (GIs), industrial designs, patents, layout-designs of integrated circuits and protection of undisclosed information, and contains further provisions relating to anti-competitive practices in contractual licences and enforcement of IP rights. Further, much like other covered agreements of the WTO, the most-favoured-nation (MFN) and national treatment (NT) principles lie at the heart of the Agreement.

Where the TRIPS Agreement is perhaps unusual is that it establishes standards of IP protection that each WTO Member must accord to nationals of other Members.[1] Such a regulatory, harmonised approach is different from the approaches of the other covered agreements of the WTO and might have prevented further developments outside of the multilateral forum. However, Members are specifically permitted under the Agreement to apply higher levels of protection if they so desire, as long as the principles of MFN and NT are respected.[2] Thus unlike Article XXIV of the GATT, Article 4 of the TRIPS Agreement does not exempt Preferential Trade Agreements (PTAs) from the operation of MFN – any Member which grants 'any advantage, favour, privilege or immunity' to the nationals of *any* other country (whether a WTO Member or not) must accord the same treatment to the nationals of other WTO Members.

---

1 TRIPS Agreement, Article 1.3. The Agreement also requires that Members comply with certain provisions of other international IP agreements, most notably the Paris Convention for the Protection of Industrial Property (1967) (TRIPS Agreement, Article 2.1) and the Berne Convention for the Protection of Literary and Artistic Works (1971) ('Berne Convention') (excluding Article 6*bis*) (TRIPS Agreement, Article 9.1).
2 TRIPS Agreement, Article 1.1.

Such higher standards of IP protection than those mandated by the TRIPS Agreement are often called 'TRIPS-Plus' provisions. Members may negotiate PTAs which provide for TRIPS-Plus provisions that require, *inter alia*, the inclusion of additional protectable subject matter, broader and more extensive standards of protection, stronger enforcement mechanisms, and a weakening of 'flexibilities' and 'special and differential treatment' granted to developing and least developed countries in the TRIPS Agreement. The effect of these provisions is, in part, to 'ratchet up' international IP standards, as the more PTAs are negotiated, the more far-reaching the implications of the PTA provisions become. In such a circumstance, it appears that if enough PTAs are negotiated containing TRIPS-Plus provisions, some of these may well become the new minimum standards from which any future WTO trade round will proceed.[3]

This chapter does not attempt to analyse comprehensively all recent negotiations involving TRIPS-Plus provisions. Instead, it seeks to illustrate certain trends by highlighting and considering some of the more frequently used, important and potentially far-reaching TRIPS-Plus provisions that have recently been negotiated. Our analysis in this chapter will therefore focus on three areas of IP – copyright, GIs and patents – as well as briefly considering overarching issues of enforcement, focusing on criminal measures.[4]

II. Subject area analysis

A. Copyright

While numerous PTAs contain references to copyright law, sometimes imposing a small number of obligations in relation to highly technical issues,[5] it is in those PTAs negotiated by the United States (US) and, to a lesser extent, the European Union (EU) that we see the imposition of the most significant and extensive obligations going beyond those required by the TRIPS Agreement. Two of the most notable areas in this regard relate to the term of copyright protection and to the protection of technological protection measures.[6]

---

3 See Bryan Mercurio, 'TRIPS-Plus Provisions in PTAs: Recent Trends', in Lorand Bartels and Federico Ortino (eds.), *Regional Trade Agreements and the WTO Legal System* (Oxford: Oxford University Press, 2006), pp. 215–37, at p. 223.

4 Even within this framework, considerations of space force us to narrow our scope to only some contemporary and controversial issues. For a statistical overview of PTAs containing IP provisions up to March 2013, see Xavier Seuba, 'Intellectual Property in Preferential Trade Agreements: What Treaties, What Content?' (2013) 16(5–6) *Journal of World Intellectual Property* 240–61.

5 See, e.g., Japan–Malaysia EPA, Article 122; EC–CARIFORUM EPA, Article 143; and Malaysia–Australia FTA, Articles 13.14–13.16.

6 For discussion of other copyright provisions in the context of US PTAs, see Pedro Roffe, *Bilateral Agreements and a TRIPS-Plus World: The Chile–USA Free Trade Agreement*, TRIPS Issues Papers 4 (Ottawa: Quaker International Affairs Programme, 2004), at pp. 27–9 and 31–2, at http://law-wss-01.law.fsu.edu/gpc2007/materials/roffe_ottowa2004.pdf.

1. Extension of copyright term

By virtue of Article 7(1) of the Berne Convention for the Protection of Literary and Artistic Works, which is incorporated into the TRIPS Agreement through Article 9.1, WTO Members are required to grant a minimum term of copyright protection for most literary and artistic works (excluding photographs) that expires fifty years after the death of the author.[7] The TRIPS Agreement further stipulates that the minimum term of protection for certain works whose term is not calculated by reference to the life of the author (which might include collective works) is to be fifty years from the first publication or the making of the work (Article 12). In addition, it provides a minimum term for performances of fifty years from the first fixation of the performance, and for phonograms of fifty years from the first publication of the phonogram (Article 14.5). These terms broadly reflected US law as it stood in 1994.

In 1993, however, what was then the European Community (EC) required its member States to adopt a term of protection for most literary and artistic works (including photographs) of the life of the author plus seventy years, and for a range of other works of seventy years from the first lawful making available of the work.[8] Further, member States were placed under an obligation not to apply this TRIPS-Plus term to works from countries, such as the US, with shorter terms of protection. Such works were only to be protected in the EC for the shorter term provided for under the laws of their originating countries.[9] This was a significant factor that drove the US Congress to enact domestic legislation in 1998 that increased the term of protection for most works to the life of the author plus seventy years.[10] The US also took the opportunity at that time to raise the term of protection for subject matter whose term was not based on the life of a natural person to the shorter of ninety-five years from publication or 120 years from creation.

Although such domestic legislation proved controversial,[11] the US has since used Free Trade Agreements (FTAs) and Trade Promotion Agreements (TPAs) with both developed and developing countries to require the term of protection to be extended beyond TRIPS standards to approximate US standards, so that US works are protected for longer in those countries. All but one of its recent PTAs include a

---

7 More specifically, fifty years after the end of the year of the death of the author (see Berne Convention, Article 7(5)). All references to periods of years in our discussion of copyright term are calculated from the end of the year of the act or event in question.

8 Council Directive 93/98/EEC of 29 October 1993 harmonising the term of protection of copyright and certain related rights [1993] OJ L290/9, Articles 1, 2 and 13.1. This Directive has since been repealed and replaced by Directive 2006/116/EC of the European Parliament and of the Council of 12 December 2006 on the term of protection of copyright and certain related rights [2006] OJ L372/1 (and see also Directive 2011/77/EU of the European Parliament and of the Council of 27 September 2011 amending Directive 2006/116/EC on the term of protection of copyright and certain related rights).

9 Council Directive 93/98/EEC, above n. 8, Article 7.1. See also Berne Convention, Article 7(8).

10 See generally Orrin G. Hatch, 'Toward a Principled Approach to Copyright at the Turn of the Millennium' (1998) 59(4) *University of Pittsburgh Law Review* 719–57, at 729–32.

11 Apart from substantial academic criticism, the legislation was the subject of an unsuccessful constitutional challenge in the US Supreme Court: *Eldred v. Ashcroft*, 537 US 186 (2003).

requirement that for works (including photographic works), performances and phonograms where the term is to be calculated by the protecting party on the basis of the life of a natural person, the minimum term shall be the life of the author plus seventy years. This TRIPS-Plus requirement first appeared in the US–Singapore FTA (Article 16.4.4(a)) and was followed in US FTAs with Chile (Article 17.5.4(a)), Australia (AUSFTA) (Article 17.4.4(a)), Morocco (Article 15.5.5(a)), the Dominican Republic–Central America (CAFTA–DR–US) (Article 15.5.4(a)), Bahrain (Article 14.4.4(a)), Oman (Article 15.4.4(a)), Korea (KORUS FTA) (Article 18.4.4(a)) and Colombia (Article 16.5.5(a)), and in TPAs with Peru (Article 16.5.5(a)) and Panama (Article 15.5.4(a)). The exception to this trend is the US–Jordan FTA (one of the earliest PTAs), which does not address the issue.

Where the term of protection for works, performances and phonograms is to be calculated other than by reference to the life of a natural person, there is a strong, albeit surprising, consistency between the various US PTAs. In FTAs with Singapore (Article 16.4.4(b)), Chile (Article 17.5.4(b)), Australia (Article 17.4.4(b)), Morocco (Article 15.5.5(b)), Bahrain (Article 14.4.4(b)) and Colombia (Article 16.5.5(b)), in CAFTA–DR–US (Article 15.5.4(b)), and in TPAs with Peru (Article 16.5.5(b)) and Panama (Article 15.5.4(b)), the required minimum term for such works, performances and phonograms is the same: either a minimum of seventy years from the end of the year of the first authorised publication, or, failing such publication within fifty years from creation, a minimum of seventy years from the end of the year of creation.[12] This is somewhat unexpected because these are lesser terms than those provided for under US law. It is noteworthy that while the US Industry Functional Advisory Committee on Intellectual Property Rights for Trade Policy Matters, commenting in the context of what would become CAFTA–DR–US, thought that such extensions represented a 'major advance' for US interests, it also urged the US to seek to increase the minimum levels of protection in future PTAs,[13] presumably so that these aligned more closely with US standards. Thus far, only the FTA with Oman (Article 15.4.4(b)) does this, requiring a minimum term of ninety-five years from the end of the year of the first authorised publication of the work, performance or phonogram, or, failing such publication, within twenty-five years from creation, a minimum of 120 years from the end of the year of creation.

Recent EU PTAs also impose TRIPS-Plus obligations relating to the term of copyright protection. For example, under the EU–Korea FTA (Article 10.6), the EU–Central America Association Agreement (Article 234) and the EU–Colombia

---

12 Under Article 18.4.4(b) of the KORUS FTA, the '70 years from the end of the year of creation' term applies if there has been no authorised publication within twenty-five years of creation of the work.

13 Report of the Industry Functional Advisory Committee on Intellectual Property Rights for Trade Policy Matters (IFAC-3), 'The US–Central American Free Trade Agreement (PTA): The Intellectual Property Provisions' (12 March 2004), at p. 11, at www.grain.org/article/entries/3619-us-cafta-the-intellectual-property-provisions.

and Peru Trade Agreement (Article 218.1), the term of protection of a work calculated on the basis of the life of a natural person must be the life of the author plus seventy years. In the last of these PTAs, it is further provided (Article 218.4) that where the term of protection for works, other than photographs or works of applied art, is calculated on a basis other than the life of a natural person, the term shall either be seventy years from the end of the year of authorised publication, or, failing publication within fifty years from the making of the work, seventy years from the end of the year of its making.[14]

These provisions would seem to be a windfall for copyright owners in the US and EU, as well as each of the above-mentioned countries with which they have entered agreements. They have, however, been the subject of criticism in this latter group of countries. In most cases the partner countries are net importers of copyright products, meaning that the benefits of extension flow primarily to US and EU copyright owners, at the expense of such works falling into the public domain in the partner countries. This imposes additional costs on those countries. For example, in the Australian context it was suggested that as a result of the term provisions of the AUSFTA, net royalty payments were likely to increase significantly, additional compliance costs would be imposed on libraries, archives and other cultural organisations, and problems with dealing with 'orphan works' (generally, older works whose copyright owners cannot be located) would likely be exacerbated.[15] An additional concern, expressed by a number of US commentators, relates to the impoverishment of the 'public domain' that results from term extension, in that the content on which people can rely for education and future creation is limited.[16] Nevertheless, given the potential benefits that are thought to flow to copyright owners from term extension,[17] the trend for TRIPS-Plus term provisions on copyright term in PTAs is likely to continue.[18]

---

14 In contrast, under Article 235 of the EU–Central America Association Agreement (between the EU and Costa Rica, El Salvador, Guatemala, Honduras, Nicaragua and Panama), the minimum term of protection afforded to performers, producers of phonograms and broadcasting organisations is set at fifty years.

15 See, e.g., Matthew Rimmer, 'Robbery Under Arms: Copyright Law and the United States–Australia Free Trade Agreement' (2006) 11(3) *First Monday*, at http://papers.ssrn.com/sol3/papers.cfm?abstrac t_id=855805; cf. Allen Consulting Group, *Copyright Term Extension: Australian Benefits and Costs*, Report Commissioned by the Motion Picture Association (March 2003) (on file with author). For a more recent critique, see Australian Government, Productivity Commission, *Bilateral and Regional Trade Agreements* (November 2010), at pp. 165–7, at www.pc.gov.au/__data/assets/pdf_file/0010/ 104203/trade-agreements-report.pdf.

16 See, e.g., Lawrence Lessig, *Free Culture* (New York: Penguin, 2003), Chapters 13–14.

17 Cf. Paul J. Heald, 'Property Rights and Efficient Exploitation of Copyrighted Works: An Empirical Analysis of Public Domain and Copyrighted Fiction Best Sellers', in Fiona Macmillan (ed.), *New Directions in Copyright Law* (Cheltenham, UK: Edward Elgar, 2007), vol. 6, pp. 74–111.

18 See, e.g., the leaked drafts of the Trans-Pacific Partnership Agreement (TPP) (November 2013), Article QQ.G.6, at wikileaks.org/tpp/static/pdf/Wikileaks-secret-TPP-treaty-IP-chapter.pdf; (October 2014), Article QQ.G.6, at wikileaks.org/tpp-ip2/tpp-ip2-chapter.pdf. This Agreement is being negotiated between Australia, Brunei Darussalam, Canada, Chile, Japan, Malaysia, Mexico, New Zealand, Peru, Singapore, the US and Vietnam.

2. Technological protection measures

Technological protection measures (TPMs) are, in short, devices and software developed to prevent unauthorised copying of digital works.[19] The TRIPS Agreement does not deal with TPMs, which only came to prominence in the 1990s in light of advances in information and communication technology that facilitated the copying of works in digital form. The omission of the issue, however, was seen as a serious oversight by content holders and software organisations.[20] As such, these organisations lobbied for legal protection of TPMs in an alternative forum, namely the World Intellectual Property Organization (WIPO), which included provisions on TPMs in the WIPO Copyright Treaty (1996) (WCT) and the WIPO Performances and Phonograms Treaty (1996) (WPPT). These require Contracting Parties to provide 'adequate legal protection and effective legal remedies against the circumvention of effective technological measures' used by authors, performers and phonogram producers in connection with the exercise of their rights that restrict unauthorised acts in respect of their works, performances or phonograms.[21] The wording of the WCT and WPPT provisions offers a degree of flexibility for Contracting Parties as to the domestic implementation of such protection and remedies.

Almost all of the PTAs concluded by the US contain a provision requiring the parties to ratify or accede to the WCT and WPPT (or affirm that they have done so),[22] thus obliging them to afford at least the protection and remedies outlined above. However, each of these PTAs also contains further, highly detailed requirements on TPMs, similar to those contained in the US Digital Millennium Copyright Act of 1998 (DMCA). While the level of protection varies slightly between PTAs, most impose a similar, restrictive standard.

In each US PTA, apart from that with Jordan, the parties are essentially obliged to impose liability and make civil and criminal remedies available against those engaging in one of two types of conduct involving TPMs.[23] The first is the act of circumventing a TPM that controls access to a protected work, performance, phonogram, or other subject matter. The second is the manufacture of and trafficking in devices, or the provision of services, for the circumvention of all types of TPM

---

19 Two common examples are password protection systems and encryption.

20 See South Centre and Centre for International Environmental Law, 'Intellectual Property and Development: Overview of Developments in Multilateral, Plurilateral, and Bilateral Fora', South Centre and CEIL IP Quarterly Update: First Quarter 2005, at p. 7, at www.ciel.org/Publications/IP_Update_1Q05.pdf.

21 See WCT, Article 11 and WPPT, Article 18.

22 Under Article 4.1 of the US–Jordan FTA the parties are required only to 'give effect to' the substantive provisions of the WCT and WPPT. There is no mention of the issue in the US–Chile FTA (presumably because both countries were already Contracting Parties at the date of the agreement).

23 Under Article 4.13 of the US–Jordan FTA, the parties are only required to proscribe the second type of conduct.

(i.e., both access control and copy control devices).[24] This two–tiered approach closely follows that taken under the DMCA.

The PTAs also permit the parties to make available a limited number of exceptions to liability. These include reverse-engineering a computer program for interoperability purposes, encryption research by a qualified researcher, government acts undertaken for law enforcement or security purposes, access by libraries or similar institutions for the sole purpose of making acquisition decisions, and particular uses exempted by the parties following periodic government review.[25] However, in line with the position under the DMCA, not all of the exceptions can be made available in relation to both acts of circumvention and the trafficking of circumvention devices/provision of circumvention services.

One area in which the PTAs differ is in their treatment of 'knowledge' in the context of circumvention. For instance, Article 17.7.5(a) of the US–Chile FTA requires the parties to proscribe only the *knowing* circumvention of an effective technological measure. In contrast, the US–Singapore FTA (Article 16.4.7(a)), AUSFTA (Article 17.4.7(a)) and KORUS FTA (Article 18.4.7(a)) go further in requiring the prohibition of both knowing acts of circumvention and acts where the person had *reasonable grounds to know* that he or she was engaged in circumvention. The trend, however, seems to be for a knowledge requirement to be dispensed with altogether,[26] which more closely accords with the DMCA.

Laws protecting TPMs tend to receive the support of copyright owners concerned about financial losses said to be incurred by widespread and unchecked copyright piracy. Nevertheless, the inclusion of WCT and WPPT-Plus provisions on TPMs in US PTAs is highly controversial.[27] For example, it is said that US-style TPM laws

24 See US–Singapore FTA, Article 16.4.7(a); US–Chile FTA, Article 17.7.5(a)–(b); AUSFTA, Article 17.4.7(a); US–Morocco FTA, Article 15.5.8(a); CAFTA–DR–US, Article 15.5.7(a); US–Bahrain FTA, Article 14.4.7(a); US–Oman FTA, Article 15.4.7(a); US–Peru TPA, Article 16.7.4(a); KORUS FTA, Article 18.4.7(a); US–Colombia FTA, Article 16.7.4(a); and US–Panama TPA, Article 15.5.7(a). With the exception of the US–Chile FTA, the parties may exempt from criminal liability non-profit libraries, archives, educational institutions and public non-commercial broadcasting entities. Under Article 17.7.5(b) of the US–Chile FTA, '[a] Party may exempt from criminal liability, and if carried out in good faith without knowledge that the conduct is prohibited, from civil liability, acts... carried out in connection with a nonprofit library, archive or educational institution'. See also Anti-Counterfeiting Trade Agreement (ACTA), Articles 27.5–27.6 (requiring parties to provide protection against both acts of circumvention of TPMs and the provision of services designed to facilitate circumvention of TPMs) and Article 27.7 (permitting parties to 'maintain appropriate limitations or exceptions' to these provisions, with no further detail specified).

25 See US–Singapore FTA, Article 16.4.7(e)–(g); US–Chile FTA, Article 17.7.5(d); AUSFTA, Article 17.4.7(a); US–Morocco FTA, Article 15.5.8(d); CAFTA–DR–US, Article 15.5.7(d)–(f); US–Bahrain FTA, Article 14.4.7(e); US–Oman FTA, Article 15.4.7(d); US–Peru TPA, Article 16.7.4(e)–(f) and (h); KORUS FTA, Article 18.4.7(d); US–Colombia FTA, Article 16.7.4(e)–(f) and (h); and US–Panama TPA, Article 15.5.7(d).

26 See US–Morocco FTA, Article 15.5.8(a)(i); CAFTA–DR–US, Article 15.5.7(a)(i); US–Bahrain FTA, Article 14.4.7(a)(i); US–Oman FTA, Article 15.4.7(a) (i); US–Peru TPA, Article 16.7.4(a)(i); US–Colombia FTA, Article 16.7.4(a)(i); and US–Panama TPA, Article 15.5.7(a).

27 In this regard, it is interesting to note that recent EU PTAs, such as the EU–Central America Association Agreement (Article 233) and the EU–Colombia and Peru Trade Agreement (Article 221) only require

provide over-broad protection to copyright owners in that they prevent consumers from engaging in conduct with copyright works that would not in fact infringe copyright. The exceptions to circumvention liability contained in US PTAs are limited in scope – most notably, they make no provision for circumvention to allow a user to engage in general 'fair use'-type conduct with the protected work. Thus, circumventing a TPM in Chile to make a back-up copy of a protected computer program would be impermissible, even though the making of the back-up copy would not constitute copyright infringement under Chilean law. In addition, it has been argued the exceptions that are allowed under US PTAs intended to ensure access for educational, research and other legitimate interests are so narrowly drafted that they are inadequate for their stated purpose.[28]

It has also been claimed that TPM laws are being used by some copyright owners for anti-competitive purposes and to stifle free expression and scientific research.[29] For example, it has been noted that such laws have been used as part of attempts to segment global markets for films and computer games through region-coding technology, as well as in attempts to control aftermarkets in non-copyright products such as ink cartridges and garage door openers.[30] While not all of these attempts have been successful, such conduct raises questions about whether the full consequences of strong TPM laws have been appreciated.

There is thus a real apprehension that the imposition of DMCA-type provisions in US PTAs, going beyond the mere requirement to accede to the WCT and WPPT, deprives other countries of the ability to draft their TPM provisions and include exceptions that best take into account the needs and concerns of users of copyright material in those countries.[31] Strong doubts have also been raised as to whether such provisions are, in practice, likely to raise standards beyond those required by the

compliance with WCT and WPPT obligations. The EU–Korea FTA goes further, setting out more detailed obligations in relation to TPMs in Article 10.12. However, these obligations are not as extensive as those contained in the KORUS FTA, or other US PTAs.

28 See, in the context of the DMCA, Pamela Samuelson, 'Intellectual Property and the Digital Economy: Why the Anti-Circumvention Regulations Need to Be Revised' (1999) 14(2) *Berkeley Technology Law Journal* 519–66.

29 See Electronic Frontier Foundation, 'Unintended Consequences: Twelve Years Under the DMCA' (March 2010), at www.eff.org/wp/unintended-consequences-under-dmca.

30 See Dale Clapperton and Stephen Corones, 'Locking in Customers, Locking out Competitors: Anti-Circumvention Laws in Australia and Their Potential Effect on Competition in High Technology Markets' (2006) 30(3) *Melbourne University Law Review* 657–715.

31 Cf. the more liberal TPM laws adopted in countries such as New Zealand (Copyright Act 1994, sections 226–226E (introduced in 2008)); Switzerland (Federal Act of October 9, 1992 on Copyright and Related Rights, Article 39a (introduced in 2008)) and India (Copyright Act 1957, section 65A (introduced in 2012)). These might be compared with the more restrictive Canadian approach introduced in 2012 (Copyright Act (RSC, 1985, c. C-42), sections 41–41.21), drafted at the time Canada was negotiating ACTA: for criticism, see Elizabeth F. Judge and Saleh Al-Sharieh, 'Join the Club: The Implications of the *Anti-Counterfeiting Trade Agreement*'s Enforcement Measures for Canadian Copyright Law' (2012) 49(3) *Alberta Law Review* 677–744, at 734–9.

WCT and WPPT in any meaningful manner.[32] However, as with the issue of copyright term, it is probable that TRIPS-Plus provisions on TPMs, in a form similar to the DMCA provisions, will continue to be a key feature of future PTAs.[33]

B. *Geographical indications*

The TRIPS Agreement imposes complex obligations on WTO Members to protect other Members' GIs, defined in Article 22.1 as 'indications which identify a good as originating in the territory of a Member, or a region or locality in that territory, where a given quality, reputation or other characteristic of the good is essentially attributable to its geographical origin'. These obligations include providing the legal means to prevent misleading uses of GIs or uses that constitute unfair competition (Article 22.2), with a higher standard of protection that does *not* turn on consumer confusion required in respect of GIs for wines and spirits (Article 23.1). They also involve providing for the refusal or invalidation of the registration of a trademark that contains or consists of another Member's GI with respect to goods not originating in the territory indicated, provided (in the case of non-wine or spirit GIs only) that the use of the trademark would mislead the public as to the true place of origin of those goods (Articles 22.3 and 23.2). These obligations are, however, subject to a range of exceptions. For example, a Member is not required to prevent the use of another Member's GI for wines or spirits where the GI has been used in the first Member's territory in respect of goods or services either continuously or in good faith before certain dates (Article 24.4). Nor is a Member under any obligation to protect another's GI where the term has become generic in the first Member's territory (Article 24.6). Further, in implementing GI protection Members must not prejudice the eligibility for or validity of either the registration of or the right to use certain prior trademarks that are identical or similar to GIs (Article 24.5).

A number of recent PTAs contain TRIPS-Plus provisions concerning GIs. Some of these provisions are relatively minor. For example, in a number of European Free Trade Association (EFTA) Agreements, parties are simply required to make protection available for GIs in respect of *services* as well as goods.[34] However, the most noteworthy TRIPS-Plus provisions relating to GIs are those contained in PTAs entered into by the US and by the EC/EU. From the early 1990s, the EC used

---

32 See Robert Burrell and Kimberlee Weatherall, 'Exporting Controversy? Reactions to the Copyright Provisions of the US–Australia Free Trade Agreement: Lessons for US Trade Policy' [2008] *University of Illinois Journal of Law, Technology and Policy* 259–319.

33 WCT-Plus and WPPT-Plus provisions relating to TPMs have been proposed in Article QQ.G.10 of the leaked drafts of the IP Chapter of the TPP (November 2013 and October 2014).

34 See the Convention Establishing EFTA (Vaduz Convention), Annex J, Article 5; and EFTA FTAs with Croatia, Annex VII, Article 3; the Former Yugoslav Republic of Macedonia (FYROM), Annex V, Article 3; Jordan, Annex VI, Article 3; Korea, Annex XIII, Article 5; Lebanon, Annex V, Article 6; Mexico, Annex XXI, Article 3; Morocco, Annex V, Article 3; Singapore, Annex XII, Article 5; and Turkey, Annex XII, Article 3.

TRIPS-Plus provisions in bilateral agreements specifically on trade in wine and/or spirits to secure increased protection amongst certain of its trading partners for European wine and spirit GIs, in particular those that had become generic or semi-generic terms in such countries. More recently, the EU has sought to impose TRIPS-Plus levels of GI protection that apply to all goods in a number of broader PTAs. In contrast, the major aim of the US appears to be to ensure that its PTA partners implement their TRIPS obligations on GIs in a particular manner to ensure that GIs are *not* afforded extra levels of protection or given pre-eminence over trademarks.

Before separately analysing the two approaches taken by the US and the EU in detail, it is necessary to place them in a wider context. Despite the fact that the EU and US are broadly in step on many IP issues, the parties have historically disagreed over the relative importance and proper means of protecting GIs.[35] The EU has long considered the strong protection of European GIs – of which there are several thousand – to be a crucial aspect of its agricultural policy of sustaining the rural European economy. To this end it has established systems specifically regulating the use of GIs for agricultural foodstuffs, wines and spirits.[36] These provide for high levels of protection that exceed TRIPS standards. The US, on the other hand, despite its burgeoning wine industry, has not traditionally sought to promote artisanal and localised production through its rural policies. It thus has relatively few GIs of value in local or international markets and has shown little interest in regulating GIs in the same manner as the EU. This has meant that producers in the US wishing to identify their goods using GIs must, for the most part, rely on trademark laws (e.g., by obtaining certification trademark registration) or consumer protection legislation, with more detailed laws applying in respect of wines and spirits.[37]

Given these domestic attitudes, it is unsurprising that the EU and US have clashed over the international protection of GIs. The incoherence of the GI Section of the TRIPS Agreement, negotiated largely by the EU and the US – in which Members are obliged to provide different levels of protection depending on the goods to which the GI relates and in which various substantive issues were left open for further negotiation – is testament to the deep divisions between the parties on the issue. More recently, the EU has been at the forefront of a campaign at the WTO to increase the scope of protection that Members must afford to GIs. This has involved calling for the higher standard of protection currently applying only to wine and spirit GIs under

---

35 For a comprehensive analysis, see Dev Gangjee, *Relocating the Law of Geographical Indications* (Cambridge: Cambridge University Press, 2012).

36 See Regulation No 1151/2012 of the European Parliament and of the Council of 21 November 2012 on Quality Schemes for Agricultural Products and Foodstuffs [2012] OJ L323/1; Council Regulation (EC) No 479/2008 of 29 April 2008 on the Common Organisation of the Market in Wine [2008] OJ L148/1; Council Regulation (EC) No 110/2008 of 15 January 2008 on the Definition, Description, Presentation, Labelling and the Protection of Geographical Indications of Spirit Drinks [2008] OJ L39/16.

37 See generally Justin Hughes, 'Champagne, Feta, and Bourbon: The Spirited Debate About Geographical Indications' (2006) 58(2) *Hastings Law Journal* 299–386.

Article 23.1 of the TRIPS Agreement to apply to all GIs, and for Members to accept unconditionally a list of forty-one selected European GIs (including such controversial expressions as 'Feta', 'Prosciutto di Parma', 'Champagne' and 'Porto') as nongeneric, protected terms. The EU has also led the call for the establishment of a multilateral register for the notification and registration of GIs that would facilitate the international protection of its own GIs and potentially marginalise the role of the TRIPS Article 24 exceptions.[38] Not only has the US consistently opposed the EU's agenda, but it also initiated WTO dispute settlement proceedings against what was at the time the EC, claiming in part that the EC's domestic laws regulating GIs for agricultural foodstuffs violated its TRIPS obligations.[39] It is arguable that a major aim of the US in bringing such proceedings was to embarrass the EC politically by exposing deficiencies in its GI regime, potentially diminishing its credibility as an advocate for greater international GI protection.[40]

The recent attempts by the EU and the US in their bilateral PTAs to export their particular models of GI protection thus need to be seen as part of an ongoing and larger battle over the scope of GI protection that has been taking place in various international fora.

1. GIs in EC and EU PTAs

The way in which the EC and EU have sought to incorporate GI obligations in their PTAs has taken place in two phases. The first phase (from around 1994 to 2008) involved the EC entering into trade agreements specifically on wine and/or spirits, in which it sought to secure increased protection for its wine and/or spirit GIs in return for granting increased access to European markets for foreign producers. This can be seen in the various agreements on trade in wine and/or spirits into which it entered with Australia,[41] Mexico,[42] South Africa,[43] Switzerland,[44]

---

38 See Michael Handler, 'Rethinking GI Extension' in Dev Gangjee (ed.), *Research Handbook on Intellectual Property and Geographical Indications* (Cheltenham, UK: Edward Elgar, forthcoming 2016).

39 See Panel Report, *EC–Trademarks and GIs (US)*.

40 See Michael Handler, 'The WTO Geographical Indications Dispute' (2006) 69(1) *Modern Law Review* 70–80.

41 Agreement between Australia and the European Community on trade in wine [1994] OJ L86/94 ('EC–Australia Wine Agreement 1994'), superseded by the Agreement between the European Community and Australia on Trade in Wine [2009] OJ L28/3 ('EC–Australia Wine Agreement 2008'). For consideration of the latter agreement, see Vicki Waye, 'Wine Market Reform: A Tale of Two Markets and Their Legal Interaction' (2010) 29(2) *University of Queensland Law Journal* 211–44.

42 Agreement between the European Community and the United Mexican States on the mutual recognition and protection of designations for spirit drinks [1997] OJ L152/16 ('EC–Mexico Spirits Agreement').

43 Agreement between the European Community and the Republic of South Africa on trade in wines [2002] OJ L28/4 ('EC–South Africa Wine Agreement'); Agreement between the European Community and the Republic of South Africa on trade in spirits [2002] OJ L28/113 ('EC–South Africa Spirits Agreement').

44 Agreement between the European Community and the Swiss Confederation on trade in agricultural products [2002] OJ L114/132, Annex 7 ('EC–Switzerland Wine Agreement') and Annex 8 ('EC–Switzerland Spirits Agreement').

Chile[45] and Canada,[46] each containing detailed provisions on the recognition and protection of certain listed wine and/or spirit GIs. The EC and US also entered into an Agreement on trade in wine[47] which, although not dealing specifically with the issue of GIs, is significant for its requirements relating to the protection of 'names of origin' for wines, and thus merits separate consideration. The second phase (from around 2008) has involved the EU entering into far-reaching, general PTAs that contain IP chapters, or a series of IP-focused provisions, which impose obligations on the EU's partner countries to impose TRIPS-Plus levels of protection for all GIs (not merely GIs for wine and/or spirits).

Looking at PTAs in the first phase, similar TRIPS-Plus provisions are contained in the agreements with each of the first-mentioned countries in the paragraph above. Three provisions are worthy of particular discussion.

First, in each agreement the parties agree to provide either reciprocal or mutual protection to each other's listed GIs.[48] Unsurprisingly, the vast majority of the GIs required to be protected are European. Under the EC–Mexico Spirits Agreement, for example, the EC is only obliged to protect 'Tequila', 'Mezcal', 'Sotol' and 'Charanda', whereas Mexico is required to protect around 200 European terms.[49] More significant is that the protection under these agreements is to happen *automatically*. There is no scope for the protecting party to determine whether the GI in question is required to be protected under the TRIPS Agreement, and the protecting party must recognise the examination procedure of the other's authorities as sufficient for its domestic purposes.[50] In addition, most agreements impose obligations as to the levels of protection that are to be afforded to the listed GIs. Apart from the EC–Canada Wine and Spirits Agreement, each agreement provides that a party's GIs must not be

---

45 Agreement establishing an association between the European Community and its Member States, of the one part, and the Republic of Chile, of the other part [2002] OJ L352/1, Annex V: Agreement on trade in wines ('EC–Chile Wine Agreement') and Annex VI: Agreement on trade in spirit drinks and aromatised drinks ('EC–Chile Spirits Agreement').

46 Agreement between the European Community and Canada on trade in wines and spirit drinks [2004] OJ L35/3 ('EC–Canada Wine and Spirits Agreement').

47 Agreement between the European Community and the United States of America on trade in wine [2006] OJ L87/2 ('EC–US Wine Agreement').

48 EC–Australia Wine Agreement 1994, Article 6.1; EC–Mexico Spirits Agreement, Article 4.3; EC–South Africa Wine Agreement, Article 7.1; EC–South Africa Spirits Agreement, Article 5.1; EC–Switzerland Wine Agreement, Article 5.1; EC–Switzerland Spirits Agreement, Article 5.3; EC–Chile Wine Agreement, Article 5.1; EC–Chile Spirits Agreement, Article 5.1; EC–Canada Wine and Spirits Agreement, Articles 10.1, 11.1, 14.1 and 15.1; and EC–Australia Wine Agreement 2008, Article 13.2.

49 See EC–Mexico Spirits Agreement, Annexes I and II (as modified by Commission Decision 2004/785/EC of 26 October 2004 on the conclusion of an Agreement in the form of an exchange of letters between the European Community and the United Mexican States concerning amendments to Annex II of the Agreement between the European Community and the United Mexican States on the mutual recognition and protection of designations for spirit drinks [2004] OJ L346/28).

50 See David Vivas-Eugui and Christophe Spennemann, 'The Treatment of Geographical Indications in Recent Regional and Bilateral Free Trade Agreements', in Meir Perez Pugatch (ed.), *The Intellectual Property Debate: Perspectives from Law, Economics and Political Economy* (Cheltenham, UK: Edward Elgar, 2006), pp. 305–44, at pp. 315–16.

used in the other party other than under the conditions laid down in the laws and regulations of the *first* party.[51]

The above provisions alter the TRIPS Agreement standards, under which parties are free to determine under their own laws whether the sign in question satisfies the Article 22.1 definition of a GI, and are only obliged under Article 23.1 to provide the 'legal means' to prevent the misuse of the wine or spirit GI (which could well differ from the means used in the originating country). The coercive, detailed approach taken in these agreements is also highly unusual. It is rare in any international agreement dealing with IP to see requirements imposing obligations to provide automatic protection for specified examples of IP (i.e., listed names), as distinct from provisions harmonising the legal standards of the parties that would facilitate such protection.[52] Such an approach demonstrates the importance to Europe of securing as high a level of protection as possible for its wine and spirit GIs in international markets.

Second, and directly related to the first point, the EC agreements do not allow the parties to take advantage of certain key exceptions under the TRIPS Agreement. In fact, only a few exceptions are specifically preserved. All agreements allow the parties to provide dual protection for homonymous GIs (in line with Articles 23.3 and 22.4 of the TRIPS Agreement)[53] and most allow the maintenance of an exception permitting non-misleading use of a trader's personal name (Article 24.8).[54] Some also state that the parties are not obliged to protect a GI that ceases to be protected in its country of origin or has fallen into disuse in that country (Article 24.9).[55] But other TRIPS exceptions are excluded. At times this is done explicitly, such as in the

---

51 EC–Australia Wine Agreement 1994, Articles 7.2–7.3; EC–Mexico Spirits Agreement, Articles 4.1–4.2; EC–South Africa Wine Agreement, Article 7.2; EC–South Africa Spirits Agreement, Article 5.2; EC–Switzerland Wine Agreement, Article 5.2; EC–Switzerland Spirits Agreement, Articles 5.1–5.2; EC–Chile Wine Agreement, Article 5.2; EC–Chile Spirits Agreement, Article 5.2; and EC–Australia Wine Agreement 2008, Article 13.1.

52 However, this approach is taken in other PTAs not involving the EC where countries consider that they have particular indications worth protecting in foreign markets: see, e.g., Canada–Chile FTA, Annex C–11 (under which Chile is required to protect the GI 'Canadian whisky' in return for Canada protecting the Chilean wine GI 'Chilean pisco'); Chile–China FTA, Article 10 and Annexes 2A and 2B (under which Chile is required to protect 'Shaoxing wine' and 'Anxi Tieguanyin' in return for China protecting 'Chilean pisco'); and Korea–Chile FTA, Article 16.4 and Annexes 16.4.3–16.4.4.

53 EC–Australia Wine Agreement 1994, Article 6.5; EC–Mexico Spirits Agreement, Article 6; EC–South Africa Wine Agreement, Articles 7.4–7.5; EC–South Africa Spirits Agreement, Articles 5.4–5.5; EC–Switzerland Wine Agreement, Article 5.4; EC–Switzerland Spirits Agreement, Article 7; EC–Chile Wine Agreement, Articles 5.4–5.5; EC–Chile Spirits Agreement, Articles 5.4–5.5; EC–Canada Wine and Spirits Agreement, Article 34.1; and EC–Australia Wine Agreement 2008, Articles 13.6–13.7.

54 EC–Australia Wine Agreement 1994, Article 6.6; EC–Mexico Spirits Agreement, Article 7; EC–South Africa Wine Agreement, Article 7.6; EC–South Africa Spirits Agreement, Article 5.6; EC–Switzerland Spirits Agreement, Article 8; EC–Chile Wine Agreement, Article 5.6; EC–Chile Spirits Agreement, Article 5.6; EC–Canada Wine and Spirits Agreement, Article 34.2; and EC–Australia Wine Agreement 2008, Article 13.8.

55 EC–Australia Wine Agreement 1994, Article 6.7; EC–Mexico Spirits Agreement, Article 8; EC–South Africa Wine Agreement, Article 7.7; EC–South Africa Spirits Agreement, Article 5.7; EC–Switzerland

EC–Mexico Spirits Agreement and the two EC–Switzerland Agreements, each of which contain express waivers of Articles 24.4–24.7 of the TRIPS Agreement.[56] In other agreements, this exclusion is implicit in the fact that each party is obliged to provide exclusive protection to the listed GIs of the other.[57]

The significance of the EC's approach to the TRIPS exceptions is that it obliges the other parties to its agreements to protect terms that may have become generic wine or spirit descriptions in those countries (such as champagne, sherry and port), and to cancel the registration of trademarks identical with or similar to protected GIs, even if such rights were acquired before the coming into force of the TRIPS Agreement in that country. Such provisions have, however, proven to be highly contentious. For example, negotiations between the EC and South Africa in the late 1990s over the much larger Trade, Development and Cooperation Agreement almost broke down over the EC's insistence that South Africa cease using certain generic wine and spirit denominations.[58] In this regard, it is worth noting that some of the EC agreements contain detailed provisions allowing for the gradual phasing out of generic names in non-EC countries. Thus, under the EC–South Africa Agreements, South Africa is required to phase out the domestic and export use of such names as 'Sherry' and 'Ouzo',[59] while the EC–Australia Wine Agreement 2008 required the phasing out by Australian producers of 'burgundy', 'chablis', 'champagne', 'graves', 'manzanilla', 'marsala', 'moselle', 'port', 'sauterne', 'sherry' and 'white burgundy' by 1 September 2011, and 'tokay' by 1 September 2020.[60] In the area of trademarks, the EC–Chile Agreements list various registered Chilean trademarks for names such as 'Moselle' and 'La Rioja' that must be cancelled within particular periods of time.[61]

Third, EC Wine Agreements with Australia, Chile and Switzerland go further than requiring the protection of GIs in that they impose obligations to protect certain listed 'traditional expressions'. These are names legally recognised in a country that are traditionally used to refer to the production or ageing method, or the quality, colour or other traditional feature, of wine originating from that country. As with GIs, most of the traditional expressions to be protected are European – examples contained in these agreements include common words such as 'ruby', 'tawny',

Spirits Agreement, Article 9; and EC–Canada Wine and Spirits Agreement, Article 34.2; and EC–Australia Wine Agreement 2008, Article 13.9.

56 EC–Mexico Spirits Agreement, Article 4.4; EC–Switzerland Wine Agreement, Article 5.7; and EC–Switzerland Spirits Agreement, Article 5.4.

57 Cf. Articles 34.2–34.3 of the EC–Canada Wine and Spirits Agreement, which preserve some aspects of the TRIPS Articles 24.5 and 24.6 exceptions.

58 Emily Craven and Charles Mather, 'Geographical Indications and the South Africa–European Union Free Trade Agreement' (2001) 33(3) *Area* 312–20, at 313–5.

59 EC–South Africa Wine Agreement, Article 25; and EC–South Africa Spirits Agreement, Article 23.

60 EC–Australia Wine Agreement 2008, Article 15.

61 EC–Chile Wine Agreement, Article 7 and Appendix VI; and EC–Chile Spirits Agreement, Article 7 and Appendix VI (see also Article 8.4, which provides that certain trademarks may not be used to prevent the use of protected GIs).

'vintage' and 'superior'. Traditional expressions are not recognised as a form of intellectual property under the TRIPS Agreement and the requirement that non-EC countries protect European traditional expressions is a potentially onerous one in that it deprives traders in those countries of the ability to use ordinary, descriptive terms that their consumers would not associate with a particular country's wines or spirits.[62] While the EC has stated in WTO negotiations that it is not seeking to have traditional expressions included in its proposed multilateral GI register,[63] it will be worth seeing whether it seeks increasingly to protect these potentially valuable terms in future bilateral agreements.

The EC–US Wine Agreement is different from the above-mentioned agreements. It is the product of a longstanding difference of opinion between the parties over, amongst other things, whether the US provides adequate legal protection for European wine GIs. Under US law a geographical term that is also understood in the US to describe a class of wine can be designated as 'semi-generic'. Such a term may be used on wine originating other than in the geographical region suggested by the term, provided that the true place of origin is indicated. Designated semi-generic terms in the US include famous European GIs such as 'burgundy', 'champagne', 'chianti', 'madeira', 'port' and 'sherry'.[64] The key feature of the EC–US Wine Agreement that goes much of the way to resolving the conflict between the parties over this issue is the requirement under Article 6.1 for the US to seek to change the legal status of the terms currently designated as semi-generic and to restrict the use of such terms on wine labels solely to wine originating in the EC. This is subject to a 'grandfathering' provision in Article 6.2, which allows for the continued use of semi-generic names where used on wine labels bearing a certified brand name where the certification was issued before 10 March 2006.[65] In addition, under Article 7, certain listed European and US 'names of origin' are only to be used to designate wines with those geographical origins. In return for agreeing to protect or phase out the use of certain European geographical names, the US has secured more stable access to EC markets for wines made in accordance with practices not recognised in the EC.[66]

Interestingly, the Agreement refers only to 'terms' and 'names of origin', and Article 12.4 states that the names to be protected 'are not necessarily considered, nor excluded from being considered, geographical indications' under either US or EC

---

62 Vicki C. Waye, 'Assessing Multilateral vs Bilateral Agreements and Geographic Indications Through International Food and Wine' (2005) 14(2) *Currents: International Trade Law Journal* 56–68, at 60–1.

63 WTO Document TN/IP/M/5 (28 April 2003), paras. 44 and 49.

64 See 26 USC §5388(c); 27 CFR §4.24(b) (2006). See further Leigh A. Lindquist, 'champagne or Champagne? An Examination of US Failure to Comply with the Geographical Provisions of the TRIPS Agreement' (1999) 27(2) *Georgia Journal of International and Comparative Law* 309–44, at 326–9.

65 For comment, see Brian Rose, 'No More Whining about Geographical Indications: Assessing the 2005 Agreement between the United States and the European Community on the Trade in Wine' (2007) 29(3) *Houston Journal of International Law* 731–70, at 765.

66 See EC–US Wine Agreement, Article 4.2.

law. Article 12.1(a) further provides that nothing in the Agreement shall 'affect the rights and obligations of the Parties under the WTO Agreement'. Notwithstanding this, it is hard to see how the EC–US Wine Agreement could be interpreted other than to impose conditions on the US's treatment of EC GIs, and in this light it can be said to impact on and extend the US's TRIPS obligations. Further, it will be interesting to see whether the consensus reached on this issue by the two major antagonists over the international protection of GIs will have any impact on negotiations for the establishment of the multilateral GI register for wines and spirits that are currently stalled at the WTO.[67]

Turning to the second phase of European PTAs, the EU's more recent energies have been focused on securing a TRIPS-Plus level of protection for GIs for all products in foreign markets. The first manifestation of this was in a 2008 Economic Partnership Agreement with a bloc of Caribbean countries known as the CARIFORUM States.[68] Under Article 145B, the latter group agreed to afford under their domestic laws the high level of protection contained in Article 23 of the TRIPS Agreement (which, under the TRIPS Agreement, is only required to be provided in relation to GIs for wine and spirits) to GIs for all goods.[69] More recently, in the EU–Korea FTA, the Republic of Korea agreed to provide the Article 23 level of protection to a large number of listed European GIs for agricultural foodstuffs. An important consequence of this is that the Republic of Korea has agreed to protect terms that in many parts of the world are understood as generic descriptors. For example, producers of the generic cheese varieties 'feta' and 'parmesan' in third-party countries (such as the US) will be forced to rebrand their goods for export to the South Korean market, where such terms are required to be protected as European GIs.[70] This raises questions as to whether the countries that suffer loss of market access in such circumstances might be entitled to compensation.[71]

Not all recent EU PTAs contain such high level obligations. In the EU's 2012 Trade Agreement with Peru and Colombia, the latter countries are required only to prevent use that 'exploits the reputation of the geographical indication' and 'non-authorised use of geographical indications other than those identifying wines, aromatized wines or spirits drinks *that creates confusion*, including even in cases where the name is accompanied by indications such as style, type, imitation and

---

67 Timothy E. Josling, 'The War on *Terroir*: Geographical Indications as a Transatlantic Trade Conflict' (2006) 57(3) *Journal of Agricultural Economics* 337–63, at 355.
68 EC–CARIFORUM EPA. The relevant countries are Antigua and Barbuda, the Bahamas, Barbados, Belize, Dominica, the Dominican Republic, Grenada, Guyana, Haiti, Jamaica, Saint Kitts and Nevis, Saint Lucia, Saint Vincent and the Grenadines, Suriname and Trinidad and Tobago.
69 But note Article 145C, which allows such countries to apply a 'genericism' exception.
70 EU–Korea FTA, Articles 10.18.4, 10.21.1 and Annex 10-A.
71 Crina Viju, May T. Yeung and William A. Kerr, 'Geographical Indications, Conflicted Preferential Agreements, and Market Access' (2013) 16(2) *Journal of International Economic Law* 409–37.

other similar that creates confusion to the consumer',[72] which falls short of the Article 23 standard.[73] However, it is likely that the EU will seek expanded GI protection in future PTAs. For example, the recently negotiated Comprehensive Economic and Trade Agreement (CETA) between the EU and Canada contains detailed, fine-grained GI provisions, requiring Canada to raise its domestic levels of GI protection and protect certain listed EU GIs (Article 22.7.4). Interestingly, Canada has been able to carve out some degree of protection for its traders who are currently using, or might wish to use, such terms for more descriptive purposes. For example, the parties have agreed in principle that:

- some EU GIs will be protected in Canada, but such protection will not impact on the ability of Canadian producers to use specified, commonly employed terms, such as 'Valencia orange', 'Black Forest ham', 'Tiroler bacon', 'Parmesan', 'Bavarian beer' and 'Munich beer' (Article 22.7.11);
- the cheese names 'asiago', 'feta', 'fontina', 'gorgonzola' and 'munster' will be protected as GIs, but existing Canadian producers will be able to continue to use such terms as generic product descriptors, and future traders will be able to use such terms if accompanied by qualifiers such as 'type' or 'style' (Articles 22.7.6.1– 22.7.6.2); and
- certain EU GIs, such as 'noix de Grenoble' and 'Budějovické', will not be protected in Canada at all.[74]

The agreement also contains further provisions dealing with the relationship between terms recognised as GIs in the EU but which are protected as trademarks in Canada.[75]

2. GIs in US PTAs

Separate from its specific dealings with the EC on wine, the US has included detailed GI provisions in most of its recent PTAs. Unlike Europe, however, this has not been done primarily for the benefit of US producers wishing to secure stronger protection

---

72 EU–Colombia and Peru Trade Agreement, Article 210.1(a) and (b) (emphasis added).

73 Cf. Frederick M. Abbott, 'Trade Costs and Shadow Benefits: EU Economic Partnership Agreements as Models for Progressive Development of International IP Law' in Josef Drexl, Henning Grosse Ruse-Khan and Souheir Nadde-Phlix (eds.), *EU Bilateral Trade Agreements and Intellectual Property: For Better or Worse?* (Heidelberg: Springer, 2014), pp. 159–70, at p. 166.

74 See Canadian Government, 'Technical Summary of Final Negotiated Outcomes, Canada–European Union Comprehensive Economic and Trade Agreement: Agreement-in-Principle' (18 October 2013), at pp. 20–21, at http://international.gc.ca/trade-agreements-accords-commerciaux/agr-acc/ceta-aecg/understanding-comprendre/technical-technique.aspx?lang=eng.

75 See, e.g., European Commission, 'Facts and Figures of the EU–Canada Free Trade Deal', MEMO/13/1911, Brussels (18 October 2013) ('thanks to the agreement, some prominent EU GIs such as Prosciutto di Parma . . . will finally be authorised to use their name when sold in Canada, which [they have been unable to do] for more than 20 years' due to the existence of Canadian parties having trademark rights over "Parma"). For background, see Dev Gangjee, 'Quibbling Siblings: Conflicts Between Trademarks and Geographical Indications' (2007) 82(3) *Chicago-Kent Law Review* 1253–91, at 1270–6.

for their GIs in foreign countries.[76] Rather, the goal of the US appears to be to encourage other countries to adopt a particular model of protection of GIs, namely through trademark law. The hoped-for result is that such countries will not provide special treatment to GIs and, in particular, will not give GIs primacy over traditional trademarks in the event of any conflict between the two. While such parties remain free under these PTAs to implement *sui generis* systems regulating GIs that afford high levels of protection, along the lines of the European model, this is potentially made more difficult in light of the fact that they are obliged to make trademark protection available for GIs. The US approach can therefore be seen as a tactic being employed as part of its broader strategy of resisting European attempts to have its model of GI protection become a *de facto* global standard.

We now turn to the GI provisions of US PTAs. Despite some differences in structure there is a strong degree of consistency between them in terms of substance. For a start, each PTA makes clear that GIs may be protected as trademarks. In the US–Jordan FTA (Article 4.6), US–Singapore FTA (Article 16.2.1), US–Chile FTA (Article 17.2.1), AUSFTA (Article 17.2.1), CAFTA–DR–US (Article 15.2.1), KORUS FTA (Article 18.2.2) and the US–Panama TPA (Article 15.2.1), it is explicitly stated that the parties are to provide that trademarks may include GIs. FTAs with Bahrain (Article 14.2.2), Oman (Article 15.2.2) and Colombia (Article 16.2.2) and the TPA with Peru (Article 16.2.2) contain a more detailed requirement that GIs may constitute certification or collective marks (themselves a subset of trademarks).[77] In addition, a number of PTAs provide that GIs may consist of much the same subject matter as trademarks, namely words (including personal and geographic names), as well as letters, numerals, figurative elements and colours (including single colours).[78]

The approach of conflating GI and trademark protection has been criticised as 'undermining the intention of the drafters of the TRIPS Agreement, which specifically established two different categories of IPRs'.[79] However, this criticism is misplaced. Not only does it assume that a settled 'intention' of the drafters can be discerned from such a

76 The US has, however, sought specific recognition for the names 'Bourbon Whiskey' and 'Tennessee Whiskey' in the Market Access chapters of some of its PTAs: see US–Chile FTA, Article 3.15.1 (in return for the US recognising 'Pisco Chileano', 'Pajarete' and 'Vino Asoleado': Article 3.15.2); CAFTA–DR–US, Article 3.12.1; US–Peru TPA, Article 2.12.1 (in return for the US recognising 'Pisco Perú': Article 2.12.2); KORUS FTA, Article 2.13.1 (in return for the US recognising 'Andong Soju' and 'Gyeongju Beopju': Article 2.13.2); US–Colombia FTA, Article 2.12.1; and US–Panama TPA, Article 3.12.1. See also exchange of side letters between Mark Vaile, Australian Minister for Trade, and Robert B. Zoellick, USTR, 18 May 2004, at www.ustr.gov/assets/Trade_Agreements/Bilateral/Australia_PTA/Final_Text/asset_upload_file778_3889.pdf.
77 While the US–Morocco FTA does not contain such an explicit statement, it is clear that GIs may be protected as trademarks from Article 15.2.5, which states that '[e]ach Party may provide limited exceptions to the rights conferred by a trademark, including a geographical indication'.
78 See US–Chile FTA, Article 17.4.1; AUSFTA, Article 17.2.1, n. 17-5; US–Morocco FTA, Article 15.3.3; US–Bahrain FTA, Article 14.2.2, n. 4; US–Oman FTA, Article 14.2.2, n. 4; and KORUS FTA, Article 18.2.2, n. 5. See also TRIPS Agreement, Article 16.1.
79 Vivas-Eugui and Spennemann, above n. 50, at p. 327. See also Bernard O'Connor, 'The EC Need Not Be Isolated on GIs' (2007) 29(8) *European Intellectual Property Review* 303–6, at 306.

heavily compromised negotiating process in relation to the GI Section,[80] but it also pays insufficient regard to Article 1.1 of the TRIPS Agreement, which provides that 'Members shall be free to determine the appropriate method of implementing the provisions of this Agreement within their own legal system and practice'. While the US approach might cause a degree of consternation amongst those more familiar with *sui generis* models of GI protection, there is nothing illogical or conceptually problematic about protecting GIs through trademark law. What is more interesting is to explore some of the consequences of requiring countries to adopt this particular model of GI protection.

One noted outcome of the US approach is that it establishes a potentially different set of obstacles for individual traders to overcome in order to secure protection for their GIs compared with those likely to be faced under a *sui generis* system. Some of these obstacles are the result of specific terms of the PTAs which oblige countries to have particular procedures in place relating to applications for GI protection.[81] Others are simply due to the inherent requirements of trademark registration processes. For example, to obtain certification or collective trademark registration for a GI, a party would need to demonstrate that the sign is distinctive. Given that most GIs are geographically descriptive terms and thus not inherently distinctive, acquired distinctiveness would almost invariably need to be established in order to secure registration. Under a *sui generis* system for protecting GIs, no such requirement would be likely to exist.[82] However, the effect of these differences should not be overstated, for it cannot be said that obtaining trademark protection for GIs would necessarily be a more onerous process. For example, under the *sui generis* EU regime a party seeking registration of a GI for an agricultural product needs to comply with a number of detailed procedural and substantive requirements[83] that an applicant for certification or collective trademark registration in, say, the US would not need to satisfy.[84]

A different, and much more significant, consequence of the US approach to GIs in its PTAs is that it encourages countries to prioritise trademarks over GIs in the event of any conflict between them. For example, each PTA obliges countries to grant to owners of registered trademarks the exclusive right to prevent third parties from using in the course of trade identical or similar signs – specifically stated to include GIs – for goods or services related to those in respect of which the trademark is registered, where such use would result in a likelihood of confusion.[85] In addition,

---

80 See UNCTAD–ICTSD, *Resource Book on TRIPS and Development* (New York: Cambridge University Press, 2005), at pp. 279–89.

81 See US–Chile FTA, Articles 17.4.4–17.4.8; AUSFTA, Article 17.2.12; US–Morocco FTA, Article 15.3.1; CAFTA–DR–US, Articles 15.3.2–15.3.6; US–Bahrain FTA, Article 14.2.12; US–Oman FTA, Article 15.2.13; US–Peru TPA, Article 16.3.1; KORUS FTA, Article 18.2.14; US–Colombia FTA, Article 16.3.1; US–Panama TPA, Articles 15.3.2–15.3.6.

82 See Roffe, above n. 6, at p. 41.   83 Regulation No 1151/2012, above n. 36, Articles 7–8.

84 See Hughes, above n. 37, at 309–11.

85 See US–Jordan FTA, Article 4.7; US–Singapore FTA, Article 16.2.2; US–Chile FTA, Article 17.2.4 (with a limitation to 'subsequent' GIs); AUSFTA, Article 17.2.4; US–Morocco FTA, Article 15.2.4; CAFTA–DR–US, Article 15.2.3; Bahrain, Article 14.2.4; Oman, Article 15.2.4; US–Peru TPA, Article 16.2.4;

both the US–Oman FTA (Article 15.2.7) and KORUS FTA (Article 18.2.7) include a provision requiring the prohibition of the use of a mark or GI that is identical or similar to a well-known trademark if the use of the mark or GI is 'likely to cause confusion, or to cause mistake, or to deceive or risk associating the trademark or geographical indication with the owner of the well-known trademark, or constitutes unfair exploitation of the reputation of the trademark'. While these provisions might, in isolation, give trademarks precedence over conflicting GIs, most PTAs allow parties to provide exceptions to trademark owners' rights in line with Article 17.1 of the TRIPS Agreement.[86] In *EC–Trademarks and GIs*, the WTO panel determined, in effect, that a provision of EC law that allowed for the co-existence of a later GI with an earlier trademark was, in the circumstances, a permissible exception under Article 17.1, even if this resulted in a degree of consumer confusion.[87] Parties to US PTAs could potentially allow for similar exceptions, thus limiting the rights of trademark owners in relation to confusingly similar GIs.

A more telling example of the way in which US PTAs prioritise trademarks over GIs is a provision contained in all PTAs after the US–Singapore FTA that requires parties to provide certain grounds for refusing an application for protection or recognition of a GI. Two such grounds are mandated: first, that the GI is likely to cause confusion with a trademark that is the subject of a good-faith pending application or registration; and second, that the GI is likely to cause confusion with a pre-existing trademark, the rights to which have been acquired through use in good faith in that party.[88] The second of these grounds appears to be a straightforward example of the 'first in time, first in right' principle – that is, the first user of the term in question gains priority.[89] However, the first ground is different because it only requires the application for or registration of the trademark to pre-date the application for protection or recognition of the GI.[90] Thus, it may be the case that a first-used GI will be denied recognition if the application for protection of the GI post-dated the application for registration of a confusingly similar trademark. In either situation,

---

KORUS FTA, Article 18.2.4; US–Colombia FTA, Article 16.2.4; and US–Panama TPA, Article 15.2.3. In the FTAs with Morocco, Australia, Oman and Korea, CAFTA–DR–US and the TPA with Panama it is further stipulated that a likelihood of confusion shall be presumed 'in the case of the use of an identical sign, including a geographical indication, for identical goods or services'.

86 See US–Singapore FTA, Article 16.2.3; US–Chile FTA, Article 17.2.5; AUSFTA, Article 17.2.5; US–Morocco FTA, Article 15.2.5; CAFTA–DR–US, Article 15.2.4; US–Bahrain FTA, Article 14.2.5; US–Oman FTA, Article 15.2.5; US–Peru TPA, Article 16.2.5; KORUS FTA, Article 18.2.5; US–Colombia FTA, Article 16.2.5; and US–Panama TPA, Article 15.2.4.

87 Panel Report, *EC–Trademarks and GIs (US)*, paras. 7.644–7.687. See further Handler, above n. 40, at 75–7.

88 See US–Chile FTA, Article 17.4.10; AUSFTA, Article 17.2.12(b)(v); US–Morocco FTA, Article 15.3.2; CAFTA–DR–US, Article 15.3.7; US–Bahrain FTA, Article 14.2.13; US–Oman FTA, Article 15.2.14; US–Peru TPA, Article 16.3.2; KORUS FTA, Article 18.2.15; US–Colombia FTA, Article 16.3.2; and US–Panama TPA, Article 15.3.7.

89 See Stephen Stern, 'The Conflict Between Geographical Indications and Trade Marks or Australia Once Again Heads Down the Garden Path' (2005) 61 *Intellectual Property Forum* 28–37, at 31–2.

90 For an example of this ground in application under Australian law, see *Rothbury Wines Pty Ltd* v. *Tyrell* [2008] ATMOGI 1, at www.austlii.edu.au/au/cases/cth/ATMOGI/2008/1.html.

co-existence of conflicting GIs and trademarks is not contemplated, and trademarks are given primacy over GIs.

In summary, it can be seen that the US is taking a consistent approach to GIs in its PTAs in that it is encouraging other countries to adopt a minimalist, trademark-oriented model of legal regulation of GIs, as distinct from a *sui generis* scheme of protection as exists under EU law.[91] Thus, the divergent approaches currently taken by the EU and US to GIs in the bilateral context (apart from in the Wine Agreement between them), and the fact that these approaches are unlikely to change in the foreseeable future, undoubtedly make common understanding on GIs at the multi-lateral level less likely,[92] short of serious political compromise.[93]

C. Patents

While the EU has essentially been the only WTO Member pushing for increased protection of GIs in its PTAs, the US was for some time the only major WTO Member actively negotiating for TRIPS-Plus provisions in the area of patents, particularly in the area of medicines. In recent years, however, the EU, the European Free Trade Association (EFTA) (Iceland, Liechtenstein, Norway and Switzerland) and others have likewise begun negotiating for TRIPS-Plus patent provisions in PTAs. Thus, while most PTAs either do not directly mention IPRs or simply re-affirm that both parties agree to abide by their TRIPS commitments,[94] PTAs containing provisions relating to patents that have the potential to impact significantly upon the provision of health services in signatory countries are becoming increasingly common. Not surprisingly, several of these provisions remain controversial. Moreover, it is worth noting that while pressure from a Democratic controlled Congress in 2007 led to a pullback from the US on certain provisions and slightly less onerous commitments in a number of areas (including pharmaceutical patents) in PTAs with Peru, Colombia and Panama,[95] the Obama administration appears to have abandoned this position in

91 See also Articles QQ.D.1–QQ.D.14 of the leaked drafts of the IP Chapter of the TPP (November 2013 and October 2014).

92 Vivas-Eugui and Spennemann, above n. 50, at p. 338.

93 The issue is likely to be highly controversial in negotiations over a Transatlantic Trade and Investment Partnership between the US and EU: see 'EU in Food Fight with US over Cheese Names', *Los Angeles Times* (13 March 2014), p. B6 ('[a]s part of trade talks, the EU wants to ban the use of names like Parmesan, feta and Gorgonzola on cheese made in the United States').

94 This ranges from agreements between developing countries (e.g., Armenia–Kazakhstan FTA, Article 11; Bulgaria–Bosnia and Herzegovina FTA, Article 26; and Chile–Costa Rica FTA (no specific provision)), to agreements negotiated between developed and developing nations (e.g., EU–Jordan Association Agreement, Article 27; EFTA–Tunisia FTA, Article 1; and Japan–Mexico EPA, Article 73), to agreements between developed countries (e.g., New Zealand–Singapore Closer Economic Partnership Agreement, Part 9; and Australia–New Zealand Closer Economic Relations Trade Agreement (no specific provision)).

95 See Office of the USTR, *Bipartisan Agreement on Trade Policy: Intellectual Property Provisions*, 11 May 2007, at https://ustr.gov/archive/assets/Document_Library/Fact_Sheets/2007/asset_upload_file945_11283.pdf.

subsequent negotiations. This shift can be seen in the leaked drafts of the IP Chapter of the Trans-Pacific Partnership Agreement (TPP). Despite the fact that the TPP is being negotiated with several developing country partners the US has continuously requested provisions which seek to maximise IP protection to the fullest possible extent.

Owing to space restrictions, this chapter limits the survey of PTAs to patent provisions relating to pharmaceuticals, and even then to only a few select issues.

1. Patent term extensions

The TRIPS Agreement requires Members to grant patent protection for a period of at least twenty years from the date of filing of an application for a patent (Article 33). This is a minimum period of protection and, like other aspects of the TRIPS Agreement, Members can offer more protection if they so desire. While the grant of a patent entitles most patentees the exclusive right to market and distribute their inventions for the entire twenty-year period, the pharmaceutical industry and other medical researchers do not benefit from the entire period of protection. This is due to the fact that in order to protect their potential medical invention from competitors, those wishing to apply for patent protection must do so at a very early stage of basic research, many years before filing an application for regulatory approval. However, as drugs, vaccines and other medicinal products require lengthy testing periods (often lasting between eight and twelve years) to secure regulatory approval before they can be marketed and distributed to the public, pharmaceutical patent holders do not get the full benefit of the twenty-year term.

While the TRIPS Agreement does not oblige Members to 'compensate' patent holders for 'unreasonable' delays in approving a patent or registering the product, several Members do attempt to rebalance the effects of the time delay and 'compensate' the pharmaceutical patentee for any 'unreasonable' delay caused by the national drug regulatory authority in examining an application for registration or a patent office in assessing the application for a patent. Such 'compensation' occurs by extending the patent term for the same amount of time as the 'unreasonable' delay.[96] For example, Article 17.10.2 of the US–Chile FTA states:

> With respect to pharmaceutical products that are subject to a patent, each Party shall:
> (a) make available an extension of the patent term to compensate the patent owner for unreasonable curtailment of the patent term as a result of the marketing approval process.

A similar clause appears in the US–Singapore FTA (Article 18.8.4(a)), AUSFTA (Article 17.10.4), US–Morocco FTA (Article 15.10.3), CAFTA–DR–US (Article 15.10.2), US–Bahrain FTA (Article 14.8.6), US–Oman FTA (Article 15.8.6 (a)) and

---

96 The provisions negotiated by the US reflect domestic American law and have their origins in the US Drug Price Competition and Patent Term Restoration Act of 1984 (Hatch–Waxman Act).

346 MICHAEL HANDLER AND BRYAN MERCURIO

KORUS FTA (Article 18.8.6 (b)). Interestingly, in each FTA, the term 'unreasonable' is not defined.[97]

Such an approach is distinct from that of EFTA, which generally provides a compensatory term of protection for pharmaceuticals (and plant protection products) if more than five years have elapsed between the filing date of the patent application and the date of market authorisation, subject to certain conditions.[98] Likewise, the EU approach provides for a set maximum period of extension. For example, Article 10.35.2 of the EU–Korea FTA provides:

> The Parties shall provide, at the request of the patent owner, for the extension of the duration of the rights conferred by the patent protection to compensate the patent owner for the reduction in the effective patent life as a result of the first authorisation to place the product on their respective markets. The extension of the duration of the rights conferred by the patent protection may not exceed five years.

A similar provision is found in Article 11.31 of the draft EU–Singapore FTA. Interestingly, while the provision requires the parties to 'make available an extension of the duration of the rights conferred by the patent protection to compensate the patent owner for the reduction in the effective patent life as a result of the administrative marketing approval process ... [that] may not exceed five years', footnote 26 also explicitly obliges Singapore to protect 'substances for diagnosis or testing and authorised as a medicinal product'.

With respect to 'unreasonable' delays in the issuance of a patent, US PTAs provide for an additional period of patent protection, with the term 'unreasonable' being defined in the relevant agreement. For example, Article 17.9.6 of the US–Chile FTA states:

> Each Party *shall* provide for the adjustment of the term of a patent, at the request of the patent owner, to compensate for unreasonable delays that occur in granting the patent. For the purposes of this paragraph, an unreasonable delay shall be understood to include a delay in the issuance of the patent of more than five years from the date of filing of the application in the Party, or three years after a request for examination of the application has been made, whichever is later, provided that periods of time attributable to actions of the patent applicant need not be included in the determination of such delays.[99]

---

97 In the KORUS FTA, however, Article 18.8.6(b), n. 21 limits the patent term extension to new pharmaceutical products only if the drug 'at least contains a new chemical entity that has not been previously approved as a pharmaceutical product in the territory of the Party'.

98 See, e.g., EFTA FTAs with Albania (Annex V, Article 4), Montenegro (Annex VI, Article 5) and Ukraine (Annex XIII, Article 4). Curiously, Article 117.6(c) of the Japan–Switzerland FTA provides differing levels of protection for each of the parties, with additional protection being a maximum of five years for Japan and a maximum of 'at least five years' for Switzerland.

99 Emphasis added. See also KORUS FTA, Article 18.8.6(a); and CAFTA–DR–US, Article 15.9.6.

Other US PTAs have similar provisions, with the only variation being the number of years considered 'unreasonable'. For example, the US–Singapore FTA (Article 16.7.7), AUSFTA (Article 17.9.8), US–Morocco FTA (Article 15.9.7), US–Bahrain FTA (Article 14.8.6) and US–Oman FTA (Article 15.8.6(a)) refer to four years from filing and two years from a request for examination, respectively, while the later US–Colombia FTA (Article 16.9.6 (b)), US–Peru TPA (Article 16.9.6(b)) and US–Panama TPA (Article 15.9.6(b)) are slightly more permissive and refer to five and three years, respectively. The subsequently negotiated KORUS FTA (Article 18.8.6(a)) deems an unreasonable delay to be four and three years, respectively. It has been reported that the US has made a similar request in the ongoing TPP negotiations. Neither the EU nor EFTA has sought to provide for an additional period of patent protection due to delays in the issuance of the patent in recent PTAs.

The aforementioned agreement between the Democratic Party and the Bush Administration in 2007 altered the standard language used in US agreements to take into account the challenges faced by developing countries. More specifically, the US–Peru TPA (Article 16.9.6), US–Colombia FTA (Article 16.9.6) and US–Panama TPA (Article 15.9.6) modify the requirement that each party '*shall*' provide for the adjustment of the term of a pharmaceutical patent to '*may*', indicating a more flexible approach to the issue.[100] Additionally, the above provisions of these agreements now also state that parties should use their 'best efforts' to process applications expeditiously with a view to avoiding unnecessary delays, and call on both parties to co-operate and provide assistance to meet these objectives.

Finally, it is worth noting that some agreements, such as the US–Singapore FTA (Article 16.7.8), provide for a five-year extension of the patent term when a patent is granted based on the examination conducted in another country.[101] The extension will be awarded when it has also been awarded in the other country. Interestingly, the US–Jordan FTA, while containing the extension provision relating to unreasonable delays resulting from the marketing approval process, does not contain an extension provision relating to unreasonable delays in the issuance of a patent.

These provisions are unlikely to have much impact in the developed world. In fact, as noted above, it is common international practice to grant extensions for delays caused by registration and examination, especially in developed countries. The concern, however, relates to developing countries with scarce economic resources that may take more time in approving the marketability of drugs and processing patent applications. In the case of the former, how long a delay is to be considered 'reasonable' under a PTA with the US? One would imagine it will be answered on a case-by-case basis, but would the issuing country and the US agree on the result (especially if the delay is five or six years)? In relation to delays in the issuance of a

---

100 See Office of the USTR, Statement and *Bipartisan Agreement*, above n. 95. The more permissive term, 'may', is also found in some EFTA PTAs: see, e.g., Article 6.9.5 of the EFTA–Colombia FTA.
101 This provision also appears to be in the proposed US–Andean TPA.

patent, the time lines assist in the determinative process, but can a delay over and above the timeline set out in the various agreements ever be considered 'reasonable'? It does not appear so.

The extra years added to a patent may also have serious consequences for public health in poorer developing countries.[102] Poorer countries rely on lower prices generated by generic competition in order to supply their populations with many life-saving drugs. Delays in allowing generic competition could prevent large portions of the population from accessing needed drugs.

It seems entirely sensible to extend patents when 'unreasonable' delay prevents the patent holder from exploiting their invention, and it is easy to imagine abuse from patent offices and regulatory authorities. However, the undefined nature over what is considered 'unreasonable' as it relates to delays caused by the regulatory process and the strict timeline as relating to delays caused by the patent office are both potentially troublesome. Perhaps more worrying is the fact that other countries have now also begun negotiating for patent term extensions in PTAs. With the EU and EFTA now negotiating patent term extensions for delays in the granting of marketing approval in all of their PTAs, the practice and the obligations are likely to become even more common in future.

2. Protection of test data

As discussed in the preceding section, before marketing or distributing a drug the manufacturer must apply for regulatory/marketing approval with a national drug regulatory authority to ensure that the drug is safe, effective and of sufficient quality. The regulatory authority does not undertake clinical trials or otherwise test the drugs; instead, it relies on the clinical trials and other data conducted and submitted by the applicant. When a later applicant (a generic manufacturer) seeks registration of the same drug, it need not re-conduct the same clinical trials but must only submit and prove that the drug it seeks to distribute is of the same quality and therapeutically equivalent to the previously approved drug. This process facilitates the introduction of generic drugs to the market and, without having to conduct any clinical trials, generic manufacturers save resources and can introduce their drug on the market at a reduced rate.

The TRIPS Agreement does not explicitly require WTO Members to provide any period of data exclusivity to an original applicant – that is, it does not explicitly prevent others from using the data of the patent holder in gaining marketing approval. While the interpretation of the TRIPS Agreement on this point is contentious, the wording of Article 39.3 merely states the need to protect 'undisclosed test or other data' from 'unfair commercial use' and 'disclosure', provided that the

---

102 See Ruth Mayne, *Regionalism, Bilateralism, and 'TRIP Plus' Agreements: The Threat to Developing Countries*, UN Human Development Report Office Occasional Paper 2005/18 (2005), at p. 14, at http://hdr.undp.org/en/content/regionalism-bilateralism-and-%E2%80%9Ctrip-plus%E2%80%9D-agreements.

data required 'considerable effort' to generate, that it is undisclosed and that the product involves a 'new chemical entity'.[103] The provision does not dictate how protection should occur, the limit of such protection or a time period for the protection. On the contrary, the text indicates that it is up to the individual Member to determine what constitutes 'unfairness'.[104] In addition, the provision does not define what is meant by a 'new chemical entity'.

Recent US PTAs, however, seek to bring the US's partners into line with US domestic law by preventing the later applicant and the national authority from relying on the clinical studies and data provided by the original applicant when seeking to register the generic version of the drug for a given period of time following the first registration.[105] US PTAs generally seek a five-year period of exclusivity for a new pharmaceutical product (ten years for a new agricultural chemical product). For instance, Article 17.10.1(a) of the AUSFTA reads:

> If a Party requires, as a condition of approving the marketing of a new pharmaceutical product, the submission of undisclosed test or other data concerning safety or efficacy of the product, the Party shall not permit third persons, without the consent of the person who provided such information, to market a same or similar product on the basis of (1) such information or (2) the approval granted to the person who submitted such information for at least five years from the date of marketing approval in the Party.

Other US FTAs, such as those with Singapore (Article 16.8.1), Bahrain (Article 14.9.1) and Oman (Article 15.9.1), and CAFTA–DR–US (Article 15.10.1), contain similar provisions. Of note, however, is that some US PTAs confine data exclusivity protection to pharmaceutical products utilising new chemical entities. This can be seen in the US–Chile FTA (Article 17.10.1), US–Morocco FTA (Article 15.10.1) and KORUS FTA (Article 18.9.1). That being said, the KORUS FTA adds a further twist to the protection of test data by differentiating between pharmaceutical products containing a new chemical entity that has been earlier approved for marketing in another pharmaceutical product and drugs that do not contain a previously approved chemical entity. In the former, data exclusivity term is limited to three years from the date of obtaining marketing authorisation (Article 18.9.2(a)), whereas

---

103 Commentators such as Carlos Correa strongly assert that Article 39.3 is not a limit on generic manu-facturers, but rather a requirement that, when data has been submitted to the regulatory agency, it must be protected against 'unfair commercial use': see Carlos M. Correa, *Protection of Data Submitted for the Registration of Pharmaceuticals: Implementing the Standards of the TRIPS Agreement* (Geneva: SADAG, 2002), at www.who.int/medicines/areas/policy/protection_of_data.pdf.

104 Indeed, during TRIPS negotiations, negotiators rejected the option to include stronger 'data exclusivity' provisions, as originally proposed by the US: see UNCTAD–ICTSD, above n. 80, at pp. 522–6.

105 See Jayashree Watal, *Intellectual Property Rights in the WTO and Developing Countries* (Oxford: Oxford University Press, 2001), at p. 200. US FTAs with Singapore, Article 16.7.5; Chile, Article 17.9.4; Morocco, Article 15.9.6; and Bahrain, Article 14.8.5; and CAFTA–DR–US, Article 19.5.3 also limit the availability of data to after the expiry of the patent, and if the party permits exportation, the product shall only be exported outside the territory of that party for purposes of marketing approval requirements of that party.

in the latter a five-year term of protection applies (Article 18.9.1(c)). The exceptions to standard US practice regarding test data are in the PTAs with Peru, Colombia and Panama, which provide not for a set period of protection but only for a 'reasonable period' of time.

Some FTAs negotiated by the EU and EFTA adopt the same five-year standard as seen in most US PTAs (e.g., EU–Korea FTA, Article 10.36; EFTA–Colombia FTA, Article 6.11.2). However, the more recent EFTA FTAs extend data exclusivity protection to eight years for pharmaceutical products. This is the case with FTAs with Hong Kong (Annex XII, Article 4.2), Montenegro (Annex VI, Article 6.2) and Serbia (Annex VI, Article 5.2). That being said, other EFTA FTAs do not state a set period of protection but instead apply a cost-sharing or compensatory liability scheme. For example, Annex XIII, Article 3 of the EFTA–Korea FTA states:

> The Parties shall prevent applicants for marketing approval for pharmaceutical and agricultural chemical products from relying on undisclosed test or other undisclosed data, the origination of which involves a considerable effort, submitted by the first applicant to the competent authority for marketing approval for pharmaceutical and agricultural chemical products, utilizing new chemical entities, for an *adequate number of years* from the date of approval, except where approval is sought for original products. *Any party may instead allow in their national legislation applicants to rely on such data if the first applicant is adequately compensated.*[106]

Moreover, certain agreements contain an additional provision which keeps the data exclusivity period intact even after the expiration of the patent. Thus, while provisions requiring a period of data exclusivity normally operate concurrently with the patent period of the pharmaceutical, such provisions implicitly add a new form of TRIPS-Plus protection by explicitly allowing the period of data exclusivity to continue even if patents covering a particular pharmaceutical expire. For instance, Article 17.10.3 of the AUSFTA states:

> When a product is subject to a system of marketing approval pursuant to Article 17.10.1 or 17.10.2 as applicable and is also subject to a patent in the territory of that Party, the Party shall not alter the term of protection that it provides pursuant to Article 17.10.1 and 17.10.2 in the event that the patent protection terminates on a date earlier than the end of the term of protection specified in Article 17.10.1 and 17.10.2, as applicable.

This is also the case in US FTAs with Singapore (Article 16.8.1), Morocco (15.10.1, note 11), Oman (Article 15.9.3) and the KORUS FTA (Article 18.9.4). Again, the amended language in PTAs with Peru, Colombia and Panama alters the general data exclusivity provision for a country that relies on the US Food and Drug

---

106 Emphasis added. See also Article IV, Annex V of the EFTA–Lebanon FTA, which grants a period 'of at least six years [protection], except where approval is sought for original products, *or unless the first applicant is adequately compensated*' (emphasis added).

Administration for marketing approval and grants approval within six months of a US firm's application. In such a circumstance, the period of exclusivity required to be maintained would run 'concurrent' with that in the US, meaning that, no matter when the test data is registered in the PTA-partner country, the exclusivity period expires at the time it would in the US.[107] Moreover, these agreements also contain an exception to the data exclusivity provision for measures to protect public health in accordance with the Doha Declaration and subsequent implementing protocols. The latter exception also appears in the KORUS FTA.[108]

As a result of provisions requiring the protection of test data, generic manufacturers wishing to market and distribute a generic whilst the period of data exclusivity is in force must conduct their own clinical trials and submit their own findings to the national authority. Such an approach is troublesome, not least because conducting tests and generating clinical data is extremely expensive (sometimes costing into the tens of millions of dollars).[109] The generic industry will find it difficult to implement such onerous requirements, and therefore from a public health perspective, this requirement is difficult to justify.[110] Even if generic manufacturers were able to generate this data, the cost of the resulting drugs produced would rise considerably as well as delay the introduction of the generic into the marketplace. Moreover, such duplication of testing could be viewed as unethical, as it simply repeats the testing and clinical trials where safety and efficacy have already been determined.[111]

Even more, some US regional PTAs include provisions which apply a period of data exclusivity from the approval date of another country even if the manufacturer has not sought to register the drug in that particular country.[112] In such a circumstance, the generic manufacturer would still be prohibited from relying on the data for a certain time period, with the end result being that the country does not have access to that particular drug until the expiration of the data exclusivity period.

Several US PTAs also effectively prohibit generic manufacturers from using evidence of registration of the originator drug in another country to prove the safety and efficacy of their version. The only condition that can be imposed on the originator is to require that marketing approval be sought within five years of registering the

---

107 See Office of the USTR, Statement and *Bipartisan Agreement*, above n. 95.
108 KORUS FTA, Article 18.9.3.
109 Ravikant Bhardwaj, K. D. Raju and M. Padmavati, 'The Impact of Patent Linkage on Marketing of Generic Drugs' (2013) 18(4) *Journal of Intellectual Property Rights* 316–22 (2013).
110 Sisule F. Musungu and Cecilia Oh, *The Use of Flexibilities in TRIPS by Developing Countries: Can They Promote Access to Medicine*, Commission on Intellectual Property Rights, Innovation and Public Health (CIPIH), Study 4C (August 2005), at p. 66, at www.who.int/intellectualproperty/studies/TRIPSFLEXI.pdf.
111 MDF, 'Trading Away Health' MSF Access Campaign Issue Brief, August 2012, p 11, at http://aids2012.msf.org/wp-content/uploads/2012/07/TPP-Issue-Brief-IAC-July2012.pdf.
112 See, e.g., Article 15.10 of CAFTA–DR–US.

product in a country other than a party to that particular PTA.[113] Depending on how the originator times its entry into the market, the effect of the provision could result in ten years of test data protection. For example, a pharmaceutical company could register the original drug in one of the PTA countries but wait five years before submitting the market approval application in another PTA-member country. It would then be entitled to a further five years of exclusivity from that date.

In addition, most US PTAs eliminate the Article 39.3 requirement in the TRIPS Agreement which protects data only in cases where the pharmaceutical in question utilises 'new chemical entities' and where the generation of data involves considerable effort.[114] The provision in these PTAs requires data protection with respect to any new product (with 'new product' being loosely defined as 'one that does not contain a chemical entity that has previously been approved by the Party').[115] The effect of this provision is to allow a first registrant of a new pharmaceutical product to obtain protection even in the case of old and well-known products, and such protection may be sought irrespective of whether any effort was spent in generating the data.[116]

Finally, as noted above, data protection could act to prevent a generic manufacturer from obtaining marketing approval at any time during the patent period, even when a compulsory licence is issued and even in preparation to enter the market upon expiration of the patent (both of which are allowed under the TRIPS Agreement).[117] A period of data exclusivity increases the final cost of the marketed product and possibly delays its entry onto the market. Data exclusivity can also act as a *de facto* patent, ensuring a minimum period of monopoly for pharmaceutical companies, preventing competition and, in some instances, even prohibiting a generic manufacturer from seeking registration in a country. Furthermore, a period of exclusivity relying upon the registration in another country potentially deprives a country of the drug for the entirety of that period. It is also important to note that the period of data exclusivity negotiated in PTAs is independent from the patent process and applies regardless of whether the drug is patented in the country. Thus, the effect

---

113 These provisions are found in the US–Singapore FTA, Article 16.8.2; AUSFTA, Article 17.10.1(c); US–Morocco FTA, Article 15.10.1; CAFTA–DR–US, Article 15.10.1(b); US–Bahrain FTA, Article 14.9.1(b); US–Oman FTA, Article 15.9.1(b); and KORUS FTA, Article 18.9.1 (b).

114 See AUSFTA, Article 17.10.1(d); US–Morocco FTA, Article 15.10.1; CAFTA–DR–US, Article 15.10.1(c); US–Bahrain FTA, Article 14.9.1(c); US–Oman FTA, Article 15.9.1(c); and KORUS FTA, Article 18.9.1(c).

115 This extends the provision found in Article 4.22, n. 10 of the US–Jordan FTA which restrictively defined 'new chemical entity' as including 'protection for new uses for old chemical entities for a period of three years'.

116 See Frederick M. Abbott, 'The Doha Declaration on the TRIPS Agreement and Public Health and the Contradictory Trend in Bilateral and Regional Trade Agreements', Quaker United Nations Office Occasional Paper 14 (April 2004), at p. 8, at http://papers.ssrn.com/sol3/papers.cfm?abstract_id=1977300.

117 These rules are embodied in the US–Singapore FTA, Article 16.8.4(c); AUSFTA, Article 17.10.4; US–Morocco FTA, Article 15.10.4; CAFTA–DR, Article 15.10.2; US–Bahrain FTA, Articles 14.9.4; US–Oman FTA, Article 15.9.4; and KORUS FTA, Article 18.9.5.

of a period of data exclusivity where a patent does not exist serves to maintain an artificial barrier to entry into the marketplace and higher prices to consumers.

As with the linkage of market approval to patent status, a period of data exclusivity could be detrimental to countries taking advantage of a compulsory licence. Again, a manufacturer granted authority to produce a generic drug under compulsory licence must still be registered by the national drug regulatory authority and if the generic manufacturer cannot rely on existing data to gain regulatory approval it cannot respond to the compulsory licence and supply the needed drug. Thus, where a medicine is protected by patent, data exclusivity could effectively render the compulsory licence meaningless if the generic manufacturer has to repeat time-consuming and costly tests to obtain marketing approval of its drug.[118]

The US has countered this argument by contending that 'if circumstances ever arise in which a drug is produced under a compulsory license, and it is necessary to approve that drug to protect public health or effectively utilize the TRIPS/health solution, the data provision provisions in the PTA would not stand in the way'.[119] Leaving aside the legal effect of such statements, the meaning from a US standpoint is if a compulsory licence fits within the US view of what is 'necessary', then it would not allow the PTA to stand in the way of the licence. Such a stance removes the ability to protect public health from the signatory country and shifts it to the US.

Test data protection is an integral part of US PTAs, and it is likely that future agreements will expand upon the protections granted in current PTAs. This can be seen in the TPP negotiations, where not only is the US requesting a five-year period of exclusivity but also the protection of regulatory data specifically for biological drugs. There, the US has proposed a twelve-year data exclusivity term.[120] If included in the final agreement, this will be the first US PTA to include such protection. The US proposals for the TPP appear to abandon the flexibilities granted to Peru, Colombia and Panama. While maintaining its position in regard to a period of 'at least' five years of test data exclusivity, the TPP proposals also revert to the more traditional American position in not limiting data exclusivity to new chemical entities. Likewise, the TPP proposal does not include a provision which has the data exclusivity protection beginning as of the date of marketing approval by the US Food and Drug Administration if the partner country grants approval within six months of an application for marketing approval and relies on evidence of marketing approval being granted in the US. The relevant date is therefore the registration in the country concerned, not the registration date in the US as per the agreements with Peru, Colombia and Panama.

Perhaps more worrying is that others, such as the EFTA negotiating bloc, are successfully negotiating periods of protection of eight years for test data. Given this, it

---

118 Some PTAs limit the use of compulsory licensing to emergency situations. In such circumstances, due to time constraints, it will be impossible to conduct the necessary tests and obtain registration of the drug.

119 Letter from USTR General Counsel John K. Veroneau to Congressman Sander M. Levin, 19 July 2004 (in the context of the US–Morocco FTA).

120 See the leaked draft of the IP Chapter of the TPP (October 2014), Article QQ.E.20.

seems likely that it is only a matter of time before other nations likewise negotiate for longer periods of exclusivity in their PTAs.

3. Linkage of patent status and regulatory approval

Several US PTAs introduce provisions which prevent national drug regulatory authorities from granting marketing approval to generic versions of a drug that is under patent in the country without the consent of the patent holder. While such patent linkage provisions are prohibited in the EU and not negotiated into agreements by other countries, they are becoming commonplace in many countries due to the negotiation of PTAs with the US. A typical patent linkage provision is Article 16.8.4 of the US–Singapore FTA, which requires both notification and consent before the regulatory authority can grant marketing approval to a pharmaceutical product under patent. The provision reads:

> With respect to pharmaceutical products that are subject to a patent:
>
> . . .
>
> (b) the patent owner shall be notified of the identity of any third party requesting marketing approval effective during the term of the patent; and
>
> (c) the Party shall not grant marketing approval to any third party prior to the expiration of the patent term, unless by consent or acquiescence of the patent owner.

Similar provisions appear in the AUSFTA (Article 17.10.5), CAFTA–DR–US (Article 15.10.2) and the US–Oman FTA (Article 15.9.4).[121] The US–Morocco FTA contains a similar provision but may go further and limit applications to the regulatory authority during the patent term to those that are consistent with the research and testing exemption (commonly known as a 'Bolar' provision) contained earlier in the FTA.[122] On the other hand, the temporary shift in US policy means that US PTAs with Peru, Colombia and Panama do not contain the requirement that the country's regulatory agency withhold approval of a generic drug until it can certify that no patent would be violated if marketing approval were granted for the generic.[123] In the TPP negotiations, the US has reverted to its more traditional position.

The typical provision reproduced above represents a significant shift from traditional operating standards, where the market approval of a drug – that is, the regulatory approval granted to a product which proves its safety and efficacy – has

---

121 Interestingly, Article 4.23 of the US–Jordan FTA contains the notification language identified above but does not link approval to consent or acquiescence of the patent owner. Likewise, Article 18.9.5 of the KORUS FTA merely calls for the prevention of marketing a product without the consent of the patent owner when an applicant relies on the information/evidence of safety and efficacy submitted by the originator.

122 See Article 15.10.4, n. 15 of the US–Morocco FTA.

123 However, each party must provide procedures and remedies for adjudicating patent infringement or validity disputes which, *inter alia*, respect due process and offer effective rewards. See Office of the USTR, Statement and *Bipartisan Agreement*, above n. 95.

been entirely separate to a drug's patent status. Thus, the patent status of a drug has always been irrelevant to whether a drug is of sufficient quality, safety and efficacy to be marketed in a particular nation or region. The separation of patent status and regulatory approval is due to the fact that the authorities granting patents and those granting regulatory and marketing approval have very different areas of expertise and competency. Authorities assessing and granting patents decide whether the drug at issue is novel and inventive and otherwise meets the criteria for a patent in that country, whereas national drug regulatory authorities simply assess whether the drug at issue is of sufficient quality, safety and efficacy to be marketed as a potential medical treatment. As a result, national drug regulatory authorities have traditionally not been concerned with the patent status of a drug they are assessing and the potential infringement of a patented drug by the applicant generic manufacturer has never had a bearing on decisions of such authorities.

Therefore, if a patent holder believes that its patent is being infringed, it traditionally has had the responsibility of enforcing its rights. In practice, this entails the patent holder bringing suit against the alleged infringer in an effort to prevent further sales of the infringing product and recover damages. This process can be lengthy and costly, but it ensures the validity of a patent before enforcing the rights asserted by the plaintiff. In addition, IPRs have always been recognised as 'private rights' (the TRIPS Agreement supports this position) and it seems logical that the owner of private rights should be responsible for their enforcement. The newly delegated role of the regulatory authority as an 'enforcer' of a private right is therefore of significant benefit to the rights holder.

Not only will these provisions delay access to generic drugs, the linkage between market approval and patent status could also be detrimental to countries taking advantage of the TRIPS-recognised flexibility of a compulsory licence.[124] More specifically, it is unclear whether a compulsory licence may be issued to provide entry of generic drugs where the law does not allow registration prior to the expiration of the patent. This potential impediment is caused by the fact that a manufacturer granted authority to produce under compulsory licence still must be registered by the national drug regulatory authority. Thus, if the regulatory authority is prohibited from registering generics until the patent expires, the compulsory licence will be prevented from coming to fruition.

4. Limits on compulsory licences

Compulsory licensing is recognised in the TRIPS Agreement as a public health safeguard temporarily allowing a government to override a patent and authorise

---

124 It is well established that the introduction of generic drugs results in lower prices. See, e.g., Patented Medicines Price Review Board, Treasury Board of Canada, *A Study of the Prices of the Top Selling Multiple Source Medicines in Canada* (November 2002), at www.ibrarian.net/navon/paper/A_Study_of_the_Prices_of_the .pdf?paperid=3539401.

the production of generic versions of a patented product.[125] Despite the Doha Declaration, which affirmed countries' rights to use compulsory licensing and to determine the circumstances warranting this action,[126] this safeguard is being restricted in numerous US PTAs.

The restrictions placed on compulsory licensing are two-fold. First, US PTAs indirectly restrict compulsory licensing as a result of the data exclusivity provisions discussed above. Second, direct restrictions limit the grounds on which compulsory licences can be issued. For instance, and unlike in the TRIPS Agreement, these provisions are stated in the negative and confine the use of compulsory licences to specified cases (such as remedying an anti-competitive practice, public non-commercial contexts, national emergencies and other cases of extreme urgency, and the failure to meet working requirements). For example, Article 4.20 of the US–Jordan FTA states:

> Neither Party shall permit the use of the subject matter of a patent without the authorization of the right holder except in the following circumstances:
>
> (a) to remedy a practice determined after judicial or administrative process to be anti-competitive;
> (b) in cases of public non-commercial use or in the case of a national emergency or other circumstances of extreme urgency, provided that such use is limited to use by government entities or legal entities acting under the authority of a government; or
> (c) on the ground of failure to meet working requirements, provided that importation shall constitute working.[127]

Moreover, while the TRIPS Agreement mandates that 'adequate' remuneration be paid to the patent holder, the US–Singapore FTA raises the level of compensation required to 'reasonable and entire' (Article 16.7.6(b)(ii)), terms which are undefined. The FTA also expressly restricts the transfer of 'know how' (Article 16.7.6(b)(iii)), a term not found in the TRIPS Agreement.[128] This latter restriction is important because 'know how' licensing agreements frequently accompany a licensing arrangement and enable the licensee to make efficient use of the patent. Without access to 'know how', the commercial value of access to a patent is often worth much less to a licensee.

It should be noted that the above agreements are not necessarily indicative of the US imposing restrictions on compulsory licensing across its PTAs. In fact, US FTAs with Morocco and Chile, and CAFTA–DR–US, do not contain any language directly

---

125 See further Carlos M. Correa, 'Intellectual Property Rights and the Use of Compulsory Licenses: Options for Developing Countries', Trade-Related Agenda, Development and Equity Working Paper 5, South Centre (1999), at www.iatp.org/files/Intellectual_Property_Rights_and_the_Use_of_Co.pdf.
126 The US unsuccessfully negotiated for such provisions in the TRIPS negotiations. See Watal, above n. 105, at p. 320.
127 Similar provisions also appear in the US–Singapore FTA, Article 16.7.6; and AUSFTA, Article 17.9.7.
128 See also Article 17.9.7(b)(iii) of the AUSFTA.

relating to compulsory licensing, and the US proposals in the ongoing TPP negotiations are tame in comparison to the FTAs with Australia and Singapore. Perhaps the FTAs with Australia and Singapore are distinguishable as those nations already restricted the use of compulsory licences to cases of emergency or other circumstances of extreme urgency prior to their FTAs with the US.[129]

On the other hand, PTAs negotiated by some countries (including Singapore, Switzerland, EFTA and the EU) not only do not restrict compulsory licensing but explicitly recognise the principles established in the Doha Declaration.[130]

5. Limitations on 'flexibilities'? Side letters and general understandings on public health

The above demonstrates that certain requirements imposed on the US's PTA partners pose a threat to public health and welfare by removing the flexibilities granted in the TRIPS Agreement and mandating a more restrictive system of healthcare.[131] The US has asserted, however, that certain side letters and general understandings on public health contained in some of its PTAs ensure the right of partner countries to adopt measures which protect public health.

The US negotiated a 'Side Letter on Public Health' with Morocco, Bahrain and Oman, and an 'Understanding Regarding Certain Public Health Measures' with CAFTA–DR. The substantive wording of these four documents is identical. And while it is true that the side letters/understanding reserve to the parties the ability to protect public health, they also contain a potentially restrictive understanding of public health. It is worth setting out in full:

> The obligations of [the Intellectual Property Chapter] of the Agreement do not
> affect the ability of either Party to take necessary measures to protect public

129 That being said, it should also be noted that US PTAs often provide similar treatment to countries of vastly differing levels of development. For instance, the US attempts to restrict and/or prohibit parallel importation of patented products or products produced from patented processes: see, e.g., US–Morocco FTA, Article 15.9.4; and AUSFTA, Article 17.9.4. However, it should be noted that both FTAs provide that the prohibition may be limited to cases where the patent owner has placed restrictions by contract or other means. Notwithstanding this, the provisions may effectively prohibit parallel importation and essentially allow patent holders, through contract law, to segment markets and maintain price discrimination. The US–Singapore FTA, Article 16.7.2, also restricts parallel importation by allowing patent holders to block parallel importation into either country when the same is done in violation of a distribution agreement anywhere in the world. Interestingly, a number of US PTAs with developing countries, including FTAs with Chile and Jordan, and CAFTA–DR–US, are silent on the exhaustion of patent rights; thus, these countries have retained the flexibility granted by TRIPS.
130 See, e.g., Singapore–Costa Rica FTA, Article 13.4; Switzerland–China FTA, Article 11.5; EFTA–Peru FTA, Article 6.2.5; EFTA–Colombia FTA, Article 6.2.5; EU–CARIFORUM EPA, Article 147(B); EU–Korea FTA, Article 10.34.
131 In addition, the 'net gains analysis' presumes that earnings in agriculture or other sectors due to increased market access translate into ability to afford higher priced medicine; this presumption is questionable: Musungu and Oh, at p. 55. For other concerns, see above n. 110; and Commission on Intellectual Property Rights, *Integrating Intellectual Property Rights and Development Policy*, 3rd edn (London: Commission on Intellectual Property Rights, 2003), at www.iprcommission.org/papers/pdfs/final_report/CIPRfullfinal.pdf.

health by promoting access to medicines for all, in particular concerning cases such as HIV/AIDS, tuberculosis, malaria, and other epidemics as well as circumstances of extreme urgency or national emergency.

In recognition of the commitment to access to medicines that are supplied in accordance with the Decision of the General Council of 30 August 2003 on the Implementation of Paragraph Six of the Doha Declaration on the TRIPS Agreement and Public Health (WT/L/540) and the WTO General Council Chairman's statement accompanying the Decision (JOB(03)/177, WT/GC/M/82) (collectively the 'TRIPS/health solution'), [the Intellectual Property Chapter] does not prevent the effective utilisation of the TRIPS/health solution.

With respect to the aforementioned matters, if an amendment of the WTO Agreement on Trade-Related Aspects of Intellectual Property Rights (1994) enters into force with respect to the Parties and a Party's application of a measure in conformity with that amendment violates [the Intellectual Property Chapter] of the Agreement, our Governments shall immediately consult in order to adapt [the Intellectual Property Chapter] as appropriate in the light of the amendment.[132]

There is no reason to believe that the side letters/understanding are less than a genuine attempt at providing comfort and certainty to partner countries that the US does not intend to use the agreement to prevent the adoption of public health measures. That being said, the information contained in the side letters themselves presents interpretative difficulties. For example, some disagreement still exists as to what constitutes a 'TRIPS/health solution'. The lack of clarity of the term could allow the US to apply pressure on partners to submit to its understanding of the terms or initiate dispute settlement proceedings for clarification of the understanding. More specifically, and importantly, the side letters/understanding state that the PTA does not affect 'necessary' measures to protect public health. Such terminology is not used in the Doha Declaration and could be interpreted restrictively to limit many health alternatives. Moreover, it is unclear whether the side letters/understanding restrict the ability of parties to issue a compulsory licence to protect public health where 'necessary' and to situations of 'extreme' urgency.[133] The World Bank has recognised potential difficulties with the side letters in stating:

Notwithstanding the potential flexibilities provided by these side letters, they raise several questions. How widely will the parties to the [four] agreements define the 'protection of public health' – or, what definitions would an

132 The letters can be found at www.ustr.gov/sites/default/files/uploads/agreements/fta/morocco/asset_upload_file258_3852.pdf; www.ustr.gov/sites/default/files/uploads/agreements/fta/bahrain/asset_upload_file447_6296.pdf; www.ustr.gov/sites/default/files/uploads/agreements/fta/oman/asset_upload_file44_8808.pdf and www.ustr.gov/sites/default/files/uploads/agreements/cafta/asset_upload_file697_3975.pdf, respectively.
133 More broadly, this is merely an example of an unfortunate trend in many negotiating areas, where PTA texts are increasingly dependent upon the interpretation of complex and vaguely worded side letters of understanding.

arbitration panel use? Uncertainty, in this respect may become itself a barrier to making use of the flexibilities and may open the door for restrictive interpretations by vested interest. Also, several of the other US PTAs do not contain comparable side letters, raising questions about conflicts between intellectual property obligations and public health objectives in at least some of the affected countries.[134]

Another issue with the side letters/understanding is their interpretative value. In particular, as the side letters/understanding are not part of the actual text, their legal weight in a dispute settlement proceeding is questionable. At best, a tribunal would find the side letters to be in context within the meaning of Article 31(2)(b) of the Vienna Convention on the Law of Treaties, which includes 'any instrument which was made by one or more parties in connection with the conclusion of the treaty and accepted by the other parties as an instrument related to the treaty'. To some, the side letters/understanding are unquestionably part of the broader 'agreement' and therefore would carry full weight in a dispute settlement proceeding. Such a view may well be correct, but one then wonders what if any difference there is (or stated differently, what value is there) between a provision in the text and a side letter or understanding.

While the side letters/understanding provide some comfort, as did the assertion from the then-United States Trade Representative (USTR) that 'the United States has no intention of using dispute settlement to challenge any country's actions that are in accordance with that solution',[135] other questions remain. For instance, is there any legal difference between the 'Side Letter on Public Health' signed by the parties in agreements with Morocco, Bahrain and Oman and the 'Understanding Regarding Certain Public Health Measures' with CAFTA–DR? If not, why did the agreement with CAFTA–DR not make use of a 'side letter' for this issue as it did for many other issues? Another lingering question is whether the addition of the phrase in the concluding sentence that the side letter 'shall constitute an agreement' has any interpretive value. The phrase appears in the side letter with Morocco, but in no other side letter/understanding. The side letter with Morocco is otherwise an exact replica of the other side letters/understanding. One can also query whether the additional phrase contemplates a separate agreement or merely an agreement as part of the larger agreement.

Perhaps as a result of the uncertainty surrounding the side letters/understanding, the US shifted its position on the issue and agreed to include the contents of its side letters/understanding in the text of its PTAs with Peru (Article 16.13.2(b)), Colombia (Article 16.13.2(b)) and Panama (Article 15.12.2(b)), and, to a lesser extent, the KORUS FTA (Article 18.11.2(b)).[136] More specifically, the US policy shift calls for

---

134 World Bank, *Global Economic Prospects 2005: Trade Regionalism and Development* (Washington, DC: World Bank, 2004), at p. 110, at http://siteresources.worldbank.org/INTGEP2005/Resources/gep2005.pdf.

135 Letter from Veroneau, above n. 119. Of course, such a statement is non-binding and cannot be relied upon in dispute settlement proceedings.

136 See Office of the USTR, Statement and *Bipartisan Agreement*, above n. 95.

an affirmation of the Doha Declaration, a clarification that the agreement does not and should not prevent the parties from taking measures to protect public health or from utilising the TRIPS/health solution, and the inclusion of an exception (for Peru, Colombia and Panama) to the data exclusivity provision for measures to protect public health in accordance with the Doha Declaration and subsequent implementing protocols. The US negotiating position at the TPP appears to pull somewhat back from the latter provision but still favours inclusion of the former.

D. Enforcement: criminal measures

The TRIPS Agreement contains detailed provisions relating to enforcement of IP rights, set out in Articles 41 to 61. However, the most noteworthy provision relates to the making available of criminal procedures and penalties for certain conduct. Article 61 requires WTO Members to provide for criminal procedures and penalties in cases of 'wilful trademark counterfeiting or copyright piracy on a commercial scale'. Members are specifically permitted to make such procedures and penalties available in relation to infringements of other IP rights, in particular those committed wilfully or on a commercial scale. The Article also provides that remedies shall include imprisonment and/or fines sufficient to provide a deterrent, consistent with the level of penalties applied for crimes of a corresponding gravity, and may also include the seizure, forfeiture and destruction of infringing goods.[137]

While many PTAs contain a provision obliging parties to provide for enforcement measures in line with the TRIPS Agreement standards,[138] relatively few require parties to go further and impose stronger enforcement measures than those required by TRIPS, particularly in the context of criminal procedures and measures. The major exception here is the US,[139] whose PTAs require parties to implement their TRIPS obligations in specific ways and also impose additional, TRIPS-Plus obligations.

Many US PTAs set forth in detail the sort of conduct that parties must consider to be 'wilful copyright piracy on a commercial scale' and thus made subject to criminal

---

137 For detailed consideration of Article 61 of the TRIPS Agreement, see Panel Report, *China–Intellectual Property Rights*.

138 This is a feature of PTAs involving the EFTA: see the Convention Establishing EFTA (Vaduz Convention), Annex J, Article 7; and FTAs with Chile, Annex XII, Article 8; Croatia, Annex VII, Article 5; FYROM, Annex V, Article 5; Jordan, Annex VI, Article 5; Korea, Annex XIII, Article 7; Lebanon, Annex V, Article 8; Mexico, Annex XXI, Article 5; Morocco, Annex V, Article 5; Singapore, Annex XII, Article 8; Tunisia, Annex V, Article 8; and Turkey, Annex XII, Article 5. See also Korea–Chile FTA, Article 16.5; and Panama–El Salvador FTA, Articles 17.02–17.03.

139 See, however, Japan–Thailand EPA, Article 140.1 (both parties 'shall provide for criminal procedures and penalties to be applied at least in cases of infringement of patents, utility models, industrial designs, trademarks, copyrights and related rights, layout-designs of integrated circuits and rights relating to new varieties of plants, committed wilfully and on a commercial scale'); EU–Korea FTA, Article 10.55 ('[s]ubject to its national or constitutional law and regulations, each Party shall consider adopting measures to establish the criminal liability for counterfeiting geographical indications and designs').

measures. For example, under Article 17.11.26(a) of the AUSFTA such conduct must include:

   (i) significant wilful infringements of copyright, that have no direct or indirect motivation of financial gain; and
   (ii) wilful infringements for the purposes of commercial advantage or financial gain.

Virtually identical provisions are contained in the US–Singapore FTA (Article 16.9.21), US–Morocco FTA (Article 15.11.26(a)), CAFTA–DR–US (Article 16.11.26(a)), US–Bahrain FTA (Article 14.10.26), US–Oman FTA (Article 15.10.26), US–Peru TPA (Article 16.11.26), KORUS FTA (Article 18.10.26), US–Colombia FTA (Article 16.11.26) and US–Panama TPA (Article 15.11.26).[140] Such provisions are noteworthy because they require parties to implement their TRIPS obligations so as to require them not only to criminalise conduct that is objectively on a 'commercial scale' but also conduct involving particular commercial 'purposes'.[141] More recently, we can see provisions requiring parties to criminalise copyright piracy irrespective of whether it is on a commercial scale or not. Article 18.10.29 of the KORUS FTA obliges the parties to:

> provide for criminal procedures to be applied against any person who, without authorization of the holder of copyright or related rights in a motion picture or other audiovisual work, knowingly uses or attempts to use an audiovisual recording device to transmit or make a copy of the motion picture or other audiovisual work, or any part thereof, from a performance of the motion picture or other audiovisual work in a public motion picture exhibition facility.[142]

This provision thus requires the parties to adopt standards going well beyond those contained in the TRIPS Agreement.

In addition, most US PTAs specify that criminal measures must be available for conduct that is related to copyright piracy and trademark counterfeiting. For instance, many PTAs provide that the wilful importation or exportation of pirated copyright goods or trademarked counterfeit products is to be criminalised.[143] More tellingly, some PTAs also cover conduct that may occur in the absence of copyright

---

140 Article 4.28 of the US–Jordan FTA defines 'wilful copyright piracy on a commercial scale' only by reference to the conduct in paragraph (i). Article 17.11.22(a) of the US–Chile FTA refers only to the conduct in paragraph (ii) but, unlike any other PTA, further stipulates that such piracy must include 'willful infringing reproduction or distribution, including by electronic means, of copies with a significant aggregate monetary value, calculated based on the legitimate retail value of the infringed goods': for comment, see Roffe, above n. 6, at p. 45.

141 Article 23.1 of ACTA contains similar (although not quite as extensive) obligations, in providing that 'acts carried out on a commercial scale include at least those carried out as commercial activities for direct or indirect economic or commercial advantage'.

142 A similar, although optional, obligation is contained in Article 23.3 of ACTA.

143 See AUSFTA, Article 17.11.26(b); US–Morocco FTA, Article 15.11.26(a); CAFTA–DR–US, Article 16.11.26(a); US–Bahrain FTA, Article 14.10.26; US–Oman FTA, Article 15.10.26; US–Peru TPA,

piracy or trademark counterfeiting. For example, Article 15.11.27 of the US–Morocco FTA requires the criminalisation of the:

(a) knowing trafficking in counterfeit labels affixed or designed to be affixed to: a phonogram, a copy of a computer program, documentation or packaging for a computer program, or a copy of a motion picture or other audiovisual work; and

(b) knowing trafficking in counterfeit documentation or packaging for a computer program.

Similar provisions are contained in the AUSFTA (Article 17.11.28), US–Bahrain FTA (Article 14.10.28), US–Oman FTA (Article 15.10.28), US–Peru TPA (Article 16.11.26), KORUS FTA (Article 18.10.27(f)) and the US–Colombia FTA (Article 16.11.28).[144]

The US regards the enforcement of its nationals' IP rights in foreign countries as a major concern, and has used a variety of tactics to attempt to force such countries to provide stronger and more effective protection against copyright piracy and trademark counterfeiting.[145] The PTA provisions discussed above are a relatively new aspect of its larger strategy to increase enforcement standards at an international level. Clearly, it is hoped that by entering into bilateral agreements with developing countries, not only will levels of IP infringement decrease in those countries, but also that there might be 'flow-on' effects in that such countries might co-operate with their regional neighbours in an attempt to reduce piracy in the broader region.[146] However, it is well recognised that in such countries there may continue to be a discrepancy, for cultural and other reasons, between the strong enforcement measures that exist on the books and the actual levels of, and resources allocated to, enforcement of IPRs. In addition, it has also been doubted that enforcement provisions in US PTAs with developed countries that already have criminal measures and procedures in place will have much meaningful impact at all.[147] Nevertheless, the clear trend is for detailed enforcement provisions to be an integral part of US PTAs.[148]

III. Conclusion

While numerous PTAs contain TRIPS-Plus provisions, the US is the main party that has sought higher and stronger standards of IP protection and enforcement in its

---

Article 16.11.26; KORUS FTA, Article 18.10.26; US–Colombia FTA, Article 16.11.26; and US–Panama TPA, Article 15.11.26. See also ACTA, Article 23.1, n. 9.

144 See also ACTA, Article 23.2.

145 See Executive Office of the President of the United States, *2007 Trade Policy Agenda and 2006 Annual Report of the President of the United States on the Trade Agreements Program* (March 2007), at https://ustr. gov/archive/Document_Library/Reports_Publications/2007/2007_Trade_Policy_Agenda/ Section_Index.html.

146 See Assafa Endeshaw, 'Intellectual Property Enforcement in Asia: A Reality Check' (2005) 13(3) *International Journal of Law and Information Technology* 378–412, at 396–7.

147 See Burrell and Weatherall, above n. 32.

148 See Article QQ.H.7 of the leaked draft of the TPP (November 2013).

bilateral agreements. In bypassing the WTO, the US has in its recent PTAs served to entrench amongst a growing number of developed and developing countries (although not its major trading partners) ever-higher minimum standards of IP protection and the removal of certain flexibilities made available under multilateral instruments.[149] This can be seen particularly in the areas of copyright and patents. However, it is important to recognise that despite the close similarities in the form and substance of the IP Chapters of US PTAs (at least after the US–Jordan FTA), the provisions of these agreements are not identical to each other, some key differences between the agreements exist and there does not appear to be a trend emerging for ever-increasing standards across all areas of IP.

Other major producers and exporters of IP-protected products have not, for the most part, sought to use bilateral agreements to increase standards of IP protection in the same manner as the US. As has been seen, the EU's approach in particular has, until recently, been more targeted, focusing largely on securing greater protection for European wine and spirit GIs amongst key trading partners. However, in the last five or so years, the EU's approach has been more like that of the US, as it has sought to impose more comprehensive obligations on its trading partners in relation to IP protection and enforcement. These developments will be worth watching closely, particularly as the EU and the US seek to enter into new PTAs such as the TPP, CETA, and the Transatlantic Trade and Investment Partnership between the EU and the US, to see what impact this might have on future multilateral negotiations on IP rights.

149 See Peter Drahos, 'BITs and BIPs: Bilateralism in Intellectual Property' (2001) 4(6) *Journal of World Intellectual Property* 791–808, at 798–9.

13

Social issues: Labour, environment and human rights

LORAND BARTELS*

I. Introduction

A. Trade and social issues

International trade agreements have numerous – but also sometimes conflicting – effects on the ability of countries to protect social values, including labour and environmental standards and human rights. The preamble of the WTO Agreement claims as one of its primary objectives the 'raising [of] standards of living', and it is widely recognized that, as said by the World Commission on the Social Dimension of Globalisation, 'wisely managed, [the global market economy] can deliver unprecedented material progress, generate more productive and better jobs for all, and contribute significantly to reducing world poverty'.[1] But as this very statement recognizes, the potential of trade liberalization to improve social protections does not always translate into actual improvements.

This is for several reasons. At a general level, trade can lead to increased efficiencies, with benefits for the environment, governments and consumers. But increased export opportunities can also put pressure on local environments and people living on land coveted by exporters.[2] There are also costs for any country pursuing a policy of trade liberalization. Liberalization leads to unemployment and reduced income in inefficient sectors and, while this is supposed to be only a short-term problem, structural adjustment has proven to be a challenge even for the wealthiest of countries.[3] Legally, it is relevant that these negative effects can disproportionately affect minorities and women, who are specially protected by international human rights treaties.[4] The trilateral relationship between intellectual property, trade and social

---

* I am grateful to those who read and commented on this version and the version of this chapter in the first edition of this volume. These include Morten Broberg, Franz Ebert, Meredith Kolsky Lewis, Andrew Lang, Armand de Mestral and Jeffrey Vogt. Thanks also to Stephanie Mullen for excellent research assistance.

1 World Commission on the Social Dimension of Globalization, *A Fair Globalization – Creating Opportunities for All* (Geneva: ILO, 2004), at x.
2 Smita Narula, 'The Global Land Rush: Markets, Rights, and the Politics of Food' (2013) 49 *Stanford Journal of International Law* 101.
3 Cf *The Full Monty* (Redwave Films and Channel Four Films, 1997).
4 Marzia Fontana, 'The Gender Effects of Trade Liberalization in Developing Countries: A Review of the Literature' in Maurizio Bussolo and Rafael De Hoyos (eds.), *Gender Aspects of the Trade and Poverty Nexus:*

protection is also complex. Intellectual property protections can promote trade in goods and services containing intellectual property, thereby enabling individuals to enjoy the fruits of their labours. But the very same protections can also hinder a country's ability to meet its social objectives, as the debate on TRIPS and essential medicines has amply demonstrated.

Government efforts to achieve social protection in *other* countries can also impact on trade. Market access restrictions, whether unilateral or agreed (and this by no means excludes some degree of coercion), are frequently applied to products from countries involved in human rights abuses, as well as to products from countries that do not comply with environmental or public morals norms. They may also be applied to protect high domestic standards of social protection (to prevent so-called 'social dumping').[5] The reasons for imposing these restrictions may be moral, political or economically protectionist, or a combination of all three.[6] Trade restrictions with protectionist effects are especially controversial, as the country imposing the restrictions will usually justify its restrictions as a legitimate means of achieving worthy objectives, while the recipient country will see them as illegitimate ('blue' or 'green') protectionism in another guise.[7]

B. Links between trade and non-trade issues in the WTO

Inspired by the 1927 Convention for the Abolition of Import and Export Prohibitions and Restrictions (the first multilateral trade agreement),[8] most of the WTO

A Macro-Micro Approach (Washington, DC: World Bank/Palgrave, 2009), 26; Gillian Moon, 'Fair in Form, but Discriminatory in Operation – WTO Law's Discriminatory Effects on Human Rights in Developing Countries' (2011) 14 *Journal of International Economic Law* 553.

5 The Preamble of the 1919 Constitution of the International Labour Organization (ILO) states that 'the failure of any nation to adopt humane conditions of labour is an obstacle in the way of other nations which desire to improve the conditions in their own countries', and efforts to reduce competition by means of low labour standards date back to Daniel Legrand in 1840. See Steve Charnovitz, 'The Labor Dimension of the Emerging Free Trade Area of the Americas' in Philip Alston (ed.), *Labour Rights as Human Rights* (Oxford: Oxford University Press, 2005), 164. The empirical evidence on whether countries with low social standards have an advantage in the competitiveness of their traded goods and services is equivocal: for a survey of the literature, and the conclusion that there is no 'race to the bottom' see Keith Maskus, 'Trade and Competitiveness Aspects of Environmental and Labor Standards in East Asia' in Kathie Krumm and Homi Kharas (eds.), *East Asia Integrates: A Trade and Policy Agenda for Shared Growth* (Washington, DC: World Bank/Oxford University Press, 2004), 115–134 and Brian Langille, 'What is International Labor Law For?' (2009) 3 *Law and Ethics of Human Rights* 47, especially at 68.

6 Steve Charnovitz, 'The International Labour Organization in its Second Century' (2000) 4 *Max Planck YBIL* 147, 167, discussing the ILO.

7 See eg Gregory Shaffer, 'The Under-Examined Trade-Environment Linkage: Domestic Politics and WTO Disputes', 2005, available at http://www.researchgate.net/publication/267861297_The_Under-Examined_Trade-Environment_Linkage_Domestic_Politics_and_WTO_Disputes.

8 Article 4 of this Convention inspired the 'General Exceptions' in Article XX GATT 1947, which has itself served as the chief inspiration for all such clauses in regional trade agreements. The Convention never came into force due to Poland's non-ratification. See, further, Steve Charnovitz, 'Exploring the Environmental Exceptions in GATT Article XX' (1991) 25 *Journal of World Trade* 37.

agreements contain express rights to regulate for public policy purposes,[9] including what we would now recognize as environmental protection. The last twenty years have shown these to be widely used, and critical parts of the trade liberalization package. But these provisions are limited in a number of important respects. First, they only permit WTO members to act unilaterally, and even then not in all cases where social protection might be desirable. In particular, it is not clear how far a WTO member can protect social values in other countries (other than by means of labelling or in cases justified on the basis of public morals).

There has also been a notable failure to grapple with these issues at the WTO. Admittedly, the issue is less sensitive in relation to environmental issues. The preamble of the WTO Agreement contains a reference to sustainable development, and the Appellate Body has said that achieving 'sustainable development' is one of the objectives of the WTO itself, basing itself on the questionable argument that 'WTO objectives may well be pursued through measures taken under provisions characterized as exceptions'.[10] There is also a WTO Committee on Trade and Environment, which has done some useful work in identifying the relationship between trade and environmental issues.[11] But for all this, virtually no progress has been made in reconciling the more difficult aspects of the relationship between trade and social protection, including environmental protection. The 2001 Doha Ministerial Declaration required negotiations on a number of environmental matters,[12] including, at the EU's urging, 'the relationship between existing WTO rules and specific trade obligations set out in multilateral environmental agreements',[13] but this mandate has produced almost nothing of substance.

More obviously still, the topic of labour standards has barely been mentioned at the WTO since the 1996 WTO Singapore Ministerial Conference issued a Declaration punting the issue to the ILO,[14] and adding, for good measure, that high labour

---

9 A rare exception is the 2006 China–Pakistan agreement, which contains no general or security exceptions: http://fta.mofcom.gov.cn/topic/enpakistan.shtml. Article 14 of the 1958 Benelux Treaty (renewed in 2008) has a single exception for 'vital interests'.

10 WTO Appellate Body, *EC – Tariff Preferences*, WT/DS246/AB/R, adopted 20 April 2004, para 94. It would be more accurate to say, as the Appellate Body did in an earlier report, that sustainable development is one of the objectives of WTO *Members*: WTO Appellate Body, *US – Shrimp*, WT/DS58/AB/R, adopted 6 November 1998, para 154. WTO Members committed themselves to this objective in the Doha WTO Ministerial Declaration, WT/MIN(01)/DEC/1, 20 November 2001, para 6.

11 Minisha Sinha, 'An Evaluation of the WTO Committee on Trade and Environment' (2013) 47 *Journal of World Trade* 1285.

12 Doha Declaration, *ibid.*, paras 31, 32, 33 and 51.

13 Doha Declaration, *ibid.*, para 31(i). On the EU's role in the adoption of this statement see Bart Kerremans, 'What Went Wrong in Cancun? A Principal-Agent View on the EU's Rationale Towards the Doha Development Round' (2004) 9 *European Foreign Affairs Review* 363, 378.

14 Ironically, this had the effect of boosting that organization's profile. See Steve Charnovitz, above at n 6, 158–159 and 163.

standards should not be used for protectionist purposes.[15] And while there has been a fruitful joint report by the WTO and ILO Secretariats on the links between trade and employment,[16] at the diplomatic level the relationship remains cool. The Singapore Ministerial Conference was marked by the embarrassing withdrawal, at the request of some developing countries, of an unofficial speaking invitation to the Director-General of the ILO,[17] and two decades later the ILO enjoys neither regular observer status at WTO meetings[18] nor speaking rights at WTO Ministerial Conferences.[19] At the more general level, despite UN reports on the potentially negative effect of the WTO on human rights,[20] there has been no systematic attempt in the WTO to consider these issues.[21]

Since its founding, then, social issues have been left to one side of the main WTO agenda, much to the relief no doubt of those who were at one stage concerned about its 'contamination' by 'non-trade issues'.[22] And there matters might have remained, but for the sudden increase in the number of regional trade agreements being negotiated and concluded, from the early 1990s to today, which gave an opportunity

---

15 WTO Singapore Ministerial Declaration, WT/MIN(96)/DEC, 18 December 1996, para 4. The statement is repeated in the ILO Declaration on Fundamental Principles and Rights at Work, 18 June 1998 (1998) 37 *ILM* 1233, para 5. Even the mention of labour standards was too much for India, Pakistan and Sri Lanka, which consented only very reluctantly: see Kevin Kolben, 'The New Politics of Linkage: India's Opposition to the Workers' Rights Clause' (2006) 13 *Indiana Journal of Global Legal Studies* 225, 241.

16 WTO/ILO, *Trade and Employment: Challenges for Policy Research* (Geneva: WTO/ILO, 2007). The Singapore Ministerial Declaration, *ibid.*, para 4, also promised that 'the WTO and ILO Secretariats will continue their existing collaboration'.

17 Chakravarthi Raghavan, 'EC Labour Standards Move Trashed', *Third World Network*, 8 November 1999, available at www.twn.my/title/trashed-cn.htm.

18 A list of WTO observers is available at www.wto.org/english/thewto_e/igo_obs_e.htm.

19 The ILO has always been invited to attend WTO Ministerial Conferences.

20 Eg the following UN ECOSOC documents: *Human Rights and Intellectual Property – Statement by the Committee on Economic Social and Cultural Rights*, E/C.12/2001/15, 14 December 2001; *Globalisation and its Impact on the Full Enjoyment of Human Rights – Report of the High Commissioner for Human Rights*, E/CN.4/2002/54, 15 January 2002; *The Impact of the Agreement on Trade-Related Aspects of Intellectual Property Rights on Human Rights – Report of the Commissioner*, E/CN.4/Sub.2/2001/13, 27 June 2001; *Liberalisation of Trade and Services and Human Rights – Report of the High Commissioner*, E/CN.4/Sub.2/2002/9, 25 June 2002; *Human Rights, Trade and Investment – Report of the High Commissioner*, E/CN.4/Sub.2/2003/9, 2 July 2003; *Mainstreaming the Right to Development into International Trade Law and Policy at the World Trade Organization – Note by the Secretariat*, E/CN.4/Sub.2/2004/17, 9 June 2004; see also the Activity Report by the UN Special Rapporteur on the Right to Food: Olivier de Schutter, *The World Trade Organization and the Post-Global Food Crisis Agenda*, Activity Report, November 2011.

21 See the discussion on the proposed ILA Declaration on Trade and Human Rights in ILA, *Report of the International Trade Law Committee*, Toronto Conference (2006), 18–21; also Ernst-Ulrich Petersmann, 'The WTO and Regional Trade Agreements as Competing Fora for Constitutional Reforms: Trade and Human Rights' in Lorand Bartels and Federico Ortino (eds.), *Regional Trade Agreements and the WTO Legal System* (Oxford: Oxford University Press, 2006), Ch 12. An exception is the rebuttal of de Schutter, *ibid.*, in an open letter by the WTO Director-General, Pascal Lamy, on 14 December 2011, at www.wto.org/english/news_e/news11_e/agcom_14dec11_e.htm#letter; on which cf 'WTO Defending an Outdated Vision of Food Security – UN Food Expert Responds to Pascal Lamy', Press Release, Office of the High Commissioner for Human Rights, 16 November 2011.

22 See the statement signed by 103 intellectuals in 'Third World Intellectuals and NGOs' Statement Against Linkage (TWIN-SAL)', 15 November 1999, available at www.cuts-international.org/Twin-sal.htm.

to those countries with an interest in linking trade and social issues for negotiating corresponding provisions in their new regional trade agreements.

II. Social issues in regional trade agreements

A. Introduction

Against this background, the phenomenon of regional trade agreements has offered countries an opportunity to experiment with different means of regulating the protection of social issues. These have taken several distinct forms. One involves not just the incorporation of the ordinary WTO exceptions for unilateral measures, but modifications and enhancements to these exceptions. Another involves the express subordination of the trade agreement to other international agreements between the parties, including those specifically concerned with social protection (such as multilateral environmental agreements). A third technique has been to include in the trade agreement certain obligations requiring the parties to comply with human rights, and labour and environmental standards.[23] This section discusses these models and their variants, as these have evolved over the past two decades.

B. Exceptions

Many regional trade agreements simply adopt the list of general exceptions found in Article XX GATT, sometimes even incorporating this provision by reference.[24] However, a number of countries have modified these clauses to provide greater policy space, and they have done this in four main areas: environment, labour, culture and indigenous rights. By contrast, and no doubt reflecting the greater sensitivity of these issues, there have been fewer efforts to amend clauses to measures designed to protect human rights. Whether this changes remains to be seen.[25]

---

23 See also Marie-Claire Cordonier Segger, 'Sustainable Development in Regional Trade Agreements' in Bartels and Ortino, above at n 21, Ch 13 and Petersmann, above at n 21.

24 Eg Art 12 Australia–Singapore (reiterating Art XX GATT), Art 1601 Australia–Thailand (incorporating by reference), Art 22.1 Australia–US (incorporating by reference with some modifications, as discussed below); Art 15.1 NZ–Thailand (reiterating Art XX GATT), Art 11.22(2) NZ–Transpacific (reiterating with some modifications, as discussed below), Art 19.02 Mexico–Chile, Art 19.02 Mexico–Uruguay, Art 168.1 Mexico–Japan (all incorporating by reference), Art 9.16 Mexico–Costa Rica (reiterating) and Art 19.2(2) Japan–Singapore, Art 10 Japan–Malaysia, Art 23 Japan–Philippines (all incorporating by reference), Art 99 Chile–China, Art 20.02 Chile–Costa Rica, Art 20.01 Chile–Korea (all incorporating by reference), Art 18 China–Macao and Art 18 China–Hong Kong (both incorporating by reference).

25 For a proposal to include such an exception in the EU's free trade agreements, see Lorand Bartels, *Human Rights Clauses in Trade and Investment Agreements After the Lisbon Treaty: Implications for the European Parliament*, Committee on International Trade and Subcommittee on Human Rights, Committee on Foreign Affairs, European Parliament, DROI/2012/09, January 2014.

1. Environment

Article XX GATT is a conditional exception for measures including those (b) 'necessary to protect human, animal or plant life or health' and (g) 'relating to the conservation of exhaustible natural resources if such measures are made effective in conjunction with restrictions on domestic production or consumption'. The word 'environment' does not appear, for the obvious reason that the concept of environmental protection did not exist in 1947, when these words were drafted.

The 1993 NAFTA incorporated these clauses by reference but subject to this modification:

> The Parties understand that the measures referred to in GATT Article XX(b) include environmental measures necessary to protect human, animal or plant life or health, and that GATT Article XX(g) applies to measures relating to the conservation of living and non-living exhaustible natural resources.[26]

This wording has been adopted in subsequent agreements by the NAFTA parties[27] as well as by some others.[28] Whether it changes much, on the other hand, is doubtful. The express reference to 'environmental measures' does not increase its scope, and the clarification that the term 'exhaustible natural resources' includes living resources merely repeats what the WTO Appellate Body said in *US – Shrimp*.[29] It is highly unlikely that identical treaty wording between identical parties would mean something different in the context of a regional trade agreement.

Another model clause, taken from Article 36 of the Treaty on the Functioning of the European Union (TFEU), states as follows:

> The Agreement shall not preclude prohibitions or restrictions on imports, exports, goods in transit or trade in used goods justified on grounds of public morality, public policy or public security; the protection of health and life of humans, animals or plants; the protection of national treasures possessing artistic, historic or archaeological value; or the protection of intellectual, industrial and commercial property or rules relating to gold and silver. Such prohibitions or restrictions shall not, however, constitute a means of arbitrary or unjustifiable discrimination where the same conditions prevail or a disguised restriction on trade between the Parties.

This provision is found in early EU and EFTA regional trade agreements[30] and in a number of agreements concluded by Balkan countries (in almost all cases with the addition of a reference to measures 'justified on grounds of ... protection of the environment').[31]

---

26 Art 2101 NAFTA.
27 Art 22.1 Australia–US; Art 21.1 CAFTA; Art O-01 Canada–Chile; Art 10.1 Canada–Israel; Art 11.02 Mexico–Israel; Art 12 US–Jordan; Art 21.1 US–Morocco and side letter; Art 21.1 US–Singapore; Art 22.1 US–Peru; Art 22 EFTA–Canada.
28 Art 16.2 Singapore–Chinese Tapei; Art 22.1(1) Korea–Australia; Art 18.1(1) Hong Kong–Chile.
29 *US – Shrimp*, above at n 10, para 131.   30 Eg Art 17 EFTA–Croatia.   31 Eg Art 23 Croatia–Albania.

Needless to say, the EU Court of Justice (CJEU) has produced a rich jurisprudence on the interpretation of Article 36 TFEU, which implies, at least in theory, a 'strict' proportionality test involving a balancing of the benefits of the measure against the resulting detriment to trade. This is a more intrusive test than under WTO law, which, even in theory, never second-guesses the level of protection which a measure is intended to achieve.[32] Where the CJEU has exercised jurisdiction over such clauses in the EU's regional trade agreements, it has interpreted this wording in the same way as under EU law,[33] but it is not certain that other tribunals would apply the CJEU test.

Other agreements have amended the GATT model in ways that are not easy to follow. Australia's 1983 agreement with New Zealand abandons the GATT requirement that a measure to conserve exhaustible natural resources must be taken in conjunction with domestic restrictions,[34] while India's agreements with Sri Lanka and Nepal[35] and the many agreements concluded by countries of the former Soviet Union (now the Commonwealth of Independent States, or CIS) omit any reference to such an exception at all.[36] There are also several examples of ad hoc exceptions clauses. For example, the Egypt–Jordan agreement allows measures 'for religious, hygienic, security or environmental reasons' so long as they are 'in conformity with the applicable laws and regulations in both countries',[37] which is not much of a condition.

2. Labour

It is rare for regional trade agreements to contain exceptions for unilateral measures in relation to labour issues, these being more commonly addressed by positive obligations, as discussed below. The 2008 Cariforum–EC Economic Partnership Agreement is therefore unusual in containing a footnote to its general exceptions stating that '[t]he Parties agree that ... measures necessary to combat child labour shall be deemed to be included within the meaning of measures necessary to protect public morals or measures necessary for the protection of health.'[38] This may have been inspired by the 2001 Treaty of Chaguaramas Establishing the Caribbean Community, which permits the adoption of measures 'relating to child labour'.[39]

---

32 Jan Neumann and Elisabeth Türk, 'Necessity Revisited: Proportionality in World Trade Organization Law After *Korea – Beef, EC – Asbestos* and *EC – Sardines*' (2003) 37 *JWT* 199.
33 Case C-340/97, *Nazli* [2000] ECR I-957, paras 55–56.   34 Art 18 ANZCERTA.
35 Art IX India–Nepal; Art IV India–Sri Lanka (which adopts a subjective test for measures 'which [the party] considers necessary for ... the protection of human, animal or plant life and health').
36 Eg Art 10 Armenia–Georgia.   37 Art 8 Egypt–Jordan.
38 Fn 1 to Art 224(1) Cariforum–EC Economic Partnership Agreement.
39 Art 226(1)(g) Revised Treaty of Chaguaramas Establishing the Caribbean Community. I am grateful to Franz Ebert for this reference.

3. Culture

Another modification concerns the GATT exceptions available for the protection of cultural heritage. Article XX(f) GATT permits measures 'imposed for the protection of national treasures of artistic, historic or archaeological value', but this does not protect domestic content not rising to the level of a 'national treasure'. To remedy this perceived deficiency, beginning with its 1988 agreement with the US, Canada has sought in all of its regional trade agreements to protect 'cultural industries', defined in terms of persons engaged in the production, distribution or exhibition of print, audio and audio-visual materials.[40] Such a clause has not been adopted by other countries, with the exception of New Zealand, which includes an exception in its trade agreements for measures to support 'creative arts of national value'.[41]

4. Indigenous and minority rights

New Zealand is also responsible for a general exceptions clause allowing affirmative action measures to support its indigenous population. This clause states that:

> Provided that such measures are not used as a means of arbitrary or unjustified discrimination against persons of the other Parties or as a disguised restriction on trade in goods and services, nothing in this Agreement shall preclude the adoption by New Zealand of measures it deems necessary to accord more favourable treatment to Maori in respect of matters covered by this Agreement including in fulfilment of its obligations under the Treaty of Waitangi.[42]

Other regional trade agreements also make allowance for positive discrimination, but in the more limited contexts of schedules of concessions for cross-border services, investment and government procurement. As in many other areas, the NAFTA parties led the way. For services and investment, Canada was permitted 'the right to adopt or maintain any measure denying investors of another Party and their investments, or service providers of another Party, any rights or preferences provided to aboriginal peoples', and the US and Mexico were permitted 'to adopt or maintain any measure according rights or preferences to socially or economically disadvantaged minorities [Mexico: groups]'.[43] In relation to government procurement measures, NAFTA contains an exception 'relating to goods or services of handicapped

---

40 Art O-07 Canada–Chile.
41 Eg Ch 15, Art 1(3) and (4) ASEAN–Australia–New Zealand Free Trade Agreement. Footnotes define this to include 'the performing arts – including theatre, dance and music – visual arts and craft, literature, film and video, language arts, creative on-line content, indigenous traditional practice and contemporary cultural expression, and digital interactive media and hybrid art work, including those that use new technologies to transcend discrete art form divisions. The term encompasses those activities involved in the presentation, execution and interpretation of the arts; and the study and technical development of these art forms and activities.'
42 *Ibid.*, Art 5(1).   43 Annex II NAFTA.

persons, of philanthropic institutions or of prison labor'.[44] There are similar provisions in agreements with Australia and Chile.[45]

In NAFTA and certain later agreements the United States included an exemption for 'small and minority businesses',[46] and Canada, Japan and South Korea have followed suit. But this has not been uncontroversial. When the US included a similar exemption to its commitments in the WTO Government Procurement Agreement the EU objected by exempting its own bid challenge procedures in relation to these countries' small and medium enterprises.[47]

5. Modifications to the 'Chapeau' conditions

In a number of agreements, the parties to regional trade agreements have also relaxed the strict conditions set out in the Chapeau to Article XX GATT that measures not amount to arbitrary or unjustifiable discrimination or a disguised restriction on international trade.[48] Some agreements omit (or almost omit) any Chapeau-type conditions. The Caricom–Dominican Republic agreement is an example. Others use different formulations. The regional trade agreements concluded by the CIS countries allow for:

> measures ... which are considered by the Contracting Party necessary for the protection of its vital interests or which are undoubtedly necessary for the implementation of international agreements of which [the party] is a signatory or intends to become a signatory if these measures concern ... health protection of people, animals and plants.[49]

Doing away with the traditional non-discrimination conditions, this provision adds two alternatives. One is that, in the opinion of the relevant party, the measure is necessary for the protection of its 'vital interests', a test which, despite its subjectivity, is set high for a measure designed, for example, to protect a minor species of animal. A subset of these agreements (with Kyrgyzstan and Georgia)[50] add that such

---

44 Art 1018.2(d) NAFTA. The same phrase is found in Article XXIII of the original WTO Government Procurement Agreement and, with 'handicapped' changed to 'persons with disabilities', Article III of the revised Government Procurement Agreement, in force since April 2014.

45 Annex II (investment and services) and Annex 15A, Section 7, General Notes (government procurement), Australia–US; Ch 6 Art 15 (government procurement) and Annex 4-II(A) (investment and services), Australia–Singapore; Annex on Australian commitments on services and investment, Australia–Thailand (this agreement contains no substantive obligations on government procurement); Annex 11.6 Chile–Hong Kong.

46 Annex II NAFTA.

47 Christopher McCrudden and Stuart Gross, 'WTO Government Procurement Rules and the Local Dynamics of Procurement Policies: A Malaysian Case Study' (2006) 17 *European Journal of International Law* 151, at 158.

48 On this see Lorand Bartels, 'The Chapeau of the General Exceptions in the WTO GATT 1994 and GATS Agreements: A Reconstruction' (2015) 109 *American Journal of International Law* (forthcoming).

49 Art 11 Kyrgyzstan–Moldova. On these agreements generally, see Rilka Dragneva and Joop de Kort, 'The Legal Regime for Free Trade in the Commonwealth of Independent States' (2007) 56 *International and Comparative Law Quarterly* 233.

50 Eg Art 11 Kyrgyzstan–Moldova.

measures must also be 'general[ly] accepted in the international practice'. It is not entirely clear what this might mean. Second, measures are permitted if they are 'undoubtedly necessary' for the implementation of an international agreement. This is also a relatively high standard to meet.

C. Conflicts clauses and other international agreements

Many regional trade agreements have made use of conflicts clauses to protect rights and/or obligations under other international agreements with social objectives. Such conflicts clauses have effect under Article 30(2) of the Vienna Convention on the Law of Treaties, which provides that '[w]hen a treaty specifies that it is subject to, or that it is not to be considered as incompatible with, an earlier or later treaty, the provisions of that other treaty prevail'.[51]

A well-known example is Article 104 of NAFTA, which states that certain environmental treaties[52] are to take priority in the event of any inconsistency, 'provided that where a Party has a choice among equally effective and reasonably available means of complying with such obligations, the Party chooses the alternative that is the least inconsistent with the other provisions of this Agreement'.[53] The US abandoned this clause in subsequent agreements[54] but resurrected a version of the clause following the May 2007 change in US policy on social issues (discussed below). The agreements concluded since then contain the following clause:

> In the event of any inconsistency between a Party's obligations under this Agreement and a [listed environmental] agreement, the Party shall seek to balance its obligations under both agreements, but this shall not preclude the Party from taking a particular measure to comply with its obligations under the covered agreement, provided that the primary purpose of the measure is not to impose a disguised restriction on trade.[55]

The traditional clause survived in the practice of the two other NAFTA parties, being adopted in Canada's agreements with Chile and Costa Rica and Mexico's agreement with Chile. Chile evidently found this clause to its liking, taking it up in its agreement with Costa Rica, and it has also surfaced in an agreement between Panama and Taiwan.[56]

---

51 See the International Law Commission Commentary on (then) Art 26(2) of the draft Vienna Convention on the Law of Treaties, in ILC, *Report of the International Law Commission on the work of the second part of its seventeenth session*, Document A/6309/Rev.l, (1966) II *YILC* 214–216.

52 CITES, the Montreal Protocol, the Basel Convention, and two bilateral environmental agreements.

53 Art 104 NAFTA. The clause was very briefly considered in *S.D. Myers, Partial Award*, 13 November 2000, para 215, available at www.state.gov/s/l/c3746.htm.

54 The 2001 US–Jordan agreement contained nothing on point, and later agreements contain statements on 'the mutual supportiveness' of environmental and trade agreements and promises to consult on this matter within the WTO: eg Art 19.8 AUSFTA.

55 Art 20.10 US–Korea, Art 18.13 US–Colombia, Art 17.13.3 US–Panama and Art 18.13 US–Peru.

56 Art A-04 Canada–Chile, Art I.3 Canada–Costa Rica, Art 1-06 Chile–Mexico, Art 1.03 Panama–Taiwan.

There are also examples of more wide-ranging conflicts clauses, such as the clause in the EFTA–Singapore FTA stating that '[t]he provisions of this Agreement shall be without prejudice to the rights and obligations of the Parties under the [WTO Agreement] *and any other international agreement* to which they are a party'.[57] In addition, there are instances of a more targeted use of this formulation. Thus, in the Australia–Thailand FTA the parties 'affirm with respect to each other their existing rights and obligations relating to technical regulations' not only under the TBT Agreement but also under 'all other international agreements, including environmental and conservation agreements, to which the Parties are party'.[58]

Also worth noting are a number of ambiguous conflicts clauses, as in the China–Pakistan agreement, in which the parties 'confirm' (or 'affirm') their rights and obligations under other agreements.[59] It is not clear whether this means that the treaty 'is not to be considered as incompatible' with the other agreements, as required by Article 30(2) of the Vienna Convention. An alternative reading would be that the provision amounts to an unenforceable political statement of the 'mutual supportiveness' of the different regimes. In the same way, treaties sometimes reiterate commitments under other regimes, for instance human rights regimes, but this does not necessarily mean that those regimes prevail in cases of conflict. The preambular recitals found in many EFTA (and now Balkan) agreements that 'no provision of this Agreement may be interpreted as exempting the Contracting Parties from their obligations under other international agreements' are of similarly ambiguous legal effect. Here the language is clearer, though there are limits to how far mere 'interpretation' can avoid a conflict, but the fact that the language is located in a preamble weakens the binding force of the statement.

D. Positive social obligations

Provisions in regional trade agreements allowing the parties free scope to take protective measures go part of the way to resolving any problems between trade and social protection. Some countries however have decided on a more complete solution, which is to use regional trade agreements as a platform for the positive regulation of social protection. Many agreements contain provisions on cooperation on these matters, but these provisions are not further discussed in this chapter.

---

57 Emphasis added. Art 4 EFTA–Singapore. See also Art 1.3 Chile–Korea; Art 18.2 NZ–Transpacific; Art 3 China–Pakistan; Art 20.1 China–Hong Kong; Art 20.1 China–Macao; cf Art 4.2 EFTA–SACU (which covers only 'obligations').

58 Art 703(1) Australia–Thailand.

59 Art 3 China–Pakistan; Art 4 EFTA–Chile; Art 42.4 EFTA–Tunisia; also Art 3 China–Chile; Art 1.1(2) Singapore–Jordan.

1. NAFTA

NAFTA was ground-breaking in linking the regulation of social matters to trade obligations. It did this by means of two side agreements imposing substantive obligations on the parties, and these established a template that has influenced almost every subsequent set of provisions on and environmental and labour standards in regional trade agreements.

The obligations are of several distinct types. One is a minimum standard: the parties 'shall ensure' that their laws provide for high levels of environmental and labour protection, in the latter case defined by reference to eleven labour 'principles'.[60] Second is an obligation concerning the enforcement of domestic laws: in NAFTA the parties must promote compliance with and enforce their domestic environmental and labour legislation[61] subject to a responsible exercise of discretion and a bona fide decision to allocate resources to other relevant matters.[62] Third is an aspirational obligation: the parties 'shall strive' continually to improve their existing laws.

These side agreements were also innovative in terms of their mechanisms for enforcing these obligations. Both side agreements provided for a complaints mechanism triggered by 'citizen submissions'. Under the environment side agreement, a citizen submission is lodged with the secretariat of the body administering the agreement (the Commission for Environmental Cooperation);[63] under the labour agreement the submissions are lodged with the relevant party itself.[64] These complaints can ultimately lead to inter-state enforcement, although not in respect of all obligations.[65] Simplifying somewhat, consultations are available for any matter under these agreements, but formal dispute settlement is available only for the failure to enforce domestic environmental laws and labour laws, and even then only in relation to occupational safety and health, child labour or minimum wage labour standards. There are also two conditions: the failure to enforce

---

60 Annex 1 North American Agreement on Labor Cooperation (NAALC) lists these principles as: (i) freedom of association and protection of the right to organize; (ii) the right to bargain collectively; (iii) the right to strike; (iv) prohibition of forced labour; (v) labour protection for children and young persons; (vi) minimum employment standards, such as minimum wages and overtime pay, covering wage earners, including those not covered by collective agreements; (vii) elimination of employment discrimination on the basis of such grounds as race, religion, age, sex, or other grounds as determined by each party's domestic laws; (viii) equal pay for men and women; (ix) prevention of occupational injuries and illnesses; (x) compensation in cases of occupational injuries and illnesses; and (xi) protection of migrant workers.

61 Art 5 North American Agreement on Environmental Cooperation (NAAEC); Art 3 NAALC. They must also publicize their laws and provide for private party enforcement of these laws before impartial tribunals: Arts 4, 6–7 NAAEC; Arts 4–7 NAALC.

62 Art 45(1) NAAEC; Art 49(1) NAALC.   63 Arts 14 and 15 NAAEC.

64 Art 16(3) NAALC. There have been around eighty citizen submissions under the environment agreement, and around half that under the labour agreement: See the lists at www.cec.org/Page.asp?PageID=1226&SiteNodeID=545 and www.dol.gov/ilab/trade/agreements/naalc.htm respectively.

65 Parts 4 and 5 NAAEC; Parts 4 and 5 NAALC.

domestic laws must be trade-related[66] and must represent a 'persistent pattern' of behaviour.[67] In such cases arbitral panels may award a monetary penalty, collected if necessary by suspending trade concessions, though the labour side agreement limits this remedy cases involving occupational safety and health, child labour or minimum wage standards.[68] The monetary penalty is to be spent on environmental or labour law enforcement (or also environmental improvements) in the territory of the party in default.[69]

2. United States

Because of the absence of 'fast track' negotiating authority between 1994 and 2002, the US only negotiated one regional trade agreement during this period, namely with Jordan in 2001. This agreement included social provisions based on the NAFTA side agreements, although with some differences.

In relation to labour standards, the parties 'reaffirm their obligations as members of the International Labor Organization ("ILO") and their commitments under the ILO Declaration on Fundamental Principles and Rights at Work and its Follow-up'.[70] It is unclear whether this represents an independently enforceable obligation. In light of the next obligation, it must be considered unlikely. This next obligation is to 'strive to ensure that such labor principles and [a list of] internationally recognized labor rights … are recognized and protected by domestic law'.[71] This is a minimum standards obligation but is weaker than the equivalent in NAFTA in two respects.

---

66 In a complaint against Guatemala, the US states that 'the ordinary meaning of the phrase "in a manner affecting trade" in Article 16.2.1(a) of the CAFTA–DR FTA, on which see below at n 84, encompasses any course of action or inaction by a Party that has a bearing on, influences or changes – i.e., affects – cross-border economic activity, including by influencing conditions of competition within and among the CAFTA-DR Parties.' See *In the Matter of Guatemala – Issues Relating to the Obligations Under Article 16.2.1(a) of the CAFTA–DR, Initial Written Submission of the United States*, 3 November 2014, at www.ustr.gov/sites/default/files/US%20sub1.fin_.pdf.

67 Art 24 NAAEC; Art 17 NAALC.

68 Canada is not subject to trade sanctions, and has arranged that any fines will be enforced domestically by Canadian courts: Annex 36A NAAEC; Annex 41A NAALC.

69 Annex 34(3) NAAEC; Annex 39(3) NAALC.

70 Art 6(1) US–Jordan. Philip Alston has sparked a debate on whether the ILO Declaration (and the use of this Declaration in US regional trade agreements) threatens the ILO regime. See Philip Alston, '"Core Labour Standards" and the Transformation of the International Labour Rights Regime' (2004) 15 *EJIL* 457 and responses: Brian Langille, 'Core Labour Rights – The True Story (Reply to Alston)' (2005) 16 *EJIL* 409, Francis Maupain, 'Revitalization Not Retreat: The Real Potential of the 1998 ILO Declaration for the Universal Protection of Workers' Rights' (2005) 16 *EJIL* 439, Philip Alston, 'Facing Up to the Complexities of the ILO's Core Labour Standards Agenda' (2005) 16 *EJIL* 467 and Jordi Agustí-Panareda, Franz Christian Ebert and Desirée LeClercq, 'Labour Provisions in Free Trade Agreements: Fostering their Consistency with the ILO Standards System', ILO Background Paper, March 2014, 16-19, at www.ilo.org/wcmsp5/groups/public/—dgreports/—inst/documents/genericdocument/wcms_237940.pdf.

71 Art 6(1) US–Jordan. It is going too far to say that 'Article 6(1) requires parties to enact domestic legislation to provide for a minimum wage': Roman Grynberg and Veniana Qalo, 'Labour Standards in US and EU Preferential Trading Arrangements' (2006) 40 *JWT* 619, at 630. Art 6(3) adds, seemingly redundantly, that 'each Party shall strive to ensure that its laws provide for labor standards consistent with the internationally recognized labor rights set forth in paragraph 6.'

First, the list of rights is more limited: it misses the ILO core labour standard on discrimination.[72] Second, the parties are only obliged to 'strive to ensure' that they will meet these standards, which is weaker than the 'ensure' obligation in NAFTA.[73] The minimum environmental standards are similar in both agreements, although again the 'ensure' obligation has become 'strive to ensure'.[74]

In relation to existing laws, the US–Jordan agreement adds a new provision stating that 'it is inappropriate to encourage trade by relaxing domestic [environmental/labor] laws',[75] although what this means is that 'each Party shall strive to ensure that it does not waive or otherwise derogate from, or offer to waive or otherwise derogate from, such laws as an encouragement for trade with the other Party.'[76] This may be best understood as targeting specific regulatory subsidisation in relation to specific geographical areas (as, for example, Special Economic Zones) or types of enterprise. The agreement does not remove the ability of the parties to modify their laws in a general manner. It reproduces the NAFTA obligations on enforcement of domestic laws, but now adds as substantive conditions what were previously dispute settlement conditions: the parties must not fail to effectively enforce domestic environmental and labour legislation through a sustained or recurring course of action or inaction in a manner affecting trade.[77] It also contains an aspirational obligation to the effect that 'each Party shall strive to continue to improve those [environmental and labour] laws.'[78] Finally, the agreement provided that all of its labour and environmental obligations – relevantly, its minimum standards – are subject to the same dispute settlement provisions as the economic aspects of the agreement, with 'any appropriate and commensurate measure' as an available remedy.[79] In practice, however, this amounted to nothing, as side letters between the US and Jordan ruled out this option.[80]

The Trade Promotion Authority Act of 2002, which granted fast-track negotiating authority for another year, set out negotiating objectives on a range of matters, including on environmental and labour provisions.[81] It required negotiators to

---

72 Art 6(6) US–Jordan. The list does however include a non-ILO right to minimum wages. This list, and the omission of non-discrimination, has its origins in the US GSP program of the early 1980s. For the history, see Lance Compa, 'From Chile to Vietnam: International Labour Law and Workers' Rights in International Trade' in Claire Kilpatrick and Joanna Scott (eds.), *Critical Legal Perspectives on Global Governance: Liber Amicorum David M Trubek* (Oxford: Hart, 2013), at 146–147.

73 The US Department of Labor concluded that Bahrain had violated 'strive to ensure' obligations in the US–Bahrain agreement in US Department of Labor, Public Report of Review of US Submission 2011-01 (Bahrain), at www.dol.gov/ilab/reports/pdf/20121220Bahrain.pdf.

74 Art 5(2) US–Jordan.   75 Arts 5(1) and 6(2) US–Jordan.   76 *Ibid.*

77 Arts 5(3) and 6(4) US–Jordan.   78 Arts 5(2) and 6(3) US–Jordan.   79 Art 17(2)(b) US–Jordan.

80 See the side letters dated 23 July 2001, in which the representatives of the US and Jordan each promised that 'my Government would not expect or intend to apply the Agreement's dispute settlement enforcement procedures to secure its rights under the Agreement in a manner that results in blocking trade.' For discussion of the relevance of these side letters for the enforcement of the labour provisions of the agreement, US Congressional Record, Proceedings and Debates of the 107th Congress, First Session, House of Representatives, 31 July 2001, H4871–H4881 (text of letters at H4874–H4875).

81 19 USC 3802.

'seek provisions in trade agreements under which parties to those agreements strive to ensure that they do not weaken or reduce the protections afforded in domestic environmental and labor laws'[82] and – along the lines of the US–Jordan agreement – to seek equal dispute settlement mechanisms for all obligations in the agreements.[83] US regional trade agreements were negotiated pursuant to this mandate with Singapore, Chile, Morocco, CAFTA–DR, Bahrain and Oman, but these agreements do not fully correspond to these demands. While they revert to the higher NAFTA minimum standard in requiring the parties to 'ensure' high levels of environmental protection (labour remains with 'strive to ensure' the minimum standard), the obligations concerning domestic laws remain essentially the same as before. In particular, there is no lock-in of existing standards, but only a prohibition on waiving or derogating from an existing law.[84] There is also a qualification to the effect that 'labor standards should not be used for protectionist trade purposes'. Furthermore, contrary to the US–Jordan agreement, and contrary also to the mandated negotiating objectives, these agreements offer dispute settlement only in relation to the domestic enforcement obligations.[85]

There was a significant shift in policy in May 2007, when both Democrat and Republican parties agreed on strengthened social provisions in future regional trade agreements.[86] This produced a new template for social provisions that has been adopted in all subsequent US agreements. In these agreements, there is a new minimum standard consisting of an obligation requiring each party to 'adopt and maintain in its statutes and regulations, and practices' a list of labour rights, which are said to be 'as stated in' the 1998 ILO Declaration on Fundamental Principles and Rights and Work and its Follow-Up.[87] The list now includes non-discrimination but no longer includes 'acceptable standards of work'. There is an equivalent obligation to implement obligations in a list of multilateral environmental agreements. On the other hand, by way of a footnote, this minimum standard is now only applicable when it affects trade or investment between the parties. The provisions on existing laws and domestic enforcement obligation continue much as before, but with a reduced discretion to allocate resources in relation to minimum labour standards. The other major change is that the same dispute settlement options are available for all obligations, including removal of the cap on fines.

---

82 19 USC 3802(a)(7).   83 19 USC 3802(b)(12).
84 These clauses have generated several claims, including one formal invocation of dispute settlement proceedings in relation to Guatemala. See https://ustr.gov/issue-areas/labor/bilateral-and-regional-trade-agreements.
85 For a critical view see Labor Advisory Committee for Trade Negotiations and Trade Policy, *Report to the President, the Congress and the United States Trade Representative on the US–Chile and US–Singapore Free Trade Agreements*, 28 February 2003.
86 USTR, Press Release, 'Bipartisan Trade Deal', May 2007, at www.ustr.gov/sites/default/files/uploads/fact sheets/2007/asset_upload_file127_11319.pdf.
87 By means of a footnote the agreement ensures that the obligation does not cover the Follow-Up to the 1998 ILO Declaration, which concerns reporting requirements. As to whether there might be any significance to the use of the word 'rights' as opposed to 'principles', see Agustí-Panareda *et al.*, above at n 70, 16–19.

These agreements have generated a number of formal complaints, leading in some cases to improvements in labour conditions.[88]

3. Canada

Canada followed NAFTA with agreements with Israel, Chile and Costa Rica. Its agreement with Israel contains no social clause, while its agreement with Chile is accompanied by environment and labour side agreements very much on the NAFTA model. Its agreement with Costa Rica is similar but has a reduced system of inter-state enforcement. Enforcement under the labour agreement is limited to 'reasonable and appropriate measures, exclusive of fines or any measure affecting trade, but including the modification of cooperative activities ... to encourage the other Party to remedy that persistent pattern',[89] while the environment agreement replaces enforcement with a system of implementation by 'government to government coordination'.[90] The environment agreement also adds in its preamble that 'it is inappropriate to relax environmental laws in order to encourage trade'.

Nonetheless, Canada's subsequent side agreements with Peru (2009), Colombia (2011), Jordan (2012) and Panama (2010) strengthened labour (though not environmental) protections in several ways in a manner that was clearly influenced by developments in US practice.[91] These agreements now contain an obligation to implement ILO principles, including the core labour rights as well as acceptable minimum employment standard and non-discrimination in respect of working conditions for migrant workers, and soft language on improving these protections. They also contain a clause prohibiting derogation from domestic laws in order to encourage trade or investment.[92] Formal dispute settlement with sanctions is available for violations of core labour rights or a persistent pattern of failure to comply with domestic laws on all labour matters.[93] There are also remedies, including enforcement of an action plan recommended by the panel or, if a party fails to implement the action plan, a monetary fine. In the Canada–Panama, Canada–Peru and Canada–Colombia agreements, any monetary assessment made is limited to US$15m. The Canada–Jordan agreement places no limitations on the amount awarded by the review panel but the fine must be paid into a special labour fund to implement an action plan.

---

88 See ILO/International Institute for Labour Studies, *Social Dimensions of Free Trade Agreements* (ILO: Geneva, 2013), Ch 2 and Jeffrey Vogt, 'Trade and Investment Arrangements and Labor Rights' in Lara Blecher *et al.* (eds.), *Corporate Responsibility for Human Rights Impacts: New Expectations and Paradigms* (Chicago: ABA Publishing, 2014).
89 Art 23(5) CCRALC.   90 Art 7(1) CCRAEC.
91 The 2009 Canada–EFTA agreement seems not to have included any social provisions.
92 Eg Arts 1 and 2 Canada–Peru.   93 Eg Art 13 Canada–Peru.

4. Chile

Chile has also adopted elements of the post-NAFTA model in a number of its free trade agreements. The 2007 Chile–Panama side agreements on labour and environment contain soft obligations affirming the parties' ILO obligations along with obligations to 'strive to ensure' that their laws implement these obligations. There is also a soft statement to the effect that it is inappropriate to use waivers and derogations of labour and environmental laws to encourage trade and investment. The only concrete obligation is to enforce existing labour laws. There is a contact point for disputes but no formal dispute settlement. The 2008 Chile–Colombia agreement is somewhat stronger, insofar as it contains in addition an obligation to ensure high levels of environmental protection.[94] The 2009 Chile–Peru side agreement is similar to the Chile–Panama side agreement, although it additionally refers to the 1990 UN International Convention on the Protection of the Rights of All Migrant Workers and Members of Their Families. The 2009 Chile–Turkey agreement also extends the existing model insofar as it adds that a party 'shall not fail to effectively enforce its labor laws, in a manner affecting trade between the Parties'.[95] When it comes to the environment, on the other hand, the provisions are hortatory.

5. The European Union

The approach of the European Union to social issues consists of two main components. On the one hand, it has a long-standing practice of including 'human rights clauses' in its international agreements (including regional trade agreements) which allow for the suspension of the agreement in the event that one of the parties violates human rights or democratic principles. Traditionally, the EU preferred to deal with 'softer' social issues, including labour and environment, by way of cooperation, entailing also where necessary financial and technical assistance. Since 2008, however, the EU has also adopted provisions on labour and environmental protection based on the post-NAFTA model.

(a) Human rights clauses

Human rights clauses have their origins in the Lomé Conventions of the 1970s and 1980s, but the EU decided in 1995 on a systematic policy of including such clauses in all future international trade agreements, including regional trade agreements.[96] Clauses of this type are now found in the nine regional trade agreements between the EU and its European and Mediterranean neighbours, as well as in regional trade agreements with numerous other countries. It is also found in the Cotonou Agreement,[97] which governs

---

94 Art 18.2(2) Chile–Colombia FTA.   95 Art 37(7) Chile–Turkey.
96 For a full analysis of these clauses see Lorand Bartels, *Human Rights Conditionality in the EU's International Agreements* (Oxford: Oxford University Press, 2005).
97 The Cotonou Agreement is a framework trade and development agreement between the EU and seventy-eight developing countries, mainly former colonies.

relations with seventy-eight African, Caribbean and Pacific countries and in a large number of non-preferential trade and cooperation agreements.

The core of the human rights clause is an 'essential elements' clause stating that:

> Respect for the democratic principles and fundamental human rights established by the Universal Declaration of Human Rights shall inspire the domestic and international policies of the Parties and shall constitute an essential element of this Agreement.

This basic provision is given its main operative effect via a 'non-execution' clause, which states that a failure to fulfil an obligation under the agreement, including human rights obligations, entitles the other party, subject to a consultation procedure, to take 'appropriate measures'. To date, human rights clauses have been applied in cases involving gross human rights violations and military coups,[98] but they have the potential to cover a range of matters, including any violations of labour or environmental rights that rise to the level of 'human rights'.[99]

(b) Sustainable development chapters

Since 2008, the EU has also introduced labour and environmental provisions in its trade agreements, based very much on the post-2007 United States model. In so-called 'sustainable development chapters', these agreements contain minimum obligations to implement listed multilateral ILO and environmental obligations,[100] and above this a set of other obligations concerning domestic legislation. Some agreements require the parties to 'strive for' high levels of protection, subject to a proviso that this is not done for protectionist purposes.[101] The Cariforum agreement goes further in two respects. First, the obligation is to 'ensure' high levels of protection.[102] Second, there is an innovative obligation 'not to encourage trade or foreign direct investment to enhance or maintain a competitive advantage by ... lowering the level of protection provided by domestic [environmental and public health/social and labour] legislation'.[103] This wording locks in existing levels of protection in a way that the other versions of these 'do not waive or derogate' clauses do not, albeit only in relation to the purposes mentioned. Ironically, then, it is the EU that ended up implementing what was a negotiating objective for the US in 2002. Further significant differences from the North American model concern enforcement. The EU agreements provide for varying degrees of civil society involvement in monitoring of these provisions,[104] but ultimately there is no equivalent to 'citizen submissions' nor to inter-state enforcement by means of dispute settlement. In this respect, the EU model falls far short of the North American model.

---

98 Johanne Døhlie Saltnes, 'The EU's Human Rights Policy: Unpacking the Literature on the EU's Implementation of Aid Conditionality', *Arena Working Paper No 2*, March 2013, at 7 (Table 1).
99 Lorand Bartels, 'Human Rights and Sustainable Development Obligations in the EU's Free Trade Agreements' (2013) 40 *Legal Issues of Economic Integration* 297.
100 Eg Arts 286 and 287 EU–Central America.   101 Eg Art 285 EU–Central America.
102 Art 192 EU–Cariforum.   103 Arts 188(1)(a) and 193(1)(a) EU–Cariforum.
104 See, eg, Woolcock *et al.*, *European Union: Trade Agreement with Colombia and Peru*, European Parliament, March 2012, www.europarl.europa.eu/committees/en/studies.html, Ch 6.

6. Other countries and regions

Other countries and regions have been inspired by these approaches. EFTA presents an interesting case, as it tends to follow the EU model, at least to some extent. Early EFTA agreements contain a type of human rights clause on the model of the EU agreements, but this practice petered out.[105] In 2010 EFTA adopted a new policy, again taking the EU's lead, of including 'sustainable development chapters' in future trade agreements.[106] This policy has now been reflected in an agreement with Montenegro and a labour side agreement with Hong Kong. These provisions are slightly weaker than their EU counterparts. First, the parties merely 'recall' and 'reaffirm' their multilateral obligations without incorporating these into the agreement. Second, while these agreements include a variant of the EU–Cariforum provision on not weakening existing protections, the prohibition applies only when the measure is for the '*sole* intention to encourage investment from another Party or to seek or to enhance a competitive trade advantage of producers or service providers operating in its territory'.[107] Protections can be lowered so long as there is another reason for doing so.

Concrete obligations in relation to environmental and labour standards are also found in some other agreements, again based on the NAFTA or post-NAFTA model.[108] One interesting example is the 2006 Nicaragua–Republic of China (Taiwan) agreement, which adopts the US model of that era. The post-NAFTA practice of the US has also influenced New Zealand,[109] which has negotiated several labour and environment side agreements in the context of free trade agreements with countries in the region. In these side agreements the parties promise that they will 'not seek to gain trade or investment advantage' by weakening or derogating from

105 Art 1.2 of EFTA–Jordan, EFTA–Morocco, EFTA–Palestinian Authority, and EFTA–Macedonia. Another permits 'rebalancing measures' in the event of a failure to fulfil an obligation: Arts 1.2 and 33 EFTA–Lebanon. The preamble to the EFTA–Tunisia agreement refers to 'the observance of human rights and political and economic freedom, which form the very basis for co-operation between the EFTA States and Tunisia'. The EFTA agreements with Turkey, Israel, Mexico, Singapore, Chile, Singapore and SACU have no operative human rights provisions.

106 The policy is summarized in SECO, *Conclusion of EFTA work on trade, environment and labour standards*, 30 August 2010. I owe this reference to Ioana Cismas, 'The Integration of Human Rights in Bilateral and Plurilateral Trade Agreements: Arguments for a Coherent Relationship with Reference to the Swiss Context' (2012–13) 21 *Currents: International Trade Law Journal* 3, at 18 n 56.

107 Art 4(2)(a) EFTA–Hong Kong Labour Side Agreement; Art 34(2)(a) EFTA–Montenegro (emphasis added). These agreements also state that '[t]he violation of fundamental principles and rights at work shall not be invoked or otherwise used as a legitimate comparative advantage.' It is not clear what this adds or even means.

108 For a very useful list and analysis, see Franz Ebert and Anne Posthuma, 'Labour Provisions in Trade Arrangements: Current Trends and Perspectives', *IILS Discussion Paper, No 205* (Geneva: IILS, 2011), although it should be noted that the categorization of provisions in this publication differs somewhat from that adopted here.

109 In 2001 New Zealand adopted frameworks for integrating labour and environment issues into its regional trade agreements. See www.mfat.govt.nz/Trade-and-Economic-Relations/NZ-and-the-WTO/Trade-Issues/0-environment-framework.php.

their labour or environment legislation, and reaffirm (or, in the case of non-Members, affirm) ILO obligations and commitments. They also promise to 'work actively to ensure' that their legislation is 'in harmony' with 'internationally recognised labour principles and rights' and 'internationally accepted levels of environmental protection such as those established by multilateral environment agreements to which the Participants are party', and 'to promote public awareness of [their] environmental laws, regulations, policies and practices domestically'. Similar to at least some of the US agreements, these also state that each party will 'ensure' (this being notably stronger than the previous terminology of 'work actively to ensure') that its trade and environmental legislation and policies are not used for trade protectionist purposes.[110] But practice is not uniform: the New Zealand side agreements with Hong Kong, for instance, are largely hortatory.

III. WTO issues

A final issue also deserves consideration, which is the effect of these regional rules in WTO law. In principle, while Article XXIV GATT requires the parties to a regional trade agreement to eliminate 'duties and other restrictive regulations of commerce' with respect to 'substantially all the trade' in products originating in their territories, there is an exception for measures 'permitted under . . . Article XX'.[111] But many of the provisions discussed in this chapter go beyond Article XX. The simple answer would be that under the WTO, a measure not covered by a relevant WTO exception is simply not permitted. Indeed, in the WTO case *Canada – Periodicals*,[112] Canada failed to mention the NAFTA 'cultural industries' exception, even though this was undoubtedly relevant to the subject matter of the dispute. At one point it seemed possible that the WTO dispute settlement system would take account of such law 'applicable between the parties'.[113] But recent developments have shown the WTO system to be conservative in this regard.[114] The answer will have to await a future defendant in WTO dispute settlement

---

110 Eg NZ–Malaysia Agreements on Labour and Environmental Cooperation.

111 Art XXIV:8(a)(i) GATT for customs unions and Art XXIV:8(b) GATT for free trade areas. Two additional points: first, it is difficult to see the lexical relevance of the apparent condition 'where necessary' in these paragraphs; second, the security exception in Art XXI GATT, which is not included in the list of permitted exceptions in Art XXIV, also overrides Art XXIV by its own terms. This reduces the value of the argument that the treaty drafters cannot have intended to prohibit parties from taking security measures under regional trade agreements, and therefore that the list in Art XXIV is not exclusive. This argument is usually made in support of the legality of other non-listed trade restrictions under regional trade agreements, in particular trade remedies. On the other hand, this does not explain the inclusion of Art XX in the list.

112 WTO Appellate Body Report, *Canada –Periodicals*, adopted on 30 July 1997, WT/DS31/AB/R.

113 Joost Pauwelyn, *Conflict of Norms in Public International Law: WTO Law Relates to Other Rules of International Law* (Cambridge: Cambridge University Press, 2003).

114 See Chapter 6 of this volume.

proceedings invoking a clause in a regional trade agreement between the same parties as a defence to the WTO claim.

IV. Prospects for social issues in future regional trade agreements

The relationship between trade and social issues has – at least for some countries – become less sensitive over the past decade. Some countries are committed to negotiating a link between trade and social protection, others are feeling their way, and yet others remain sceptical. There is an evident interest from developed countries in these matters, but this is not fixed. Some developing countries (most particularly Chile) also see the merit in permitting themselves – and sometimes obliging themselves and their partners – to act to protect social values. And some developed countries, such as Australia and Japan, are still reluctant to connect trade with what at one time were considered to be 'non-trade' issues.

Where agreements do seek to promote rules on environment and labour, one can see certain trends emerging in terms of the approach and wording adopted. At the general level, there is some modest effort to expand on the general exceptions, and to work with conflicts clauses to ensure that obligations in other agreements take priority over the trade agreement. There is also a more or less fixed menu of provisions that are now regularly used to establish positive social obligations covering minimum standards, non-derogation clauses, non-'fail to enforce' clauses, and, more recently, lock-in clauses. The practice of the EU in relation to human rights clauses is also settled, although it does not seem to have caught on with other countries, which do not advertise an external human rights policy to quite the same degree.

14

Dispute settlement

VICTORIA DONALDSON AND SIMON LESTER

I. Introduction

As international trade disputes have shifted over the years from diplomatic exercises to more legalistic contests,[1] the dispute settlement procedures set out in trade agreements have taken on a more important role. The dispute provisions of the GATT 1947 were a mere two paragraphs.[2] Over the years, these provisions were supplemented with additional rules, eventually developing into the detailed procedures of the WTO's Dispute Settlement Understanding. And in the 350-plus WTO disputes that have been brought since the WTO's inception, these rules have been elaborated by panels and the Appellate Body. The result is that today the WTO's dispute procedures are well-developed, widely studied, and generally considered reliable and credible by governments and other actors.

Not surprisingly, then, in drafting the preferential trade agreements (PTAs) discussed in this book, the state parties to these agreements came up with dispute provisions that are similar in many ways to the WTO rules. As a result, for many of the topics discussed in this chapter, we note the related WTO provisions and offer comparisons. However, there are differences as well. These differences may reflect the various opinions among WTO Members as to what the rules should be, as well as new thinking about the best approach to certain issues based on the experience at the WTO.

In this chapter, we examine the following aspects of the dispute procedures in recent bilateral and regional PTAs. First, we look at the *administration* of dispute settlement procedures. At the WTO, administration of the DSU is carried out by the Dispute Settlement Body, which is made up of all the WTO Members. In addition, the WTO has a Secretariat that provides various services in support of this administration. In this section, we examine whether and to what extent PTAs have similar bodies and support.

---

1 See generally, Robert E. Hudec, *Enforcing International Trade Law: The Evolution of the Modern GATT Legal System* (Salem, NH: Butterworth, 1993).

2 In fairness, the GATT was originally intended to be one chapter in the larger International Trade Organisation (ITO), which had six full articles setting out dispute settlement procedures. But the ITO never came into force, and the GATT thus had to function on its own.

Second, we address the relationship of PTA dispute settlement to other dispute settlement, such as the DSU. A key aspect of this issue is the recent talk about the 'spaghetti bowl' or 'noodle bowl' of trade agreements that now exist, with a great deal of overlap among the countries who have signed agreements with each other. In this context, we examine the rules these PTAs establish for addressing the options for bringing disputes in different fora.

Next, we turn to the details of bringing a complaint. In this section, we try to explain how agreements differ in the extent to which they set out specific rules in this regard, and also how they address certain systemic issues relating to the complaints that can be brought.

We then turn to the process of selecting the 'judges' who will hear the case. Trade disputes differ from most domestic judicial systems in that they do not have a standing body of judges who will hear cases. Rather, the disputing governments themselves choose the judges (for the most part).

We also examine the details of the panel process, comparing and contrasting the different rules that have been chosen.

Finally, we discuss several aspects of the rules on implementation of adverse decisions, that is, where a violation has been found. This is an area in which there has been some new thinking in recent years, as governments try to work out the most effective rules possible for ensuring that adverse judgments are followed.

Before turning to the substance, we note two overarching points at the outset. First, we are not dealing here with *all* dispute settlement under the PTAs at issue. Rather, we are focusing on government-to-government dispute settlement over 'trade' issues, which is generally the subject of a separate chapter in these agreements. In addition to this type of dispute settlement, some agreements have special dispute procedures in areas such as investment, environment and labour. These areas will be not be covered here, but will be discussed, albeit briefly, in the substantive chapters of the book covering these topics.

Second, we note that at the time of this writing there have been no disputes under the recent bilateral and regional trade agreements that are the focus of this book. Some older agreements, like the North American Free Trade Agreement (NAFTA) and the United States–Israel Free Trade Agreement, have seen a handful of government-to-government disputes, several of which resulted in panel reports being issued. For the more recent agreements, however, there has been nothing so far. As a result, there is no dispute settlement practice to look at, which creates some important gaps in the understanding of how the process will actually work.

II. Administration of dispute settlement

We first examine the various types of institutional frameworks created under PTAs for the administration of dispute settlement. Before doing so, we recall how this is handled in the context of the WTO.

The administration of dispute settlement is expressly identified in the WTO Agreement as one of the functions of the WTO.[3] Formally, all WTO functions are carried out, at the highest level, by the Ministerial Conference, which is composed of all WTO Members and which meets at least once every two years.[4] Between such meetings, responsibility for WTO functions lies with the General Council, also composed of representatives of all WTO Members.[5] The WTO Agreement further provides that the General Council is to convene as the Dispute Settlement Body, with its own chairman and rules of procedure, to discharge the responsibilities assigned to that Body under the DSU.[6]

Thus, it is the DSB which administers dispute settlement in the WTO on a day-to-day basis. The DSB has a formal role throughout the process, beginning with the requirement that it be notified of all requests for consultations through to its surveillance and monitoring of the implementation of adopted panel and Appellate Body reports. The findings set out in panel and Appellate Body reports bind the parties to the dispute only once those reports have been adopted by the DSB, and DSB authorisation is required before a complaining party may impose trade sanctions against a responding party who has not brought its inconsistent measure into conformity with its obligations. In this regard, the DSU expressly assigns to the DSB 'the authority to establish panels, adopt panel and Appellate Body reports, maintain surveillance of implementation of rulings and recommendations, and authorise suspension of concessions and other obligations'.[7] The DSB is directed to meet as often as necessary to carry out its functions.[8] In practice, this means that it meets regularly once a month, supplemented by special meetings from time to time.

The DSB takes decisions by consensus.[9] However, this decision-making rule is reversed at the following key stages of the dispute settlement system: the establishment of a panel,[10] the adoption of panel and Appellate Body reports,[11] and the authorisation of the suspension of concessions.[12] The fact that a 'negative consensus' decision-making rule applies at these vital steps in the proceedings operates to make it almost inconceivable that a responding party or its allies would succeed in getting the DSB to block any of these decisions. This, in turn, has the consequence that the essential responsibility for driving proceedings forward rests with the complaining party, who may request the DSB to take the necessary decisions to keep the process moving.[13]

---

3 Article III.3.   4 Article IV.1.   5 *WTO Agreement*, Article IV.2.   6 Article IV.3.
7 DSU, Article 2.1.   8 *Ibid.*, Article 2.3.
9 *Ibid.*, Article 2. Footnote 1 to that Article defines consensus to mean that no Member present when the decision is taken formally objects to the proposed decision.
10 DSU, Article 6.2.   11 *Ibid.*, Article 16.4.   12 *Ibid.*, Article 22, paras. 6 and 7.
13 The DSU imposes a 'negative consensus' rule by providing, in each case, that a decision 'shall' be taken unless the DSB decides by consensus otherwise.

As far as institutional support for dispute settlement is concerned, Article 27 of the DSU provides that the WTO Secretariat has the responsibility 'of assisting panels, especially on the legal, historical and procedural aspects of the matters dealt with, and of providing secretarial and technical support'.[14]

A. The administration of PTAs

None of the PTAs examined has as elaborate an institutional system as the WTO. Various arrangements exist. Most PTAs provide for some sort of joint committee or commission to deal with administration of the agreement.[15] This body may be at the cabinet or ministerial level, or at a lower level, or both.[16] Some PTAs create a single administrative body, but specify that it may meet either at the level of Ministers or of senior officials.[17] Yet other PTAs do not provide for any body to administer the agreement at all. Instead, they combine a requirement that each party identify a 'contact point' to facilitate bilateral communication on issues related to the PTA with a requirement for a periodic meeting of Ministers to review the operation of the agreement.[18] The PTAs that contemplate the creation of a joint administrative body provide for decision making to be achieved through consensus or mutual agreement. Typically, the joint administrative body or ministerial meeting is also empowered to establish additional committees, sub-committees or working groups as necessary.

14 DSU, Article 27.1. Paragraphs 2 and 3 of Article 27 provide for the WTO Secretariat to make a qualified legal expert available to assist developing countries with dispute settlement – while ensuring the continued impartiality of the Secretariat – and contemplate the provision of special training courses on dispute settlement procedures and practices to WTO Members. Article 17.7 contains a similar provision regarding the support to be provided to the Appellate Body, which has an administratively separate secretariat. Article VI of the WTO Agreement deals with the WTO Secretariat more generally.

15 These bodies have a variety of names, including the Joint Committee (EFTA–Chile Free Trade Agreement, Article 85), the Free Trade Co-ordinators (Canada–Costa Rica Free Trade Agreement, Article XIII.2); the Free Trade Commission (United States–Chile FTA, Article 21.1) and the Association Committee (European Union–Chile Association Agreement (EU–Chile AA), Article 6). Most agreements provide for regular meetings to be held annually, with an additional possibility to call additional special meetings. Some PTAs call for only biennial meetings/reviews (e.g., the New Zealand–Singapore Closer Economic Partnership Agreement (NZ–Singapore CEPA), Article 68.1; and EFTA–Chile FTA, Article 85.6).

16 Some agreements name these cabinet or ministerial-level bodies (e.g., the Free Trade Commission created in Article XIII.1 of the Canada–Costa Rica FTA and the Association Council created in Article 3 of the EU–Chile AA).

17 For example, the Closer Economic Partnership Joint Commission created in Article 16 of the New Zealand–Thailand Closer Economic Partnership Agreement (NZ–Thailand CEPA); the Free Trade Commission created in Article 18.1 of the Korea–Chile Free Trade Agreement; and the Free Trade Agreement Joint Commission created in Article 1701 of the Thailand–Australia Free Trade Agreement.

18 See, e.g., Singapore–Australia Free Trade Agreement, Chapter 17, Articles 2 and 3. The NZ–Singapore and Korea–Singapore PTAs do not create any joint body to oversee implementation of the agreement, although they do provide for consultations in certain substantive areas (not including dispute settlement) as well as periodic review of the agreement at the Ministerial level and the possibility to create committees and working groups (Article 68.1 and Article 22.1, respectively).

Although a few PTAs expressly provide a joint high-level body with the power to issue interpretations of the agreements,[19] many others are silent on this issue. Some PTAs provide that when an issue relating to the agreement arises in a domestic court or tribunal of either party, the relevant joint body created under that agreement is to submit an agreed interpretation of the PTA to that domestic court or administrative tribunal.[20]

With respect to the administration of dispute settlement under these agreements, only a few PTAs identify this as a discrete function to be carried out by a body created pursuant to the agreement.[21] Similarly, only a few PTAs refer to a secretariat that will be involved in administration of the agreement or in supporting a dispute settlement mechanism. However, even the agreements that do contemplate the provision of such support do not appear to envisage the creation of a new and autonomous entity so much as require each party to identify an existing body or individual within its territory that will serve as part of a 'secretariat' in order to provide support and co-ordinate, as necessary, with its counterpart in the territory of the other party to the PTA.[22]

B. The role of administrative bodies in dispute settlement

Generally speaking, the level of formal involvement of any administrative body in dispute settlement is significantly lower than is the case within the WTO, and in many PTAs there is no role for such bodies in individual disputes.[23] Many PTAs do,

---

19 An example is contained in Article 19.2.2(e) of the United States–Morocco Free Trade Agreement. Along the same lines, Article IX:2 of the WTO Agreement provides that '[t]he Ministerial Conference and the General Council shall have the exclusive authority to adopt interpretations of this Agreement and of the Multilateral Trade Agreements'.

20 E.g., Korea–Chile FTA, Article 19.16; US–Chile FTA, Article 22.19; Central American–Dominican Republic–United States Free Trade Agreement (CAFTA–DR–US), Article 20.20; and Canada–Costa Rica FTA, Article XIII.19. Such provisions usually also allow each party to submit its own interpretation to the domestic tribunal in the event that the joint administrative body is unable to reach agreement.

21 See, e.g., Canada–Costa Rica FTA, Article XIII.3. The PTAs to which the US is party contain specific provisions entitled 'Administration of Dispute Settlement Proceedings'. However, these provisions state only that each party to the agreement is to designate an office to provide administrative assistance to panels, notify the location of such office, and be responsible for its operation and costs as well as a share of the expenses of panellists (CAFTA–DR–US, Article 19.3; Australia–United States Free Trade Agreement (AUSFTA), Article 21.3; US–Chile FTA, Article 21.2; United States–Singapore Free Trade Agreement, Article 20.2; US–Morocco FTA, Article 20.3). The Japan–Singapore Economic Partnership Agreement (Japan–Singapore EPA) provides for the establishment of a Consultative Committee to 'facilitate the implementation of' Chapter 21 on dispute settlement, and requires that the Committee include 'one legal expert designated by each Party' (Article 140.4).

22 Canada–Costa Rica FTA, Article XIII.3; CAFTA–DR–US, Article 19.3; AUSFTA, Article 21.3; US–Chile FTA, Article 21.2; US–Singapore FTA, Article 20.2; US–Morocco FTA, Article 20.3; EFTA–Chile FTA, Article 86; and Korea–Chile FTA, Article 18.2 and Annex 18.2.

23 At first glance, the terms of the PTA between the European Communities (EC) and Israel appear to give a prominent role to its ministerial-level Association Council in assigning to that body responsibility for

however, provide for the relevant joint administrative body to adopt rules of procedure and/or codes of conduct for panels.[24] Below we survey the types of involvement
provided for in certain PTAs.

Several PTAs provide for the relevant joint body or secretariat to be notified of
certain steps in the resolution of an individual dispute.[25] In the early stages of a
dispute, quite a few PTAs require or allow a dispute to be referred to the joint body
created under the agreement at the outset of the dispute, either in lieu of[26] or
following bilateral consultations[27] and before the establishment of a panel. The
EFTA–Chile FTA provides for bilateral consultations between the disputing parties,
but adds that such '[c]onsultations shall take place before the Joint Committee unless
the Party or Parties making or receiving the request for consultations disagree'.[28]
A few PTAs allow a joint administrative body to provide or have recourse to good
offices, conciliation or mediation.[29]

Another approach is to give joint bodies a role in sending the dispute to a panel
and/or selecting the panellists. The India–Sri Lanka Free Trade Agreement provides for
its Joint Committee to be notified if the parties are unable to negotiate a solution to
their dispute, and then for a panel to be constituted by its Joint Committee 'in
consultation with the relevant Arbitration Bodies in the two countries'.[30] The
European Union–Israel Association Agreement (EU–Israel AA) provides for each
party to the dispute to appoint an arbitrator and for the third arbitrator to be appointed
by its ministerial-level Association Council, and the European Union–Chile
Association Agreement (EU–Chile AA) provides for an Association Committee to
establish a list of at least fifteen arbitrators and, upon receipt of a request to establish a
panel, to select three names by lot from that list.[31]

As far as the work of panels is concerned, a number of agreements make some
provision for administrative support. For example, the Canada–Costa Rica Free

---

settling disputes referred to it by either party. However the agreement also provides for the dispute to be
referred to a three-person arbitration in the event that the Association Council is unable to resolve the
dispute through a decision (European Union–Israel Association Agreement (EU–Israel AA), Article 75).
The European Union–South Africa Trade, Development and Co-operation Agreement (EU–SA TDCA)
contains similar provisions in its Article 104.

24 For example, Turkey–Morocco FTA, Article 33.9; Canada–Costa Rica FTA, Article XIII.12; CAFTA–DR–
    US, Article 20.7.2(d) and Article 20.10; AUSFTA, Article 21.7.5(b) and 21.8; US–Morocco FTA,
    Article 20.7.5(c) and Article 20.8; US–Singapore FTA, Article 20.4.4(b)(ii) and (d); US–Chile FTA,
    Articles 22.7.2(b) and 22.10; and EC–SA TDCA, Article 104.8.
25 See Canada–Costa Rica FTA, Articles XIII.7.2 (request for consultations) and XIII.8.3 (request for
    establishment of a panel); EFTA–Chile, Article 96.5 (implementing measure); and EU–Chile AA, Article
    188.5 (implementing measure).
26 Turkey–Morocco FTA, Article 33.2; EU–Chile AA, Article 183; and EU–Mexico FTA, Articles 42.2 and
    42.3.
27 CAFTA–DR–US, Article 20.5.1; US–Singapore FTA, Article 20.4.2(a); AUSFTA, Articles 21.6 and 21.7;
    US–Chile FTA, Article 22.5; US–Morocco, Article 20.6; and Japan–Singapore EPA, Article 140.3.
28 Article 90.1.   29 E.g., CAFTA–DR–US, Article 20.5.4(b); and US–Chile FTA, Article 22.5.4(b).
30 India–Sri Lanka FTA, Article XIII.1 and XIII.2.
31 EU–Chile AA, Articles 185.2 and 185.3. Article 104.7 of the EU–SA TDCA contains a similar provision.

Trade Agreement provides for its Secretariat to provide administrative assistance to panels.[32]

Although none of the PTAs have a formal procedure for adopting panel reports analogous to the WTO process, a few do stipulate that the panel report shall be delivered to the relevant joint administrative body.[33] Among these, a small number also provide for that joint body to then take a decision on the basis of the panel report which will bind the parties insofar as implementation is concerned.[34] In addition to requiring panel reports to be delivered to the Association Committee, the EU–Chile AA requires that all rulings on compliance measures and the level of suspension of benefits be provided to that Committee and made publicly available.[35] That agreement also requires responding parties to notify the Association Committee of implementing measures and complaining parties are to notify benefits that they propose to suspend.[36]

Most PTAs do not assign any joint body a role as far as the surveillance of panel rulings is concerned, but the Canada–Costa Rica FTA provides for its Free Trade Commission to include on its agenda the implementation of adopted recommendations or rulings whenever the measure found to be inconsistent has not been brought into conformity with the agreement.[37]

Lastly, as explained further in Part VI below, the Commissions/Joint Committees created in the various PTAs to which the United States (US) is party are given a special role in the collection and disbursement of monetary assessments in cases where there has been no implementation and the responding party elects to pay a monetary assessment rather than be subject to the suspension of concessions,[38] and in disputes relating to the enforcement of labour or environmental laws in which there has been no implementation.[39]

III. Relationship with other trade agreements and dispute settlement provisions

Possibly the most interesting, and thorniest, issues that arise in connection with the proliferation of PTAs concern how those agreements relate to each other and to the WTO's multilateral system. The substantive obligations created under the agreements are often similar or identical to those found in the WTO, and specific acts or measures taken by one country may give rise to a course of action under multiple

32 Canada–Costa Rica FTA, Article XIII.3.3(a).   33 E.g., Turkey–Morocco FTA, Article 33.6.
34 Turkey–Morocco FTA, Articles 33.7 and 33.8.   35 EU–Chile AA, Article 188.11.
36 *Ibid.*, Articles 188.5 and 188.8.
37 Canada–Costa Rica FTA, Article XIII.18.7. The reference to 'adopted' recommendations or rulings in this provision is puzzling because the agreement does not set out any procedure for the adoption of panel reports.
38 See US–Morocco FTA, Article 20.11.6; AUSFTA, Article 21.11.6; US–Chile FTA, Article 22.15.6; US–Singapore FTA, Article 20.6.6; and CAFTA–DR–US, Article 20.16.7.
39 See US–Morocco FTA, Article 20.12.4; AUSFTA, Article 21.12.4; US–Chile FTA, Article 22.16.4; US–Singapore FTA, Article 20.7.4; and CAFTA–DR–US, Article 20.17.4.

agreements. In such circumstances, it is far from clear which dispute settlement mechanism an affected trading party can or should seek recourse to, and whether there is any relationship or hierarchy of norms among the various obligations created under the myriad of overlapping bilateral, regional and multilateral agreements.

The DSU does not expressly refer to other dispute settlement fora, identify any hierarchy of international law norms[40] or offer disputing parties any choice of forum. Article 23 of the DSU does, however, include a provision that was intended to reinforce the obligation to use the WTO's multilateral dispute settlement system and prevent Members from taking unilateral action in relation to alleged violations of WTO obligations.[41] This provision requires WTO Members to seek redress for any violation of the covered agreements exclusively through the dispute settlement mechanism contained in the DSU, including the procedures for determining the reasonable period of time for implementation and for obtaining authorisation to suspend concessions. In addition, Members are prohibited from making any unilateral determination that a violation has occurred. Instead, Members must pursue their concerns through the DSU, following the adoption of, and consistent with, the findings contained in a panel or Appellate Body report. Although Article 23 was by all accounts designed to prevent unilateral action by WTO Members, it seems possible to argue that the provision would preclude *any* determination, other than pursuant to the DSU, that a violation of a WTO obligation has occurred, including by panels operating pursuant to PTAs. This could raise interesting questions given the extensive incorporation by reference of WTO obligations found in many PTAs although, as discussed below, several PTAs themselves preclude panels from making determinations concerning WTO obligations.

In contrast to the DSU, many PTAs explicitly acknowledge the existence of legal obligations under multiple agreements (in particular the WTO) as well as the existence of multiple dispute settlement mechanisms (in particular that of the WTO) that may be available in respect of the same set of circumstances. Some of the ways in which PTAs address these issues are examined below.

A. Obligations in other agreements and conflicting norms

1. References to WTO obligations

Nearly all of the PTAs examined contain extensive references to, or incorporation by reference of, substantive WTO obligations. These range from statements that the PTA is established 'consistent with Article XXIV' of the GATT and Article V of the

---

40 Except that Article 3.2 of the DSU prescribes the use of customary rules of interpretation of public international law and Article 1.2 makes clear that certain special and additional rules and procedures contained in other WTO agreements prevail over those contained in the DSU.

41 Article 23 was widely seen as a reaction to an attempt to constrain the US use of Section 301 of its Trade Act of 1974, which allowed the President to make a determination of inconsistency with a trade agreement and to take retaliatory action against the foreign country or entity responsible.

GATS,[42] to statements that the PTA shall not diminish or reduce rights and obligations under the covered agreements,[43] and include statements confirming rights and obligations under the WTO Agreement[44] or under specific covered agreements;[45] as well as the wholesale incorporation of specific obligations, such as the rules on national treatment set out in Article III of the GATT 1994 and its interpretative notes,[46] or Article XX of the GATT and its interpretative notes.[47] The incorporation of WTO rights and obligations relating to the use of safeguards and antidumping measures is common in many of the PTAs examined,[48] and many also refer to WTO obligations in respect of SPS and TBT measures and customs valuation.

A few of these agreements direct panels to take account not only of the substantive WTO obligations, but also of the interpretation of those obligations in WTO dispute settlement.[49] The New Zealand–Singapore, Canada–Costa Rica, and Central American–Dominican Republic–United States (CAFTA–DR–US) PTAs state that

42 Thailand–Australia FTA, Article 101; and CAFTA–DR–US, Article 1.1.

43 For example: 'This Agreement shall not diminish the scope of any commitment made by either Party under GATS to which the other party has access' (Thailand–Australia FTA, Article 816); 'Nothing in this Article shall be construed so as to derogate from the obligations of the Parties' under the Agreement on Trade Related Investment Measures in Annex 1A to the WTO Agreement, or as parties to the Agreement on Government Procurement in Annex 4 to the WTO Agreement (Japan–Singapore EPA, Articles 75.3 and 101.5 respectively).

44 For example: 'The Parties confirm their rights and obligations under the Marrakesh Agreement establishing the World Trade Organization and the other agreements negotiated thereunder . . . to which they are party, and under any international agreement to which they are a party' (EFTA–Chile FTA, Article 4); 'The Parties affirm their existing rights and obligations with respect to each other under the WTO Agreement and other international agreements to which both Parties are party' (Korea–Chile FTA, Article 1.3.1.). See also US–Morocco FTA, Article 1.2.1; US–Singapore FTA, Article 1.1.2; US–Chile FTA, Article 1.3; AUSFTA, Article 1.1.1.2; CAFTA–DR–US, Article 1.3.1; and Canada–Costa Rica FTA, Article I.3.1.

45 For example: 'With respect to matters related to this Chapter [III on Trade in Services] the Parties confirm the rights and obligations existing under any bilateral or multilateral agreements to which they are a party' (EFTA–Chile FTA, Article 43); 'Nothing in this Chapter shall be construed so as to affect the rights and obligations that either Party has as a party to the Agreement on Technical Barriers to Trade in Annex 1A to the WTO Agreement' (Japan–Singapore EPA, Article 55.3. Article 8.8.2 of the Korea–Singapore FTA contains similar language); and '[T]he Parties affirm their existing rights and obligations with respect to each other under the TBT Agreement' (US–Morocco FTA, Article 7.2).

46 One of many such examples may be found in Article 3.2.1 of the CAFTA–DR–US.

47 CAFTA–DR–US, Article 21.1. In addition to incorporating Article XX, this provision records the parties' understanding 'that the measures referred to in Article XX(b) of the GATT 1994 include environmental measures necessary to protect human, animal, or plant life or health, and that Article XX(g) of the GATT 1994 applies to measures relating to the conservation of living and non-living exhaustible natural resources'.

48 The Turkey–Morocco FTA makes extensive reference to the covered agreements as the basis for its obligations with respect to such matters as SPS measures (Article 13.2), anti-dumping and countervailing duty measures (Article 18), safeguards (Article 19.1), balance of payments measures (Article 26), and technical barriers to trade (Article 34.3).

49 See, e.g., Article 4.2 of the Japan–Singapore EPA, which states that 'In the application of [the previous paragraph setting out security and general exceptions] the relevant interpretations and operation of the WTO Agreement shall, where appropriate, be taken into account'. Articles 19.2 and 69.2 of that Agreement contain similar provisions.

they are each to be interpreted in accordance with international law and with the objectives set out in that agreement.[50]

2. Provisions relating to conflicting norms

Several PTAs contain 'conflicts' provisions stipulating which, as between the PTA in question and another international agreement, is to prevail in the event of a conflict. As mentioned above, several such provisions are cast as 'confirming' rights under WTO agreements or clarifying that the PTA should not be construed as derogating from WTO rights and obligations. It is, however, interesting to survey a few of the different types of priorities that parties to PTAs have attached to potentially conflicting norms.

The New Zealand–Singapore Closer Economic Partnership Agreement (NZ–Singapore CEPA) makes clear that nothing in that agreement is to be regarded as exempting either party from its obligations under any other international, regional or bilateral agreement, and provides that any inconsistency between such other agreement and the PTA 'shall be resolved in accordance with the general principles of international law'.[51] The US agreements with Morocco, Singapore and Australia include a general provision that these agreements 'shall not be construed to derogate from any legal obligation between the Parties that entitles goods or services, or suppliers of goods or services, to treatment more favourable than that accorded' under those agreements.[52] Singapore's PTAs with Australia, Japan and Korea acknowledge the possibility of a conflict between an obligation assumed by the parties under another agreement and an obligation under the PTA and provide that, in such a situation, the parties shall consult and seek to find a mutually satisfactory solution, taking account of international law.[53] The Korea–Chile Free Trade Agreement appears to go even farther in providing that, in the event of an inconsistency between that agreement and another international agreement to which both parties are party, the Korea–Chile FTA 'shall prevail to the extent of the inconsistency, except as otherwise provided in this Agreement'.[54] The same agreement also includes a rather unique provision deeming its SPS rules and disciplines to be consistent with the SPS Agreement.[55]

---

50 NZ–Singapore CEPA, Article 58.2; Canada–Costa Rica FTA, Article 1.2.2; and CAFTA–DR–US, Article 1.2.2. The Singapore–Australia FTA also provides that panels 'shall clarify the provisions of this Agreement in accordance with customary rules of interpretation of public international law' (Chapter 16, Article 1.5).
51 NZ–Singapore CEPA, Article 80.
52 US–Morocco FTA, Article 1.2.2; US–Singapore FTA, Article 1.1.3; and AUSFTA, Article 1.1.3.
53 Singapore–Australia FTA, Chapter 17, Article 5; Japan–Singapore EPA, Article 6.1; and Korea–Singapore FTA, Article 1.3.2. However, Article 1.3.3 of the Korea–Singapore FTA adds that such general duty of consultation does not apply where there are express provisions of the Agreement regarding inconsistencies between that agreement and another international agreement. Article 18.6 of the NZ–Thailand CEPA also provides for consultations between the parties in the event that either one of them considers that there is an inconsistency between that agreement and any other agreement to which both are party.
54 Article 1.3.2.
55 Article 8.2.3 of that Agreement reads: 'The framework of rules and disciplines that guide the adoption and enforcement of the sanitary and phytosanitary measures included in this Chapter is deemed to be consistent with the SPS Agreement.'

The agreement between Canada and Costa Rica also provides that it is to take precedence over any other agreement to which both countries are party 'except as otherwise provided'. That agreement then goes on to identify three multilateral environmental treaties that would prevail in the event of any inconsistency. However, the privileged position afforded the norms set out in those three environmental treaties is subject to the condition that 'where a Party has a choice among equally effective and reasonably available means of complying with such obligations, the Party chooses the alternative that is the least inconsistent with the other provisions of this Agreement'.[56] Korea's PTA with Singapore provides that its provisions on customs valuation 'shall take precedence over' the Customs Valuation Agreement.[57] Article 2(a) of the Japan–Mexico Economic Partnership Agreement (Japan–Mexico EPA) provides that 'Nothing in this subparagraph shall affect the rights and obligations of the Parties under the United Nations Convention on the Law of the Sea, as may be amended'. The PTAs to which the US is party all contain a hortatory article entitled 'Relationship to Environmental Agreements' that acknowledges the important role of multilateral environmental agreements, and commits the parties to 'continue to seek means to enhance the mutual supportiveness of multilateral environmental agreements to which they are both party and trade agreements to which they are both party',[58] and/or to consult regularly on negotiations in the WTO regarding multilateral environmental agreements and on the extent to which the outcome of such negotiations may affect those PTAs.[59] Several PTAs also provide that their provisions do not apply to tax measures and that, in the event of an inconsistency between the PTA and a tax convention, the tax convention shall prevail to the extent of the inconsistency.[60]

Lastly, it is worth noting that many of the PTAs examined contain certain rules regarding which norm is to prevail in the event of an internal conflict between chapters of the agreement.[61] As regards such conflicts within a PTA, it is quite common, in those agreements that contain chapters on investment, to include a provision to the effect that in the event of a conflict between the provisions of the chapter on investment and the provisions of any other chapter, the provisions of the

---

56 Canada–Costa Rica FTA, Article I.4. The three treaties listed are: the Convention on International Trade in Endangered Species of Wild Fauna and Flora (CITES); the Montreal Protocol on Substances that Deplete the Ozone Layer (Montreal Protocol); and the Basel Convention on the Control of Transboundary Movements of Hazardous Wastes and Their Disposal (Basel Convention).
57 Korea–Singapore FTA, Article 4.17(b).   58 US–Morocco FTA, Article 17.8; and AUSFTA, Article 19.8.
59 US–Morocco FTA, Article 17.8; US–Singapore FTA, Article 18.8; US–Chile FTA, Article 19.9; and AUSFTA, Article 19.8. The wording of the relevant provisions in the CAFTA–DR–US differs slightly, but appears to be of similar effect (Article 17.12).
60 CAFTA–DR–US contains one such example in Article 21.3.2.
61 The WTO contains a similar rule in the General Interpretative note to Annex 1A of the World Trade Agreement, which provides: 'In the event of conflict between a provision of the General Agreement on Tariffs and Trade 1994 and a provision of another agreement in Annex 1A to the Agreement Establishing the World Trade Organisation (referred to in the agreements in Annex 1A as the "WTO Agreement"), the provision of the other agreement shall prevail to the extent of the conflict.'

other chapter will prevail.[62] In contrast, in those PTAs which contain chapters on telecommunications, it is more common to include a provision that in the event of a conflict between chapters, the chapter on telecommunications shall prevail.[63] Interestingly, Article 57.1 of the Japan–Singapore Economic Partnership Agreement (Japan–Singapore EPA) provides that in the event of a conflict between a Sectoral Annex and the provisions of the agreement dealing with mutual recognition, it is the provisions of the Annex that shall prevail.

B. Recourse to other dispute settlement fora and the consequences of choosing a forum

As mentioned above, when two countries are parties to a PTA as well as WTO Members, the same set of facts or circumstances may be actionable both in a WTO dispute settlement proceeding and using a PTA dispute settlement mechanism. Many PTAs strive to prevent the same dispute from being pursued in different fora, but the achievement of this objective is complicated by difficult questions including: when is a dispute the 'same' if the legal source of the obligations is different or the obligations themselves differ in some respects; and what is the relevance of the priority afforded to multilateral dispute settlement in Article 23 of the DSU when rights and obligations under PTAs are in dispute?

Many PTAs examined contain an express statement to the effect that the PTA does not affect the rights of the parties to the agreement to have recourse to dispute settlement available to them under other international agreements.[64] These often make clear that the choice of forum rests with the complaining party, and that once a particular dispute has been initiated under *either* the PTA or another international agreement, recourse to the other forum is precluded.[65] Notwithstanding this general rule, some PTAs allow the parties to agree to pursue disputes simultaneously in two

---

62 Japan–Mexico EPA, Article 69; Korea–Chile FTA, Article 10.3.1; US–Morocco FTA, Article 10.2.1; US–Singapore FTA, Article 15.3.1; AUSFTA, Article 11.2.1; and CAFTA–DR–US, Article 10.2.

63 E.g., Korea–Chile FTA, Article 12.8; US–Morocco FTA, Article 13.16; US–Singapore FTA, Article 9.15; US–Chile FTA, Article 13.16; AUSFTA, Article 12.24; and CAFTA–DR–US, Article 13.16.

64 Thailand–Australia FTA, Article 1801.2; EU–Mexico FTA, Article 47.4; Japan–Singapore EPA, Article 139.2; Japan–Mexico EPA, Article 151.1; NZ–Thailand CEPA, Article 17.1.2; and NZ–Singapore CEPA, Article 58.1. The NZ–Singapore CEPA is the only one of those listed that does not also impose a 'single exclusive forum' requirement on parties to a dispute that could be pursued under more than one agreement.

65 Thailand–Australia FTA, Article 1801.4; EFTA–Chile FTA, Article 88.1; EU–Mexico FTA, Article 47.4; Japan–Singapore EPA, Article 139.2; Japan–Mexico EPA, Article 151.2; Korea–Chile FTA, Article 19.3.2; Korea–Singapore FTA, Article 20.3.2; US–Morocco FTA, Articles 20.4.1 and 20.4.3; US–Singapore FTA Article 20.4.3(a) and (c); US–Chile FTA, Article 22.3; AUSFTA, Article 21.4; CAFTA–DR–US, Article 20.3; NZ–Thailand CEPA, Article 17.1.4; and Canada–Costa Rica FTA, Articles XIII.6.1 and XIII.6.4. The choice of forum rules contained in Article 22.3 of the US–Chile FTA and Article 20.3.1 of CAFTA–DR–US apply in circumstances where a dispute arises under the PTA and under 'another *free trade* agreement' (emphasis added), which may suggest that the choice afforded the plaintiff and the ensuing exclusivity of forum rule would not apply where, for example, the other available forum is under a multilateral environmental

fora.[66] The PTAs that preclude the parties from having recourse to two different dispute settlement mechanisms typically define the 'initiation' of a dispute in the WTO context – i.e., the step that, once taken, would block recourse to the dispute settlement mechanism in the PTA – as the complaining party's request for establishment of a panel.[67] Certain PTAs also require a party planning to initiate recourse to dispute settlement under another agreement to first notify the other party of its intention to do so.[68]

PTAs containing such choice of forum clauses vary in their designation of the type of dispute that, once initiated in one forum, would preclude recourse to a second forum. Some refer to disputes on the 'same matter' or on a 'particular matter'.[69] Thailand's PTAs with Australia and New Zealand refer to 'a dispute', but clarify that the bar on having recourse to two distinct mechanisms 'does not apply if substantially separate and distinct rights or obligations under different international agreements are in dispute'.[70]

In apparent acknowledgement of Article 23 of the DSU, several PTAs expressly prohibit panels constituted pursuant to those agreements from making determinations or considering issues regarding the parties' rights and obligations under the WTO Agreement.[71] Certain PTAs seek to have the parties give priority to WTO dispute settlement when WTO obligations or WTO-like obligations are at stake. Thus the EU–Chile AA provides that when one party seeks redress for a violation of an obligation under that agreement that is 'equivalent in substance' to a WTO obligation, then that party must resort to WTO dispute settlement.[72] This rule in favour of WTO dispute settlement can, however, be overcome if the parties otherwise

agreement. Similarly, Article 21.4 of the AUSFTA refers to 'this Agreement and under another *trade agreement*' (emphasis added).

66 Thailand–Australia FTA, Article 1801.5; NZ–Thailand CEPA, Article 17.1.5; and Japan–Singapore EPA, Article 139.4.

67 Thailand–Australia FTA, Article 1801.6; NZ–Thailand CEPA, Article 17.1.6; EFTA–Chile FTA, Article 88.3; EU–Mexico FTA, Article 47.4; Japan–Singapore EPA, Article 139; Japan–Mexico EPA, Article 151.4; Korea–Chile FTA, Article 19.3.3; Korea–Singapore FTA, Article 20.3.3; US–Morocco FTA, Article 20.4.4; US–Singapore FTA, Article 20.4.3(d); US–Chile FTA, Article 22.3.2; and Canada–Costa Rica FTA, Article XIII.6.5. A smaller number of PTAs also define the step which, if taken under the PTA in question, would trigger the 'exclusive forum' rule, which is also the request for establishment of a panel. See, e.g., Japan–Mexico EPA, Article 151.3; Korea–Singapore FTA, Article 20.3.2; US–Morocco FTA, Article 20.4.4; US–Singapore FTA, Article 20.4.3(d); and US–Chile FTA, Article 22.3.2.

68 Thailand–Australia FTA, Article 1801.3; NZ–Thailand CEPA, Article 17.1.3; EFTA–Chile FTA, Article 88.4; US–Morocco FTA, Article 20.4.2; and US–Singapore FTA, Article 20.4.3(b).

69 E.g., EFTA–Chile FTA, Article 88.1; and EU–Mexico FTA, Article 47.4.

70 Thailand–Australia FTA, Article 1801.4, and NZ–Thailand CEPA, Article 17.1.4. Similarly, Article 139.3 of the Japan–Singapore EPA and Article 151.2 of the Japan–Mexico EPA both clarify that the requirement of exclusivity of forum 'does not apply if substantially separate and distinct rights or obligations under different international agreements are in dispute'.

71 E.g., EU–SA TDCA, Article 104.10; and EU–Mexico FTA, Article 47.3. As discussed below, some PTAs also simply exclude disputes relating to certain subject areas – such as safeguards – from the scope of their dispute settlement mechanism and provide instead that such disputes are to be resolved in the WTO.

72 Article 189.4(c).

agree. The relevant provision of the EU–South Africa Trade, Development and Co-operation Agreement (EU–SA TDCA) also pulls in opposite directions. It states that arbitration proceedings under that agreement 'will not consider issues relating to each Party's WTO rights and obligations', but allows the parties to refer any such issues to arbitration. It states that the parties 'shall endeavour to settle disputes relating to specific obligations' under the agreement through recourse to the dispute settlement procedures under that agreement, but adds that this is '[w]ithout prejudice to their right to have recourse to WTO dispute settlement procedures'.[73] The Japan–Mexico EPA specifies that nothing in its chapters on Trade in Goods, Investment or Services shall prevent either party from applying retaliatory measures in accordance with Article 22 of the DSU.[74]

A few agreements contain special rules regarding forum in the case of disputes relating to the environment. The United States–Chile Free Trade Agreement contains a provision suggesting that environmental disputes are to be referred for action under multilateral environmental agreements rather than under that bilateral agreement. However, this is subject to the condition that the parties agree that the matter 'is more properly covered' by such other environmental agreement to which they are party.[75] The agreement between Canada and Costa Rica contains a unique provision that allows the responding party to control the forum for certain types of environmental disputes. Where the respondent's defence is based on Convention on International Trade in Endangered Species of Wild Fauna and Flora (CITES), the Montreal Protocol on Substances that Deplete the Ozone Layer (Montreal Protocol), or the Basel Convention on the Control of Transboundary Movements of Hazardous Wastes and Their Disposal (Basel Convention), the respondent may, within fifteen days of the complainant's initiation of dispute settlement (e.g., in the WTO), make a written request that the dispute be considered under the Canada–Costa Rica FTA. Upon receipt of such a request, the complainant is required to withdraw from participation in the other proceedings and may initiate dispute settlement proceedings under the bilateral PTA. This agreement is therefore notable because it provides for the norms set out in three listed environmental agreements to prevail in the event of any inconsistency, and allows the responding party to force the interpretation and application of those norms to be carried out in a dispute settlement proceeding under the bilateral trade agreement rather than, for example, in the WTO.[76]

73 Article 104.10.
74 Article 167.2 provides: 'Nothing in Chapters 3, 7 and 8 shall be construed to prevent either Party from taking any necessary action as may be authorised by Article 22 of the Understanding on Rules and Procedures Governing the Settlement of Disputes in Annex 2 to the WTO Agreement, as may be amended.'
75 Article 19.6.10. The CAFTA–DR–US contains a similar provision in Articles 16.6.9 (relating to labour) and 17.10.9 (environment).
76 Canada–Costa Rica FTA, Article XIII.3, read together with Article I.4.

Many of the PTAs examined also contain restrictions on the use of their own dispute settlement mechanism. The substantive areas most frequently excluded from dispute settlement are investment, competition,[77] government procurement[78] and financial services,[79] as well as 'soft' obligations on co-operation and consultation.[80] The PTAs to which the US is party and which contain obligations relating to labour and the environment often limit resort to dispute settlement and provide for special rules relating to remedies for alleged breaches of those obligations in respect of which recourse to dispute settlement is permitted.[81] Such exclusions are sometimes set out in the substantive chapters concerned, sometimes in the chapter on dispute settlement,[82] and sometimes in both. Several PTAs also impose, in specific subject areas, additional requirements of consultation or efforts to reach a mutually agreed solution before allowing recourse to the standard dispute settlement mechanism.[83]

C. Preclusion of a private right of action

Several PTAs expressly forbid the parties to provide for a right of action for private parties against the other party to the PTA under its domestic law for failure on the

77 E.g., Thailand–Australia FTA, Article 1208; EFTA–Chile FTA, Article 78; EU–Mexico FTA, Article 180; Japan–Singapore EPA, Article 105; Japan–Mexico EPA, Article 135; Korea–Singapore FTA, Article 15.8.2; Canada–Costa Rica FTA, Article XI.6.3; and Singapore–Australia FTA, Chapter 12, Article 8.2.

78 E.g., Thailand–Australia FTA, Article 1505.

79 Japan–Mexico EPA, Article 109. Although they do not preclude resort to dispute settlement regarding financial services, many PTAs impose additional requirements regarding the composition of panels and the sectors in which retaliation may be undertaken in the event of non-compliance. See, e.g., Korea–Singapore FTA, Article 12.12; US–Morocco FTA, Article 12.17; US–Singapore FTA, Article 10.18; and AUSFTA, Article 13.18.

80 E.g., Japan–Mexico EPA, Articles 138 (with respect to improvement of the business environment) and 148 (with respect to bilateral co-operation); and Korea–Singapore FTA, Article 18.1 (with respect to co-operation). Other examples include: Article 610.2 of the Thailand–Australia FTA, and Article 15 of the Japan–Mexico EPA, which preclude resort to the dispute settlement mechanism under those agreements for SPS matters; Article 1109 of that Agreement, which limits resort to dispute settlement in respect of electronic commerce; and several agreements that impose limitations where the dispute concerns provisions on the entry and temporary stay of nationals for business purposes, including an 'exhaustion of local remedies' requirement (e.g., Japan–Mexico EPA, Article 118; Korea–Chile FTA, Article 13.7.1; Korea–Singapore FTA, Article 13.6.1; US–Singapore FTA, Article 11.8.1; US–Chile FTA, Article 14.6; and Singapore–Australia FTA, Chapter 11, Article 6). Safeguards and trade remedies are also often removed from the reach of PTAs. The Canada–Costa Rica FTA, for example, does not allow its dispute settlement mechanism to be used in respect of safeguards (Article VI.4), anti-dumping measures (Article VII.1.5), and sanitary and phytosanitary measures (Article IX.5.1.2). Instead, the parties agree to use WTO dispute settlement to resolve disputes in these subject areas.

81 US–Morocco FTA, Articles 16.6.5 and 17.7.5; US–Singapore FTA, Articles 17.6.5 and 18.7.5; US–Chile FTA, Articles 18.6.7–18.6.8 and 19.6.8–19.6.9; AUSFTA, Articles 18.6.5 and 19.7.5; and CAFTA–DR–US, Articles 16.6.7–16.6.8 and 17.10.7–17.10.8. For more details on the special remedies that may be awarded in such disputes, see below.

82 E.g., Thailand–Australia FTA, Article 1801.1; and EFTA–Chile FTA, Article 87.3.

83 E.g., Japan–Singapore EPA, Article 52.4 ('Without prejudice to Chapter 21 [on Dispute Settlement], if any problem arises as to the interpretation or application of this Chapter [on Mutual Recognition], the Parties shall, first of all, seek an amicable solution through the Committee.')

part of the latter to comply with its obligations under the PTA.[84] A number also provide that if an issue of interpretation or application of the agreement arises in a domestic judicial or administrative proceeding of one party, then that party should notify the other, and the two parties should endeavour through the joint administrative body of the PTA to submit an agreed interpretation of the PTA to the relevant court or tribunal failing which either party may, in accordance with the rules of that court or tribunal, submit its own views to that body.[85]

IV. Bringing a complaint

We now turn to several practical issues relating to how a complaint is brought. In this regard, we first offer a general overview of the dispute process. We then discuss the various types of complaints that can be made, followed by a brief consideration of whether 'proposed measures' can be challenged. Next, we examine the requirements for the documents that constitute the initiation of a dispute: the consultations and panel requests. Finally, we discuss the issue of the role of private lawyers in the process.

A. Overview of the first steps in the dispute process

The basic dispute settlement process is similar across PTAs, with several steps that come into play. Disputes always begin with a request for consultations, with consultations between the parties then taking place soon after. However, there is then a split into two groups of agreements, taking different approaches. In the first group, if the consultations do not resolve the complaint, the complaining party may then request a panel on the matter immediately.[86] This process mirrors that of the WTO.

By contrast, in the second group, if consultations fail to resolve the matter, the dispute is referred to a body headed by the parties themselves (referred to as a Joint Committee or Commission or Association Committee in various agreements).[87] The dispute will be referred to a panel only if this body cannot resolve the dispute itself. In a sense, this step forces the dispute to be examined by high-ranking officials of the parties one more time to see if a resolution can be reached. At the very least, it delays the process a bit to give the parties time to think more about a negotiated solution. All of the recent US agreements fall into this category.

In addition, many agreements provide for the option of good offices, conciliation or mediation. This is a less formal means of resolving disputes, in which suggestions

---

84 E.g., Korea–Chile FTA, Article 19.17; US–Morocco FTA, Article 20.15; US–Singapore FTA, Article 20.10; US–Chile FTA, Article 22.20; AUSFTA, Article 21.15; CAFTA–DR–US, Article 20.21; and Canada–Costa Rica, Article XIII.20.

85 E.g., Korea–Chile FTA, Article 19.16.   86 See, e.g., Korea–Singapore FTA, Article 20.6, para. 1.

87 See, e.g., US–Singapore FTA, Article 20.4, paras. 2–4; and US–Chile FTA, Article 22.6, para. 1.

for resolution are made by a neutral party without a finding of wrongdoing. The possibility of such a process also exists at the WTO, but the procedure has rarely been used,[88] so it is not clear how big a role it will play in PTA dispute settlement. The PTAs do not specify who would preside over the mediation. In the WTO context, the Director-General is mentioned as someone who might provide these services,[89] but there is no counterpart to the Director-General in the context of PTAs. It is possible that the WTO Director-General or someone of a similar stature could preside in the context of PTAs. In general, good offices, etc. may take place before or after the panel process has started.[90] If the parties agree, the two processes may take place simultaneously.[91]

B. Types of complaints

Under the GATT, Article XXIII provides only limited guidance on disputes. With regard to the types of complaints, paragraph 1 states the following:

> If any Member should consider that any benefit accruing to it directly or indirectly under this Agreement is being nullified or impaired or that the attainment of any objective of the Agreement is being impeded as the result of:
>
> (a) the failure of another Member to carry out its obligations under this Agreement; or
> (b) the application by another Member of any measure, whether or not it conflicts with the provisions of this Agreement; or
> (c) the existence of any other situation.

Based on this language, there are a number of possible complaints that could be made under the GATT: the phrases 'any benefit accruing to it directly or indirectly under this Agreement is being nullified or impaired . . . as the result of' and 'the attainment of any objective of the Agreement is being impeded as the result of' can be paired with any of the three sub-paragraphs (a), (b) and (c), leading to six possible complaints. In practice, however, the vast majority of complaints have been that 'any benefit accruing to it directly or indirectly under this Agreement is being nullified or impaired . . . as the result of (a) the failure of another Member to carry out its obligations under this Agreement'. There have been a few high-profile complaints which refer to 'benefits accruing' as the result of '(b) the application by another Member of any measure, whether or not it conflicts with the provisions of

---

88 To date, there has been one 'mediation' in the context of the WTO that made reference to DSU Article 5, although the parties stated that the matter was not a 'dispute' in terms of the DSU. WT/GC/66, 16 October 2002, Request for Mediation by the Philippines, Thailand and the European Communities.

89 DSU, Article 5.6.

90 Korea–Singapore FTA, Article 20.5: '[Good offices, conciliation or mediation] may begin at any time and be terminated by either Party at any time.'

91 Singapore–Australia FTA, Chapter 16, Article 3, para. 2. 'If the Parties agree, procedures for good offices, conciliation or mediation may continue while the dispute proceeds for resolution before an arbitral tribunal appointed under Article 4 (Appointment of Arbitral Tribunals)'.

this Agreement' ('non-violation' complaints) and an occasional complaint under (c) related to 'other situations' ('situation' complaints), but there is limited jurisprudence on these other types of complaints.

The PTAs covered here take several different approaches to the types of complaints that can be brought. There are usually some parallels with the GATT language, but the PTA language is never identical.

We begin with the agreements involving the US, as these all use similar language setting out several possible complaints: a measure being 'inconsistent' with the obligations of the agreement, a Party 'otherwise fail[ing] to carry out its obligations' under the agreement, or certain 'benefit[s] the Party could reasonably have expected to accrue to it under [certain designated provisions] [are] being nullified or impaired as a result of a measure that is not inconsistent with this Agreement'.[92] Some agreements have similar language, but do not limit the nullification or impairment remedy to specific provisions, but rather provide this as a general remedy.[93]

The agreements not involving the US also set out a variety of possible complaints, including: 'any matter affecting the implementation, interpretation or application' of the agreement; 'any measure or any other matter that is inconsistent with the obligations of this Agreement'; 'any measure or any other matter that . . . causes nullification or impairment of any benefit accruing to it directly or indirectly' under certain provisions or as a general matter; 'any benefit accruing to it directly or indirectly under this Agreement is being nullified or impaired as a result of the failure of the Party complained against to carry out its obligations'; 'any benefit accruing to it directly or indirectly under this Agreement is being nullified or impaired, or that the attainment of any objective of this Agreement is being impeded, as a result of the failure of the other Party to carry out its obligations under this Agreement'. The various agreements include some or all of these phrases. We set out the following agreements as examples of the language used:

- *Korea–Singapore FTA*: 'any matter affecting the implementation, interpretation or application of this Agreement or whenever a party considers that any measure or any other matter that is inconsistent with the obligations of this Agreement or causes nullification or impairment of any benefit accruing to it directly or indirectly under' certain provisions.[94]
- *Singapore–Australia FTA*:

  > Any Party which considers that any benefit accruing to it directly or indirectly under this Agreement is being nullified or impaired, or that the attainment of *any* objective of this Agreement is being impeded, as a result of the failure of the

---

92 See, e.g., US–Morocco FTA, Article 20.2.   93 See, e.g., CAFTA–DR–US, Article 20.2, para. (c).
94 Korea–Singapore FTA, Article 20.4.

other Party to carry out its obligations under this Agreement, may, with a view to achieving satisfactory settlement of the matter, make representations or proposals to the other Party, which shall give due consideration to the representations or proposals made to it.[95]

- *EFTA–Chile FTA*: 'A Party may request in writing consultations with another Party whenever it considers that a measure applied by that Party is inconsistent with this Agreement or that any benefit accruing to it directly or indirectly under this Agreement is impaired by such measure.'[96]

Thus, many of the elements of GATT legal complaints are also present in the PTA dispute settlements provisions, although the phrasing and order of the provisions vary. In addition, some of the PTA provisions are more general and vague than others, whereas some are more limiting in the scope of the complaints (especially with regard to the scope of non-violation nullification or impairment claims). As with GATT/WTO dispute settlement, the most prevalent form of complaint is likely to be that a party has acted inconsistently with the provisions of the agreement (there are different characterisations of this type of complaint in the various PTAs, but the essence is the same). The various other types of complaints still exist as an option where proving inconsistency is considered difficult, but their precise scope is unclear and will have to be defined through actual disputes. There is a good chance that panels faced with such complaints will look to GATT/WTO practice for guidance.[97]

C. Challengeability of proposed measures

An issue related to the types of complaints that may be brought is the scope of the 'measures' that may be challenged. In the WTO context, this is a broad topic with a number of elements.[98] We focus here on one narrow aspect: the ability to challenge 'proposed measures'. A number of agreements make reference to the term 'proposed measures', in different ways. In some agreements, consultations may be requested for both actual and proposed measures, but a panel request can only be made for actual measures.[99] By contrast, other agreements refer to the possibility of consultations on actual or proposed measures, but do not explicitly exclude claims against proposed

---

95 Singapore–Australia FTA, Article 16.2, para. 2.   96 EFTA–Chile FTA, Article 90, para. 1.
97 In this regard, one PTA, the Chile–Costa Rica FTA, makes reference to GATT case law with respect to nullification or impairment: 'To determine the elements of nullification or impairment, the Parties may take into account the principles deriving from case law on Article XXIII, paragraph 1(b), of the GATT 1994' (Chile–Costa Rica FTA, Article 19.03 and Annex 19.03, para. 3).
98 For example, there is a great deal of debate on the scope (and even existence) of the so-called 'mandatory/discretionary' distinction.
99 CAFTA–DR–US, Article 20.4, para. 1: 'Any Party may request in writing consultations with any other Party with respect to any actual or proposed measure or any other matter that it considers might affect the operation of this Agreement'. Article 20.6, para. 6: 'An arbitral panel may not be established to review a proposed measure'.

measures.[100] In this latter situation, whether a panel may be requested to examine such measures is not completely clear, but there is no express statement that this cannot happen.

In terms of policy considerations, there are a number of arguments that can be made for and against allowing challenges to proposed measures. For example, an argument against such challenges is the waste of resources in having panels consider measures that may never come into effect. On the other hand, examining such measures early on could limit trade damage where the measure would be found in violation, by recommending its removal earlier, and could also help Members ensure that their laws are consistent with trade agreements.

We also note that the scope of the term 'proposed' may be open to interpretation. A question arises as to when in the legislative or executive process a measure has been 'proposed'. Would the suggestion for a measure in a parliamentary speech qualify? Or would there have to be a more formal proposal, such as the introduction of a bill in the US Congress or the submission of regulations by a government agency for public comment? What about a measure that has been adopted by the legislature but has not yet come into force?

D. Requirements for consultations and panel requests

In the context of the WTO, the DSU contains provisions that help ensure clarity in consultations and panel requests. For example, Article 4.4 of the DSU requires that '[a]ny request for consultations shall be submitted in writing and shall give the reasons for the request, including identification of the measures at issue and an indication of the legal basis for the complaint'. Similarly, Article 6.2 of the DSU requires that '[t]he request for the establishment of a panel ... shall indicate whether consultations were held, identify the specific measures at issue and provide a brief summary of the legal basis of the complaint sufficient to present the problem clearly'. These requirements define the mandate of a panel and reflect a due process objective of giving responding parties knowledge of the case to which they are responding.

In the PTAs at issue, most agreements have requirements similar to those in the DSU, either for the consultations request or the panel request, or both. For example, with regard to panel requests, CAFTA–DR–US states that '[t]he requesting Party ... shall set out the reasons for the request, including identification of the measure or other matter at issue and an indication of the legal basis for the complaint'.[101] Other agreements use language that is a bit more general, such as

---

100 See, e.g., Canada–Costa Rica FTA, Article XIII.7, para. 1: 'A Party may request in writing consultations with the other Party regarding any actual or proposed measure or any other matter that it considers might affect the operation of this Agreement'.

101 CAFTA–DR–US, Article 20.6, para. 1.

the following in the Singapore–Australia agreement: 'The request [for Arbitral tribunal] shall include a statement of the claim and the grounds on which it is based.'[102]

The interpretation and application of these provisions will quite possibly follow the same trend as in WTO dispute settlement, where challenges to panel requests are frequent and a detailed jurisprudence has developed. Given the similarities in the provisions, PTA panels may look to WTO case law for guidance.

E. Role of private counsel

An important aspect of bringing any legal complaint is which lawyers may be involved. The disputes dealt with in this chapter are, formally speaking, between governments. As a result, government lawyers, as well as other officials, are involved in all aspects of the litigation process. By contrast, the role of private lawyers in these kinds of trade disputes is less clear. In most instances, there are commercial entities involved in influencing governments to adopt measures that are the subject of trade disputes, and also in the decision to file a complaint. These commercial entities generally have lawyers advising them on the relevant legal issues. As a result, it is natural, and perhaps unavoidable, for these lawyers to be involved in some way in the government-to-government litigation, assisting or even leading the process.

In GATT/WTO dispute settlement, private lawyers have long played a role in 'behind-the-scenes' work, such as preparing written submissions and responses to panel questions. In the early years of WTO dispute settlement, several panels and the Appellate Body ruled that these private lawyers could participate in panel meetings and Appellate Body oral hearings as well, thus crossing the 'final frontier' of private lawyer participation in trade disputes.[103] Today, private lawyers can and do play a role in all aspects of WTO proceedings, and are bound by the same rules (e.g., confidentiality) as government lawyers.

For the most part, the PTAs examined here do not address explicitly the issue of the role of private lawyers. It is almost a certainty that the 'behind-the-scenes' type work done by private lawyers is permissible, as there would be no way to monitor or stop it even if that were desired. With regard to the participation of private lawyers in panel hearings, it is probably a safe assumption that this will be permitted, on the basis of the same reasoning used in the context of the WTO. There are occasional exceptions to this general rule, though. For example, in the Model Rules for the European Union–Mexico Free Trade Agreement, it is stated:

---

102 Singapore–Australia FTA, Article 16.4.
103 See Appellate Body Report, *EC–Bananas III*, paras. 5–12; and Panel Report, *Indonesia–Autos*, paras. 14.1–14.2.

The following persons may attend a hearing:

    ...

    (b) advisers to a Party, provided that they do not address the arbitration panel and provided further that neither they nor their employers, partners, business associates or family members have a financial or personal interest in the proceeding;[104]

An 'adviser' is defined in paragraph 1 as 'a person retained by a party to advise or assist the Party in connection with the arbitration panel proceeding'. Thus, this provision appears to limit the role of private lawyers during the hearing, allowing them to attend the hearing but not permitting them to speak to the panel. Presumably, however, they can discuss issues with the government counsel during the hearing and offer advice on what to say. The reasons for the approach taken in this agreement are not clear, and most other agreements do not seem to have similar language.[105]

V. Selection procedures for panels/tribunals

Various names are given to the group of 'judges' who hear complaints under PTAs: Panel, Arbitration Panel, Arbitral Panel, Arbitral Tribunal and Arbitration Tribunal. For ease of reference, we will refer to these bodies using the term 'Panel', the term used at the WTO, except where necessary to distinguish among them. In this section we discuss a number of issues related to the process parties follow when selecting members of these panels.

A basic question at the outset is, how many people serve on a panel? Virtually all PTAs specify that the Panel shall be composed of three members, with one member serving as Chair. However, there are a couple of PTAs involving the US that establish three as the default number but allow the parties to agree on a different number.[106] In addition, a slightly older FTA, from 1997 between Canada and Chile, establishes a five-member panel.[107]

With regard to the process of selecting individuals to serve on a panel, there are several key issues, some of which overlap to an extent:

(1) whether a 'roster' or 'list' of possible panellists is to be maintained;
(2) qualifications and requirements for panel service;
(3) the appointment process;
(4) procedures to prevent parties from blocking the appointment process.

We discuss each issue in turn.

---

104 EU–Mexico FTA, Annex XVI to Decision No. 2/2000 of the EC–Mexico Joint Council of 23 March 2000, para. 25; see also Decision of the Joint EFTA–Singapore Committee No. 2 of 2004, adopted on 26 May 2004, para. 23; and Decision of the EFTA–Mexico Joint Committee No. 3 of 2002, adopted on 22 October 2002, para. 25.
105 In contrast to the limiting language in the EFTA–Singapore and EFTA–Mexico agreements, the EFTA–Chile Model Rules allow for advisers to address the panel. See Annex XVII, para. 20.
106 See, e.g., AUSFTA, Article 21.7, para. 3.   107 Canada–Chile FTA, Article N-11, para. 1.

1. Roster or list

About half of the agreements examined provide for a 'roster' or 'reserve list' or 'contingent list' of people who can serve on panels. These 'rosters' and 'lists' are made up of qualified candidates, and are to be referred to in the panel composition process. Generally speaking, but not in all cases, where the term 'roster' is used in the agreement, this indicates that the panellists are 'normally' to be selected from the roster.[108] In addition, many of these agreements state that a party 'may exercise a peremptory challenge against any individual not on the roster who is proposed as a panellist by the other disputing Party'.[109] By contrast, where a 'contingent' or 'reserve' list is used, the list is used to help fill slots when the parties are having difficulty agreeing on panellists.[110] For these agreements, it is up to the parties to propose candidates for panel service, with no limitations on choosing candidates aside from the various qualifications and requirements described in the next section.

The number of people included on the 'roster' or 'list' ranges considerably, from five[111] to seventy[112] in the agreements examined. The duration of the list is usually a specific period, e.g. three years, and the persons on the list may be re-appointed. Often some number of people on the roster/list must be nationals of one of the parties, whereas another group is required to be non-nationals of either party.

2. Qualifications

The panellists chosen must meet certain qualifications. There are three broad categories in this regard: expertise, character and nationality. In terms of expertise, most agreements include a requirement to the effect that panellists have 'expertise or experience in law, international trade, other matters covered by this Agreement or the resolution of disputes arising under international trade agreements'.[113] Others are sometimes more general, such as the Japan–Singapore EPA, which requires only 'relevant technical or legal expertise';[114] or more specific, such as the NZ–Singapore CEPA, which states that, in addition to having 'relevant technical or legal expertise', they 'must be a well-qualified governmental or non-governmental individual, and can include persons who have served on or presented a case to a WTO panel, served in the Secretariat of the WTO, taught or published on international trade law or policy, or served as a senior trade policy official of a Member of the WTO'.[115] This latter provision mirrors Article 8.1 of the DSU. Finally, one agreement prefers a diverse group, noting that '[t]he members shall have sufficiently diverse background and a wide spectrum of experience'.[116]

---

108 See, e.g., Chile–Costa Rica FTA, Article 19.11, para. 3.
109 See, e.g., Canada–Chile FTA, Article N-11, para. 2.
110 See, e.g., US–Singapore FTA, Article 20.4, para. 4(a).   111 *Ibid.*, para. 4(b).
112 CAFTA–DR–US, Article 20.7, para. 1.   113 See, e.g., NZ–Thailand CEPA, Article 17.5, para. 6(a).
114 Japan–Singapore EPA, Article 143, para. 7.   115 NZ–Singapore CEPA, Article 61, para. 5.
116 EFTA–Chile FTA, Annex XVII, para. 49.

With regard to character, the provisions do not vary much, usually stating that the panellists be chosen on the basis of factors like objectivity, reliability, sound judgement, independence and impartiality, and requiring that panellists comply with a code of conduct.

Finally, nationality requirements vary considerably. Some agreements include only a general requirement that panellists serving as the Chair 'be independent of, and not be affiliated with or take instructions from, any Party'.[117] This does not appear to make nationality a criterion for service, as it focuses more generally on the panellist's independence from the governments involved. Other agreements, however, do set nationality restrictions, especially with regard to the Chair, requiring, for example, that the Chair not be a national of, and shall not have his or her usual place of residence in the territory of, nor be employed by, either Party.[118]

3. The appointment process

With regard to the appointment process, there are various approaches that have been taken. With most agreements, the disputing parties each appoint a member of the panel. Then, the parties either try to decide jointly on a third member to Chair the panel, or the first two members pick the Chair. For other agreements, by contrast, the parties pick the Chair first. The time frames for appointment vary somewhat.

4. Blocking the appointment process

An important aspect of the appointment process is whether the rules prevent the party complained against from blocking the establishment of a panel by refusing to take required actions. It has been alleged that blocking of the appointment process for a panel was a problem in a NAFTA dispute between the US and Mexico on sugar imports.[119]

Most of the agreements examined prevent blocking, using a variety of means to do so. For example, the following provisions have been used in this regard:

- *CAFTA–DR–US*: If the parties cannot agree on a Chair, the Chair shall be selected 'by lot' from 'among the roster members who are not nationals of a disputing Party'. Similarly, if a party fails to select a panellist within the designated period, the panellist 'shall be selected by lot within three days from among the roster members who are nationals of such Party or Parties'.[120]
- *New Zealand–Thailand CEPA*: If within the time periods for appointment 'the necessary appointments have not been made', either Party may invite the President

---

117 See, e.g., US–Morocco FTA, Article 20.7, para. 5(b).
118 See, e.g., EFTA–Singapore FTA, Article 60, para. 6.
119 See Mexico's arguments in this regard as part of a WTO proceeding on a related mater. Panel Report, *Mexico–Taxes on Soft Drinks*, para. 4.223.
120 CAFTA–DR–US, Article 20.9, para. 1(b).

of the International Court of Justice to make the appointments (a less senior member of the ICJ may take on this task if the President is a national of either Party).[121]

- *Korea–Chile FTA*: If the Parties are unable to agree on the Chair, the chairperson of the Commission for the agreement shall select by lot the Chair of the panel from among the roster members who are not nationals of either Party; similarly, if a Party does not select its panellist, the chairperson of the Commission shall select by lot the panellist, from among the roster members who are nationals of that Party.[122]
- *EFTA–Singapore FTA*: If the panel members and Chair have not been appointed within the mandated time periods, 'the necessary designations shall be made at the request of any Party to the dispute by the Director-General of the World Trade Organization'.[123]

Thus, some agreements arrange for automatic appointment of panellists from the 'rosters' and 'contingent/reserve lists' that were created (or in some instances from the candidates proposed), whereas others provide for an outsider to appoint the panellists.

Some agreements do not explicitly provide for a means to prevent blocking. For example, the Korea–Singapore FTA provides: 'Each Party shall appoint a member within thirty (30) days of the receipt of the request under Article 20.6.'[124] Thus, there is no means for ensuring that parties appoint a member (although there is such a means for the selection of the Chair in that agreement). It remains to be seen how language of this sort will be interpreted and applied. It may be possible that the parties will not engage in or allow this kind of blocking even though no explicit language prevents the tactic.

VI. The panel process

Once the panel has been appointed, the next step is to begin the dispute process, which, like any legal process, involves written submissions and a hearing before the panel. In this section, we discuss several aspects of the process: the timetable for reports; the existence of working procedures for the panel; the existence of an interim report; treaty interpretation; the ability of the panel to seek expert advice; external transparency of the panel process, that is, the ability of non-parties to participate and observe; the panel voting process; and the ability of the panel to make recommendations to help resolve the dispute.

A. Timetable for reports

All PTAs attempt to set limits on the length of the panel process, in the interest of a speedy resolution of disputes. Usually, the agreements set out a time period for

---

121 NZ–Thailand CEPA, Article 17.5, para. 3. 122 Korea–Chile FTA, Article 19.9, paras. 3 and 4.
123 EFTA–Singapore FTA, Article 60, para. 5. 124 Korea–Singapore FTA, Article 20.7, para. 1.

issuance of the interim report to the parties, a short additional time for issuance of the final report to the parties, and then a shorter additional time for circulation of the report to the public. For example, CAFTA–DR–US establishes time periods of 120 days between panel selection and issuance of the interim report; thirty additional days for issuance of the final report to the parties; and fifteen additional days for circulation of the final report to the public.[125] Some agreements have slightly longer time periods, while some are slightly shorter.

WTO dispute settlement procedures have similar limits. However, at the WTO these limits are not met in many cases. This is largely due to the complexity of many disputes, the increasing number of disputes involving large numbers of claims, and the time needed for translation of reports into all three official WTO languages. While the latter may not be an issue in PTAs, the other issues might lead to similar delays. As a result, it remains to be seen whether these time limits will be respected.

B. Existence of panel working procedures

The dispute settlement provisions of most agreements provide only some basic information on the procedures to be followed in disputes. Most of the agreements surveyed attempt to supplement these rules with detailed procedures to be followed in the form of 'Model Rules of Procedure', available in an Annex to the agreement. However, while many agreements refer to such Model Rules in their text, only a few of these agreements appear to have actually developed such rules at the time of this writing.[126]

In the context of the WTO, both the Appellate Body and panels have working procedures they follow. The Appellate Body has an established set of rules it follows each time,[127] while individual panels adjust theirs for each dispute.[128]

C. Interim report

During the Uruguay Round of GATT negotiations, two innovations were added to dispute settlement in the hopes of improving the quality of reports: issuance of an 'interim report' to the parties, on which they could provide comments; and an appeal mechanism. The use of interim reports gives parties the chance to offer additional insights to the panel before the process is completed, allowing the panel to provide better reasoned opinions. The appellate mechanism gives a new group of judges a chance to review the reasoning of the panellists.

In PTAs, while there is no appeal process, the interim report mechanism has generally been used. This report is normally referred to as the 'initial' report, although

---

125 CAFTA–DR–US, Articles 20.14 and 20.15.   126 See, e.g., EFTA–Chile FTA, Annex XVII.
127 Working Procedures for Appellate Review, WTO Doc. No. WT/AB/WP/5 (4 January 2005).
128 Appendix 3 of the DSU sets out basic procedures for panels to follow, but over the years panels have modified these procedures to address a number of issues that have arisen.

it is sometimes called a 'draft'. A short period of time, usually fourteen days, is allotted for the parties to provide comments on the initial report.

In WTO dispute settlement, there has been fairly extensive use of the interim review process. The parties appear to offer quite a few substantive criticisms, as well as more basic suggestions such as corrections of typographical errors. In many instances, panels will offer further explanations of their views in response to the parties' substantive criticisms, but they rarely change their findings. In two disputes, panels have actually changed their findings at the interim review stage.[129]

There have been suggestions that parties in WTO disputes are reluctant to provide too much in the way of substantive criticism of panel reports during the interim review stage, due to the fear that a panel may shore up its reasoning, thus making an appeal of the issue more difficult. There is some logic to this view, although whether it is true as an empirical matter is not clear. Regardless, the situation is different in PTAs, as there is no appeal process. Thus, parties will likely set forth detailed criticisms as part of this process. At the very least, it offers a defending party who expects to lose a chance to extend the process a bit.

D. Treaty interpretation

Article 3.2 of the DSU states that clarification of WTO rules is to be carried out in accordance with 'customary rules of interpretation of public international law'. Virtually everyone agrees, and the jurisprudence clearly establishes, that such interpretation should be based on Articles 31 and 32 of the Vienna Convention on the Law of Treaties (Vienna Convention).[130]

For the PTAs covered here, some, but not all, specify treaty interpretation rules, but there is some variety in the way they do it.[131] Many PTAs state that interpretation is to be 'clarified' under the 'customary rules of interpretation of public international law', or 'interpreted' under the 'applicable rules of international law' or the 'customary rules of interpretation of public international law'. One agreement, the Australia–United States Free Trade Agreement (AUSFTA), refers to the 'rules of interpretation under international law as reflected in Articles 31 and 32 of the Vienna Convention on the Law of Treaties'.[132] On occasion, agreements also refer to the 'objectives' of the agreement as a basis for interpretation and application of the provisions.[133]

---

129 See Panel Report, *US–Carbon Steel*, paras. 7.24 and 8.133–8.145; and Panel Report, *Korea–Paper AD Duties*, paras. 6.3–5 and 7.108–111.
130 Of course, while the general interpretative principles are agreed upon, the specific application of these rules is often contested.
131 Agreements involving the US and Canada tend not to specify any such rules, whereas most others do.
132 AUSFTA, Article 21.9, para. 2.   133 See Korea–Singapore FTA, Article 20.2, para. 5.

With regard to those PTAs that do not specify any such rules, the panels may have a bit more flexibility in terms of the interpretation rules they apply, but most likely they will gravitate towards rules that are the same as, or similar to, those in the Vienna Convention.

E. Expert advice

Like Article 13 of the DSU, most PTAs allow panels to request additional information to help them decide a case. Generally, PTAs state that panels may request this information upon the request of a party or on their own initiative, and the panel's request may be made to any person or body in relation to any information or technical advice.[134] Some agreements do provide limitations, such as requiring that the parties agree to the process[135] and be permitted to submit comments.[136] Others limit the scope of the information at issue to 'scientific information and technical advice from experts'[137] or provide separate, additional provisions on scientific/technical information.[138] Aside from these few limitations, however, these provisions are quite broad in terms of the scope of the information that may be requested.

F. External transparency

'External transparency' is a term that refers to making the procedures of an agreement, both in regard to disputes and other decision-making, accessible to those outside the government of the state parties. In relation to disputes, there are three aspects of this idea that have been included in various agreements: making panel hearings open to the public; making the parties' submissions to the panel available to the public; and allowing non-governmental entities to make *amicus curiae* submissions to the panels.

1. Open panel hearings

The recent PTAs involving the US indicate that the panel hearings shall be open to the public, subject to provisions on protecting confidential information.[139] Agreements to which the US is not party tend not to have explicit provisions of this kind, although it is possible that the parties could agree to open panel hearings for a particular dispute if they chose to do so. One agreement states that hearings are to be closed to the public 'unless the Parties decide otherwise', and notes that if hearings are opened

---

134 See, e.g., CAFTA–DR–US, Article 20.12: 'On request of a disputing Party, or on its own initiative, the panel may seek information and technical advice from any person or body that it deems appropriate, provided that the disputing Parties so agree and subject to such terms and conditions as such Parties may agree.'

135 *Ibid.*   136 NZ–Thailand CEPA, Article 17.7.   137 EFTA–Singapore FTA, Article 61.

138 Korea–Singapore FTA, Article 20.10, para. 2.   139 See, e.g., CAFTA–DR–US, Article 20.10.

to the public 'part of the hearing may . . . be closed to the public' and the hearing shall be closed if business confidential information is at issue.[140]

2. Making submissions public

Generally speaking, most PTAs make clear that parties can make their own written submissions to the panel available to the public, provided that they ensure that any confidential information of another Party is not disclosed. For example, the NZ–Thailand CEPA states: 'Nothing in this Article shall preclude a Party from disclosing to the public statements of its own positions or its submissions, but a Party shall not disclose information submitted by the other Party to an arbitral tribunal which the latter Party has designated as confidential.'[141] Agreements involving the US go even further, *requiring* that various submissions be made public (confidential information excepted).[142] Finally, the Korea–Singapore FTA provides that the transcript of the hearing can be made available as well,[143] something that does not occur in WTO dispute settlement.

3. Allowing *amicus curiae* submission

In WTO dispute settlement, the acceptance and consideration of *amicus curiae* submissions has been very controversial. The Appellate Body has ruled that these submissions may be taken into account in appellate proceedings[144] and by panels,[145] but the issue is a sensitive one, and most panels and Appellate Body divisions receiving such submissions explicitly make a statement to the effect that they did not find it necessary to take the submissions into account.[146]

Several PTAs provide explicit rules on this issue. For example, CAFTA–DR–US provides that 'the panel will consider requests from non-governmental entities in the disputing Parties' territories to provide written views regarding the dispute that may assist the panel in evaluating the submissions and arguments of the disputing Parties'.[147] All of the other US PTAs contain similar language. The Korea–Singapore FTA also has such language, but instead uses the words 'may consider', giving the panel some additional discretion.[148]

There are two key aspects of these provisions. First, panels need only 'consider' requests to make *amicus* submissions. They are not required to grant such requests, although presumably they must consider the request in good faith and provide some reasoning as to their decision. And second, only entities 'in the disputing Parties'

140 EFTA–Chile FTA, Annex XVII, para. 22.   141 NZ–Thailand CEPA, Article 17.7, para. 2.
142 See, e.g., CAFTA–DR–US, Article 20.10, para. 1(c): '[E]ach participating Party's written submissions, written versions of its oral statement, and written responses to a request or questions from the panel shall be public.'
143 Korea–Singapore FTA, Annex 19.10, para. 36(b).
144 Appellate Body Report, *US–Lead and Bismuth II*, paras. 36–42.
145 Appellate Body Report, *US–Shrimp*, paras. 99–110.
146 See, e.g., Appellate Body Report, *Mexico–Taxes on Soft Drinks*, para. 8.
147 CAFTA–DR–US, Article 20.10, para. 1(d).   148 Korea–Singapore FTA, Article 20.9, para. 1(e).

territories' may make these submissions. It is not clear how much of a restriction this will be in practice, as an organisation interested in the issue could probably set up a new office in one of the disputing parties or find an entity located within a disputing party to make the submission on its behalf.

Finally, the EFTA–Chile FTA goes into more detail than other agreements, placing a number of conditions on *amicus* submissions. This agreement requires that such submissions be made 'within 10 days following the date of the establishment of the arbitration panel, that they are concise and in no case longer than 15 typed pages, including any annexes, and that they are directly relevant to the factual and legal issue under consideration by the panel'. Furthermore, the submission must 'contain a description of the person, whether natural or legal, making the submission, including the nature of its activities and the source of its financing, and specify the nature of the interest that that person has in the arbitration proceeding', and 'shall be made in English and Spanish languages'. Even if these conditions are fulfilled, though, the panel 'shall not be obliged to address, in its ruling, the factual or legal arguments made in such submissions'.[149]

Of course, where no rules are provided, it may still be possible for panels to take such submissions into account, as there are no explicit rules on this in the WTO either, and the Appellate Body nevertheless decided, based on various contextual provisions, that these submissions were allowed.

G. Panel voting

As noted above, there are generally three members on a panel, as is also the case at the WTO. As a result of this structure, several questions arise: Should decisions be made by consensus or majority vote? May panellists issue separate opinions? And where separate opinions are issued, are they to be attributed to specific panellists or remain anonymous?

Most agreements have something to say about some of these questions, but rarely are all three covered. Some agreements encourage consensus but allow for majority voting;[150] others simply assume that sometimes the decision will be based on majority voting;[151] still others just require a majority vote.[152]

Some agreements state explicitly that where members disagree, a separate opinion may be issued.[153] While not all refer to this possibility, it may simply be assumed that

---

149 EFTA–Chile FTA, Annex XVII, paras. 34–6.
150 See, e.g., Korea–Singapore FTA, Annex 20a, para. 20: 'The panel shall take its decisions by consensus; provided that where a panel is unable to reach consensus it may take its decisions by majority vote.'
151 See, e.g., CAFTA–DR–US, Article 20.13, para. 5: 'Panelists may furnish separate opinions on matters not unanimously agreed.'
152 See, e.g., Japan–Mexico EPA, Article 154, para. 7: 'The arbitral tribunal shall take its decisions including its award by majority vote.'
153 See, e.g., EFTA–Singapore FTA, Article 61, para. 6: 'Panelists may furnish separate opinions on matters not unanimously agreed.'

this can be done, and it is not prohibited expressly in any agreement. Where separate opinions are to be issued, it is always indicated that the individual opinions are not to be attributed to specific panel members.[154]

H. Recommendations

Most of the PTAs covered make some reference to a panel making recommendations to the parties in the event of a finding of violation. Such a recommendation goes beyond simply 'bringing the measure into conformity'. Rather, this kind of recommendation relates to 'resolution of the dispute' or, in several agreements, 'suggested implementation options for the Parties to consider'.[155] In all agreements, the panel is not required to make such a recommendation, but simply has the discretion to do so. For some agreements, it is up to the panel whether to make any recommendations; for other agreements, a panel may do so only if the parties agree.[156]

VII. Implementation

Once the DSB adopts panel and Appellate Body reports containing findings of inconsistency, the WTO Member whose measure has been found to be inconsistent becomes subject to various obligations with respect to implementation. Article 3.7 of the DSU sets out certain relevant principles, namely that, in the absence of a mutually agreed solution, the withdrawal of a measure found to be inconsistent is the desired outcome, that compensation is to be temporary and only resorted to when the immediate withdrawal of the inconsistent measure is impracticable, and that the suspension of concessions is considered the 'last resort' of a complaining Member and is subject to DSB authorisation. Articles 21 and 22 of the DSU, entitled 'Surveillance of implementation of recommendations and rulings' and 'Compensation and the suspension of concessions', respectively, set out the detailed mechanics of implementation. These include: how the reasonable period of time for implementation is to be determined; the procedure to be followed when the parties to a dispute disagree over whether implementation has occurred; the reporting (by the Member whose measure has been found inconsistent) and monitoring (by the DSB) of implementation; the procedures and principles that are to be followed in the event that compensation or the suspension of concessions is sought; and associated procedures and timeframes.

---

154 See, e.g., EFTA–Singapore FTA, Article 61, para. 6: 'No arbitration panel may disclose which panellists are associated with majority or minority opinions.'
155 See, e.g., Japan–Singapore EPA, Article 144, para. 1(d).
156 The Korea–Singapore FTA says that panels are to provide 'recommendations, if any, on the means to resolve the dispute' (Article 20.11, para. 2(c)); by contrast, CAFTA–DR–US provides that the report shall contain 'recommendations, if the disputing Parties have requested them, for resolution of the dispute' (Article 20.13, para. 3(c)).

Articles 21 and 22 of the DSU are often pointed to as containing certain lacunae,[157] and as ripe for improvement. They have been the subject of many proposals and much discussion in the context of the ongoing negotiations on reform of the DSU, as well as of much academic commentary. Interestingly, variants of several of the proposals that have been made during these WTO negotiations have been adopted in some PTAs. Overall, however, most PTAs follow the WTO implementation model fairly closely, with a few additional innovations or improvements.

A. Start of the implementation phase

In WTO dispute settlement, the step that triggers the implementation process and associated obligations is the adoption of a panel and, if applicable, Appellate Body report by the DSB. This step has no equivalent in any of the PTAs examined. The Turkey–Morocco FTA does, however, appear to interject an additional step between the delivery of a panel report to the parties and the triggering of implementation obligations. Paragraph 7 of Article 33 of that Agreement requires the Joint Committee, to which the final panel report is presented, to 'take a decision to settle the dispute on the basis of the final report of the panel' and requires the parties 'to take the necessary steps required to implement this decision'. The following paragraph reinforces that it is the decision of the Joint Committee (rather than the panel report directly) with which the parties must comply, and also implies that such a decision will also set out the measures that may be taken by a complaining party in the event of non-implementation of such decision.[158] In most PTAs, however, the implementation phase begins upon the receipt by the parties of the report of the panel. In many cases it is the receipt of this report that starts the clock for the notification(s) required of responding parties whose measures have been found to be inconsistent. Several PTAs expressly state that the parties are bound by the final report and/or required to take the implementation measures necessary to comply with the ruling, and many also require the parties to consult in an effort to agree on specific implementation measures.[159] Korea's agreements with Chile and Singapore expressly state that a panel's final report shall not be subject to appeal.[160]

---

157 In particular the so-called 'sequencing' issue, or the fact that Articles 21 and 22 do not address the temporal relationship between compliance proceedings under Article 21.5, on the one hand, and negotiations for compensation and arbitration proceedings under Article 22, on the other.

158 Turkey–Morocco FTA, Article 33.8 provides that 'If the Party complained against fail[s] to implement . . . the decision mentioned in paragraph 7 of this article, the complaining Party shall be entitled to take measures in line with the decision of the Joint Committee'.

159 EU–Mexico FTA, Title VI, Chapter III, Article 46.4; and US–Morocco FTA, Article 20.10.1 (the parties 'shall agree on the resolution of the dispute, which normally shall conform with the determinations and recommendations, if any, of the panel'). See also US–Singapore FTA, Article 20.5.1; US–Chile FTA, Article 22.15.1; AUSFTA, Article 21.10.1; and CAFTA–DR–US, Article 20.15.1.

160 Korea–Chile FTA, Article 19.14.1; and Korea–Singapore FTA, Article 20.13.1.

B. *The period of time allowed for implementation*

Many PTAs mirror the DSU in providing that compliance with recommendations and rulings is to be 'prompt'. Like the DSU, most set out a mechanism for determining what the period of time for implementation should be in a specific dispute. In the majority of cases, this period is to be determined either by mutual agreement of the parties to the dispute or through recourse to the original panel.[161] Some envisage a single arbitrator making this determination, with the relevant individual to be selected either on agreement of the parties or by lot among the original panellists.[162] A few PTAs provide that the reasonable period of time is to be notified by the responding party (sometimes subject to guidelines) and that, if such period is not acceptable to the complaining party, then either: that complainant retains the option of referring the issue to the original panel;[163] or the parties are to enter into consultations on the issue.[164] Some PTAs do not prescribe a time within which the reasonable period of time for implementation must be set,[165] and some simply state that, if a party considers prompt compliance impracticable, then the parties must enter into consultations with a view to developing a mutually acceptable resolution and a reasonable period to implement such resolution.[166]

The PTAs to which the US is party are silent on the issue of the period of time for implementation. This may be an issue on which the parties could agree to request the panel to make a determination on in its initial report,[167] even though it is not expressly identified as such.[168] In the PTA between Korea and Chile, parties are directed to implement the final report of the panel 'within the time-frame that it

---

161 Article 20.13.2(b) of the Korea–Singapore FTA and Article 46.4 of Chapter III of the EU–Mexico FTA require the tribunal to determine the reasonable period of time within fifteen days of a request from a party.

162 See Canada–Costa Rica FTA, Section II, Article XVIII.16, Article 2(b) and footnote thereto.

163 Japan–Mexico EPA, Chapter 15, Article 156.2; EU–Chile AA, Articles 188.3 and 188.4; and EFTA–Chile FTA, Chapter X, Articles 96.3 and 96.4.

164 Japan–Singapore EPA, Chapter 21, Article 147.1(c).

165 See Turkey–Morocco FTA, Chapter 16, Article 9.1; and Korea–Singapore FTA, Article 20.13.2(b), which sets no time limit for the agreeing of a reasonable period of time, but allows either party to request the original panel to make such a determination and allows only fifteen days for the panel to do so.

166 NZ–Thailand CEPA, Article 17.10.3.

167 The relevant agreements authorise the parties to agree to request the panel to make 'any other determination' or recommendation. This would seem to encompass the possibility of asking a panel to make a determination as to the period of time for implementation – provided that the parties agree. See CAFTA–DR–US, Article 20.10.6; AUSFTA, Article 21.10.1; US–Chile FTA, Article 22.14.1, US–Singapore FTA, Article 20.5.1; and US–Morocco FTA, Article 20.10.1.

168 In contrast, the US–Chile FTA and CAFTA–DR–US expressly identify a finding as to the degree of adverse trade effects caused by a measure found to be inconsistent as an issue on which a party may request a panel to make a finding, and require the panel's terms of reference to reflect such a request (US–Chile FTA, Article 22.10(6); CAFTA–DR–US, Article 20.10(6)).

orders', which implies that the panel is empowered or expected to set implementation deadlines.[169]

As regards the length of the reasonable period of time for implementation, some PTAs follow the DSU in setting fifteen months as an outside guideline, or as the default period which may be modified by mutual consent.[170] The Japan–Singapore EPA provides that the period may 'extend to twelve months only if administrative or legislative measures have to be undertaken' but also allows this period to be extended or shortened if the parties agree that such modification is warranted by special circumstances.[171] The NZ–Singapore CEPA states that the period shall not exceed twelve months unless the responding party advises the complainant that 'primary legislation' is required for implementation, in which case the period is not to exceed fifteen months.[172] Quite a few PTAs are altogether silent on the issue.

C. Notification obligations and surveillance of implementation

Given that very few PTAs contemplate that a joint body will administer dispute settlement, there is little 'surveillance' of implementation that corresponds to the role of the DSB in this regard in the WTO. Yet a large number of PTAs do impose notification obligations on parties whose measures have been found by a panel to be inconsistent. The notification requirements generally attach shortly after receipt of the panel report and, in some cases, once the implementing measure has been adopted. A few PTAs also prescribe in some detail what such notifications must contain.

1. Prior to implementation

Several PTAs require responding parties found to have acted inconsistently to notify their intentions regarding implementation.[173] Some contain fairly specific details as to the required content of such notifications, including the reasonable period of time needed for implementation, the specific implementation measures, and a 'concrete proposal' for 'temporary compensation' until full implementation has been achieved.[174] A time limit of thirty days following receipt of the panel report is the norm for notifications of implementing action,[175] although only twenty days is

---

169 Korea–Chile FTA, Article 19.14.1. Neither the provisions of that Agreement nor the Model Rules of Procedure annexed to it specifically mention that a panel may, or may be requested to, fix a reasonable period of time for implementation, although Rule 7 of the Model Rules allows a party to request the panel to make findings as to the degree of adverse trade effects of an inconsistent measure.

170 EU–SA TDCA, Article 104.9(e).   171 Chapter 21, Article 147.1.   172 Part 10, Article 65.

173 E.g., Thailand–Australia FTA, Article 1810.2; and NZ–Thailand CEPA, Article 17.10.2.

174 EFTA–Chile FTA, Article 96.3; and EU–Chile FTA, Article 188.3.

175 EU–SA TDCA allows sixty days for such notification (Article 104.9(b)).

typically allowed if the only matter to be notified is the period of time proposed for implementation.[176]

The agreement between Canada and Costa Rica sets out additional notification/ reporting obligations. Like Article 21.6 of the DSU, that agreement requires a responding party that has not yet achieved implementation to provide periodic status reports.[177] In addition, if that party has not already notified the other of compliance it is under an obligation, no later than twenty days before the expiry of the reasonable period of time, to provide a written notification of the measures that it has taken or expects to have taken by the end of the reasonable period of time.[178]

2. Upon implementation

A few PTAs require a responding party to notify its implementing measure to the complainant.[179] The Canada–Costa Rica FTA contains rather detailed notification obligations regarding a party's implementation measures. The notification must 'include a detailed description as well as the text of the relevant measures the Party complained against has taken', or the measures that it expects to take before the end of the reasonable period of time.[180]

D. Compliance disputes and the 'sequencing' problem

Within the WTO, the brief two sentences that comprise Article 21.5 of the DSU have raised a number of questions regarding compliance disputes. In the earlier years of WTO dispute settlement, most of the questions related to two broad themes: (1) What is the relationship between compliance proceedings under Article 21.5 and the various proceedings contemplated under Article 22 of the DSU – the so-called 'sequencing' issue, discussed below and (2) Which aspects of an original dispute settlement proceeding are encompassed by the phrase 'these dispute settlement procedures' and may or must therefore form part of a compliance proceeding?[181] Over time, WTO Members have managed to conduct their disputes notwithstanding the apparent lacunae or ambiguous language in the relevant DSU provisions, often on the basis of bilateral agreements between the parties. Yet, in what seems probably the result of a heightened awareness of the uncertainties associated with Articles 21 and 22, several recent PTAs include

---

176 Japan–Mexico EPA, Article 156.2; and Japan–Singapore EPA, Article 147.1.
177 Canada–Costa Rica FTA, Article XIII.16.4(b), requires such status reports to be provided, beginning six months after the date of the final panel report, until such time as the parties agree, or a compliance panel finds, that compliance has been achieved.
178 Canada–Costa Rica FTA, Article XII.16.(c)(ii).   179 E.g., EU–Chile AA, Article 188.5.
180 Article XIII.16.4(c)(iii).
181 Thus, in the early years of WTO dispute settlement Members expressed differing opinions as to whether consultations on an implementing measure were required before the consistency of that measure could be referred to a compliance panel, and as to whether an appeal was possible in proceedings under Article 21.5 of the DSU.

provisions that seem designed to clarify the sequence of and steps involved in compliance proceedings. More recently within the WTO, a number of compliance proceedings have raised issues relating to possible limits that may apply to the scope of proceedings under Article 21.5 of the DSU, and concerning the relationship between Article 21.5 proceedings and original panel proceedings. So far, such issues have arisen in specific disputes and been decided as necessary by panels and the Appellate Body. Such issues have not been expressly dealt with in the text of the PTAs examined.

1. Compliance procedures

A few of the less detailed PTAs make no express reference to the issue of compliance.[182] This is also true of the Korea–Chile FTA, even though that agreement has a more elaborated dispute settlement mechanism. It is not clear on the face of the agreement whether implementing measures alleged to be inconsistent would be subject to new dispute settlement proceedings or whether the authority which the agreement gives to a panel asked to determine 'whether the level of benefits suspended by the complaining Party is excessive' would imply authority, as well, to examine the consistency of an implementing measure.[183]

A small number of PTAs explicitly address the issue – which has been controversial in the WTO context – of whether it is necessary to engage in consultations before referring a compliance measure to a compliance panel. The Canada–Costa Rica FTA states that while consultations are 'desirable, they are not required prior to a request for a compliance panel'.[184] Thailand's agreements with Australia[185] and New Zealand,[186] along with the Japan–Singapore EPA, however, appear to make consultations a prerequisite to recourse to a compliance panel.[187] Virtually all of the PTAs with some provisions on compliance proceedings provide expressly for, or appear to contemplate, that it is the original panel that will hear the compliance dispute.

The time afforded a compliance panel to complete its work varies among the agreements, and may be thirty,[188] forty-five,[189] sixty[190] or ninety[191] days from the date of the request or date of which the compliance panel is established or composed. The PTAs which provide for a single panel to decide both compliance issues and the level of suspension of concessions simultaneously (see below) typically provide two time limits: ninety days if the panel is asked to address compliance *or* the appropriate level of suspension of concessions, and 120 days if the panel is asked to

182 E.g., Turkey–Morocco FTA; EU–Israel AA; EU–SA TDCA; and India–Sri Lanka FTA.
183 Article 19.15.   184 Article XIII.17.3.   185 Article 1810.3.   186 Article 17.10.3.
187 See Article 147, paras. 3 and 4.
188 Japan–Mexico EPA, Article 156.8; and Korea–Singapore FTA, Article 20.14.6.
189 EU–Chile AA, Article 188.5.
190 EU–Mexico FTA, Article 46.5; Korea–Chile FTA, Article 19.15.5; and Singapore–Australia FTA, Article 9.2.
191 Canada–Costa Rica FTA, Article XIII.17.7.

address compliance *and* the appropriate level of suspension,[192] although this is not always the case.[193] One PTA expressly states that when an implementing measure is found by a compliance panel to be inconsistent, the respondent is not entitled to any further period of time for implementation.[194]

The wording of some PTAs may suggest that the scope of *measures* that a compliance panel may examine is intended to be different than is the case under the DSU. For example, it is possible, under a few PTAs, to request a compliance panel to make a determination as to the conformity of a *proposed* implementing measure,[195] even if that measure is not yet in force. A second example is that the wording of certain PTAs might restrict the implementing measures that may be referred to a compliance panel to measures that are adopted *during the period of time for implementation*.[196] Whether such a restriction is created is unclear, and it is also uncertain what the purpose of such a restriction might be – for example, to preclude a compliance panel from examining implementing measures adopted once that period of time has expired, to preclude 'serial' compliance proceedings as has happened in a few instances in the WTO context,[197] or for some other reason.

2. The 'sequencing' problem

The so-called 'sequencing' problem is rooted in the lack of any express indication, in the text of the DSU, of the relationship between Article 21.5, dealing with compliance disputes, and Article 22, dealing with compensation and the suspension of concessions. This is compounded by the time limits imposed for the initiation of negotiations on compensation and for a request for authorisation to

192 US–Morocco FTA, Article 20.11.3; US–Singapore FTA, Article 20.5.5; AUSFTA, Article 21.11.3; and CAFTA–DR–US, Article 20.16.3.
193 Thailand's PTAs provide that the panel shall be reconvened within thirty days of a request and present its determination within ninety days after it reconvenes (Thailand–Australia FTA, Article 1811.3; NZ–Thailand CEPA, Article 17.11.3).
194 Canada–Costa Rica FTA, Article XIII.17.9.
195 EU–Chile FTA, Article 188.4; and EFTA–Chile FTA, Article 96.4. Other PTAs authorise the complainant to request consultations with respect to a proposed implementing measure and further allow the complainant to seek the suspension of concessions in the event that such consultations do not lead to a mutually acceptable resolution. If the responding party objects to the level of the proposed suspension, then the resulting panel examination may cover both the level of suspension of concessions as well as the conformity of the proposed measure (see, e.g., Thailand–Australia FTA, Article 1810.3 and Article 1811, as well as NZ–Thailand CEPA, Articles 17.10.3 and 17.11).
196 For example, Article 9.2 of the Singapore–Australia FTA, which closely follows Article 21.5 of the DSU in most respects, contains the additional qualifying phrase 'within the reasonable period of time' to its introductory phrase: 'Where there is a disagreement as to the existence or consistency with this Agreement of measures taken *within the reasonable period of time* to comply with the recommendations' (emphasis added).
197 There were two consecutive Article 21.5 proceedings in each of the *US–FSC* and *Canada–Dairy* disputes. In addition, an Article 21.5 panel is currently considering Ecuador's claims against the European Communities' modified banana import regime, eight years after adoption of the first Article 21.5 panel's report and nearly ten years after the adoption of the report in the original proceedings.

suspend concessions set out in Article 22.2 of the DSU. Both deadlines are calculated with reference to the date of expiration of the reasonable period of time for implementation, and make no allowance for a longer period of time in the event that a compliance proceeding is ongoing. The issue first came to a head in the *EC–Bananas III* dispute. Since that time, most disputing parties who are involved in compliance proceedings under Article 21.5 of the DSU have concluded bilateral procedural agreements between themselves. Typically, these stipulate that the complaining party will request both the establishment of a compliance panel under Article 21.5 of the DSU and the suspension of concessions under Article 22. Such agreements further provide that the DSB will both establish the compliance panel and refer the level of suspension of concessions to an arbitral panel, but that the latter proceeding will be suspended until the former has been completed. These arrangements have the consequence that the complaining party may have to wait much longer than the expiry of the reasonable period of time before obtaining DSB authorisation to suspend concessions.

A few PTAs follow the DSU structure quite closely and may, therefore, contain their own sequencing issues. The agreement between Chile and Korea appears to eliminate sequencing issues by omitting altogether the possibility to refer compliance disputes back to the panel.[198] A number of PTAs, however, include provisions that appear designed to avoid the sequencing problem. The Korea–Singapore FTA, for example, authorises a complainant to begin suspending benefits thirty days after it has given notice of its intention to do so or after delivery of a panel report on the issue of compliance, 'whichever is later'.[199] The Singapore–Australia FTA contains a provision that closely resembles Article 21.5 of the DSU,[200] along with a subsequent provision that links the deadlines for requesting compensation and arbitration on the level of suspension of concessions to the date of circulation of the compliance panel report, rather than to the expiration of the reasonable period of time.[201]

A significant number of the PTAs examined sidestep the sequencing problem by combining the functions that, in the WTO, are dealt with separately in Article 21.5 and paragraphs 2–6 of Article 22. Such mechanisms differ in two significant respects from the DSU. First, under the DSU compliance disputes are conducted separately from arbitrations on the level or nature of suspension of concessions, whereas many

---

198 Article 19.15 of that allows the complainant to suspend benefits if there is no implementation of the panel report within thirty days following the expiration of the implementation period, but does not address the issue of a possible disagreement over whether such implementation has occurred.

199 Article 20.15.6.   200 Singapore–Australia FTA, Chapter 16, Article 9.2.

201 Chapter 16, Article 10.1. This type of mechanism seems to imply that a complaining party must have recourse to a compliance panel even when there is no disagreement as to whether or not implementation has occurred (e.g., if the responding party has taken no action) because, at least on the face of the relevant provision, compensation negotiations can only be initiated *after* the report of the compliance panel and the suspension of concessions can, in turn, only be sought twenty days after a request for such negotiations has been made.

PTAs assign to the same panel both the task of assessing the conformity of an implementing measure as well as the task of determining the appropriate level of suspension of concessions in the event of non-implementation. Secondly, in contrast to Article 21.5 of the DSU, pursuant to which responsibility for referring a matter to a compliance panel rests primarily – if not exclusively[202] – with the complaining party, many of the PTAs examined assign to the responding party the responsibility of referring compliance issues to a panel. This is achieved by allowing a complaining party dissatisfied with an implementing measure to request consultations and, if those consultations do not yield a mutually acceptable resolution, to notify its intention to suspend concessions. At that point, the responding party may refer issues of compliance and/or the level of suspension to the original panel. Five of the agreements which allow a responding party to refer compliance issues and the level of suspension of concessions to an original panel contain an additional, separate provision that allows a responding party to request the original panel to determine the consistency of an implementing measure even in the absence of a request by the complainant to suspend concessions,[203] although others do not.[204]

E. Remedies available in the event of non-compliance

As indicated, most PTAs indicate that implementation of the recommendations and rulings of the panel (or the resolution agreed by the parties upon receipt of such report) is the preferred outcome in the event that a panel finds that a measure does not conform to a party's obligations under the PTA. At the same time, nearly all provide for other remedies which are, in most cases, expressly characterised as 'temporary' pending implementation. In those PTAs which provide some explanation of the available remedies, these tend to replicate those found in the DSU, namely agreed compensation (meaning the grant by the responding party that is not yet in compliance of additional benefits or concessions under the agreement) or the suspension of concessions by the complaining party. The PTAs to which the US is party contain a third remedy, namely the possibility for the responding party to pay an

---

202 WTO Members have in the past debated whether the DSU allows a responding party to refer its implementing measure to a panel to determine its consistency with the covered agreements. Such a referral was made, in one instance, by the European Communities. In that case, however, the panel determined that the implementing measure was not consistent with the European Communities' obligations, and neither the European Communities nor any other WTO Member put the report on the agenda of the DSB for adoption. Thus, the Report in *EC–Bananas III (Article 21.5–EC)* remains the only panel report never to have been adopted by the DSB.

203 CAFTA–DR–US, Article 20.18; AUSFTA, Article 21.13; US–Chile FTA, Article 22.17; US–Singapore FTA, Article 20.8; and US–Morocco FTA, Article 20.13. As discussed below, such provisions provide a means for a respondent to terminate the suspension of concessions or its duty to pay an annual monetary assessment in the event that it has achieved implementation after the imposition of such measures.

204 NZ–Thailand CEPA; Korea–Singapore FTA; Thailand–Australia FTA; and Japan–Singapore EPA.

annual monetary assessment. Some PTAs contain no express reference to remedies that might be available in the absence of implementation, although their terms often contain language that might allow a variety of such remedies to be adopted.[205]

1. Compensation

Although a few of the PTAs examined contain no express reference to compensation as a possible remedy,[206] a large majority clearly indicate that it is an option. Among these, many also make clear that, as under the DSU, compensation is a temporary measure pending the preferred outcome of implementation of the panel report. The principal differences among the agreements with respect to compensation include: whether there is a specified time for initiating negotiations on compensation and, if so, whether it is calculated with reference to the date of delivery of the final panel report or the date of the expiration of the period of time for implementation; whether the onus is on the complaining party or the respondent to initiate discussions on compensation or present a proposal; and whether compensation is to be negotiated or proposed by the complainant and then subject to a panel determination in the event that the respondent does not agree, and to the deadlines for the various steps in the process. The PTAs typically provide that a complaining party may proceed to the suspension of concessions if no agreement on compensation is reached and, in some cases, if an agreement is reached but subsequently breached by the responding party.

Like the DSU, several PTAs link the initiation of discussions on compensation to the end of the reasonable period of time for implementation.[207] In contrast, the EU–Mexico FTA authorises the complainant to request consultations on compensation if the respondent has failed to notify its implementing measure before the end of the reasonable period of time *or* if a compliance panel has ruled that the implementing measure is inconsistent.[208] The two PTAs to which Thailand is party make clear that compensation discussions can occur within an implementation period, but do not necessarily tie such discussions to dates calculated in relation to the panel's final ruling. These agreements require 'consultations with a view to developing a mutually acceptable resolution, such as compensation or any alternative arrangement and agreeing on a reasonable period to implement such resolution' whenever the responding party considers that prompt compliance is 'impracticable' or if the complaining party considers that a proposed or adopted implementing measure does not constitute implementation. They provide for direct recourse to an arbitral panel (which may also determine the consistency of an implementing measure) in the

---

205 Turkey–Morocco FTA, Article 33.8 allows a complaining party to take measures 'in line with the decision of the Joint Committee' but provides no indication of what those might be.
206 Korea–Chile FTA; and EU–SA TDCA.
207 Canada–Costa Rica FTA, Article XIII.18.1; Korea–Singapore FTA, Article 20.14.1; Japan–Mexico EPA, Article 156.3; and EU–Mexico FTA, Article 46.4.
208 EU–Mexico FTA, Article 46.6.

event that such consultations do not lead to a mutually acceptable resolution.[209] These agreements make clear that compensation is to be temporary and that full implementation is a preferred resolution.[210]

Several PTAs provide for consultations on compensation within twenty,[211] thirty[212] or forty-five[213] days of the date of delivery of the final panel report. These then afford the parties a period of twenty[214] or thirty[215] days after which, if there is no agreement on compensation, the complaining party may notify its intention to suspend concessions.[216] Several of these agreements also allow a complaining party to make such a notification if an agreement on compensation has been reached but the complaining party subsequently considers that the responding party has failed to comply with the terms of such agreement.[217]

Chile's agreements with both the EU and EFTA place the onus on the party whose measure has been found inconsistent to notify the other party of, *inter alia*, 'a concrete proposal for a temporary compensation until the full implementation of the specific measures required for compliance with the ruling'.[218] The notification must be made within thirty days of the ruling of the panel and, in the event of a disagreement on the content of such notification, the complainant shall request that the original panel rule on 'whether the compensation proposal is manifestly disproportionate'.[219] This ruling is to be made within forty-five days.

2. Suspension of concessions

Nearly all of the PTAs with more elaborate dispute settlement mechanisms follow the WTO model on suspension of concessions fairly closely. Key differences include the fact that, under the PTAs, there is no need for the authorisation of a body equivalent to the DSB in order to suspend concessions. In addition, some PTAs – in particular

---

209 NZ–Thailand CEPA, Article 17.10.3; and Thailand–Australia FTA, Article 1810.3.

210 The two Thai agreements provide for such consultations in the event that *prompt* compliance is impracticable. In contrast, Article 147.2 of the Japan–Singapore EPA calls for consultations on a mutually acceptable resolution 'through compensation or any alternative arrangement' when the implementing party considers that 'compliance with the original award is *impracticable*' (emphasis added). The Japan–Singapore EPA does not contain any statement to the effect that compensation is temporary. The significance of these differences – if any – is unclear.

211 Singapore–Australia FTA, Article 10.1.   212 Korea–Singapore FTA, Article 20.14.1.

213 AUSFTA, Articles 21.11.1 and 21.11.2; US–Singapore FTA, Articles 20.6.1 and 20.6.2; and US–Morocco FTA, Articles 20.11.1 and 20.11.2.

214 Singapore–Australia FTA, Article 10.1; Korea–Singapore FTA, Article 20.14.1; Japan–Mexico EPA, Article 156.3; and EU–Mexico FTA, Article 46.4.

215 AUSFTA, Articles 21.11.1 and 21.11.2; US–Singapore FTA, Articles 20.6.1 and 20.6.2; and US–Morocco FTA, Articles 20.11.1 and 20.11.2.

216 AUSFTA, Articles 21.11.1 and 21.11.2; US–Singapore FTA, Articles 20.6.1 and 20.6.2; and US–Morocco FTA, Articles 20.11.1 and 20.11.2.

217 AUSFTA, Articles 21.11.1 and 21.11.2; US–Singapore FTA, Articles 20.6.1 and 20.6.2; US–Morocco FTA, Articles 20.11.1 and 20.11.2; and Japan–Singapore EPA, Article 147.2.

218 EU–Chile AA, Article 188.3(c); and EFTA–Chile FTA, Article 96.3(c).

219 EU–Chile AA, Article 188.4; and EFTA–Chile FTA, Article 96.4.

those that do not incorporate the notion of a reasonable period of time for implementation – appear to allow for benefits to be suspended more quickly following the issuance of the panel report than would generally be the case in the WTO.

PTAs which expressly include the possibility of suspending concessions typically authorise a complaining party to initiate the use of this remedy. In most instances the complainant does so by notifying its intention to suspend concessions, although in some agreements it does so by directly requesting the original panel to determine the appropriate level of suspension of concessions.[220] The complainant may take the relevant step either upon expiration of the time allowed for negotiations on compensation,[221] or where an agreement on compensation or resolution of the dispute has been reached but the complainant subsequently considers that the respondent has failed to observe such agreement.[222] Examples include:

- The Japan–Singapore EPA allows a complaining party to notify its intention to suspend concessions within thirty days of the determination of a compliance panel that implementation has not been achieved or within thirty days of the expiration of the implementation period.[223]
- Chile's agreements with the EU and EFTA authorise a complainant to notify its intention to suspend concessions in the event that the responding party has failed to notify implementing measures before the expiration of the implementation period, or, in the event that an implementing measure does not constitute implementation, if there is no agreement on compensation.[224]

The agreements that provide for the complaining party to first notify its intention to suspend concessions provide a period – five,[225] ten[226] or thirty[227] days – within which a responding party may, if it objects to the proposal, refer the matter to the original panel.

Most PTAs prescribe a time limit within which the panel must complete its assessment of the appropriate level and/or nature of suspension of concessions, for example in thirty,[228] forty-five,[229] sixty[230] or ninety[231] days, although some are silent

---

220 See, e.g., Singapore–Australia FTA, Article 10.2.
221 *Ibid.*, and Korea–Singapore FTA, Article 20.14.2.
222 See, e.g., the PTAs to which the US is party; and Korea–Singapore FTA, Article 20.14.2.
223 Article 147, paras. 5 and 6.   224 EU–Chile AA, Article 188.6; and EFTA–Chile FTA, Article 96.6.
225 EU–Chile AA, Article 188.8.   226 Canada–Costa Rica FTA, Articles XIII.18.3 and XIII.18.4.
227 Singapore–Australia FTA, Article 10.2; see also the PTAs to which the US is party.
228 Korea–Singapore FTA, Article 20.14.6.
229 Canada–Costa Rica FTA, Article XIII.18.5(c); EU–Chile AA, Article 188.8; and EFTA–Chile FTA, Article 96.8.
230 Korea–Chile FTA, Article 19.15.5.
231 NZ–Thailand CEPA, Article 17.11.3; and Thailand–Australia FTA, Article 1811.3. The PTAs to which the US is party allow a panel ninety days in the event that it is only making a determination regarding the level of benefits to be suspended, but 120 days in the event that it is asked, at the same time, to make a determination regarding the conformity of a measure taken to comply with the panel report.

on the permissible duration of such proceedings.[232] Many also stipulate that the complainant must await the decision of that panel before proceeding to suspend concessions,[233] although some are silent on this issue. In contrast, the Korea–Chile FTA appears to allow a complaining party to suspend benefits at any time once thirty days after the time-frame for implementation fixed in the panel report has elapsed.[234] The wording of that agreement appears to assume that a panel will be activated only *after* the complaining party has suspended benefits.[235] Similarly, the two PTAs examined to which Thailand is party allow the complaining party to suspend benefits thirty days after it has given notice of its intention to do so *even if* panel proceedings are ongoing relating to compliance or the level of suspension.[236]

Most PTAs do not contain detailed rules regarding the procedures that are to be followed by a panel that has been asked to make a determination regarding the appropriate level and/or nature of suspension of concessions, although the Model Rules of Procedure annexed to some PTAs do address this issue. The Annex to the Korea–Chile FTA, for example, sets time limits for the first submissions of each party and provides that the panel may, unless the parties decide otherwise, decide not to convene a hearing.[237]

As for substantive principles governing the suspension of concessions, nearly all of the PTAs provide rules regarding the *level* of suspensions. They typically convey, although not always with the same language, the general principle that the level of suspension of concessions should be equivalent to the level of nullification and impairment caused by the measure found to be inconsistent.[238] As mentioned above, the PTAs to which Thailand is party authorise the suspension of concessions even while panel proceedings to determine the appropriate level of such suspension are ongoing. However they also each contain a unique provision which seems to be designed to impose some discipline on such unilateral action. These provisions allow a panel, in fixing the appropriate level of suspension of concessions, to adjust the level

---

232 See, e.g., Singapore–Australia FTA, Article 10.

233 Japan–Mexico EPA, Article 156.6(a); Japan–Singapore EPA, Article 147.4(a); EU–Chile AA, Article 188.8; and EFTA–Chile FTA, Article 96.8.

234 Article 19.15.

235 Korea–Chile FTA, Article 19.15.4: '[T]he original panel shall determine whether the level of benefits *suspended* by the complaining Party is excessive.'

236 NZ–Thailand CEPA, Article 17.11.3; and Thailand–Australia FTA, Article 1811.3.

237 Annex 19.10, Rule 42.

238 Thus, for example the NZ–Thailand CEPA refers to 'benefits of equivalent effect to the non-conformity found' (Article 17.11.1 and 17.11.2(c)); the PTAs to which the US is party as well as the Korea–Singapore FTA refer to 'benefits of equivalent effect'; the Canada–Costa Rica FTA directs the panel to determine 'whether the level of such suspension is equivalent to the level of nullification or impairment' (Article XIII.18.5); and the Japan–Mexico and Japan–Singapore EPAs refer to 'level of nullification or impairment that is attributable to the failure to comply' with the panel report (Articles 156.5(c) and 147.4(c), respectively). Although the Singapore–Australia FTA contains no explicit requirement of equivalency, this is in all likelihood implicit in the provision that the panel is to determine the 'appropriate' level of suspension of benefits, Article 10.2.

of 'equivalent' benefits 'to reflect any loss sustained' by a respondent 'as a result of excessive suspension'.[239]

Many of the PTAs also set out rules governing the *nature* of the concessions which may be suspended, and these tend to follow the WTO model in specifying that the complaining party should first seek to suspend benefits in the same sector or sectors as those affected by the inconsistent measure, and that only if it is not practicable or effective to suspend benefits in the same sector should recourse be had to other sectors.[240] Most of the PTAs which contain such provisions appear to also allow a panel to pronounce on whether or not these principles have been respected,[241] although some appear to limit the role of the panel to determining simply the *level* of the benefits that may be suspended.[242] Other PTAs are silent on the issue of whether a panel is to address the nature of the concessions to be suspended,[243] and one expressly prohibits a panel from doing so.[244] As explained below, several agreements have special provisions regarding the suspension of concessions when the dispute relates to financial services.

Many PTAs contain a statement to the effect that only benefits accruing or obligations owing under that specific agreement may be suspended,[245] and that the suspension of benefits is to be temporary.[246] A few also contain a provision analogous to Article 22.9 of the DSU, making clear that the suspension of concessions may be undertaken in disputes where the non-conformity of the measure derives from measures taken by regional or local government entities.[247]

3. Monetary assessments

Among the PTAs examined, all of the ones to which the US is party contain an additional potential remedy which has no current equivalent in the WTO, namely monetary assessments.[248] Pursuant to these agreements, in the event of

---

239 NZ–Thailand CEPA, Article 17.11.3, and Thailand–Australia FTA, Article 1811.3, provide: 'If the tribunal determines that the level of benefits proposed to be or actually suspended is excessive, it shall determine the level of benefits it considers to be of equivalent effect to the non-conformity found by the tribunal, adjusted to reflect any loss sustained by a Party as a result of excessive suspension.'

240 See, e.g., Singapore–Australia FTA, Article 10.4; Korea–Singapore FTA, Article 20.14.4; Korea–Chile FTA, Article 19.15.1; Japan–Mexico EPA, Article 156.6; NZ–Thailand CEPA, Article 17.11; Thailand–Australia FTA, Article 1811.2; and EFTA–Chile FTA, Article 7. The EU–Chile AA refers to the suspension of benefits in 'the same Title or Titles of this Part of the Agreement as that affected by the measure' (Article 188.7). The relevant Part of the agreement dealing with trade is Part IV, and it is divided into eight titles. Thus, for example, Title II deals with trade in goods, Title III with trade in services, and Title V with intellectual property rights.

241 See EU–Chile AA, Article 188.8; and EFTA–Chile, Article 96.8.

242 See, e.g., Korea–Chile FTA, Article 19.15.

243 See, e.g., the PTAs to which the US is party; and the Korea–Singapore FTA.

244 Canada–Costa Rica FTA, Article XIII.18.5.   245 See, e.g., Singapore–Australia FTA, Article 10.3.

246 *Ibid.*, Article 10.5; Canada–Costa Rica FTA, Article XIII.18.6; Japan–Singapore EPA, Article 147.7(b); Japan–Mexico EPA, Article 156.6(b); EU–Chile AA, Article 188.9; and EFTA–Chile FTA, Article 96.9.

247 See, e.g., Canada–Costa Rica FTA, Article XIII.18.9.

248 See US–Morocco FTA; AUSFTA; US–Chile FTA; US–Singapore FTA; and CAFTA–DR–US.

non-implementation, a complaining party has a right to suspend benefits either within thirty days after having notified its intention to do so, or twenty days after a panel's determination of the appropriate level and nature of suspension, *unless* the responding party provides written notice that it will pay an annual monetary assessment within that twenty- or thirty-day period. A complaining party that receives such a notice is then precluded from suspending benefits – at least until the responding party has failed to pay the monetary assessment. The amount is to be fixed by agreement of the parties or, failing such agreement, shall be equal to 50 per cent of the level of benefits that either: (1) a panel has determined to be of equivalent effect to the nullification and impairment or, if the level of suspension has not been referred to a panel; (2) the level that the complaining Party proposed to suspend. The monetary assessment is to be paid in quarterly instalments beginning sixty days after the responding party gives notice that it intends to pay an assessment. Although the default rule is that the monetary assessment will be paid to the complaining party, each of these PTAs also provides that, if the relevant Commission or Joint Committee under the PTA so decides, the assessment is to be paid into a fund established by that Commission or Joint Committee, and may be spent by that body 'for appropriate initiatives to facilitate trade between the Parties, including by further reducing unreasonable trade barriers or by assisting a Party in carrying out its obligations under the Agreement'. The agreements impose no limit on the length of time for which such monetary assessments may be paid.

4. Special remedies for disputes related to specific subjects

Several PTAs to which the US is party contain a special provision relating to non-implementation in disputes where a panel has determined that the responding party is not enforcing its domestic environmental or labour laws as required under the PTA.[249] These agreements specify that the general provisions on non-implementation do not apply. Instead, a separate article, entitled 'Non-Implementation in Certain Disputes', sets out the only remedy that may be available in the event that, following delivery of the final panel report, the disputing parties are unable to reach agreement on a resolution of the dispute, or the parties do reach such agreement but the complaining party considers that the responding party has breached that agreement. In such circumstances, the relevant PTAs authorise the complaining party to request that the panel be reconvened to impose an annual monetary assessment on the other party. The panel is then to reconvene as soon as possible and, within ninety days thereafter, determine the amount of the assessment. In making its determination, the panel is

---

249 See US–Morocco FTA; AUSFTA; US–Chile FTA; US–Singapore FTA; and CAFTA–DR–US.

instructed to take into account six listed factors,[250] and its determination may not exceed a ceiling of 15 million US dollars annually, adjusted for inflation. Once the panel has determined the amount of the annual assessment or at any time thereafter, the complaining party is entitled to provide notice in writing demanding payment. The assessment is payable in equal quarterly instalments beginning sixty days after the later of the panel's determination or the delivery of the notice demanding payment.

The monetary assessment is not, however, payable to the complaining party. Instead, it is to be paid into a fund established by the relevant Joint Committee/ Commission of the relevant PTA, and may be spent by that body 'for appropriate labour or environmental initiatives, including efforts to improve or enhance labor or environmental law enforcement, as the case may be, in the territory of the Party complained against, consistent with its law'. The PTAs further provide that, in 'deciding how to expend monies paid into the fund, the [Commission or Joint Committee] shall consider the views of interested persons in the disputing Parties' territories.'

In the event that a monetary assessment is not paid, the relevant PTAs also authorise the complaining party to take 'other appropriate steps to collect the assessment or otherwise secure compliance'. Such steps may include the suspension of tariff benefits under the Agreement, as necessary to collect the assessment, while bearing in mind the Agreement's objective of eliminating barriers to bilateral trade and while seeking to avoid unduly affecting parties or interests not party to the dispute. Three of the five agreements which contain these special rules for non-implementation in specific environmental or labour related disputes also provide that, in the event of non-payment of a monetary assessment the complaining party shall, before having recourse to any other measure, seek to obtain the funds from an escrow account, if one exists and has been funded by the other party to ensure payment of any assessments against it.[251]

In addition, although some PTAs exclude trade in financial services altogether from the dispute settlement mechanisms they contain,[252] others authorise the resolution of disputes, but set out special provisions relating to disputes concerning financial services. Insofar as the remedies are concerned, such PTAs provide specific rules regarding the type of benefits that may be suspended in the event of non-implementation. More specifically, they provide that when a measure has been found by a panel to be inconsistent with the PTA, the complaining

---

250 These are: the bilateral trade effects of the Party's failure to effectively enforce the relevant law; the pervasiveness and duration of the Party's failure to effectively enforce the relevant law; the reasons for the Party's failure to effectively enforce the relevant law; the level of enforcement that could reasonably be expected of the Party given its resource constraints; the efforts made by the Party to begin remedying the non-enforcement after the final report of the panel; and any other relevant factors.

251 US–Morocco FTA, Article 20.12.5; US–Singapore FTA, Article 20.7.5; and AUSFTA, Article 21.12.5.

252 E.g., Japan–Mexico EPA, Article 109.

party: may suspend benefits in the financial services sector if the measure affects *only* the financial services sector; may suspend benefits in the financial services sector that have an effect equivalent to the effect of the measure in that party's financial services sector if the measure affects *both* the financial services sector and any other sector; and may *not* suspend benefits in the financial services sector if the measure affects *only* a sector other than the financial services sector.[253]

5. 'Appropriate' measures

Lastly, we mention briefly two agreements to which the EU is party and their reference to the possibility for one party to the agreement to take 'appropriate measures'. The EU agreements with Israel and Chile each provide that, in the event that one party considers that the other has failed to fulfil an obligation under the agreement, then the party 'may take appropriate measures'.[254] However, before doing so, the party which considers the other party not to have fulfilled an obligation must supply the Association Council with all relevant information required to enable the Association Council to undertake a thorough examination of the situation with a view to seeking a solution acceptable to the parties. The agreements do not define what may constitute 'appropriate measures', but do specify that, in the selection of such measures priority must be given to those which least disturb the functioning of the agreement.[255] Such measures must be notified to the Association Committee and are to be the subject of consultations within that Committee if the other party so requests.

The EU–Chile AA contains two further provisions '[b]y way of derogation from' the above. One of these restricts the potential scope of application of such 'appropriate measures' by clarifying that, when the obligation alleged to have been breached is contained in Part IV of that agreement – which deals with trade and trade-related matters – then the party which considers the other party to be in breach must 'exclusively have recourse to, and abide by, the dispute settlement procedures' contained in that Part of the agreement.[256] The second derogation authorises a party to 'immediately' take 'appropriate measures in accordance with international law' in two circumstances: (1) denunciation of the agreement that is not sanctioned

---

253 E.g., Korea–Singapore FTA, Article 12.12.5; US–Morocco FTA, Article 12.17.4; US–Singapore FTA, Article 10.18.4; US–Chile FTA, Article 12.17.6; and CAFTA–DR–US, Article 12.18.5. The AUSFTA has a similar provision in Article 13.18.4.

254 These agreements each impose a requirement on the parties to adopt any general or specific measures required to fulfil their obligations under the agreement and to ensure that they comply with the objectives in the agreement (EU–Israel AA, Article 79.1; EU–Chile AA, Article 200.1).

255 EU–Israel AA, Article 79.2; and EU–Chile AA, Article 200.2.

256 EU–Chile AA, Article 200.4. The other Parts of the agreements deal with: General and Institutional Provisions (Part I); Political Dialogue (Part II); Co-operation (Part III); and Final Provisions (Part VI).

by the general rules of international law;[257] and (2) violation 'of the essential elements' of the agreement.[258]

F. Post-retaliation proceedings

Certain PTAs, in particular those to which the US is party, contain provisions allowing for post-retaliation compliance proceedings.[259] Such proceedings enable a respondent that did not implement and was subjected to the suspension of concessions to seek to have those sanctions lifted in the event that it subsequently achieves implementation. This is a concept that has been proposed in the context of the negotiations on the clarification and improvement of the DSU, but which does not currently exist in the WTO. This lacuna arguably explains the *raison d'être* of the *Canada–Continued Suspension (EC–Hormones)* and *US–Continued Suspension (EC–Hormones)* disputes.[260]

The PTAs that include post-retaliation proceedings provide that, if the disputing parties disagree on whether implementation has been achieved, the respondent can request a compliance panel to make a ruling on this issue. If the panel finds that there has been compliance, then the complaining party must lift its sanctions and/or, in the PTAs to which the US is party, the respondent is relieved of its obligation to pay a monetary assessment. Panels are to make such determinations within thirty,[261] forty-five[262] or ninety[263] days.

VIII. Conclusion

Dispute settlement under PTAs is in its infancy. Rules have been established, but they have not been applied, as cases have not yet arisen. The reasons for the absence of

---

257 EU–Chile AA, Article 200.3(a).
258 EU–Chile AA, Article 200.3(b). The 'essential elements' are defined as those contained in paragraph 1 of Article 1 of that agreement, which reads as follows: Respect for democratic principles and fundamental human rights as laid down in the United Nations Universal Declaration of Human Rights and for the principle of the rule of law underpins the internal and international policies of the Parties and constitutes an essential element of this Agreement.
259 CAFTA–DR–US, Article 20.18; AUSFTA, Article 21.13; US–Chile FTA, Article 22.17; US–Singapore FTA, Article 20.8; US–Morocco FTA, Article 20.13; Canada–Costa Rica FTA, Article XIII.18.10; EU–Chile AA, Article 188.8; and EFTA–Chile FTA, Article 96.10.
260 These disputes were initiated by the EC, the respondent in an earlier dispute, *EC–Hormones*, against the two complaining parties in those earlier disputes, the US and Canada. Both had – with the authorisation of the DSB and following an arbitration on the level of suspension – suspended concessions *vis-à-vis* the EC. Subsequently, the EC considered that it had implemented the DSB's recommendations and rulings. However, because the US and Canada disagreed with this assessment, they declined to remove the sanctions or to seek compliance proceedings under Article 21.5 of the DSU. Accordingly, the EC initiated a new dispute claiming that the continued suspension of concessions by the US and Canada was inconsistent with the DSU.
261 EFTA–Chile FTA, Article 96.10.   262 EU–Chile AA, Article 188.10.
263 CAFTA–DR–US, Article 20.18.1; AUSFTA, Article 21.13.1; US–Chile FTA, Article 22.17.1; US–Singapore FTA, Article 20.8.1; and US–Morocco FTA, Article 20.13.1.

cases are unclear. Perhaps governments generally prefer the WTO dispute settlement process where it is available for particular trade barriers, as this process is well understood. However, PTA obligations go beyond those of the WTO in many areas, so one would expect disputes under PTAs to occur eventually.

Although it may only be a minor factor, notably absent with PTA dispute settlement is the equivalent of the Advisory Centre on WTO Law (ACWL). The ACWL provides low-cost assistance to developing countries in relation to their disputes at the WTO. As many PTAs involve developing countries, such an organization would also be valuable in the PTA context.

It has been suggested that PTA disputes could be handled by the WTO dispute settlement process. There is some sense to this proposal. It may be, however, that little effort will be made to evaluate and consider the PTA dispute settlement process until disputes arise.

INDEX